Warman's

JEWELRY

3rd EDITION

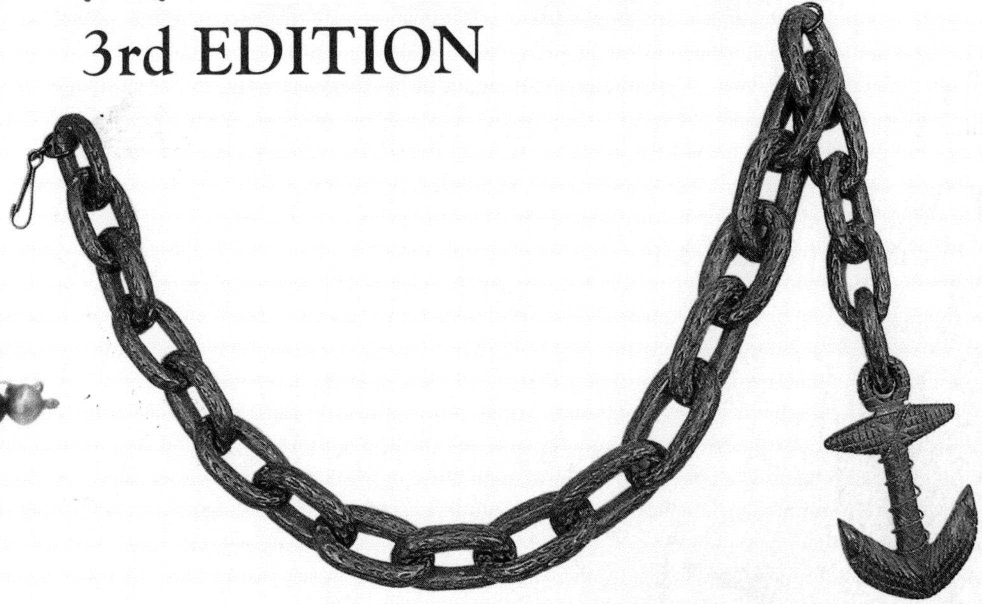

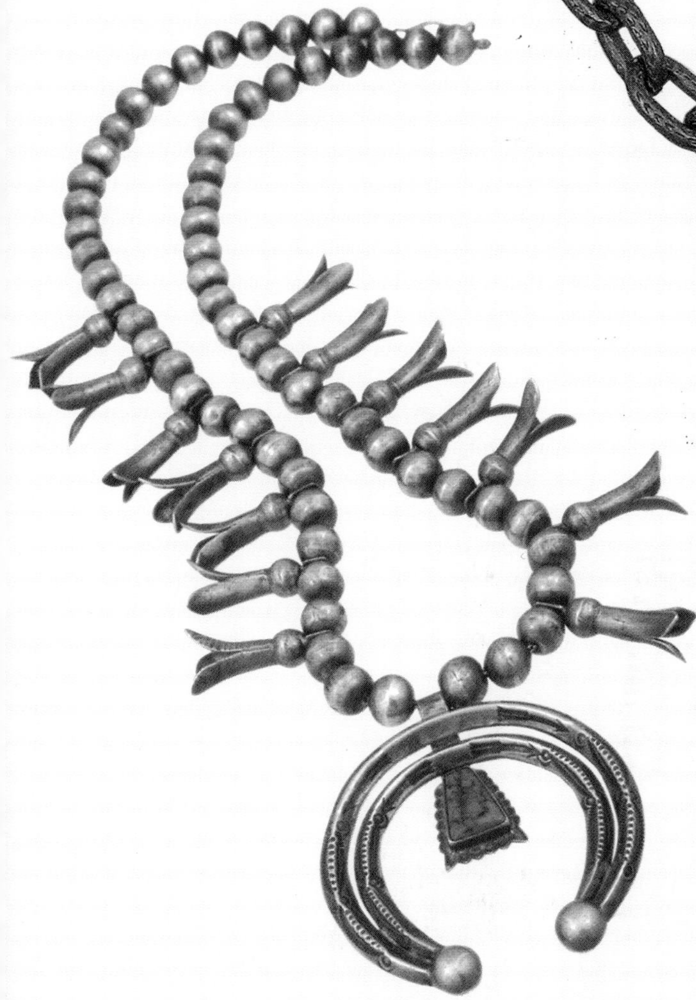

A Fully Illustrated Identification and Price Guide to
18th, 19th & 20th Century Fine and Costume Jewelry

CHRISTIE ROMERO

Published by

krause publications
An F&W Publications Company

700 East State Street • Iola, WI 54990-0001
715-445-2214 • 888-457-2873
www.krause.com

Please call or write for our free catalog.
Our toll-free number to place an order or obtain a free catalog is 800-258-0929 or please use our regular business telephone 715-445-2214 for editorial comment and further information.

ISBN: 0-87349-328-1
Library of Congress: 2002105098

Information on the photos pictured on the cover and title page can be found on the following pages: **Front cover**, clockwise from top right: brooch/pin, page 122; brooch/pin, page 115; charm bracelet, page 130; brooch/pin, page 227; pendant, page 88; pendant, page 248; clip, page 195; and brooch/pin, page 37. **Back cover:** the top photo is a general "timeline" photo showing the different periods of jewelry featured in the book; bottom photos, from left: pendant and cord, page 172; brooch/pin, page 41; and pendant and chain, page 94. **Title page:** ring, page 161; necklace, page 220; and brooch/pin, page 152. The watch chain at top right, not featured in the book, is a piece of black jewelry from the Mid-Victorian period: bog oak, wm, c. 1860-70, 21 grad hand-carved links, carved in three- to four-link sections, each from a single piece, joined with seams (most links are seamless), terminating in a carved anchor fob entwined with wm corded wire, black-lacquered wm jump rings, snap hook on opposite terminal, anchor 1¾" w x 3", chain 21½" tl, widest link 1" w, $350. (Author's collection)

Acknowledgments

For this third edition of *Warman's Jewelry*, in addition to faithful friends, colleagues, and students who have continued to generously provide me with information and jewelry, the list of those to be thanked has grown longer. I feel fortunate to have made contact with many who have contributed much to the field, and who were willing to assist me. Their names, contact information, and areas of expertise can be found on the Board of Advisers pages. I thank them one and all.

I am especially indebted to the readers of the first two editions of *Warman's Jewelry*, whose favorable response has prompted the writing of the third with the desire to make it even better. This book would not have been published without their support.

For support *and* advice above and beyond the call of duty, I am indebted once again to my dear friend Sherry Shatz, who also cheerfully volunteered to do "grunt work," as well as some serious research on a number of wide-ranging topics. I thank Nancy Shadforth for willingly subjecting herself to my editorial eye and tackling the daunting task of caption descriptions. Nancy's computer and proofreading skills also helped greatly when it came time to pull all the captions together in an orderly fashion. Patrick Kapty was a lifesaver for pitching in with jewelry for photos, database entry, evaluations, discussions, and assorted other cries for help. Gene Ratcliffe certainly deserves mention for accompanying me to auction previews, taking notes, doing gem i.d.s, measuring jewelry, and entering information in my database.

Dealers and collectors provided a sizable portion of the items pictured in this edition. Globetrotter Sam Gassman again proved to be a bottomless source of jewels shipped from points east, and information e-mailed or phoned from everywhere. Jane Clarke came to the rescue with many beautifully photographed examples for the costume jewelry sections, and with a market analyzer's "take" on prices. Matt Burkholz provided me with a number of expertly photographed slides of deliciously colorful Bakelite, along with well-detailed descriptions that made my job of captioning much easier. Pat Seal and her extensive collection of vintage jewelry advertising added much-needed primary documentation to the costume jewelry manufacturers' list. Pat was also a contributor of a number of great examples for the photos this time around. Lynne Arkin allowed me to set up a makeshift digital photo studio in her show booth on setup day to capture images of some of her and Lenore Dailey's fine inventories. Lynne, Lenore, and husband Jerry Baird were, as always, pillars of support. Didier Haspeslagh was likewise most accommodating in allowing me to photograph some superb pieces from his inventory "on site" at the L.A. Modernism show, and in providing information and advice. Margot Conté saved the day with digital images of pieces from her micromosaic collection. Recently acquired examples from the Healy collection found their way into these pages, thanks to Bruce's photographs and information. Shari Miller was once again a much-appreciated dispenser of information, and this time also contributed her photographic talents, as well as fine examples for the Native American and Studio Artists sections. Gilly Phipps, my forever friend, sent love and support along with a great variety of "shtuff." Fellow "Antiques Roadshow" appraisers and friends Karen Lorene and Barry Weber offered advice and counsel; Facèré Jewelry Art manager Helen Brooks sent images the "high-tech" way, through cyberspace. Colleagues Elise Misiorowski and Janet Zapata took time away from their busy schedules to ponder questions and solve mysteries. Amanda Triossi, formerly of Sotheby's Institute, was a long-distance supporter, friend, and adviser via e-mail, and in person at Jewelry Camp. Ever-supportive friends Gail Gerretsen, Gail Levine, Chuck Pinkham, Julie Robinson, and Terrance O"Halloran all gave generously of their time, expertise, and jewelry or photos. Aram Berberian gave advice and sent splendidly photographed examples for the Arts & Crafts section. Jewel Stern aided me in research for that section as well.

While all my contributors have my deepest appreciation, I am especially grateful to those who trustingly brought or sent me mass quantities of their treasured collections (and/or inventory) to be photographed: Kymm Arbiso, Chris Enebo, Caren Fine, Lisa Johnson, Carrie Leeper, Dawn Lowe, Munir Meghji, Elaine Sarnoff, Vickie Vega, and Diane White.

On a sad note, I must thank one three-time contributor posthumously. Hairwork collector extraordinaire Carmelita Johnson passed away in March 2002, only days after I had come to her "open house" to view and photograph pieces from her fabulous collection. Her daughter Andrea Tice is now the caretaker of this important collection, and I commend her for handling it so well.

Although I did not know her personally, I was also saddened to hear of the passing of Carla Genelli Brunialti, wife of Robert Brunialti. As collectors and researchers of American costume jewelry, and authors of two books, the Brunialtis have contributed much-needed information to the field.

Again there were several contributors who did not wish to have their names published, but whose contributions are just as much valued as any other. They filled many a "hole" in several categories.

Some sections of this edition would have been sparse indeed if it hadn't been for the cooperation and assistance of auction houses and their jewelry department personnel. Heartfelt thanks go to friend and colleague Peter Shemonsky at Butterfields; Mary Borchert, formerly at Beverly Hills Auctioneers (now closed); Debbie Bloom at Christie's and Jane Padelford at Christie's Images; Daniela Mascetti at Sotheby's London; Gloria Lieberman and her staff at Skinner, Inc.; Ron Dupuis and staff at Dupuis Jewellery Auctioneers; Jan Glier Reeder in the Couture department at William Doyle; Julie Munn and staff at R.G. Munn.

Jewelry history education and information dissemination would be sorely lacking were it not for the efforts of a few "movers and shakers" in the field. Joyce Jonas, director of the annual Antique & Period Jewelry & Gemstone conference on the East Coast, has brought the greatest number of jewelry lovers together in one place to teach, learn, network, and endlessly discuss their mutual passion. I thank Joyce for making me a "regular" on her faculty, and for her friendship. Jewelcollect and SilverForum are two Internet e-mail discussion groups that have brought people together in cyberspace who never would have met otherwise. Liz Bryman of Jewelcollect and co-moderators Patrick Kapty and Marbeth Schon of SilverForum have ably administered to their respective groups. I'm pleased to have taken part in both of them.

The staff at Olson Photo and Imaging of Anaheim, California, continued to be helpful as I made the transition from slide film to digital images. Artist and teacher Brad Pettigrew also helped out with scans of marks, and taught me Adobe Photoshop basics in a few easy lessons, faster than any book or online course.

Kris Manty at Krause Publications, a glutton for punishment, took on the job of editing this edition as capably as she did the last. I would not have had it any other way. My appreciation of her knows no bounds.

My family, as always, monitored my progress with love and concern, as only those who have firsthand familiarity with the stresses of writing can. Peggy and Norm Levine, mother and "step," Sam and Ron Schultz, father and brother, Laura Sanderford, sister-in-law, and my precious teen-age nieces, Johana and Emily: thank you one and all. I thank my in-laws, stepchildren, and grandchildren for understanding why I couldn't always participate in family gatherings, and for asking, "How's the book going?"

Saving the best for last, to my Computer Wiz husband Jimmie, who simultaneously handled my book-writing, class-teaching, Roadshow travels, *and* the restoration of our beloved bungalow with patience, a sympathetic ear, and a helping hand: I give my undying love and gratitude, and dedicate this book to you.

Christie S. Romero

Contents

Introduction 6
Organization of the Book 7
Price Notes 10
Board of Advisers 11
Other Contributors 11
Comments Invited 11
State of the Market 12
Board of Advisers 13
Auction Houses 15
Abbreviations 15
Timeline 16

Part 1—Late Eighteenth and Nineteenth Century Jewelry

Introduction 23
Late Georgian Jewelry, c. 1760-1837 24
Cut Steel, Berlin Iron, Silesian Wire Work 30
Memorial, Mourning, and Hair Jewelry 34
Miniatures 37
Early Victorian (Romantic Period) c. 1837-1861 39
Coral 43
Hairwork 44
Scottish Jewelry 47
Mid Victorian (Grand Period) c. 1861-1880 49
Black Jewelry 50
Tortoiseshell and Piqué 54
Revivalist Jewelry 55
Etruscan 55
Renaissance 55
Egyptian 56
Cameos and Intaglios 60
Mosaics in Jewelry 65
Manufactured Gold, Gold-Filled, Gold-Plated Jewelry 68
Late Victorian (Aesthetic Period) c. 1880-1901 74
Early Celluloid 76
Silver and Mixed Metals 77
Diamonds and Colored Gemstones 82

Part II
Turn-of-the-Century Jewelry

Introduction 92
Arts and Crafts c. 1890-1920 92
Great Britain 93
Germany and Austria 94
The United States 95
Art Nouveau c. 1895-1910 107
Beaux-arts and "Neo-Renaissance" c. 1890-1920 115
Edwardian c. 1890-1920 119

Part III

Twentieth-Century Jewelry

Introduction 126
Fine Jewelry c. 1920-1935 126
Costume Jewelry c.1920-1935 136
Plastics and Other Novelty Jewelry c. 1920-1970 145
Celluloid and Cellulose Acetate 145
Bakelite and Casein 146
Lucite 147
Fine Jewelry c. 1935-1945 157
Mid-Century Modern-American Studio Jewelry c. 1945-1965 163
Fine Jewelry c. 1945-1960 175
Fine Jewelry 1960-1975 180
Costume Jewelry (Designer/Manufacturer Signed and Other)
Section One: c. 1935-1950 187
Section Two: c. 1950-1975 200

Part IV

Special Collectible Jewelry

Introduction 212
Native American Jewelry 212
Mexican Jewelry c. 1930-1970 222
Scandinavian Jewelry 232
Denmark 232
Norway 240
Sweden 244
Finland 246

Appendices

Marks on Metals 251
American Manufacturer's Marks 252
Mid-Century Modern-American Studio Jewelry 253
Twentieth Century American Costume Jewelry Manufacturers/Designers 253
Marks and Names on Mexican Silver Jewelry and Metalware c. 1930-1990 255
Twentieth Century Jewelry Designers and Manufacturers in Scandinavia 257
Basic Hallmark Identification 259
References 261
Glossary 265
Index 269

Introduction

A quick glance through these pages will make it readily apparent to the reader that *Warman's Jewelry*, 3rd edition is more than an update of the second edition. It is an *all color* new edition that contains *all* new photographs, as well as new information, marks, and references.

Thanks to technology and digital photography, new features have been added, as well as new categories and style classifications. However, the basic purpose of this book remains the same: it is a "field guide" to styles and types of antique, period, and vintage collectible jewelry currently on the market. It is for anyone who owns old jewelry, whether it is a collector's collection, a dealer's inventory, an heir's inheritance, a packrat's accumulation, or a garage-saler's finds. No matter how they've acquired it, most people want to know the same basic things about a piece: how old it is, where and how it was made, who made it, what it is made of, and the ubiquitous bottom line, what it is worth. Jewelry has always been kept and worn, for many different reasons, but only within the last 20 years or so has conscientious collecting (by style or period, material, country of origin, etc.) become a major reason to buy. As greater numbers of collectors have entered the field, there has been a growing need for more information about the many varieties of collectible jewelry being bought and sold today. *Warman's Jewelry* was written in response to that need. The third edition continues in that tradition.

Past editions have focused on American-made pieces currently available in the United States. But with the explosive growth of the Internet and the globalization of the marketplace since the publication of the second edition, that focus is no longer necessary. Nonetheless, the categories that are primarily American, or include many American examples, have been retained: American Arts & Crafts, mid-century modernist American studio artists, 1950s and 1960s fine and costume jewelry, and the Special Collectibles section which covers Native American jewelry, as well as the product of two regions which are closely tied to the U.S.: Mexican and Scandinavian jewelry. New to this edition are separate divisions for each of the Scandinavian countries, and a chronological division of designer/manufacturer signed costume jewelry. A new category, Beaux-arts and Neo-Renaissance, which includes both American and European jewelry, has been added to Part II, Turn of the Century.

Jewelry is the only art form where the "intrinsic" value of the materials from which it is made can have greater value than the work itself. Many beautiful and historically significant pieces have been destroyed for their stones and metal, particularly after a certain style becomes "outdated" or "old-fashioned." This usually happens before there is retrospective appreciation for the style, before it becomes "collectible."

Stones and metal are paint and canvas. Rare and beautiful stones can be used to great effect to enhance a jewel. However, supply and demand, and the public's perceptions, can alter value. For example, aluminum was once a rare and valuable metal, and platinum was looked down upon as "unripe gold." While our culture has consistently placed a higher value on gold and precious gemstones (diamonds, rubies, sapphires, and emeralds), other factors, such as craftsmanship, design and designer, and provenance, as well as rarity and desirability, can outweigh intrinsic value. The following table of seven criteria (3 **C**s, 2 **D**s, 2 **S**s), with questions to ask when evaluating a piece of jewelry, can be a useful aid:

<u>C</u>raftsmanship	Is it well-made, with attention to details and finish?
<u>C</u>ondition	Are there any cracks, chips, dents, missing parts, metal corrosion, or other damage? Are all parts original? Has it been repaired? Is there evidence of lead solder on precious metal?
<u>C</u>olor	Especially important in costume jewelry, is/are the color(s) currently fashionable, popular? In gemstones, is the color desirable for its kind?
<u>D</u>esign	Can the style be attributed to the period in which it was made? Can it be attributed to a particular maker? Is the piece balanced and proportioned? Does it have "eye appeal (this is a subjective evaluation)? Is it *wearable*?
<u>D</u>emand	Is the piece highly sought-after, currently in vogue?
<u>S</u>carcity	Is this a rare item, or is it commonly avail able?
<u>S</u>ize	Is it a large or small piece? Is the size appropriate for the style? (Large size is usually more desirable, but style and the wearer's proportions should also be taken into consideration)

Note that age alone does not make a piece valuable. A badly made and designed 150-year-old piece is worth no more today than it was when it was first produced. If it is in poor condition, it is probably worth less! A loupe or magnifier is an essential tool for examining a piece of jewelry. Ten power (10x) is the standard magnification. In addition to detecting alterations and repairs, a loupe is necessary to read hallmarks and maker's marks, to evaluate condition, and to analyze materials (stones, metal, enamel, etc.) and construction. It is important to scrutinize a piece thoroughly, both front *and* back, in order to detect the clues that will tell you what you need to know before you buy.

A word of caution is in order when buying gemstone-set jewelry. The public has been conditioned to believe that the intrinsic value of all gemstones is high and that jewelry set with them is expensive. To some extent this is true, but the range of gemstone values is wide and variables are many. Unless you have some gemological knowledge and have studied the complexities of the market carefully, you can easily get burned. Your best defense against rip-off is your *own* knowledge, but when in doubt, consult a gemologist (G.G., F.G.A., or C.G.A.) for gemstone identification, a qualified gemstone appraiser (who should also be, or be associated with, a gemologist) for values. Another caveat: Appraisers are not licensed or regulated by law, but some of them are credentialed by recognized national appraisal organizations. Make sure the appraiser you choose has had the proper training and experience.

In order to truly understand old jewelry, you must see and handle a *lot* of it. Readers are encouraged to avail themselves of every opportunity to do so, including attending shows, flea markets, museum exhibitions, and seminars, conferences, and classes on antique jewelry. A unique opportunity to enhance one's knowledge with lectures and hands-on experience takes place annually in July, formerly at the University of Maine, now held at Hofstra University Conference Center in Hempstead Long Island, NY: the Antique & Period Jewelry and Gemstones Course, directed by Joyce Jonas. Inquiries about the course may be sent to Joyce Jonas & Associates, Inc., 215 East 80th St., Suite 5K, New York, NY 10021-0539, (212) 535-2479, Fax: (212) 988-0721 , e-mail: JWLRYCAMP@aol.com, Web site: www.jewelrycamp.org.

The Gemological Institute of America (www.gia.edu) and three national appraisal organizations—the American Society of Appraisers (www.appraisers.org), International Society of Appraisers (www.isa-appraisers.org), and the National Association of Jewelry Appraisers—respectively provide specialized instruction in gemology and gems and jewelry valuation theory and techniques. A correspondence course in jewelry appraisal, The Master Valuer Program, is also available (www.mastervaluer.com).

My own classes in antique, period, and vintage jewelry are held in southern California at Santiago Canyon College in Orange, California, and at other locations throughout the year. Information on these is available at the Center for Jewelry Studies Web site: www.center4jewelrystudies.org.

Another opportunity to see, handle, and closely examine antique and period jewelry is the auction preview. Christie's and Sotheby's hold "important" and "magnificent" jewelry sales at which historically and gemologically significant pieces are offered. If in-person inspection is not possible, the color catalogs for these sales, which include biographical and other pertinent information, are excellent reference resources. These and the other auction houses whose names, addresses, and Web sites appear on a following page, also offer a wide range of antique, period, and contemporary jewelry, and were the sources for much of the fine jewelry pictured and listed in this book. All of them hold previews of upcoming sales which are well worth attending. Their catalogs, with prices realized, provide up-to-date market information. They also post their sales on their Web sites, and archive prices realized from past sales. Because the Internet has made them much more accessible, British and Canadian auctions are included in this edition (**all prices realized are given in U.S. dollars**).

ORGANIZATION of the BOOK

Warman's Jewelry, 3rd edition, is divided into four main sections: Late Eighteenth and Nineteenth Century, Turn of the Century, Twentieth Century, and Special Collectibles. Within each section, the photographs are arranged by category in the manner most appropriate and conducive to locating a particular type of piece. Within each category, the photos are alphabetical by type of piece (bracelet, brooch/pin, etc.). A timeline precedes, and a glossary follows the main body of the book. The index cross-references by type of piece (e.g., all earrings), name of maker/designer (e.g., all pieces made by Eisenberg), material (e.g., all pieces made of jet), and motif (e.g., animals).

Timeline: One of the unique features of *Warman's Jewelry* is the Timeline. Its purpose is to aid in circa-dating and put jewelry in context with other relevant historical events, discoveries, and inventions. It also summarizes some of the information included in the text of each section. The dates can be used to set the earliest and/or latest possible circa date for a piece. For example, the lowering of karatages of gold to 15, 12, and 9 karat was made legal in Great Britain in 1854. Therefore, gold jewelry with the British designation "9 ct" would date to after 1854. In 1932, the British law was changed, eliminating 15 and 12 karat in favor of 14 karat gold, which gives us the latest date for a piece marked "15 ct" or "12 ct."

Construction methods, materials and findings, if unaltered, can also be helpful circa-dating clues. For example, commercially-made safety catches for brooches were introduced around the turn of the century (one version was patented in 1901, another in 1911). An original safety catch on a brooch, then, is a telltale sign of twentieth century manufacture. Care must be taken, however, to ascertain that the finding is in fact original. Alterations on old pieces are common.

Patents are another useful circa-dating tool, when used as a clue to a piece's age in addition to other factors, such as style and manufacturer's dates of operation. In the captions, if a patent number is found on the back of a piece, it is given along with the corresponding year in which the patent was issued. (In the case of design patents, the name of the designer to whom the patent was issued is also given, where known.) Prior to the 1930s, the patent's actual date of issue is more often stamped on a piece, rather than the number. This is not necessarily the year in which the piece was made, as patents are valid for 17 years (design patents for a maximum of 14; some terms were shorter). The piece could have been made later, but it certainly could not have been made *earlier* than the year the patent was issued. Patent searches can now be done online at the U.S. Patent and Trademark Office's Web site (www.uspto.gov/patft/#notices).

Clothing styles have often dictated or at least influenced types and styles of jewelry, so it is helpful to have some knowledge of fashion history when researching and dating a piece. Significant specific events related to fashion are listed in the Timeline, but space did not permit the inclusion of every stylistic change in clothing and jewelry fashion. Some of this information can be found in the text of each section, and, for further information, books on fashion history are included in the references.

The dates given in the Timeline are as accurate as could be ascertained. I attempted to confirm each date in two or more sources, using original sources or notations whenever possible. Research is never complete, however. New information continues to be discovered which sometimes contradicts previously published "facts." Indeed, the Timeline in this edition of *Warman's Jewelry* includes some newly researched dates for discoveries and inventions, which were not known when the second edition was published.

Different dates are often given in various sources for the same event. Sometimes there is a span of a number of years between date of first invention and dates of patenting, perfecting, publishing results, commercialization, and common use. One source may cite, for example, the date a new manufacturing process was *patented*, but another may give the date it was *invented*, perhaps five years earlier. Or it may have taken its inventor five years to perfect, and may not have been available to the public for another five. The difficult task for historians is to decide which date is the most accurate, significant and helpful. We don't always agree. Analysis of history is often a matter of subjective interpretation.

History: Jewelry does not exist in a vacuum. Fashion and history have a cause-and-effect relationship to jewelry designs. Events, discoveries, inventions, social trends, and fads play important roles in jewelry history. Each category of this book is prefaced by an encapsulated history, so that readers will understand why a particular piece of jewelry was made and worn during a given period. Design elements that identify a particular style or period, and well-known designers and manufacturers are also included.

It is not always possible to pinpoint the age of a piece exactly. A dated publication can help to circa-date a piece, but relying on only one piece of evidence can also be misleading. Some "models" (manufacturers' name for designs) continued to be made for many years, even decades, as long as they were popular and sold well. There is a "bell curve" to every style or trend—an ascension, peak, and tapering off in popularity. Styles evolve, coexist, and overlap. This is better understood when history is viewed as a continuum of *simultaneous* events, rather than as a linear succession of events.

Improved methods of communication have hastened the rate of influence and change over the past two centuries; today, trends come and go at breakneck speed. Historians used to record changes in fashion by the decade; now changes occur annually.

References: For further information, the references that were consulted for the text for each section and category are listed in the appendix. Additional sources are available through the Center for Jewelry Studies Web site, www.center4jewelrystudies.org. This appendix also includes periodicals, collectors' clubs, Internet sites, and museums. Because of growing interest and the constant need for updated information, new titles and new editions appear every year. At press time, the following books of a general nature were in print. Some of these and some out-of-print and specialized publications may only be available through book dealers who specialize in books on antiques and/or gems and jewelry. Many of them publish catalogs of their inventory, run ads in antiques trade papers, or sell at shows. Nowadays, the Internet has made both in-print and out-of-print books much easier to obtain. Many booksellers list their inventory on one or more book sites that specialize in used, out-of-print, and hard-to-find books. One good search engine that compiles the listings of several sites is www.bookfinder.com.

Listed are author, title, most recent edition, publisher (if self-published, listed as "published by author"), and date of publication.

Howard L. Bell, Jr., *Cuff Jewelry*, published by author, 1994.

C. Jeanenne Bell, *Answers to Questions About Old Jewelry, 1840-1950*, 5th edition, Krause Publications, 1999.

David Bennett & Daniela Mascetti, *Understanding Jewellery*, 2nd ed., Antique Collectors' Club, 2000.

Roseann Ettinger, *Popular Jewelry, 1840-1940*, Schiffer Publishing, revised ed., 2002.

Richard E. Gilbert and James H. Wolf, *Complete Price Guide to Antique Jewelry*, Ashland Publications, 1998.

Stephen Giles, consultant, *Miller's Antiques Checklist: Jewellery*, Reed International Books Ltd., 1997.

Duncan James, *Antique Jewellery: Its Manufacture, Materials, and Design*, Shire Publications Ltd., Buckinghamshire, UK, 1999.

Jean-Noel Liaut and Bertrand Pizzin, *Cuff Links*, Assouline, 2002.

Karen Lorene, *Buying Antique Jewelry: Skipping the Mistakes*, Lorene Publications, 1987.

Daniela Mascetti and Amanda Triossi, *Earrings: From Antiquity to the Present*, Thames & Hudson, 1999.

Mascetti and Triossi, *The Necklace From Antiquity to the Present*, Harry N. Abrams, 1997.

Donald S. McNeil, *Jewelers' Dictionary*, 3rd ed., Chilton Book Co., 1979.

Anna M. Miller, *Buyer's Guide to Affordable Antique Jewelry*, Carol Publishing Corp., 1993.

Harold Newman, *An Illustrated Dictionary of Jewelry*, Thames & Husdson, 1987.

Clare Phillips, *Jewels and Jewelry*, Watson-Guptill Publications, 2000.

Dorothy T. Rainwater, *American Jewelry Manufacturers*, Schiffer Publishing, 1988.

Sheryl Gross Shatz, *What's It Made Of? A Jewelry Materials Identification Guide*, 3rd ed., published by author, 1996.

Oppi Untracht, *Jewelry Concepts and Technology*, Doubleday, 1985.

Sarah Hue-Williams, *Christie's Guide to Jewellery*, Assouline, 2001

Numerous books on diamonds and colored gemstones have been published, some of them consumer-oriented and non-technical. The catalog of the G.I.A. (Gemological Institute of America) Bookstore, 5355 Armada Drive, Suite

300, Carlsbad, CA 92008-4698, (800) 421-8161, lists the ones in print, which can be ordered by mail. Its online catalog is on its Web site: www.gia.edu/geminstrument/index.cfm (click on Product Catalog, then Books).

The video cassette is another medium for disseminating information in the antiques field. My video, "Hidden Treasures, A Collector's Guide to Antique and Vintage Jewelry of the 19th and 20th Centuries," produced by Venture Entertainment Group, is the first of its kind on the subject.

Periodicals: Specialized periodicals are listed in the appropriate categories. Some that cover a broad range of jewelry topics are:

Gems & Gemology, the quarterly journal of the Gemological Institute of America (see address above). Occasionally includes articles on period jewelry.

Jewelers' Circular-Keystone, 1018 W. Ninth Ave., King of Prussia, PA 19406. Internet Web site: www.jckgroup.com. Monthly trade publication of the retail jewelry industry that includes articles on antique and period jewelry and watches in most issues.

Professional Jeweler, Bond Communications, 1500 Walnut St., Suite 1200, Philadelphia, PA 19102; (215) 567-0727. Internet Web site: www.professionaljeweler.com Published monthly, occasional articles on period jewelry.

Maine Antique Digest, P.O. Box 1429, Waldoboro, ME 04572, (207) 832-4888. Internet Web site: www.maineantiquedigest.com. Peter Theriault, FGA, GG, writes a monthly column on antique and collectible jewelry. He welcomes questions and press releases on related topics, addressed to him at 58 Bayview St., Camden, ME 04843; phone/fax: (207) 236-3933, e-mail: gemlab@midcoast.com.

Jewelry Connoisseur, 3930 Howard Hughes Parkway, Suite 230, Las Vegas, NV 89195-9199; (877) 987-3400; Web site URL for subscribing online: www.jewelrymag.com/subscriptions.html. A Rapaport quarterly publication, with articles on antique and period jewelry in every issue.

Collectors' Clubs: Perhaps as an indication of the newness, and/or the diversity of the field, there is no national organization with local chapters of jewelry collectors in general. However, a number of specialized jewelry-related clubs and societies exist in the United States. Most of these can be found listed under the appropriate category in the References appendix. A few for which there is no category, or which span several categories, are listed here:

American Hatpin Society, c/o Virginia Woodbury, 20 Montecillo Drive, Rolling Hills Estates, CA 90274 (further information about the club can be found at www.collectoronline.com/AHS/; related Hatpin Collectors Web site: http://members.aol.com/frankie854/index.html).

The American Society of Jewelry Historians (semiannual newsletter), #103, 1333A North Ave., New Rochelle, NY 10804-2120, (914) 235-0983, e-mail: info@jewelryhistorians.com; Web site: www.jewelryhistorians.com. One regional chapter has been formed in New England; others may follow.

Bead Societies are located in a number of U.S. cities. A comprehensive listing can be found in Peter Francis, Jr.'s *Beads of the World*, Schiffer Publishing, 1994.

National Antique Comb Collectors Club International (and newsletter), Belva Green, editor, 90 S Highland Ave. #1204, Tarpon Springs, FL 34689, Web site: www.geocities.com/heartland/pointe/5350.

National Cuff Link Society (newsletter "The Link"), Eugene Klompus, president, P.O. Box 346, Prospect Heights, IL 60070, (708) 632-0561, Web site: www.cufflink.com.

Internet: The growing number of jewelry-related Web sites on the Internet is mind-boggling. Sites containing information pertinent to a particular category are listed under that category's References. Many other Web sites offer a broad range of information, including links to other sites (which can lead to an understanding of why it's called "the World Wide Web!"). My own Web site, www.center4jewelrystudies.org, has a Reference page of relevant links to many of these educational and informational sites.

Museums: As of yet, the U.S. does not have a museum with an extensive *permanent* collection of jewelry on display, comparable to museums in Great Britain and Europe. But with the recent creation of a yet-to-be-named museum at the Gemological Institute of America in Carlsbad, California (under the able direction of Elise B. Misiorowski), there is great hope. Specialized collections can be found listed in the References appendix under the appropriate category (museums' Web sites are listed where available). A few other museums with unique collections are:

The Bead Museum, Prescott, Arizona; Miller Comb Museum, Homer, Alaska; Providence Jewelry Museum, Providence, Rhode Island (old jewelry-making equipment and other items related to the area's costume jewelry manufacturing industry).

Reproductions: Fakes, reproductions, and stylistic copycats are rampant in jewelry. Whenever a particular style or type of jewelry becomes popular, knockoffs proliferate. This has long been a common practice. Reproductions become especially problematic when they enter the secondary market after a number of years, with signs of wear making them difficult to distinguish from an original of the period. Notations on reproductions are included in the categories when applicable.

Marks: Categories with numerous makers' marks appear separately in an appendix, as do marks that span more than one category. A new feature of the third edition is the inclusion of the mark as struck on a piece within its photograph, wherever possible. Some of these "thumbnails" are also included in the marks appendices.

Attribution of unsigned pieces must rely on provenance, or documentation such as company catalogs or archives, sales receipts or owners' records, and fashion magazines or trade publications which picture the item in question along with its maker's name. Most old jewelry is unmarked and unattributable, and must be evaluated solely on its own merits. Ideally, the same should be true of "signed" pieces, but the fact is that an "important" name on a piece scores points with collectors and adds value. Nevertheless, the name itself should not be the only or even the first thing taken into consideration when evaluating a signed piece. Marks and attributions are "the frosting on the cake," and are therefore listed at the end of the captions descriptions.

Photos and captions: The variety of jewelry is so great that it would be impossible to include examples of every kind. Unlike some other collectibles, with jewelry, there is less likelihood of finding pieces identical to those shown. In certain categories, such as mass-produced costume jewelry of the mid-20th century, multiples of the same design can still be found. What you will find more often are comparable pieces—from the same period, of the same style, made from the same materials. The prices listed are for specific pieces of specific quality and condition. It is important to make sure you are comparing "apples to apples." Although they may be beyond most budgets, "high-end" pieces are pictured as a basis for comparison, and as sought-after examples. They set standards by which other pieces of their genre can be measured. However, it must be noted that the pieces in this book are not all necessarily the very best examples of their kind; rather, they are representative of what is on the market today.

Although a watch can often be a jewel as well as a timepiece, the factors that determine value and collectibles are too complex and specialized to fit within the scope of this book. Watch collectors already have a number of fine references at their disposal. However, watch accessories, such as chains, fobs, and pins, are included, as well as a few watches that function primarily as jewelry rather than as timepieces. Of necessity, some other categories were also omitted: most "generic" (undatable or otherwise unidentifiable) jewelry, and ethnic jewelry (indigenous Middle Eastern, Oriental, African, etc.). Several other jewelry books include pieces from the '80s and the '90s. While it is important to stay abreast of recent developments, it is often difficult to determine what tomorrow's collectibles will be from today's vantage point. Thirty years is considered a sufficient span of time for a clear perspective on what has "staying power" for jewelry collectors. Now that the '60s are a firmly established era, collectors and historians are beginning to look at the '70s. The first edition of *Warman's Jewelry* covered the 20th century up to circa 1965. The second edition extended its coverage to circa 1975. The third edition includes some pieces from the late '70s and early '80s.

Every effort was made to be consistent in the captions descriptions. However, it was not always possible to examine the jewelry firsthand, and information provided in catalogs was not always complete (e.g., weights, numbers, and cuts of stones). The most detailed information on pieces sold at auction came from a semiannual report, *Auction Market Resource for Gems and Jewelry,* a comprehensive compilation of recent auction results from a dozen different houses, published by Gail Levine, GG. Auction house condition reports also provided additional information.

Due to space constraints, the photographs are not all to scale, but measurements are included in the captions to give readers an idea of actual size. Measurements are in inches, rounded to the nearest eighth. Width or diameter is at the widest point; total length includes any findings. Inside diameter is given for cuff and bangle bracelets. Rings are measured shoulder to shoulder and top to bottom. Necklace and flexible bracelet lengths are clasp to clasp. Width of brooches, clips, earrings, and pendants is side to side; length is top to bottom as the piece is worn. Stone measurements are usually given in millimeters, weights in carats. Total weight for the entire piece, metal, and gemstones, if any, is in pennyweights.

Unless otherwise credited, photographs were taken by the author. The captions for the photographed pieces in *Warman's Jewelry* are as detailed as possible. The reasoning behind this is threefold. First, the reader will more clearly understand the terms used to describe a piece when they can be correlated to the photo. Second, because we often look but don't see, the captions will call the reader's attention to details that might otherwise be missed, as well as to details not visible in the photos, such as findings, marks, and cuts of stones. Finally, these descriptions are given in hopes that they will help to further a common usage of terms whenever we attempt to describe an unseen piece. Terms that may be unfamiliar to the reader are further explained in the glossary.

Glossary: Jewelry has its own lexicon. Many jewelry terms are derived from the French, which became the language of choice when jewelry-making terminology was adopted internationally in the eighteenth century. This glossary lists terms used in *Warman's Jewelry*, and is necessarily incomplete. The general references list jewelry dictionaries that the reader can use as supplements. Some jewelry-related Web sites have glossaries as well. Often there is more than one word that can be used to describe a piece of jewelry. For example, the word used to describe a piece of jewelry fastened to clothing by means of a pinning device is either *brooch* or *pin*. Some say that size determines which word is used, but no one has determined at exactly what size a brooch becomes a pin. Others say that *brooch* is the only correct term and *pin* is the word for the mechanism itself, the hinge or joint, pinstem, and catch. In this book, whenever more than one word can be used for a jewelry form, both are included in the listings, e.g., "Brooch/Pin."

PRICE NOTES: BUYER'S GUIDE, NOT SELLER'S GUIDE

Most of the pieces pictured in this book were for sale, or sold at auction, within the past two years. Those that are from private collections were usually acquired at antiques shows, shops and malls, auctions, flea markets, and yard sales over the past several years, but are valued at current levels. Prices listed are *average retail,* the median of prices noted in various parts of the U.S. (if and when comparables could be found), except for auction results, designated by **[A]**, which are actual, rounded to the nearest dollar, including the 10 percent to 17.5 percent buyer's premium charged by the auction house. Regional retail prices may be higher or lower than average retail, and often depend upon the individual dealer. Auction prices are subject to a number of variables, and are not considered retail or wholesale. They represent the price that one person—a dealer *or* private party—paid at the time and place the piece was offered for sale.

In most cases, the prices in this book are those a buyer should expect to pay for a piece in excellent to very good condition. Pieces with flaws that affect value are so noted in the descriptions. Because prices are *average* retail (except for auction results), some collectors will consider the price on a particular piece a bargain and others will say it is exorbitant. Everyone likes to think they are getting "a deal" when they buy. The tendency for most jewelry price guides is to overstate values, which has conditioned the collecting public to expect to see higher prices listed than what was actually paid for a piece. This is not the case with *Warman's Jewelry*. "Average retail" means just that: there will be times and places when *higher* prices will be asked and paid, as well as lower than what is listed here.

The marketplace where a piece is sold affects price as much as other criteria, i.e., design, craftsmanship, condition, demand and scarcity, and intrinsic value of metals and stones in fine jewelry. Pricing data was gathered from all over the country, and from Canada and the UK, but differences were often a result of the *type* of marketplace (e.g., an urban retail shop versus a rural flea market), rather than its region or locale. Prices were compiled from a number of sources, including auction houses, appraisers, dealers, jewelry store owners, collectors, and that newest and most pervasive of marketplaces, the Internet.

If you see one of your possessions in this book (or a similar one) and wish to sell it—as a private party to a dealer, or as a dealer to a dealer—you should expect to receive approximately 35 percent to 40 percent of the value listed. If it cannot be resold quickly, expect even less; and it is possible that a dealer may not wish to purchase it at all. Collectors are very specialized; dealers work for years to assemble a list of collectors who will pay top dollar for an item. Try to be as objective about your item as possible. If it is an heirloom, its sentimental value may be greater than any dollar amount you could get for it.

BOARD of ADVISERS

One person cannot be an expert in every type of jewelry. Many "specialists"—dealers, collectors, gemologists, appraisers, auction house directors, museum curators, researchers, and historians—were consulted for the sections relating to their specialty. Some provided expertise in more than one field, or general gemological and/or historical information, as well as photos or items for photos. Their names appear in the captions and in their respective categories in the References appendix. Mailing and/or e-mail addresses and/or phone numbers are listed in the front of this book. If you wish to buy or sell an item in their field or fields of expertise, send a note, with a photograph or photocopy, description, and self-addressed stamped envelope (call or e-mail if no address given). If time and interest permit, they will respond.

OTHER CONTRIBUTORS

Other dealers and collectors who provided jewelry for the photos are listed here. Correspondence to any of them may be addressed in care of the author (see below).

Dealers: Kymm Arbiso and Barbara Warren (Ocean Eyz Antique Jewelry), D. Brett Benson, Peggy Dunner, Chris Enebo, Andrea Fatell, Bill Faust (Faust Gallery), Richard Fauteux, Betty Kalousek and Carrie Leeper (Generations), Gloria Karp, Sam Kusler, Dawn Lowe (Xcentricities), Lisa Mercer (Déja Vu Antiques), Mehrdad Moghadam (Jewelry Forever), Linda Morgan (Linda Morgan Antiques), Gilly Phipps (Phipps Antiques), Diane Richardson (The Gold Hatpin), Nancy Shadforth, Ellen & Ned Solway (Deja Voodoo), Mike Spent (Postmodern), Julia Stayden, Denese Strand, Mary Williamson, and Sharen and Nicholas Wood.

Several of my dealer-contributors, including some advisers, are members of the Internet e-mail listserv Jewelcollect and most of them also have Web sites: Martha Exline (Metique), Beegee McBride (South Texas Trading Co.), and Elizabeth Nyland. Links to their sites and many others can be found on the Jewelcollect Web site: www.jewelcollect.org.

Collectors: Gudrun Baxter, Dorothy Blandi, Victoria Palzkill Bonanno, Jon Bonnell, Jill Crawford, Marisela Doria, Gail Eastman, Gail-Marie Enos, Caren Fine, Scott Grodsky, Alice and Charlotte Healy, Ellen and Mal Hoffs, Sue James, Lisa Johnson, Bob and Diane Kusek, Kim Lord, Watters O. Martin, Jr., Tela Palmer, Kathleen Peterson, Catherine Ratcliffe, Gene Ratcliffe, Marne Ryan, Elaine Sarnoff, Maryann Schneider, Tamara Torino, Teri Vaughn, Vickie Vega, Diane White, Sandra Willard, and Sue Ellen Yoho.

COMMENTS INVITED

Readers are encouraged to send their comments and suggestions to Christie Romero, Center for Jewelry Studies, P.O. Box 424, Anaheim, CA 92815-0424. E-mail: CR4jewelry@aol.com; Web site: www.center4jewelrystudies.org.

State of the Market

Crystal balls are in short supply, but a combination of firsthand observations and opinions gathered from a cross-section of advisers has yielded a "snapshot" of market conditions in mid-2002. These are subject to change over a relatively short period of time.

The wavering state of the economy may have much to do with the state of the antique and period jewelry market. On some levels, a pervasive sense of uncertainty seems to have prompted cautiousness, but the "upper echelons" continue to flourish. In a departure from the "trendy" behavior of the past few years, the sharp dichotomy between what sells and what doesn't has less to do with "what's hot and what's not" than it does with quality, rarity, and in most cases, name recognition. No one style or period dominates the market, but "important" names still carry clout.

Another surprising dichotomy exists between types of market*places*. Antiques show dealers are reporting a drop in traffic and sales, whereas auction houses are for the most part doing well at their live auctions. Online auctions are a mixed bag, as are other Internet sales. The online auction behemoth eBay has seen a slump in sales as the number of offerings grows to overwhelming proportions, with the exception of the rare and desirable. But competitive bidding for these items still stops short of record highs. It is definitely a buyer's market in cyberspace these days. However, buyers must have the patience to sift through a lot of "chaff" to find choice "wheat kernels" worth bidding on or purchasing.

Show dealers and shopkeepers are finding that they must actively cultivate their customer base in order to stay afloat. Those who are successful make sure their customers know where they will be selling and/or what they have for sale that might be of interest. Collectors continue to buy from trusted dealers who carry good examples of what they collect.

Marketplace principles have not changed, but rather have become more exaggerated. Whereas an average middle-market period piece may once have sold if the price was right, in many cases now it simply does not sell. The "gotta have it" syndrome is no longer fueled by strong trends, and impulse buys are no longer as prevalent, so a piece must be special indeed to generate the burning desire to own it. Competition for desirable pieces still drives the auction market, and is perhaps why sales are up at auctions and down at shows. "The Name Game" is going stronger than ever, with the "magic" names of Tiffany, Cartier, and Lalique dominating fine jewelry. In costume jewelry, the big names alone are not enough, but "top of the line" and "rare" pieces by Chanel, Schiaparelli, Coro, Trifari, Miriam Haskell, Boucher, and a few others can still start collectors' hearts racing. Mexican silver is another name-driven collectible, with William Spratling leading the pack. The opening of a major exhibition in October 2002 should have an upward effect on prices for pieces by Spratling and other well-known names, but those by the lesser-knowns and unknowns may not be as fortunate.

Where names are not commonly a factor, which is often the case with older antique jewelry, color and fashion come into play, and trends still have some effect. Turquoise and coral are back in style, so pieces set with these materials are cropping up more often, and selling well. But platinum and diamonds are also holding their own, and Edwardian and Art Deco pieces are still in demand at auction. In costume jewelry, Bakelite is now a well-established collecting category in which color plays an important part. However, demand and rarity are equally overriding principles here as well.

In theory, the Internet should have been the great leveler, creating a certain amount of homogeneity in what is being sought, bought, and sold. However, in spite of the Internet and eBay, and a globalized marketplace, regionalism is still alive and well. Certain categories of jewelry still sell more readily, and sometimes for higher prices, in some markets than in others.

One thing is clear: The best defense against the vagaries of the marketplace for dealers, collectors, and private inheritors trying to sell or buy at the best price, and auctioneers or appraisers needing to get a handle on the market's ups and downs, is to arm oneself with information. A number of ways to do that are available today. This book is one of them.

BOARD OF ADVISERS

Lynne Arkin, G.G.
Apriori Antiques
3484 Sacramento St.
San Francisco, CA 94118
(415) 440-3000
e-mail: lynarkin@aol.com
Marsh & Co.

Aram Berberian
ARK Antiques
P.O. Box 3133
New Haven, CT 06515
(203) 498-8572
e-mail:
ark_antiques@yahoo.com
American Arts & Crafts

Roberto Brunialti and Carla Ginelli Brunialti
e-mail:
r.brunialtigriffani@unindustria.co.it
20th century costume (c. 1935-50)

Isabelle "Liz" Bryman
Liz Collectible Jewelry
P.O. Box 1368
Levittown, PA 19058
e-mail:
lizbryman@lizjewel.com
Web site: www.lizjewel.com
20th Century costume

Matthew Burkholz
Route 66 Antiques
P.O. Box 198
Chatham, NY 12037
(518) 392-9177
e-mail: bigmlb@aol.com
Bakelite

Steven Cabella
The Modern i Gallery
500 Red Hill Ave.
San Anselmo, CA 94904
(415) 456-3960
e-mail: moderni@slip.net
Mid-Century American Modernist

Jane Civins, Curator
Providence Jewelry Museum
P.O. Box 9650
Providence, RI 02940
(401) 785-8762
e-mail:
jewelsandtools18@hotmail.com

Jane Clarke
Morning Glory Antiques
12815 Central NE
Albuquerque, NM 87123
(505) 296-2300
e-mail:
jane@morninggloryantiques.com
Web site:
www.morninggloryantiques.com
20th Century costume

Margot Conté, Collector
e-mail: MargotC@aol.com
Micromosaics

Jill Crawford, Collector
(310) 457-8076
e-mail: lambie55@aol.com
Mexican silver, mid-century modern

Neil and Natasha Cuddy
N&N Vintage Costume Jewelry
Toronto ONT, Canada
e-mail: sales@trifari.com
Web site: www.trifari.com
20th Century costume

Lenore Dailey
The Raven's Nest
100 S. Sunrise Way, #482
Palm Springs, CA 92262
(760) 413-9705
e-mail:
RAVENANTQ@aol.com
18th century and Victorian mourning

Ulysses G. Dietz
The Newark Museum
P.O. Box 540
Newark, NJ 07101
(973) 596-6661
e-mail:
UDietz@newarkmuseum.org

Samuel C. Gassman, G.G.
E. Foxe Harrell
33 Bank St. #22
New York, NY 10014
(212) 675-9968
e-mail: zfox6@hotmail.com
18th-19th century

Gail Gerretsen
c/o Blackwelders Antiques & Fine Art
25 South El Molino
Pasadena, CA 91101
(626) 584-0723
(323) 257-7009 (messages)
Arts & Crafts

Elayne Glotzer
Double Vision
1225 Abbott Kinney Blvd.
Venice, CA 90291
(310) 314-2679
e-mail: Dv2ak@aol.com
20th Century costume

Belva Green
Antique Comb Collectors Club International
90 S Highland Ave. #1204
Tarpon Springs, FL 34689
(727) 942-7354
e-mail:
belva.green@verizon.net
Hair combs

Didier Haspeslagh
Didier Antiques
58-60 Kensington Church St.
London W8 4DB, UK
e-mail:
didier.antiques@virgin.net
British and European Arts & Crafts and Art Nouveau

Bruce Healy, Collector
(303) 494-9222
Scandinavian

Laura Hiserote
Hiserote Micromosaics
P.O. Box 87872
Vancouver, WA 98687
(360) 256-3767
e-mail:
laura@micromosaics.com
Web site:
www.micromosaics.com

Mary Lee Hu
University of Washington
Art-Box 353440
Seattle, WA 98195
e-mail:
mhu@u.washington.edu
Metalworking techniques

Dorothy Kamm
P.O. Box 7460
Port St. Lucie, FL 34985
e-mail:
dorothy.kamm@usa.net
Painted porcelain

Patrick Kapty
Mad Jewelry
e-mail:
CK4ARTsAKE@aol.com
Web site:
www.madjewelry.com
20th century modern American, Mexican, Scandinavian, plastics

Ellie Laubner
(610) 432-3828
e-mail:
ellielaubner@yahoo.com
Vintage fashions

Keith Lauer
National Plastics Center and Museum
210 Lancaster St.
Leominster, MA 01453
(978) 537-9529
Web site:
http://npcm.plastics.com

Gail Brett Levine, G.G., I.S.A.
Publisher, *Auction Market Resource*
P.O. Box 7683
Rego Park, NY 11374-7683
(718) 897-7305
e-mail:
76766.614@compuserve.com
Web site:
www.AuctionMarketResource.com

Karen Lorene
Facèré Jewelry Art
City Center, 1420 Fifth Ave.
Seattle, WA 98101
(206) 624-6768
e-mail: FacereArt@aol.com
Web site:
www.facerejewelryart.com

Yvonne Markowitz
Museum of Fine Arts
Egyptian Department
465 Huntington Avenue
Boston, MA 02115
(617) 369-3348
e-mail: YMarkowitz@mfa.org

Daniela Mascetti, F.G.A.
Sotheby's
34-35 New Bond Street
London W1A 2AA, UK
e-mail:
daniela.mascetti@sothebys.com

Al Munir Meghji, Collector
(604) 251-5183
e-mail:
pioneermodern@shaw.ca
Mid-20th century modern

Anna Miller, G.G.
Director, Master Valuer Program
17314 Emerald Isle Drive
Houston, TX 77095
(281) 485 1606
e-mail:
mastervaluer@netscape.net
Web site:
www.mastervaluer.com
Cameos

Shari Watson Miller
4825 E. Earl Dr.
Phoenix, AZ 85018
(602) 952-1467
e-mail: DsrtTrader@aol.com
Mid-Century American and Native American

Amy Milner
Cini Designs
348 South Cedros Ave.
Solana Beach, CA 92075
(858) 792-0754
e-mail: AMCini58@aol.com
Web site:
www.cinijewelry.com

Elise B. Misiorowski, Museum Director
Gemological Institute of America
5345 Armada Drive
Carlsbad, CA 92008
(760) 603-4073
e-mail: emisioro@gia.edu

Penny C. Morrill
e-mail: morrillpc@yahoo.com
Mexican silver

Ginger Moro
P.O. Box 64376
West Los Angeles, CA 90064
e-mail:
modmoro@earthlink.net
European costume, Scandinavian

Terrance O'Halloran, G.G., J.M.A.
Werkstätte
P.O. Box 5344
San Pedro, CA 90733
e-mail: TWOH@aol.com
Arts & Crafts, Art Nouveau

Susan Oakes Peabody and John Peabody
Oakes Studios
P.O. Box 69 Route 117
Franconia, NH 03580
(603) 823-5994
American Arts & Crafts (Oakes)

B. Lennart Persson and Svein G. Josefsen
Effie-graa.com
e-mail: post@effie-graa.com
Web site: http://effie-graa.com
Scandinavian

Sigi Pineda
Reforma #52
Taxco, Gro. CP40230, Mexico
52 (762) 2-15-91
Mexican silver

Charles Pinkham, Dealer
(909) 620-5805 (by appointment)
e-mail:
pinkham950@earthlink.net
20th Century costume and silver

Benjamin Randolph
The Eden Sterling Co.
7672 Montgomery Rd. #244
Cincinnati, OH 45236
(800) 385-3336
e-mail: info@edensterling.com
Web site:
www.SilverCollecting.com
Early 20th century American silver

Fred Rezazadeh
e-mail: FredReza@aol.com
Scandinavian

Julie P. Robinson, Historian and Restorer
P.O. Box 117
Upper Jay, NY 12987
(518) 946-7753
e-mail:
celuloid@frontiernet.net
Plastics

Marbeth Schon
M. Schon Antiques
110 South Second St.
Bay St Louis, MS 39520
(228) 467-9890
e-mail: Marbeth1@aol.com
Web site: www.mschon.com
20th century modern silver

Patsy Sanders Seal, Collector-Dealer
Treasures from Yesterday
10 Rosewood Place
Joshua, Texas 76058
(817)295-4569
e-mail: PATSTFY@aol.com
20th Century costume

Sheryl Gross Shatz, C.G., SCC, Historian
e-mail: SGShatz@aol.com

Peter Shemonsky, G.G., I.S.A.
Butterfields
220 San Bruno Ave.
San Francisco, CA 94103
(415) 503-3306
e-mail:
pshemonsky@butterfields.com

Elle Shushan
Augustus Decorative Arts, Ltd.
Box 700
New York, NY 10101
(212) 333-7888
e-mail:
elle@portrait-miniatures.com
Web site:
www.portrait-miniatures.com
Miniatures

Bobye Syverson
The Enchanted Castle
2627 Chamberlain Ave.
Madison, WI 53705-3717
(608) 238-7993
e-mail: BOBYE@Prodigy.net
20th century costume (Eisenberg)

Lucille Tempesta, Publisher/Editor
Vintage Fashion & Costume Jewelry Newsletter
P.O. Box 265
Glen Oaks, NY 11004
Fax: (718) 939-7988
e-mail: VFCJ@aol,com

Amanda Triossi, M.A., F.G.A.
Vicolo del Cedro 36
Rome 00153, Italy
e-mail: amanda@triossi.com

Ramona Tung, Collector
e-mail: that_rat@yahoo.com
Early 20th century Arts & Crafts, Art Deco, Theodor Fahrner

Joanne Valentine
Almost Antiques
47-0420 Waihee St.
Kaneohe, HI 96744
e-mail:
valsplace@hawaii.rr.com
Ming's of Honolulu

Barry Weber
Edith Weber & Associates
994 Madison Ave.
New York, NY 10021
(212) 570-9668
e-mail:
barry@antique-jewelry.com
Web site:
www.antique-jewelry.com
Late 18th-19th century

Colin Williamson
Plastics Historical Society
1 Carlton House Terrace
London SW1Y 5DB England
e-mail: SmilePlas@aol.com
Web site:
www.plastiquarian.com
Plastics, Victorian compositions

Mike Woshner
2306 Spokane Ave.
Pittsburgh, PA 15210
e-mail:
mwoshner@bellatlantic.net
Vulcanite and other compositions

Janet Zapata
Decorative Arts Consultant
(973) 376-7608 (by appointment)
e-mail:
JanetZapata@comcast.net
American fine and silver, Tiffany

AUCTION HOUSES

Bonham's
Montpelier Street
Knightsbridge, London SW7 1HH
UK
Tel: 44 20 7393 3900
Fax: 44 20 7393 3905
www.bonhams.com/jewellery.shtm

Butterfields
Peter Shemonsky, Jewelry
220 San Bruno
San Francisco, CA 94103
(415) 503-3306
Fax: (415) 861-8951
www.butterfields.com/areas/jewelry.html

Butterfields
Dana Ehrman, Jewelry
7601 Sunset Blvd
Los Angeles, CA 90046
(323) 436-5406
Fax: (323) 850-5843

Christie's
Simon Teakle, Jewelry
20 Rockefeller Plaza
New York, NY 10020
(212) 636-2300
(212) 636-2399
www.christies.com/departments/overview.asp?DID=33

Christie's Los Angeles
Debbie Bloom, Jewelry
360 North Camden Dr.
Beverly Hills, CA 90210
(310) 385-2666
Fax: (310) 385-9292

William Doyle Galleries
Berj Zavian, Jewelry
Jan Glier Reeder, Couture (& Costume Jewelry)
175 East 87th St.
New York, NY 10128
(212) 427-2730
Fax: (212) 369-0892
www.doylenewyork.com

Joseph DuMouchelle Auctioneers
5 Kercheval
Grosse Ponte Farms MI 48236
(313) 884-4800
Fax: (313) 884-7662
www.dumouchellejewelers.com

Dupuis Jewellery Auctioneers
94 Cumberland St., Suite 908
Toronto, Ont Canada M5R 1A3
(416) 968-7500
(416) 968-7739
www.dupuisauctions.com

R. G. Munn Auction
Native American & Western Art
P.O. Box 705
Cloudcroft, NM 88317
(505) 687-3676
Fax: (505) 687-3592
www.members.tripod.com/~RGMunn

Skinner, Inc.
Gloria Lieberman, Jewelry
The Heritage on the Garden
63 Park Plaza
Boston, MA 02116
(617) 350-5400
Fax: (617) 350-5429
www.skinnerinc.com

Sotheby's London
Daniela Mascetti, Jewelry
34-35 New Bond St.
London W1A 2AA
UK
Tel: 44 20 7293 5308
Fax: 44 20 7293 5964
www.sothebys.com

Sotheby's New York
Carol Elkins, Jewelry
1334 York Ave. (at 72nd St.)
New York, NY 10021
(212) 606-7000
Fax: (212) 606-7107

Sotheby's Beverly Hills
Lisa Hubbard, Jewelry
9665 Wilshire Blvd
Beverly Hills, CA 90210
(310) 274-7863
Fax: (310) 274-0899

Sotheby's Chicago
Eve Reppen Rogers, Jewelry
215 West Ohio St.
Chicago, IL 60610
(312) 670-0010
Fax: (312) 670-4248

Weschler's
John S. Weschler, Jewelry
909 E. St. NW
Washington, DC 20004
(202) 628-1281
Fax: (202) 628-2366
www.weschlers.com

Please note: Beverly Hills Auctioneers is no longer in business.

ABBREVIATIONS

Am	American
appl	applied
approx	approximately
bc	brilliant cut
bg	background
cab	cabochon
ct, cts	carat, carats (gem stones)
ct or c	karat gold (Eng)
C	century
c.	circa
circ	circular
constr	construction
curv	curvilinear
dam	damaged
dk	dark
diag	diagonal
dia	diameter
dwt	pennyweight
emb	embossed
Eng	English
engr	engraved
Fr	French
f.w.	freshwater (pearls)
geo	geometric
Ger	German
gf	gold-filled
gp	gold plated
grad	graduated
hmk	hallmark
hp	hand painted
h	height
imp	impressed
irid	iridescent
Ital	Italian
k	karat (gold)
lg	large
l	length
lt	light
mfr	manufacturer
mk	mark
mkd	marked
mm	millimeter(s)
mono	monogram
MOP	mother of pearl
No	number
#	numbered
oe	old European cut
om	old mine cut
orig	original
pr	pair
pat	patent
pc, pcs	piece, pieces
pl	plated
plat	platinum
ptd	painted
rect	rectangular
rev	reverse
r.s.	rhinestone(s)
rh pl	rhodium-plated
rc	rose cut
sgd	signed
sp	silver plated
st yg	silver-topped yellow gold
sm	small
sc	single cut
sq	square
ster	sterling silver
syn	synthetic
sz	size
tl	total length
tw	total weight
turq	turquoise
wg	white gold
wm	white metal
w	width
yg	yellow gold
ym	yellow metal

PHOTO POSITION ABBREVIATIONS

L - Left
C - Center
R - Right
T - Top
B - Bottom
TL - Top Left
TC - Top Center
TR - Top Right
CL - Center Left
CR - Center Right
BL - Bottom Left
BC - Bottom Center
BR - Bottom Right

More than one piece in a position is assigned a number, reading left to right (or top to bottom), e.g., BL-1 is the first piece on the left at the bottom, BL-2 is the second piece on the left at the bottom (to the right of the first piece).

TIMELINE

Late Georgian Period

Date	General History, Discoveries & Inventions
1760	George III becomes king of Great Britain
1774	Louis XVI becomes king of France
1775	American Revolution begins, Congress adopts the Declaration of Independence, 1776
1782	French scientist Antoine Laurent Lavoisier succeeds in melting platinum from its ore using pure oxygen
1789	French Revolution begins, ends 1799
	George Washington elected first President of the United States, dies 1799
1799-1815	Napoleonic Wars
1800	Thomas Jefferson elected President of the U.S.
	Alessandro Volta invents the first battery, the Volta Pile
	Metallurgist Wm. H. Wollaston, chemist Smithson Tennant begin collaboration, create commercial-grade platinum, discover platinum family of metals (palladium, rhodium, 1802; iridium, osmium, 1803)
1801	Robert Hare of Philadelphia invents oxyhydrogen ("gas") blowpipe
1804	Napoleon crowns himself Emperor of France
1811	George III declared insane; Regency period begins in Britain
1812-1815	War between U.S. and Great Britain
1813-1815	Prussian War of Liberation against Napoleon
1815	Kingdom of France (Bourbon dynasty) restored, Louis XVIII becomes king
1820	George III of Great Britain dies, George IV becomes king
	Platinum discovered in Russian Ural Mountains
1824	Charles X becomes king of France
1829-1837	Andrew Jackson is President of U.S.
1830	"India rubber" elastic first appears in women's clothing
	Godey's Lady's Book first published
	Louis-Philippe I becomes king of France
	George IV of Great Britain dies, William IV becomes king
1836	Edmund Davey discovers and identifies acetylene
	U.S. Patent Act passed. U.S. Patent Office issues Patent Number 1

Date	Jewelry & Gemstone History, Discoveries & Inventions
1730	Georges Frédéric Strass becomes famous for paste jewelry (c.)
1760	American goldsmith Paul Revere begins making jewelry (c.)
1764	Josiah Wedgwood introduces fine ceramic known as jasper ware in plaques with relief decoration resembling cameos, mounted in cut steel, manufactured by Matthew Boulton beginning in 1773
1769	Die-stamping machine patented by John Pickering, adapted for inexpensive jewelry in 1777
1780	Burmese jadeite imported into China
1785	eye miniatures popularized by Prince George of England
1786	Marc Étienne Janety, goldsmith to Louis XVI of France, crafts a sugar bowl out of platinum
1793	Seril Dodge of Providence, RI, advertises offering of jewelry items made to order, sells business to half-brother Nehemiah, 1796
1795	Diamonds begin to be set *à jour* (c.)
1799	Amethysts discovered in the Ural Mountains of Russia
1800	*À jour* settings for colored stones begin to appear (c.)
	Cannetille filigree developed by Parisian jewelers (c.)
1801	E. Hinsdale establishes first American factory for the manufacture of fine jewelry in Newark, NJ
1804	Royal Ironworks of Berlin opens, jewelry production begins 1806
1813-1815	Berlin iron jewelry made in Germany as patriotic gesture during War of Liberation: "*gold gab ich fur eisen*" [I gave gold for iron]
1815	Fortunato Pio Castellani established in Rome, begins study of granulation in ancient goldwork, 1827
1819	*The Gas Blowpipe* by E.D. Clarke is published
1820s	Ancient goldwork discovered in Etruscan excavations
1824	Pinmaking machine for straight pins patented in England by Lemuel Wellman Wright, by John Howe in U.S. 1832
1829	Sir Walter Scott's *Anne of Geierstein* is published, describing the opal as "misfortune's stone"
	French square hallmark for *doublé d'or* (rolled gold) introduced by Paris Mint
1830	Claw/coronet settings of the Middle Ages revived

Early Victorian (Romantic) Period

Date	General History, Discoveries & Inventions
1837	Victoria becomes Queen of Great Britain
	Louis J. M. Daguerre perfects daguerreotype photographic process

Date	Jewelry & Gemstone History, Discoveries & Inventions
1837	Enameled garter armlet made for Queen Victoria; Order of the Garter strap and buckle motifs become popular

The telegraph is patented by Cooke and Wheatstone, improved by Samuel Morse, first message sent 1844

1839 Charles Goodyear invents and patents (1844) vulcanized rubber; displays products at Crystal Palace (1851)

1840 Victoria weds Prince Albert

1842 Gutta percha introduced in Paris
Excavations of ancient Assyrian capital of Nineveh begin
British kite-shaped registry mark introduced

1848 Balmoral Castle in Scotland purchased by Queen Victoria
Formation of the Pre-Raphaelite Brotherhood in England
Gold discovered in California

1849 California Gold Rush
The safety pin invented and patented by Walter Hunt of New York (patent #6,281)

1850 High tariff placed on foreign goods imported into U.S.

1851 First international exhibition, the Great Exhibition of the Works of Industry of All Nations, held at The Crystal Palace in London
Gold and diamonds first discovered in Australia
Hard rubber (vulcanite) patented by Nelson Goodyear

1852 Louis Napoleon becomes Napoleon III, beginning of French Second Empire

1853 Commodore Matthew Perry sails American fleet into Japan, opens East-West trade relations
Crystal Palace Exhibition held in New York, modeled after London exhibition

1854 Results of first commercially successful aluminum reduction process published by Henri Ste. Claire Deville

1855 Paris *Exposition Universelle*
Aluminum articles first exhibited
R.W. Bunsen begins using gas-air burner that is his namesake

1856 Wm. Perkin accidentally discovers the first synthetic aniline (coal-tar) dye, mauve

1857 Financial "Panic of 1857" affects all U.S. industries
Furnace to melt platinum and its alloys developed by Henri Ste. Claire Deville

1858 First attempted laying of a transatlantic cable

1859 Construction of the Suez Canal begins
Comstock Lode (silver) discovered in Nevada

Charles Lewis Tiffany founds company in New York City; becomes Tiffany & Co. 1853

1840 Electroplating commercialized, patented by Elkingtons of Birmingham. Large-scale jewelry manufacturing begins in U.S.
Process for permanently foiled pastes (faceted glass) discovered
Steam power first used for diamond cutting in Amsterdam

c. 1840 Scottish motifs in "pebble" (agate) jewelry popularized, continuing through the rest of the century
Repoussé and machine stamping replace *cannetille* (gold filigree)
Algerian knot motif introduced in Paris

1841 Duty on imported jewelry and mounted gemstones levied by U.S.

1846 Riker, Tay & Searing founded in Newark, NJ, become Riker Bros. 1892

1847 Cartier founded in Paris

1848 Caldwell & Bennett becomes J.E. Caldwell & Co., Philadelphia
Thomas H. Lowe of Birmingham introduces rolled gold plating process (a.k.a. gold filled) to Providence, RI, manufacturers

1849 Gold electroplating patented
Opals first discovered in Australia, first with play of color, 1863

1850 Tube-shaped ("trombone") safety catch patented by Charles Rowley of Birmingham England
Brooches with swiveling compartments introduced (c.)
Garnet-glass doublets introduced (c.)

1851 Artificial aventurine ("goldstone") exhibited at Crystal Palace

1852 Tiffany & Co. introduces the English sterling standard to the United States
Machine for heat-pressing bog oak patented

1853 Demantoid garnets discovered in Ural Mountains, identified as green andradite, 1864, named demantoid, 1878
Process for "bloomed gold" documented

1854 Use of 15-, 12-, and 9-karat gold made legal in England

1855 Theodor Fahrner founds jewelry factory in Pforzheim, Germany
First aluminum jewelry made in France (c.)
Patents for Bois durci, Parkesine, and artificial coral issued

1857 Snake-chain making machine patented in U.S.

1858 Boucheron founded in Paris

1859 Jewels of Queen Ah-Hotep of Egypt discovered
First attempt at organized jewelers' union in U.S., not successful until 1900 (International Jewelry Workers Union of America)

1860 Henry D. Morse opens first American diamond-cutting factory in Boston, develops standards for American round brilliant cut, 1872-75
English patent for machine to manufacture stamped settings (collets) for stones granted to Frenchmen Bouret and Ferré

Mid Victorian (Grand) Period

Date	General History, Discoveries & Inventions
1861	U.S. Civil War begins [1861-1865]; Lincoln inaugurated
	Prince Consort Albert dies; Victoria enters prolonged period of mourning
1862	International Exhibition held in London
1863	Edward, Prince of Wales, marries Alexandra of Denmark
1865	Lincoln assassinated
1866	First successful transatlantic cable laid
1867	Paris *Exposition Universelle*
1868	Celluloid, the first successful semi-synthetic thermoplastic, invented in U.S. by John Wesley Hyatt; commercial production begins in 1872; trade name registered, 1873

Date	Jewelry & Gemstone History, Discoveries & Inventions
1861	Fortunato Pio Castellani turns business over to son Augusto
1861-c.1880	Wearing of mourning (black) jewelry required at British court
1862	Archeological Revival gold jewelry exhibited by Castellani of Rome at International Exhibition
	Reverse crystal intaglios by Charles Cook shown at Exhibition
	Japanese decorative arts exhibited for the first time in the West
1865	Sapphires found in Missouri River in Montana
1867	Egyptian Revival jewelry exhibited at Paris Exposition
	First authenticated diamond, the Eureka, discovered in South Africa
	Parisian firm Boucheron begins production of *plique à jour* enamels
1868	Gorham Mfg. Co., Providence RI, adopts sterling standard of 925 parts per thousand

1869	First transcontinental railroad from Omaha to San Francisco Suez Canal opened	1869	Henry D. Morse cuts the Dewey diamond, largest found in America to date (23.75 cts, cut to 11.70 cts) "Diamond rush" begins in South Africa with discovery of the "Star of Africa" *American Horological Journal* first published, merges with *The Jewelers' Circular* to become *The Jewelers' Circular and Horological Review*, 1873
1870	Fall of the French Empire British metallurgist George Matthey perfects lime furnace for platinum refining	1870	*The Jewelers' Circular* founded, first issue published February 15 Peter Carl Fabergé takes over father's business Diamonds discovered in Kimberley, South Africa
1870s	Recession in Europe	1870s	Influx of European craftsmen and designers into U.S. Japanese craftsmen introduce metal-working techniques and designs to the West
1872	International Exhibition held in London	1872	Black opals first discovered in Queensland, Australia Ferdinand J. Herpers of Newark, NJ, patents six-prong setting for diamonds, introduced as the "Tiffany setting" by Tiffany & Co., 1886
1873	Universal Exhibition held in Vienna	1873	Henry D. Morse and Charles M. Field obtain British and U.S. (1874, 1876) patents for steam-driven bruting (diamond-cutting) machines
1874	Gold discovered in Black Hills of Dakota Territory		
1875	Arthur Lazenby Liberty founds Liberty & Co. of London	1875	The Celluloid Mfg. Co. begins jewelry production in Newark, NJ
1876	Centennial Exposition held in Philadelphia Wearing of swords banned in Japan Queen Victoria becomes Empress of India Alexander Graham Bell patents the telephone	1876	Alessandro Castellani presents and lectures on Etruscan Revival jewelry at Centennial Exposition
1877	Advent of bottled oxygen (liquefied and compressed)	1877	Successful experiments with chemical manufacture of very small rubies and sapphires in Paris, published by Frémy
1878	Paris *Exposition Universelle*	1878	Tiffany & Co. awarded gold medal for encrusted metals technique in the "Japanesque" style at Paris Exposition Tiffany Diamond discovered in South Africa Unger Bros. of Newark, NJ, begins the manufacture of silver jewelry Earring covers for diamond earrings patented Patent for platinum-tipped prongs for setting diamonds (#202,402)
1879	T. A. Edison patents incandescent light bulb	1879	Gem expert George F. Kunz joins Tiffany & Co. Hiddenite, green variety of spodumene, found in North Carolina

Late Victorian (Aesthetic) Period

Date	General History, Discoveries & Inventions	Date	Jewelry & Gemstone History, Discoveries & Inventions
1880	Rational Dress Society founded in Britain	1880	Cecil Rhodes establishes the De Beers Mining Company in South Africa (renamed De Beers Consolidated Mines in 1888) Mass production of wrist watches begins in Switzerland, introduced in U.S. 1895, U.S. manufacture 1907 (c.)
1881	The first electrically-lit theatre, The Savoy, opens in London		
1883	Metropolitan Opera House opens in New York City		
		1885	First appearance of the "Geneva" synthetic ruby
1886	Gold discovered in South Africa (Transvaal) Statue of Liberty dedicated	1886	Tiffany setting for diamond solitaires introduced Richard W. Sears starts a mail-order company to sell watches (second company to sell jewelry and watches founded in 1889)
1887	Queen Victoria's Golden Jubilee Hall-Héroult process for refining aluminum developed; first commercial production in Switzerland, value drops Celluloid photographic film invented by Hannibal W. Goodwin	1887	Gold extraction by cyanide process invented by John Stewart Macarthur and the Forrest brothers Tiffany & Co. purchases French crown jewels Birmingham (England) Jewellers' and Silversmiths' Association formed by manufacturers Tiffany & Co. purchases French crown jewels Black opals discovered in New South Wales, Australia; commercial mining at Lightening Ridge mine begins 1903 The Belais brothers of New York begin experimenting with alloys for white gold (c.); David Belais introduces his formula to the trade in 1917 (referred to as "18k Belais")
1888	George Eastman introduces the first commercial box camera, the Kodak	1888	C.R. Ashbee's Guild of Handicraft founded in London, the first crafts guild to specialize in jewelry-making and metalwork
1889	Paris *Exposition Universelle* - Eiffel Tower constructed, first structure to serve as landmark for an exposition	1889	Tiffany & Co. exhibits enameled orchid jewels by Paulding Farnham at the Exposition Universelle Sapphires found in Dry Cottonwood Creek, Montana
1890	Sarah Bernhardt plays Cleopatra on stage Charles Dana Gibson's "Gibson Girl" first appears in the humor magazine *Life*		
1891	The marking of foreign imports with the name of the country of origin in English required by the enactment of the McKinley Tariff Act, October, 1890	1891	Power-driven bruting (girdling) machine for cutting diamonds patented in England
1892	*Vogue* Magazine founded in U.S.	1892	Marcus & Co., formerly Jaques & Marcus, established in New York
1893	World's Columbian Exposition in Chicago	1893	Cultured pearls first developed by K. Mikimoto in Japan; first spherical pearls grown 1905 "Platingeld" introduced, used for simulated gold and platinum chains

1894	Thomas Edison's Kinetoscope Parlor ("peepshow") opens in New York City	1894	Screwback earring finding for unpierced ears patented (U.S.)
1895	Sigfried (aka Samuel) Bing opens his new Paris gallery of decorative art called "*L'Art Nouveau*" American Consuelo Vanderbilt marries the British Duke of Marlborough The wireless telegraph invented by Guglielmo Marconi (first transatlantic wireless signal in 1901) Bonanza Creek Gold Rush in Klondike (Yukon, Canada)	1895	René Lalique exhibits jewelry at the Bing gallery and the Salon of the *Societé des Artistes Français*; begins work on a series of 145 pieces for Calouste Gulbenkian Daniel Swarovski opens glass stone-cutting factory in Tyrol, Austria Blue sapphires discovered in Yogo Gulch, Montana
1897	Queen Victoria's Diamond Jubilee Casein plastics marketed in Germany Boston and Chicago Arts and Crafts Societies founded	1897	Lacloche Frères established in Paris
1898	Alaska Gold Rush Spanish-American War	1898	Commercial sapphire mining begins in Rock Creek, Montana
1899-1902	Boer War (South Africa)	1899-1902	Diamond supplies curtailed by Boer War; prices for De Beers' reserve stock rise

Edwardian Period (*Belle Époque*)

Date	General History, Discoveries & Inventions	Date	Jewelry & Gemstone History, Discoveries & Inventions
1900	Paris *Exposition Universelle* U.S. officially adopts the gold standard with McKinley's signing of the Gold Standard Act (monometallism) Oxyacetylene torch invented by Edmund Fouché	1900	Synthetic rubies exhibited at Paris Exposition; Tiffany & Co. exhibits a life-size iris corsage ornament set with Montana blue sapphires Boucheron, Fouquet, Lalique, Vever and other French jewelers display their Art Nouveau jewels at Paris Exposition The Kalo Shop founded by Clara Barck Welles in Chicago, begins jewelry-making 1905, closed 1970 The diamond saw is invented by a Belgian working in the U.S. (c.)
1901	Queen Victoria dies. Edward VII becomes king McKinley assassinated. Theodore Roosevelt becomes President Pan-American Exposition held in Buffalo NY Gustav Stickley begins publishing his periodical, *The Craftsman* (until 1916)	1901	Lever safety catch for brooches patented by Herpers Brothers of Newark Tiffany & Co. exhibits at Pan-American Exposition, special mark (beaver) used on exhibition pieces
1902	Vienna Secession Exhibition Edward VII coronation	1902	Flame-fusion process for synthesizing rubies presented in Paris by Verneuil, published and patented 1904 Joseph Asscher develops the Asscher cut for diamonds Cartier opens a London branch Pink variety of spodumene, kunzite, discovered in California, identified by and named for George F. Kunz Process for setting rhinestones or metal in celluloid patented
1903	Wiener Werkstätte founded in Vienna, Austria by Koloman Moser and Josef Hoffmann	1903	Fabergé opens London branch, selling mostly "gentlemen's things"
1904	Louisiana Purchase Exposition held in St. Louis New York City subway opens Construction begins on the Panama Canal	1904	Louis Comfort Tiffany exhibits his jewelry for the first time at the St. Louis Exposition Marshall Field & Co., Chicago, establishes a craft shop for jewelry and metalware (closed c. 1950) Georg Jensen opens his silversmithy in Copenhagen, Denmark
1905	Albert Einstein proposes his theory of relativity Henri Matisse and other fauvist artists exhibit at *Salon d'Automne* in Paris	1905	Forest Craft Guild founded by Forest Mann in Grand Rapids MI The Kalo Shop begins jewelry-making in Chicago Cullinan diamond (3,106 carats) discovered in Transvaal So. Africa, presented to Edward VII 1907 First spherical cultured pearls grown in Japan by Mikimoto, patented 1908, U.S. patent, 1916
1906	San Francisco earthquake and fire Finland is first European country to grant women's suffrage	1906	National Stamping Act passed in U.S., requiring marking of gold and silver content Van Cleef & Arpels founded in Paris
1907	First exhibition of cubist paintings held in Paris, including works by Pablo Picasso and Georges Braque Suffragettes demonstrate for the right to vote in London	1907	Tiffany & Co. establishes Art Jewelry Dept. with Louis Comfort Tiffany as director Benitoite discovered in California, declared official state stone, 1985
1908	Henry Ford introduces the first mass-produced automobile, the Model T Couturier Paul Poiret opens "Boutique Chichi," introduces corsetless dresses and the vertical line in fashion (c.)	1908	First spherical cultured pearls patented in Japan by Mikimoto (first grown in 1905, American patent granted in 1916) Synthetic spinel accidentally produced by flame fusion process
1909	Leo H. Baekeland patents first entirely synthesized plastic, Bakelite The Wright brothers begin large-scale manufacture of the airplane (first flight 1903, patented 1906) Copyright symbol © introduced for printed works	1909	Cartier New York opens

1910	The *Ballets Russes* production of *Schéhérazade* presented in Paris Edward VII dies, George V becomes king of Great Britain First major American women's suffrage parade held in New York City, demonstration in Washington DC, 1913 France classifies platinum as a precious metal, new hallmark (dog's head) issued 1912	1910	Eugene Morehouse invents the "bullet" safety catch for brooches, patented for B.A. Ballou & Co 1911
		1910-1920	Suffragette jewelry in green, white, and violet (first initials for "give women votes") is popular in Britain and U.S.
1911	George V coronation	1911	George V has Cullinan I and II set in Imperial State crown and scepter The Hope Diamond is purchased by Ned and Evalyn Walsh McLean Synthetic blue sapphires patented in U.S by Verneuil
1912	The *Titanic* sinks	1912	Oscar Heyman & Bros. founded in New York
1914	World War I begins First ship through Panama Canal (completed 1913) The first U.S. fashion show is staged by Edna Woolman Chase, editor of *Vogue*	1914	Platinum declared a "strategic metal" during wartime, use in jewelry diminished
1915	Panama-Pacific International Exposition held in San Francisco Panama-California Exposition held in San Diego	1915	U.S. patent #1165448 granted to Karl Gustav Paul Richter of Pforzheim Germany, for a white gold alloy of gold, nickel and palladium
1917	Theda Bara plays Cleopatra in first (silent) film version The U.S. enters the war Russian Revolution begins	1917	David Belais of New York introduces his formula for 18k white gold to the trade, known as "18k Belais" Cartier designs the Tank wristwatch, first public sale 1919
1918	First regular airmail service, between Washington DC and New York City, begins, New York to San Francisco 1921 World War I ends Bohemia, Moravia and Slovakia become the Republic of Czechoslovakia		

The "Modern" Era

Date	General History, Discoveries & Inventions	Date	Jewelry & Gemstone History, Discoveries & Inventions
1919	Bauhaus founded in Germany by Walter Gropius The Eighteenth Amendment to the U.S. Constitution is ratified (Prohibition)	1919	Marcel Tolkowsky publishes *Diamond Design*, detailing the cut and proportions of the modern brilliant ("American" or "ideal" cut), following scientific standards first discovered and developed by Henry D. Morse
1920	The Nineteenth Amendment, giving women the right to vote, is ratified First regular radio programs begin broadcasting in Pittsburgh		
1922	Howard Carter discovers King Tutankhamun's tomb in Egypt	1922	Raymond C. Yard, Inc. founded in New York City
1923	Cartoonist John Held Jr's "Betsy Co-ed" and "Joe College" first appear on the cover of humor magazine *Life* (c.)	1923	Frederik Lunning comes to New York City, opens a shop for Georg Jensen, 1924 Synthetic pearl essence for simulated pearls invented, called "H-scale"
		1924	Egyptologist Caroline R. Williams discovers the granulation technique used by ancient goldsmiths
1925	*Exposition Internationale des Arts Decoratifs et Industriels Modernes* held in Paris Josephine Baker appears in the *Revue Nègre* in Paris	1925	Synthetic spinel, inadvertently produced by flame fusion process 1908, in wide commercial use (c.) Firm of Trifari, Krussman & Fishel established
1926	The first commercial injection molding machine patented by Eckert and Ziegler in Germany		
1927	Charles Lindbergh flies solo nonstop New York to Paris Motion pictures with sound first publicly shown (Al Jolson in "The Jazz Singer") Cellulose acetate, trade name Lumarith, introduced by Celluloid Corp.	1927	Cartier patents model with spring system for double clip brooch
		1928	Schiaparelli establishes "Maison Schiaparelli" in Paris Paul Flato opens salon in New York
1929	The Great Depression begins with stock market crash	1929	Trabert & Hoeffer, Inc.-Mauboussin merger agreement Black, Starr & Frost merger with Gorham Corp., until 1966
1930	Formation of the *Union des Artistes Modernes* in Paris Construction completed on Chrysler Building in New York		
1931	Empire State Building becomes New York's tallest	1931	The "Duette" pinback mechanism for double clip brooches patented by U.S. costume jewelry manufacturer Coro William Spratling opens the first silver workshop in Taxco, Mexico
1932	Franklin D. Roosevelt elected President Radio City Music Hall opens	1932	14k gold replaces 12k and 15k in Britain, by decision of the Worshipful Company of Goldsmiths, London Harry Winston opens a retail jewelry business in New York City

1933 Construction begins on Golden Gate Bridge in San Francisco (completed 1937)
Prohibition repealed
Gold taken out of circulation
"Century of Progress" World's Fair opens in Chicago

1934 Cecil B. De Mille's "Cleopatra" starring Claudette Colbert in title role
Salvador Dalí exhibits surrealist paintings in New York City

1935 French luxury cruise ship *Normandie* arrives in New York
U.S. Works Progress Administration inaugurated

1936 George V dies. Edward VIII of Britain abdicates the throne to marry American-born divorcée Wallis Simpson, becomes Duke of Windsor, succeeded by George VI
Margaret Mitchell's novel, *Gone With the Wind*, is published
BBC inaugurates television service; general broadcasting begins in U.S. 1941
Life magazine founded by Henry Robinson Luce

1937 Du Pont de Nemours & Co. introduces acrylic plastic, trade name "Lucite"; also patents nylon fiber
The International Exhibition of Arts and Techniques in Modern Life held in Paris
First feature-length animated film, Walt Disney's "Snow White and the Seven Dwarfs"

1939 "Gone With The Wind" premiers
World War II begins in Europe
First nylon stockings marketed
The New York World's Fair, titled "The World of Tomorrow," opens

1940 France falls under German occupation

1941 The U.S. enters the war with the Japanese bombing of Pearl Harbor
Craft Horizons, the first national magazine for crafts, is published by the Handcraft Cooperative League
First U.S. television broadcasting begins

1942 Rationing of consumer products (sugar, coffee, gasoline) begins in U.S.
Polyethylene formulated by Earl S. Tupper and DuPont, Tupperware introduced 1946

1943 Postal zones added to addresses of large cities in U.S.

1945 Roosevelt dies. Harry Truman becomes President
World War II ends
United Nations is formed, holds first session 1946

1947 Couturier Christian Dior introduces "The New Look"
Copyright laws re-enacted by U.S. Congress, expanded to include illustrations of merchandise and designs for art works

1948 Jewish State of Israel declared, admitted to U.N. 1949
Truman elected to full term as President

1949 German Federal Republic (West Germany) proclaimed

1951 Color television is introduced in U.S.

1952 George VI of Britain dies; succeeded by Elizabeth II
Dwight D. Eisenhower elected President

1953 Marilyn Monroe sings "Diamonds Are a Girl's Best Friend" in "Gentlemen Prefer Blondes"

1933 The "invisible setting" (*serti invisible*) patented by Cartier and Van Cleef & Arpels (introduced in U.S. 1936)
Lost wax process, used in dentistry since c.1910, reintroduced for mass production of jewelry castings with vulcanized rubber molds (c.)

1934 Ernest Oppenheimer creates the De Beers Consolidated Mines Ltd. diamond cartel
Synthetic emeralds ("Igmerald") developed by IG-Farben, Germany, first seen by gemologists
Van Cleef & Arpels introduces the "Ludo" flexible strap bracelet
Patent for clipback earring finding for unpierced ears granted to Eugene Morehouse for B.A. Ballou

1935 D. Lisner & Co. introduces "Bois Glacé" jewelry, their trade name for colorless phenolic plastic (Bakelite) laminated to wood
The Jewelers' Circular merges with *The Keystone* to become *Jewelers' Circular-Keystone*

1937 Van Cleef & Arpels makes "marriage contract" bracelet for Wallis Simpson, the Duchess of Windsor
Boucheron, Cartier, Mauboussin, Van Cleef & Arpels and others display figural jewels of colored gold and gemstones at Paris exhibition
Paul Flato opens his Los Angeles establishment
Double-pronged hinged (dress) clip introduced (c.)

1939 First commercially successful synthetic emerald process marketed by Carroll Chatham of San Francisco, CA ("Chatham Created Emerald" term first used 1963)
The House of Jewels at the New York World's Fair is sponsored by Tiffany & Co., Black, Starr & Frost-Gorham, Udall & Ballou, Marcus & Co., and Cartier New York
Van Cleef & Arpels opens an office in New York City
Verdura opens his own shop in New York
Sam Kramer opens shop in Greenwich Village

1940 The Bank of France bans all gold trading

1941 10% luxury tax on jewelry in U.S., raised to 20% 1944
Jean Schlumberger opens shop in New York, joins Tiffany & Co. 1956

1942 Use of platinum for jewelry prohibited in U.S.
White metal restricted by U.S. government, sterling silver used as substitute in costume jewelry

1945 Suzanne Belperron forms partnership Herz-Belperron with Jean Herz in Paris
Mexican government requires marking of sterling silver with "spread eagle" assay mark (c.)

1946 Opal doublets first made in Australia, triplets c. 1960
First national exhibit of American studio artists' jewelry held at Museum of Modern Art in New York City
Jerry Fels founds "Renoir of Hollywood" in Los Angeles, CA
David Webb opens office in New York, salon in 1963

1947 Synthetic star rubies and sapphires ("Linde") first marketed
Costume jewelry manufacturers begin abandoning design patents in favor of copyrights, using © as part of maker's mark
Synthetic rutile introduced as a diamond simulant
Metalsmithing workshop series for war veterans begins, ends 1951

1948 De Beers Diamond Corp. launches the slogan "a diamond is forever"

1949 Harry Winston purchases Hope diamond. His "Court of Jewels" exhibit opens in New York, tours U.S. for the next four years

1951 The Metal Arts Guild organized in San Francisco

1952 Italian jewelers Buccellati establish a salon in New York City

1953 Mamie Eisenhower wears Trifari faux pearls to inaugural ball

1955 Atomically generated power first used in the U.S.
Disneyland amusement park opens

1957 The U.S.S.R. launches the first "Sputnik" satellite on Oct. 4
Jack Kerouac's *On the Road* published, coins the term "Beat Generation"

1958 Universal Exhibition opens in Brussels, Belgium

1960 John F. Kennedy elected President of U.S.
Birth control pills introduced to the public

1961 Audrey Hepburn stars in "Breakfast at Tiffany's"
Soviets, U.S., put first men in space

1963 Kennedy assassinated. Lyndon Johnson becomes President
U.S. Post Office introduces the ZIP code
Elizabeth Taylor stars in "Cleopatra"

1964 The Beatles perform live for the first time in the U.S.
Vietnam War begins

1969 U.S. moon landing
Woodstock music festival

1972 Richard Nixon re-elected

1974 Nixon resigns as a result of Watergate (1973)

1976 U.S. bicentennial
The microprocessor is introduced; Apple II personal computer, 1977

1954 De Beers institutes the annual Diamonds International Awards for original designs in diamond-set jewelry
First successful production of synthetic diamonds at General Electric, process patented 1960, large gem-quality crystals produced 1970

1955 Swarovski Corp introduces the "aurora borealis" color effect for rhinestones and crystal in collaboration with Christian Dior
Strontium titanate introduced to the public as a diamond simulant

1961 International Exhibition of Modern Jewelry (1890-1961) held in London
U.S. National Stamping Act amended, requiring a maker's trade mark

1967 Tanzanite discovered in Tanzania

1972 Cubic zirconia "skull melt" process patented, CZs commerically commercially marketed, 1976
Gilson produces synthetic opal and synthetic turquoise

1974 Tsavorite garnet (green) discovered in Kenya, Africa

1976 National Stamping Act amendment introduces the marking of "plumb" gold (e.g., "14 KP"), meaning exact (no tolerance)

1979 Main pipe of the Argyle Diamond Mine in Australia discovered, mining company commissioned in 1985
Sugilite, named for Professor Ken-ichi Sugi, begins appearing on the market (discovered 1944)

TIMELINE REFERENCES

David Bennett & Daniela Mascetti, *Understanding Jewelry*, 2nd edition, Antique Collectors' Club, 1994.

Shirley Bury, *Jewellery 1789-1910, The International Era*, Vols. I & II, Antique Collectors' Club, 1991.

Ulysses G. Dietz, ed., *The Glitter & The Gold, Fashioning America's Jewelry*, The Newark Museum, 1997.

Martha G. Fales, *Jewelry in America 1600-1900*, Antique Collectors' Club, 1995.

Gemological Institute of America, *Gems & Gemology*, Vol. 23 #2 Summer 1987, Vol. 24 #1, Winter 1988, Vol. 32 #2, Summer, 1996, Vol. 33 #3, Fall, 1997.

Bernard Grun, *The Timetables of History*, revised 3rd ed., Simon & Schuster/Touchstone, 1991.

David Federman, "American Diamond Cutting: The Untold Heritage," *Modern Jeweler*, Vol. 84 E1 (January, 1985).

Derric Mercer, ed. in chief, *Millennium Year by Year*, Dorling Kindersley, 1999.

Hans Nadelhoffer, *Cartier, Jewelers Extraordinary*, Harry N. Abrams, 1984.

Kurt Nassau, *Gems Made By Man*, Chilton Book Co., 1980.

National Geographic, *Eyewitness to the 20th Century*, National Geographic Society, 1999.

Richard Platt, *Smithsonian Visual Timeline of Inventions*, Dorling Kindersley, 1994.

Penny Proddow, Debra Healy, Marion Fasel, *Hollywood Jewels, Movies, Jewelry, Stars*, Harry N. Abrams, 1992.

Dorothy Rainwater, *American Jewelry Manufacturers*, Schiffer Publishing, 1988.

Diana Scarisbrick, *Jewellery in Britain 1066-1837*, Michael Russell Publishing Ltd., 2000.

Erika Speel, *Dictionary of Enamelling: History and Techniques*, Brookfield, 1998.

Joseph W. Tenhagen, "What is the 'Ideal Cut' Diamond Today?" prepared for the National Association of Jewelry Appraisers Conference, 1998.

Laurence Urdang, ed., *The Timetables of American History*, updated edition, Simon & Schulter/Touchstone, 1996.

Alfred M. Weisberg, *Why Providence?*, Providence Jewelry Museum, 1992.

Information Please Almanac, Houghton Mifflin Co., 1991.

Microsoft Encarta Multimedia Encyclopedia, 2000 (CD-ROM).

Internet Web sites: (http://inventors.about.com),
Virtual Reference Desk (www.loc.gov//rr/askalib/virtualref.html),
Innovation Timeline (www.ideafinder.com/history/timeline.html)

Advisors: Karen Lorene, Elise Misiorowski, Peter Shemonsky, Joseph W. Tenhagen, Janet Zapata.

Part I

Late Eighteenth and Nineteenth Century Jewelry

Jewelry has always been worn for many purposes. In addition to social status, it can serve as a memento of loved ones living or dead. It also has a role as decorative and/or functional parts of clothing. A jewel can be worn as an expression of religious faith, and as a talisman or amulet to ward off evil and disease.

Souvenir jewelry, and traditional jewelry symbolic of national or cultural origin or group membership, are also common. In fact, more non-status antique jewelry, often made from non-precious materials, survives today in its original form than does gemstone and gold jewelry. Anything with components of value was more likely to be broken up for its gemstones and precious metal and reworked into pieces in keeping with current fashion.

Fine and expensive high-karat gold and gemstone pieces from the late eighteenth and early nineteenth centuries certainly do turn up at auctions and high-end antiques shows. However, most of the earliest accessible and affordable jewelry that exists today is memorial and sentimental jewelry.

The first section is divided accordingly, covering what is known as the Late Georgian and Regency periods in Great Britain (the reigns of Georges III and IV), circa 1760-1837 (William IV reigned 1830-1837, but there is no "William period"). In the U.S., these periods correspond roughly to the late Colonial and Federal periods.

Although it may seem arbitrary, the year 1837 is generally recognized by jewelry historians as the beginning of a new era, although some types and styles of jewelry carried over from the previous decade. The time span of the period is lengthy, so it is usually divided into three sub-periods. While there is a difference of opinion as to the exact years when one sub-period ends and the next begins, there is general recognition of their names: They are called the Early or Romantic, the Middle or Grand, and the Late Victorian or Aesthetic Period.

In order to more easily understand the great diversity and quantity of Victorian jewelry, the photographs in this section have been grouped by types and/or materials. Each category is listed under the sub-period most closely associated with it, but individual photos may have earlier or later circa dates.

Jewelry doesn't always fit neatly into one or another time-slot or category. Styles tend to overlap, and newer versions of old designs continued to be made in later periods. Many materials were worn throughout the late eighteenth and nineteenth centuries, e.g., coral, cut steel, and diamonds; many motifs recurred, such as snakes, flowers, and hands, and many types or forms of jewelry continued to be worn, like watch chains, bracelets, and cameos.

Precise dating can be difficult, unless there are clues like maker's marks, hallmarks with date letters, or engraved dated inscriptions. More often than not, late eighteenth and nineteenth century jewelry is unmarked. Identifying construction techniques and original findings can help to narrow the date range. Some findings, however, like the "C"-catch (a simple hook) and the "tube" hinge of brooch pin assemblies, were in use for the entire period, and often continued to be used in the twentieth century. Furthermore, pieces with intrinsic value—precious metals and stones—do not always survive intact. Alterations are common.

Several thematic threads were woven into the fabric of society. Nature, history, symbolism, and above all, sentiment, were sometimes inextricably intertwined.

In Victorian times, naturalism was expressed in jewelry with exact depictions of flora and fauna in gold and gemstones or other materials. Distasteful as it may seem today, real insects and birds' heads were sometimes made into jewelry. Flowers were symbols of sentiment and nature. Every flower had a specific meaning, and their definitions were catalogued in several flower dictionaries. One book, published in 1866, was appropriately called *The Language and Sentiment of Flowers* (several versions are still available today).

The second half of the nineteenth century was the age of the international exhibition—what later came to be known as World's Fairs and Expos. Their historical importance should not be underestimated. In a period lacking mass communications media like television, exhibitions were the mass marketing tool of the era. They made it possible for manufacturers and merchants to display their wares over a period of six months or more to hundreds of thousands of potential customers.

The latest discoveries and developments, styles, and tastes were introduced to the general public at exhibitions. Instead of "as seen on TV," an item would be touted, for example, "as seen at the Paris Exposition." To have a booth at an exhibition conferred the highest status upon the goods and their maker. Jewelry was exhibited by such prestigious firms as Froment-Meurice of Paris and Phillips of London at London's Crystal Palace Exhibition in 1851, Castellani of Rome exhibited at the International Exhibition in London in 1862 and at the Philadelphia Centennial Exposition in 1876, and Tiffany & Co. of New York was also at the Philadelphia Centennial and the Paris Exposition in 1867, 1878, 1889, and 1900.

The designs of these and other exhibitors became fashionable by word of mouth and through reports in periodicals. They inspired many imitators.

The period 1837-1901 is called Victorian in the United States, as well as Great Britain. In spite of our country's independence from hers, Victoria's tastes influenced Americans, as well as her own subjects. While the Western world looked to Paris for the latest styles and trends, English interpretations of French styles were acceptable to the more conservative American temperament. At times, these styles were modified even further by American artisans and manufacturers.

When the young Queen ascended the throne of Great Britain in 1837, the United States was still a young country. Machine-made jewelry production had begun in New England and New Jersey, but a distinct American style had yet to emerge. Most of it was imitative of the English or French. Some jewelers, in fact, tried to "pass" their items as European. Other types of jewelry that were worn were usually imported from Britain and the Continent.

In the early years of this country's history, patriotism and lifestyles in general discouraged ostentatious displays of wealth. Aristocracy and all that symbolized it, like jewelry, was out. The Puritan work ethic was in. Many Americans wore little, except sentimental jewelry, until after the Civil War.

Wives of statesmen and presidents, the elite of Boston, New York, and Philadelphia, and other well-to-do Americans were the exception to this rule. Dolley Madison was known for her jeweled turbans, sent from Paris—the War of 1812 notwithstanding.

In the 1840s, President John Tyler's new wife, Julia, was the closest thing to royalty this country ever saw. She wore crowns and diamond tiaras.

Reproduction Alert

Manufacturers in Portugal, South America, Germany, Thailand, and the U.S. can and do reproduce late eighteenth and nineteenth century style pieces to any specification, using stones and findings identical to the originals. Unless you have one of their catalogs or are aware of the provenance of a piece, it is often extremely difficult to differentiate new from old.

LATE GEORGIAN JEWELRY, C. 1760-1837

A quick look at the beginning of the Timeline in the front of this book will hint at the social and political upheaval that took place in Europe and America during this time period: The American and French Revolutions, England at war with France, France with the United States. George III was declared insane. Louis XVI was beheaded. Napoleon overran Europe and crowned himself Emperor. Little wonder that changes in social customs, fashion, and attitudes about personal adornment occurred at the same time.

At the beginning of the period, royalty and nobility were the primary wearers of jewels of high intrinsic value. In 1762, Queen Charlotte, wife of George III, posed for her portrait wearing, among other jewels, a diamond stomacher which covered her entire V-shaped bodice. (Evidence that diamond-set jewels were made and worn in America in pre-Revolutionary times has been presented, but little of it survives or is documented.) Low necklines and upswept hair suggested long earrings and short necklaces. The *girandole* (French for chandelier) and *pendeloque* were popular shapes for earrings and pendants. The former usually consist of three pear-shaped diamond (or colored gemstone) drops suspended from a central element and small surmount (see photo below). Pendeloques are single pear-shaped drops, sometimes suspended from a central bow and single-stone or cluster surmount (page 27). Short necklaces of graduated collet-set diamonds or other gemstones, known as *rivières*, were worn through the first two or three decades of the 19th century (this necklace style was revived in the 1880s; see page 87). Diamonds began to be set *à jour* (open-backed) at this time, but colored gemstones such as garnets and topaz continued to be mounted in closed back settings lined with

Pendant, diamonds, wm, ym, c. 1790, *girandole* of stylized floral and foliate design, pierced and set throughout with om, rc and sc diamonds in closed wm and ym settings, later-added bail, fitted case, 2" w x 3¼" tl, **$2,520** [A]. (Photo courtesy of Sotheby's, London, 6/20/01)

colored foil to enhance their natural color. Open settings for colored stones began appearing around the turn of the 19th century, but were not in the majority until the 1840s.

Large diamond-set bow brooches, known as *sévigné*, were fashionable when tight bodices were in style in the late eighteenth century, but when fashions changed, they were no longer wearable. The bow motif itself remained, however. Floral spray and feather brooches were also set with diamonds. These tended to be stylized and flat until Early Victorian naturalism gave them dimension and a realistic look.

The eighteenth century is commonly called the Age of Diamonds, but it could also be called the "Age of Paste" (a high lead content glass, invented by Georg Frédéric Strass in 1730). Those who could not afford to emulate the aristocracy still strove to imitate their style. Paste jewels were set in silver or gold closed-back mounts and foiled for added sparkle (see photo below). A black spot was often painted on the culets of colorless brilliant-cut stones to further emphasize the look of diamonds of the period (now called "old mine cut," cushion-shaped with a small table and large culet, or bottom facet). The jewelry forms were identical to those set with diamonds and colored gemstones. Paste jewels were prized in their own right, not merely as a substitute or imitation, and were sold by many of the "best" jewelers of England, France, and in the Colonies before the American Revolution.

Brooches/Pins, late 18th–early 19th C:
TL, pastes, silver, c. 1800-1820, a lg circ-cut paste center stone encircled by smaller circ-cut and pear-shaped pastes in a scalloped-edge convex closed-back silver mount, C-catch, tube hinge, extended pinstem, 1⅛" dia, **$200**.
TR, pastes, rc diamonds, gilt brass, c. 1830, a six-petal flowerhead formed of pear-shaped pink foiled pastes in pronged bezels with bead-tipped ropetwist borders, alternating with sm collet-set rc diamonds, center an om diamond, in a flat closed-back mount, C-catch, tube hinge, extended pinstem, 1" dia, **$500**.
B, silver, rubies, pearls, green beryls, 1790-1820, rubbed-over collet-set gemstones, pearls in flowerheads, in an elliptical openwork closed-back silver mount, suspending a ruby-set drop, later-added trombone catch with Fr import mk, pinstem mkd 800, probably Austro-Hungarian, 1½" w x 1¾", **$400**. (Lisa Johnson collection)

Hair Ornament, yg, carnelian, c. 1810, in the Neo-classical style, carnelian intaglio of a female figure, lyre, and cherub set in openwork foliate border, loop for safety chain on stem, unmkd, probably French, 8½" tl, head 1⅜" w x 3¼", **$2,600**. (Courtesy of E. Foxe Harrell, New York, NY)

The American and French Revolutions, like most wars, were an impetus for change. Jewelry, a non-essential luxury, was one of the first things to go, sold or melted down for the war effort, or survival. In France, anything that smacked of aristocracy was frowned upon. Jewels were not part of the new republic's ideology. But by the end of the eighteenth century, a desire for personal adornment had returned, albeit in new forms.

Fashion changed drastically at the turn of the nineteenth century, when Napoleon's First Empire held sway. The late eighteenth century's full skirts, tight bodices, and three-quarter sleeves with deep lace ruffles, gathered draped collars (berthas), or ruffled lace necklines were discarded in favor of the Neo-classical look of filmy, high-waisted, and draped Grecian-style dresses with short puffed sleeves and deep *décolletage*. The style's simplicity and the fabrics' delicacy required changes in jewelry forms: out went stomachers and large, heavy brooches. In came necklaces of plaques and draped chains, small buckles for sashes worn just under the bosom, smaller gem- or paste-set brooches, narrow link bracelets worn in multiples, aigrettes, and hair ornaments (see photo above). Interest in Greek and Roman antiquities had been heightened by new archeological discoveries at Herculaneum and Pompeii in the mid-eighteenth century, and was kept alive by Empress Josephine's preoccupation with classical motifs. Cameos and mosaics were worn as necklaces *en esclavage*, the plaques joined with two or three lengths of swagged chain encircling the base of the neck.

In the 1820s, fashions underwent another change. Sleeves were longer and grew larger toward the end of the decade. Waists remained high but skirts were fuller and heavier, embellished with ruffles and trimmings. By 1830, the waist had returned to its natural position, tightly sashed and buckled. Tight bodices returned. Sleeves were voluminous, necklines cut straight across. Jewelry forms included

Chain, yg, c. 1830, each rounded circ link decorated with star motifs, links ¼" dia, approx 44" tl, **$3,024** [A]. (Photo courtesy of Sotheby's, London, 6/20/01)

long draped chains, wide buckles and bracelets, long earrings (the "torpedo" shape was popular), and fancy combs in elaborately dressed hair. Cross pendants were also popular, especially Maltese crosses, which could be set with diamonds, colored gemstones, or pastes, carved from chalcedony or made entirely of gold (see page 29). Gold was in short supply in the early 19th century, but the decorative technique known as *cannetille*, a type of scrolled filigree with tightly coiled spirals or rosettes, was used to make a small amount of gold go a long way (see necklace on page 27, pendant/necklace below). Substantial-looking chains were made of stamped thin gauge gold, and very lightweight (see photo, left). In the 1820s and 1830s, the romantic notion of the "language of stones," like that of flowers, gave rise to pieces with messages spelled out by the initial letter of the stone's name, known as "acrostic jewelry." "Regard," the most commonly expressed sentiment, was represented by ruby, emerald, garnet, amethyst, ruby, and diamond. "Dearest" was another favorite "acrostic" (see rings in photo below).

As the Industrial Revolution gave rise to more mechanized methods of production in the first three decades of the nineteenth century, more jewelry was made for the middle classes, making way for the profusion and variety of the Victorian era.

Rings, "dearest" acrostics:
T, yg, diamond, emeralds, amethyst, ruby, sapphire, topaz, enamel, c. 1846, a half hoop of circ-cut stones, the first letter of each stone spelling "DEAREST," the sides decorated with enameled forget-me-nots and the shank engraved "FORGET ME NOT MY DEAREST 1846," enameling imperfect, ¼" w, sz 5¼, **$4,200** [A].
B, yg, diamond, emeralds, amethyst, ruby, sapphire, topaz, c. 1820, set at the center with an om diamond bordered by a mixed-cut emerald, amethyst, ruby, emerald, sapphire and topaz, the first letter of each stone spelling "DEAREST," ½" top, sz 4½, **$2,688** [A]. (Photo courtesy of Sotheby's, London, 6/20/01)

Pendant/Necklace, 18k yg, c. 1830, central *girandole* pendant with floret and scroll motif *cannetille* decoration, suspended from a spiral double ropetwist chain with two slides, pendant 1⅞" w x 2⅛", 19" tl, **$2,185** [A]. (Photo courtesy of Skinner, Inc., Boston, MA, 9/25/01)

Brooch/Pin, amethysts, 15k yg, c. 1810, 12 circ-cut amethysts surrounding a lg faceted oval amethyst set à jour in cut-down yg collets, C-catch, tube hinge, later-added safety pin on chain, 1¼" w x 1⅛", **$400**. (Courtesy of E. Foxe Harrell Jewelers, New York, NY)

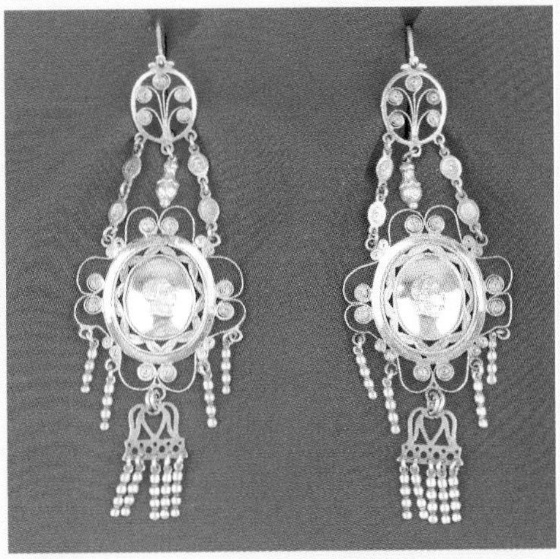

Earrings, pendent, 14k yg, c. 1810, openwork surmounts with wiretwist decoration, each suspending an oval medallion surmounted by the profile of a classical male within similarly decorated frames, fringe terminals, 1⅜" w x 4⅞", **$690** [A]. (Photo courtesy of Skinner, Inc., Boston, MA, 9/25/01)

Earrings, pendent, diamonds, st yg, c. 1800, *pendeloque*, each drop a cut-down collet-set pear-shaped diamond suspended within a frame of om diamonds, from a collet-set om diamond and an inverted pear-shaped surmount, later findings, ⅞" x 2¼" tl, **$127,000** [A]. (Copyright Christie's Images, New York 2002©, Christie's New York, NY, 10/23/01)

Brooches/Pins, flower motifs:

TL, garnet, seed pearls, yg, c. 1830, cut-down collet-set garnet encircled with split pearls, engr yg stem and leaves set with two split pearls, closed convex yg back, C-catch, tube hinge, extended pinstem, ½" w x 1", **$550**. (Lisa Johnson collection)

TR, spinel, pastes, silver, late 18th C, depicting a flower-filled urn, the center set with a pear-shaped natural pink spinel, the flowers set with pink, green, and colorless pastes in a closed-back silver mount, C-catch, tube hinge, extended pinstem, 1" w x 1¼", **$1,800**.

B, coral, rhodolite garnet, yg, wm, c. 1820, carnation of carved coral with a rhodolite garnet center encircled by yg stamens, riveted to a yg stem with engr leaves, C-catch, tube hinge, wm pinstem, 1" w x 1¼", **$400**. (Courtesy of E. Foxe Harrell, New York, NY)

Earrings, garnets, yg, c. 1830, cruciform, collet-set with circ-cut stones, closed backs, later-added earwires, ½" w x ⅞" tl, **$400**. (Lisa Johnson collection)

Necklace, yg, seed pearls, emeralds, diamonds, c. 1820, a row of yg lozenge-shaped plaques with *cannetille* decoration, set with seed pearls and mixed-cut emeralds, suspending a similarly decorated detachable pendent drop on three rows of chains, 2" T to B at center, approx 19" tl, **$4,200** [A]. (Photo courtesy of Sotheby's, London, 6/20/01)

Necklace, diamonds, silver, c. 1760, ropetwist set throughout with rc diamonds, decorated at the front with a twisted knot design, suspending a tasseled pendant with vertical rows of ribbon bow motifs, fitted case, 3" T to B at center, 17" tl, **$12,600** [A]. (Photo courtesy of Sotheby's, London, 6/20/01)

Pendants, mid-18th C, gemstones or paste in convex closed-back settings:
L, silver, rc diamonds, rose gold, openwork silver lozenge shape decorated with rose gold floral motifs set with sm rc diamonds, suspending a similarly decorated articulated cruciform and pear-shaped drop, two loops for ribbon on rev, possibly Ger, 1⅝" w x 3", **$1,200**.
C, silver gilt, paste, openwork bow-shaped top suspending openwork cruciform and ovoid drops, set throughout with emerald-colored pastes, probably Spanish, later-added pin assembly (converted from pendant), lead solder on rev, 2" w x 3⅝", **$900**.
R, gilded brass, garnets, openwork gilt metal top with scrollwork and angel motifs, bezel-set with circ-cut garnets, suspending two drop-shaped garnets and a similarly decorated openwork crucifix, probably Austro-Hungarian, 1¾" w x 2¾", **$500**. (Courtesy of E. Foxe Harrell, New York, NY)

Pendant, garnet, yg, seed pearls, c. 1830, cruciform, two circ-cut and two pear-shaped collet-set garnets encircled with seed pearls (three pearls missing) in convex closed-back yg setting with yg bail, ¾" w x 1¾", **$300**. (Lisa Johnson collection)

Pendant, cross, amethysts, silver gilt, rc diamonds, early 19th C, bezel-set with 12 cushion-shaped, oval and round amethysts in an open-backed silver gilt mount, interspersed with sm rc diamonds (sold with a 24" 14k yg modern rope chain), 2⅜" w x 3", **$673** [A]. (Photo courtesy of Dupuis Jewellery Auctioneers, Toronto, ONT, Canada, 6/11/01)

Pendant, foiled pastes, silver, c. 1770, Maltese cross with foiled pink pastes cut to fit the closed silver mount, surmounted by an integral bail stamped with an illegible hmk, 2" x 2", **$1,100**. (Courtesy of E. Foxe Harrell, New York, NY)

Ring, garnet, pastes, silver, yg, c. 1800, center collet-set cushion-cut garnet (chipped), encircled by circ-cut colorless pastes, flanked by clusters of three pastes, in closed-back cut-down silver collets, yg mount, split shank, ¾" w x ½", sz 7, **$400**. (Lisa Johnson collection)

Ring, enamel, glass, pastes, yg, st yg, 1787, royal presentation ring set with the carved profile of Prince William (later William IV) on a blue enamel ground within a border of circ-cut pastes, engraved on the rev "The gift of his Royal Highness Prince William Henry 12 July 1787," original leather case, ⅞" w x 1⅛", **$3,360** [A]. (Photo courtesy of Sotheby's, London, 6/20/01)

Ring, diamonds, rubies, emerald, silver, 18k yg, c. 1780, an oval-cut ruby in yg, circ-cut emerald, and om diamond in silver cut-down collets with closed backs, around a sm fleur-de-lis set with a rc diamond, surmounted by a st yg arch set with diamonds and rubies, flanked by circ-cut rubies in rubbed-over collet settings, engr foliate design on shank, ½" dia at center, sz 8½, **$3,500**. (Courtesy of E. Foxe Harrell, New York, NY)

Suite: Pendant and Pendent Earrings, silver, diamonds, c. 1780-1800, pendant a six-rayed foliate star shape suspending an openwork pear-shaped drop, set with eight sm flat-cut diamonds in closed back settings, matching pear-shaped earrings with circ surmounts, later-added yg earwires, pendant 1⅛" w x 2" tl, earrings ½" w x 1¼" tl, **$900**. (Lisa Johnson collection)

CUT STEEL, BERLIN IRON, SILESIAN WIRE WORK

Jewelry made from riveted faceted beads or studs of polished steel dates at least as far back as the 16th century. Cut steel jewelry had its heyday in the late eighteenth century, when some of the most delicate and intricate ornaments were made to imitate the sparkle of diamonds. But it persisted as a craft and a fashion into the twentieth century. Much of what survives today was made in France, especially in the form of buckles for shoes and waists.

Some sources say that circa dating can be determined by construction methods and the number of facets on the studs. Earlier pieces have numerous (up to 15) facets, while later ones have as few as five. Machine-stamped strips instead of individually riveted studs are an indication of later, lower-quality, manufacture. But, according to other sources, multi-faceted, individually studded examples of higher quality can also date as late as the 1900s. England was a primary source for cut steel in the eighteenth century, the most well-known manufacturer being Matthew Boulton of Soho, near Birmingham. But factories in France were still turning out cut steel trinkets as recently as the 1940s.

Although buckles are the form most often seen today (for which there is less demand), bracelets, brooches, earrings, chains, chatelaines, and necklaces can also be found (see pages 32 and 33). Considering the intricacies of their design and craftsmanship, and their relative scarcity, prices on these pieces remain quite reasonable.

Most of the black lacy cast iron jewelry known as Berlin iron was made in the early nineteenth century. Its manufacture began around 1806, but a quantity of it was made in Germany during the Prussian War of Liberation against Napoleon (1813-15). Some pieces continued to be made in the 1850s and were exhibited by German manufacturers at the Crystal Palace in 1851. Berlin iron was sand-cast, then lacquered black. Earlier pieces tended toward the Neo-classical, with cast cameo-like profiles mounted on polished steel plaques, sometimes framed in gold (see necklace on page 32). By the '30s, Gothic Revival was the stylistic influence. Gothic arches and tracery were cast into lace-like necklaces, bracelets, earrings, cross pendants, and chains (see necklace on page 32). Today, Berlin iron in any style is extremely scarce and expensive, but the Neo-Gothic forms are in the greatest demand.

Another unique type of iron and steel jewelry, associated with a part of Eastern Europe then known as Silesia (now mostly part of Poland, and parts of the Czech Republic and eastern Germany), is sometimes referred to as Silesian wire work. Wrapped and woven iron or steel wire mesh was fashioned into bracelets, necklaces, brooches, and earrings, sometimes decorated with cutout polished steel shapes known as "sequins" or *paillettes*. Little documentation or information is available about this work, including where it was made and by whom (the name "Silesian wirework" is itself of questionable origin, possibly a term coined by collectors). Although a number of examples are shown in Anne Clifford's *Cut Steel and Berlin Iron Jewellery*, cited in the References (including the identical twin of the necklace in the photo below), the author can only conjecture about its origin. As yet, 31 years after that book's publication, no one has come up with any further information. Some theorize the work was done in England or France, but to date, no documentation supports this theory.

The woven wire mesh was machine-made, which circa-dates the pieces to no earlier than the first quarter of the 19th century. The bracelet on page 31 contains lithographs of the Princess Royal Victoria and her fiancé, the future Frederick III of Prussia. Their engagement began in 1856, which dates this piece quite closely (they married in 1858).

Regardless of its origin, the intricacy of the workmanship is something to marvel at. Coupled with its rarity, Silesian wirework is certainly deserving of greater appreciation and respect than to be called "Brillo pad" jewelry, as once source would have it.

A more readily available type of iron jewelry dates to the latter part of the nineteenth century. It is inaccurately called "gunmetal," perhaps because its smooth burnished bluish-graey surface resembles the barrel of a gun. Chains and lockets are the predominant forms, but accessories and chatelaine appendages are also found on the market (see Late Victorian section, page 75).

Necklace, Silesian wirework, c. 1820, 12 bow-shaped links of black-lacquered fine wire mesh with wirework rosette centers flanking a central looped knot motif with a wirework rosette, suspending a trefoil cross pendant, hook and eye clasp, 16" tl, 2¼" T to B, cross ⅞" x 1⅛", **$900**. (Tamára Torino collection)

Bracelet, link, Berlin iron, cut steel, early 19th C, five links of black-lacquered open scrolled wirework surmounted by polished cut steel star, crescent and lozenge shapes, v-spring clasp, 2½" w, 7" tl, **$1,000**. (Photo courtesy of Linda Morgan Antiques, New York, NY)

Bracelet, Silesian wire, c. 1820, wire mesh strap, ornamental mesh slide, cut steel beads and bow-shaped twisted wire clasp, polished steel rosette with center fringe of five rod and coiled wire drops, 7" tl, clasp 2¼" w x 1⅛", **$750**. (Courtesy of E. Foxe Harrell, New York, NY)

Bracelet, Silesian wire, lithographs, c. 1856, a foliate wreath surmounted by a crown motif in fine woven wire mesh (rusted), central woven wire frames enclosing lithographs of the engagement portraits of Princess Royal Victoria (oldest daughter of Queen Victoria) and Crown Prince Frederick of Prussia, surmounting a narrow braided wire band with integral hook fastener, 2½" ins dia, center 2½" w x 1½", **$1,800**. (Courtesy of E. Foxe Harrell, New York, NY)

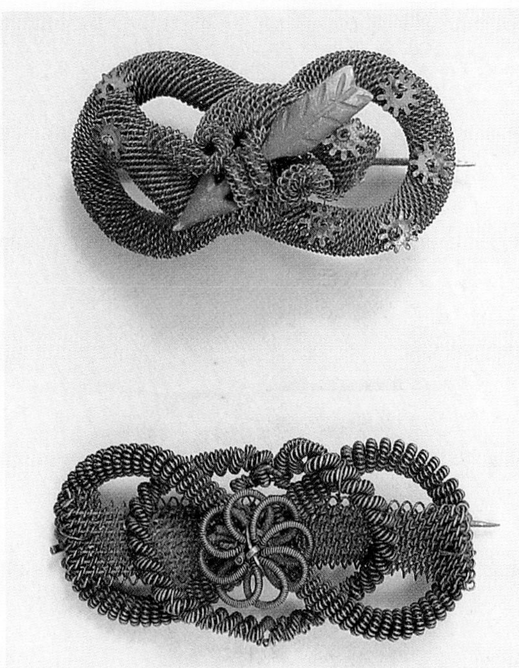

Silesian wirework brooches, c. 1830-40:
T, woven mesh bow shape decorated with "sequins" (some missing), pierced by a carved coral arrow, wire C-catch, wrapped wire hinge, 1⅝" w x ⅞", **$200**.
B, coarse wire mesh bow shape, wire C-catch, wrapped wire hinge, 2⅛" w x 1", **$150**.
(Author's collection).

Brooch/Pin, Silesian wire, bone, c. 1840, a twisted Silesian wire frame decorated with "sequins" (some missing) enclosing a pierced and carved oval bone plaque depicting a deer in foliage (a piece missing from center), 2⅜" w x 1⅞", **$210**. (Diane White collection)

Chatelaine, watch, cut steel, late 18th C, a segmented horizontal bar mounted on a fixed long narrow waist hook, the center bar suspending articulated rows of cut steel clusters and chain links interspersed with oval spacers, terminating in swivel hooks and cut steel tassels, flanked by shorter chains suspended from the outer bars, terminating in larger looped tassels (for a similar example, see p. 49 in *Chatelaines, Utility to Glorious Extravagance*, cited in References), 7" tl, **$800**. (Photo courtesy of Linda Morgan Antiques, New York, NY)

Necklace, Berlin iron, polished steel, c. 1840, open lacy quatrefoil links terminating in a v-spring and hand clasp, suspending a girandole pendant with Gothic arches above and below a polished steel disk surmounted by a rosette, flanked by foliate motifs, three open pear-shaped drops, 16" tl, pendant 1½"w x 3" tl, **$1,800**. (Courtesy of E. Foxe Harrell, New York, NY)

Earrings, pendent, cut steel, polished steel, c. 1820-30, open triangular surmount suspending a lg open pear-shaped drop enclosing a free-swinging smaller pear-shaped drop, riveted throughout with sm circ and larger navette-shaped faceted cut steel studs, polished steel backing, shepherd's hook earwires, 1" w x 3⅛" tl, **$400**. (Author's collection)

Necklace, festoon, Berlin iron, polished steel, c. 1820, swagged chains of coiled wirework rosette links suspending an oval polished steel plaque surmounted by a cast iron classical figure within a lacy openwork beaded cast iron frame, plaque 1⅛" w x 1⅞", 15" tl, **$1,265** [A]. (Photo courtesy of Skinner, Inc., Boston MA, 9/25/01)

Necklace, cut steel, MOP, early Victorian, three flowerhead motifs with MOP petals flanked by openwork cut steel medallions and prong-set MOP disks, continuing to a cable link steel chain, MOP-set clasp, 17" tl, flowers 1½" dia, **$1,600**. (Photo courtesy of Linda Morgan Antiques, New York, NY)

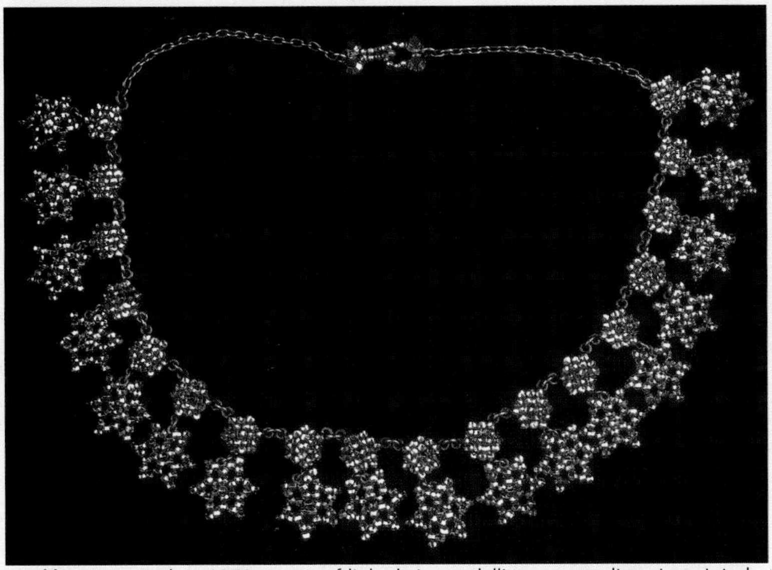

Necklace, cut steel, c. 1850, a row of linked circ medallions suspending six-pointed star motifs, continuing to a cable link chain, hook and eye clasp, 18" tl, stars ½" dia, **$1,800**. (Photo courtesy of Linda Morgan Antiques, New York, NY)

Suite: Bracelet and Brooch, Silesian wire, c. 1840, bracelet an openwork coiled wire strap, hook closure under gathered and coiled wire mesh surmount in grape cluster motif, matching brooch, C-catch, tube hinge, bracelet 8" tl, top 1⅝" w x 2", brooch 1⅞" w x 2¼", **$750**. (Courtesy of E. Foxe Harrell, New York, NY)

Pendant, cross, Berlin iron, cut steel, early 19th C, black-lacquered scrolled wirework cross surmounted by cut steel bars, stars, and a central equilateral cross, suspended from a steel mesh rod and circ jump ring chain, 2¼" w x 3", **$650**. (Photo courtesy of Linda Morgan Antiques, New York, NY)

MEMORIAL, MOURNING, and HAIR JEWELRY

One of the most popular expressions of sentimentality, on both sides of the Atlantic, was the making and wearing of jewelry containing human hair, a practice which originated in the seventeenth century. These pieces were worn as memento mori (mourning) and also as love tokens.

The earliest type of hair jewelry was made with glass or rock crystal-covered compartments to hold the hair of a loved one, living or deceased. These continued to be made and worn through the greater part of the nineteenth century, with some alterations in style. Eighteenth and early to mid-nineteenth century mourning brooches might depict an entire funereal scene painted on ivory, complete with weeping willow, urn, and a despondent maiden standing forlornly by. The sepia tones of the paint were often derived from using macerated hair as a pigment. This was strictly for reasons of sentiment, not because the hair provided a superior form of paint. Sometimes the scene was made three-dimensional with snippets of hair forming, for example, the branches of the willow (see page 35).

Handkerchief pins, hair, c. 1800-1820:
1st, convex elliptical gf frame with raised rim, central compartment containing braided blond hair, rock crystal cover, rev engr with initials "AA," C-catch, tube hinge, extended pinstem, 1" w x ½", **$165.**
2nd, oval glazed compartment containing two knots of hair, blond surmounting brown, set in convex-backed yg frame, C-catch, tube hinge, extended pinstem, ¾" w x ½", **$200.**
3rd, rounded rect glazed compartment containing braided blond hair, stamped and engr gf frame, C-catch, tube hinge, extended pinstem, 1" w x ½", **$175.**
4th, rect glazed compartment containing braided hair, stamped and engr frame, scalloped edge, C-catch, tube hinge, extended pinstem, ⅝" w x ½", **$190.**
5th, rounded rect central compartment containing brown hair, crystal cover, seed pearl and yg frame, initials "MAB" engr on rev, C-catch, tube hinge (on plate mounts), extended pinstem, ¾" w x ⅝", **$225.** (Courtesy of E. Foxe Harrell, New York, NY)

In some pieces, the hair is formed into curls, called "Prince of Wales plumes," (see reverse of miniature on page 37), or made into wheat sheaves, mounted on a white background. Another technique was to lay strands of hair flat on "goldbeater's skin," a type of adhesive backing, and cut out individual floral motifs which were then assembled as a three-dimensional "picture" under glass.

More commonly, locks of hair were simply braided or coiled, sometimes using more than one color (from different family members), and placed in compartments set into a frame and covered with glass.

On mourning pieces, the outer or inner frame could include a snake motif, symbolizing eternity. Seed pearls, symbolic of tears, were sometimes added, along with gold thread or wire tied around the lock of hair. In late Georgian and early Victorian pieces, the backs are gold or gold-filled, and slightly convex. They were often engraved with names or initials, and dates of birth and/or death. This personalization of a piece is desirable to collectors, and of course it takes the guesswork out of placing the piece in its time-frame.

Late Georgian mourning brooches or pins were often navette-shaped, oval, or oblong; circa 1820-40, they were small rounded rectangles, ovals, or crescents, often worn pinned to black ribbon as a necklace or bracelet. They were bordered with pearls, garnets, coral, French jet (black glass), or black enamel around the glass-covered compartment (according to Shirley Bury [op. cit. References], these were sometimes called "handkerchief pins," later known as "lace pins." (See this page and page 35). Later brooches were larger, worn at the throat or in the center of the bodice. Black onyx plaques or black enameled borders inscribed "In Memory Of" around a central hair compartment became standardized forms for mourning pieces (see page 35).

Double-sided rock crystal lockets with gem-set frames were popular in the mid to late eighteenth century. They could contain a lock of hair or other memento of a loved one (see page 35).

Late Georgian mourning rings, like brooches, could also be navette-shaped or oblong, or wide bands with inscriptions encircling the outer surface (see page 36, ring, top left). Others bore inscriptions around the outside of a narrow black-enameled shank surmounted by a hair compartment framed in garnets or pearls, or a gemstone (see page 36). Some mourning rings have swiveling compartments, one side containing hair (see page 36, ring, top right). Victorian mourning rings might be simple bands with woven hair channel-set around the outside, or an enameled inscription. Fancier rings had cutout or enameled names on compartments containing hair (see page 36, bottom photo).

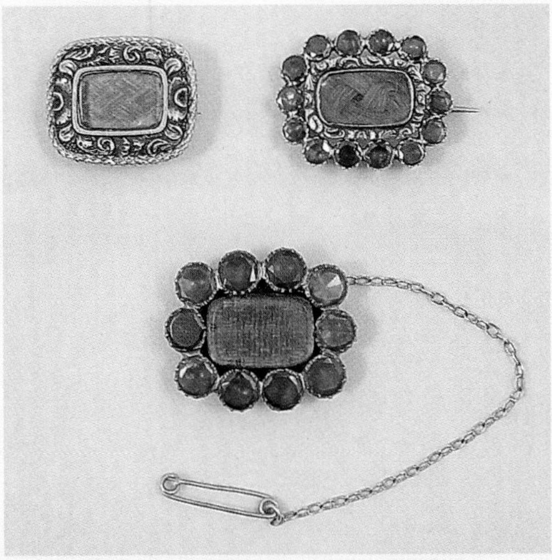

Handkerchief pins, hair, glass, c. 1830:
TL, glazed compartment containing tightly woven brown hair inside a rounded rect chisel-engr yg frame, C-catch, tube hinge, ⅞" w x ¾", **$350**.
TR, collet-set circ-cut garnets framing a glazed compartment containing braided brown hair, convex yg back, engr yg border, C-catch, tube hinge, extended pinstem, 1" w x ¾", **$375**. (Lisa Johnson collection).
B, rounded rect glazed compartment containing tightly woven brown hair, bordered with circ-cut garnets in cut-down collets, rolled gold convex back, later-appl jump ring on rev, safety chain and safety pin, C-catch, tube hinge, 1" w x ⅞", **$300**. (Author's collection).

Pendant, 12k rose gold, ivory, hair, enamel, glass, c. 1800, polychrome depiction on ivory of a woman leaning against an urn and tomb surrounded by foliage, within a black and white enameled border with gold accents, glass cover, set within a plain rose gold frame, rev with flat-woven hair surmounted by mono on oval ivory plaque within concentric oval gold frames set in a cobalt blue *basse-taille* enameled surround, 2½" w x 3½" tl, **$2,950**. (Courtesy of Lenore Dailey, The Raven's Nest, Palm Springs, CA).

Brooch/Pin, yg, glass, hair, enamel, c. 1840-50, tubular yg frame, an Algerian knot motif, decorated with engr and *taille d'épargne* enameled foliate scrolls, enclosing an oval glazed compartment containing a mourning scene (urn and weeping willow) in sepia-toned paint and snippets of hair, on a milk glass plaque set in a yg collet with three projecting soldered yg wire loops on rev holding it in place, C-catch, tube hinge, extended pinstem, 2¼" w x 1⅝", **$700**. (Courtesy of Lenore Dailey, The Raven's Nest, Palm Springs, CA)

Lockets, rock crystal, gemstones, late 18th C:
T, ovoid rock crystal within a yg garnet-set frame, hinged at the top, surmounted by a garnet-set flower motif and bail, ½" w x ⅞" h, **$650**.
B, faceted-edge rounded shield-shaped rock crystal set in a yg cut-down collet, hinged at the top, surmounted by an openwork design, rc diamonds set in st yg flanking a yg X shape set with green and red pastes, 1" w x 1⅛" tl, **$1,000**. (Courtesy of Chris Enebo Antique Jewelry, Tualatin, OR)

Pendant, yg, enamel, hair, wire, porcelain, c. 1800, large oval yg frame, *basse-taille* cobalt blue enameled ground, the front and back with an engr inner yg frame enclosing a glazed compartment with a bowknot of hairwork and wirework over a porcelain ground, surmounted by a hinged pendant bail, 2⅜" w x 3⅝" tl, **$1,645** [A]. (Photo courtesy of Dupuis Jewellery Auctioneers, Toronto, ONT, Canada, 6/12/01)

Pendant, ivory, 9k rose gold, hair, gold wire, white beads, MOP, c. 1800, circ polychrome miniature on ivory of a mourning scene depicting a woman standing beside a tomb inlaid with MOP and gold threads (slight damage), a cherub in flight holding a flower wreath and an arrow, in a sylvan landscape, beveled glass cover, rose gold frame, glazed rev containing a curl of hair decorated with gold threads and sm white beads, 1¾" dia, bail ¼," **$1,200**. (Courtesy of Chris Enebo Antique Jewelry, Tualatin, OR)

Brooch/Pin, enamel, hair, yg, glass, c. 1843, blonde and white braided hair enclosed in a glazed compartment, "IN MEMORY OF" Old English lettering through black enamel on frame with chisel-engr inner and outer borders, engraved on rev: "Ms Buchannan died 12th Nov 1843 John Wilson died 4th June 1843," C-catch, tube hinge, extended pinstem, 1⅞" w x 1½," **$425**. (Photo courtesy of Morning Glory Antiques, Albuquerque, NM)

Rings, yg, enamel:
L, c. 1779, narrow yg band, black enameled raised center inscribed "SAML BALL OB 9 JAN 1779 AE: 61," illegible hmks on inside, ⅛" w, sz 8, **$425**. (Courtesy of E. Foxe Harrell, New York, NY)
C, c. 1768, oval-cut amethyst bezel-set in a closed back setting, openwork shoulders continuing to a black-enameled shank inscribed "THO FLOWER OB 16 AUG 1766 AE 66," inside engr "Jane Flower OB 9 Mar 1768," ¼" w at center, sz 8, **$850**.
R, c. 1803, plain yg band, narrow bands of white enamel flanking black enameled center inscribed "DOROTHEA WYLDE OB 14 SEP 1803 AE 37," Eng hmks, ¼" w, sz 7-1/2, **$725**. (Catherine Ratcliffe collection).

Rings, yg, enamel:
L, date letter for 1825-26, wide band with chisel-engr 18k yg borders enclosing black enameled "IN MEMORY OF" in Old English lettering, inside engr with inscription "John Craig Esq, Obit 1 May 1826, Aet 75," stamped with London hmks, maker's mk WE, ⅜" w, sz 8, **$750**.
R, c. 1810, swiveling rect compartment, rock crystal-covered center on one side containing braided blond hair and framed with sq-cut garnets, black enameling on rev inscribed "ANNE BUXTON OB 5 NOV 1808 AET 85" inside white enameled border, mounted on narrow yg shank, ⅛" w x ⅛", sz 7, **$1,100**.
(Courtesy of Chris Enebo Antique Jewelry, Tualatin, OR)

Rings, yg, ivory, sepia-tone paint, glass:
L, c. 1784, navette-shaped engr frame bezel set with ivory plaque painted with funereal symbols: urn, two doves, weeping willow, initials "RT" flanking urn, rev engr "Frances Cumbers Ob 5 Novr 1784" mounted on engr shoulders tapering to narrow shank, approx size 7½, head ¾" w x 1¼", **$1,800**.
R, c. 1783, elongated octagonal plaque with mourning scene of a weeping man standing beside an urn surmounting a pedestal inscribed "SARAH STARR OB 5 MAY 1783 AE 12 YRS" mounted in engr yg frame, glass cover, engr shoulders tapering to narrow shank, approx size 4½, head ¾" w x 1¼", **$1,895**. (Courtesy of Lenore Dailey, The Raven's Nest, Palm Springs, CA)

Ring, yg, hair, enamel, rock crystal, c. 1820, rounded rect yg compartment containing braided blond/gray hair, rock crystal cover, mounted on black enameled yg band, inscribed on outside: "JOHN BAYLIES OB 12 NOV:1777 AE:50" (top line) and "ELIZ. BAYLIES OB 22 JAN 1816 AE:85" (bottom line), approx size 8½, ½" w x ⅜," shank ¼" w, **$325**. (Carmelita Johnson collection)

Ring, black glass (Fr jet), turquoise, glass, gf, rock crystal, hair, c. 1830-40, eight circ-cut black glass stones set in cut-down collets around a central glazed compartment containing braided brown hair, shank of grad turq and turq-colored glass cabs set in cut-down collets, approx sz 5, ⅝" x ½," **$495**. (Courtesy of Lenore Dailey, The Raven's Nest, Palm Springs, CA)

Rings, yg, enamel, hair, c. 1830:
T, black enameled rounded rect with central glazed compartment containing woven dk brown hair, continuing to tapered shank, black enameled block letters "IN MEMORY OF" around outside, mkd "18ct" on inside shank, approx sz 9½, ½" w x ½", **$395**.
B, bowed, cusped rect frame with black enameled Old English lettering "IN MEMORY OF" around central rect glazed compartment containing woven strands of brown hair, rev engr "Sarah Roper Parnell, Oct 29th, 1830," continuing to a pierced and engr tapered shank, approx sz 6, ⅝" w x ½", **$495**. (Courtesy of Lenore Dailey, The Raven's Nest, Palm Springs, CA)

Rings, yg, hair, c. 1850-70:
T, tightly braided rows of blond and brown hair channel-recessed in yg band surmounted by engr yg plaque with mono, ½" w, sz 6, **$200**.
BL, "Lottie" engr on scrolled yg plaque covering braided brown hair channel-recessed in yg band, ⅜" w, sz 5, **$200**.
BR, yg band, hollow construction, inside lined with tightly braided brown hair, L-shaped cutouts on engr top surface, illegible mono, ⅜" w, sz 6½, **$250**.
(Private collection).

MINIATURES

Before the advent of photography, the miniature portrait was the only way to capture a wearable likeness of a loved one. This was another popular form of sentiment in the eighteenth and early to mid-nineteenth centuries.

Some miniatures were worn as memorials to a deceased spouse or parent, but others were simply a way of keeping a likeness as a reminder of the object of one's affections. Queen Victoria wore a portrait of Albert as a bracelet clasp from the beginning of their marriage, which she of course continued to wear after his death. Bracelets and pendants were the most common way of wearing a miniature, but brooches were also worn. Portrait miniatures in painted enamel often have a lock of the portrayed loved one's hair enclosed in a compartment on the reverse.

Portraits are relatively easy to circa-date, if one is familiar with fashion history, and notes the clothing, hair, and other details of the person depicted. These are usually rendered in the styles of the times.

Other types of miniatures have religious themes, some simply depict a pretty scene. The Swiss were known for painted enamels (sometimes called Geneva or Swiss enamel), most often depicting people, usually women, in regional dress against a scenic background (see bracelet, top right). These were at the height of fashion in the 1830s. Sylvan scenic Swiss landscapes were also rendered in enamels during this period.

One of the rarest and most desirable forms of miniature is the eye miniature, said to have originated with George IV in 1785, while he was Prince of Wales. He sent a miniature of his eye in a letter to the widow Maria Fitzherbert, whom he later secretly married. The eye portrayed was difficult to identify, giving rise to the idea of a "secret lover," always watching (see page 38). Eye miniatures were worn through the first half of the nineteenth century, although by the 1820s, the fashion had waned considerably. They are not often seen on the market today (see Reproduction Alert).

The masked ball was another context in which anonymity was sought as a form of amusement. These were a popular diversion among the wealthy of the late nineteenth century, who often dressed in pre-Revolutionary eighteenth century costume. Portraits of masked revelers were sometimes made in miniature (see brooch, right, and stickpin on page 38).

By the second half of the nineteenth century, photographs began to supersede portrait miniatures, and were often inserted into one side of the swiveling compartment of a large gold or gilt metal brooch (see Manufactured Gold and Gold-filled section, page 70). The other side might contain a lock of the loved one's hair or a swatch of his or her clothing. Photographs were also contained in lockets, a tradition that continues to this day.

Reproduction Alert

Because they are scarce and sought-after, eye portraits have been faked, usually by taking the hair out of a brooch with a glazed compartment and replacing it with an eye. Some of the eyes aren't even actual paintings, rather they are printed. The small screened dots making up the picture are the giveaway.

Bracelet, hinged bangle, Swiss enamel, yg, c. 1830, oval miniature depicting a seated lady with two children, within a scalloped border decorated with black and white enamel motifs on a similarly decorated bangle, enamel imperfect, 2½" inside dia, 2⅛" T to B at center, **$2,016** [A]. (Photo courtesy of Sotheby's, London, 6/20/01)

Brooch/Pin, painted ivory, yg, glass, c.1850, polychrome portrait of a young girl, glass cover, chamfered-corner rect yg frame and convex backing, C-catch, tube hinge, extended pinstem, ⅞" x 1", **$1,500**. (Courtesy of Lenore Dailey, The Raven's Nest, Palm Springs, CA).

Brooch/Pin, bisque, enamel, gilt brass, c. 1850, oval plaque, ptd enamel scene of a girl with cat and chicks, set in gilt brass frame (enamel damaged), 2" w x 1½", **$100**. (Vickie Vega collection)

Brooch/Pin, 18k yg, enamel, rc diamonds, st yg, late 19th C, polychrome enamel depicting the head of a masked woman in 18th C costume set within a yg bg, rc diamond eyes and border, Fr hmk (eagle's head) on C-catch, extended pinstem, tube hinge, 1⅛" dia, **$2,900**. (Courtesy of Lenore Dailey, The Raven's Nest, Palm Springs, CA)

Brooch/Pendant, painted ivory, yg, beveled lead crystal, hair, gold thread, seed pearls, c. 1840, ptd portrait of a woman set in a beveled glass-covered yg frame, engr scrollwork at compass points, glazed compartment on rev containing Prince of Wales plumes of hair and gold thread with three seed pearls, slight damage/repair on frame, later-added trombone catch, tube hinge, 2¼" w x 2¾", **$2,250**. (Courtesy of Lenore Dailey, The Raven's Nest, Palm Springs, CA)

Brooch/ Pendant, 15k yg, ivory, pearls, c. 1870-80, portrait bust of a woman in mid-Victorian dress and hairstyle painted on ivory, in a yg backing and frame set with a border of sm pearls, larger pearls at compass points, rev engr "Mary Augusta Andruss, wife of Charles C. Lathrop, Newark, N.J.," C-catch, tube hinge, hinged bail, 1⅞" x 2¼", **$1,500**. (Marne Ryan collection)

Pendants, eye miniatures, ptd ivory, gold:
T, early 19th C, a ptd eye and a lock of hair on ivory in a heart-shaped glazed yg frame encircled by prong-set rc garnets, a glazed compartment on rev containing white cloth, suspended from a detachable garnet-set bail, ¾" w x 1¼" tl, **$2,300**.
BL, Brooch/Pendant, c. 1830-40, a ptd eye in a rect yg frame, beveled glass cover, encircled by split pearls in cut-down collets, convex pink gold back, loops for bail and safety chain on top and bottom rev, C-catch, tube hinge, extended pinstem, 1⅛" w x ⅞" l, **$2,500**.
(Courtesy of Apriori Antiques, San Francisco, CA)
BR, early 19th C, a ptd eye in an oval yg mount, beveled glass cover, within a lozenge-shaped frame formed from flowerheads set with pear-shaped garnets and sm turq cabs alternating with grad rows of circ-cut garnets, turq cabs and seed pearls, cut-down collets, slightly convex yg backs, oval glazed compartment on rev containing braided blond hair, pendant hook, 1½" w x 1⅜", **$3,200**. (Courtesy of Lenore Dailey, The Raven's Nest, Palm Springs, CA)

Pendant, ptd ivory, seed pearls, yg, glass, hair, c. 1800, circ eye miniature bordered with seed pearls set in yg, pearl-set hinged bail, hinged glazed compartment on rev containing braided brown hair, ⅞" w x 1⅛" tl, **$2,985**. (Courtesy of Lenore Dailey, The Raven's Nest, Palm Springs, CA)

Pendant, ptd ivory, silver, yg, seed pearls, late 18th C, depicting a putto with harp ptd *"en grisaille,"* yg frame with silver border and bow motif bail set with seed pearls, double loops on rev for suspending from a ribbon, ⅞" w x 1⅞", **$800**. (Vickie Vega collection)

Pendant, ivory, silver, 14k yg, seed pearls, c. 1800, an oval miniature depicting a young country girl with a basket and flowers, set in a yg bezel encircled by a foliate motif silver frame and bow-shaped detachable bail set with seed pearls, hinged glazed compartment on rev containing hair, Fr hmks, 1⅛" w x 2⅜" tl, **$1,410** [A]. (Photo courtesy of Butterfields, San Francisco and Los Angeles, CA, 9/25/01)

Scarf Pin/Stickpin, yg, enamel, rc diamonds, late 19th C, polychrome enamel depicting the head of a masked woman in 18th C costume, rc diamond-set eyes, set in a yg frame, mounted on a yg pinstem, fitted case, head ⅝" w, 3½" tl, **$1,607** [A]. (Photo courtesy of Sotheby's, London, 11/27/01).

EARLY VICTORIAN (ROMANTIC PERIOD) c. 1837-1861

Queen Victoria set the tone for the era as the first female to rule Great Britain since Queen Anne (d. 1714). Like most women of her time, she was an incurable romantic—and she *loved* jewelry! The early years of her reign are aptly called The Romantic Period (also known as the Victoria and Albert period). In 1840, Victoria married Albert, who became Prince Consort in 1857, and died suddenly in 1861. The 21 years of their marriage were filled with love, devotion, and the births of nine children. Symbols of romance were predominant in the jewelry that Albert designed and had made for Victoria. Her betrothal ring was in the form of a snake with its tail in its mouth, symbol of everlasting love, a motif that recurs throughout the nineteenth century. The snake also symbolized eternity, guardian spirit, and wisdom. Snake (or serpent) jewelry was especially popular in the 1840s. Gold snake necklaces, bracelets, and rings were set throughout with small turquoise cabochons or partly enameled and gem-set (see page 42 and below).

Flowers in jewelry were both symbolic of Victorian sentiment and a reflection of interest in nature. Flower motif brooches in diamonds and paste carried over from Georgian times, but became more three-dimensional and realistic. Flower heads were often set *en tremblant*. Gold and colored gemstone flowers were also realistically rendered (see brooch at top right and page 41).

The hand is another recurring romantic symbol in Victorian jewelry. It had a variety of meanings depending on how it was depicted. Hands holding flowers conveyed the flower's message. Yew wreaths symbolized mourning. Clasped hands symbolized friendship. Good luck and "evil eye" hand gesture amulets were carved in coral, ivory, jet, and mother-of-pearl (see pendant on page 43). Hands were also used as clasps for bracelets and neckchains, especially in earlier period pieces (see necklace on page 32).

Brooch/Pin, yg, turquoise, c. 1835-1840, high karat yg in a realistic ivy leaf and forget-me-not flower design, buds set with sm turq cabs, engr and textured surface, C-catch, flanged hinge, 2" w x 1⅛", **$600**. (Private collection)

Sentiment prevailed in the gifts of jewelry Victoria exchanged with others. She fostered the widespread practice of giving and wearing jewelry made with the hair of the giver as a memento or love token. And no one thought it at all strange that she had a bracelet made from her children's baby teeth.

The Great Exhibition of the Industry of All Nations, held in London in 1851, was perhaps the single most important event of the early Victorian period. It was dubbed "The Crystal Palace" after the gigantic all-glass structure that housed it. Never before had there been a multinational exhibit of any kind, held anywhere. This monumental spectacle has been called "the focal point for the Victorian culture of the Western world." Its success spawned "Crystal Palace" offspring in Cork in 1852, New York and Dublin in 1853, Munich in 1854, and Paris in 1855. In 1854, the Crystal Palace itself was recreated at Sydenham, outside London. The jewelers who took part in these exhibitions were the most highly esteemed trendsetters of jewelry fashion. If it had been seen at the Crystal Palace, it was "in." In 1851, naturalistic diamond flower brooches and hair ornaments, Celtic annular (ring) brooches, and Scottish "granite" bracelets, Berlin iron jewelry, and gemstone and enameled bracelets were among the jewels shown.

Early Victorian fashions determined the ways in which jewelry was or was not worn. The dresses of the period were full-skirted, worn with petticoats, and often had long sleeves. Lace collars with brooches pinned at the throat were common. Necklines on dresses worn by younger women were cut low and wide across the shoulders. Velvet or silk ribbons were sometimes worn around the neck,

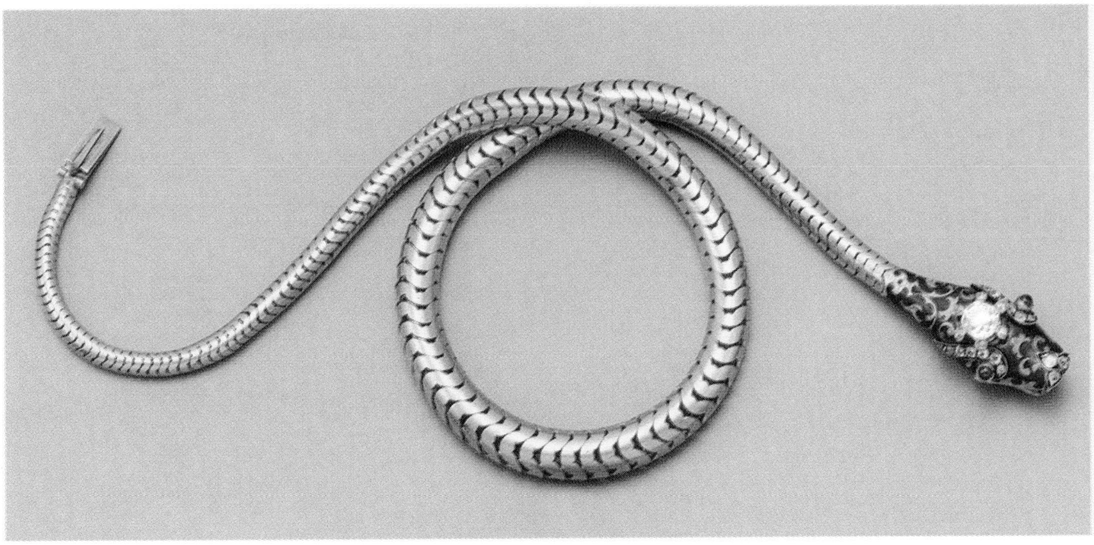

Necklace, snake, yg, enamel, diamonds, garnets, c. 1840s, the clasp depicting a serpent's head decorated with royal blue enamel and set with om and sc diamonds, the reverse inscribed "CKC TO DPC JAN 31ST 1844" on a graduated flexible chain of Brazilian linking, fitted case by Wartski, head ⅝" w x 1¼", approx 17" tl, **$6,384** [A]. (Photo courtesy of Sotheby's, London, 6/20/01)

crossed in front and pinned with a small brooch. Large jeweled brooches with pendent drops, called bodice brooches, were worn on low-cut gowns in the evening (see this page). Unless otherwise altered, early Victorian brooches usually have an extended pinstem (meant to be pushed back through the clothing to keep the brooch in place), C-catch, and tube hinge.

In the late 1840s and early 1850s, bonnets were worn during the day, and for evening wear, center-parted hair covered the ears in loops or ringlets, trimmed in ribbons or flowers. Consequently, earrings were seldom worn. Bracelets, worn in multiples on both wrists, were the most popular form of jewelry, especially snake-shaped coils or bangles. "Stretchy" expandable bracelets were introduced in the early 1840s, thanks to the invention of elastic, c. 1830. In spite of their prevalence, relatively few early Victorian bracelets survive today, having been subjected to considerably more wear and damage than brooches or necklaces might have been.

Romanticism inspired the beginnings of a revival of medieval and Renaissance motifs and decorative elements that was to continue throughout the century. Gothic architecture was translated into jewels. Gold was still in relatively short supply at the onset of the Early Victorian period. In the 1830s, gold was mostly hand-wrought filigree (*cannetille*), but by the 1840s, filigree was out and hollow stamped or repoussé thin gauge metal was in, used as settings for gemstones, or as frames for portrait miniatures and enamels. While *à jour* settings for faceted gemstones were now common, foiled stones in closed-back mounts continued to be seen, especially "pinked" topaz (colorless topaz with pink foil backing, see brooch on page 41).

Seed pearl jewelry was often made with little, if any, gold at all. Tiny pearls strung on horsehair and mounted on cut-to-shape mother-of-pearl backings were made into entire suites of delicate and fragile jewels, typically of floral and foliate design. It is unusual to find individual pieces intact, and even rarer to come across intact suites, many of which were made in England in the first half of the nineteenth century (see tiara on page 42). The fashion for seed pearls persisted longer in the United States (see suite on page 42). It was traditionally worn as bridal jewelry, but seed pearl jewelry items were still being offered for sale for everyday wear in American trade cataologs of the nineteen-teens (see brooches on page 83).

Bracelet, bangle, *doublé d'or* (rolled gold), silver, c. 1835, heraldic shield flanked by silver rampant hounds surmounting engr scrollwork, continuing to a band with raised engr foliate scroll decoration on a textured ground, adjustable keyhole clasp, French hmks for silver before 1838, and rolled gold after 1829 ("DOUBLÉ R" in a square) on outside near clasp, 1⅞" T to B at center, 2¾" inside dia, **$1,800**. (Courtesy of E. Foxe Harrell, New York, NY)

Bracelets, link, Swiss enamel, 18k yg, c. 1840, hollow links of opposed C-scrolls terminating in a rounded and waisted rect clasp, with allover black and white Swiss enameled floral/foliate motif decoration, flat backing, safety chain, 7⅜" tl, clasps 1⅜" x 1", **$4,000**/pr. (Courtesy of E. Foxe Harrell, New York, NY)

Brooch/Pin, bodice, aquamarine, yg, glass, c. 1840, stylized trefoil design, set with three mixed-cut aquamarines and aquamarine pendent drop (detachable), set in repoussé scrollwork with chain swags, glazed hair compartment on rev, 2⅜" w x 3⅜", **$1,607** [A]. (Photo courtesy of Sotheby's, London, 11/27/01)

Brooch/Pin, bodice, yg, amethysts, c. 1840, navette-shaped die-stamped yg scrolled openwork with central faceted oval amethyst in open-backed pronged collet, suspending a scrolled openwork drop similarly set with an elongated faceted pear-shaped amethyst, flat backing, C-catch, tube hinge, extended pinstem, safety chain with safety pin, 1⅞" w x 2½" tl, **$550**. (Courtesy of E. Foxe Harrell Jewelers)

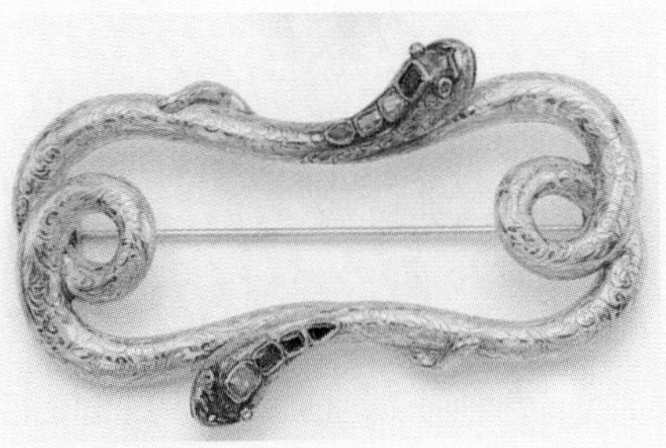

Brooch/Pin, yg, rubies, emeralds, sc diamonds, c. 1840, an openwork design of two undulating serpents, their heads set with emeralds and rubies, their eyes with diamonds and their bodies decorated with stylized plume and foliate motifs, originally a buckle, later pinback assembly, 3¼" w x 1⅝", **$1,176** [A]. (Photo courtesy of Sotheby's, London, 6/20/01)

Brooch/Pin, chalcedony, enamel, turquoise, yg, c. 1840-50, concave oval chalcedony plaque inlaid with a yg forget-me-not motif set throughout with sm turq cabs, the plaque held by fluted prongs within a blue-enameled scallop-edge yg frame with foliate decoration, C-catch, tube hinge, extended pinstem, 2" w x 1⅝", **$450**. (Photo courtesy of Morning Glory Antiques, Albuquerque, NM)

Brooch/Pin, yg, foiled "pinked" topaz, c. 1840, die-struck and engr floral and scrolled foliate yg lozenge shape, the center set with a lg oval faceted foiled colorless topaz in a pronged bezel, glazed compartment on closed-back rev containing tightly woven brown hair, the mount unbacked, C-catch, tube hinge, extended pinstem, 2¼" w x 1⅜", **$500**. (Courtesy of Patrick Kapty, Palm Springs, CA)

Brooch/Pin, coral, turquoise, seed pearls, silver, yg, rubies, c. 1840-50, depicting a three-dimensional bird in st yg, pavé-set with sm turq cabs and seed pearls, ruby eyes, with a seed pearl-set yg floral/foliate branch in its beak, on a carved pink coral leaf riveted to a yg backing, suspending two articulated drops with yg beads, turq-set leaves, and prong-set seed pearls, C-catch, tube hinge, extended pinstem, 1⅛" w x 2½", **$1,500**. (Courtesy of Xcentricities, Beverly Hills, CA)

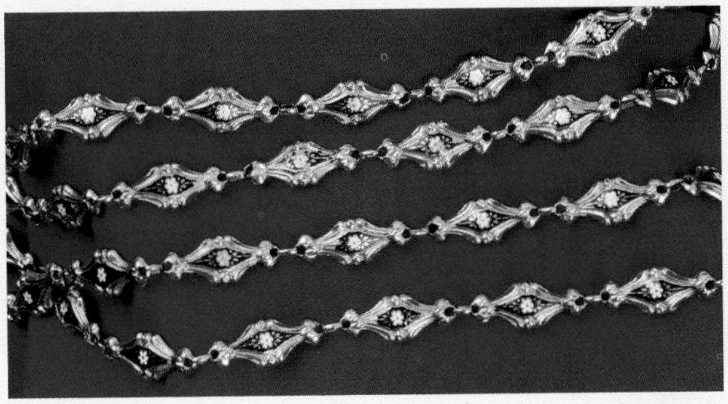

Chain, 18k yg, Swiss enamel, c. 1840, fifty-one lozenge-shaped hollow links, raised ridged borders with black and white floral and foliate Swiss enameled decoration in the centers, some wear to enamel, 54" tl, **$3,290** [A]. (Photo courtesy of Skinner, Inc., Boston, MA, 12/11/01)

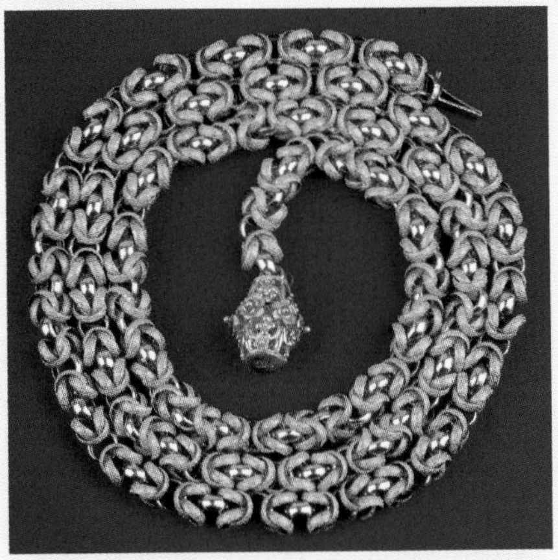

Chain, 14k yg, early Victorian, textured and polished interwoven fancy links terminating in a v-spring and barrel clasp decorated with flowerheads and beading, original fitted box, 60.1dwt, ⅜" w x 46½" tl, **$7,590** [A]. (Photo courtesy of Skinner, Inc., Boston, MA, 9/25/01)

Necklace, turquoise, mine-cut diamonds, st yg, c. 1840, composed of grad floret links, the centers set with an oval turq cab, encircled by om diamonds, the connecting links of om diamonds, retailed and accompanied by sgd, original fitted box from S.J. Phillips Ltd. London, 16" tl, ⅝" w at center, **$19,925** [A]. (Photo courtesy of Butterfields, San Francisco and Los Angeles, CA, 9/25/01)

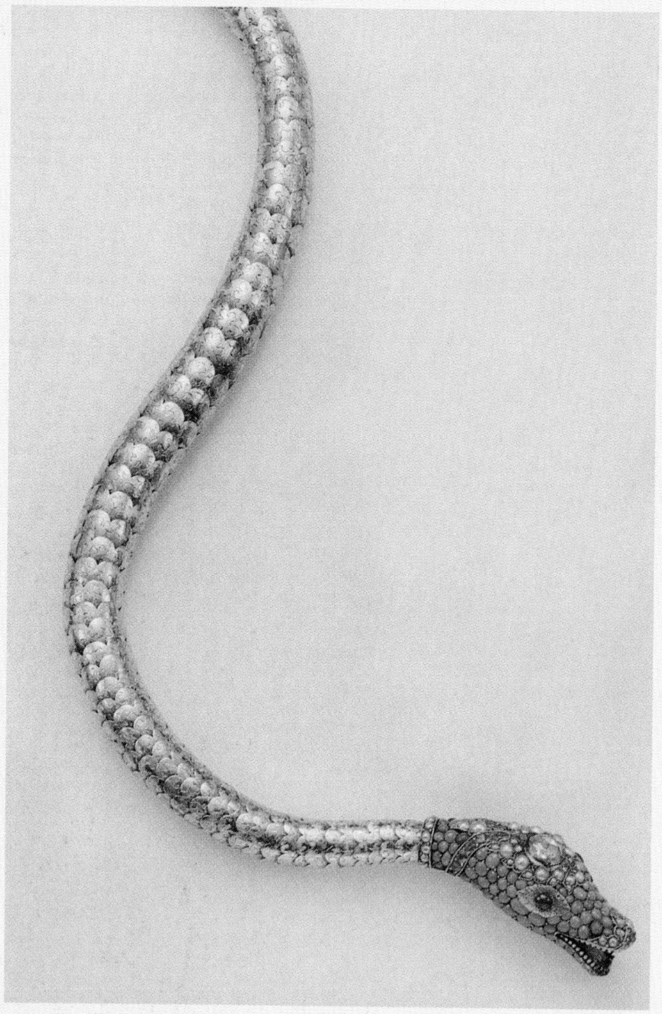

Necklace, snake, yg, turquoise, rc diamond, half pearls, garnets, rubies, c. 1845, the head pavé-set with turq cabs, seed pearls, rubies, garnet eyes, and a lg rc diamond, continuing to an articulated engr snake-scale linking, head ¾" w 1⅝", approx 16" tl, **$6,768** [A]. (Photo courtesy of Sotheby's, London, 11/27/01)

Rings, c. 1830-40:
L, a cluster of opals and seed pearls encircling a rect-cut garnet in an engr yg flowerhead and openwork foliate mount, hinged compartment, ½" dia, sz 7½, **$500**.
R, three-color gold, in the shape of an envelope, top-hinged "flap" with appl green gold leaves around a sm bezel-set turq cab, bottom-hinged "flap" underneath, opens to reveal a compartment, flanked by turq-set flowerheads, ⅜" w x ¼" h, sz 6, **$900**. (Courtesy of Chris Enebo Antique Jewelry, Tualatin, OR)

Tiara, seed pearls, MOP, horsehair, 9k yg, c. 1850, grad floral sprays of seed pearls of varying size strung on horsehair and mounted on MOP plaques, yg wire mounts attaching sprays to yg circlet, looped terminals for ribbon attachment, in orig box, Eng, 12" circumference, 3¾" at center tapering to 1¼", **$1,800**. (Photo courtesy of Sharen and Nicholas Wood, London)

Suite: Necklace and Brooch/Pin, seed pearls, yg, c. 1861, necklace of grad oval and circ plaques of seed pearls set in concentric circles within crimped gold mountings with closed backs, brooch a single oval plaque, in a fitted Tiffany box. Note: once thought to have been worn by Mary Todd Lincoln, wife of the President, at his inauguration, later discovered to be a nearly identical copy, sold by Tiffany & Co, necklace 22" tl, 2½" T to B at center, brooch 2" w x 1⅞", **$11,163** [A]. (Photo courtesy of Skinner, Inc., Boston, MA, 12/11/01)

CORAL

Coral was popular throughout the nineteenth century. Children wore coral necklaces to fend off disease and evil spirits, because the Victorians held on to the ancient belief that coral had curative and protective powers. It also appealed to their interest in nature. Beads, carved cameos, floral motifs, good luck charms, and natural branches were made into jewelry of all types. Italy, particularly Naples, was the primary source for coral, and most carvers were Italian. Desirable, but rarer, colors were deep red and pale pink.

The most prevalent surviving forms are those in which the coral is protected by a metal mounting or frame, and beads. Intact examples of delicately carved all-coral pieces are more difficult to find.

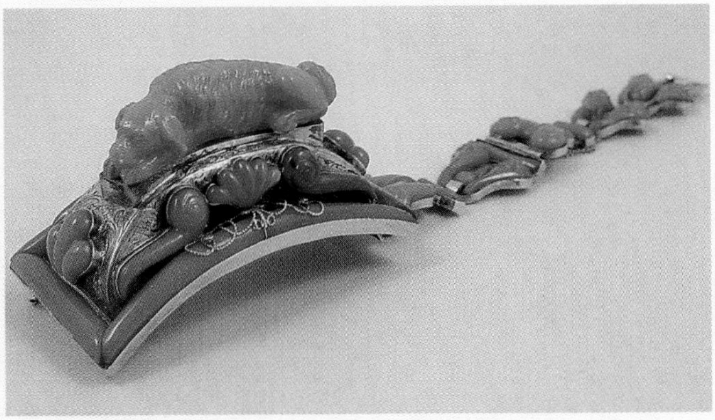

Bracelet, link, c. 1850, detailed realistic carving depicting a reclining dog in high relief on an engr yg plinth set with carved coral scrolls and shells, surmounting a convex rect clasp framed in coral with yg wire decoration, joined to hinged yg U-shaped links set with carved coral alternating with coral rods (one coral piece missing from link), v-spring clasp and safety chain, probably from Southern Italy, 6½" tl, clasp 2⅝" x 1⅜" x approx 1¾" h, **$2,500**. (Courtesy of E. Foxe Harrell, New York, NY)

Brooch/Pin, yg, black enamel, rc diamonds, seed pearls, c. 1850, lozenge-shaped, made up of oblate (slightly flattened round) coral beads surmounted by rc diamonds in star-shaped settings on black-enameled disks, mounted on a yg framework above yg S scrolls suspending a fringe of five inverted coral teardrops capped with seed pearls, C-catch, tube hinge, extended pinstem, 1¾" w x 2⅜" tl, **$500**. (Sue Ellen Yoho collection)

Brooch/Pin, c. 1850-60, carved flowers and leaves mounted on silver wires (a few leaves missing), C-catch, tube hinge, 2½" w x 1½", **$200**. (Author's collection)

Pendants, coral, yg:
TL, c. 1840, carved amuletic hand wearing a yg bracelet set with a turq bead, suspending a carved coral shoe and brush from yg jump rings, ⅜" w x 1¾" tl, **$450**. (Lisa Johnson collection)
TR, Brooch/Pendant, c. 1850, carved Medusa head mounted on a yg framework suspending swagged yg chains, C-catch, tube hinge, extended pinstem, freeswinging bail on loop, 1⅛" w x 1¼" tl, **$1,200**.
B, c. 1820-40, cross of faceted round coral beads, engr bail, pivot link under top bead, X-shaped yg center set with split pearl, smaller beads suspended from yg loops at terminals, 2¼" w x 4¼", **$750**. (Courtesy of E. Foxe Harrell, New York, NY)

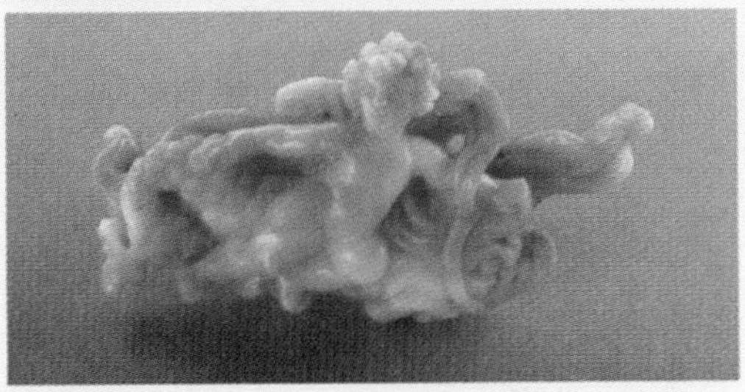

Brooch/Pin, c. 1860, three-dimensional carving of a cherub and a fish in waves of water ("boy on a dolphin"), variegated pale pink to orange, yg C-catch and tube hinge, 1¼" w x ⅝", **$688**. (Photo courtesy of Karen Lorene, Facèré Jewelry Art, Seattle, WA)

Brooch/Pin, bar, late Victorian, three flowerheads of carved pink coral mounted on wm bar with pin assembly, C-catch, tube hinge, 1⅝" w x ⅝", **$100**. (Courtesy of Chris Enebo Antique Jewelry, Tualatin, OR)

Pendant, stanhope, coral, yg, seed pearls, glass, late Victorian, a cross of coral rods held by yg cylinders, central engr yg foliate decoration with seed pearls around a stanhope viewing lens, depicting a Madonna with baby and child, mounting imperfect. 1" w x 1⅞" tl, **$275**. (Courtesy of Ocean Eyz Antique Jewelry, Orange, CA)
Note: According to an Internet Web site biography of inventor Lord Charles Stanhope (1753-1816, www.acmi.net/au/AIC/STANHOPE_BIO.html), photomicrography (first used 1853) made possible the production of the tiny transparent photos needed for the Stanhope Viewers. Lenses and photos were usually made in France, the earliest date from 1860s, and were made well into the 20th century. The majority date from 1890s and later, and contain photos with one to a dozen different views.

HAIRWORK

Hairwork is a second type of hair jewelry, in which the entire piece is made of woven hair with the addition of gold or gold-filled fittings and decorative elements. These pieces were not necessarily meant for mourning. They were made by and for women and men out of their own or a loved one's hair and given as mementos or love tokens.

The technique involved the use of a type of worktable where individual strands of hair were weighted and woven together to form hollow tubes around a solid core of cording and/or wire. This core was sometimes removed, and the tubes were then tied or enclosed with gold rings at intervals to form spherical or elliptical hollow "beads" (see earrings on page 45).

After processing and weaving, the hairwork could then be made into necklaces, bracelets, earrings, or brooches. A commonly found form is a watch chain in which the tube or rope of hair is woven in a spiral pattern, with an added gold or gold-filled swivel hook, bar, and fob charms (sometimes also made of hair).

Recently published information indicates that hairwork jewelry dates back further than was previously thought. Documented examples survive going back to the late eighteenth century. But the height of hairwork's popularity was during the mid-nineteenth century, when it was made commercially, as well as by "loving hands at home" from instructions found in women's magazines of the day, such as *Godey's Lady's Book* or *Peterson's Magazine*. Fittings for hair watch chains were advertised in Sears catalogs as late as 1911, but the practice of making and wearing hair jewelry had waned considerably by the 1880s.

While the thought of human-hair jewelry may be distasteful to some, collectors find both the idea and its execution fascinating. In recent years, there has been a growing appreciation for this lost art, as well as interest in reviving it.

The value of hair jewelry is in the workmanship: solid gold fittings enhance value only slightly over gold-filled. Watch chains are the form most usually found, while necklaces and earrings are scarce. Brown is the most common hair color; blond and white are scarce, and red is rare, not only because redheads are in the minority, but also because red hair was attributed to women of ill repute.

Damaged pieces are difficult to repair, so be sure to check condition carefully.

Bracelets, snakes, c. 1840-60:
T, dk brown hair woven in a tapering expandable pattern, engr gp tail and head with red and turq-colored glass stones and a seed pearl, v-spring on tail terminal clasps into head, 7" tl, **$250**.
B, tightly woven lt brown hair over a central core, yg tail and head with engr diaper pattern and ornate foliate scrolls, open mouth with serrated teeth, aquamarine cab eyes, coiled 2⅝" dia, head ⅝" w, **$400**. (Carmelita Johnson collection).

Bracelet, gf, c. 1870, gray-brown hair woven in an expandable pattern, floral engr gf terminals hinged to loop-in-loop gf center with soldered ring for charm (bracelet stretches to go over hand), center 2" x ⅝", **$275**. (Carmelita Johnson collection).

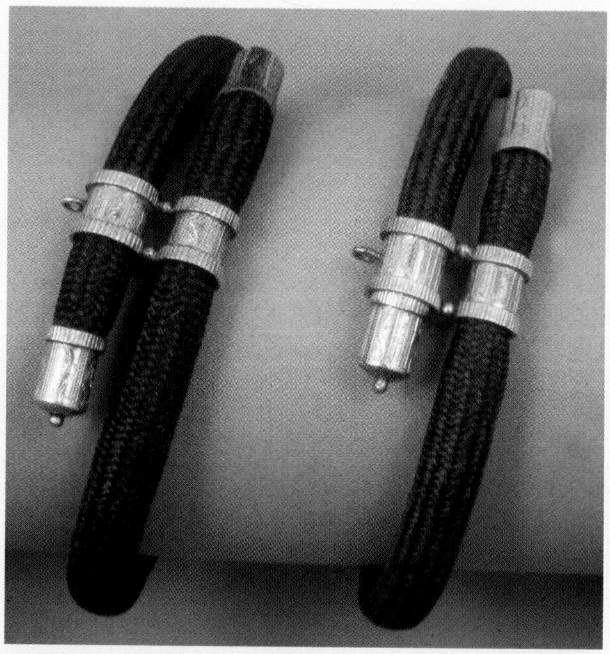

Bracelets, yg, c. 1880-90, bypass (crossover) bangles, tightly woven dk brown hair, engr yg terminals and sliding tubes, soldered loops for suspending charms, 2¼" inside dia, ¾" at center, pr, **$650**. (Carmelita Johnson collection)

Brooch/Pin, yg, c. 1870, in the shape of a harp, engr yg "strings," yg frame, dk brown woven hair inserts, C-catch, tube hinge, ⅞" w x 1½", **$475**. (Carmelita Johnson collection)

Earrings, gp metal, c. 1870-80, lt brown hollow hairwork hoops, each suspending a hairwork acorn with a gp metal cap from a metal wire, earwires attached to metal end caps, 1¼" w x 1¾", **$225**. (Carmelita Johnson collection)

Earrings, pendent, gold, c. 1870:
L, *girandole* style, each with three horizontal rods of dk brown hair woven around solid cores with rose gold capped terminals, surmounted by a gold branch with gold-capped hollow round hairwork berries, suspending three hollow hairwork pear-shaped drops with rose gold caps from gold beads and jump rings, shepherd's hook earwires, 1" w x 2" tl, **$375**.
R, circ lt brown hairwork rosette surmounts with yg bead centers suspending tassels of yg bead-tipped foxtail chains, kidney earwires, ½" w x 2¼" tl, **$350**. (Carmelita Johnson collection)

Earrings, pendent, hollow hairwork, c. 1870:
L, tapered hollow tubes, pear-shaped drops with later-added yg earwires, ⅛" w x 2⅞" tl, **$225**.
R, a yg flower cap surmounting a hollow tube with yg rings forming three segments, yg bead terminal, later-added yg earwires, ½" w x 2½" tl, **$255**.
(Courtesy of Lenore Dailey, The Raven's Nest, Palm Springs, CA)

Necklace, gf, c. 1870, tightly woven rope of dk brown hair in linked sections with gf caps, front clasp suspending a gf heart framing a hollow open hairwork center, 17¼" tl, heart ½" w x ¾", **$225**. (Carmelita Johnson collection)

Pendant, yg, glass, c. 1850-60, spiral-shaped snake pendant of hair woven around solid core, blue glass cab eyes, engr yg head and tail, jump ring suspended from mouth, soldered ring at end of tail, ⅝" w x 2¾" tl, **$250**. (Elaine Sarnoff collection)

Necklace, horsehair, c.1880, unbroken chain of woven black horsehair links, interspersed with three-link sections of white horsehair, ornamental loop at center, 27" tl, **$100**. (Courtesy of Gilly Phipps, Philadelphia, PA)

Suite: Brooch/Pin and Earrings, c. 1860, brooch of hollow-woven white hair arranged in loops forming an equilateral cross with yg flowerheads at compass points, surmounted by a cluster of hairwork beads and an oval banded agate cab set in a six-pointed yg star, matching pendent earrings of hairwork bead clusters surmounted by circ agate in five-pointed stars, suspended from oval agate cab surmounts, shepherd's hook earwires, brooch 1⅜" sq, earrings ½" w x 1½" tl, **$3,000**. (Courtesy of Gloria Karp Antique Jewelry, Riverdale, NY)

Suite: Brooch/Pin and Earrings, c. 1880, engr yg brooch in the shape of a butterfly, inserts of woven brown hair in wings, flat yg backing, replaced safety catch, matching earrings with orig kidney wires, brooch 1½" w x 1⅝", earrings ½" w x 1⅝" tl, **$500**. (Carmelita Johnson collection)

SCOTTISH JEWELRY

Gothic and Celtic Revivals were already well under way when Victoria ascended the throne. Her own romantic attachment to ancient and medieval history was certainly influential in furthering the public's preoccupation with the past. Britain's, particularly Scotland's, past was romanticized by historical novels, like those of Sir Walter Scott. And after Victoria purchased Balmoral, a castle in Scotland, in 1848, everyone became enamored of Scottish motifs. Circular Scottish plaid pins (sometimes called "target" brooches, see below right and page 48), heraldic crests, dirks and claymores (knives and swords, see page 48), thistles and St Andrew's crosses (Scottish national emblems), the Order of the Garter strap and buckle (symbol of the chivalric order headed by Victoria, see bracelet, right)—all were made into jewelry with varieties of agates, malachite, cairngorms (dark yellow-amber faceted quartz), and amethysts set in engraved silver or gold.

Unless a piece is hallmarked with a British date letter (and many pieces are not; in fact, "purist" collectors say that "real" Scottish agate jewelry is never hallmarked), precise dating of Scottish jewelry is difficult. Earlier pieces tend to be more faithful to traditional Scottish motifs. Mid- and Late Victorian pieces incorporated anchors, hearts, serpents, arrows, and other non-Scottish forms. Subtle differences can be seen in later nineteenth century pieces, such as the cut of the stones and the absence of ornate engraving. Some traditional forms continued to be made, and C-catches and tube hinges continued to be used as brooch findings well into the twentieth century (see bar brooch on page 48). But rhodium plating and cast mountings are sure signs of more recent vintage and lesser quality. Brooches are the most common form; bracelets are scarcer, but they do turn up; necklaces, earrings, and buckles are rare. Scottish jewelry is very wearable with today's fashions and, consequently, demand is high, especially for larger, less-common pieces.

Brooches/Pins, sterling:
L, c. 1870-80, in the shape of an anchor (symbol of hope), malachite inlaid flush into engr ster, surmounted by a ring, ropetwist wire spiraling around the shank to the base, C-catch, tube hinge, extended pinstem, 1½" w x 2⅜", **$300**.
R, c. 1860-70, "target" brooch, a circ-cut citrine in the open center, encircled by cut-to-shape flat sections of agate and bloodstone (jasper), alternating with silver beads and circ-cut pink stones in an engr ster mount, C-catch, tube hinge, extended pinstem, appl jump ring for safety chain, 1½" dia, **$400**. (Courtesy of Chris Enebo Antique Jewelry, Tualatin, OR).

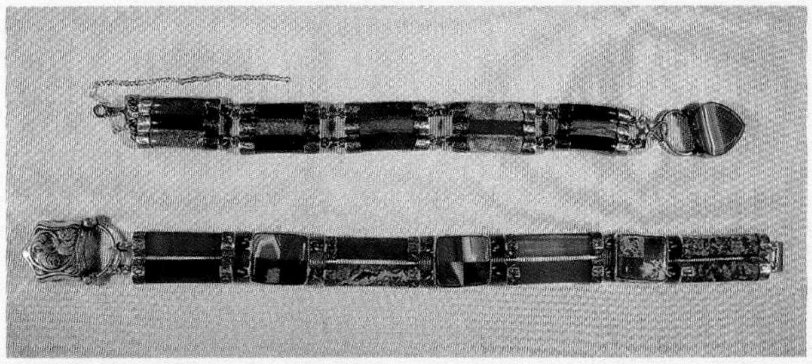

Bracelets, link, silver mounts:
T, c. 1880, links made up of three curved vari-colored agate and jasper rods on slate backings, engr silver caps, heart-shaped banded agate padlock clasp, engr silver rev, ⅝" w x 6⅞" tl, **$800**.
B, c. 1895, rect plaques inlaid with four quadrants of vari-colored agate and bloodstone (jasper), alternating with paired carnelian and agate cylinders with faceted sides, engr silver padlock clasp, silver caps and bezels, ⅝" w x 8" tl, clasp ¾" w x 1⅛", **$1,000**. (Courtesy of Lenore Dailey, The Raven's Nest, Palm Springs, CA)

Bracelet, link, malachite, silver, c. 1860-70, buckle and strap (garter motif) hinged sq silver links inlaid with malachite (one plaque cracked) in engr silver frames, terminating in a buckle clasp with hasp and "grommets" (adjustable), ¾" sq links, buckle 1¼" w, 8" tl, **$400**. (Author's collection)

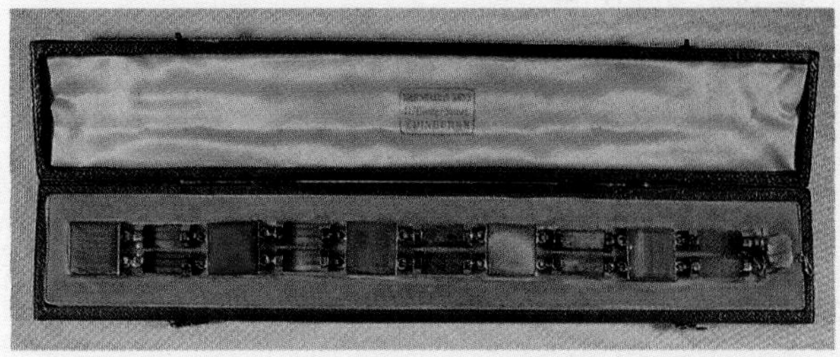

Bracelet, link, agate, jasper, amethyst, smoky quartz, chalcedony, 15k yg, c. 1875, square stone plaques alternating with paired faceted cylinder stone links, mounted in yg, safety chain, in original box mkd "MARSHALL AND SONS, 87 George St, EDINBURGH," ⅝" w x 8" tl, **$2,500**. (Courtesy of Lenore Dailey, The Raven's Nest, Palm Springs, CA)

Bracelet, link, agate, jasper, gp brass, hair, c. 1880, eight ridged hexagonal agate plaques set in gp brass backings with prongs, suspending a circ charm containing braided brown hair in a glazed compartment, brass frame, v-spring and box clasp, 7½" tl, ¾" w, **$475**. (Courtesy of Deja Voodoo, Santa Cruz, CA)

Brooch/Pin, agate, citrine, silver, c. 1850, outer ring of green agate with four oval faceted cairngorms (citrines) in pronged bezels interspaced between arms of an appl silver cross inlaid with striated gray agate, engr silver mount, C-catch, tube hinge, 1¾" dia, **$350**. (Courtesy of E. Foxe Harrell, New York, NY)

Brooch/Pin, jasper, bloodstone, agate, slate, silver, c. 1870, "target" brooch with inlaid bloodstone and red jasper in a star pattern around an open center with engr silver scallop edge within a ring of banded agate, mounted on a slate backing, silver frame, C-catch, tube hinge, 1¾" dia, **$385**. (Courtesy of Deja Voodoo, Santa Cruz, CA).

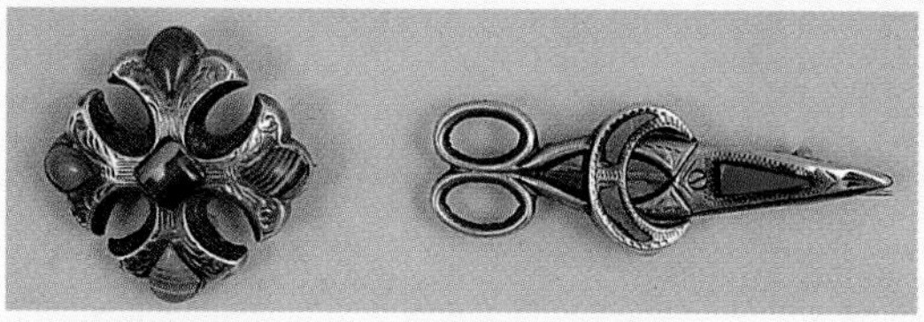

Brooches/Pins, silver, agate, late Victorian:
L, stamped and engr moline cross (equilateral with each arm forked and curved back at terminals) set with gray and brown banded agate, flat backing, C-catch, tube hinge, 1" w x 1," **$85**. (Diane White collection)
R, in the shape of scissors, engr silver inlaid with flat shaped pieces of green and red agate, C-catch, tube hinge, 2" w x ⅝", **$135**. (Courtesy of E. Foxe Harrell, New York, NY)

Brooch/Pin, bar, silver, faceted glass, 1951 date letter, opposed thistle motifs prong-set with citrine-colored oval faceted glass, Glasgow hmks, illegible maker's mk, "SCOTLAND," C-catch, tube hinge, 3" w x ⅜", **$100**. (Lisa Johnson collection)

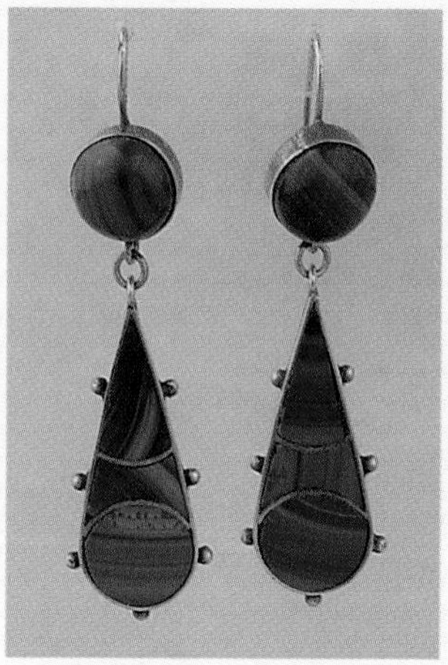

Earrings, pendent, malachite, silver, c. 1870, each teardrop-shaped drop inlaid with malachite in three curved sections, set flush in silver frames with beaded edges, suspended from a bezel-set circ malachite cab surmount, shepherd's hook earwires, ⅝" w x 2¼" tl, **$375**. (Author's collection)

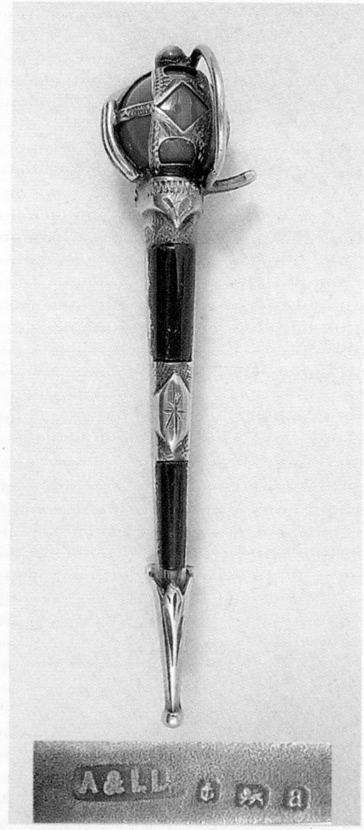

Brooch/Pin, sterling, bloodstone, red jasper, date letter for 1900, in the shape of a claymore (Scottish broadsword), circ hilt of red jasper overlaid with engr ster, tapered blade of bloodstone inlaid in engr ster, Birmingham (Eng) hmks, maker's mk "A & L Ld," C-catch, tube hinge, ½" w x 2½", **$250**. (Author's collection)

MID VICTORIAN (GRAND PERIOD) c. 1861-1880

The Romantic Period ended abruptly with the death of Prince Albert in 1861, and the beginning of the Civil War in the U.S.—causes for deep mourning on both sides of the Atlantic. Wearing black was more than a correct form for mourning; it became fashionable. Fashion, as always, played an important role in the changing look of jewelry. The voluminous skirt, supported by crinolines, or hoops, was introduced in the mid-1850s, and became the look of the 1860s. This wider silhouette required larger jewelry. Brooches were massive, bracelets widened, and were often worn in pairs, one on each wrist. Lower necklines prompted the wearing of necklaces and large lockets. Lockets and brooches often contained photographs, which gradually overtook portrait miniatures as a form of memorial jewelry. Hairstyles changed to once again reveal the ear; and earrings returned, growing to greater lengths towards the end of the period. Trains, bustles, ruffles, pleats, flounces, and fringe adorned the skirts of the 1870s. Tassels and fringe appeared in jewelry to compliement the look.

For those who weren't in mourning, it was a colorful period. William Perkin discovered coal tar in 1856, which led to his accidental discovery of the first synthetic aniline dye. The first color he produced was purple, or mauve, which created such a sensation that it ushered in the era that followed, called the "Mauve Age." The fashion for bright colors continued through the 1870s. Colored gemstones and enamels complimented the look.

By the 1860s, Revivalism was in full swing. Women were piling on Etruscan-style amulets and other "classical" ornaments to the point of being satirized by the press. Revivalist Castellani's goldwork was displayed at the International Exhibition in London in 1862. Egyptian-style jewels were seen at the *Exposition Universelle* in Paris in 1867. Enameled Renaissance Revival jewels were seen in fashionably colorful social circles as well.

International exhibitions whetted appetites for exotic jewels from exotic places, like India. Mogul jewelry, Jaipur enamel, and gold-mounted tiger's claws from Calcutta became the rage in the 1870s, especially after Queen Victoria was proclaimed Empress of India in 1876 (see brooches below). These pieces also inspired the work of English, European, and American jewelers.

After the Civil War, it became acceptable for American women to wear jewelry in greater quantities. Prosperity was growing, and with it the desire to display signs of wealth. What better way for a man to proclaim his status than to bedeck his wife in jewels? For the upper classes, at least, The Grand Period was indeed grand.

Working-class women were also decking themselves in baubles, bangles, and beads, although they were of the mass-produced "imitation" variety. Frankly fake costume jewelry was still an unheard of idea. Even if it wasn't "real," women wanted it to look like it was. Manufacturers were now capable of turning out machine-made goods in quantity to satisfy their demand. Electroplated trinkets set with glass "stones" were made to look like gold and diamond jewels.

Men continued to drape their vests with the requisite watch chains and fobs. Cuff links, also known as sleeve buttons, tie pins (also called scarfpins, stickpins, stockpins, cravat pins), signet rings, collar buttons, and shirt studs were additional forms of male adornment. Most of these were gold or gold-filled. Gemstones were added on occasion, particularly to stickpins.

By the 1860s, Tiffany & Co. had established itself as America's most prestigious and reputable firm, first by importing the best of European goods, then by manufacturing their own wares of the highest quality. From 1867 until the end of the century, Tiffany exhibited and won medals at international expositions in Paris and the U.S. They promoted an appreciation of American craftsmanship and resources by exhibiting pieces with American themes, and newly discovered American gemstones, like Montana blue sapphires and Maine tourmalines. They also displayed newly discovered diamonds from South Africa and opals from Australia.

The Centennial Exposition in Philadelphia was a landmark event in American jewelry history. It gave Tiffany and other American jewelers the opportunity to "strut their stuff" in a grand manner and capture the world's attention. It furthered the recognition of the United States as an industrial nation with a talent for invention and production.

Brooches/Pins, tiger claws, yg, c. 1850-60:
T, a single claw mounted in yg, surmounting a ball-tipped rod, the yg cap decorated with yg scrolled wire and leaves, a circ-cut citrine prong-set in center, C-catch, flanged hinge, 1½" w x 1½", **$325**. (Courtesy of Xcentricities, Beverly Hills, CA)
B, opposed tiger claws in 18k yg setting surmounted by a yg scrolled wire, a yg filigree insect and floral/foliate motifs, suspending two yg tassels from chain, C-catch, tube hinge, mkd "18 WN" on appl rect plaque, made in India, 2⅜" w x ¾", 1¾" tl, **$300**. (Author's collection)

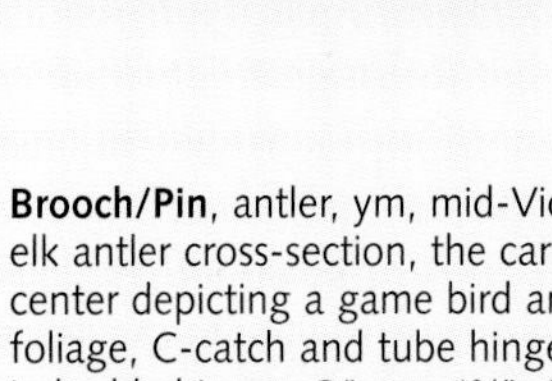

Brooch/Pin, teeth, yg, mid-Victorian, feline teeth, possibly tiger, mounted in yg with engr "AGR" mono in central yg band with engr scalloped border, engr terminals, later-added safety catch with lead solder, 2¾" w x ⅝", **$300**. (Elaine Sarnoff collection)

Brooch/Pin, antler, ym, mid-Victorian, elk antler cross-section, the carved center depicting a game bird amid foliage, C-catch and tube hinge imbedded in rev, 2" w x 1¾", **$150**. (Courtesy of E. Foxe Harrell, New York, NY)

BLACK JEWELRY

Sentiment was the glue that held Victorian lives together. It was also the preservative that has saved many pieces of jewelry from being discarded or sold for scrap. Surely one prevailing sentiment was that of bereavement. Victoria had an unswerving sense of propriety, and issued rules and regulations governing strict codes of behavior for herself, her family, her court and her subjects. These rules of etiquette included dress codes for all occasions, particularly for mourning, including the proper jewelry to be worn.

After Prince Albert died, Victoria went into a period of mourning that lasted for the rest of her life, a full 40 years. For much of this time, all members of the royal court were required to wear black. This funereal atmosphere spread throughout the populace, creating a demand for black jewelry, the only color permitted during periods of full mourning. Jet was the material of choice. An entire industry grew up around the mining and carving of jet, a fossilized coal found near the town of Whitby in England. The area became famous for its artisans, and tourists went to Whitby to watch them work. They brought home jet souvenirs (see brooch on page 51, center), sometimes personalized with the names of loved ones, not necessarily departed.

Brooches, bead necklaces, and bracelets were the most commonly worn types of jet jewelry. Bracelets were often of the "stretchy" type, strung on elastic (see below), and usually worn in pairs (as were many types of bracelets). Pendent earrings were worn, but are not found as often today as are brooches and bracelets.

Jet jewelry became so popular that it spawned a number of imitations. Two of the most common were black glass, misleadingly called "French jet" (also known as "Vauxhall glass," see earrings on page 52), and vulcanite, a hardened (vulcanized) rubber that is sometimes mistakenly called gutta-percha (see pages 52 and 53). Gutta-percha is a natural substance from the Malayan palaquium tree. It was occasionally used for jewelry, but it is not stable in air, so little

Bracelets, jet, elastic, c. 1860-70:
T, carved V-shaped segments flanking central ornament, an oblate sphere within fluted and ridged hemispheres, continuing to narrow rounded rect segments, strung on elastic, 1⅛" at center to ⅜" at back, **$125**.
B, rect segments divided into faceted pyramids, strung on elastic, ¾" w, **$175**. (Courtesy of Richard Fauteux, San Pedro, CA)

Watch Key, yg, steel cable, gutta percha, c. 1858, a circ cross-section of steel cable, the inner portion coated with gutta percha, set in a yg bezel with a yg chain-link frame, repoussé foliate scrolls above and below, surmounted by a circ bail, terminating in a tapered yg tube lined with steel, attributed to Tiffany & Co., sold on the occasion of the first (unsuccessful) completion of the Transatlantic Cable by Cyrus Field on August 5, 1858, ¾" w x 1⅞" tl, **$150**. (Courtesy of Peter Shemonsky, San Francisco, CA)

survives (see above). Other materials are also erroneously labeled gutta-percha, including shellac-based compositions molded into daguerreotype ("union") cases, hand mirrors and brushes, buckles, and other jewelry (see buckle on page 51), and pressed horn (processed and dyed black), often seen in mourning jewelry (see page 51, BL and BR, and page 53, left) . Bog oak, from the peat bogs of Ireland, is sometimes included in this group of jet imitations, but although it is black to dark brown, and carved (usually with Irish motifs) or heat press-molded, it was never meant as a substitute for jet (see bracelet and brooches, TL and TR, page 51, and locket on page 52).

True jet tends to command higher prices than do comparable pieces made from its imitations. Many dealers do not know how to tell the difference. The word "jet" has become synonymous with "black," so any black shiny jewelry material may be misidentified as jet (See References: *What's It Made of?* for identifying those materials).

Black onyx is another material used in mourning jewelry, and about which there is some confusion. Gemologically, the correct name is dyed black chalcedony. Onyx by definition is a banded, or layered, stone, most often seen carved into cameos. The black color is almost always a result of soaking in sugar solution and heating in sulfuricsulphuric acid, a process that was known to the Romans (see earrings on page 52).

Black enamel was often the material of choice for mourning jewelry, usually applied to gold brooches and rings (see pages 51 and 53). The surface might be smooth or engraved, sometimes with the words "In Memory Of" in old English lettering on the enameled ground (see pages 35 and 36).

At times it can be difficult to determine where mourning left off and fashion began in black jewelry. Massive necklaces, diamond-enhanced brooches, and elaborately carved bracelets might lead one to question the depth of the wearer's mourning. But considering that some women wore black for most of their adult lives, it is not surprising that they would want to enliven their "toilet" with a bit of fashionable elegance. Because it *was* fashionable, black jewelry was also worn by women who were not in mourning.

Bracelet, French jet (glass), c. 1880, wraparound, faceted and molded black glass beads strung on wire, forming a snake, 10" tl, head ⅜" w, **$150**. (Courtesy of Generations, La Verne, CA)

Bracelet, bog oak, elastic, c. 1860-80, central domed disk, a lg press-molded shamrock in the open center with a ropetwist patterned frame, encircled by smaller shamrocks within cross-hatched border, continuing to a bracelet of 13 carved I-beam shaped segments, each with two opposed press-molded shamrocks, drilled and strung on black elastic, center 1⅜" dia, segments ¾" w, **$300**. (Author's collection)

Brooch/Pin, glass, yg, ym, early Victorian, oval rev-molded and white-ptd clear glass depicting an urn and a weeping willow, engr yg frame within a radiating border of circ-cut faceted black glass ("French jet"), black lacquered ym backing, C-catch, tube hinge, 1" w x 1⅛", **$425**. (Courtesy of Lenore Dailey, The Raven's Nest, Palm Springs, CA)

Brooch/Pin, 15k yg, seed pearls, enamel, hair, c. 1870, convex oval with star center accented by nine seed pearls and black enamel, framed by corded wire and trefoil border, glazed compartment containing braided hair on rev, upturned hook for pendent watch on rev, 1¾" w x 1½", **$259** [A]. (Photo courtesy of Beverly Hills Auctioneers, Beverly Hills, CA, 4/1/01)

Brooches/Pins, bog oak, jet, pressed horn:
TL, c. 1870-80, carved and pierced bog oak oval, a castle and thatched-hut village within a laurel wreath border, appl brass pin assembly on rev, 1¾" w x 1½", **$125**. (Lisa Johnson collection)
TR, c. 1860, cutout and carved bog oak castle motif within circ cross-hatched border, C-catch, tube hinge, 1½" dia, **$95**.
C, c. 1870, flat oval jet plaque carved with bas-relief of Whitby Abbey on textured ground, the name encircling upper portion, new brass pin assembly appl to wm oval plate on rev, sm chips on edge, 2¼" w x 1⅝", **$150**.
BL and BR, c. 1880, Eng, pressed horn, flat-backed brass pin assembly mounted on rev, mkd with Eng kite-shaped registry mark for 1880 (IV material category, ceramic), C-catches, tube hinges:
BL, molded in the shape of a hand holding a floral/foliate wreath (symbol of mourning), 2⅞" x 1¼", **$155**.
BR, molded wheat sheaf (Christian symbol of hope of new life. It is often used to mark the passing of a loved one because of its symbolic relationship to life eternal after death) with molded egg-and-dart border, extended pinstem, 1⅝" x 2", **$125**.
(Author's collection)

Brooches/Pins, crosses, c.1850-60:
T, jet cross with engr yg bead-tipped terminals, C-catch, tube hinge, ¾" w x 1¼", **$125**. (Author's collection)
BL, black-enameled circ domed disk, inlaid yg cross set with seed pearls, within an engr texture and fretwork yg frame, silk-lined glazed compartment on convex rev, C-catch, tube hinge, 1⅜" dia, **$300**.
BR, jet cross with engr yg bead-tipped terminals mounted on a diaper-pattern engr open-backed oval yg plaque, engr foliate border, C-catch, tube hinge, ring for safety chain on rev, 1" w x 1⅜", **$185**.
(Courtesy of E. Foxe Harrell, New York, NY)

Buckle, shellac composition, brass, c. 1865, two rect plaques surmounted by smaller octagonal plaques, with molded relief floral/foliate decoration, border of quatrefoils, Xs and acorns, attached to lacquered black flat brass hook-and-eye closure with cutout openings for belt at each end on rev,
3½" w x 2¼", **$125**. (Author's collection)

Earrings, pendent, black glass, black painted base metal, c. 1870, circ, oval and marquise-cut "French jet" faceted flat-backed glass beads mounted on black-lacquered metal backings, forming articulated pear-shaped fringed pendants, later-added surmounts and post findings, ⅞" w x 2¾" tl, **$300**. (Sue Ellen Yoho collection)

Earrings, pendent, vulcanite, yg, c. 1870, a ring-shaped (annulus) surmount with a cube attached at the base, suspending another annulus and three ridged, tapered and cusped drops, yg shepherd's hook earwires and findings, ½" w x 2¼" tl, **$350**. (Author's collection)

Earrings, pendent, Vauxhall glass, painted metal, molded glass, c. 1870, each a molded glass "cameo" encircled by prong-set circ-cut glass, suspending three drops of prong-set grad circ-cut glass mounted on black-lacquered metal backing, suspended from circ-cut surmount, shepherd's hook earwires, ⅞" w x 2⅜", **$400**. (Courtesy of E. Foxe Harrell, New York, NY)

Earrings, drop, black onyx, yg, seed pearls, c. 1880, each an inverted ridged drop suspended from a trefoil surmount, yg chain and seed pearl, later-added screwbacks, ⅜" w x 1¾" tl, **$1,195**. (Courtesy of Apriori Antiques, San Francisco, CA)

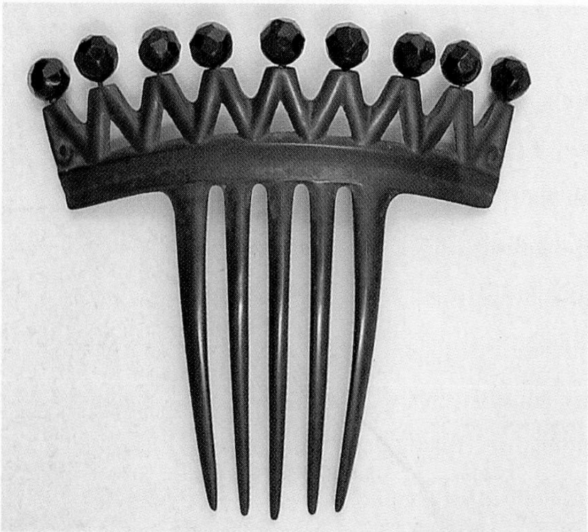

Hair Comb, vulcanite, French jet (glass), c. 1860-70, lg molded vulcanite comb, open saw-tooth pattern decoration surmounted by a row of round faceted black glass beads, 4½" w x 4½", **$100**. (Private collection)

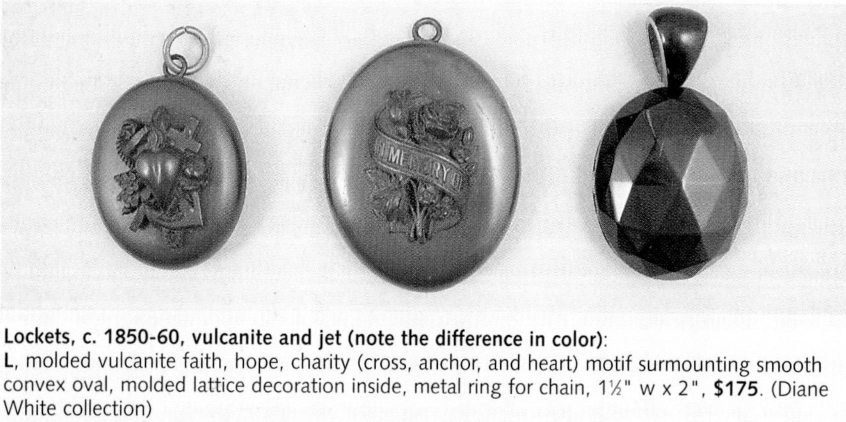

Lockets, c. 1850-60, vulcanite and jet (note the difference in color):
L, molded vulcanite faith, hope, charity (cross, anchor, and heart) motif surmounting smooth convex oval, molded lattice decoration inside, metal ring for chain, 1½" w x 2", **$175**. (Diane White collection)
C, smooth domed oval locket surmounted by an appl molded floral motif enclosed by scrolled ribbon reading "In Memory Of," locket interior imp with fleur-de-lis and scroll pattern on ridged ground, 1⅞" w x 2⅜", **$275**.
R, one side a convex faceted jet oval appl to wm liner mkd "TSTPATENT" on the opening opposite the hinge, engr mono on flat textured ground within jet oval on rev, bail a single piece of carved jet inlaid into brass, 1½" w x 2¾" tl, **$375**.
(Author's collection)

Locket, jet, hair, glass, c.1870, plain oval locket, front glazed compartment with brown and blond braided hair, jet bail, 1⅝" w x 2¾" tl, **$495**. (Courtesy of Lenore Dailey, The Raven's Nest, Palm Springs, CA)

Locket, bog oak, yg, c. 1875, each side a circ domed disk of bog oak set in a yg frame, one side carved with an American eagle symbol (as shown on an Am dollar bill), the other possibly the seal of a fraternal order (a central triangular symbol above drapery and tassels, a cannon below, flanked by spears or arrows and flames), both carvings with a floral/foliate border, inside unlined, 1¼" dia, **$250**. (Author's collection)

Pendants, crosses, c. 1860-70:
L, pressed horn, c. 1860-70, press-molded Celtic cross with wheat and poppy motifs (damaged on bottom end), circ horn bail, later-added ym jump ring, 2¼" w x 3¾", **$70**.
C, jet, wm, c. 1860-70, three-dimensional, deeply carved allover geo and foliate motifs, made up of five pieces, bulbous arms joined to the spherical center, surmounted by a wm eyepin and bail, 3¼" w x 5½", **$400**.
(Diane White collection)
BR, bog oak, glass, yg, c. 1860-70, cruciform, allover crosshatching, centering a stanhope showing scenes of Ireland, mkd "MADE IN FRANCE," yg bail, ⅝" w x 1¼", **$75**. (Lisa Johnson collection)

Ring, 18k yg, seed pearls, enamel, c. 1850-60, Maltese cross within a circ disk flanked by enameled shoulders, accented with seed pearls and black enamel on yg, center ⅜" dia, **$201** [A]. (Photo courtesy of Beverly Hills Auctioneers, Beverly Hills, CA, 4/1/01)

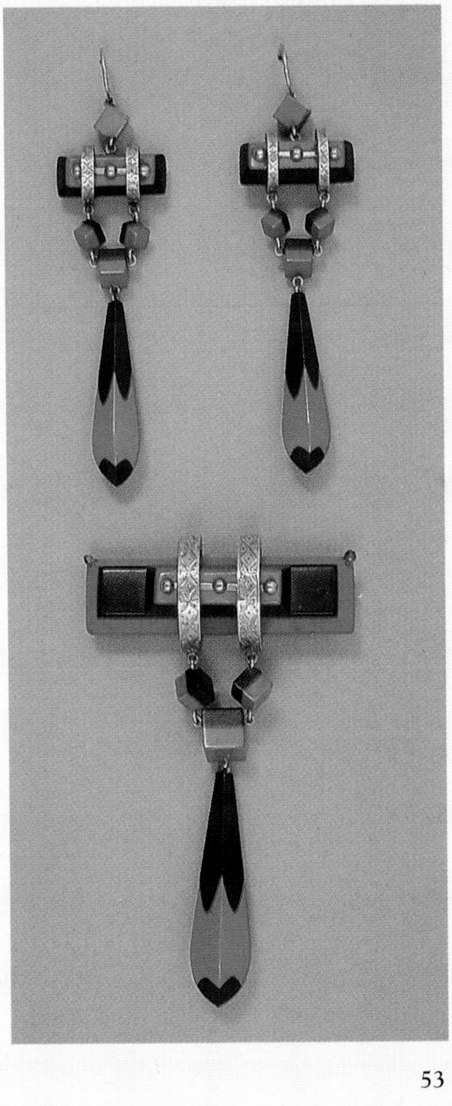

Suite: Brooch/Pin and Pendent Earrings, vulcanite, yg, c. 1870, unusual combination of contrasting colors, laminated layers of orange and black vulcanite, brooch a tapered rect bar surmounted by a smaller bar with yg trim, and two half-round black vulcanite arcs covered with engr yg strips, suspending three cubes and a ridged, tapered and cusped drop, later-added pin mechanism, matching pendent earrings, cube surmounts suspended from yg shepherd's hook earwires, brooch 1⅞" w x 3⅛", earrings ⅞" w x 3" tl, **$2,500**. (Gloria Karp collection)

TORTOISESHELL and PIQUÉ

Tortoiseshell was another popular nineteenth-century jewelry material. It was also considered suitable for half-mourning. Lockets, hair combs, and bracelets were made from this natural plastic taken from the shell of the hawksbill turtle (now an endangered species).

A technique known as piqué, originally used in ornamental objects in the seventeenth century, was applied to jewelry and popularized in the mid- to late-nineteenth century. After softening it with heat, the tortoiseshell was inlaid with gold and/or silver in floral or geometric patterns. The technique using inlaid strips of metal cut into ornate designs is called *piqué posé*. *Piqué point* refers to dots or other small geometric shapes inlaid in an overall pattern.

Animal rights were not a big issue in Victorian times. Animals or parts of animals were used with impunity. It is now illegal to buy or sell tortoiseshell in this country. Antique pieces are exempt, but there are restrictions regarding import and export to and from other countries. Not all mottled brown lightweight material is tortoiseshell, however. Toward the end of the century, many hair combs and other jewelry and objects were made of celluloid in imitation of tortoiseshell (see Early Celluloid in Late Victorian section).

Bracelet, link, yg, brass, early Victorian, oval double-pierced blonde tortoiseshell links, modified heart clasp framed in yg, joined with brass jumprings (possibly later-added), ⅝"w x 7", heart ¾", **$600**. (Lisa Johnson collection)

Bracelets, hinged bangles, yg, c, 1880, *piqué point*, pr of rounded-edge dark brown tortoiseshell bangles inlaid with diagonal rows of six-pointed stars alternating with serrated geo strips, ½" w, 2⅛" inside dia, **$600/pr**. (Courtesy of Richard Fauteux, San Pedro, CA)

Brooches/Pins, piqué, silver, yg, c. 1860-70:
L, *piqué posé*, domed tortoiseshell circle with flat back (hollow), inlaid with two intersecting quatrefoils of foliate and floral motifs in yg and silver, C-catch, tube hinge, extended pinstem, 1⅝" dia, **$300**. (Author's collection)
R, *piqué point*, interlaced tortoiseshell strand forming a trefoil knot inlaid with a line of six-pointed yg stars, larger star in the center, C-catch, tube hinge imbedded into rev, 1¾" dia, **$275**. (Catherine Ratcliffe collection)

Earrings, c. 1870, in the shapes of amphorae suspended from round bead surmounts, yg shepherd's hook earwires, ½" w x 2⅛" tl, **$750**. (Courtesy of Chris Enebo Antique Jewelry, Tualatin, OR)

Earrings, piqué, silver, yg, c. 1860-70:
L, *piqué posé*, dk brown double hoops inlaid with silver and yg floral motifs, yg borders, later-added posts, ⅞" w x 1⅜", **$600**.
R, *piqué posé*, pierced pear-shaped drops with scalloped edges, inlaid with silver and yg flowers, S-scrolls and geo motifs, suspended from similarly decorated lobed surmounts, shepherd's hook earwires, ¾" w x 2" tl, **$900**. (Courtesy of Lenore Dailey, The Raven's Nest, Palm Springs, CA)

Necklace, yg, silver, c. 1870, *piqué posé*, a strand of hollow round beads with an allover inlaid gold and silver pattern of flowerheads within circles, suspending a fringe of 11 inverted hollow teardrop shapes with similar circ pattern flanking floral/foliate motifs from silver jump rings and yg bails, 1¾" T to B at center, 13½" tl, **$1,528** [A]. (Photo courtesy of Skinner, Inc., Boston, MA, 3/17/02)

REVIVALIST JEWELRY

Victorians were fascinated with ancient history. For them, history meant revivals. Archeological discoveries and published accounts of ancient historical events and epics prompted revivals of jewelry styles from ancient and medieval cultures: Assyrian, Celtic, Egyptian, Etruscan, Gothic, Hellenistic and Roman, Mogul (India), Moorish, and Renaissance. Exact copies were favored over interpretations. With some exceptions, originality and creativity were not notable characteristics of Revivalist style, although exquisite workmanship and attention to details often were.

A number of noted jewelers of the mid- to late-nineteenth century worked in the Revivalist mode, copying ancient forms. Among these, the most famous were the Castellani family of Rome, and Carlo Giuliano (c.1831-1895) and sons Carlo and Arthur of London.

Etruscan

Revivalism reached its height during the 1860s and 1870s. A mania for all things Italian promoted the popularity in particular of Etruscan Revival jewels, most closely associated with what is generically called the "archaeological style," which also includes copies of Roman cameos and intaglios, mosaics, and "Hellenistic" (of Greek history, language and culture, 4th to 1st century BC) gold jewelry. The discovery of gold treasures from antiquity in Tuscany, in west-central Italy, near Rome, instigated the attempt to copy the ancient technique of granulation. Minute beads of gold were applied side-by-side to a gold surface to create a design. The difficulty lay in soldering the beads to the surface without melting them. Fortunato Pio Castellani (1794-1865), while unable to duplicate the technique exactly, came closest to perfecting it (see shell cameo brooch with gold frame by Castellani on page 61). Twisted, or "corded," wirework was also applied to gold jewels in the Etruscan style. Others made the attempt at granulation and wirework, but were not always as successful.

The ancient jewels themselves were copied by the Castellani, as well as the techniques. The bulla, a two-sided round pendant worn by the Etruscans as an amulet (see Mosaics in Jewelry, page 66), and the fibula, a safety-pin type of brooch used to fasten garments, were among the favorite forms.

The popularity of the Castellani's work was of course a motive for their imitators—copyists of copyists, as it were. Skill in craftsmanship, or the lack of it, is what separates the "wheat from the chaff." Some craftsmen were very skilled indeed, but the range of quality in Etruscan-style jewels is wide (for a fine example of Etruscan Revival by an unknown maker, see hinged bangle on page 56). Although quality workmanship is of primary consideration, a signature can add a great deal of value. The Castellani marks, back-to-back overlapping Cs, are important ones to know. It is also important to note that their marks, as well as their techniques, were copied, but some unsigned pieces can be attributed to the Castellani (see necklace on page 58).

Large numbers of pieces in the archaeological style were produced by anonymous manufacturers throughout the last half of the nineteenth century. Many unsigned examples of varying quality can be found today of Etruscan decoration on gold and gold-filled pieces.

Renaissance

The Giulianos were Revivalists of another sort. They specialized in jewels in the Renaissance style, and were famous for their enameling. One trademark was an enameled white background with black dots, or black with white dots. Carlo Giuliano's work reached its peak in the 1870s. Although he, too, employed granulation as well as other ancient techniques, unlike most Revivalists, he was an interpreter of the style. He improved upon techniques and forms with original ideas rather than exact copies. He signed his pieces C.G. in an applied or impressed oval plaque (see hinged bangle and necklace on page 57).

Sons Carlo and Arthur (mark: C.& A.G.) carried on after their father's death in 1895, but changing styles affected their business. Early 20th century pieces were not as successful. The business closed in 1914, the year of Arthur's death. Both Giuliano marks have been counterfeited.

Locket and Necklace, 14k yg, enamel, diamonds, c. 1885, Fr, polychrome enamel depicting a mythological scene, attributed to Eugène Richert, framed by rc and table-cut diamonds, decorated with granulation and wirework, locket attributed to Eugène Fontenay, suspended from an omega-style collar accented with wirework, locket 1¼" w x 2¼" tl, collar 14½", **$9,988** [A]. (Photo courtesy of Butterfields, San Francisco and Los Angeles, CA, 9/25/01)

Other noted archaeological and Renaissance revivalist jewelers were John Brogden of London (see hinged bangle on page 57), Ernesto Pierret (1824-1870) of Rome, and Eugène Fontenay (1823-1887, see locket on page 55), Froment-Meurice (1802-1855, see bracelet, right), Jules Wièse (1818-1890) and son Louis of Paris (see brooch on page 56).

Enamel, colored gemstones, and pearls are characteristic materials for Renaissance Revival jewels (see pendants on page 59). Austrian and Hungarian Renaissance Revival jewelry was produced in quantity in the late nineteenth and early twentieth centuries (see Beaux-Arts and Neo-Renaissance Jewelry in Part II). It is cruder in execution and materials—usually silver gilt, enamel, low-quality gemstones (sometimes glass) and freshwater pearls. Nevertheless, these pieces have a certain appeal, and are of growing interest, particularly among collectors of costume jewelry. Accordingly, prices have risen. Most pieces are unmarked, but sometimes a piece will have an Austro-Hungarian silver quality hallmark, usually a dog's head in a coffin-shaped lozenge (see Marks on Metals appendix; for other less commonly seen Austrian hallmarks, see Tardy, *International Hallmarks on Silver*, English translation, Paris, 1985.)

Egyptian

The discovery of the tomb and treasures of Queen Ah-Hotep and the start of construction of the Suez Canal in 1859 (completed 10 years later), inspired the return of the Egyptian style, which had been revived once before in the late eighteenth and early nineteenth centuries. Familiar Egyptian symbols—scarabs, pharaohs, lotus blossoms, falcons, and vultures—found their way into jewels by Castellani, Giuliano, Brogden, Robert Phillips, and several famous French jewel houses, including Froment-Meurice and Boucheron. These pieces were worked in gold, enamel, gemstones, and mosaics (see earrings on page 66) in much the same manner as other Revivalist jewelry.

Revivalism caught on in the United States, too, although somewhat later. When Alessandro Castellani exhibited his family's work at the 1862 International Exposition in London, America was in the throes of the Civil War. But in 1876, at the Centennial Exposition in Philadelphia, Castellani presented his ideas and his jewelry to the receptive American public.

Soon after, classical motifs and "Etruscan" worked gold began making their appearance in American-made jewelry, most of it mass-produced.

Today it is not unusual to find American pieces, both signed and unsigned, that reflect the widespread appeal of the past during the mid- to late-Victorian era.

Reproduction Alert

Faked signatures and reproductions are common. Signed pieces should be authenticated by an expert.

Bracelet, yg, silver, enamel, pearls, rubies, mid-19th C, Renaissance Revival, a grad line of openwork plaques of enameled ivy leaves set with pearls and foiled rubies and decorated with winged female figures and putti in silver and yg, attributed to Froment-Meurice, 2⅛" at center, 6¾" l, **$7,056** [A]. (Photo courtesy of Sotheby's, London, 6/20/01)

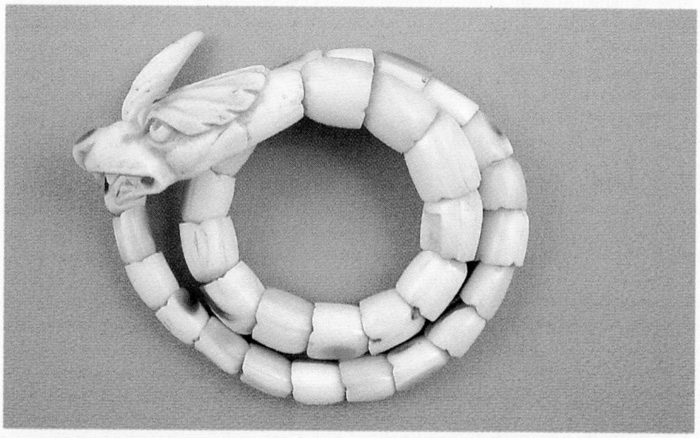

Bracelet, wraparound, shell, c. 1850, carved segments strung on wire, in the form of a serpent or chimera, probably from Southern Italy, head ½" w x 1½", **$475**. (Courtesy of E. Foxe Harrell, New York, NY)

Bracelet, hinged bangle, 18k yg, c. 1860, Etruscan Revival, a circ center panel with raised concentric rings within a granulated and scrolled wirework ground, completed by a similarly decorated double-hinged band with balustered finial decoration, centering the Latin letters "AEI" (an abbreviation for *"aeternitas,"* meaning eternity or immortality and symbolizing a title of the emperor), maker's mk and Vatican assay mk, ⅝" w, 2¼" inside dia, 1¾" dia at center, **$2,542** [A]. (Photo courtesy of Dupuis Jewellery Auctioneers, Toronto, ONT, Canada, 6/12/01)

Bracelet, hinged bangle, yg, enamel, opal, diamonds, c. 1870s, a wide band set with an oval compartment, the lid decorated with an opal within a border of rc diamonds and royal blue enamel in a twisted wire and beadwork frame, opening to reveal a portrait miniature, flanked by collet-set om diamonds within star-shaped plaques of royal blue enamel, enamel imperfect, makers mk "JB," fitted case by John Brogden, 16 Henrietta Street, Covent Garden, London, 1½" T to B at center, **$4,200** [A]. (Photo courtesy of Sotheby's, London, 6/20/01)

Bracelet, hinged bangle, lapis lazuli, yg, c.1870, Etruscan Revival, the front set with five cut-corner rect lapis lazuli tablets, each within a chased gold frame with wirework batons and borders joined to three tapered gold arched bands, sgd "C.G." for Carlo Giuliano, 1¼" w, 2½" inside dia, **$10,575** [A]. (Copyright Christie's Images, New York 2002©, Christie's New York, NY, 10/22/01)

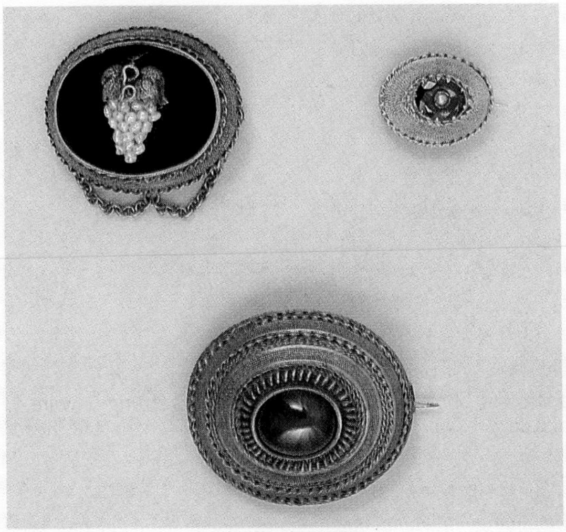

Brooches/Pins, yg, c. 1860-80:
TL, a cluster of seed pearl grapes with engr yg leaves riveted to a black onyx plaque mounted in a yg wiretwist frame with chain festoons, C-catch, tube hinge, loop for safety chain, 1¼" w x 1¼", **$300**.
TR, sm oval faceted garnet surmounted by a seed pearl, set in a twisted wirework frame, C-catch, tube hinge, extended pinstem, ¾" w x ⅝", **$200**.
(Lisa Johnson collection)
B, an oval carbuncle bezel-set in a domed oval wiretwist frame, C-catch, tube hinge, 1½" w x 1⅜", **$300**. (Courtesy of E. Foxe Harrell, New York, NY)

Brooch/Pin, enamel, rhodolite garnets, glass, silver, yg, mid-19th C, Renaissance Revival, Limoges enamel depicting a blackamoor mounted in a silver frame, encircled by tiny enameled yg blackamoor heads between each collet-set garnet, glazed compartment lined with silk on rev, replaced pin assembly with lever safety catch, 1⅜" w x 1⅝", **$950**. (Courtesy of E. Foxe Harrell, New York, NY)

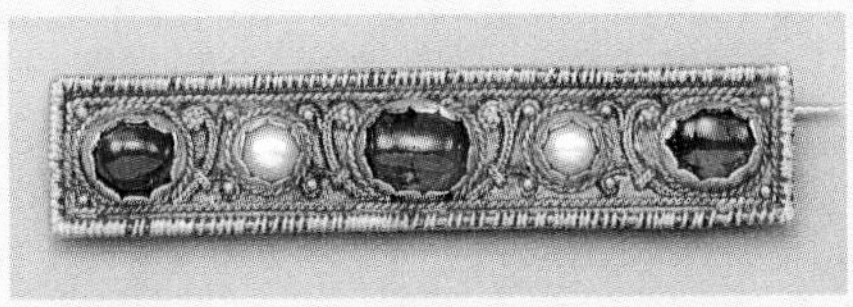

Brooch/Pin, bar, yg, pearls, sapphires, c. 1880, a rect plaque set with pearls and foiled sapphire cabs in a border of corded decoration, signed "Wièse," maker's mk for Wièse (a star within a lozenge), case by Wièse, 90 Rue de Richelieu, 3" w x ⅝", **$7,560** [A]. (Photo courtesy of Sotheby's, London, 6/20/01)

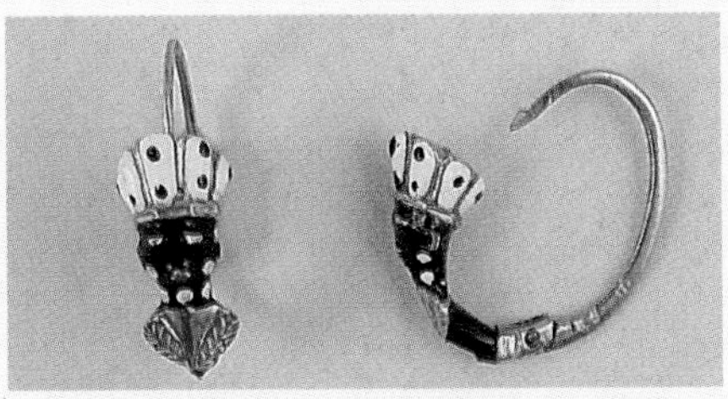

Earrings, yg, enamel, mid-19th C, Renaissance Revival, enameled heads of blackamoors on hoops, Fr earwires, ⅝" dia, **$750**. (Courtesy of E. Foxe Harrell, New York, NY).

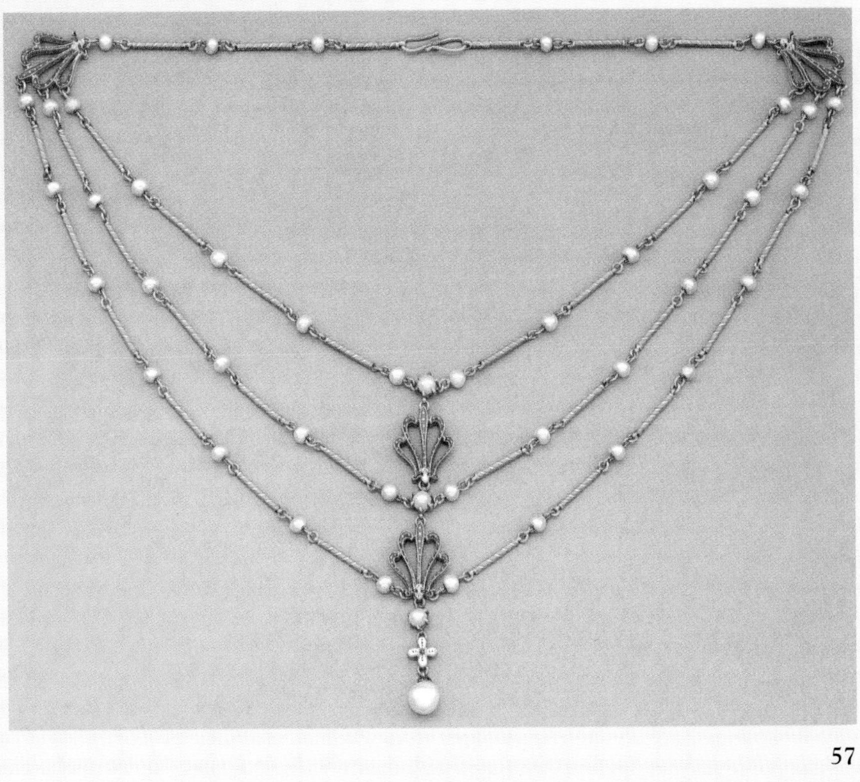

Necklace, enamel, yg, pearls, c. 1870, Renaissance Revival, triple festoon, blue-enameled spiral patterned baton links alternating with pearls, red-enameled open anthemion motif (flat floral/foliate decoration) connectors with white dots, pearl drop suspended from white-enameled quatrefoil with black dots, S-clasp stamped "CG" for Carlo Giuliano on both sides, in fitted case (necklace has been shortened), 18" longest festoon, 2⅝ " T to B @ center, **$7,106** [A]. (Photo courtesy of Sotheby's, London, 11/27/01)

Necklace, yg, glass beads, c. 1870, Archaeological Revival, a woven yg chain suspending vine leaf motifs alternating with purple glass bead bunches of grapes, S-hook clasp, attributed to Castellani, unsgd, 1" at center, approx 16" tl, **$20,020** [A]. (Photo courtesy of Sotheby's, London, 6/20/01)

Necklace, silver, pink stones, silver gilt, c. 1870, Renaissance Revival, five shield-shaped links with scrolled foliate openwork around masks alternating with smaller fleur-de-lis links set with pink stones, continuing to a fringe of quatrefoil links suspending silver drops, 1" T to B at center, 16" tl, **$1,344** [A]. (Photo courtesy of Sotheby's, London, 11/27/01)

Necklace, festoon, 18k yg, amethysts, c. 1880, swags of fine cable-link chain joining angular and circ plaques engr with foliate motifs, scrolled wirework and beaded edges, and centering three circ-cut amethysts, approx 15.00 cts tw, in multiple-pronged settings, 16½" tl, 2⅛" T to B at center, **$1,944** [A]. (Photo courtesy of Dupuis Jewellery Auctioneers, Toronto, ONT, Canada, 6/12/01)

Pendant, yg, enamel, garnets, c. 1860, Renaissance Revival, cross made up of black and white enameled blackamoor heads with gem-set enameled turbans, 1¼" w x 1¾", **$2,600**. (Photo courtesy of Facèré Jewelry Art, Seattle, WA)

Pendant and Chain, enamel, pearls, diamonds, yg, c. 1860, Renaissance Revival, Holbeinesque design, a button pearl in a scalloped blue-enameled setting, in the center of a polychrome enameled floral motif oval plaque encircled by six om diamonds in carré settings, engr floral motifs on rev, suspending a pearl drop from an enameled cap, surmounted by a geo enameled bail, suspended from a fine yg chain, 1⅛" w x 2⅝" tl, chain 17" tl, **$5,376** [A]. (Photo courtesy of Sotheby's, London, 6/20/01)

Pendants, silver, enamel, pearls, gemstones, Renaissance Revival, c. 1870:
L, a three-dimensional polychrome enameled swan set with sm rubies within enameled scrollwork, suspending a seed pearl, suspended from double chain joined with a jump ring bail (neckchain not original), unmkd, possibly Austrian, 1¼" w x 2½", **$300**.
R, c. 1870, Austrian, polychrome enamel on a three-dimensional depiction of St. George and the Dragon, silver gilt, the dragon's body a blister pearl, suspending a f.w. pearl, hmkd "A" for Vienna before 1872 on suspension loop, with another illegible hmk, suspended from a double seed pearl and silver chain joined with a jump ring bail (neckchain not original), 1¼" w x 2⅛", **$500**. (Elaine Sarnoff collection)

Watch Fob, satin glass, yg, seed pearls, red stones, mid-19th C, depicting a blackamoor female bust in lampworked black glass, with glass eyes and lips, wearing a gem-set yg crown, yg earrings, and gem-set yg collar, the base set with an uncut disk of banded agate (for a seal), 1¼" tl, ⅝" w at base, **$1,100**. (Courtesy of E. Foxe Harrell, New York, NY)

CAMEOS and INTAGLIOS

The cameo has come to be known as a classic form of jewelry, the epitome of the "old-fashioned" look. But its widespread popularity began in the nineteenth century as a tourist souvenir. Hardstone cameos date to ancient Rome; shell cameos to the Renaissance. Late eighteenth century Neo-classicists revived the art, inspired by Napoleon's preoccupation with Roman Imperialism. But it was the Victorians who popularized (some say vulgarized) the cameo made from a variety of materials—shell, lava, coral, ivory, jet, as well as gemstones—as a part of a Greco-Roman Revival that remained in vogue from mid-century onward.

Travelers touring Europe (on guided excursions organized and conducted by the West's first travel agent, Thomas Cook), helped promote cameo-carving to the point of mass production. Italy was a favorite destination, especially, due to the Victorian preoccupation with ancient history, the ruins of Pompeii at Mount Vesuvius. "Lava" cameos were purchased as souvenirs. The material, actually a form of limestone mixed with volcanic particles called "pyroclastics" (real lava is molten rock), was found in the region, and associated with the volcano that was Pompeii's downfall. Nearby, in the seaside town of Torre del Greco, Italian cameo carvers made shell and coral cameos for the tourists, as they continue to do today.

A true cameo is a miniature sculpture in relief, carved from a single piece of material. When the material is layered, as are agate (onyx) and shell, the carver uses the light and dark layers as contrasting background and foreground. When a design is carved into only the thin white layer of onyx with a thick black layer underneath, the background of the design appears translucent bluish-white. This is called "nicolo." The subject matter of cameos can range from classic mythological and Biblical scenes, floral bouquets and landscapes, to the more commonly seen heads or busts of women or men. Male cameos predominate the Neo-classical period.

A woman's profile is the motif most closely associated with cameos by their wearers today. These can date anywhere from 1840 to the present. Their look is usually in keeping with the style of the times.

One favorite technique for circa-dating is to look at the nose of the woman in profile. Aquiline, or Romanesque, noses are found on the classic beauties of the mid-nineteenth century. Pert, turned-up noses are found on twentieth-century interpretations of female attractiveness. It's important to remember that carvers could only carve what they knew; hairstyles and attire can also help in circa-dating.

The most common material for cameos is shell, which is soft and easy to carve. Portrait cameos were sometimes made with the depicted woman wearing a necklace or other jewelry set with a small diamond. These are called cameos *habillés* (French for "dressed up"), and are still being made. Hardstone "blackamoor" cameos *habillés* of the mid-nineteenth century, depicting the profiles of African women, are much less commonly seen, and highly desirable collector's items (see page 61).

Nineteenth century lava and coral cameos are also found today, although not as abundantly (see lava and coral cameos on pages 61 and 63). While most shell cameos are carved in bas-relief, due to the relative shallowness of the material's layers, lava and coral, being monochromatic, can be and often are carved in high relief. The protruding noses on these cameos are most susceptible to damage.

Some of the best and most highly prized cameos are made from hardstone. These cameos are more difficult and time-consuming to fashion, and require a great deal of skill with lathe-held tools. Cameo experts point out that the word "carved" is technically incorrect when applied to stone cameos and intaglios. The correct word is "engraved." The art of engraving gemstones is called "glyptics" or "the glyptic arts." Hardstone cameos are occasionally engraved within a concave depression in the stone, where the edge of the stone is level with the highest part of the cameo itself. *Chevet* or *chevée*, *cuvette*, or *curvette* are the terms, used interchangeably, for this type of cameo. The British term is *dished*.

The quality of a cameo's carving can range from breathtaking to abysmal. Values also range widely, depending on the skill of the carver, depicted subject, size, and the materials used for the cameo and the mounting or frame. Quickly-made mass-produced shell cameos—most of which come from Idar-Oberstein, Germany, not Italy—are of little value. Ultrasonic machine-made stone cameos have been produced for the past 30 years. These have a faintly textured surface referred to as the "fresh-fallen snow" syndrome by author Anna Miller (see References). Their quality and value are low. Pseudo or assembled cameos are molded from natural or synthetic materials and laminated to a backing or set in a metal frame.

Brooches are the usual form, but cameos can also be found set into necklaces, bracelets, earrings, rings, and stickpins.

Intaglios, which actually preceded cameos in ancient times, are the opposite of cameos, in that the design is recessed, engraved into the stone, below the surface. The most common association is with fob seals, or signet rings, in which the intaglio is used to create an impression in relief when pressed into sealing wax (see page 64). These fobs and rings are also worn for ornamental purposes, but the design is less perceptible than that of a cameo. Intaglios are engraved in hardstone, never shell or other soft material. Molded glass imitation intaglios are found in inexpensive jewelry.

Reverse-painted rock crystal intaglios were popular from the time of their invention circa 1862 well into 20th century, especially in sporting jewelry featuring animal motifs (see Edwardian Jewelry in Part II). Dogs, horses, or other animals were engraved into the backs of rock crystal quartz cabochons. The intaglios were then painted in realistic colors and backed with mother-of-pearl before setting. From the front, the animals appear three-dimensional. These were imitated with molded and painted glass in the twentieth century.

Bracelet, link, lava, yg, c. 1850-60, six linked oval cameos in varied colors, three facing left, three facing right, high-relief male heads of famous literary figures, including Dante, Homer, and Shakespeare, set in plain yg bezels, v-spring and box clasp, 7¾" tl, cameos 1⅛" w x 1⅜", **$1,600**. (Courtesy of E. Foxe Harrell, New York, NY)

Brooch/Pin, hardstone, seed pearls, yg, glass, c. 1870, the profile of a Bacchante set in a twisted wire yg frame set with pearls, compartment with photo, hook on rev, damage to bg stone, 1¾" w x 2⅛", **$150**. (Diane White collection)

Bracelet, link, lava, 800 silver, c. 1940, 12 lava cameos depicting heads of Roman gods and goddesses in various colors, set in 800 silver frames, post-1938 Italian hmks on v-spring clasp (cameos possibly carved earlier), ⅝" w x 7" tl, **$350**. (Author's collection)

Brooch/Pin, lava, yg, c. 1860-70, high-relief front-facing cameo of a Bacchante, C-catch, tube hinge, extended pinstem, 1½" w x 2", **$800**. (Elaine Sarnoff collection)

Brooch/Pin, coral, yg, mid-Victorian, set in a deep oval wiretwist Etruscan Revival style frame, loop for safety chain on rev, C-catch, tube hinge, extended pinstem, 1⅛" w x 1⅜", **$325**. (Courtesy of E. Foxe Harrell, New York, NY)

Brooch/Pin, hardstone, 14k yg, rc diamonds, 10k yg, c. 1860, cameo *habillé*, profile of a young African woman (blackamoor) wearing a 14k yg diadem, diamond earrings, and choker, set in a 10k yg frame, 1" w x 2", **$2,585** [A]. (Photo courtesy of Skinner, Inc., Boston, MA, 12/11/01)

Brooch/Pin, coral, 14k yg, c. 1870, front-facing head of a woman set in a multi-pronged beaded frame mounted on a lobed and cusped engr yg plaque with appl foliate decoration suspending a detachable pendant with foxtail chain tassel grad toward the center, flanked by beads, C-catch, tube hinge, 1⅜" w x 3" tl, **$500**. (Courtesy of Chris Enebo Antique Jewelry, Tualatin, OR)

Brooch/Pin, shell, yg, c. 1860, oval shell cameo depicting a female figure as Spring set within a yg frame decorated with granulation and twisted wirework, maker's mk for Castellani on rev, extended pinstem, 1¾" w x 2⅜", **$6,475** [A]. (Photo courtesy of Sotheby's, London, 11/28/00)

Brooch/Pin, shell, yg, c. 1870, the profile of an angel facing right, bezel-set in yg frame with an appl border of corded wire, C-catch, tube hinge, extended pinstem, fitted case, 2½" w x 3", **$1,042** [A]. (Photo courtesy of Sotheby's, London, 6/20/01)

Brooch/Pin, hardstone, 9k rose gold, c. 1860, an allegorical depiction of Psyche (on left) and Apollo (on right), with the central figure conveying the message that "music feeds the soul," set in a plain gold frame, C-catch, tube hinge, loop for safety chain on rev, 2¼" w x 1⅞", **$1,500**. (Courtesy of Chris Enebo Antique Jewelry, Tualatin, OR)

Brooch/Pin, sardonyx, rc diamonds, 18k yg, c. 1900, depicting a female profile, framed in rc diamonds, Fr hmks, ⅞" w x 1⅛", **$1,645** [A]. (Photo courtesy of Butterfields, San Francisco and Los Angeles, CA, 9/25/01)

Brooch/Pendant, hardstone, 14k yg, c. 1870, a classical female profile mounted in a tubular frame, flanked by Brazilian chain suspending yg beads and *"pampilles,"* an engr yg convex cartouche surmounting the base of the frame, and suspending a lg yg bead and a *"pampille,"* compartment on rev (missing glass cover), C-catch, tube hinge, pendant hook, loop for safety chain, in fitted box, 2" w x 3¼" tl, **$4,000**. (Courtesy of Chris Enebo Antique Jewelry, Tualatin OR)

Brooch/Pendant, queen conch shell, 14k wg, c. 1915-20, a woman's profile set in a filigree wg frame with floral/foliate motifs at compass points, retractable bail, lever catch, 1½" w x 2", **$200**. (Vickie Vega collection)

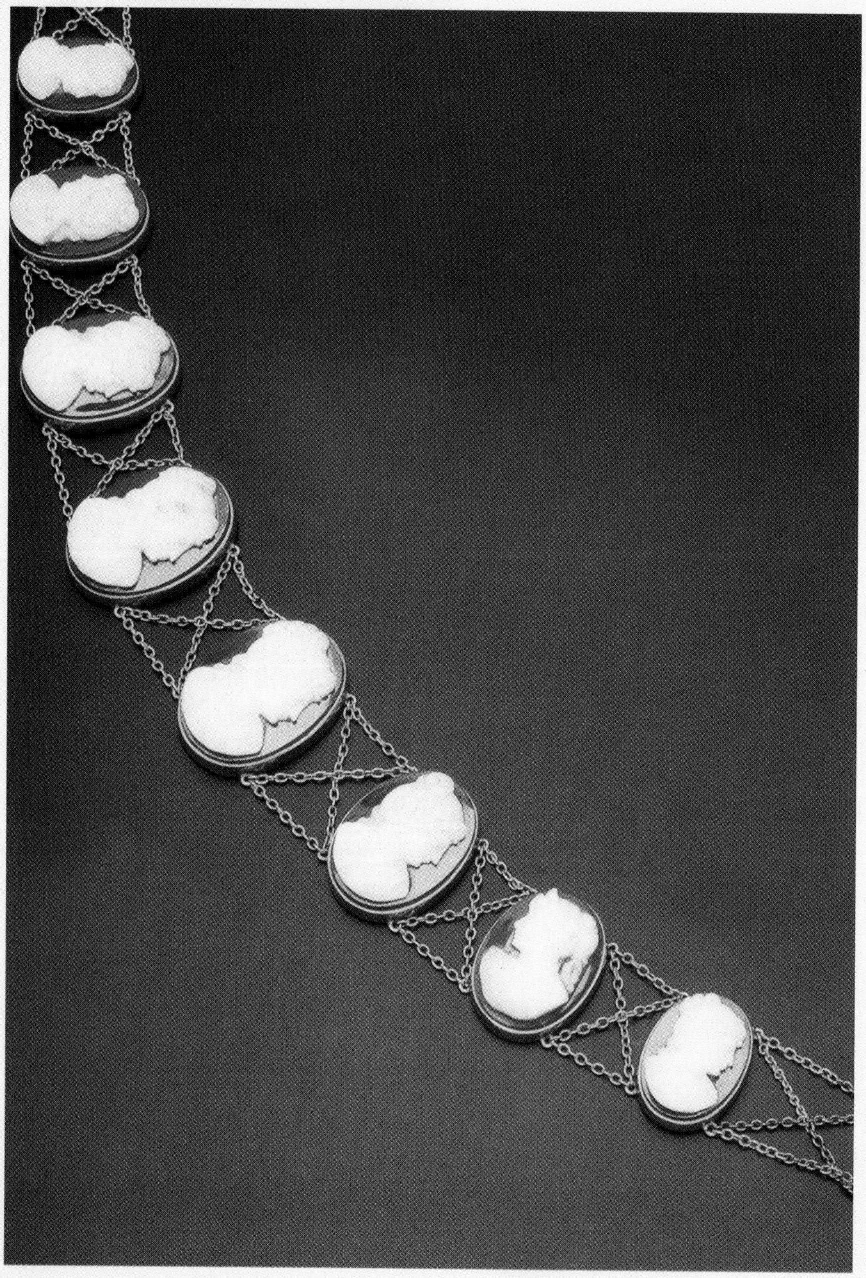

Pendant, hardstone, rc diamonds, yg, c. 1860, oval, depicting the profile of a classical warrior with a masked helmet, set within conforming frame and suspended from a ribbon bow motif bail, set throughout with rc diamonds in yg, glazed compartment on rev, 1¼" w x 2¼" tl, **$897** [A]. (Photo courtesy of Dupuis Jewellery Auctioneers, Toronto, ONT, Canada, 6/12/01)

Necklace, hardstone, yg, c. 1890, a grad row of ten oval hardstone cameos depicting maidens in profile and mounted in simple bezel frames, all joined by crossed cable-link chains, in a case stamped "HENRY BIRKS & SONS, LTD. MONTREAL," 13¾" tl, 1¼" at center, **$3,588** [A]. (Photo courtesy of Dupuis Jewellery Auctioneers, Toronto, ONT, Canada, 6/12/01)

Pendant/Necklace, shell, glass, gp brass, f.w. pearls, c. 1900-10, shell cameo of Diana set in a gp brass frame with beaded scrolls at compass points set with circ coral-colored glass cabs, suspending a pear-shaped coral glass drop, suspended from a spring ring clasp and a chain of beaded scrolls flanking bezel-set glass cabs alternating with f.w. pearls, pendant 1⅛" w x 3½" tl, chain 18" tl, **$375**. (Courtesy of Generations, La Verne, CA)

Rings, hardstone, yg:
L, c. 1870, circ black and white onyx cameo of the front-facing head of a woman, set in a multipronged 18k yg bezel, ropetwist frame, mounted on a flat band shank, ¾" dia, sz 8, **$700**.
R, c. 1880, carved white bust of a woman imbedded into dk rust-brown material within a ropetwist frame, engr shield-shaped mount, beaded shoulders, wide shank, ⅝" x ½", sz 8, **$125**.
(Lisa Johnson collection)

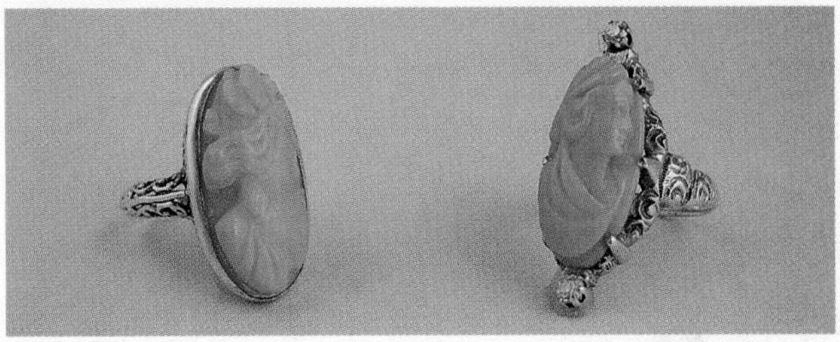

Rings, coral, yg:
L, c. 1900, an oval cameo (worn) bezel-set in a 10k yg frame with open gallery, openwork shank, mkd "A *10" for Allsop Bros., Newark, NJ (first known as such in 1894), sz 5½, center ½" w x ⅞", **$125**.
R, c. 1890, an elliptical carved coral cameo (worn) in a sculpted yg mount, a sc diamond prong-set above and below, sz 6, center ⅜" w x 1⅛", **$200**. (Vickie Vega collection)

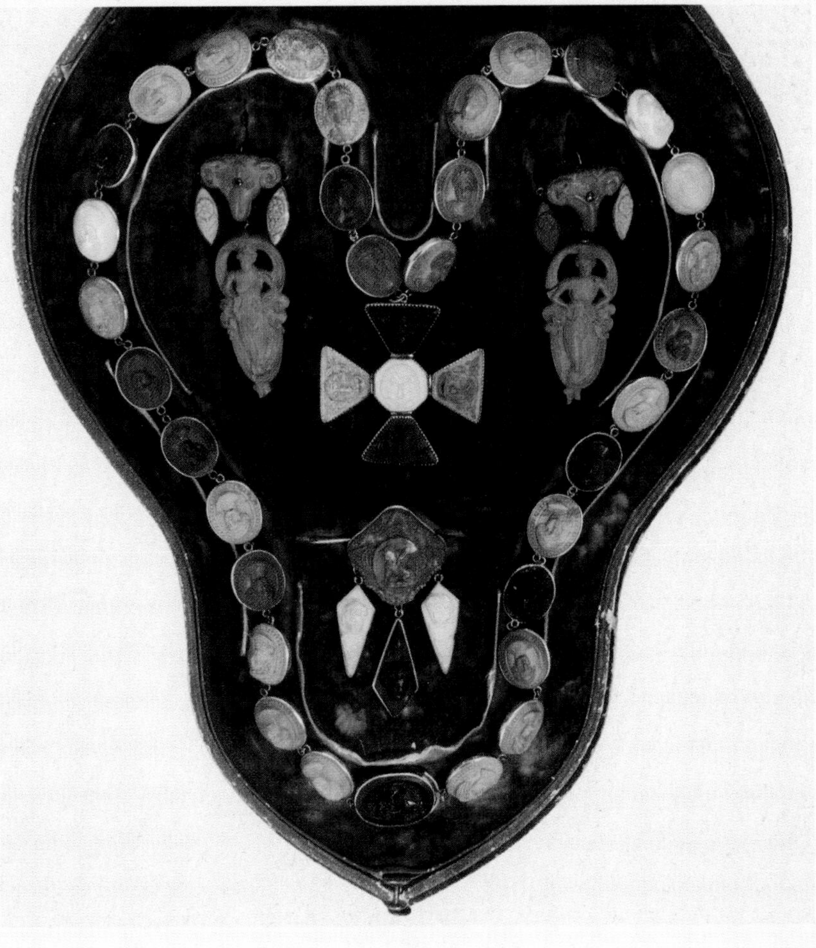

Suite: Necklace, Pendent Earrings, and Brooch/Pin, lava cameos, 10k yg, ym, c. 1860, necklace of oval lava cameos set double-sided within collets of 10k yg, suspending a Maltese cross set with lava cameos depicting mask faces; a 10k yg brooch with a central ornament depicting a griffin, suspending three kite-shaped cameos, and a pr of pendent earrings, each surmounted by a carved ram's head suspending a carved maiden, flanked by two smaller navette-shaped floral lava cameos, mounted in ym, in original fitted box, necklace 24" tl, cross 1½" sq, earrings 1" w x 2¼" tl, **$4,994** [A]. (Photo courtesy of Butterfields, San Francisco and Los Angeles, CA, 6/19/01)

Suite: Necklace and Earrings, hardstone cameos, diamonds, st rose gold, c. 1860, necklace front suspending three cameos depicting cherubs playing musical instruments, mounted in rose gold, surmounted by rc diamond-set wreaths, the lower portion of each a grad row of om diamonds in a cusped frame suspending three diamond-set drops, joined with diamond-set bows and swags to the hinged wire work gold frame set with om diamonds, the back an engr yg and silver crossbar collar, diamond-set clasp; matching pr of pendent earrings, cameos of cherubs offering a toast, diamond-set bow surmounts with later screwbacks, necklace 2¾" center drop, earrings 2⅜" tl, **$11,750** [A]. (Copyright Christie's Images, New York 2002©, Christie's Los Angeles, CA, 10/4/01)

Watch Fobs, gemstones and ym, c. 1840-50, $750 each:
L, 1, gp brass, set with uncarved amethyst, ⅞" x ¾".
L, 2, gp brass, carnelian, uncarved rect stone, ⅞" x ¾".
C, yg, carnelian, lg intaglio seal of a bearded man's profile, surmounted by a ring-shaped yg fob with foliate decoration, ⅞" x ¾", 1¾" h.
R, 1, gp brass, carnelian, ribbed bail, profile facing left, ¾" w x ⅞".
R, 2, vermeil, carnelian, carved with monogram "WHJ," ¾". (Courtesy of E. Foxe Harrell, New York, NY)

MOSAICS IN JEWELRY

The rise and fall of mosaics developed along parallel lines to that of cameos. Also based on ancient Roman techniques and revived by Neo-classicists, mosaics of the late eighteenth and early nineteenth centuries were miniature works of art in glass or stone, resembling paintings.

Like cameos, mosaics reached their height of popularity in the mid-nineteenth century, during the Revivalist rage for all things Italian. And like cameos, too, it was the tourist trade that brought them to that height, and was their downfall in terms of quality.

There are two types of Italian mosaics: Roman, or micromosaics, in which tiny bits of colored glass called *tesserae* are pieced together to form a picture, held in place with cement in a glass or stone background; and Florentine, or *pietra dura* (literally, "hard stone," plural: *pietre dure*), in which thin slices of colored stones are cut in shapes and fitted together like a jigsaw puzzle to produce a picture, usually using a bed of black marble as the foundation.

The subject matter for mosaics is also of two distinct types. Roman mosaics, catering to the tourist trade, often depict Roman ruins and landscapes (see this page and page 67), or are copies of ancient mosaics, like the Capitoline doves, often called "Pliny's doves."

King Charles spaniels were another favorite motif. Mythological and religious figures are also seen in Roman mosaics. Florentine mosaics most commonly have floral motifs, but other figurative motifs, such as butterflies and birds, are found as well (see this page and page 66).

Value depends on quality of workmanship and condition. Mosaics are easily cracked or otherwise damaged. In Roman mosaics, the size of the tesserae helps determine age and quality. Micromosaics that look less like pieces of glass and more like a painting to the naked eye are usually earlier, and better.

Entire parures, or suites, of jewelry were made from both types of mosaics. Demi-parures of pendant or brooch and earrings are also found.

The brooch is the most common single form of mosaic jewelry. Mosaics continue to be made in Italy today, still for tourists, but with much larger tesserae and much lesser workmanship.

Brooch/Pin, micromosaic, black glass, gf, c. 1850-60, rect black glass ground inlaid with an oval mosaic of a building, stamped scrollwork gf frame, C-catch, tube hinge, 1⅞" w x 1⅝", **$950**. (Courtesy of E. Foxe Harrell Jewelers, New York, NY)

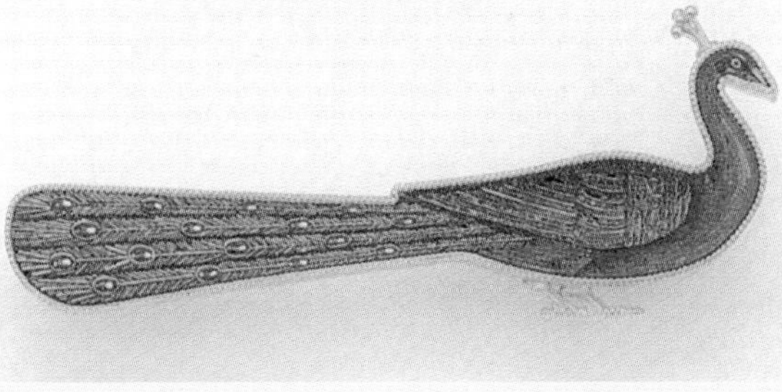

Brooch/Pin, micromosaic, yg, c. 1870, in the shape of a peacock, body and tail set with tesserae resembling plumage, within a yg ropetwist border, sgd with maker's mk for Castellani, a few tesserae deficient, 3" w x 1⅛", **$18,542** [A]. (Photo courtesy of Sotheby's, London, 11/27/01)

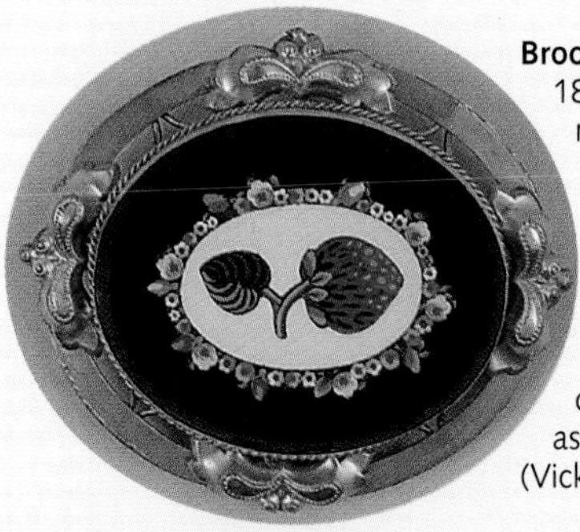

Brooch/Pin, micromosaic, yg, c. 1860, depicting a strawberry in mosaic on a white ground encircled by mosaic floral/foliate motifs within a bezel-set oval black glass plaque with wiretwist decoration within a later yg frame with die-stamped floral/foliate motifs at compass points, later-added pin assembly, 2¼" w x 2", **$700**. (Vickie Vega collection)

Brooches/Pins, *pietra dura*:
L, c. 1900, bar, iris motif on black marble ground, brass findings, 1⅝" w x ½", **$200**. (Courtesy of E. Foxe Harrell, New York, NY)
R, c. 1880-90, circ disk of black marble inlaid with a crocus motif set in a silver frame with gf beaded edge, brass backing, C-catch, tube hinge, extended pinstem, 1" dia, **$175**. (Author's collection)

Brooch/Pin, *pietra dura*, brass, c. 1915, circ disk of black marble, inlaid with a mosaic depicting a pink rose, lily-of-the-valley, forget-me-not and morning glory bouquet, mounted on a brass disk, C-catch, tube hinge, 1" dia, **$165**. (Photo courtesy of Morning Glory Antiques, Albuquerque, NM)

Bulla, micromosaic, 18k yg, c. 1840-60, two-sided, hinged at the top, each side a convex cusped plaque inlaid with polychrome geo mosaics, surmounting a convex disk, polychrome micromosaics of the heads of winged cherubs on white ground one side, two doves with olive branch and cross on blue ground on the other, encircled by geo mosaic patterns enclosed in yg wiretwist and beadwork, 1¼" w x 2", **$4,500**. (Margot Conté collection, photo by Margot Conté)

Buckles, clasps, micromosaic, gp brass:
TL, c. 1900, two-pc opposed arrowhead shapes in polychrome floral, foliate and geo patterns, some within ropetwist wire cells, set into a gp brass beaded-edge frame, hook and eye closure, bars for belt attachment on rev, 4¼" w x 2¼" at center, **$375**.
TR, c. 1880-1900, two-pc, circ plaques bisected by a lozenge-shaped center, blue and white with touches of yellow, red and green floral/foliate mosaics forming two opposed faces within ropetwist wire cells, set into a gp brass beaded-edge frame, hook and eye closure, bars for belt attachment on rev, 4" w x 1⅝" at center, **$450**.
C, c. 1860-80, two-pcs forming openwork opposed C-scrolls decorated with floral motif polychrome mosaics bisected by a central vertical bar with mosaics of daisies and teardrop-shaped foliate motif terminals, 3¼" w x 2" at center, **$850**.
BL, c. 1900, two-pc, opposed spade-shaped plaques, predominantly green with white and blue foliate pattern within ropetwist wire cells enclosing a central polychrome floral design on each pc, set into a gp brass beaded-edge frame, hook and eye closure, bars for belt attachment on rev, 4½" w x 2½" at center, **$850**.
BR, c. 1880-1900, two-pcs forming a cusped and lobed polygon, shades of blue with white, red, yellow and green, daisies and other floral/foliate motifs outlined in geo mosaics flanked by foliate scrolls, hook and eye closure, bars for belt attachment on rev, 3¼" w x 2½" at center, **$775**. (Margot Conté collection, photo by Margot Conté)

Earrings, micromosaic, yg, c. 1850:
T, Egyptian Revival, pharaoh's heads within equilateral crosses in polychrome micromosaic on geo-patterned ground, later-added screwbacks, 1⅛" dia, **$1,400**.
B, convex disks, each with a pr of doves on flowering branches on blue ground within an 18k yg frame encircled by a geo-patterned quatrefoil, later-added screwbacks, 1" dia, **$1,650**. (Margot Conté collection, photo by Margot Conté)

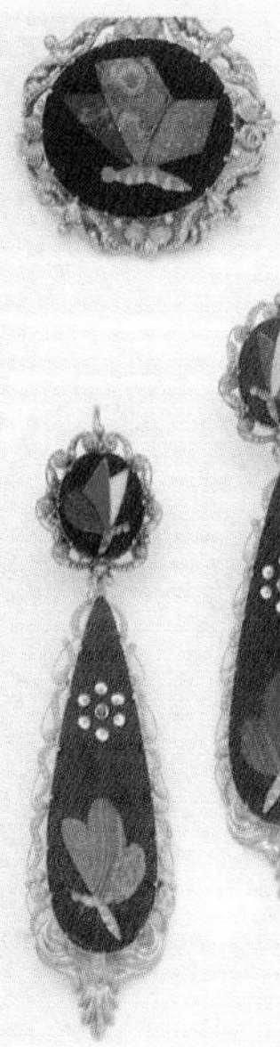

Suite: Brooch/Pin and Earrings, *pietra dura*, yg, c. 1830, butterfly motif in lapis lazuli, malachite, chalcedony and other stones, inlaid in a black stone ground, within a border of repoussé and *cannetille* goldwork, fitted case, brooch 1⅛" w, earrings 1" w x 3⅞", **$3,892** [A]. (Photo courtesy of Sotheby's, London, 11/27/01)

Suite: Brooch/Pin and Pendent Earrings, mosaic, gp brass, c. 1880, brooch with oval black glass ground inlaid with a mosaic depicting the Temple of Vesta, set in a plain gp brass frame, C-catch, tube hinge, extended pinstem, matching pear-shaped earrings inlaid with oval mosaics, one depicting the Temple of Vesta, the other the Coliseum, new gold earwires, brooch $1\frac{3}{4}$" w x $1\frac{1}{2}$", earrings $\frac{5}{8}$" w x $1\frac{3}{8}$", **$750**. (Author's collection)

Suite: Brooch/Pin and Earrings, micromosaic, 18k yg, MOP, c. 1870, brooch decorated with three circ micromosaic panels each depicting a butterfly, backed by MOP, bezel-set within a foliate scrolled repoussé frame, and a pr of pendent earrings of similar design, Fr hmks, ear wires and pin back missing, $2\frac{1}{2}$" w x $1\frac{1}{4}$", earrings 1" w x $1\frac{1}{4}$" tl, **$2,938** [A]. (Photo courtesy of Butterfields, San Francisco and Los Angeles, CA, 6/19/01)

Suite: Brooch/Pendant and Pendent Earrings, micromosaic, 14k yg, c. 1870s, brooch set with a mosaic depicting a pastoral gentleman in a revival costume (later pin assembly with lead solder, discolored yg), matching earrings set with mosiacs of gentlemen's profiles, brooch $1\frac{3}{8}$ w x $4\frac{5}{8}$" tl, earrings $\frac{5}{8}$" w x $3\frac{3}{4}$" tl, **$2,644** [A]. (Photo courtesy of Butterfields, San Francisco and Los Angeles, CA, 9/25/01)

Suite: Necklace and Pendent Earrings, micromosaic, gp brass, c. 1880-90, a row of five shamrock motifs in shades of green mosaic, alternating with sm circ red, white and blue geo-patterned disks, suspending a larger shamrock pendant, joined to a cable-link chain and spring ring clasp, matching earrings, each a single shamrock surmounted by a circ disk, with later-added screwbacks, necklace 18" tl, 2" T to B at center, earrings, $1\frac{1}{2}$" tl, **$900**. (Margot Conté collection, photo by Margot Conté)

MANUFACTURED GOLD, GOLD-FILLED, GOLD-PLATED

The Revivalists inspired an interest in goldwork. All-gold jewelry was a novelty in the mid-nineteenth century. Before discoveries in California and Australia in 1849 and 1851 made larger quantities of gold more accessible, gemstones were the focal point of most jewelry. Gold was used sparingly in very thin filigree (*cannetille*) or repoussé work in the early part of the century (see Late Georgian and Early Victorian sections). Later, heating, rolling and pressing, and electroplating, made a little gold go a long way, and gave machine-made articles the look of gold without the expense.

By the 1830s, the Industrial Revolution had come to jewelry manufacture. Birmingham became a major center for machine-made goods in England. The invention of electroplating in 1840 helped launch what was to become a huge costume jewelry industry in England and the United States (although the term "costume" jewelry wasn't coined until the early twentieth century).

The rolled gold-plating process was brought to the U.S. from Great Britain in 1848 and was a big hit with New England jewelry manufacturers. Unlike electroplating, which was applied to a finished base metal article, rolled gold was a mechanical process for sheet and wire which was then used to manufacture a finished piece. The technique was derived from Sheffield plate, developed in 1743, which was copper clad with silver and rolled to the desired thickness. Rolled gold is copper or brass clad with gold, known as gold-filled in the U.S., and called *doublé d'or* by the French, who began using the technique as early as the 1820s (see bracelet on page 40). The metal "sandwich" was treated exactly the same as karat gold: stamped, engraved, and fashioned into pieces that were identical to their solid gold counterparts.

In the U.S., manufacturing centers grew along the Eastern seaboard: in Philadelphia, New York, Boston, and especially, in Providence, Rhode Island, and the neighboring towns of Attleboro and North Attleboro, Massachusetts, and in Newark, New Jersey. Some of these manufacturers are still in business today.

It is worth noting that during the height of mid-Victorian Revivalism, several Newark firms produced quality pieces in Revivalist styles, comparable to those made in Europe. These jewels met with acceptance, however, only when they were sold as French or English-made (makers' marks were often absent at this time). America's well-to-do believed their own country's product was inferior to that of Europe. Perhaps this was because Americans excelled in the mass production of inexpensive gold and gold-filled or plated items. Many of the factories that made these items were in Providence and the Attleboros, but Newark produced a sizable portion of them as well. Although the pieces were mass-produced, there was still some craftsmanship involved. The forms may have been die-stamped by machine (the preferred method at the time), but engraving, enameling, and finishing were done by hand.

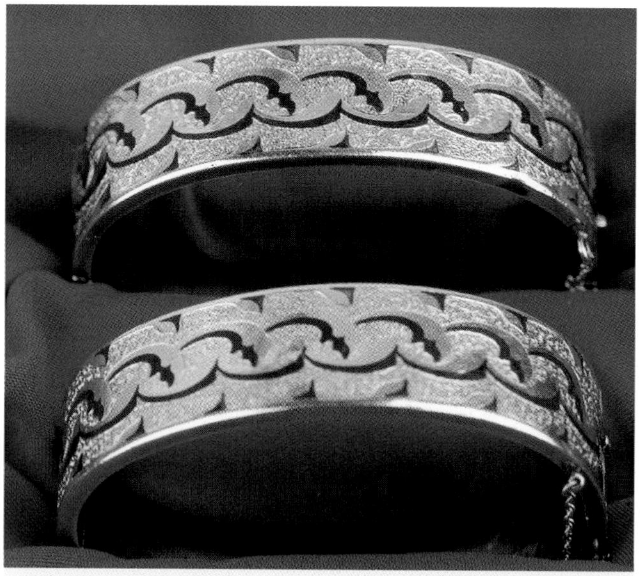

Bracelets, hinged bangles, 14k yg, enamel, c. 1870, matched pr, black *taille d'épargne* enamel decoration in a bold geo scalloped design on engr textured ground, minor interior dents, ⅝" w, 2⅛" inside dia, **$1,093** [A]. (Photo courtesy of Skinner, Inc., Boston, MA, 9/25/01)

Stamped jewelry backed with a flat plate is sometimes called "hollow work," and resembles hand-raised repoussé metalwork, in which the metal is worked from the back to create a design in relief. Engraving or chasing may be added to the front of the piece. This is the type of work that many people today consider typically Victorian, probably because it was produced in such quantities that a great deal of it has survived. Often, particularly in American pieces, the engraved depressions were partly filled with black enamel to enhance the design, called *taille d'épargne*, or "black enamel tracery" (see bracelets above and page 69, left, brooches and chatelaine on page 71, and sleeve buttons on page 73).

The addition of gold fringe or bead-tipped foxtail chain tassels was common in pieces of the 1870s, a time when women's dresses were trimmed with abundant quantities of fringe (see brooch on page 71). Long pendent earrings were in vogue, and were especially well-suited to tassels and fringing (see earrings in Hairwork section, page 45).

Garter bracelets, or *jarretières*, of gold or gold-plated brass mesh with fringed and tasseled ends, were worn in pairs. The bracelets were secured with an ornamental slide, often engraved and enameled, or set with a small cameo. They are sometimes referred to as slide bracelets, which can be confusing. Another type of bracelet is also called a slide bracelet, because it is made up of a collection of slides from longchains—a practice that began earlier in this century, after longchains went out of fashion. These slide bracelets became, and still are, popular enough to have been reproduced. The reproductions are fairly easy to detect. They don't have the "hodgepodge" look of a piece made up of old parts, as the originals are. Sometimes each slide is hallmarked in exactly the same way—a dead giveaway.

Hinged hollow bangles, both gold and gold-filled, are

Bracelets, hinged bangles, matched prs, c. 1870-80:
L, rose gf, engr and *taille d'épargne* enameled floral/foliate and geo design on textured ground, safety chains, 2¼" inside dia, ⅜" w, **$300**. (Diane White collection)
R, gf, crossover tubular bangles surmounted by stamped and engr hollow sq and semicirc ornaments with appl wiretwist, bead, and raised decoration, safety chains, 2¼" inside dia, ½" w, **$350**. (Courtesy of Andrea Fatell, Wellsley, MA)

another kind of bracelet that remained popular throughout the Victorian period. They have become a classic form, and are still made today. Widths and decorative elements vary from wide and ornately engraved or decorated to narrow and plain. The "bypass" or "crossover" design, in which decorated ends of a narrow tubular bangle cross parallel to one another at the top, gained favor in the later part of the century (see above).

With the discovery of diamonds in South Africa in 1867 leading to a greater supply—and demand—a clever American invention was patented in 1878 that was designed to protect diamond drop earrings from being lost or stolen: a spherical hinged hollow cover that snapped on over the diamond and concealed it from view. These were usually made of plain yellow gold, sometimes enameled or repoussé (see page 72).

Another unique mid-to-late Victorian ornament involved the recycling of an outdated component of eighteenth century pocket watches, the escapement cover, or "watchcock." These gilt brass inner parts were actually rather decorative, each one engraved with a variety of floral and foliate motifs, and other embellishment, including faces. In the 1880s, they were linked together to form necklaces or bracelets, or joined for brooches. Today these are quite scarce and collectible (see page 72).

One variety of necklace of typically Victorian manufacture is called a "bookchain" necklace. Stamped, flat, folded-over rectangles, resembling the shape of a book, form the links of a double-sided chain, usually engraved or decorated on both sides. The chain is held together in front by an ornate clasp or slide, often with a small cameo set in it, the ends extending like tassels. The design may have evolved from the practice of wearing a ribbon around the neck, pinned with the ends crossed in front. Another variety of bookchain has a front spring ring clasp with an extension and a second spring ring for suspending a locket or pendant (see photo at right).

Lockets, another classic jewelry form, were popular in the nineteenth century, varying in size and shape. Large oval gold and gold-filled lockets on wide or thick chains were in keeping with style proportions of the Grand Period, 1860-80. Round and somewhat smaller lockets appeared toward the end of the century (see page 72).

Gold and gold-filled longchains and slides were practical, as well as popular. A watch, lorgnette, or other useful (or decorative) item could be attached by means of a swivel hook and suspended from the chain. The ornamental slide was drawn up and the pendent piece pinned or tucked into a pocket or belt, causing the chain to drape attractively.

Gold-filled and electroplated jewelry was affordable to nearly everyone. Since it was manufactured in the same forms and styles as solid gold jewelry, unless there is enough wear on a piece to reveal base metal (usually brass), jewelry should be tested to determine if it is gold or gold-filled, as it is seldom marked. Gold-filled pieces sell for a little more than half the price of their all-gold counterparts.

Occasionally, one hears the term "pinchbeck" used to refer to gold-filled or gold-plated brass jewelry (more commonly heard in Britain). This is a word that has taken on mystic proportions. In reality, pinchbeck is an alloy of copper and zinc formulated in the early eighteenth century by Christopher Pinchbeck as an inexpensive imitation gold. It fell out of favor as a substitute for gold when electroplating was invented (c. 1840), and truly met its demise when 9 karat gold was made legal in Britain in 1854. Most pinchbeck jewelry was made in England. It was imported by American jewelers, although some work was done here. Pre-Victorian pieces made from pinchbeck are rarely seen

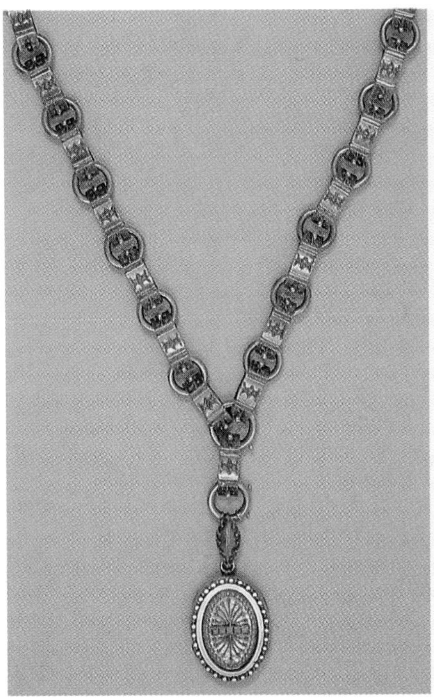

Locket and Chain, gf, turquoise, glass, c. 1870-80, bookchain with applied wiretwist and beading, double spring rings and extension suspending a similarly decorated oval locket with a central horizontal row of Fr cut turq, chain 22", locket 1" w x 2" tl, **$400**. (Courtesy of Pat Seal, Treasures From Yesterday, Fort Worth, TX)

today, despite some dealers' claims. If they are of the period, they are highly collectible, and expensive. The problem for collectors is one of circa-dating. There is no readily available test for pinchbeck, as it is really one of several alloys of brass, all of which differ only in percentages of copper to zinc.

The California Gold Rush of 1849 was followed by gold discoveries in Australia in 1851, the Black Hills of the Dakota territory in 1874, South Africa in 1886, and Alaska in 1898, thus ensuring a more plentiful supply of gold for the rest of the century. Two unique types of gold jewelry are directly connected to gold discoveries in the above-mentioned places, and to gold mining in general. A sort of commemorative or souvenir jewelry came out of the mining industry. Pieces sometimes depicted picks and shovels and other accouterments of mining, and/or were set with small gold nuggets. These can be marked "Native Gold," "Alaska Gold," or other place name phrase. Other "souvenirs" were made with compartments containing ore samples (see page 71).

Jewelry set with gold-in-quartz is a second type of mining-related jewelry, most closely associated with California. Quartz is the usual host mineral for gold, but it was more expensive to extract gold from the hard-rock mines than from placer mining, where natural forces had already separated the metal from its matrix. Gold-in-quartz was therefore called "rich man's gold." Jewelry set with polished pieces of it was considered status-symbol jewelry, now highly collectible, especially in California (see page 71).

Nineteenth century gold jewelry is often unmarked. If hallmarks are present, however, they can help determine age and country of origin. The U.S. had no legal standards until 1906, but 14 and 10 karats were the most common alloys for mass-manufactured gold of the Victorian period. A few prestigious firms, such as Tiffany & Co., used 18k exclusively, others used it occasionally. The British used 9, 12, and 15 karat gold after 1854, when standards were lowered from 18 karat. According to some experts, unassayed (unmarked) gold before 1854 can be lower than 18k. Britons spell karat with a c; the abbreviation is "c" or "ct." If a British piece is hallmarked, the date of assay is indicated by a letter.

Assayed French gold is never lower than 18k; the hallmark is an eagle's head. Makers' marks are in a lozenge. Other European countries use three-digit numbers that are karat equivalents in thousandths, e.g., 750 equals 18k, 585 is 14k, etc. (see appendices, Marks on Metals and Basic Hallmark Identification).

Bracelets, link, c. 1890:
T, gf, three stamped and engr circ disks flanked by textured fancy links, sliding ball and chain guard on clasp, ⅜" w x 7½", **$150**.
BL, yg, stamped and engr curb links with heart-shaped padlock clasp, engr initials on rev, ⅝" w x 8¼" tl, **$500**.
(Diane White collection)
BR, gf, textured curb links, die-stamped scrollwork on heart-shaped padlock clasp with key, ¼" w x 7½", **$150**. (Lisa Johnson collection)

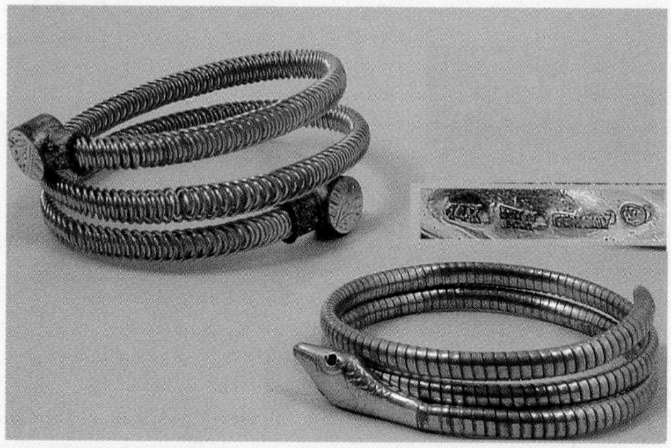

Bracelets, gf wraparound; late 19th and early 20th century:
L, c. 1890, spiral wire around central core, engr circ disk terminals, ⅛" w, 14" (extended), **$125.**
R, c. 1920s, wraparound snake motif, engr head with blue stone eyes, mkd "14K ROLLED GOLD, GERMANY," illegible maker's mk, ⅛" w, 17" tl (extended), **$150**. (Lisa Johnson collection)

Brooch/Pin, gilt metal, tinted photograph, glass, cloth, c. 1860-70, oval swivel with hp photograph of a mustachioed gentleman set under glass, glazed compartment containing cloth on rev within scalloped hollow tube outer frame, C-catch, tube hinge, 1⅝" w x 1⅞", **$235**. (Courtesy of Lenore Dailey, The Raven's Nest, Palm Springs, CA)

Brooch/Pin, yg, enamel, ore samples, c. 1870, Am, a cusped convex oval yg plaque engr with Greek key, foliate and diaper pattern motifs accented with black *taille d'épargne* enamel, enclosing an elliptical central glazed compartment divided into eight sections, each containing a different mineral or ore sample, 2½" w x 1⅜", **$1,250.** (Courtesy of Generations, La Verne, CA)

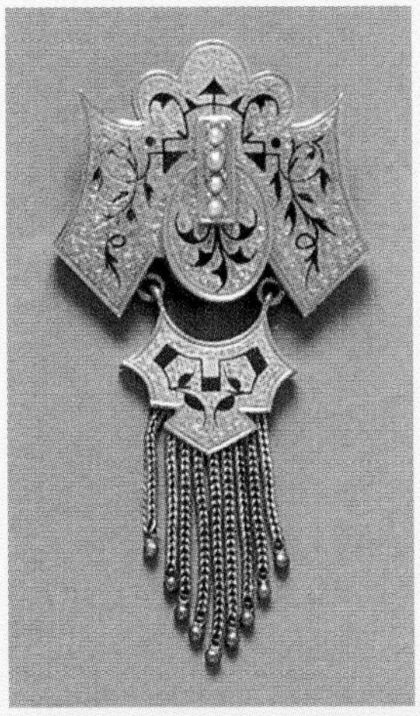

Brooch/Pin, 14k yg, seed pearls, enamel, c. 1870, scrolled and cusped shield-shaped plaque, engr foliate design accented with four seed pearls and *taille d'épargne* black enamel, suspending an engr and enameled plaque terminating in bead-tipped foxtail fringe, 1⅛" w x 2¼" tl, **$144** [A]. (Photo courtesy of Beverly Hills Auctioneers, Beverly Hills, CA, 4/1/01)

Brooch/Pin, bar, gf, yg, c. 1880, notched and cusped bar, engr yg front depicting a singing bird holding sheet music, perched on a branch, being "conducted" by a little girl, flanked by floral/foliate motifs, central circ compartment on rev mkd "PAT. JUNE 5, 1877," removable gf ring (glass cover missing), C-catch, tube hinge, 2¼" w x ⅞", **$250**. (Maryann Schneider collection)

Brooch/Pin, gf, glass, c. 1890, a "Nanny" pin in the shape of an openwork butterfly prong-set with colored and colorless circ-cut glass, surmounting a tubular bar with ball terminals, one terminal with stickpin inserted into tube, attached to safety chain, 2⅛" w x 1", **$225**. (Courtesy of E. Foxe Harrell, New York, NY)

Brooches/Pins, gold in quartz, yg, c. 1860-80:
L, an oval plaque of gold in white matrix quartz, bezel-set in an engr yg frame surmounted by an undulating ribbon of black enamel, C-catch, tube hinge, extended pinstem, 1¼" w x 1", **$650**.
R, an oval plaque of gold in black matrix quartz, bezel-set in a textured ropetwist and engr yg frame, C-catch, tube hinge, 1⅜" x 1", **$600**.
(Courtesy of Generations, La Verne, CA)

Brooches/Pins, bar, gold, c. 1880:
T, wiretwist S-scroll decoration, beaded edge, trefoil terminals set with a seed pearl, later-added safety catch, 2" w x ⅝", **$225.** (Courtesy of Xcentricities, Beverly Hills, CA)
B, yg, rose gold, green gold, black enamel, *japonaiserie* motifs of a cutout crane amid foliage within a central oval beaded frame surmounting an engr bar with fancy-shaped terminals and appl tapered half-cylinders, *taille d'épargne* enameled geo and foliate motifs, in three colors of gold, slight losses to enamel, C-catch, tube hinge, 2⅜" w x ⅜", **$250**. (Courtesy of E. Foxe Harrell, New York, NY)

Brooch/Pendant, 14k yg, gold-in-quartz, enamel, seed pearls, mid-Victorian, engr yg circ disk decorated with black and white *taille d'épargne* enamel intersected by a rectangular gold in quartz plaque surmounted by a central horizontal row of four seed pearls, 1½" w x 1⅜", **$881** [A]. (Photo courtesy of Skinner, Inc., Boston, MA, 12/11/01)

Chatelaine, handkerchief holder, 14k yg, enamel, seed pearls, c. 1880, engr and *taille d'épargne* enameled cusped convex tongs set with a seed pearl in a rect enameled plaque on each side, sliding ring closure, suspended from cable link chain and finger ring, sz 6, 4⅝" tl, **$400**. (Courtesy of Gilly Phipps, Philadelphia, PA)

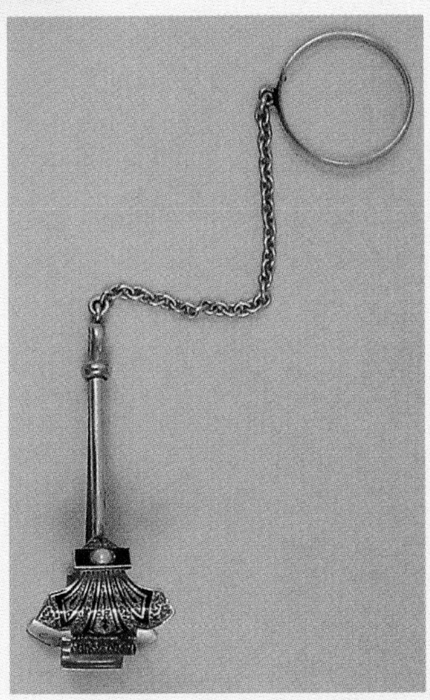

Earring covers, yg, c. 1880, each a pr of hinged yg hemispheres for enclosing a diamond (or other gemstone) drop earring, with an opening to accommodate the upper part, two projecting bead thumbpieces for separating the two halves, ½" dia, **$600**. (Courtesy of Chris Enebo Antique Jewelry, Tualatin, OR)

Locket, 14k yg, 18k yg, diamond, c. 1870-80, an om diamond in a star-cut 18k yg setting in the center of an engr and corded border, surmounting an oval-shaped convex polished 14k yg double locket, 1⅜" w x 2⅜" tl, **$460** [A]. (Photo courtesy of Beverly Hills Auctioneers, Beverly Hills, CA, 4/1/01)

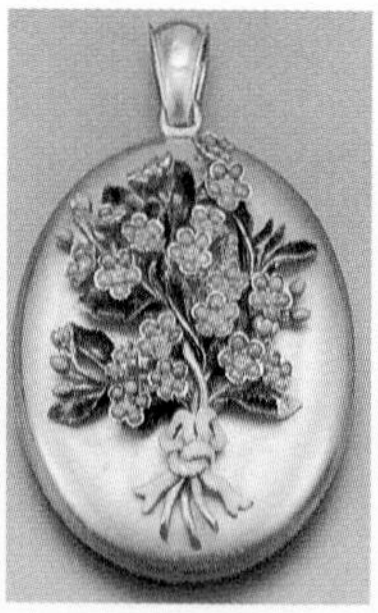

Locket, yg, turq, enamel, glass, c. 1880, plain convex oval, the front with an appl bouquet of forget-me-nots set with sm turq cabs, enameled leaves and bowknot, opening to reveal a glazed compartment, fitted case by Frazer & Haws, from Garrards 21 Regent Street, Picadilly, 1½" w x 2½" tl, **$4,200** [A]. (Photo courtesy of Sotheby's, London, 6/20/01)

Locket, 14k yg, diamond, glass, c. 1880, circ locket, concave center with raised coiled snake design, green glass eye, circ-cut diamond held in open jaws, ⅞" dia, **$980**. (Photo courtesy of Facèré Jewelry Art, Seattle, WA)

Necklace, gp brass, gp wm, c. 1880, made up of late 18th C brass watch cocks (escapement covers from pocket watches), each one with a different engr and pierced floral/foliate openwork design, three with faces at the base, v-spring clasp, 1" w x 16¼" tl, **$500**. (Courtesy of Pat Seal, Treasures From Yesterday, Fort Worth, TX)

Pendant and Chain, 14k yg, mid-Victorian, cross decorated with wirework concentric circles and beads, suspended from a chain of elongated hollow links, embellished with wirework, alternating with large rings, can be worn as a bracelet and choker, with original box, chain 21" tl, cross 2" w x 3½", **$2,350** [A]. (Photo courtesy of Butterfields, San Francisco and Los Angeles, CA, 9/25/01)

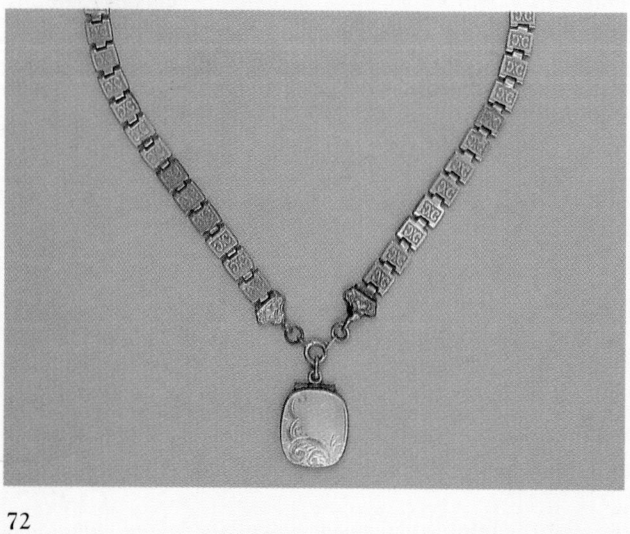

Locket and Chain, rolled gold, gf, c. 1880, rect-link bookchain decorated with die-stamped C-scrolls suspending an engr gf cushion-shaped locket (not original), lead solder at chain terminal, chain ¼" w x 17", locket ¾" w x 1¼", **$145**. (Lisa Johnson collection)

Sleeve Buttons, gf, enamel, c. 1880, a pr of two gf circ disk buttons with metal loop connectors, engr and *taille d'épargne* enameled bird, foliate and geo motifs, one side detachable, stickpins and safety chains on detachable buttons, ½" dia, 1½" w, **$150**. (Diane White collection)

Suite: Brooch/Pin and Earrings, yg, rose gold, wm, seed pearls, turq glass beads, taille d'epargne enamel, c. 1880, die-stamped and engraved, brooch a lg oval within a cusped, scrolled, and beaded-edge shield suspending a fringe of five balustered hollow drops, central motif of an anchor surmounted by a cuffed hand holding foliage, decorated with seed pearls, turq-colored glass beads, and taille d'epargne enamel in yellow and rose gold, beveled glass-covered compartment on rev, C-catch, tube hinge, matching earrings of similar design with three drops, circ surmounts on long earwires, in orig fitted leather-covered box, brooch 1⅞" w x 4¼", earrings ¾" w x 2¾" tl, **$2,000**. (Courtesy of Ocean Eyz Antique Jewelry, Orange, CA)

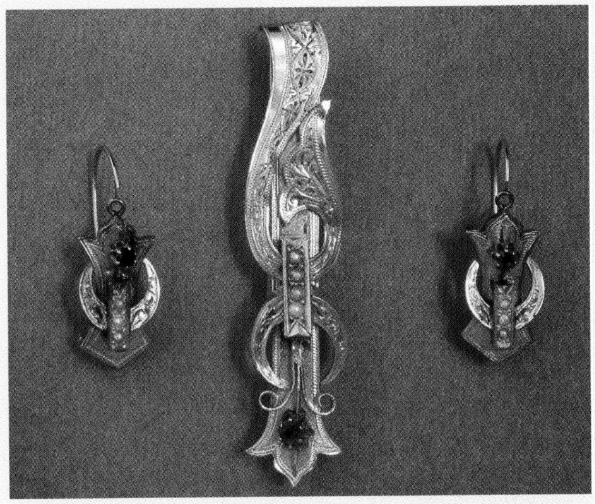

Suite: Bar Brooch/Pin and Earrings, yg, blue glass, seed pearls, c. 1880, brooch a die-stamped, pierced and engr curved and cusped floral/foliate motif surmounted by a short bar set with a row of seed pearls, a prong-set circ-cut blue glass stone in flower center, matching earrings suspended from long kidney wires, brooch 2¼" x ½", earrings ⅜" w x 1⅛" tl, **$450**. (Courtesy of Generations, La Verne, CA)

Watch Fob/Key, yg, c. 1850, an engr yg cross motif with bead-tipped horizontal terminals, engr bail, retractable key, ⅞" w x 1⅜", **$250**. (Courtesy of E. Foxe Harrell, New York, NY)

Suite: Brooch/Pin and Earrings, yg, rhodalite garnets, seed pearls, c. 1880, brooch a lobed and cusped engr yg plaque surmounted by engr foliate motifs bezel-set with lozenge-cut garnets and a seed pearl, matching pendent earrings suspended from engr circ disk surmounts, later-added clipbacks, brooch 1½" w x 1¼", earrings 1⅞" tl, **$600**. (Courtesy of E. Foxe Harrell, New York, NY)

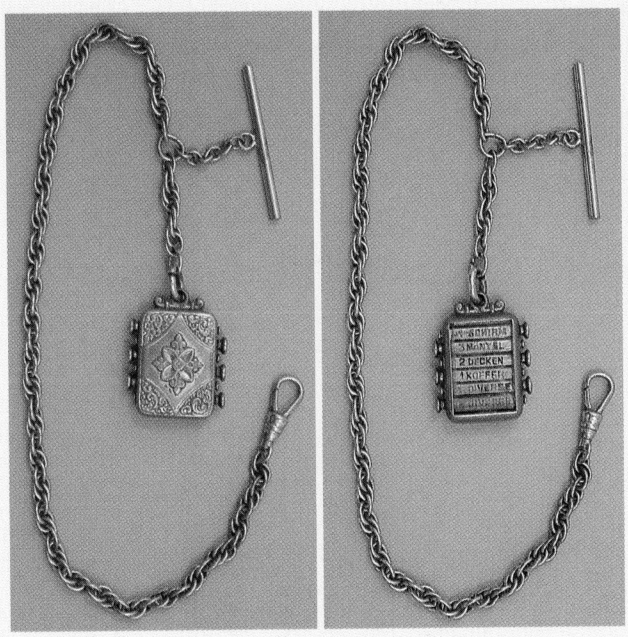

Watch Fob and Chain, gp brass, late Victorian, "gentleman's reminder" rect fob containing six square bars marked with Ger words for men's accoutrements (umbrella, coat, galoshes, suitcase, and two "various"), with projecting knobs for turning (no longer working) within a glazed compartment, stamped scrolled foliate design on rev, fob ⅞" w x 1⅜" tl, chain 11⅞" tl, **$300**. (Courtesy of Chris Enebo Antique Jewelry, Tualatin, OR)

LATE VICTORIAN (AESTHETIC PERIOD) c. 1880-1901

By the 1880s, Victorian society was beginning to change. In celebration of 50 years on the throne in 1887, Queen Victoria was willing to relax her strict rules of mourning a little, much to the relief of her subjects. Fashions had changed, too. Victoria was no longer as influential as her beautiful daughter-in-law, Princess Alexandra, who was already a trend-setting fashion plate.

In keeping with a new "aestheticism," lines were simpler, fabrics lighter. Flounces and trains were abandoned in favor of smooth curves. Delicate lace replaced heavy fringe. After a short period of protruding emphasis, the bustle became a vestige of its former self as fullness transferred to "leg-o'-mutton" and "balloon" sleeves. Collars grew higher and tighter. The tailored look was in vogue. Women were becoming more active, in the work force and at leisure, and required proper attire. Their only remaining extravagance was their headgear. Hats were large and decorated profusely with bows, ribbons, lace, flowers, plumes, and feathers—sometimes entire birds. Ornamental hatpins grew to great lengths to keep them in place.

Attitudes about jewelry were also affected. Elaborate ostentation gave way to refined simplicity. Heavy, dark, somber, massive, and ornate jewelry was losing favor. Lighthearted, light-colored, and delicate pieces took its place. Silver replaced gold for daytime wear. Many female aesthetes—early feminists rebelling against constricting fashions and protesting the notion of woman as decorative object—no longer wore any jewelry at all during the day. Diamonds continued to be the evening jewels of choice amongst most ladies of wealth and status, however.

Jewelry in general was reduced in dimension even when worn in quantity. Brooches were smaller, often worn in multiples. Crescents and stars were popular motifs. Some had utilitarian purposes as veil, lace, hat, bodice, skirt, or cuff pins. These were also called "handy pins" or "beauty pins." Earrings shrank to diminutive proportions. Sometimes they were nothing more than a single small stone, pearl, or stud. Until the 1890s, earrings were made for pierced ears. By the end of the century, however, women were beginning to look upon ear-piercing as a barbaric practice. The screwback finding was invented as a solution. The earliest "attachment for holding ear-jewels" for unpierced ears was patented in 1894. Its use gradually superseded the earwire and stud post; by the 1920s, screwbacks were predominant.

Necklaces were fringes or festoons of linked gemstone drops and chains. Princess Alexandra was the instigator of the dog-collar necklace, a high, wide choker, usually of diamonds and/or pearls, which became an Edwardian trademark when she became Queen. In the U.S., the American "royal," Consuelo Vanderbilt, who became the Duchess of Marlborough in 1895, popularized the look with her dog collar of 19 rows of pearls and diamond clasps. Both ladies had the requisite long slender necks for wearing such a jewel. Bracelets continued to be worn in multiples, growing narrower toward the end of the period. Bangles were tubular or open knife-edge wires joined by an ornamental device in front. Curb-link bracelets in gold or silver were also fashionable, often joined with a heart-shaped padlock clasp. Small waists were a fashion focal point; wide belts and ornamental buckles were commonly worn.

Chatelaines, derivatives of a chain worn by medieval keepers of keys, were once again in fashion, having returned in a slightly altered state from those of the early nineteenth century. Perhaps this was because of the focus on the waist, but it was also because Alexandra favored them. Late nineteenth century chatelaines performed a number of different specialized utilitarian and decorative functions. Various implements were suspended by chains from a decorative clasp that hooked over a belt or waist sash. They were a sort of housewife's tool kit. Scissors, needle cases and other

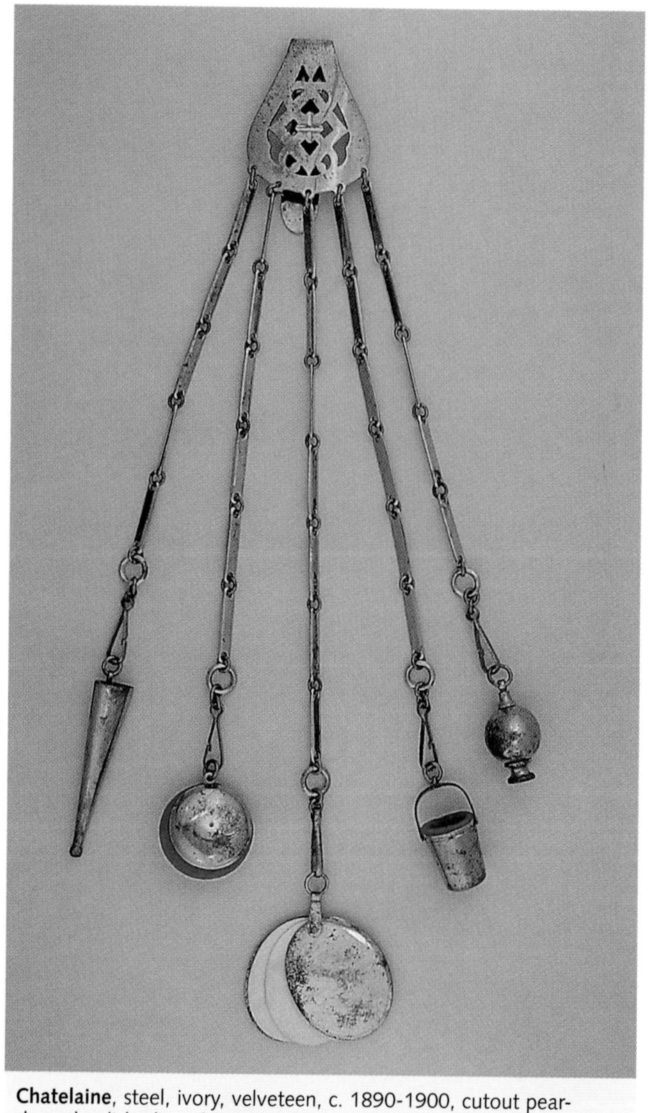

Chatelaine, steel, ivory, velveteen, c. 1890-1900, cutout pear-shaped polished steel waist plaque suspending five flat strip and circ ring chains with swivel hooks and appendages: 1" l lined thimble bucket, ¾" dia tape measure sphere (inoperative), 2½" l scissors scabbard, 1¼" dia pincushion, 1½" w x 2" ivory-leafed oval notepad with steel covers, plaque 1¾" w x 2¼", 13½" tl, **$1,000**. (Courtesy of E. Foxe Harrell, New York, NY)

sewing tools, notepads and pencils, match safes, coin purses, spectacles cases, and other assorted useful items could be hung from swivel hooks on a chatelaine (see photo below). Most of these were decorated with repoussage, stamping or engraving. Those made of silver appealed to aesthetic tastes, especially after the trend-setting Princess Alexandra was seen wearing one (see page 81).

Sporting jewelry grew in popularity as women became more involved in outdoor activities. Horseshoes and animal motifs—fox and hounds, horses, game birds, etc.— were worn with tailored clothing. Both women and men wore reverse-painted crystal intaglios, an often-used decoration for stickpins, cuff links, and small brooches.

Animal and bird motifs showed up in gem-set novelty brooches and stickpins. The ubiquitous snake was joined by lizards and salamanders, bats, frogs, mice, butterflies and other insects, and swallows (see below right).

Japanese motifs and designs gained approval after new trade relations were opened with Japan in the 1850s, and Japanese decorative arts and crafts were introduced to the West at international exhibitions in the 1860s and 1870s. Interest in things Japanese coincided with the growth of the Aesthetic Movement in Britain, France, and the U.S. The tenets of the movement embraced the Oriental approach to design: simplicity of form and inspiration from nature. Japanese fans, bamboo, scenes, and other ornamental devices, collectively referred to as *japonaiserie* (also called "Japanesque" and "japonisme"), began to crop up in jewelry, particularly in silver and mixed-metals (see page 77), imitating metalworking techniques used in Japanese sword-making. Tiffany & Co. won the Grand Prix for its "Japanesque" mixed-metals designs in silverware at the Paris Exposition of 1878. They applied the same techniques to jewelry.

International expositions continued to play an important role in the dissemination and marketing of new ideas and trends in fashion and jewelry. Two more *Expositions Universelles* were held in Paris in 1889 and 1900. The World's Columbian Exposition in Chicago in 1893 was another exhibition that brought international prestige and recognition to the U.S. Tiffany and Gorham each had their own pavilion, and numerous other American and European manufacturers were well represented with displays of jewelry.

Pendants and Chains, gunmetal, c. 1900:
L, ribbon threader, a tapered and rounded bar with an elliptical opening at one end, engr with the name "May" on one side, suspended from a yg swivel hook on a loop-in-loop link chain interspersed with black beads flanked by yg links, ½" w x 2½", chain 46" tl, **$400.**
R, coin holder, heart-shaped hinged pendant containing three gp brass coin holders, suspended from a swivel hook and curb link chain interspersed with round beads flanked by elongated links, 2¼" x 2½", chain 60" tl, **$795**. (Courtesy of Chris Enebo Antique Jewelry, Tualatin, OR)

Cosmetic Pot, chatelaine appendage, gunmetal, guilloché enamel, split seed pearls, mirror glass, c. 1900, a circ container with a hinged lid, the lid mirrored on the inside, the outside decorated with the depiction of a bird in flight set with seed pearls, a red cab eye, on a blue and white engr and enameled ground encircled by seed pearls, a suspension loop and jump ring mounted on the side of the pot, 1⅜" dia, ⅞" h, **$495**. (Courtesy of Chris Enebo Antique Jewelry, Tualatin, OR)

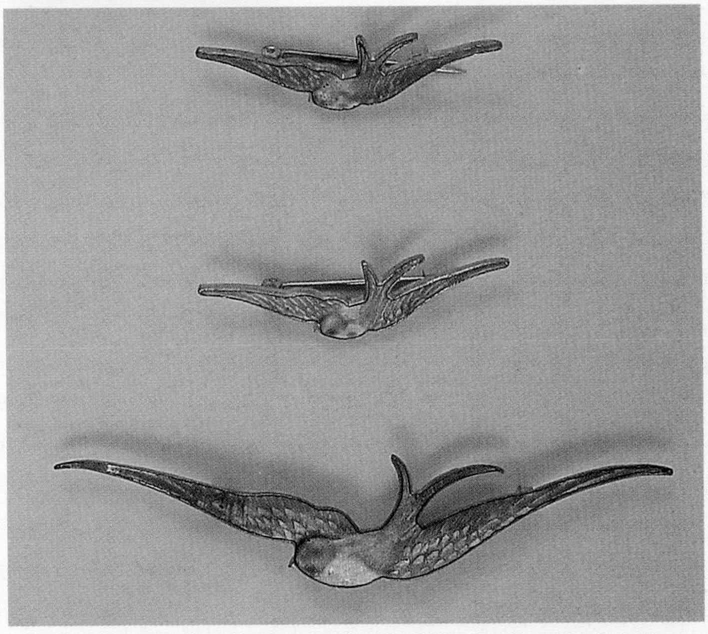

Suite: "waist set," brooches/pins, gp brass, blue enamel, c. 1900, three swallows, two sm, one lg, some loss to enamel, C-catches, flanged hinges, lg 2⅛" w x ⅝", sm 1½" w x ½", **$100**. (Vickie Vega collection)

EARLY CELLULOID

The first uses for the first commercially successful semi-synthetic plastic, invented in 1868 and dubbed "celluloid" by its inventor, John Wesley Hyatt, were utilitarian. The initial motive for its invention was as a substitute for ivory billiard balls.

Although that use proved impractical, celluloid was in fact an acceptable material for other uses, such as for detachable collars and cuffs, piano keys, and hair combs. Manufacturers of the latter took advantage of celluloid's ability to imitate tortoiseshell, a natural plastic.

Makers of inexpensive jewelry found a use for celluloid, too, as imitation coral and ivory. The earliest jewelry was made by the Celluloid Manufacturing Co. in 1875.

It wasn't until the 1920s that "frankly fake" celluloid jewelry was made (see Plastics and Novelty section).

Brooch/Pin, c. 1887, ivory-colored bow marked "WCTU" (Women's Christian Temperance Union), C-catch, extended pin-stem, 1" x 1", **$75**. (Photo courtesy of Julie Robinson, author, *Celluloid Collector's Reference and Value Guide,* Collector Books, 1999)

Hair Comb, c. 1900, imitation tortoiseshell, curv top with molded swags and leaves on stippled ground, 3" x 3", **$45**. (Photo courtesy of Julie Robinson, *Celluloid Collector's Reference and Value Guide*)

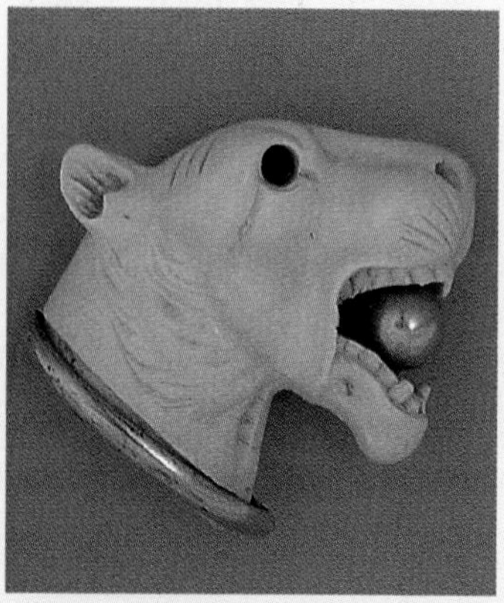

Brooch/Pin, wm, glass, c. 1900, solid molded and carved imitation ivory panther head with wm sphere in its mouth, black glass eyes, wm collar, C-catch, tube hinge, pin assembly on wm plate mounted with screws, 2⅛" w x 2", **$250**. (Courtesy of Xcentricities, Beverly Hills, CA)

Hair Comb, tinted metal, rhinestones, late 19th C, Egyptian Revival, imitation tortoiseshell, the top decorated with tinted metal floral/foliate and scarab motifs, surmounted by a row of prong-set colorless r.s., 5¼" w x 4", **$150**. (Photo courtesy of Julie Robinson, *Celluloid Collector's Reference and Value Guide*)

Celluloid-coated photographs in jewelry, c. 1900:
L, scarf pin/stickpin mounted on a pinstem, ½" dia, 2" tl, **$20**.
R, circ brooch/pin, photo set into a black celluloid frame, C-catch, ⅞" dia, **$20**. (Photo courtesy of Julie Robinson)

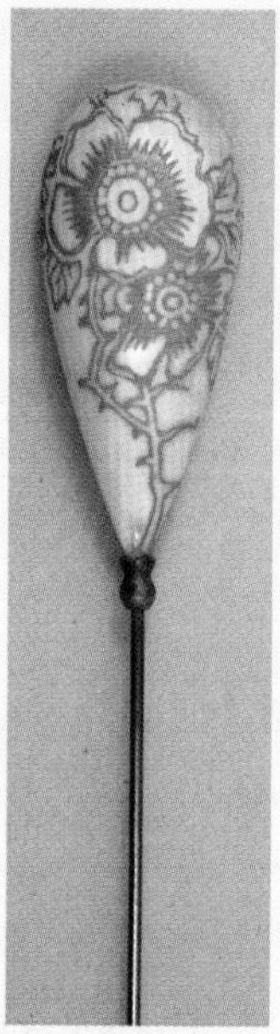

Hatpin, c. 1890-1900, blow-molded hollow pear-shaped top, wild rose motif incised into imitation ivory-grained celluloid, top ⅞" x 1⅞", 6½" tl, **$65**. (Teri Vaughn collection)

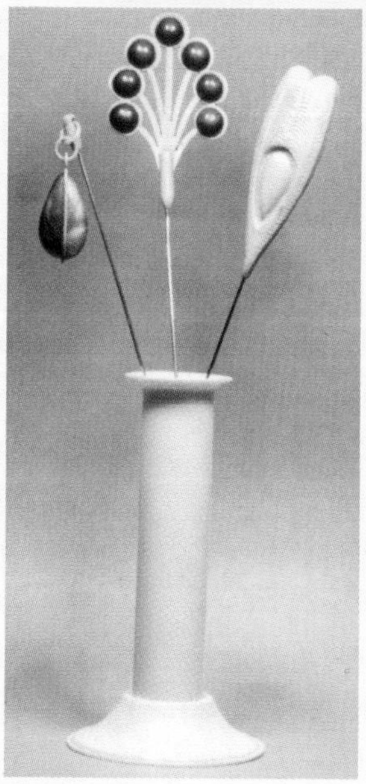

Hatpin Holder and Hatpins, celluloid, metal, c. 1900: Ivory-colored tubular container, 5" tl, **$50**.
L, blow-molded green pearlescent celluloid dangling egg decoration suspended from jump rings attached to metal pin shaft, 6¼" tl, **$55**.
C, ivory and green celluloid, fan-shaped pattern of balls on spires, 7" tl, **$75**.
R, blowmolded (hollow) pale green elongated heart with incised center, 7¼" tl, **$65**. (Photo courtesy of Julie Robinson, *Celluloid Collector's Reference and Value*)

SILVER and MIXED METALS

Silver as a metal for jewelry has fluctuated in popularity and application. In the eighteenth and nineteenth centuries, it was customarily used for setting diamonds and colorless paste, or, disguised with gilding, for making "imitation" jewels look "real." It wasn't until the latter part of the nineteenth century that silver came into its own as a material to be used for its aesthetic and sculptural qualities alone. Changing fashions, historical events and discoveries, and the Aesthetic Movement itself contributed to the metal's appreciation.

In 1876, Japan banned the wearing of swords and ended the feudal system, thus sounding the death knell for the samurai warrior. But the masterful metalwork of Japanese sword makers lived on in jewelry. Sometimes the sword fittings themselves became jewelry, and were exported to the West. The Japanese also made jewelry to suit Western tastes. It is important to clarify the meanings of the Japanese words "*shakudo*" and "*shibuichi*": these are words for Japanese metal alloys (not the decorative metalwork technique itself), similar to the English word "sterling" for an alloy of silver and copper. Japanese metalworking techniques have a number of different names, but what Westerners erroneously refer to as "*shakudo*" is usually a raised design with gold and silver inlaid into (or overlaid onto) a background metal (*shakudo* or *shibuichi*). The inlay technique is known as "damascene work" in Western culture. The general Japanese term for this type of work is "*zogan*," but each variation of the technique has a different name. Japanese inlay is often imitated with die-stamped designs in *shakudo* or *shibuichi* overlaid with thin gold and silver foil accents (see below and page 80).

The discovery of the Comstock Lode in Nevada in 1859 made silver readily available to manufacturers in the U.S. and Britain. Its relatively low cost meant that silver jewelry was now affordable to almost everyone. The *japonaiserie* craze of the 1870s and early 1880s led British and American manufacturers to produce stamped silver "trinkets" engraved with Japanese motifs. In the U.S., it was permissible to include copper in a fashion similar to the way in which Japanese alloys of copper and silver (*shibuichi*) and copper and gold (*shakudo*) were used, but assay laws prohibited British manufacturers from doing so. Touches of rose and yellow gold were added to silver for a "mixed-metals" effect (see above right and pages 79 and 80).

Brooch/Pin, *shibuichi*, yg, silver, c. 1880-90, circ *shibuichi* disk, inlaid gold and silver decoration depicting a man pulling a rickshaw with a woman holding a parasol, floral sprays in bg, C-catch and tube hinge appl to cruciform yg pronged mount on rev, loop for safety chain, 1⅛" dia, **$400**. (Courtesy of Patrick Kapty, Mad Jewelry, Palm Springs, CA)

Bracelets, hinged bangles, sterling, yg, rose gold, Eng:
L, c. 1890, engr foliate and sawtooth design accented with rose and yg floral motifs, beaded edges, v-spring and box clasp, unmkd, probably Eng, ¾" w, 2¼" inside dia, **$300**. (Courtesy of Chris Enebo Antique Jewelry, Tualatin, OR)
R, date letter for 1885, stamped and engr, with appl rose and yg floral, foliate, and C-scroll motifs, beaded edges, Birmingham hmks, illegible maker's mk, safety chain, ¾" w, 2⅜" inside dia, **$300**. (Diane White collection)

The locket and the hinged bangle were favorite forms in silver (see above and page 81). They were stamped, engraved, and embellished with beaded edges and applied motifs such as buckles, flowers and leaves, crosses, and anchors. Pastes continued to be set in silver brooches and buckles.

After a decline in the wearing of daytime jewelry in the mid 1880s, silver jewelry regained favor in the waning years of the century. Message and "love brooches" were all the rage amongst the working class. These were stamped and engraved with the names of loved ones or other endearing terms. A Biblical reference, "Mizpah," sent the message: "The Lord watch between me and thee when we are absent one from another." The language of flowers was also used to send sentimental signals to loved ones—forget-me-nots (remembrance), ivy (friendship), and a different meaning for every variety of rose. Other popular symbols were the anchor of hope, the cross of faith, the heart of charity, the good-luck horseshoe, and lovebirds (see page 79, BR). Silver coins were also used for "love tokens," engraved with ciphers or names of family members or loved ones and made into bracelets or brooches (see below). Jubilee jewelry was another sentimental working-class favorite, commemorating Queen Victoria's Diamond Jubilee, the 60th anniversary of her reign. Brooches would usually bear Victoria's cipher (VR or VRI) and the years 1837 and 1897 along with other

Brooch/Pin, bar, silver, c. 1880-90, narrow half-cylindrical bar, center appl strip of raised sq beading, suspending three "love tokens," U.S. coins dated 1873, 1875, 1877, one side of each engr with different ciphers, C-catch, tube hinge, 2¼" w x 1" tl, **$125.** (Author's collection)

engraved decoration. Touches of gold might be added. Those who could afford it wore gem-set versions.

Silver belts, buckles, clasps, and chatelaines were frequently worn during the Aesthetic period, emphasizing the tiny corseted waist that women suffered so much to achieve (see pages 80 and 81).

Only a few American makers are associated with silver jewelry of this period. Those that are made jewelry as an adjunct to their other silver wares, notably Tiffany, Gorham, and George W. Shiebler. Tiffany's and Gorham's pieces were generally in keeping with the style of the times, mostly buckles and bracelets in the aesthetic taste. Shiebler's work followed a different bent, which proved successful enough to be imitated by others (see page 80). Most well known is Shiebler's "curio medallion" series, depicting profiles of Greek and Roman deities, which can be found on brooches, bracelets, cuff links, and also on the handles of flatware. Greek lettering was sometimes added (see bracelet, right). According to an article on Shiebler by Janet Zapata and D. Albert Soeffing (cited in the References), this series was produced from about 1880 to 1900. A quote from an 1892 article about the firm in Jeweler's Circular says that the pieces were designed to look like they had been "unearthed at Pompeii and Herculaneum." It seems Revivalism was still alive and well in the 1880s and 1890s, but in a new form, with hand-crafted overtones. The company also produced quirky designs from nature, such as insects and spiders on leaves, sea shells and sea creatures, and other flora and fauna (see pages 79 and 80). Shiebler pieces are usually marked "sterling" with a winged S (see appendix, American Manufacturers, and photos with marks in this section), and numbered.

A technique known as "niello" was applied to silver ornaments in the late nineteenth century. Based on a medieval Russian technique, niello is a grayish-black mixture of silver, lead, copper, and sulfur that is applied to engraved designs on the silver's surface, then fired and polished smooth. Allover geometric or floral patterns yielded the best effect. An alloy of 800 silver (parts per thousand) was usually used because it withstands firing temperatures better than higher grades of silver (see pages 79 and 81).

Like gold, nineteenth century silver jewelry is not always hallmarked. When marks are found, however, they can be helpful clues. The American standard for silver was 900 parts per thousand until 1906. Pieces marked "standard" or "coin" are 900 silver of American origin. Some manufacturers, such as Tiffany, Gorham, and Shiebler, used the British sterling standard of 925 considerably earlier, and marked pieces "sterling." The British mark for sterling is a "lion passant," or walking lion. The place of assay and date letter hallmarks correspond to those used on gold. European countries used alloys ranging from 750 to 950 with various devices as indications of silver content for hallmarks (see appendix, Marks on Metals).

Bracelet, charm, sterling, c. 1880-90, curb link chain with alternating polished and textured links, suspending a single irregular circ charm medallion of woman's profile at end of chain, incised letters "TOEV" on rev, mkd "STERLING #8," maker's mk for George Shiebler, charm 1¼" dia, chain ¼" w x 8," **$400**. (Elizabeth Nyland collection)

Bracelet, charm, sterling, glass, enamel, c. 1900, collection of 16 stamped and engr puffed hearts, some with enamel or glass stone accents, most mkd "STERLING" and engr with names or initials on rev, suspended from engr curb-link chain with heart-shaped padlock clasp, 7¼" tl, 1¼" at center, **$400**. (Courtesy of Pat Seal, Treasures From Yesterday, Fort Worth, TX)

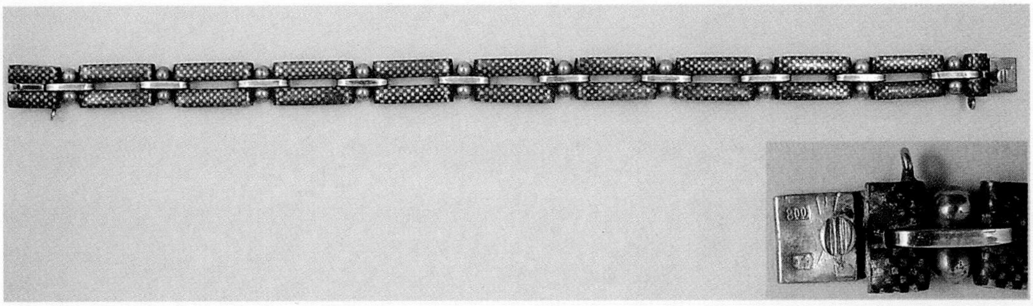

Bracelet, link, 800 silver, niello, rose gp, c. 1900, niello checkerboard patterned rect links connected by rose gp curved bars flanked by spheres, mkd "800" and unknown maker's mk on v-spring clasp, ⅜" w x 7½" tl, **$200**. (Courtesy of Denese Strand, Laguna Hills, CA)

Bracelet, 935 sterling, red stones, c. 1900, wire mesh coiled snake with die-stamped and engr head and smooth shaped tail, red stone eyes, appl plate on underside of head mkd "STERLING 935," 2" inside dia, **$450**. (Courtesy of E. Foxe Harrell, New York, NY)

Brooch/Pin, sterling, yg, rose gold, date letter for 1894-95, a scalloped, cusped and tapered lozenge-shaped plaque surmounted by a three-dimensional openwork basket motif trimmed in rose gold, flanked by colored gold floral/foliate motifs, engr and beaded edge, rev edges imp with Registry mk 241912 (1894), and Chester (Eng) hmks, C-catch, tube hinge, 1¾" w x ¾", **$250**. (Courtesy of Chris Enebo Antique Jewelry, Tualatin, OR)

Brooch/Pin, silver, c. 1890, die-stamped and engr, depicting a rowboat with two men rowing, a woman steering, and a dog, appl flat backing on rev, C-catch, tube hinge, 1⅞" w x ⅞", **$225**. (Courtesy of E. Foxe Harrell, New York, NY)

Brooch/Pin, sterling, c. 1885-95, three-dimensional beetle on a branch with leaves, maker's mk for George Shiebler, New York, NY, mkd "STERLING #2," C-catch, 3" w x 1", **$650**. (Janet Zapata collection)

Brooches/Pins, silver, Eng:

T, possibly Edwardian (c. 1901-1910), scallop-edged disc, stamped, engr and enameled, depicting a crowned lion atop a crown above the symbols for the UK: rose, shamrock, and thistle, encircled by the Latin motto "BRITANNIARUM REX FIDEI DEFENSOR" (Britain's king, defender of the faith), deep open back, cover missing, C-catch, tube hinge, extended pinstem 1⅜" dia, **$80**.

BL, date letter for 1900, stamped and engr, two open hearts joined with a bow and a swag of flowerheads and leaves, appl surface layers of rose and yg, Birmingham hmks, maker's mk "K & CO.," C-catch, tube hinge, 1¾" w x ⅞", **$125**. (Diane White collection)

BR, date letter for 1887, octagonal beaded-edge plaque, stamped and engr faith, hope, and charity symbols (cross, anchor, heart) in the center encircled by floral/foliate garland, maker's mk "P & CO.," Birmingham hmks, C-catch, tube hinge, extended pinstem, 1⅛" dia, **$75**. (Lisa Johnson collection)

Brooch/Pin, *shakudo*, yg, c. 1890, *shakudo* plaque depicting three overlapping fans, folding and circ, uppermost fan in center decorated with a marsh scene, water bird and foliate motifs, flanked by floral and foliate motifs, raised design accented with yg overlay, 2¾" w x 1", **$1,100**. (Photo courtesy of Karen Lorene, Facèré Jewelry Art, Seattle, WA)

Buckle, sterling, c. 1880-1900, elongated oval with open center, appl carnation motif along one side, imp with maker's mk for George W. Shiebler and Co., New York, NY, "STERLING" #3166, double hasp, 2" w x 3¼", **$350**. (Author's collection)

Brooches/Pins, sterling, American:
T, c. 1880-1890, five irregular overlapping grad plaques, each with a different classical profile, hammer-textured ground, maker's mk "W&H" for Wood and Hughes (in business until 1899), New York NY, mkd "STERLING #3731," C-catch, 2½" w x ⅞", **$450.**
B, c. 1900, two overlapping irregular circ disks with facing classical profiles, hammered detail, maker's mk for Lewis Bros, Providence RI (in business 1896-1915), mkd "STERLING," C-catch, 2½" w x 1½", **$400**. (Janet Zapata collection)

Match Safe, chatelaine appendage, sterling, "Connemara marble" (serpentine and marble), date letter for 1893, engr and inlaid shamrock motifs, Birmingham hmks, maker's mark "JC & S," loop for suspending from a watch chain or chatelaine, 1¾" w x 1⅝", **$150**. (Diane White collection)

Brooch and Earrings, silver, rose and yg, Eng:
T, c. 1880, stamped and engr ovals, crenelated and beaded edge, rose gold flowerhead, engr stems and leaves, later-added yg earwires, ⅝" w x ⅞", **$100**.
B, date letter for 1884, scalloped edge disk, stamped and engr, rose gold border, appl rose and yg floral and foliate motifs, Birmingham hmks, glazed compartment on rev, C-catch, tube hinge, 1⅜" dia, **$200**. (Diane White collection)

Watch Fob, sp brass, c. 1890, two-tiered convex disks suspended from chains with swallows in relief, swivel suspended from bottom, damage to plating in top disk, 1¼" w x 3¼", **$75**. (Vickie Vega collection)

Hatpin, sterling, enamel, c. 1900, heart-shaped top with green-enameled shamrock, lettering on scrolled ribbon reads "MY HEART'S RIGHT THERE," mkd "STERLING," maker's mk for C.H. Cooke Co., Providence, RI, in business 1896-1915, head ½" x ⅝", 5¾" tl, **$125**. (Teri Vaughn collection)

Pendant, vinaigrette, sterling, c. 1880-1900, slightly convex tapered vial, engraved foliate design, Am, marked "M" in a lozenge (possibly for the Mauser Manufacturing Co., New York, NY), "STERLING," engr mono on rev, spherical vented top with flowerhead decoration, screws off, ⅞" w x 3¾", **$250**. (Courtesy of Gilly Phipps, Philadelphia, PA)

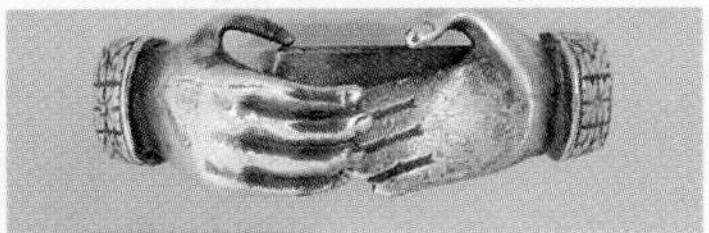

Ring, sterling, c. 1940, "gimmel/fede" ring reproduction, with swiveling concentric rings forming clasped hands with engr cuffs, engr laurel pattern on outer shanks, mkd "STERLING," pat #2220408 (1940), sz 6, **$200**. (Courtesy of Gilly Phipps, Philadelphia, PA)

Lockets, sterling, Eng:
T, date letter for 1876, convex oval, stamped, engr, and applied asymmetrical *japonaiserie* decoration on front, plain back, Birmingham hmks, maker's mk "R Co.," 1½" w x 2½", **$250**. (Diane White collection)
B, date letter for 1886, stamped and engr convex oval locket, double crenelated and beaded edge, engr foliate center, Birmingham hmks, suspended from a star punch and reeded loop chain, locket 1⅜" w x 2¼", chain 16½" tl, **$375**. (Lisa Johnson collection)

Chatelaine, sterling, coin silver, velveteen, c. 1900, waist plaque/sash pin a lion's head crest flanked by foliate scrolls, mkd "STERLING" #2343, with maker's mk for George W. Shiebler, wide flat C-catch and lg pinstem on rev, suspending seven curb link chains and swivel hooks with assorted appendages (not orig), including cast silver dog, horse (one foot broken off), and bear miniatures, an engr silver coin holder, a mechanical pencil in the shape of a champagne bottle, mkd "COIN" (900 silver), a silver needle case surmounted by a greyhound motif, and a two-sided Beaux-Arts style circ pin holder mkd "STERLING" #158, maker's mk for Gorham on one side, blue velveteen cushion in the center, 4¼" w x 7¼" at longest chain, excluding charms, **$600**. (Gail-Marie Enos collection)

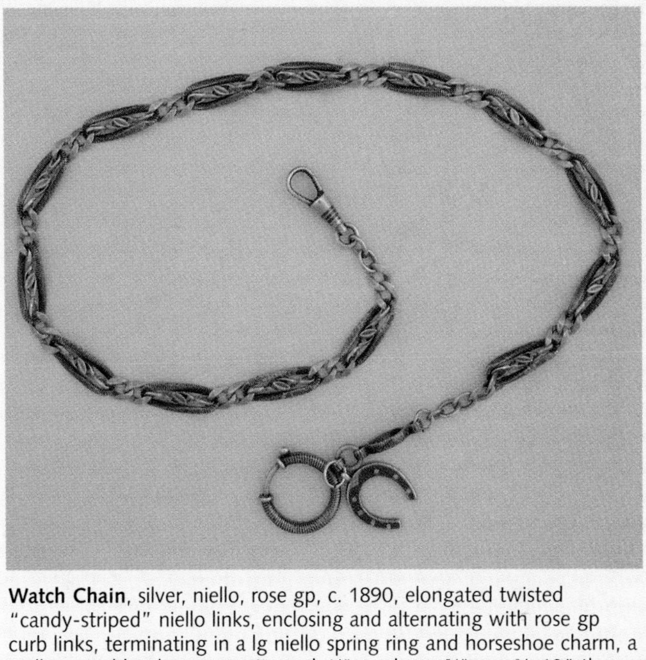

Watch Chain, silver, niello, rose gp, c. 1890, elongated twisted "candy-striped" niello links, enclosing and alternating with rose gp curb links, terminating in a lg niello spring ring and horseshoe charm, a niello swivel hook on opposite end, ¼" w, charm ⅝" w x ¾, 19" tl, **$200**. (Author's collection)

DIAMONDS and COLORED GEMSTONES

The diamond has been the stone of choice among nobility and the the wealthy for centuries. Although the eighteenth century has been called The Age of Diamonds, improved cutting and setting techniques to enhance the diamond's brilliance were developed in the nineteenth and twentieth centuries.

Until the use of platinum found favor as a metal for setting diamonds at the end of the nineteenth century, silver was used to complement the stone's whiteness, almost always laminated to a yellow gold backing, (sometimes called silver-topped yellow gold).

Closed-back and foiled settings were still in use at the beginning of the century. Open-backed (*à jour*) mounts gradually replaced them. It was discovered that brilliance was increased when light was reflected from the back, as well as the front, of the stone. The shape and cut of the diamond also evolved. Flat-backed rose cuts and cushion-shaped "old mine" cuts were eventually outnumbered (but not entirely replaced) by the circular "old European" brilliant cut toward the end of the century.

Credit for the development of the modern brilliant cut usually goes to Marcel Tolkowsky, who published his treatise *Diamond Design* in 1919. But the work of a little-known American diamond cutter, Henry D. Morse (1826-1888), preceded Tolkowsky's by more than 40 years. It was Morse who first discovered the scientific principles and precise cutting angles of what has come to be known as the "American" or "ideal" cut. And it was Morse's foreman, Charles M. Field, who developed and patented with Morse the first steam-driven diamond-cutting machines in 1874 and 1876, which preceded the European bruting (girdling) machine by 16 years. Unfortunately, to date no known pieces of nineteenth century jewelry set with Morse's brilliants have been identified.

The discovery of diamonds in South Africa in 1867 increased the stone's availability. Subsequent discoveries led to greater supplies and lower prices in the early 1880s. In spite of a world-wide depressed economy, diamond-encrusted jewels were well represented at the 1889 Paris Exposition, and found favor among the wealthy. By the 1890s, the De Beers Company had begun to control prices and dominate the South African diamond market, as it does today.

Diamonds have always been considered formal jewels for important occasions, usually reserved for nighttime wear. The Victorians had strict rules of etiquette concerning when diamonds should be worn and who should wear them. They were considered inappropriate for unmarried young women; most married matrons reserved them for balls and court appearances. However, toward the end of the century, when both diamonds and wealth were in greater supply in the United States, most rules were forgotten.

When electric lighting was introduced in the 1880s, sparkling diamond-set jewelry became even more desirable. Fashion would never be the same after electric lights began brightening up homes and public places, like the Savoy Theatre in London, opened in 1881, and the Metropolitan Opera House in New York, in 1883, where the privileged class went to see and be seen, decked in diamonds. The first tier of the Met was christened "The Diamond Horseshoe" in reference to its bejeweled patrons. At the turn of the century, the fashion for pale fabrics and colorless platinum-set jewels further heightened the demand for diamonds.

Brooch/Pin, diamonds, st rose gold, c. 1880, a spray of wild roses, set throughout with rc and om diamonds, central flowerhead set *en tremblant*, detachable segment, part of a corsage ornament, a few fragments deficient, C-catch and tube hinge, 1⅝" w x 4⅝", **$6,463** [A]. (Copyright Christie's Images, New York 2002©, Christie's Los Angeles, CA, 3/6/01)

Diamonds found their way into every conceivable form of jewelry, from tiaras to rings. The diamond brooch lent itself to a variety of motifs that reflected the Victorian preoccupation with nature.

Flower bouquets and sprays were worn throughout the nineteenth century, sometimes with parts mounted *en tremblant*, on springs or wires that trembled when the wearer moved (see above). Animal and insect motifs were popular in the 1880s and 1890s (see page 85), as were crescents and stars (see pages 83 and 84) . These were often worn scattered about the neckline, or as veil or lace pins. Figural motifs remained in vogue through the turn of the century.

In 1886, Tiffany & Co. introduced the "Tiffany setting" for diamond solitaires. The high-pronged mount elevated the stone to show off its brilliance to the best advantage. It became the standard setting for engagement rings. This type of setting was originally patented by Ferdinand J. Herpers of Newark, New Jersey, in 1872. It is perhaps not coincidental that the 14-year interval between Herpers' patent and Tiffany's setting is the length of time for which a design patent was granted.

However, if it weren't for the prestigious firm's promotions, not only of solitaires, but of all diamond jewelry (including its purchase of a major portion of the French crown jewels in 1887), Americans might have worn far fewer diamond-set jewels.

Other gemstones were in and out of style according to the vagaries of fashion.

Pavé-set small turquoise cabochons were used extensively

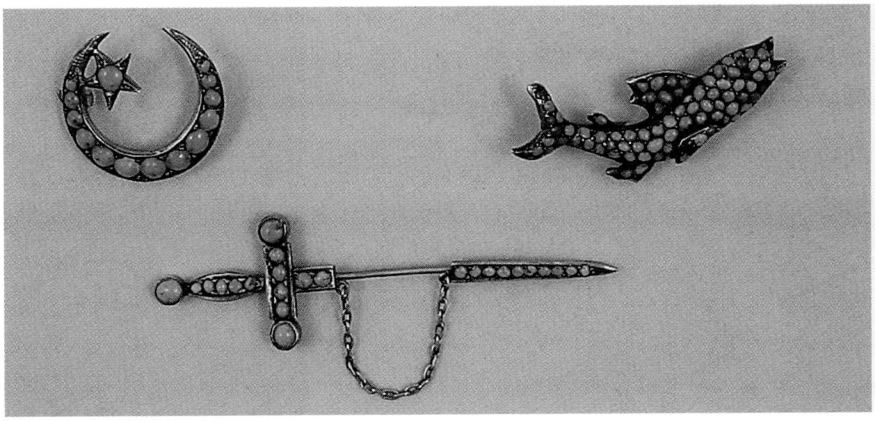

Brooches/Pins, pavé-set with turquoise, c. 1870-80:
TL, crescent and star motif, in st yg, C-catch, tube hinge, 1" dia, **$100**.
TR, fish motif in silver, one stone missing, C-catch, tube hinge, 1¾" w x ⅝", **$285**.
B, sword motif jabot pin, in silver, sheath for pinstem with chain attached, 2¾" tl, **$195**.
(Courtesy of E. Foxe Harrell, New York NY).

in jewelry of the 1840s, particularly in snake motifs. Turquoise made a return appearance in the latter part of the century (see above and pages 87 and 89). Seed pearl jewelry, a tradition since the early nineteenth century, continued to be worn (see brooches below).

Besides their familiar use in Scottish jewelry, agates, variegated varieties of quartz, are found in other types of Victorian jewelry. Factories in Idar-Oberstein Germany— the actual suppliers of many a "Scottish" pebble—have been the primary centers for the cutting and polishing of agates for three centuries. The soaking and heating processes for staining the stones has been done there as well. During the mid- to late-nineteenth century, color-enhanced banded agates were formed into beads and figural or geometric shapes. Although agate's value as a gemstone is low, Victorian agate jewelry is valued for its design, craftsmanship, and collectiblity.

Both faceted and cabochon garnets had their day at various times. There are several varieties and colors of garnets. Among them, the types most closely associated with the Victorian period are the reddish-brown pyrope, and the reddish-purple almandite.

In the early nineteenth century, memorial brooches and "handkerchief pins" were often set with flat-cut pyrope or almandite garnets around a compartment containing hair (see Late Georgian section, page 34). Large almandite cabochons, called carbuncles, are most often seen in mid-Victorian Revivalist pieces (see pages 84 and 88).

In the later part of the century, small faceted rose-cut and single-cut pyropes (also called Bohemian garnets) were set in low-karat gold and gilt base metal or silver (see page 88). This type of jewelry was mass-produced in Bohemia, and is being reproduced today.

Green demantoid garnets were discovered in the Ural Mountains of Russia in 1853, but were not identified as a variety of andradite until 1864, and not named "demantoid" (diamond-like, referring to the stone's luster) until 1878. Demantoids are found in late nineteenth and early twentieth century pieces. The green color was especially favored for the salamander and lizard brooches that were in vogue at the time (see page 85). The Russian Revolution of 1917 curtailed mining there, and by the 1920s, supply had dwindled. Demantoids are rarer, more desirable, and more costly than most other varieties of garnet.

Pyropes and almandites are the least expensive, but the quality and style of a piece set with these garnets may outweigh the stones' intrinsic value.

Opals were also popular in the late Victorian era, their wearers having overcome the superstition that the stone brought misfortune (see page 84 and page 88).

In keeping with the pale look of the period's fashions, moonstones were worn, sometimes carved as cameos (see page 123). The "man in the moon" was a favorite motif.

Pearls, another pale gem, were worn as necklaces alone or in combination with diamonds, setting the tone for what would become the classic Edwardian style of the early twentieth century (see Edwardian section in Part II).

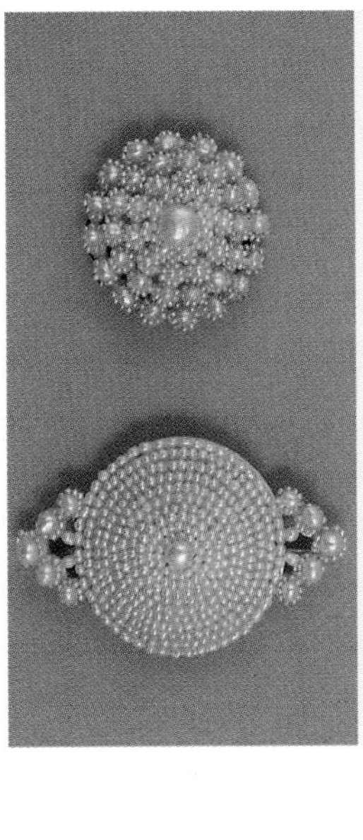

Seed pearl brooches, MOP, yg, horsehair, c. 1880-1900:
T, brooch/pendant with clusters of lg encircled by sm seed pearls in concentric rows forming a domed circ disk with a larger pearl center, strung and attached with white horsehair on a cutout scallop-edged MOP backing, appl yg pin assembly with safety pin-style catch, tube hinge, appl yg hinged bail, 2" w x 1⅛", **$300**. (Author's collection)
B, concentric rows of seed pearls forming a domed circ disk with a larger pearl center, flanked by triangular clusters of lg encircled by sm seed pearls, strung and attached with white horsehair on a cutout MOP backing, yg pinstem, C-catch, tube hinge, 2" w x 1⅛", **$400**. (Courtesy of E. Foxe Harrell, New York, NY)

Reproduction Alert

Late Victorian-style garnet jewelry is mass-reproduced. Wholesalers advertise in antique papers and on the Internet; some participate in jewelry trade shows. Most of them have catalogs with photographs. Other gemstone-set reproductions/ repros are imported from Portugal, South America, Germany, and Thailand. Some pieces are good enough to fool the experts.

Bracelet, hinged bangle, 14k yg, opals, diamonds, c.1890, a grad row of nine oval opals interspersed with om diamonds set à jour in a tapering yg bangle, safety chain, ½"w, 2¼" inside dia, **$1,196** [A]. (Photo courtesy of Dupuis Jewellery Auctioneers, Toronto, ONT, Canada, 6/12/01)

Bracelet, hinged bangle, yg, turquoise, split pearls, c. 1895, bypass design with polished ball terminals, the hinged oval form surmounted by a bird and flower motif set with split pearls and turquoise, 2¼" inside dia, 1¾" T to B at center, **$598** [A]. (Photo courtesy of Dupuis Jewellery Auctioneers, Toronto, ONT, Canada, 6/11/01)

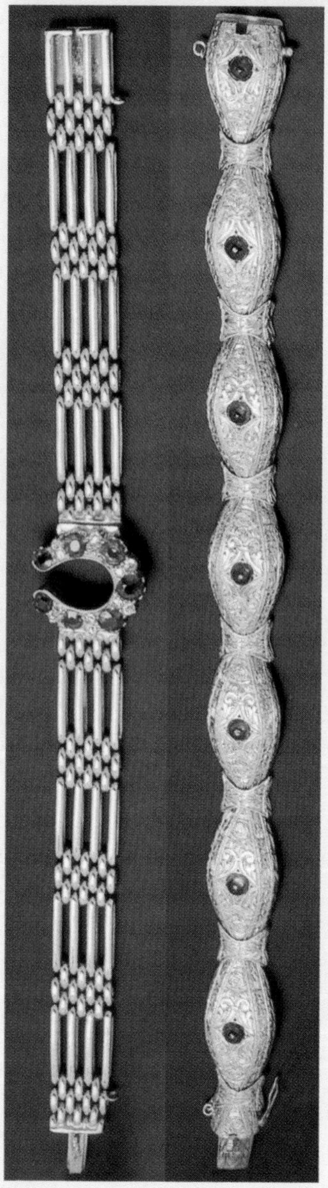

Bracelets, link, gold, c. 1880: **L**, a circ-cut sapphire and om diamond-set horseshoe motif flanked by flexible rose gold gate links, v-spring and box clasp, ¾" w at center, 7" tl, **$2,093** [A]. **R**, each of seven domed navette-shaped 18k yg segments bezel-set with a circ cabochon sapphire, joined by overlapping convex links, scrolled floral pattern chasing throughout, v-spring and box clasp with safety, ½" w x 7½" tl, **$822** [A]. (Photo courtesy of Dupuis Jewellery Auctioneers, Toronto, ONT, Canada, 6/11/01).

Brooch/Pin, 18k yg, cabochon garnets, c. 1860, stylized shield form with articulated drops, engr foliate textured yg, bezel-set with seven carbuncles (garnet cabs), in a fitted box, 1½" w x 3¼" tl, **$1,196** [A]. (Photo courtesy of Dupuis Jewellery Auctioneers, Toronto, ONT, Canada, 6/10/01).

Brooch/Pin, pink sapphire, rc diamonds, st yg, c. 1880, open circ disk encircling a flower spray motif set throughout with rc diamonds in st yg, a lg oval-cut pink sapphire (chipped) prong-set at the base of disk, tube hinge, Fr hmks (eagle's head) on pinstem and C-catch (note: yg on brooch rev tests approx 10k), 1" w x 1½", **$2,500**. (Courtesy of Jewelry Forever, San Clemente, CA)

Brooch/Pin, 10k yg, garnet-glass doublet, seed pearls, c. 1890-1900, sunburst set throughout with seed pearls, green garnet-glass doublet in center probably a replacement, C-catch, flanged hinge, 1⅛" dia, **$100**. (Teri Vaughn collection)

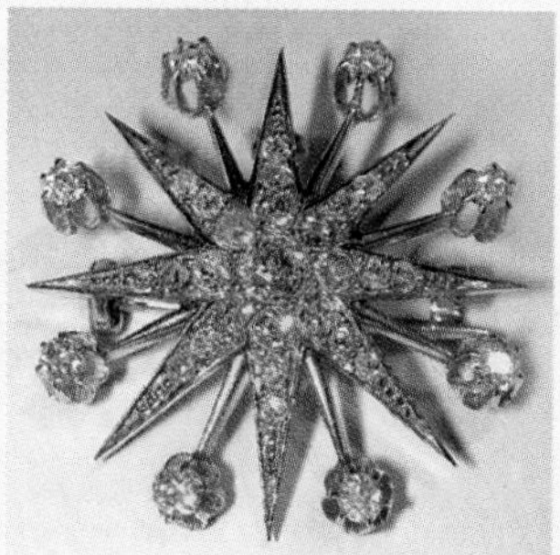

Brooch/Pin, oe diamonds, 15k rose gold, c. 1890, eight-pointed star, grad rows of pavé-set oe diamonds radiating from larger center oe diamond, star points alternating with eight flowerhead prong-set oe diamonds at the ends of eight tapered rods, approx 1.15 cts tw, C-catch, tube hinge, 1¼" dia, **$3,330**. (Photo courtesy of Karen Lorene, Facèré Jewelry Art, Seattle, WA)

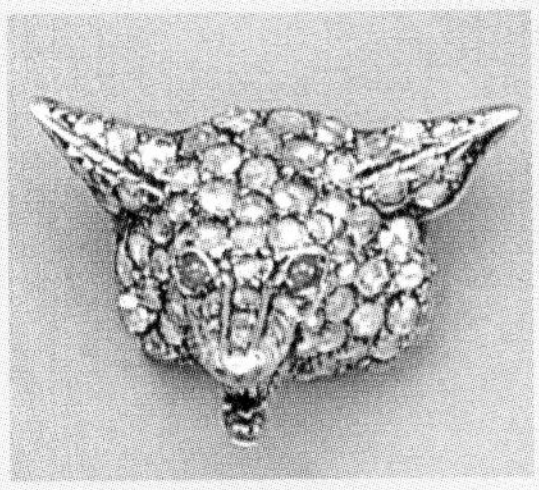

Brooch/Pin, rc diamonds, rubies, st yg, c. 1880, in the shape of a snarling fox's head, pavé-set with rc diamonds, cabochon ruby eyes, 1⅛" w x ¾", **$1,354** [A]. (Photo courtesy of Sotheby's, London, 11/27/01)

Brooch/Pin, turquoise, opals, sc and rc diamonds, st yg, late 19th C, in the shape of a bee, set throughout with turquoise and diamonds in st yg, cab opal eyes, yg legs, fitted case by The Goldsmiths & Silversmiths Company Ltd, 112 Regent Street, London, 1⅜" w x ⅞", **$2,184** [A]. (Photo courtesy of Sotheby's, London, 6/20/01)

Brooch/Pin, yg, enamel, seed pearls, c. 1890, in the shape of a beetle, green enameled wings flanking a grad row of seed pearls, body set with eight seed pearls, later-added safety catch, 1" w x 1⅝", **$300.** (Courtesy of E. Foxe Harrell, New York, NY)

Brooch/Pin, diamonds, enamel, silver, yg, c. 1895, Fr, in the shape of a swallow in flight, the head, wings, and tail pavé-set with table-cut diamonds with blue-enameled feathers, removable yg pin assembly, Fr hmks, 3¼" x 1¼", **$2,350** [A]. (Photo courtesy of Butterfields, San Francisco and Los Angeles, CA, 6/19/01)

Brooch/Pin, demantoid garnets, rubies, sc diamonds, st yg, c. 1900, in the shape of a lizard set throughout with diamonds around a center row of grad demantoid garnets, cabochon ruby eyes, ¾" w x 2½" tl, **$5,376** [A]. (Photo courtesy of Sotheby's, London, 6/20/01)

Earrings, pendent, amethysts, diamonds, st yg, yg, c. 1835-40, each pendant set with a pear-shaped amethyst within an oe diamond frame, suspended by a circular amethyst within a similar diamond frame, later screw fittings, ¾" w x 2", **$7,990** [A]. (Copyright Christie's Images, New York 2002©, Christie's New York, NY, 10/22/01)

Brooch/Pendant, diamonds, st yg, c. 1890, openwork scrolling leaves centered upon a flowerhead motif set throughout with oe diamonds, approx 6.50 cts tw, mounted in st yg, detachable pin assembly for wear as a pendant, 2¾" w x 2", **$5,606** [A]. (Photo courtesy of Dupuis Jewellery Auctioneers, Toronto, ONT, Canada, 6/12/01)

Earrings, pendent, oe, om, sc diamonds, st yg, c. 1850-60, floret surmounts suspending paired diamond-set oak leaf motifs flanking an articulated independent diamond-set frame surrounding foliate links terminating in a pear-shaped diamond, later fittings, blue leather case, 1" w x 1½" tl, **$11,750** [A]. (Copyright Christie's Images, New York 2002©, Christie's New York, NY, 10/22/01)

Earrings, pendent, om diamonds, st yg, c. 1870, revival of 18th C *girandole* style, each with three pear-shaped drops, each drop set with two grad om diamonds in cut-down collets, the center drop suspended from a single collet-set om diamond, surmounted by paired foliate motifs set with six om diamonds, and a single om diamond suspended from a circ om diamond-set flowerhead surmount, later-added findings, 1" w x 1⅞" tl, **$16,450** [A]. (Copyright Christie's Images, New York 2002©, Christie's Los Angeles, CA, 10/4/01)

Earrings, yg, turquoise, c. 1890, yg spheres, the circumference encircled with sm turq cabs, suspended from short chain, shepherd's hook earwires, ⅜" dia x 1⅛" tl, **$115**. (Vickie Vega collection)

Earrings, turq, yg, wm, c. 1900, sm turq cabs pavé-set in wm disks with yg ropetwist border, wm backing, yg frame, appl shepherd's hook earwires with rotating safety loop on rev, converted from buttons, ⅝" dia, **$450**. (Courtesy of Xcentricities, Beverly Hills, CA)

Earrings, garnets, gf, c. 1880-90, hollow die-stamped thistle motifs, each prong-set with an oval-cut rhodolite garnet, suspended from a bar below an angular surmount, kidney earwires, some lead solder repair, ½" w x 1⅜" tl, **$160**. (Diane White collection)

Necklace, diamonds, st yg, c. 1835, three detachable flowerhead pendants suspended from a leafy vine motif, set throughout with om and rc diamonds, continuing to a line of rc diamonds interspersed with om diamonds set in cut-down collets and a diamond-set clasp, in st yg, approx 15.00 cts tw, one pendant attachment missing, 15" tl, 2" T to B at center, **$16,445** [A]. (Photo courtesy of Dupuis Jewellery Auctioneers, Toronto, ONT, Canada, 6/12/01)

Necklace, *rivière*, diamonds, st yg, c. 1880, a line of 42 grad om diamonds, set in st yg cut-down collets, diamond-set clasp, sgd "Tiffany & Co.," 14" tl, ⅜" at center, **$149,000** [A]. Copyright Christie's Images, New York 2002©, Christie's New York, NY, 10/22/01).

Necklace, convertible, turquoise, diamonds, pearls, st yg, c. 1900, a grad row of openwork navette-shaped links set with pearls and rc diamonds connected by circ-cut diamonds, flanking a ribbon bow front and suspending a turq and diamond fringe; central link detaches to form a brooch accompanied by an extra fitting, the back detaches to form a bracelet, each turq and diamond fringe pendant is detachable, fitted case by H. Hoosemans, 42 Rue de l'Ecuyer, Bruxelles, 18" tl, 2¼" T to B at center, **$9,744** [A]. (Photo courtesy of Sotheby's, London, 6/20/01)

Necklace, garnets, sp brass, c. 1900, a slightly grad row of linked sm star-flowers flanking a two-layer starburst center, set throughout with Bohemian (pyrope) garnets, terminating in a garnet-set box and v-spring clasp, 16" tl, 1" dia at center, **$450**. (Courtesy of Ocean Eyz Antique Jewelry, Orange, CA)

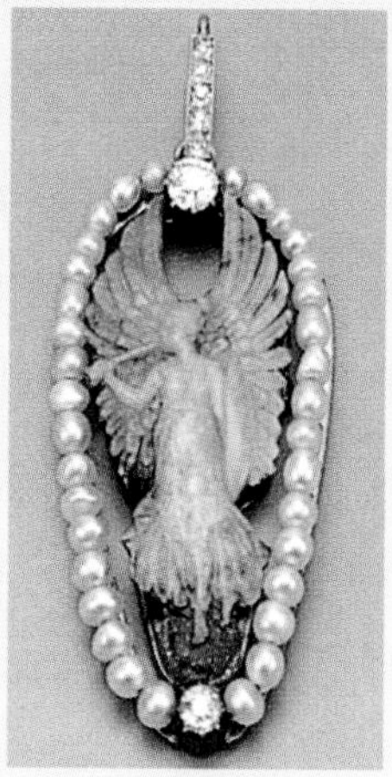

Pendant, opal, pearls, yg, c.1890, a central opal carved as a winged figure within a border of seed pearls and circ-cut diamonds, fitted case, attributed to Wilhelm Schmidt (1845-1938, cameo engraver from Idar, Germany), 1" w x 2⅝" tl, **$6,384** [A]. (Photo courtesy of Sotheby's, London, 6/20/01)

Pendant, citrine, diamonds, yg, st yg, c. 1890, Eng, an oval-cut citrine, approx 35.00 x 27.00 x 16.00 mm, bezel-set within scrolled yg wire framing, with foliate accents of st yg set with Peruzzi, om and oe diamonds, hmk for Child & Child (a daisy), Fr import mk (ET in square), diamonds approx 3.50 cts tw, 1½" w x 3½", **$4,994** [A]. (Photo courtesy of Butterfields, San Francisco and Los Angeles, CA, 9/25/01)

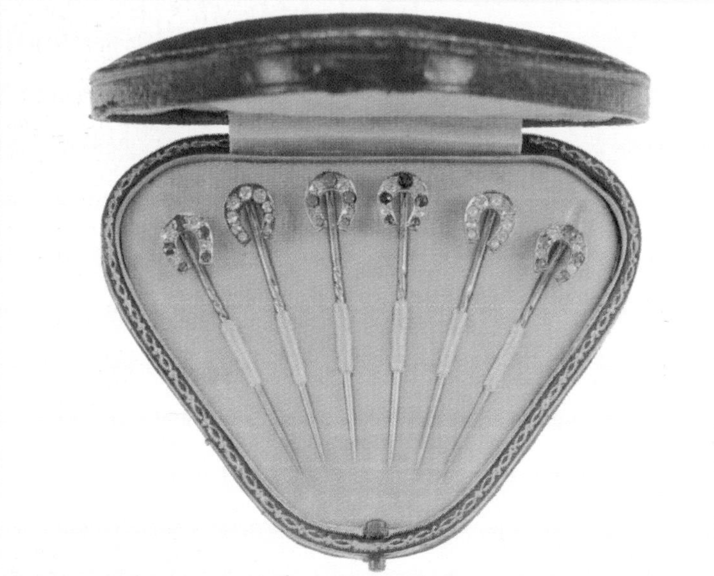

Scarf Pins/ Stickpins, yg, diamonds, seed pearls, demantoid garnets, sapphires, turq, rubies, c. 1900, a collection of six gem-set horseshoe motif stickpins in a fitted case, ⅜" x ⅜", 1⅞" tl, **$3,384** [A]. (Photo courtesy of Sotheby's, London, 11/27/01)

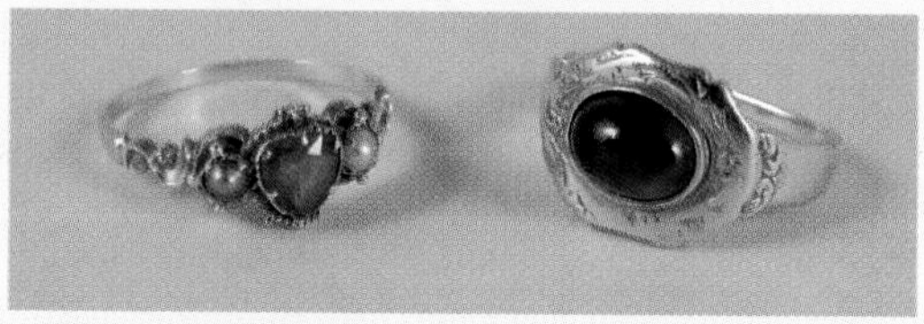

Rings, garnet and yg:
L, early Victorian, a heart-shaped garnet prong-set in yg, flanked by a gray and a white seed pearl prong-set in sculpted scrolled shoulders, continuing to a narrow shank, ½" w x ¼", sz 7, **$750**.
R, mid-Victorian, an oval carbuncle (garnet cab) bezel-set in an engr notched oval 14k yg frame surmounting engr curv shoulders, narrow shank, ½" w at center, sz 8, **$350**. (Lisa Johnson collection)

Ring, yg, rose gold, diamond, red stones, seed pearls, c. 1880, flowerhead center, yg bezel set with a sm circ-cut diamond, flanked above and below with four seed pearls and two red stones, engr rose gold shank, ¾" T to B at center, sz 7, **$300**. (Private collection)

Suite: Hinged Bangle Bracelet and Brooch/Pendant, 18k yg, om diamonds, *taille d'épargne enamel*, c. 1870, Fr, hinged bangle with five hinges and an adjustable clasp, safety chain, with engr Greek key motif borders, surmounted by a pierced, engr and enameled plaque with scroll, foliate scroll and bead decoration, a cluster of nine om diamonds in pronged flowerhead and navette-shaped mounts in the open center, eight smaller om diamonds set in enameled circ border, matching brooch surmounted by foliate scrolls and beads, with removable pendent drops on upturned hooks (originally five, one removed, one missing), long center drop surmounted by a black-enameled diamond-set bow motif, knife-edge wires set with om diamonds above C-scrolled foliate terminals, C-catch, tube hinge, Fr hmks and maker's mks on bracelet clasp, brooch catch and pinstem, bangle 1⅛" w x 2⅜" dia, brooch 2" w x 3" tl at center, **$5,000**. (Dorothy Blandi collection)

Suite: Brooch/Pin and Earrings, turquoise, diamonds, pearls, 18k rose gold, c. 1880, brooch a calibré cabochon turq shield-shaped plaque suspending rc diamond and pearl drops, rc and om diamond-set scroll surmount, matching pendent earrings, turq and diamond trefoil cluster surmounts, shepherd's hook earwires, brooch 1⅝" w x 3", earrings 2½" tl, **$7,638** [A]. (Copyright Christie's Images, New York 2002©, Christie's Los Angeles, CA, 10/4/01)

Suite: Bracelet, Brooch/Pin, Earrings, turquoise, pearls, silver, c. 1870-80, pavé-set throughout with sm turq cabs and seed pearls, belt motif hinged bangle, loop for safety and replaced pin assembly on knot motif brooch, later-added earwires on earrings, bangle ¾" w, brooch 1¼" w x 1⅞", earrings ⅞" w x 1⅛", **$1,500**. (Courtesy of E. Foxe Harrell, New York, NY)

Suite: Necklace and Earrings, diamonds, st yg, platinum, c. 1880, necklace suspending a series of grad knife-edge wire drops set with om diamonds, continuing to a plaque link back chain set with rc and om diamonds, st yg mount, matching pendent earrings, c. mid-late 20th C, set in platinum, necklace 15" tl, 2⅜" T to B at center, earrings ¾" w x 2" tl, **$51,700** [A]. (Copyright Christie's Images, New York 2002©, Christie's Los Angeles, CA, 10/4/01)

Suite: Necklace and Earrings, diamonds, garnet, emerald, aquamarine, sapphire, peridot, topaz, st yg, c. 1880, necklace a series of grad flowerhead motifs, cushion-cut colored stones encircled by om diamonds, interspersed with cut-down collet-set om diamonds, continuing to a chain of om diamonds in cut-down collets, sapphire and diamond flowerhead clasp, sapphire and diamond earrings with diamond-set stems and leaves, later-added findings, S.J. Phillips fitted leather case, necklace ⅞" w x ¾" at center, 15¼" tl, earrings ¾" w x 1", **$42,300** [A]. (Copyright Christie's Images, New York 2002©, Christie's Los Angeles, CA, 10/4/01)

Part II
Turn-of-the-Century Jewelry

The year 1900 did not signal the beginning of a new era so much as the continuation of the old and the continuing evolution of the new. The Victorian age did not end with the Queen's death in 1901; Victorianism held sway until World War I. But while a large proportion of the populace continued to cling to late Victorian fashions, three more stylistic trends emerged to establish themselves among various segments of society by the turn of the century.

This did not happen overnight. What is usually referred to as the Edwardian style had already begun to make its mark on fashionable society long before Edward became king. Aesthetic influences that led to the Arts and Crafts Movement and the beginning of modernism had made their presence felt as early as the mid-nineteenth century. And the "New Art" had made its debut in Paris in the 1890s. So, in fact, at the turn of the century, there were four concurrent jewelry styles: Victorian, Arts and Crafts, Art Nouveau, and Edwardian, plus a fifth "revivalist" style that was yet to be named.

This section is divided into four styles. As with nineteenth century jewelry, it can be difficult to clearly identify turn-of-the-century pieces as one particular style or another. At times, two or more styles are commingled in a single piece of jewelry. Historians, collectors, and dealers seem to have a need to pigeonhole and label everything. It may be hard to accept that this is not always possible. A label for a style always crops up after the style has come and gone. It is artificial by nature. While an attempt has been made to categorize the pieces in the following sections, individual interpretations vary. Up until recently, historians usually grouped all turn-of-the-century "art" jewelry under Art Nouveau. Now, most make a distinction between Art Nouveau and Arts and Crafts. (Even more recently, a new label has come into use: Beaux-arts, which is now treated as a separate style in this edition.) But one person's Arts and Crafts is another's Art Nouveau. Edwardian pieces sometimes include Art Nouveau elements, and confusion still exists over that which is neither (hence the new style designation, Beaux-arts). Some stylistic details clearly belong in one or the other camp. These will be described in the sections that follow. What is important is to understand the part that each style played in jewelry history, to recognize its characteristic components, to see how the styles influenced one another, and how designs evolved over time.

As always, events and fashion trends played an important part in the evolution of *fin de siècle* jewelry design. The pace of change was quickened by new developments. The advent of the automobile and the airplane revolutionized transportation and increased mobility. "Motoring" became a fashionable pastime. The wireless telegraph and the telephone improved communication. The motion picture industry made its humble debut as the "peepshow" at Thomas Edison's Kinetoscope Parlor in New York City. By 1910, thousands of movie theaters were showing films whose stars were already influencing fashion. Jewelers advertised their wares in the new trend-setting fashion magazine, *Vogue*.

The 1900 Paris *Exposition Universelle* heralded the pinnacle of Art Nouveau. Sarah Bernhardt's stage jewels by René Lalique and Georges Fouquet inspired many designers. The 1904 St. Louis Exposition showcased the remarkable jewels of Louis Comfort Tiffany for the first time, as well as *Jugendstil* designs from Austria.

In 1890, artist Charles Dana Gibson introduced the public to what was to become the epitome of turn-of-the-century American womanhood, the Gibson Girl. Her hair, figure, and attire were considered the height of fashion in a trend that continued through the early 1900s.

The head and neck were emphasized with large hats, upswept bouffant hairdos, and high collars for day, décolleté for evening. Hatpins, hair combs, tiaras, "dog collar" chokers, and delicate lace pins and watchpins complemented the look. Festoon necklaces, pendants and their diminutive form, the lavalier, also focused attention on the neck. The lorgnette, usually worn suspended from a chain, became a symbol of period sophistication. Corsage, or bodice, ornaments decorated "pouter pigeon" bosoms. The waist was a focal point of the "hourglass" silhouette, and anything that adorned it was fashionable. One- and two-piece buckles, sewn onto fabric or leather belts, were often-worn accessories, as were belts of swagged chains linking small plaques. Large brooches known as sash ornaments or pins were also worn at the waist. Many have open centers; some include a simulated hasp. The pinstem is invisible when the brooch is pinned to a ribbon or belt, and the brooch imitates the look of a buckle. Cuff links and scarf pins continued to be worn by both sexes. Mainstream and avant-garde designs alike were rendered in these forms, made from both precious and non-precious materials.

ARTS and CRAFTS c. 1890-1920

Arts and Crafts was more than a style. It was called a Movement, which encompassed a philosophy, an attitude, and a way of living. The practitioners of the Movement were revivalists of a sort, but unlike the Etruscan and Greco-Roman Revivalists, they were not copyists; they were interpreters of the past. They revived the *ideas* of handicraft, of medieval guilds and individual craftsmanship. Their philosophical point of view influenced their creative impulses, which found expression in a number of different forms and incorporated a variety of stylistic elements. So Arts and Crafts is not one style, but many.

Historians usually classify the various interpretations of Arts and Crafts by country of origin. While it may be that an identifiable characteristic approach to design is shared by artisans of the same nationality, it is dangerous to generalize. Without documentation or identifying marks—and many Arts and Crafts pieces are unmarked—attribution to country or maker is a guessing game at best. In terms of history, however, it can be useful to trace the movement as it developed from it origins in Great Britain and spread to Europe and the United States.

Liberty & Co. | Liberty & Co. Cymric Ltd. (1903 only) | Murrle, Bennett & Co.

Great Britain

As early as the 1870s, when Victorian Classical Revivalists were in the majority, the seeds of dissent were germinating. The dissidents were counter-revolutionaries to the Industrial Revolution. They rebelled against increased mechanization and mass-production, and the consequent loss of the human touch in the making of decorative and utilitarian objects. They also rebelled against the excesses of Victorian ornament, setting the stage for the advent of modernism at the beginning of this century. The rebellion had its roots in Great Britain, then the greatest of industrial nations. The Crystal Palace Exhibition of 1851 had shown the world the achievements of the British in the use of the machine. For some, it was the beginning of the end of craftsmanship. John Ruskin and William Morris, generally recognized as the instigators of the insurrection, went on to formulate a rather utopian philosophy which would gather steam and become the Arts and Crafts Movement. The earliest application of the philosophy was in architecture, interior design, and furnishings. Jewelry-making wasn't included until C.R. Ashbee founded his Guild of Handicraft in London in 1888.

The Aesthetic Movement of the 1870s may have given impetus to Arts and Crafts and Art Nouveau. The influence of Japanese art began with the aesthetes, and also found expression in the later styles. The adherents of the Aesthetic movement were a splinter group of intellectuals that included the Pre-Raphaelites of the art world and the advocates of dress reform, such as members of The Rational Dress Society in Britain and The Free Dress League in the U.S. While mainstream fashion kept women tightly corseted, boned, and laced into "hourglass" figures, clothing reformists attempted to liberate fashion from the confines of the corset. Reform dress for Arts and Crafts proponents was loose and high-waisted in the medieval or Renaissance style. This was part of their preoccupation with the past—recalling simpler, idealistic times in hopes of liberating themselves from the dehumanizing mechanized world. Types of jewelry made to complement the clothing were primarily necklaces and pendants, buckles, sash ornaments, and brooches. Hatpins, hair ornaments, and tiaras, an important part of period fashion, were also interpreted by Arts and Crafts designers. Rings and bracelets were less commonly made, earrings rarely.

The prime directive of the Arts and Crafts Movement purists was for one artisan to make everything entirely by hand from start to finish. No matter how varied the style, the one thing they all had in common was the desire for their handcraftsmanship to be apparent. Hammer marks and irregularities were left intact as evidence of human handiwork. Simplification of line and form, and the use of stylized organic motifs were also common threads.

Staunch social idealists, the leaders of the movement hoped to bring art to the people "in an acceptable form at realistic prices." In jewelry, the intrinsic value of the materials was of secondary importance to design and workmanship. Most Arts and Crafts artisans preferred silver to gold, and inexpensive cabochon gemstones like turquoise and moonstone to faceted diamonds and rubies. Enameling was a favorite technique of many. Some worked in brass, copper, and glass.

Although the materials were inexpensive, the time and workmanship involved in producing entirely handmade pieces made them too labor intensive to be affordable for any but the well-to-do. The rejection of the use of all machinery made production in multiples difficult and expensive. The guild artisans were unable to produce sufficient quantities of jewelry to supply the "masses." The irony of the situation was that the very manufacturers whose techniques they rejected were successful where the purists failed. British firms such as Liberty & Co., W. H. Haseler, Murrle, Bennett & Co., and Charles Horner commercialized the style, but in so doing made it affordable.

Foremost among the success stories was Liberty & Co., founded by Arthur Lazenby Liberty in 1875 as an importer of Near and Far Eastern goods, just as the *japonaiserie* craze was in full swing. The company's own popular "Cymric" (pronounced "kim´-rik," from the word for the Celts of Wales) line of metalware and jewelry was first exhibited in 1899 (see buckle on page 102). Liberty employed a number of designers to create what were then called "modern" designs. The "Liberty Style," which really *was* the people's style, was mass-produced interpretations of one-of-a-kind handmade pieces, and much more accessible and affordable to the middle and working classes. The prototypes for these pieces were designed by talented artists whose names were kept from the public at the time, but who are well-known today. Liberty's principal designer, whose work is most sought-after, was Archibald Knox (1864-1933).

Knox's work is characterized by Celtic knot motifs (also called *entrelac)* and whiplash curves in silver and enamel. In his pieces, he popularized the use of intermingled "floating" blue and green enamels pooled in central depressions. He occasionally worked in gold (see below). Some other known designer-jewelers and craftspeople who worked for Liberty were Jessie M. King of Glasgow Scotland, Oliver Baker (see pendant and chain on page 105), Arthur and Georgie Gaskin of Birmingham (see pendant on page 105), and Charles Fleetwood Varley (a scenic enamellist, see brooch on page 99). These same designers also worked independently, creating entirely handmade pieces. When Liberty appropriated their designs, the pieces were made by machine, but with hand-finished details. They retained the look of the handwrought designs, and, except by purists' standards, are still considered Arts and Crafts. Unfortunately, the pieces were only marked with one of several Liberty hallmarks ("L & Co.," "Ly & Co.," "LC&C Ld"). Attribution is based on characteristic motifs and techniques, and at times, archival documentation in the form of drawings and company records.

W. H. Haseler and Murrle, Bennett & Co. also produced designs for Liberty's retail establishment (see pendants on page 104). In 1901, W. H. Haseler, a Birmingham manufacturer, formed a partnership with Liberty to produce their Cymric line. Pieces can be marked for Liberty or "W.H.H." for Haseler. Murrle, Bennett was founded in 1884 as wholesale distributors. It was based in England, but also had manufacturing connections in Pforzheim, Germany, where it imported pieces for Liberty and also worked with Theodor Fahrner. Its mark is a conjoined "MB" inside a large C, followed by a small o, which is often used together with British hallmarks or Fahrner's marks. Some pieces are marked "M.B. & Co." World War I brought association with Fahrner to a halt, and Murrle Bennett ceased to be known as such in 1916. The company was renamed White, Redgrove and Whyte.

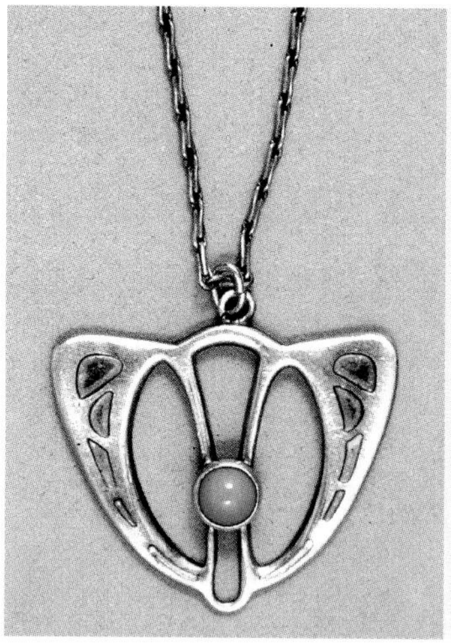

Pendant and Chain, sterling, enamel, turquoise, date letter for 1908-09, open shield-shaped pendant, foiled green and turq enameled segmented sections flanking sm circ turq cab bezel-set in center, mkd "CH" for Charles Horner, Chester hmks, chain not orig, pendant 1⅜" w x 1⅛", chain 18" tl, **$300**. (Almunir Meghji collection)

Charles Horner was a mass-marketed manufacturer in Halifax, which produced silver and enamel jewelry that was entirely made by machine, but maintained the appearance of Liberty-style Arts and Crafts. It was known for small brooches, pendants and chains (see above), and hatpins. The winged scarab, Celtic knot, and thistle were favorite motifs. Pieces are marked "C.H.," usually with Chester assay marks and date letters. For more on these four firms, see "Liberty and His Rivals" in Becker's *Antique and 20th Century Jewellery*.

Germany and Austria

By the late 1890s, The Arts and Crafts Movement had found its way across the English Channel to Europe, where it was interpreted and renamed by German, Austrian, and Scandinavian artisans. In Germany and Austria, it was called *Jugendstil* ("young style"). Scandinavians (particularly the Danes) called it *skønvirke*, which is described in the section on Danish jewelry. The Italians mostly stuck with classic revivalism, but its few practitioners called the new style *Stile Liberty*.

Theodor Fahrner (Germany)

German *Jugendstil* has been classified both as Arts and Crafts and as Art Nouveau, but it can also be viewed as the genesis of modernism. It seems best to analyze each piece individually rather than make a judgment call on the entire body of work. Certain pieces exhibit English Arts and Crafts influence while others take inspiration from French Art Nouveau. If it is possible to generalize at all, the *Jugendstil* "look," whether abstract or figural, is characterized by strong lines and bold designs. A number of individual artists worked independently or anonymously. Several manufacturers also produced *Jugendstil* jewelry. The most well-known of these was Theodor Fahrner of Pforzheim, which brought the work of many individual designers to the attention of the general public.

Brooch/Pin, boulder opal, yg, c. 1900, Eng, an oval boulder opal cab bezel-set within and behind an openwork oval *entrelac* yg frame, unmkd, attributed to Archibald Knox for Liberty, C-catch, tube hinge, 1½" w x ⅝," **$7,000**. (Caren Fine collection)

Pendant and Chain, 935 silver, turquoise, c. 1905, Ger *Jugendstil*, a convex oval plaque set with an oval turquoise cab, with cutout sections on top edge joined to a paper clip chain, appl loops on bottom edge suspending four articulated rods and an elliptical drop bezel-set with an oval turq cab, rev imp with maker's mk for Theodor Fahrner, 935, "DÉPOSÉ," 1⅜" w x 2¾", chain 18", **$2,900**. (Private collection)

Theodor Fahrner could be called the Liberty of Germany, in terms of *modus operandi*, although Fahrner manufactured jewelry exclusively, while Liberty traded in a variety of goods. What the two had in common was employing skilled freelance designers to produce "modern" designs for a commercial market. The designs themselves were sometimes the same, thanks to the connection with Murrle, Bennett & Co. Unlike Liberty, however, many of Fahrner's pieces produced between 1900-1919 were also signed by the designers. Most of these designers came from the Darmstadt Colony, an artists' community founded on the same philosophical ideals as the British guilds. It is during this period that Fahrner's *Jugendstil* jewelry was produced. Today it is highly sought-after, especially if it is artist-signed. Some important designers were Patriz Huber, Max Gradl, Franz Boeres, and Georg Kleemann.

Founded in 1855 in Pforzheim, the company's distinctive mark, a conjoined "TF" in a circle, was not introduced until 1901. The death of Theodor Fahrner (Jr.), son of the company's founder, in 1919 brought changes to the factory. Keeping up with new styles under new ownership, the company went on to become known as a producer of Art Deco fashion jewelry in marcasite, enamel, and gemstones set in silver (see Costume Jewelry, c. 1920-1935). The firm closed in 1979. A great deal of information, painstakingly compiled by its authors, can be found in the book on Fahrner cited in the References.

Heinrich Levinger (Germany)

Heinrich Levinger was another Pforzheim manufacturer which is not as well-known as Fahrner, but the pieces the company made are equally desirable to collectors. They were noted for stylized organic forms in *plique à jour* enamel and silver (see brooches on page 99). They made designs attributed to Viennese designer Otto Prutscher (1880-1949), but unlike Fahrner, no designer's mark was ever put on the pieces. In fact, sometimes the maker's mark is absent. Both Fahrner and Levinger pieces dating before 1915 can be marked with the French word "*déposé*," which means the design is registered (similar to a design patent). This mark was used for exports to both French and English-speaking countries. After World War I, the German phrase *ges. geschützt* (protected by law) replaced the French (see Ginger Moro's *European Designer Jewelry*, page 133, for a further explanation of German marks).

Wiener Werkstätte (Austria)

In Austria, Vienna was the center of *Jugendstil* activity. Among its practitioners, the best-known is a guild of multi-media craftspeople who were part of the Vienna Secession, the Wiener Werkstätte (Viennese Workshop). Founded in 1903 by Josef Hoffmann (1870-1956) and Koloman Moser (1868-1918), it was patterned after C.R. Ashbee's Guild of Handicraft. The style that evolved there is geometric and simplified, a harbinger of modernism (see brooch on page 100). Jewelry by any of the Wiener Werkstätte designers, especially the work of Hoffman and Moser, is now highly collectible. The most often-seen of the shop's marks is a superimposed "WW." An extensive history and examples of both German and Austrian Jugendstil can be found in Becker's *Art Nouveau Jewelry*, listed in the References section in the back of the book.

Some of Moser's designs were executed by the Viennese firm Georg Anton Scheid before the founding of the Wiener Werkstätte. The mark is G.A.S. with Austrian hallmarks. The Scheid pieces tended to be non-representational Art Nouveau in style.

The United States

The Art Silver Shop

British and European Arts and Crafts jewelry has been well documented in several books. American Arts and Crafts jewelry, however, has been given relatively little attention. Aside from brief chapters in two books, the only other sources of information are articles in periodicals, exhibition catalogs, and the semi-annual sales catalogs published by Aram Berberian of ARK Antiques. There are a great many more extant, accessible examples of American Arts and Crafts jewelry than some historians would lead one to believe. Some examples are by makers about whom very little published information exists, but whose work is available on the market today.

The handicraft aesthetic caught on a bit later in the United States, and lasted longer. Some say it never ended, but that is a matter of personal interpretation. It began with guilds of craftspeople inspired by and patterned after British models. The most well known are the Roycrofters and Gustav Stickley's Craftsman group. Perhaps the fact that these guilds were not known for jewelry-making explains why some collectors are unaware that American Arts and Crafts jewelry was made by many others. The movement's

Pendant and Chain, sterling, blister pearls, c. 1915, Am, symmetrically pierced and chased cusped oval frame with central oval blister pearl surmounted by two hand-wrought curling leaves and a cluster of six sm circ bezel-set blister pearls, silver leaf surmounting bail, paper clip chain, maker's mk for Josephine Hartwell Shaw ("SHAW" flanked by two hearts), Boston, MA, on rev, pendant 1½" h, chain 19" tl, **$3,200**. (Photo courtesy of ARK Antiques, New Haven, CT)

jewelry makers were concentrated in the Northeast (Boston, New York), the Midwest (especially Chicago), and California. Arts and Crafts Societies were founded in several major cities, and promoted the work of their members.

In Boston, the Society of Arts and Crafts was the guiding light of the movement. Founded in 1897, the Society began conferring the award and title of Medallist to its most highly skilled members in 1913. Four of these Medallists were jewelers whose oeuvre is recognized today as the best of American Arts and Crafts. This Boston group seems to have been directly inspired by the British in terms of design and execution, if not use of materials. Its pieces incorporate organic motifs, wire and beadwork in open, delicate, and refined designs. Unlike its British counterparts, however, the society worked primarily in gold, and used faceted stones of high intrinsic value, as well as cabochon gemstones and pearls. It relied on stones and metal for color, rather than enamel. But like the British, the group's pieces are not always signed. Documentation in the form of drawings or photographs in the Society's archives have aided attribution.

Among the earliest recipients of the Medallist award was Josephine Hartwell Shaw (1865-1941), to whom it was given in 1914. Examples of her work are rare and sought-after today (see above). Margaret Rogers (? - c. 1945) became a Medallist in 1915. She exhibited in Boston and at the annual exhibitions sponsored by the Art Institute of Chicago (see ring on page 106). Frank Gardner Hale (1876-1945) studied at C.R. Ashbee's Guild of Handicraft in England and in Europe. His work reflects the influence of his studies (see brooch on page 100 and pendant on page 104). He, too, won the Medallist award in 1915. Edward Everett Oakes (1891-1960) studied under both Shaw and Hale.

The youngest and most prolific of the four, Oakes was awarded the Society's medal in 1923. Even though he was a latecomer, his pieces retained the motifs and the aesthetic of Arts and Crafts (see dog collar on page 103). He developed distinctive repoussé leaf and flower forms that were combined with wire tendrils and beadwork in layers around gemstones. He used his own alloys of colored gold, particularly green gold, and also worked in combinations of gold and silver. His mark is his last name within an oak leaf, but, like the others, he did not always sign his work. Gilbert Oakes (1919-1987), his son, followed in his father's footsteps stylistically, and when his work is signed, it is an oak leaf with an acorn. Susan Oakes Peabody, Gilbert's daughter, still runs the Oakes Studio in Franconia, NH, with her husband John.

Laurence Foss (b. 1920) was a close friend of Gilbert Oakes who also learned jewelry-making from Edward Oakes. He was a machinist by trade, but he started making jewelry "for fun" from his own dies. He made pieces for Georg Jensen U.S.A. from the mid-1940s through the early 1950s, which he marked with his initials L/F in a shield (see bracelet and earrings on page 99). Shreve, Crump and Low in Boston also carried his work, which is not always signed (see bracelet below). He still enjoys making one-of-a-kind handwrought pieces. (Source: Interview with Laurence Foss, 6/12/02).

Stavre Gregor Panis (1889-1974) became a Craftsman member (the first of three levels of membership) of the Boston Society of Arts & Crafts in 1925. He was another latecomer whose work resembles that of the Chicago metalsmiths (especially c. 1930s Kalo) more than that of his Boston colleagues. His trademark style was hand-hammered cutout sterling plaques and figural shapes with simple engraved lines. His mark is his initials in a convex-sided triangle (see suite on page 106).

Mary Gage (1898-1993) was a woman who, like Oakes, worked in a mode that wasn't in keeping with the period in which she lived. She was behind, not ahead of, her time. Her style is much more akin to Arts and Crafts, but the period in which she worked corresponds with that of modernist studio artist-jewelers. She began silversmithing in the mid-1920s in New York City, then later moved to New England, ending up in Portland, Maine. She continued to make jewelry until her death at the age of 94 in 1993. Because her style varied little over the years, it's difficult to pinpoint circa-dates for her pieces exactly. Large flower and lily pad motifs were her specialty (see brooches on page 101).

In New York, the eccentric artistic genius Louis

Bracelet, link, silver, garnets, c. 1950, Am, rounded rect and sq hinged links, each enclosing handwrought appl leaf, acorn and berry motifs and a bezel-set circ-cut garnet, handmade v-spring and box clasp, unmkd, by Laurence Foss, ⅞" w x 7" tl, **$2,800**. (Caren Fine collection)

Brooch/Pin, 14k yg, enamel, c. 1910, Am, freeform pierced convex plaque decorated with polychrome enamel berry and foliate motifs, rev engraved "B.M.W." designed by Louis Comfort Tiffany, sgd "TIFFANY & CO.," 1⅜" w x 1¼", **$36,425** [A]. (Photo courtesy of Skinner, Inc., Boston, MA, 12/11/01)

Comfort Tiffany (1848-1933), son of the founder of Tiffany & Co., turned his attention from interior design to jewelry after his father's death in 1902. His pieces were first exhibited at the St. Louis Louisiana Purchase Exposition in 1904. Until 1907, his jewelry was made by his own firm, Tiffany Furnaces. After 1907 and until 1933, all L.C.T. pieces were made by and marked Tiffany & Co. There is ongoing controversy over the identification of L.C. Tiffany jewelry made after 1907, particularly when a Tiffany & Co. piece of the period comes up for sale at auction. An authentic, identifiable piece of Louis Tiffany jewelry sold at auction today may bring tens of thousands of dollars (see above).

Perhaps because of his association with the most prestigious jewelry firm in the country, some may find it difficult to reconcile Tiffany's jewelry with the Arts and Crafts Movement's tenets. Many classify it as Art Nouveau, along with his glass, lamps, and other decorative art objects. Jewelry historian and L.C. Tiffany biographer Janet Zapata points out that his sources and influences were many, including Oriental, Islamic, Egyptian, and Byzantine motifs, and, especially, the colors and forms found in nature. Tiffany was such an individual artist, that the diverse body of his work defies classification. However, Zapata considers his jewels to be very much in keeping with Arts and Crafts philosophy: "Louis's conception of jewelry was at odds with the pieces being made at Tiffany & Co. To him, color was paramount; gemstones were to be selected for their polychromatic effects, not for their monetary value." (p. 40, op. cit.). She further states that "each piece was hand-crafted...nothing was stamped out or cast. This craftsmanship ideal was followed at the time by Arts and Crafts designers in England and Boston..." (ibid., p. 100).

Marcus & Co. was a New York firm whose output included both British-influenced Arts and Crafts and French-influenced Art Nouveau (see brooch/pendant in Art Nouveau section, page 110). They are noted for their enameled gold, gemstone and pearl jewels. They occasionally made sterling pieces.

Another latecomer who worked in the Arts & Crafts idiom was Peer Smed (1878-1943) of Brooklyn, NY. Smed came to the United States from Denmark around 1904, having apprenticed with the well-known Danish firm A. Michelsen. Little information has been recorded about him or his work. He is known to have designed for Tiffany & Co. from his own studio in the 1930s. He made sterling flatware

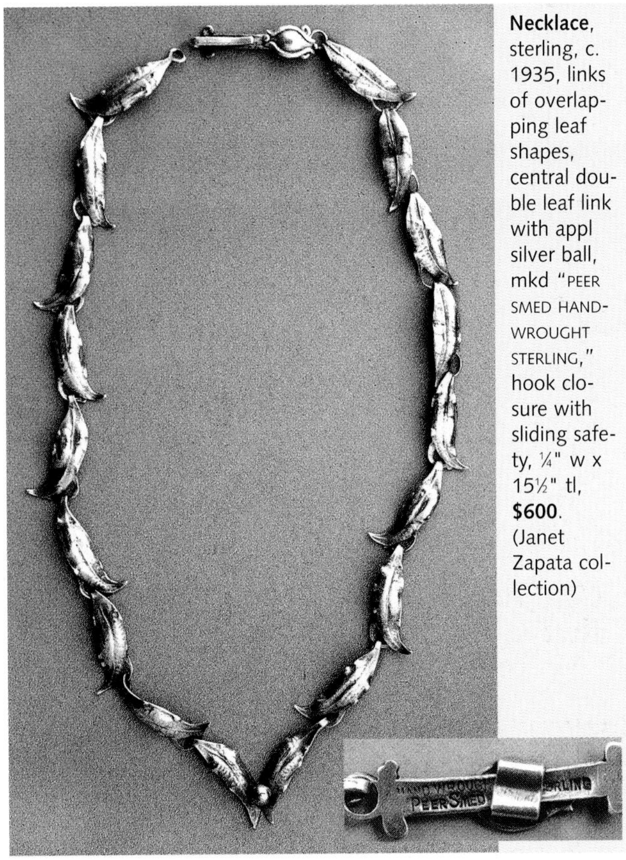

Necklace, sterling, c. 1935, links of overlapping leaf shapes, central double leaf link with appl silver ball, mkd "PEER SMED HAND-WROUGHT STERLING," hook closure with sliding safety, ¼" w x 15½" tl, **$600**. (Janet Zapata collection)

and holloware, as well as jewelry. He followed the Arts & Crafts philosophy in producing individual pieces made by hand from start to finish by one person—he employed a few Scandinavian silversmiths in his shop. He marked his pieces with his name and the words "handwrought" or "hand chased" (necklace above). According to Charles L. Venable of the Dallas Museum of Art, Peer Smed had a son named Dan, also a silversmith. He made jewelry in Los Angeles beginning in the late 1930s or very early 1940s, and died in 1951. He used his full name as his mark, "Dan Smed."

In upstate New York, Heintz Art Metal Shop of Buffalo made jewelry and decorative objects of patinated bronze with sterling overlay in cutout patterns. They were in business from 1906 to 1929. Their style is so distinctive that although their mark was not used on jewelry, it is readily identifiable (see stickpin on page 106).

The crafts community known as the Elverhöj Colony was founded in upstate New York in 1913 (the name Elverhöj comes from a Danish fairy tale). The members of the Colony followed the Arts & Crafts credo of making everything completely by hand. One of their primary products was jewelry. James Scott was a member of the Colony who made gold and silver jewelry set with gemstones; unfortunately, he did not sign his work. According to catalog #00-1 from ARK Antiques, Scott's work was among 27 items of jewelry exhibited by the Elverhöj Colony at the 13th annual exhibit of Arts & Crafts held at the Art Institute of Chicago in 1914 (see brooches on page 100).

The Chicago Arts and Crafts Society was founded in 1897, the same year as Boston's. Chicago fostered a number of Arts and Crafts silversmiths and jewelers, many of whom were both. Collectors were made aware of their work as a result of an exhibition and catalog titled, *The Chicago Metalsmiths*, sponsored by the Chicago Historical Society in 1977. The catalog is still the best source of information on this group of artisans and shops. The largest and best-known of them is The Kalo Shop, in operation from 1900 to 1970. The shop's early jewelry designs are the essence of simplicity in line and form. Most are sterling, although it made some 14k gold pieces, often set with blister or baroque pearls, mother of pearl or abalone shell, coral, moonstones, or other inexpensive gemstones. Pendants are suspended from handmade "paper clip" chains, so called because of the elongated oval shape of the links (see pendant and chain on page 105). This is a typical type of chain used by turn-of-the-century Arts and Crafts designers. In the 1920s and 1930s, the Kalo look changed to cutout and pierced repoussé floral and foliate motifs with engraved details. Later Kalo designs reflect the modern trend of the times (see brooch on page 100). The word "KALO" in block letters is found as part of the mark on all of its pieces. Some are numbered with order or design numbers.

Some other noted Chicago shops and silversmiths who also made jewelry were the Art Silver Shop (Art Metal Studios after 1934), the T.C. Shop, James H. Winn, Madeline Yale Wynne, Frances Glessner, and Matthias W. Hanck. Lebolt & Co., a retail jewelry establishment founded in 1899, installed a workshop around 1912 to produce its own line of handwrought silver and jewelry. Marshall Field & Co., a Chicago department store, catered to the demand for handcrafted metalware and jewelry by opening its own Craft Shop around 1904. It made jewelry in silver and brass using acid-etching and patination, techniques that were apparently unique to American Arts and Crafts jewelry, particularly in the Midwest. These two processes were usually combined to create a design on a shaped plaque of hammered raised metal. The effect was an "antique," aged look, more crude and rough in appearance than the polished, refined pieces of the Boston jewelers. The craft shop closed in the 1950s.

Other Midwestern shops made brass, copper, and nickel silver ("German silver") jewelry of the same genre: Carence Crafters of Chicago (who also made sterling and gemstone pieces, George W. Frost of Dayton, Ohio, and the Forest Craft Guild in Grand Rapids, Michigan, founded by Forest Mann around 1905 (see sash pins on page 101). Most, but not all, pieces are marked.

Carence Crafters

George W. Frost

The Billiken is a whimsical character that became an early twentieth century fad. He was designed and patented in 1908 by Florence Pretz, an art student from Kansas City, Missouri. She called him the "God-Of-Things-As-They-Ought-To-Be." The rights for the original design were purchased from her by the Craftsman's Guild of Chicago, which produced many different kinds of articles in the Billiken image, including buckles and sash pins of patinated and acid-etched brass with an Arts & Crafts look (see page 101). The exclusive right to manufacture Billikens in silver and gold was held by Paye & Baker silversmiths of North Attleboro, Massachusetts, (see brooch below). Today the Billiken has a devoted following.

There were a number of other lesser-known American guilds or shops based outside of Boston and Chicago. Several of them were in other parts of the northern Midwest, particularly Ohio: In Cleveland, Potter Studios, founded by Horace Potter, and the Rokesley Shop, founded around 1907. The latter produced pleasing designs in silver, enamel, pearls, and gemstones. It was one of the few American shops to use enamel in the English manner.

Pasadena, California, silversmith Clemens Friedell (1872-1963) worked for Gorham Co. in Providence, Rhode Island, before coming to California in 1910. His style has the Art Nouveau overtones of that company's "Martelé" line. His earlier work was mostly commissioned silverware. He opened a retail shop in 1929 that carried jewelry, as well as a large array of decorative silver objects and holloware.

The work of "unknowns" and unsigned pieces which exhibit an Arts and Crafts aesthetic are also illustrated in this section. As with any other type of jewelry, one should always evaluate an Arts and Crafts piece on its own merits, regardless of where, when, or by whom it was made. Because so much Arts and Crafts jewelry is unmarked, and often unattributable, this may not be just the first, but the only, method of evaluation. Many an amateur hobbyist made handcrafted jewelry in the Arts and Crafts mode. Some of it is well done; some is not.

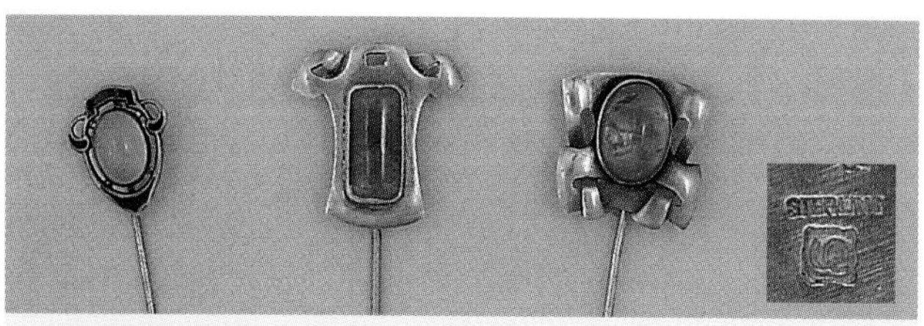

Scarf Pins/Stickpins, sterling, c. 1900-15, Am:
L, open shield-shaped head with black enameled accents, bezel-set oval chalcedony cab in the center, mkd "STERLING" on rev, 2¾" tl, head ½" w x ⅝," **$165**.
C, rect agate cab, bezel-set within an abstract cutout lobed ster frame, rev mkd "STERLING," maker's mk for Carence Crafters, Chicago, IL, 3" tl, head ⅞" square, **$450**.
R, sterling, amber, c. 1915, large oval abstract amber cab bezel-set in an interwoven cutout ster frame, rev mkd "STERLING," maker's mk for Carence Crafters, Chicago, IL, 2¾" tl, head ¾" square, **$450**.
(Courtesy of Gail Gerretsen, South Pasadena, CA)

Brooch/Pin, sterling, c. 1910-15, Am, die-stamped in the shape of a Billiken, flat backing mkd "STERLING," imp with maker's mk for Paye & Baker ("P & B" inside hearts), North Attleboro, MA, Billiken trade mark, C-catch, flanged hinge, ⅝" w x 1⅛", **$100**. (Author's collection)

Bracelets, link, silver, enamel, c. 1900, Eng:
T, blue, green and lavender enameled disks linked by double chains, unmkd, safety chain, ½" dia, 6" tl, **$400**. (Courtesy of Gail Gerretsen, South Pasadena, CA)
B, central rounded navette-shaped plaque with *entrelac* motif, turq enameled ground, flanked by flat rect links with enameled centers, mkd with maker's mk for Murrle Bennett & Co, "950" on center plaque rev, mkd "SILVER MB & CO" on clasp, safety chain, ⅝" at center, 7" tl, **$750**. (Author's collection)

Bracelets, link, sterling, Am, "late Arts & Crafts":
T, c. 1940, five domed oval plaques with raised borders, each with an appl floral/foliate motif and a bezel-set oval garnet cab at one end, appl semi-circ wires with silver bead accents at terminals joined with wide oval links, hook closure, unmkd, ⅞" w x 7¾", **$250**.
C, c. 1950, four oval openwork links, each with a repoussé curved shell shape flanked by a narrow arch of half-round beads, joined with wide connecting links, v-spring and box clasp, maker's mk for Esther Lewittes, Los Angeles, CA, 1⅛" w x 6¼", **$300**.
B, suite: link bracelet and earrings, c. 1945-50, Am, bracelet of five rounded, lobed rect plaques with upturned edges at top and bottom, each with an appl central stylized floral motif, plaques joined by wide fluted rect links, v-spring and box clasp, circ screwback earrings with similar appl floral motif, all pcs mkd "L/F" in a shield for Laurence Foss, Atkinson NH, "STERLING," #313 on bracelet and #116 on earrings, bracelet 1⅛" w x 7¼" tl, earrings ⅝" dia, **$450**. (Private collection)

Brooch/Pin, silver, enamel, c. 1910, Eng, oval plaque with a Limoges enameled waterfall and mountain landscape bezel-set in a hammered frame with strapwork corners, unmkd, enamel work attributed to Fleetwood Varley, convex back, C-catch, tube hinge, 1" w x 1⅞," **$500**. (Elaine Sarnoff collection)

Brooches/Pins, 900 silver, *plique à jour* enamel, Heinrich Levinger, Pforzheim Ger, c. 1900-1910:
L, two wing-shaped *plique à jour* enameled panels shading from lt to dk blue, intertwined at the base surmounted by a sm bezel-set oval green turq cab, and flanking a bezel-set oval green turq cab in the open center, rev mkd "900," "DÉPOSÉ," conjoined "HL" in a circle, C-catch, tube hinge, 1⅛"w x ⅞", **$1,200**.
C, open stylized foliate motif plaque, a lg collet-set oval blister pearl flanked by four triangular lt green *plique à jour* enamel panels within the open geo wire frame suspending a sm pearl drop, rev mkd "900, DÉPOSÉ," maker's mk for Heinrich Levinger, C-catch, tube hinge, 1½"w x 1⅜", **$2,500**.
R, in the shape of a two-lobed maple tree winged samara (seed), two widespread lobes of lt green *plique à jour* enamel tapering to textured silver seed pods, base of circ silver bead and stem, surmounted by circ bezel-set opal, mkd "900, DÉPOSÉ," conjoined "HL" in a circle, C-catch, tube hinge, 1½" w x ¾", **$800**. (Courtesy of Didier Antiques, London)

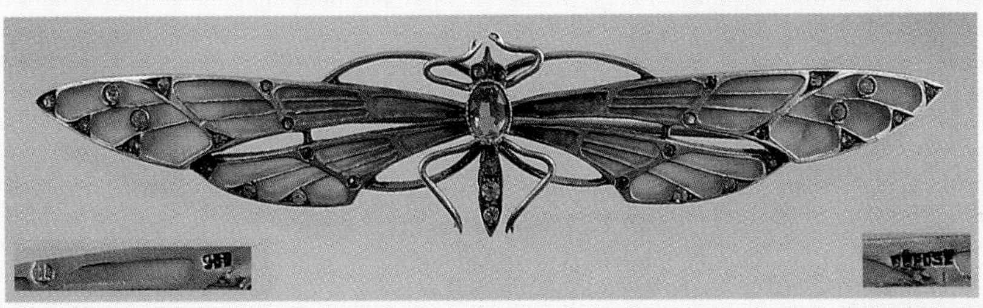

Brooch/Pin, *plique à jour* enamel, peridot, pink and colorless stones, 900 silver, c. 1900, Ger, in the shape of a stylized moth or butterfly with plique à jour wings in shades of pink, pale yellow and green interspersed with sm circ-cut colorless stones, the body bezel-set with an oval-cut peridot and circ-cut colorless stones, pink cab stone eyes, rev mkd "DÉPOSÉ, 900," maker's mk for Heinrich Levenger, Pforzheim, Ger, open tubular catch, 4⅛" w x ¾", **$2,000**. (Courtesy of Xcentricities, Beverly Hills, CA)

Brooch/Pin, bar, 14k yg, opal, c. 1910, a tapered rounded-end openwork plaque, a circ bezel-set opal in the center of appl grape leaf and spiraling bead-tipped wire vine motifs, lever catch mkd "14K," 2" w x ½", **$750**. (Courtesy of Apriori Antiques, San Francisco, CA)

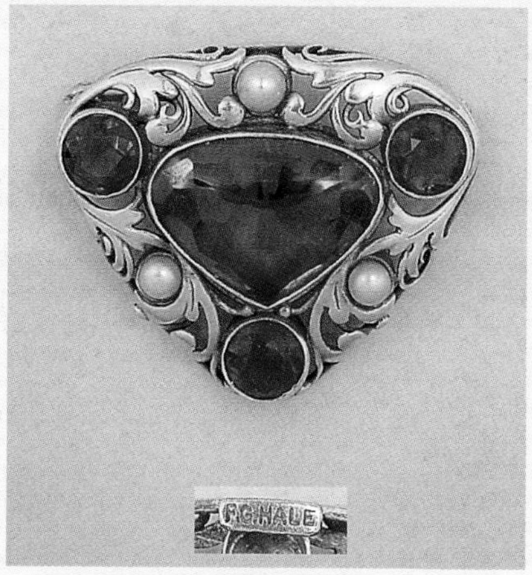

Brooch/Pin, amethysts, yg, pearls, c. 1910-20, Am, rounded inverted triangle, saw-pierced foliate scrolls enclosing a lg central bezel-set buff-top amethyst of conforming shape, a circ-cut amethyst bezel-set in each corner, and a bezel-set round pearl on each side, appl rect plaque on rev mkd "F.G. HALE" for Frank Gardiner Hale, Boston, MA, lever catch. Provenance: Hale estate, 1½" w x 1¼", **$6,500**. (Caren Fine Collection)

Brooches/Pins by James Scott, Elverhöj Colony, Milton, NY, c. 1915:
L, yg, yellow topaz, Montana sapphire, openwork navette-shaped plaque with interlocking foliate motif, central prong-set octagonal topaz flanked by two sm circ bezel-set sapphires, unsgnd, 2⅛" w x ½", **$1,600**.
R, sterling, amethyst, tourmaline, pierced and hand-wrought stepped rect plaque with finely chased interlocking and swirling strapwork motifs, lg central bezel-set pale amethyst flanked by two sm silver beads, four circ bezel-set pink tourmalines centering the four sides of the rectangle near the outer edges, 2¼" w x 1⅜", **$1,850**.
(Photo courtesy of ARK Antiques, New Haven, CT)

Brooch/Pin, brass, enamel, c. 1905, Austrian, navette-shaped brass plaque with green and white opaque *champlevé* enameled abstract foliate design, safety-pin style catch on rev, mkd "WIENER WERKSTÄTTE," 1" x ¾", **$750**. (Almunir Meghji collection)

Brooch/Pin, 18k yg, sapphire, *plique à jour* enamel, c. 1910, Am, circ openwork form centering a bezel-set circ-cut green sapphire, approx 7.6 mm, within a green plique à jour lily pad motif decorated with wiretwist, 18k yg mount, designed by LC Tiffany, signed "TIFFANY & CO.," one bead detached, minor loss to enamel, 1⅛" dia, $4,113 [A]. (Photo courtesy of Skinner, Inc., Boston, MA, 12/11/01)

Brooch/Pin, bar, sterling, carnelian cabochon, c. 1930, Am, oval carnelian cab bezel-set in an oval frame flanked by off-center horizontal hammered bars, mkd "HANDMADE, STERLING, ART SILVER SHOP," Chicago, IL, 2⅜" tl, **$200**. (Lisa Johnson collection)

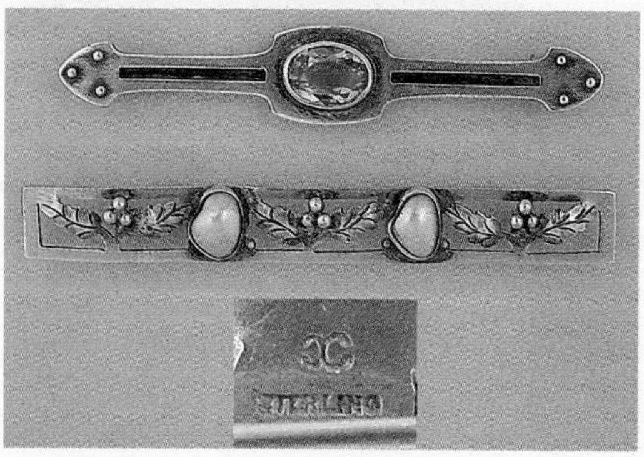

Bar Brooches/Pins, sterling, c. 1920-25:
T, shaped bar with spade-shaped terminals, each studded with three silver beads, bezel-set faceted oval amethyst in rounded rect center flanked by oxidized horizontal lines, rev mkd "HANDWROUGHT STERLING," safety catch, 2½" w x ½", **$350**. (Courtesy of Gail Gerretsen, South Pasadena, CA)
B, handwrought, cutout and engr berries and leaves motif, two bezel-set f.w. pearls, mkd "STERLING," unknown maker's mk (adorsed Cs), wide C-catch, 2¾" w x ⅜", **$250**. (Author's collection)

Brooch/Pin, sterling, enamel, c. 1950, Am, a convex circ disk, notched at compass points, with an abstract geo pattern enameled in red, blue, dk green, and black, rev mkd "KALO, STERLING," for The Kalo Shop, Chicago, IL, safety catch, 1¾" dia, **$750**. (Caren Fine collection)

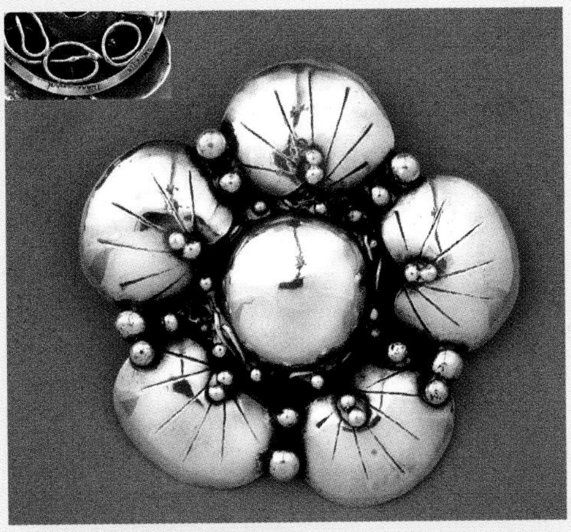

Brooch/Pin, sterling, c. 1940, five-lobed flowerhead with appl beads and engr decoration, sgd "MARY GAGE HANDWROUGHT STERLING," 2½" dia, **$200**. (Private collection)

Brooch/Pin, sterling, moonstones, c. 1940, Am, a stylized lily pad with appl bead-tipped wires and a cluster of three bezel-set oval moonstone cabs, engr radiating lines, unsgd, attributed to Mary Gage (originally purchased directly from the artist), sold together with an unattributed ster link bracelet set with moonstones, 2½" w x 2", **$518** [A]. (Photo courtesy of Skinner, Inc., Boston, MA, 9/25/01)

Brooches/Pins, sash ornaments/pins, c. 1910-20, Am:
TL, navette-shaped cusped patinated brass plaque surmounted by an appl stamped crab motif, oval cutout center on rev, wide C-catch, flanged hinge, unmkd, 2⅝" w x 2⅛", **$185**. (Author's collection)
TR, hammered German silver circ disk, a snake motif framing a bezel-set circ mottled glass cab in the center, appl disk on rev mkd "HANDWROUGHT," with an arm and hammer symbol, conjoined initials "JHP," wide C-catch, flanged hinge, 1⅞" dia, **$225**.
B, irregular cushion-shaped patinated brass plaque, acid-etched design of a face above a six-pointed star flanked by angular freeform shapes, a circ green glass cab bezel-set on one side, wide C-catch, flanged hinge, unmkd, 2¾" w x 2⅜", **$245**.
(Courtesy of Gail Gerretsen, South Pasadena, CA)

Brooches/Pins, sash ornaments/pins, patinated brass, glass, c. 1905, Am:
T, hammered convex rect plaque with two cut corners, acid-etched and patinated maze pattern, bezel-set marbled green glass cab in bottom center, maker's mk for George W. Frost, Dayton, OH on rev, wide C-catch, flanged hinge, 3" w x 2½", **$325**.
B, hammered convex rect plaque with acid-etched freeform design, circ blue glass cab center, rev mkd "FOREST CRAFT GUILD," Grand Rapids, MI, wide C-catch, flanged hinge, 2⅛" w x 1¾", **$350**. (Courtesy of Gail Gerretsen, South Pasadena, CA)

WARNING

This design is fully protected by copyright; and if infringed, the Statutes provide—Sec. 4965 — for a penalty of ten dollars for every copy possessed, sold, or exposed for sale, or for a maximum recovery of Ten Thousand Dollars.

U. S. Copyright, 1908
Also Germany, Austria, France, Italy, England, Canada, Australia and Japan

Brooch/Pin, sash ornament/pin, gp brass, c. 1910, Am, rect acid-etched and patinated plaque, a die-stamped Billiken figure in the center, appl disk on rev mkd "TRADE MARK BILLIKEN," wide C-catch, pinned to orig card, imprinted: "Copyright 1908 By The Billiken Company, Chicago, U.S.A." with rhyme: "While I'm on guard upon your sash, you'll never do a thing that's rash. - BILLIKEN." and "TRADE MARK BILLIKEN" around drawing of same, copyright warning imprinted on rev, 2⅜" w x 1⅝", **$145**. (Author's collection)

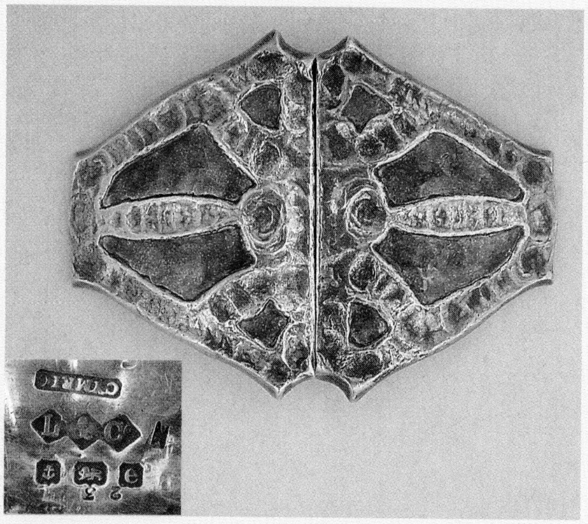

Buckle, sterling, enamel, date letter for 1905, two pieces forming a slightly convex truncated lozenge shape, cusped corners, uneven textured surface with lg and sm central depressions filled with mingled blue and green *champlevé* enamel (slight damage), rev mkd "CYMRIC," maker's mk for Liberty & Co. ("L & CO" in adjacent lozenges) on one pc, engr "London 1905" on the other, Birmingham (Eng) hmks, #23 on both pcs, appl hook and eye, bars for belt attachment, 3⅛" w x 2⅛", **$600**. (Author's collection)

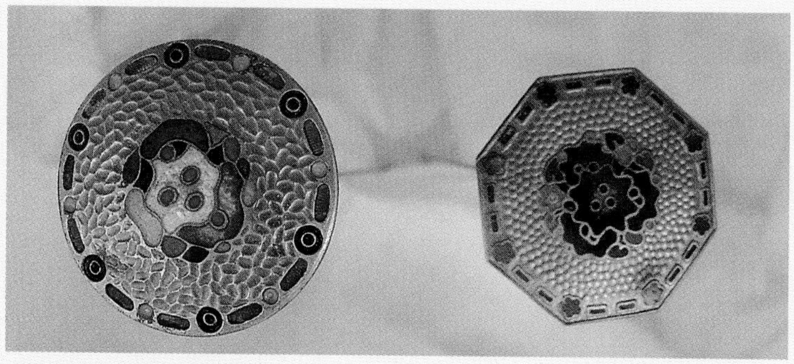

Hatpins, sp brass, enamel, unmkd, designs attributed to Hermann Häussler, Germany, c. 1910, $300 each:
L, circ raised and hammered plaque, central stylized floral design in blue, green, yellow, purple, red, and black *champlevé* enamel, border of dots, dashes, and concentric circles in blue, yellow, and black, head 1½" dia, 13⅜" tl.
R, octagonal raised and pebble-textured plaque, central stylized floral design in blue, green, yellow, and black champlevé enamel, border of dashes and flowerheads in blue and green, head 1½" dia, 12" tl. (Private collection)

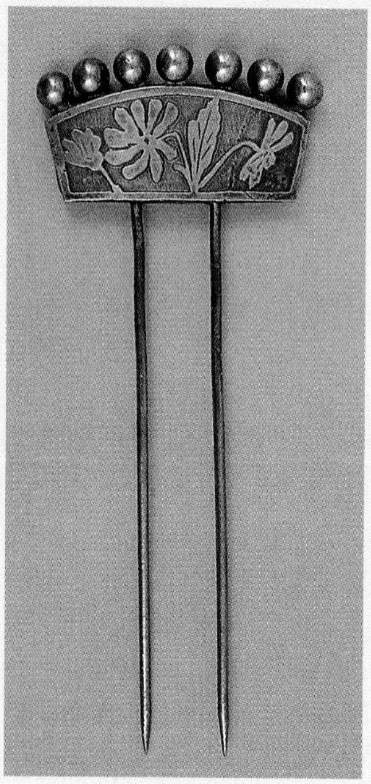

Hair Ornament, silver, c. 1910, two-pronged, acid-etched floral/foliate design on a curved rect top surmounted by a row of seven hollow spheres, unmkd, 2" w x 4½", **$300**. (Diane White collection)

Lorgnette, sterling, glass, c. 1910, raised stylized foliate branch motif on recessed ground within a raised border, enclosing folding spectacles, spring-loaded mechanism, unmkd, 2" x 6," **$365**. (Photo courtesy of Morning Glory Antiques, Albuquerque, NM)

Necklace, *négligée*, sterling, turquoise, marcasites, seed pearls, c. 1910, an irregular ovoid turq-in-matrix cab bezel-set in a sterling and marcasite frame, suspended from two lengths of cable link chain joined to a smaller bezel-set turq cab continuing to a neckchain and spring ring clasp, and suspending *négligée* two chains with two seed pearls and turq cab terminals in marcasite-set frames, mkd "sterling," illegible maker's mk, pendant center ¾" w x 2½" l, chain 17" tl, **$300**. (Private collection)

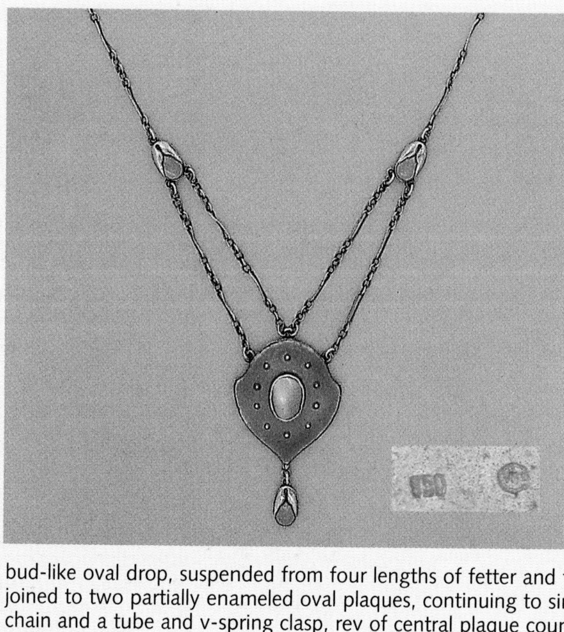

Necklace, festoon, sterling, enamel, blister pearl, c. 1900, Eng, a slightly convex, hammered texture shield-shaped plaque enameled in mingled shades of translucent turq blue and bright green, a bezel-set blister pearl in the center encircled by raised silver studs, suspending a partially enameled bud-like oval drop, suspended from four lengths of fetter and trace chain joined to two partially enameled oval plaques, continuing to single lengths of chain and a tube and v-spring clasp, rev of central plaque counter-enameled and imp with maker's mk for Murrle, Bennett & Co. "950" under the enamel, center plaque 1" w x 1½" tl, 17½" tl, **$1,250**. (Author's collection)

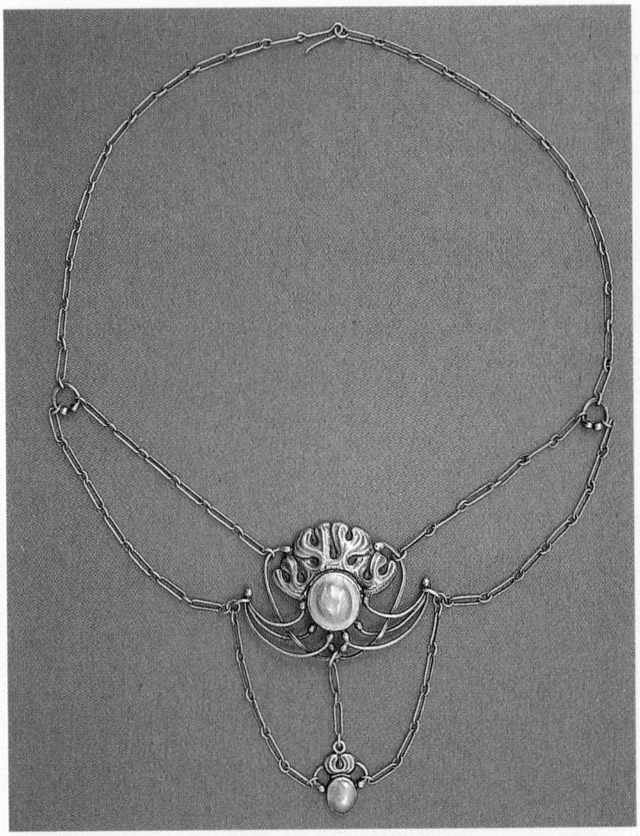

Necklace, festoon, silver, blister pearls, c. 1910, paper clip chain suspending a frame of bead-tipped wires supporting a central plaque with a bezel-set blister pearl surmounted by a repoussé stylized branch motif, swagged chains and bead-tipped wires suspending a blister pearl drop, continuing to a single chain and hook clasp, unmkd, 3" T to B at center, 17" tl, **$900**. (Gail-Marie Enos collection)

Pendant, silver, opal, f.w. pearls, c. 1910, a lg bezel-set oval boulder opal surmounted by scrolled silver wire, beads and foliate motifs, bezel-set f.w. pearl bail and drop, unmkd, attrib to Liberty, ¾" w x 2¼" tl, **$1,000**. (Courtesy of Didier Antiques, London)

Pendant, 835 silver, amber, c. 1920-30, Ger, pierced convex circ plaque with scrolling wirework base, appl beads, engr fish, starfish, and bird motifs, bail surmounted by appl fish cutout, rev mkd "835," #14, and imp fish mark inside a square for Louis Vausch, Berlin, 1½" dia, bail ⅝," **$75**. (Private collection)

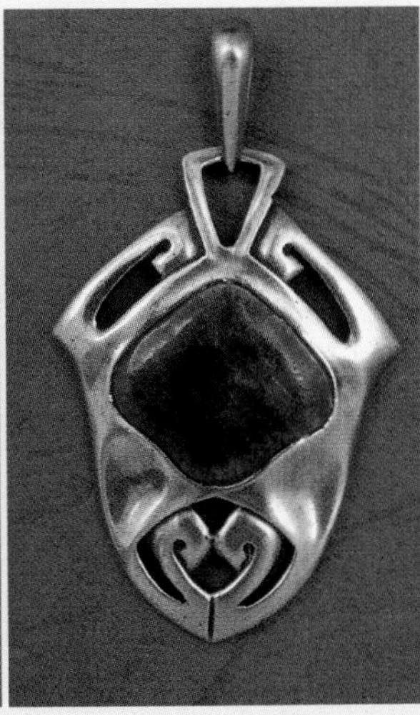

Pendants, silver, enamel, c. 1905, Eng, designs attributed to Archibald Knox:

L, shield-shaped plaque with openwork geo volutes, rounded lozenge-shaped center enameled in mingled blues and greens, rev imp with maker's mk "WHH" in a rectangle for W. H. Haseler, "SILVER," engr fancy script "K" mono, 1⅛" w x 1⅞", **$1,200**.

R, tapered rect plaque with rounded base, flanked top and bottom by open Celtic knot motifs, oval center enameled in mingled shades of blue, red, yellow, and green, rev mkd "SILVER," imp with maker's mk for Murrle, Bennett & Co., 1⅛" w x 1⅞", **$1,200**. (Private collection)

Necklace, dog collar, 14k green gold, Montana sapphires, seed pearls, diamonds, velvet ribbon, c. 1920, openwork with scrolling oak leaf foliate motifs, plaque de cou with central quatrefoil of five circ-cut bezel-set sapphires, approx 2.50 cts tw, four seed pearls between, four sm circ diamonds at compass points, flanked by two narrow side plaques, each with one central circ-cut sapphire surrounded by six seed pearls, all plaques movably attached to a black velvet ribbon with hand-wrought clasp, unmkd, by Edward Everett Oakes, Boston, MA, center plaque 1⅜" w x 1", side plaques ¼" w x 1", ribbon ⅞" w x 12" tl, **$8,800**. (Photo courtesy of ARK Antiques, New Haven, CT)

Pendant, yg, pink tourmaline, cultured pearls, baroque pearl drop, c. 1910, openwork inverted triangular plaque with appl gold beads and curv foliate motif around a central oval prong-set pink tourmaline flanked by two pearls, suspending an oval baroque pearl with foliate gold cap, mkd "F.G. HALE" for Frank Gardner Hale, Boston, MA, 1¼" w x 2⅜" tl, **$5,500**. (Gail-Marie Enos collection)

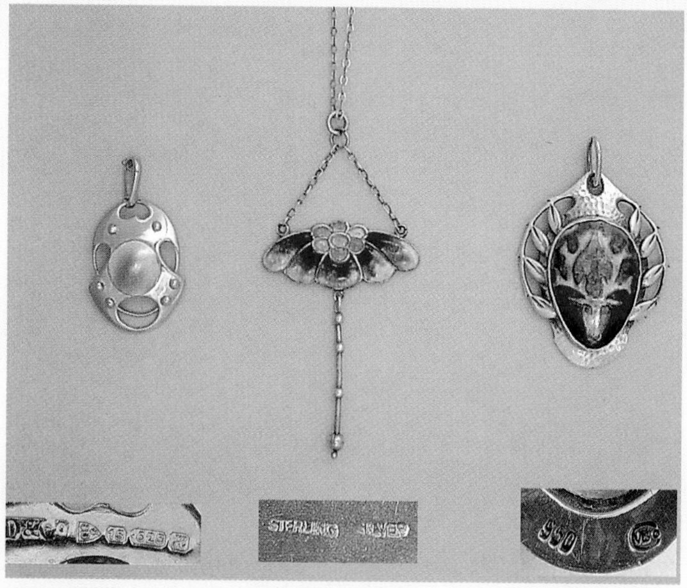

Pendants, Eng:
L, 15k yg, blister pearl, date letter for 1908-9, a convex oval with cutouts on four sides, appl bead "rivets" around a bezel-set circ blister pearl, suspended from a teardrop bail, imp with Chester [Eng] hmks, maker's mk "D&CO" on rev, ¾" w x 1¼" tl, **$900**.
C, sterling, enamel, c. 1910, stylized floral motif plaque enameled in shades of green, blue, and white, suspending a long "tail" of grad round silver beads alternating with tubular beads, suspended from two chains joined to a bail and chain, plaque mkd "STERLING SILVER" on rev, probably Eng, pendant 1⅛" w x 2½" w, chain 19" tl, **$650**.
R, 950 silver, enamel, c. 1910, inverted pear-shaped convex center enameled with a stag motif in shades of green, blue, and white, bezel-set in a hammered and openwork foliate branch motif frame, counter-enameled, frame rev mkd "950," maker's mk for Murrle, Bennett & Co, 1⅛" w x 1¾" tl, **$1,000**. (Nancy Shadforth collection)

Pendant, 14k yg, c. 1910-20, Am Gypsy pendant in the shape of a five-pointed star, gold spheres at each point, engr floral and geo motifs, suspending three heart-shaped drops at bottom, centering a bezel-set U.S. gold coin dated 1908 with the central figure (Columbia) raised, triangular incised bail, damage to gold spheres, 2½" w x 3" tl, **$500**. (Private collection)

Pendant, walrus ivory, gold nugget, brass, c. 1910, carved ivory Billiken with a gold nugget "navel," probably Eskimo, possibly an Alaska Gold Rush souvenir, ¾" w x 2⅛" tl, **$125**. (Courtesy of Ocean Eyz Antique Jewelry, Orange, CA)

Pendant/Brooch and Chain, sterling, enamel, date letter for 1910-11, a shield-shaped plaque with undulating foliate motifs framing an enameled stylized flower and leaves in a circ disk above the words "LOVE NEVER FAILETH," suspended by two short chains from a cutout plaque with the Latin phrase "FORTIS IN ARDUIS" ("valiant/courageous in the face of difficulty"), suspended from a removable long chain with hooks, pin assembly with enclosed C-catch, tube hinge on rev, both plaques imp with maker's mk for Liberty & Co. Birmingham hmks, bottom plaque rev inscribed: "NORLAND INSTITUTE AWARD OF HIGHEST MERIT TO ALICE MAKIN, FOR NOT LESS THAN 5 YEARS FAITHFUL WORK, 3 BEING UNDER ONE EMPLOYER 1902 TO 1911," center drop 1⅜" w x 1¼", chain 30" tl, **$950**. (Private collection)

Pendant and Chain, silver, enamel, f.w. pearl, c. 1900-1910, Eng, a pr of mirror-image freeform convex plaques enameled in blues and greens above two tapered horizontal bars and a curved wire, flanking a tapering vertical bar suspending a f.w. pearl, suspended from swagged silver cable link chains with sm flowerhead decorations where joined to a single chain and tube clasp, unmkd, attributed to Oliver Baker for Liberty & Co., 15½" tl, 1½" at center, **$1,200**. (Courtesy of Didier Antiques, London)

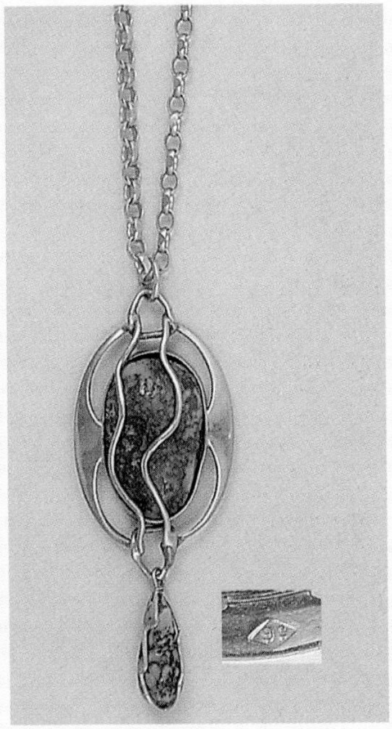

Pendant and Chain, turquoise in matrix, 9ct rose gold, c. 1900, Eng, an irregular oval turq cab bezel-set behind a rose gold "cage" of undulating wires, cutout oval frame suspending a smaller tumble-polished turq drop in an undulating wire "cage," rev mkd "9c" in a lozenge, attributed to Liberty & Co, later-added 9ct chain with Birmingham hmks, pendant ¾" w x 1⅞", chain 15-1/2", **$950**. (Courtesy of Gail Gerretsen, South Pasadena, CA)

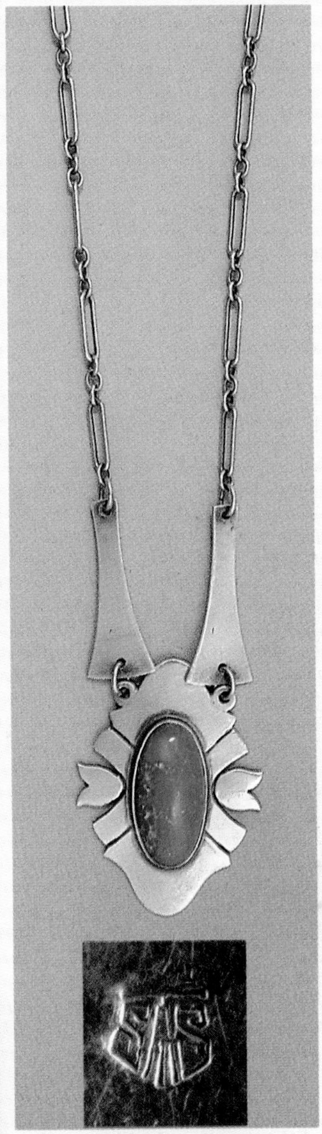

Pendant and Chain, sterling, turquoise, c. 1915-20, Am, hand-wrought, rounded navette-shaped plaque with a cutout stylized tulip motif flanking a central bezel-set oval green turq cab, suspended from two tapered rect plaques and a paperclip chain, pendant rev mkd "HANDMADE," maker's mk for The Art Silver Shop, Chicago, IL, center 1" w x 1½", chain 16" tl, **$400**. (Private collection)

Pendant and Chain, sterling, black opals, pink tourmalines, c. 1910, Eng, inverted pentagonal openwork floral/foliate plaque surmounting a wirework frame, suspended from two cable link chains, bezel-set with seven black opals and five pink tourmalines around a larger central oval black opal, suspending an oval black opal drop, rev mkd "G" in a flowerhead for Arthur and Georgie Gaskin, T-bar clasp, 1⅝" w x 1⅝", 17¾" tl, **$3,000**. (Elaine Sarnoff collection)

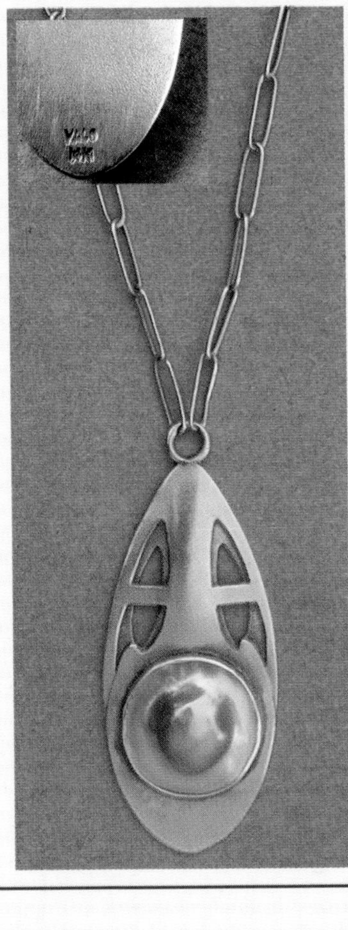

Pendant and Chain, 14k yg, blister pearl, c. 1910, Am, double-layered navette-shaped yg plaque, cutout sections above a bezel-set blister pearl, rev mkd "KALO 14K," suspended from a yg paper clip chain, pendant ¾" w x 1⅞" tl, chain 18½" tl, **$2,400**. (Courtesy of Generations, La Verne, CA)

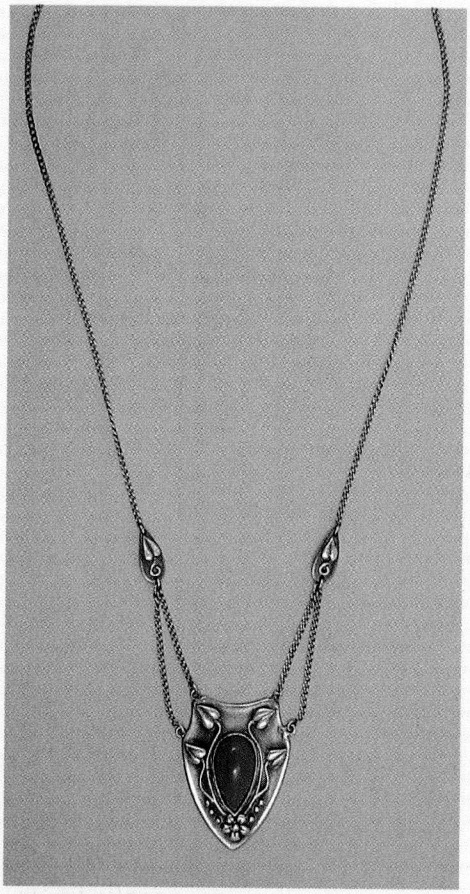

Pendant and Chain, festoon, silver, dyed blue-green chalcedony, c. 1920, a shield-shaped central pendant, appl stylized floral/foliate motifs framing an inverted teardrop-shaped center stone (chipped), suspended from swagged cable link chains joined to two sm plaques surmounted by foliate motifs, continuing to a single chain, spring ring clasp, unmkd, 1¼" w x 1¾" at center, 21" tl, **$650.** (Lisa Johnson collection)

Ring, pink, green, yg, green and pink tourmalines, c. 1910, elongated oval with appl foliate and floral motifs and beading in three colors of gold, bezel-set step-cut green tourmaline center, a circ-cut pink tourmaline above and below, mounted on a narrow shank with rolled edge, unmkd, ½" w x 1⅛", sz 7½, **$850**. (Teri Vaughn collection)

Pendant and Chain, silver, *plique à jour enamel*, c. 1915, an elongated tapered and cusped plaque suspending a shield-shaped drop within an eccentric open circle from a silver foliate motif link, in multi-colored *plique à jour* enamel, rev mkd "PM" in a lozenge on all parts, unknown maker's mk, pendant ¾" w x 2⅜" tl, chain 18" tl, **$350**. (Private collection)

Ring, demantoid garnet, 14k yg, seed pearls, c. 1915, Am, circ-cut bezel-set demantoid garnet, approx 5.71 x 4.11 mm, flanked by seed pearls, the shoulders accented by 14k yg bead and foliate motifs, mkd with a conjoined "MR" for Margaret Rogers, Boston, MA, ⅝" w x ¼", sz 6¾, **$3,290** [A]. (Photo courtesy of Skinner, Inc., Boston, MA, 12/11/01)

Ring, yg, citrine, diamonds, pearls, c. 1910-20, a bezel-set oval-cut citrine flanked by stylized yg foliate motifs, bezel-set diamonds, and pearls, surmounting a yg wire framework continuing to a narrow shank of soldered wire, unsgd, attributed to a Boston maker, possibly Edward Everett Oakes, ½" T to B at center, sz 6½, **$4,500**. (Caren Fine collection)

Ring, sterling, glass, Am, handwrought floral/foliate motifs framing an oval-cut purple glass stone, tapering to a narrow shank mkd "OKS" for Odd Krafters Shop, Chicago, IL, ¾" w x 1", sz 8, **$125**. (Private collection)

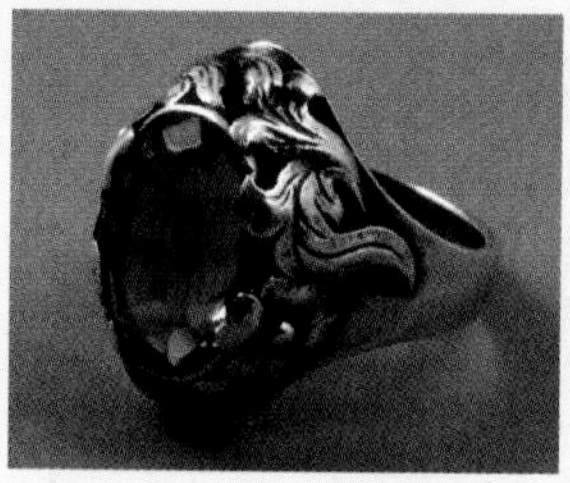

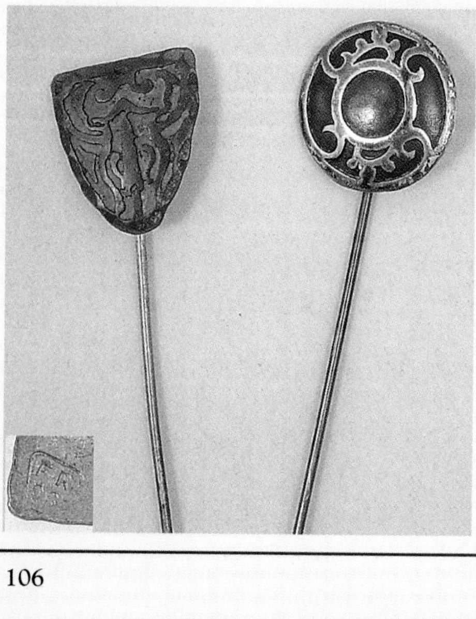

Scarf Pins/Stickpins. c. 1910, Am:
L, inverted hammered triangular brass plaque, rounded apex, acid-etched and green patinated abstract design, rev imp "FROST" in a triangle for George W. Frost, Dayton, OH, head ⅝" w x ¾", 2⅝" tl, **$100**.
R, slightly convex circ bronze disk with overlaid cutout ster foliate scroll design, unmkd, attributed to Heintz Art Metal Shop, Buffalo, NY, ¾" dia, 2⅞" tl, **$125**. (Author's collection)

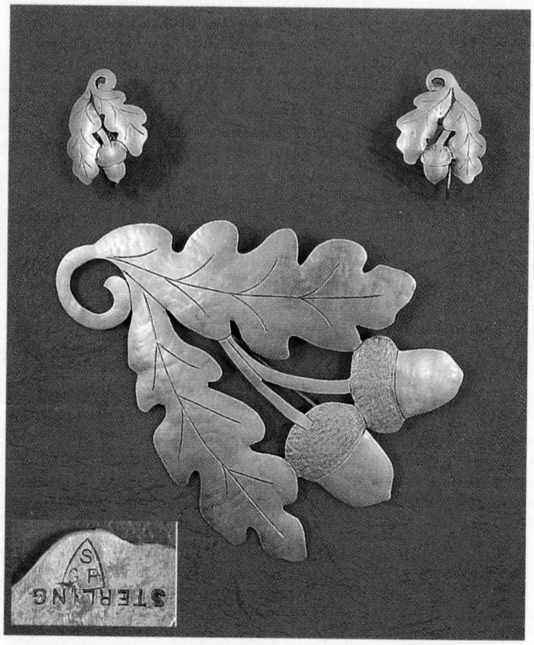

Suite: Brooch/Pin and Earrings, sterling, c. 1925-30, cutout and hand-hammered plaque in the shape of oak leaves and acorns, engr leaf veins, stippled texturing on acorn tops, matching screwback earrings, rev imp "STERLING" and "SGP" in a triangle for Stavre Gregor Panis, Boston, MA, brooch 3½" w x 2¾", earrings ¾" w x 1", **$550**. (Private collection)

ART NOUVEAU
c.1895-1910

In 1895, Sigfried (aka Samuel) Bing (1838-1905) converted his Oriental art gallery in Paris into a gallery for a new style, which gave the style its name, *L'Art Nouveau*. The Art Nouveau style caught fire and burned with a passion for a short while at the turn of the century before it flamed out and died. Its rise and fall spanned less than 20 years, but Art Nouveau had quite an impact on jewelry history. The quintessence of Art Nouveau was distilled by the French, but the ingredients for its heady mix of line and form came from the British Arts and Crafts Movement. It was the British insistence upon artistic integrity and individual expression that inspired the French to break away from constricting, traditional, imitative realism. This may explain the difficulty in determining which elements constitute which style.

The two have much in common: the use of inexpensive gemstones and other materials, enameling, the "whiplash" curve, motifs taken from nature, Japanese influence. But something changes in the translation from English to French. French pieces are figural, more three-dimensional and asymmetrical. The female face and body, naked and clothed, are predominant subjects for Art Nouveau interpretation, nearly absent in Arts and Crafts. Other Art Nouveau favorites include dragonflies and butterflies—some with female bodies—writhing snakes, and mythical creatures (chimera). The peacock and peacock feathers have been interpreted by both the British and the French in different ways. Irises, poppies, winged sycamore and maple seeds, waterlilies and trailing vines are part of the botanical repertoire of Art Nouveau.

Arts and Crafts floral and foliate motifs are stylized, the designs more abstract and controlled. Art Nouveau motifs have an element of fantasy, with exaggerated lines and sensual overtones. It might be oversimplifying to say categorically that if it's British, it's Arts and Crafts; if it's French, it's Art Nouveau. It would be fair to say, however, that the British retained too much of their Victorian sensibility to embrace Art Nouveau wholeheartedly. The French, on the other hand, were more than willing to take off in Art Nouveau's exuberant and, some say, decadent direction. Other countries followed: Belgium, Spain, and to a lesser extent, Russia. In Germany, Austria, and the United States, both British and French influences were felt.

Although there were many practitioners of the style in France, the work of one man has come to represent everything that Art Nouveau jewelry is about: René Lalique (1860-1945). His life has been well-documented and his work well-preserved (see References in the back of the book). A student of jewelry history should be familiar with his work because to understand Lalique is to understand Nouveau at its finest. Included in this section are a few examples from an important sale of Lalique pieces held at Christie's New York in October 2001 (see pages 110, 112, and 114). A number of pieces in the sale were part of a traveling 1998 exhibition of Lalique jewelry (catalog cited in the References appendix). Among the items exhibited were some of Lalique's jewels never before put on public display.

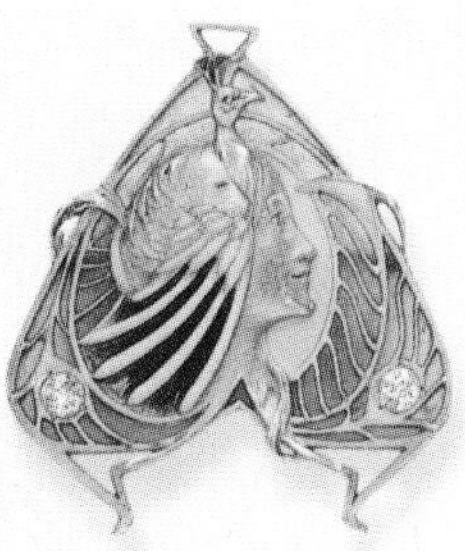

Brooch/Pin, yg, enamel, diamonds, c.1900, Fr, a woman's head in profile wearing a chased gold peacock head-dress enhanced by blue and iridescent white enameled plumes, on a backdrop of *plique à jour* feathers, accented by gold veining and two oe diamonds, sgd "L. GAUTRAIT," 1½" w x 1½", **$9,400** [A]. (Copyright Christie's Images, New York 2002©, Christie's New York, NY, 10/22/01)

Pendant, 18k yg, *plique à jour* enamel, diamonds, baroque pearl, c. 1907, Fr, openwork stylized leaves, enhanced by scrolling rc diamond trim, suspending an elongated baroque pearl accented with oe, sc, and rc diamonds, sgd "VEVER, PARIS," #2754, Fr assay mks, in orig Vever leather fitted case, 2¼" w x 3¼" tl, **$37,600** [A]. (Copyright Christie's Images, New York 2002©, Christie's New York, NY, 10/22/01)

Other important French Art Nouveau designers and houses include Maison Louis Aucoc, under whom Lalique apprenticed, Georges Fouquet, Lucien Gaillard, Lucien Gautrait, and Maison Vever. Examples by some of these artists were also offered at the Christie's October 2001 sale (see above).

The pendant on page 114 was made by Frédéric Charles Victor de Vernon (1858-1912), a medallist and engraver whose work was sold in Paris by Cartier, and made by Maison Duval and Lacloche Frères. He exhibited every year at the Paris Salons and was awarded a first-class medal in 1895. He specialized in Art Nouveau medal-jewels with religious themes, often enhanced with *plique à jour* enamel.

Enameling is one the most important decorative elements in Art Nouveau jewelry. One of the techniques that Lalique was noted for, and which became closely associated with Art Nouveau, is *plique à jour* enameling. The usual explanation is that it looks like a stained glass window; a piece has no metal backing and the enamel colors are translucent. *Plique à jour* is particularly effective when used to depict insect wings (butterflies, dragonflies) and landscapes with sky and water. It is a difficult technique, and the results are fragile. Intact pieces are scarce.

When an enameled piece does have a backing, or groundplate, there are several other possible techniques, all of which were used in Art Nouveau as well as other styles of jewelry: *basse-taille*, *champlevé*, *cloisonné*, and Limoges, or painted enamel are the ones most commonly seen. An explanation of these techniques can be found in the Glossary.

Basse-taille and *champlevé* enameled flowers on sterling or brass plaques, resembling miniature paintings, are often found in American Art Nouveau brooches and sash ornaments/pins, particularly by New England makers (see sash pins below).

The style itself was a departure from what had gone before, but jewelry forms followed fashion's dictates. Hatpins, hair combs, necklaces and pendants, ornamental *plaques de cou* for dog collars, brooches, sash ornaments/pins, and buckles, and to a lesser extent, bracelets, cuff links, rings, and stickpins, were all interpreted by Art Nouveau designers. Another commonly seen form is sometimes referred to as "medal" jewelry (see reference to Vernon on the previous page). This was a French idea (called *bijou médaille* in France, see pages 110 and 113) that was also popular in the U.S. It replaced the classic cameo with a medallion in gold or silver of the profile, full face, or torso of a woman or man in repoussé, stamped or cast relief. Borders and backgrounds were appropriately decorated with undulating vines, leaves, and flowers in the Art Nouveau style. The medallion could be a pendant, locket, brooch, or scarf pin. Less expensive versions were made in gilt base metals.

In the U.S., Americans were torn between English pragmatism and French *chic*. In New York City, Tiffany & Co. and Marcus & Co. produced beautiful enameled and gemstone-set Art Nouveau jewels that rivaled most French pieces. And, although Arts and Crafts jewelry was gaining popularity in Boston, Chicago, and other cities, Newark, New Jersey, jewelry makers were turning out pieces influenced by Art Nouveau.

In the spirit of American entrepreneurship, the style was commercialized with great, if short-lived, success, particularly by two Newark silver manufacturers, Wm. B. Kerr and Unger Bros. Both firms were noted for their die-stamped relief designs that imitated repoussé handwork. They are easily recognized and circa-dated.

The pieces are backed with flat soldered-on sterling plates that bear the companies' marks. Kerr used a fasces, a bundle of rods bound around a battle-ax; Unger Bros.' mark is its interlaced initials, UB. Typical motifs were women's faces with flowing hair, and flowers, particularly poppies, waterlilies, and irises (see belts on page 109, and buckle and lorgnette on page 112). Kerr was purchased by Gorham in 1906, retaining its name, but not its style, for some time afterward. Unger Bros. stopped making Art Nouveau designs in 1910. Brooches and buckles by either firm sell in the low to high three-figure range.

Other manufacturers, some based in Providence, Rhode Island, and Attleboro, Massachusetts, produced similar die-stamped jewelry in sterling and silver-plated brass. The quality varies. Inexpensive pieces are usually made from a single thin sheet of unbacked metal.

A grouping of American hand-painted porcelain brooches is included in this section, on page 111. This genre of jewelry is difficult to classify, although certainly the center brooch in this grouping can be called Art Nouveau in style. The craft itself, begun around 1876, has been practiced as a hobby by women for many decades, but was especially popular around the turn of the 20th century. Floral motifs were a perennial favorite. An informative and thorough book on the subject by Dorothy Kamm is cited in the References appendix.

Several notable Newark manufacturers specialized in gold jewelry in the Art Nouveau style, often enameled and/or set with gemstones: Alling & Co., Bippart, Griscom & Osborn, Carter, Howe (later Gough) & Co., Krementz & Co., Riker Bros, and Whiteside & Blank, to name the few represented in this section. See appendix, American Manufacturers, for these and additional Newark makers' marks. Many other Newark makers' marks can be found in Dorothy Rainwater's *American Jewelry Manufacturers*. Details on the companies' histories, compiled by Janet Zapata, are in *The Glitter & the Gold*, cited in the References.

The commercialization of Art Nouveau also brought about its demise. Perhaps its stylistic excesses, like a rich dessert, became cloying and difficult to digest in large quantities. After 1910, relatively little Nouveau jewelry was produced. By 1915, it was completely out of fashion.

Reproduction Alert

Since the 1960s' revival of Art Nouveau, many cast knockoffs of die-stamped period pieces have been made, especially in sterling. The reproduction pieces are solid instead of hollow, and the details are not as sharp. Reproductions of gold and gemstone Nouveau jewels can be cast or stamped, but also lack detail and signs of wear. Enameling is not as skillfully done.

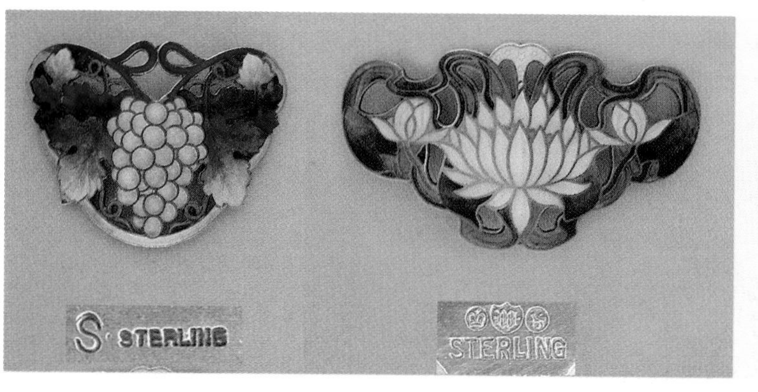

Brooches/Pins, sash ornaments/pins, sterling, enamel, c. 1910, Am:
T, a shield-shaped pierced plaque with polychrome *basse-taille* enameled grapes, leaves and vines, rev mkd "S" for Shepard Mfg. Co., Melrose Highlands, MA, "STERLING," wide C-catch, tube hinge, 2⅛" w x 1¾", **$150**.
B, a slightly convex curv pierced plaque with water lilies, leaves and vines depicted in white, green and yellow *basse-taille* enamel, rev imp "STERLING," maker's mks (pseudo hmks) for Watson, Newell & Co., Attleboro, MA, wide C-catch, flanged hinge, 2⅛" w x 1½", **$225**. (Author's collection)

Belt, "girdle," sterling, c. 1904-5, Am, central die-stamped plaque depicting the head of a woman with flowing hair, water lily motifs above and below, linked by two equal lengths of cable chain to circ discs with die-stamped heads, terminating in two circ disks with hook and eye closure, flat backing, appl bars on rev of all for attaching a ribbon backing, all pcs mkd with maker's mk for Unger Bros, Newark, NJ, "STERLING" on hook, center plaque 1⅛" w x 2¾", 26½" tl, **$1,400**. (Author's collection)

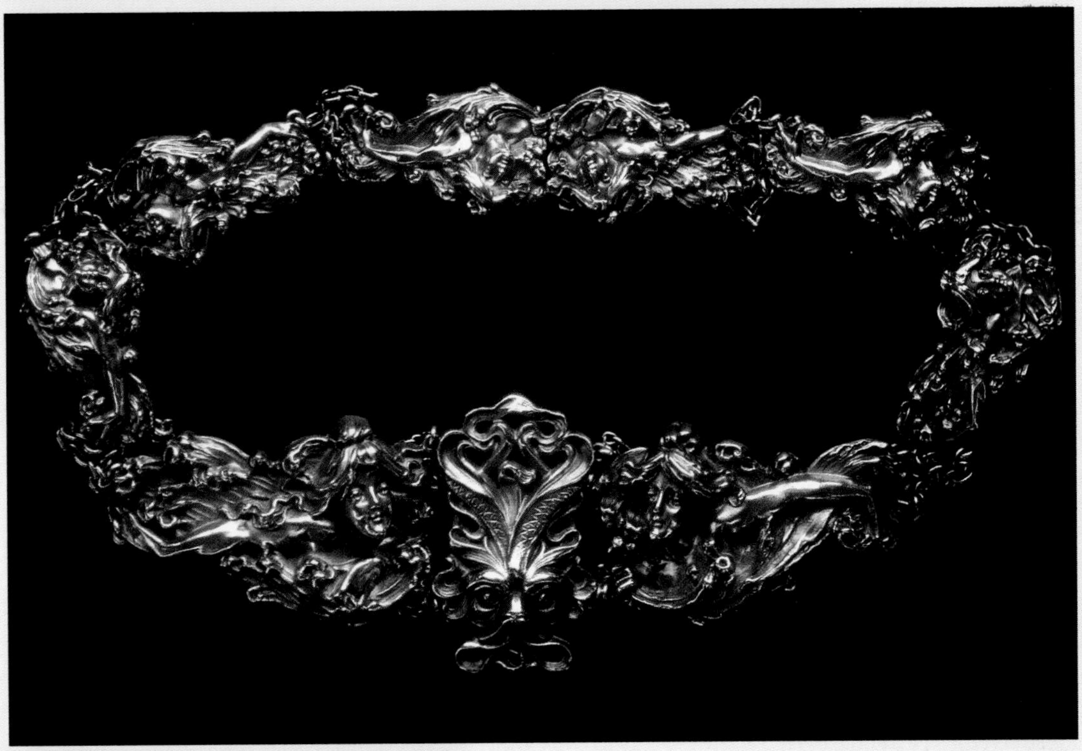

Belt, "girdle," sterling, c. 1900-1905, Am, titled "Rhine Maidens," a central die-stamped plaque of a stylized dolphin, joined by two lengths of chain to grad die-stamped plaques depicting women swimming in waves, appl bars on rev for ribbon backing, mkd "STERLING," maker's mk for Wm. B Kerr, Newark, NJ, #860, center plaque 1½" w x 2½", 32" tl, **$2,200**. (Photo courtesy of Peggy Dunner, Seattle, WA)

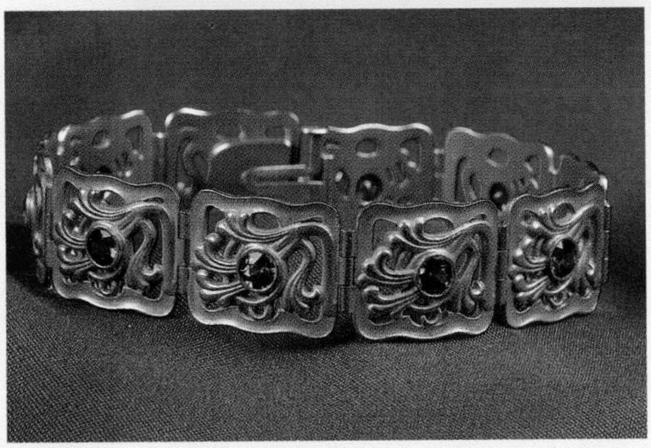

Bracelet, flexible, 14k yg, sapphires, c. 1900-10, Am, ten openwork rounded rect hinged plaques with undulating borders, each enclosing a stylized scrolled foliate motif surmounted by a collet-set circ-cut blue sapphire, maker's mk for Riker Bros, Newark, NJ, ½" w x 7" tl, **$4,348** [A]. (Photo courtesy of Skinner, Inc., Boston, MA, 3/17/02)

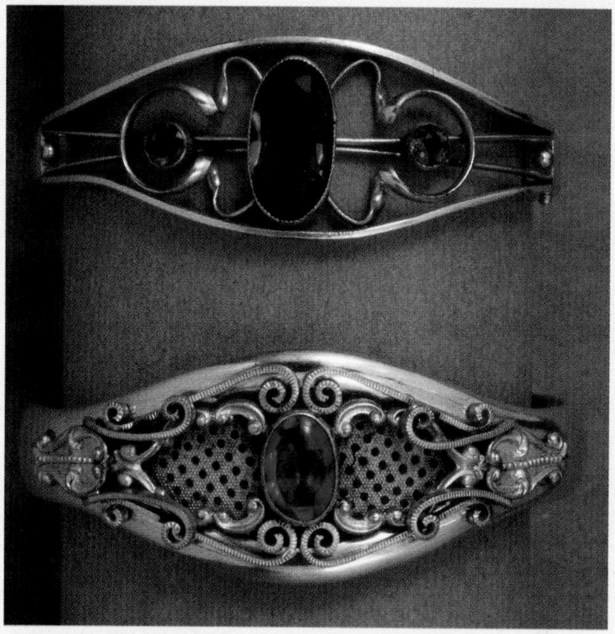

Bracelets, hinged bangles, ym and glass, c. 1910, Am:
T, tapered openwork gf frame, scrolled wire enclosing a lg oval flanked by two sm circ-cut faceted purple glass stones, ⅞" w at center, 2¼" inside dia, **$110**.
B, tapered hollow frame enclosing gp mesh surmounted by scrolled wirework, a faceted oval blue glass stone bezel-set in center, mkd "SB CO." for Standard Button Co., Attleboro MA (makers of plated jewelry), 1" w at center, 2½" inside dia, **$125**. (Courtesy of Generations, La Verne, CA)

Brooch/Pendant, carved opal, demantoid garnet, diamonds,18k yg, platinum, c. 1890, a circ carved opal depicting a sea nymph, rising/setting sun with circ-cut diamond center, and ocean waves, with grad oe diamond border above and a demantoid-set yg foliate wreath border surmounted by two stylized fish below, three hidden pendant loops, sgd "MARCUS & CO." original Marcus & Co. case, 1⅝" dia, **$35,250** [A]. (Copyright Christie's Images, New York 2002©, Christie's New York, NY, 10/22/01)

Brooch/Pin, 14k yg, diamonds, c. 1895, a *"bijou médaille,"* circ plaque with die-stamped relief depicting the profile of a woman wearing a laurel headpiece, a necklace and earring of diamonds, accented with an om diamond, the rev further decorated with engr flowers, 1" dia, **$337** [A]. (Photo courtesy of Dupuis Jewellery Auctioneers, Toronto, ONT, Canada, 6/11/01)

Brooch/Pin, 18k yg, c. 1900, *"bijou médaille,"* an irregular circ disk, depicting the profile of a young woman, a bouquet of flowers along one edge, billowing clouds on the other, stamped "JEANNE" on the front, Fr hmks, illegible maker's mk on C-catch, tube hinge, illegible mk on extended pinstem, 1" dia, **$450**. (Courtesy of Andrea Fatell, Wellsley, MA)

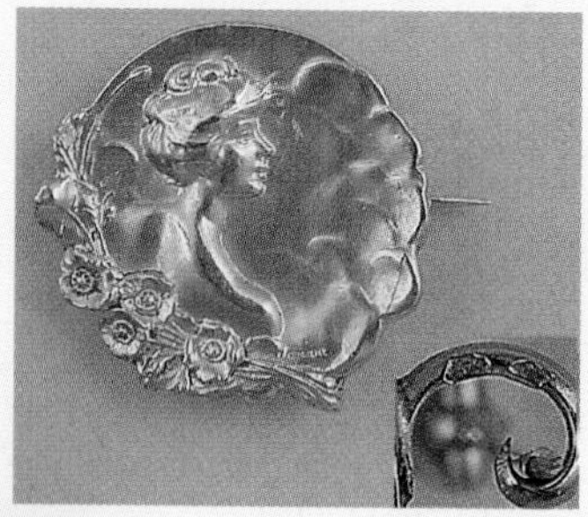

Brooch/Pin, celluloid, citrine, silver, yg, c. 1902, Fr, a central celluloid panel depicting "Dancing Nymphs" in relief, within a calibré-cut citrine frame with cusped and ridged silver corners, in a silver and yg mount, sgd "LALIQUE" for Rene Lalique, 2⅝" w x 2", **$41,125** [A]. (Copyright Christie's Images, New York 2002©, Christie's New York, NY, 10/22/01)

Brooch/Pin, 14k yg, enamel, pearl, om diamond, c. 1900, an enameled blossom encircled by a sinuous green vine and centering on a diamond, pearl accent, maker's mk for Carter, Howe & Co., Newark, NJ, 1¼" dia, **$999** [A]. (Photo courtesy of Skinner, Inc., Boston, MA, 12/11/01)

Brooch/Pin, enamel, 14k yg, pearl, oe diamonds, c. 1900, in the shape of an orchid with iridescent enamel, accented by two oe diamonds and pearl, maker's mk for Whiteside and Blank, Newark, NJ, 1⅝" w, **$2,350** [A]. (Photo courtesy of Skinner, Inc., Boston, MA, 12/11/01)

Brooch/Pin, 14k yg, enamel, red and green stones, seed pearls, c. 1900, in the shape of a dragonfly with transparent enamel on engr wings, the edges set with seed pearls, sm red stone eyes, sm green stones set in body, mkd "14k," maker's mk for Riker Bros., Newark, NJ, some crazing in enamel, repair, discoloration on rev, C-catch, tube hinge, 1¾" w x 1⅛", **$500**. (Caren Fine collection)

Brooch/Pin, brass, glass, c. 1900, in the shape of a feather with peacock-eye glass cab at one end, C-catch, flanged hinge, 1" w x 3¾", **$200**. (Courtesy of Terrance O'Halloran, San Pedro, CA)

Brooch/Pin, sash ornament/pin, brass, glass, c. 1900-1910, open rect, a snake motif forming a whiplash figure 8 around opening, oval marbled green glass cabs in two corners, 3" w x 1½", **$150**. (Courtesy of Generations, La Verne, CA)

Brooches/Pins, sash ornaments/pins, brass, glass, insect motifs, c. 1900-1910, Am:
T, a fly with purple and gold glass cab body flanked by green r.s. bezel-set in foliate motifs within an undulating open oval frame, wide C-catch, flanged hinge, 2¾" w x 2⅛", **$175**.
B, a dragonfly with openwork wings, a water lily, and a green glass cab in the open center, a die-struck crested bird with out-stretched wings on one end of a rounded rect frame with indented corners, rev mkd "J.J.S." for J. J. Sommer & Co., North Attleboro MA, unusual V-shaped safety catch, flanged hinge, 3" w x 2", **$150**. (Courtesy of Generations, La Verne, CA)

Brooches/Pins, hand-painted porcelain, c. 1900-1950, Am:
TL, c. 1910-20, circ plaque, wide gilded border appears to frame the central floral scene, inner portion of gold edging decorated with raised enamel dots in a scalloped pattern surrounding a trumpet vine in lt coral, blue, and lt green, mounted on pronged gp backing with pendant bail, C-catch, 1⅝" dia, **$55**.
TC, c. date unknown, circ frameless plaque with aster floral motif in soft pink, green, yellow, and purple, sgd "LJ," pin back attached directly to porcelain rev, 2" dia, **$50**.
TR, c. 1950, circ plaque with floral motif depicting pansies in purple, blue and soft green, set in a scalloped gp frame, sgd "Lorree Clarke," 1¼" dia, **$25**.
C, c. 1900-20, circ plaque depicting the head and shoulders of a woman with coral-colored flowers in her brown upswept hair and décolletage, lt green and yellow foliate bg, hp scalloped and scrolled gilt edging, mounted on pronged brass backing, C-catch, approx 1⅛" x 1¼", **$75**.
BL, c. 1900-20, oval plaque, red rose and foliate central motif with hp golden scrollwork with lattice accents around outer edges of disk, mounted on pronged gp backing, C-catch, 1½" w x 2", **$75**.
BR, sash pin, c. 1910-20, oval plaque depicting clusters of yellow roses and buds in yellow, green, and lt brown, mounted on pronged brass backing, C-catch, 1⅝" w x 2⅛", **$90**.
(Photo courtesy of Morning Glory Antiques, Albuquerque, NM)

Buckle, sterling, c. 1900, an open rounded rect, appl iris motif in one corner, swiveling double hasp with toothed loop for belt on rev, imp with four leaf clover mk encircled by "STERLING," for Parks Bros. & Rogers, Providence, RI, #4809, 2¼" w x 3½", **$300**. (Courtesy of Gilly Phipps, Philadelphia, PA)

Buckles, clasps, c. 1900-1905, Am:
T, sp brass, glass, die-stamped two-pc V-shaped clasp, with openwork orchid design flanking a bezel-set rounded inverted triangular peacock-eye glass cab, appl plaque on rev with maker's mk for Fishel, Nessler & Co, New York, NY, hook and eye closure, appl bars for belt attachment, 2⅞" w x 1⅜", **$175**.
B, two-pc, each pc a full-blown flowerhead and paired leaves in die-stamped high relief, hook and eye closure, appl double bars on rev for belt attachment mkd "PATENTED JUNE 25, 1901," flat backing with appl oval disk imp with maker's mk for Wm. B. Kerr & Co., Newark, NJ, "STERLING" #1564, 4⅞" w x 1½", **$450**. (Author's collection)

Cuff Links, yg, enamel, c. 1900, double circ plaques depicting cockerel heads in profile in enamel, sgd "LALIQUE" for Rene Lalique, ⅝" dia, **$19,975** [A]. (Copyright Christie's Images, New York 2002©, Christie's New York, NY, 10/22/01)

Locket, 14k yg, diamond, c. 1900, circ die-stamped relief of the bust and arm of a woman wearing a lg plumed hat, framed in lily of the valley motifs, a circ-cut diamond in her hair, 1⅛" dia, **$1,350**. (Courtesy of Apriori Antiques, San Francisco CA)

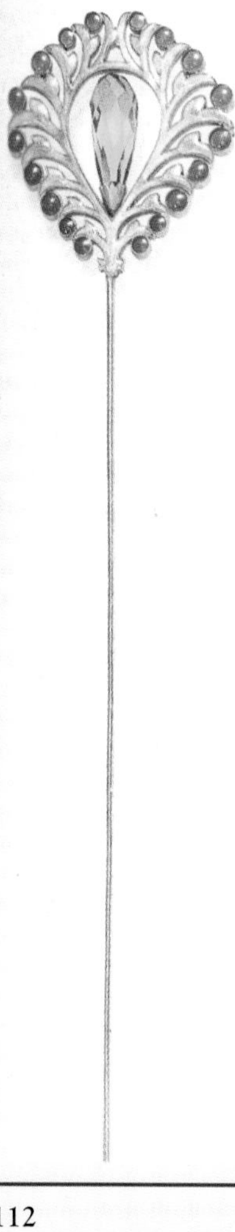

Hatpin, yg, enamel, citrine, c.1900, in the shape of a stylized peacock feather, the "eye" a briolette-cut citrine, within a sea green enameled surround and circular pink translucent terminals, sgd "LALIQUE" for Rene Lalique, 1⅜" w x 7¼", **$18,800** [A]. (Copyright Christie's Images, New York 2002©, Christie's New York, NY, 10/22/01)

Lorgnettes, sterling, c. 1900, Am:
T, enclosing a pr of folding spectacles, the case and handle decorated with a raised die-stamped female face with long flowing hair entwined with flowers, vines and leaves, mkd "STERLING," maker's mk for Unger Brothers, Newark, NJ, 4⅞", **$425**.
B, case and handle decorated with a raised die-stamped floral/foliate and ribbon design, mkd "STERLING," 5⅜", **$325**.
(Photo courtesy of Morning Glory Antiques, Albuquerque, NM)

Lorgnette, yg, diamonds, c. 1900, the smooth pear-shaped handle with a border of raised undulating lines and scrolls, set diagonally with three oe diamonds, mono on rev, the oval spectacles folded together with spring-release, 1¼" w x 5", **$561** [A]. (Photo courtesy of Dupuis Jewellery Auctioneers, Toronto, ONT, Canada, 6/12/01)

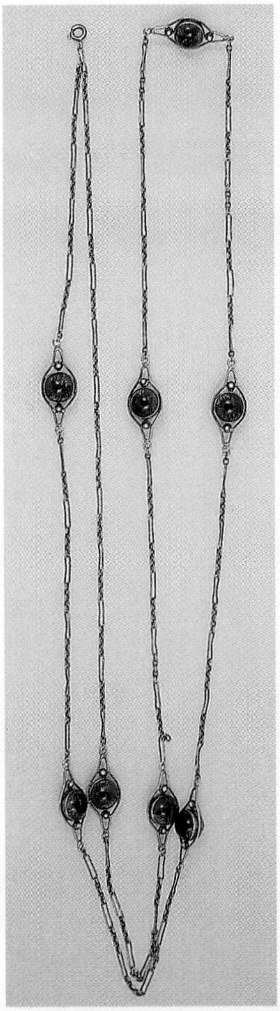

Neckchain, sterling, peacock eye glass, c. 1900, round foiled blue and green glass beads forming irises and pupils within ster wire and bead "eyes," interspersed on a fetter and cable link chain, spring ring terminal, eyes ½" w x 1⅛", 48" tl, **$150**. (Courtesy of Denese Strand, Laguna Hills, CA)

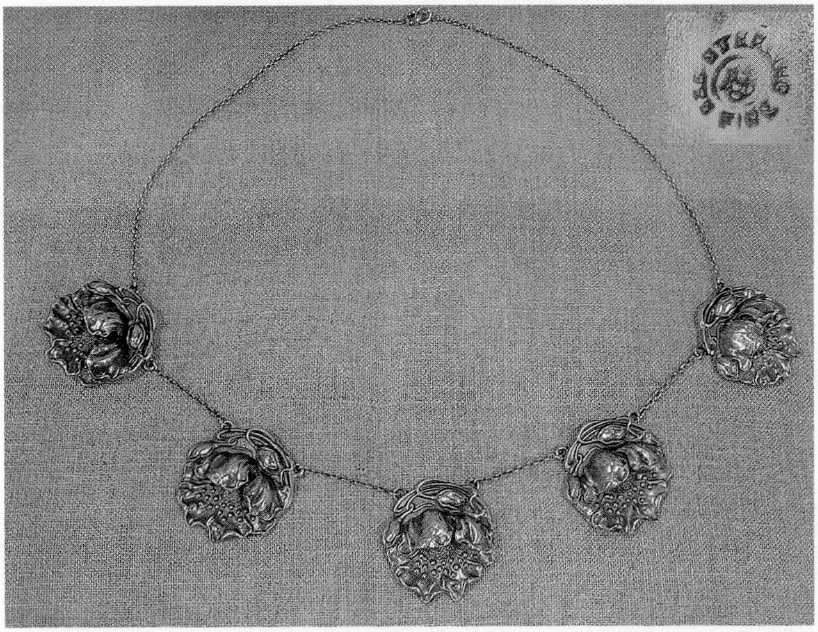

Necklace, sterling, c. 1904, Am, five die-stamped poppy motifs in high relief suspended from cable link chain with a spring ring clasp, slightly convex backs, each mkd with maker's mk for Unger Bros., Newark, NJ, possible conversion from a girdle (belt), poppies 1½" dia, 23" tl, **$950**. (Courtesy of Gail Gerretsen, South Pasadena, CA)

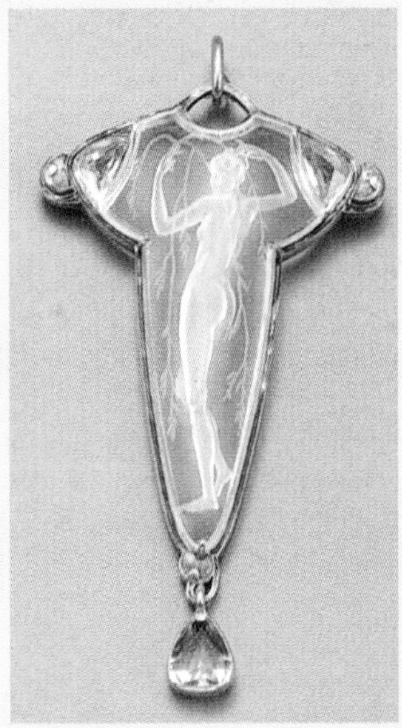

Pendant, glass, yg, enamel, citrine, c. 1900, Fr, a glass rev intaglio depicting a nude woman with engr vine motifs on the front surface, set in a yg frame with enamel accents and citrines flanking the intaglio, suspending a triangular citrine drop, sgd "LALIQUE," 1½" w x 2¾" tl, **$28,271** [A]. (Photo courtesy of Sotheby's, London, 11/27/01)

Necklace, festoon, yg, peridots, freshwater pearls, c. 1900, the openwork scrolled foliate center with a prong-set oval-cut peridot, an oval-cut peridot prong-set in openwork pear-shaped pendent drop, flanked by sm foliate scrolls, surmounted by one and suspending six natural f.w. pearls from swagged cable-link chains, 14" tl, 1⅝" T to B at center, **$1,196** [A]. (Photo courtesy of Dupuis Jewellery Auctioneers, Toronto, ONT, Canada, 6/12/01)

Pendant, silver, transparent and opaque enamel, c. 1900-1910, slightly irregular heart-shaped plaque, enameled with the upper torso and profile of a woman on a green *basse-taille* enameled ground, a silver iris along one side, #4 on rev, illegible hmks on bail, 1⅜" w x 1½", **$600**. (Courtesy of E. Foxe Harrell, New York, NY)

Pendant, 18k yg, diamonds, rubies, c. 1900, a *"bijou médaille"* circ disk depicting the profile of a woman with a headband set with circ-cut rubies and rc diamonds within a stylized foliate motif border, 1¼" dia, **$2,350**. (Courtesy of Apriori Antiques, San Francisco, CA)

Pendant, 18k yg, pink gold, green gold, diamonds, pearls, colored lead crystal, c. 1900, Fr, an oval pink crystal plaque in a reeded yg frame flanked by open yg lobes, surmounted by floral and foliate motifs in pink and green gold set with three diamonds, suspending a pearl drop with a diamond-set cap, Fr hmks (eagle's head), 1⅛" w x 2¼" l, **$4,800**. (Courtesy of Apriori Antiques, San Francisco, CA)

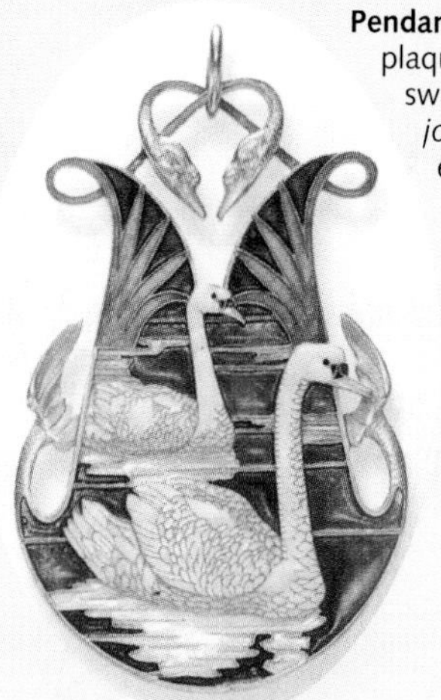

Pendant, yg, enamel, c. 1900, Fr, sculpted plaque depicting two white-enameled swans with yg detail, within a *plique à jour* enameled lake, and green-enameled foliage, the rounded bottom terminating in two yg swan's feet, a scrolling swan neck design forming the pendant hook, sgd "LALIQUE" for Rene Lalique, 1½" w x 2¼", **$64,625** [A]. (Copyright Christie's Images, New York 2002©, Christie's New York, NY, 10/22/01)

Pendant, 18k yg, *plique à jour* enamel, amethysts, pearls, diamonds, st yg, c. 1910, openwork foliate and vine motifs terminating in seed pearls, flanked by stylized *plique à jour* enameled scrolled floral motifs set with calibré-cut amethysts and rc diamonds, Austro-Hungarian hmks, 1⅛"w x 2½" tl, **$5,500**. (Courtesy of Apriori Antiques, San Francisco, CA)

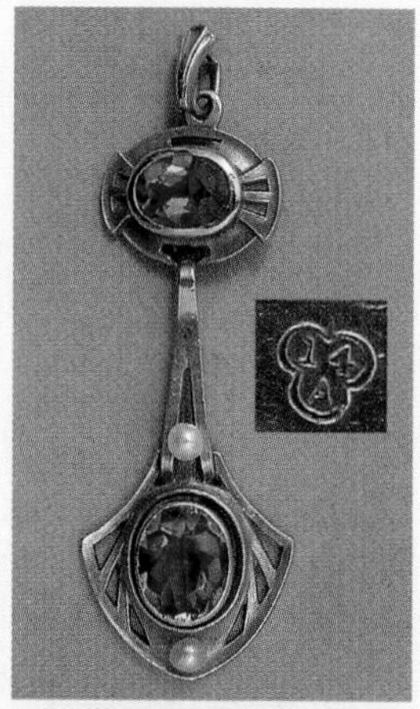

Pendant, 14k yg, citrines, seed pearls, c. 1910, Am, *Jugendstil* influence, a pierced convex oval plaque with a bezel-set oval-cut citrine flanked by cutout fan-shaped motifs, suspending a pierced tapered spade-shaped drop bezel-set with an oval-cut citrine, a seed pearl above and below, rev imp with maker's mk for Alling & Co., Newark, NJ, ⅝" w x 2" tl, **$900**. (Author's collection)

Pendant, ivory, seed pearls, diamonds, platinum, c. 1915, Fr, an oval plat plaque surmounted by a carved ivory depiction of a Madonna on a ground of pavé-set rc diamonds within a border of seed pearls, Fr plat hmk (after 1912), #2054, maker's mk, plaque sgd "VERNON" for medalist Frédéric de Vernon, 1⅜" w x 1⅞" tl, **$2,016** [A]. (Photo courtesy of Sotheby's, London, 6/20/01)

Pendant and Chain, 14k yg, enamel, amethyst, seed pearls, c. 1910, enameled leaf and pansy with a pearl center within an open shield-shaped and scrolled frame set with grad seed pearls, suspending a circ-cut amethyst and green enameled drop, removable pendant on two hooks, suspended from two chains joined to a bezel-set circ-cut amethyst suspended from chains and continuing to a spring ring clasp, threaded post on rev, missing pin assembly for brooch, suffragist colors green (enamel), white (seed pearls and enamel), and violet (amethysts), mkd "14k," maker's mk for Bippart Griscom & Osborne (a torch), Newark, NJ, ¾" w x 1¼", 18½" tl, **$1,200**. (Courtesy of E. Foxe Harrell, New York, NY)

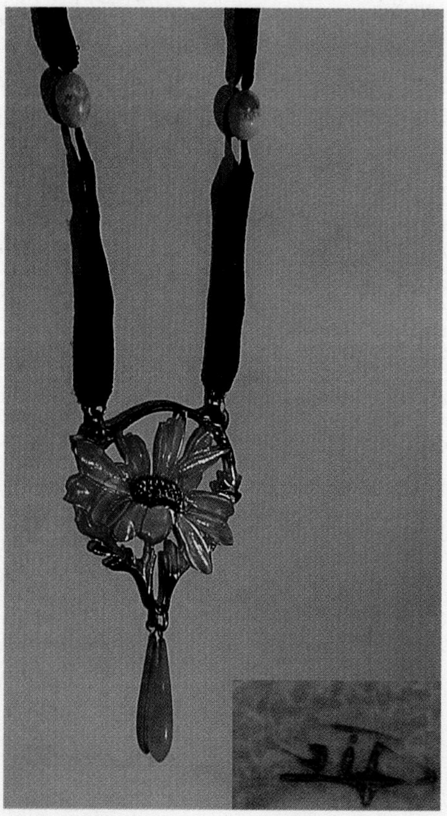

Pendant and Ribbon, clarified and dyed horn, grosgrain ribbon, c. 1900, a carved flowerhead within an open foliate branch frame, suspending an elongated hollow horn drop, suspended from a black ribbon interspersed with four hollow oval horn beads, pendant sgd "GIP" for Georges Pierre on rev, pendant 2¾" w x 4½" tl, ribbon 31" tl, **$1,200**. (Courtesy of Didier Antiques, London)

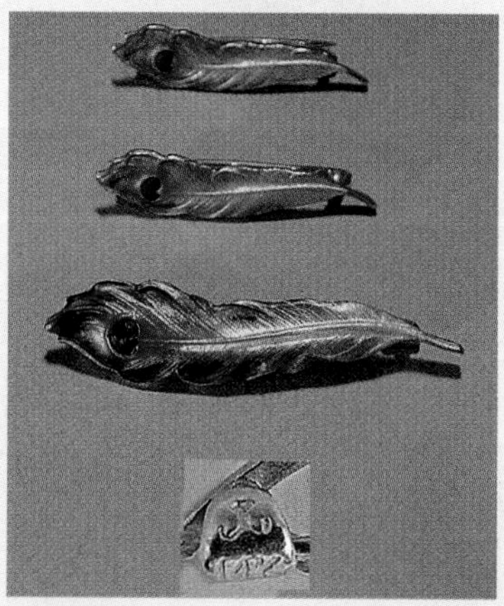

Suite: "waist set," 14k yg, enamel, c. 1910, three brooches, one lg and two sm, in the shapes of peacock feathers in polychrome enamel, catches mkd "14k," maker's mk for Krementz & Co., Newark, NJ, lg pin ⅜" w x 1½" l, smaller pair ¼" w x 1⅛" l, **$1,800**. (Courtesy of Apriori Antiques, San Francisco, CA)

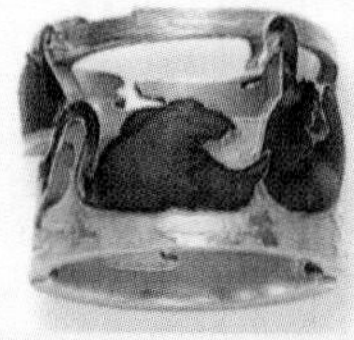

Ring, yg, enamel, c.1899, an openwork wide band with four sculpted greenish-blue enameled swans within a textured yg stylized lake, with opalescent green enameled shadows, sgd "LALIQUE" for Rene Lalique, ⅝" w, sz 9¾, **$30,550** [A]. (Copyright Christie's Images, New York 2002©, Christie's New York, NY, 10/22/01)

BEAUX-ARTS and "NEO-RENAISSANCE" c.1890-1920

All turn-of-the-century jewelry made in Newark was not made in the Art Nouveau style. A new term has entered the jewelry historian's vocabulary, taken from architecture: Beaux-arts, as delineated by Ulysses Dietz and Janet Zapata in their article on Newark jewelers for *The Magazine Antiques*, cited in the References appendix. This is a term for a turn-of-the-century style that cannot be called Art Nouveau, Arts and Crafts, or Edwardian. It is clearly derived from the Revivalist styles of the previous few decades, particularly those that came from a Viennese design source book called *Die Perle*, published in 1879 in German, English, and French. Finely detailed griffins, cherubs, and foliate scroll motifs often show up in circa 1890-1920 pieces by Wm. B. Kerr, Riker Bros., Krementz, Alling & Co., and others, which up until now have been called Art Nouveau, even though the name didn't fit. "Beaux-arts" seems to fill the need for a label for this style, and sufficient numbers of examples are on the market today to warrant giving it recognition and a separate classification.

Although they were making 90 percent of the country's karat gold jewelry at the turn of the century, Newark makers were not alone in producing the Beaux-arts style in the U.S. Gorham Manufacturing in Providence, for example, also made sterling jewelry with similar motifs and decoration (see dog collar necklace on page 117).

Considering the country of origin of one of the primary sources of these motifs (Austria), it seems logical to find similar ones cropping up in Austro-Hungarian jewelry during the same period. This is really a continuation of the Renaissance Revival style of the 1870s, hence the name "neo-Renaissance" to distinguish it from the earlier period. The turn-of-the-century pieces tend to be heavier in style and execution than earlier examples, but still feature enamel on silver-gilt, low-quality gemstones, and freshwater pearls, materials that are not usually seen in American Beaux-arts jewelry.

Bracelet, hinged bangle, 14k yg, diamonds, c. 1900, Am, an appl die-stamped lion's head, oe diamond eyes and mouth, flanked by foliate scrolls and beading, surmounting a narrow double-tubular bangle, minor dents, maker's mk for Alling & Co., Newark, NJ, 1⅜" T to B at center, **$588** [A]. (Photo courtesy of Skinner, Inc., Boston, MA, 12/11/01)

Brooch/Pin, 800 silver, turquoise, pearl, c. 1915, Ger or Austrian, parcel-gilt, a pr of griffins and openwork scrolls flanking a bezel-set pearl and two turq cabs, two turq cabs in wings and three oval turq cab drops, mkd "800, *GESETZ-GESCHÜZT* [Ger, protected by law]," and a conjoined "HM," C-catch, tube hinge, 1⅛" w x 1½", **$300**. (Courtesy of Xcentricities, Beverly Hills, CA)

Brooch/Pin, sterling, c. 1900, Am, die-stamped in the shape of a winged cupid's head, flat backing on rev mkd "STERLING," maker's mk for Wm. B. Kerr Co., Newark, NJ, # 94, C-catch, flanged hinge, 2" w x 1", **$350**. (Photo courtesy of Lisa Mercer, Deja Vu Antiques, Portland, OR)

Brooch/Pin, sash ornament/pin, brass, glass, c. 1900-1910, an open rounded navette shape surmounted by die-stamped opposed heads of snarling wolves with green glass eyes, an oval marbled green glass cab bezel-set above and below, flanked by appl scrolled wire, C-catch, flanged hinge, 2¾" w x 2", **$200**. (Courtesy of Martha Exline, Metique, Laguna Hills, CA)

Brooch/Pin, sterling, c. 1900, Am, die-stamped and engr open circ floral/foliate wreath, rev mkd "COPYRIGHTED 1901," maker's mk for Gorham Mfg. Co., "STERLING, B1420," C-catch, tube hinge, 2¼" dia, **$300**. (Author's collection)

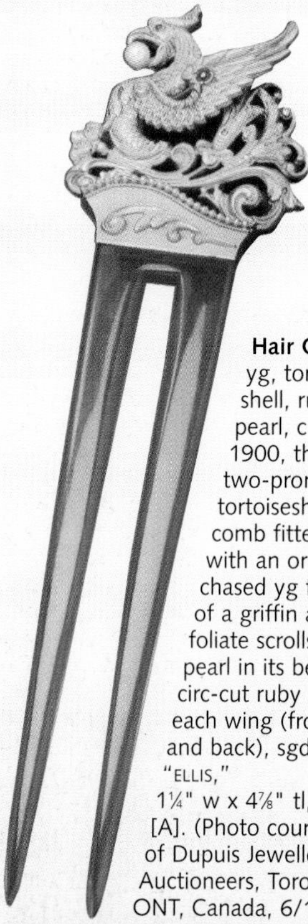

Hair Comb, yg, tortoiseshell, rubies, pearl, c. 1900, the two-pronged tortoiseshell comb fitted with an ornately chased yg figure of a griffin amid foliate scrolls, a pearl in its beak, a circ-cut ruby set in each wing (front and back), sgd "ELLIS," 1¼" w x 4⅞" tl, **$449** [A]. (Photo courtesy of Dupuis Jewellery Auctioneers, Toronto, ONT, Canada, 6/12/01)

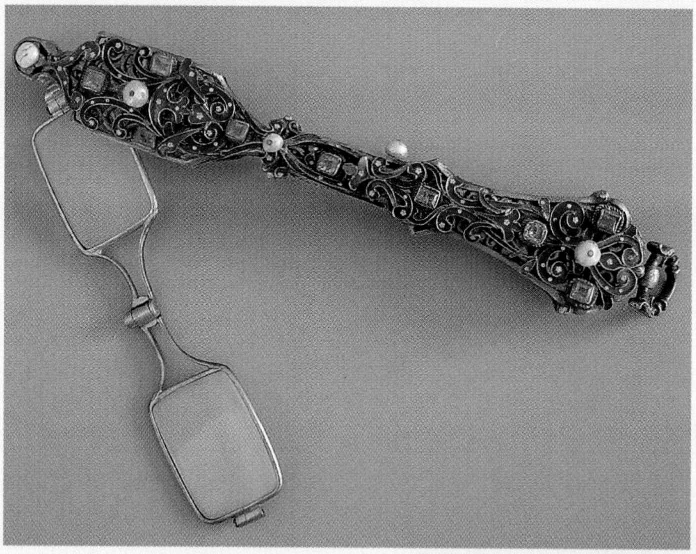

Lorgnette, 800 gp silver, enamel, green beryls, citrines, peridot, pearls, ym, yg, glass, c. 1890-1900, Austrian, an openwork silver gilt frame surmounted by polychrome enameled scrolls decorated with tiny yg flowerheads and dots, studded throughout with bezel-set rect-cut gemstones and peg-mounted pearls, mkd 800 on the hinge with a partially obscured hmk, probably an A for the Vienna Assay Office before 1901, rect folding spectacles, 1¼" x 5½", **$750**. (Photo courtesy of Morning Glory Antiques, Albuquerque, NM)

Cuff Links, sterling vermeil, red stones, c. 1900, Am, oval "dumb bell"-style links depicting a knight's head and scrolled shield within foliate border, set with a circ-cut reddish purple stone, maker's mk for Unger Bros on rev, ½" w x ¾", **$350**. (Courtesy of Andrea Fatell, Wellsley, MA)

Lavalier, coral, 14k yg, seed pearls, c. 1900-1910, Am, a circ coral cab bezel-set in the center of a yg foliate wreath frame, surmounted by a pearl, a grad line of pearls below, suspending a coral drop, rev mkd "14 B" in an oval for the Brassler Co., Newark, NJ, ¾" w x 1¾" tl, **$800.** (Courtesy of Generations, La Verne, CA)

Locket, 14k yg, c. 1900, Am, circ, with a die-stamped griffin or chimera on the front surmounted by a pendant bail, engr mono on rev, maker's mk for Whiteside & Blank, Newark, NJ on inside rim, 1" dia, **$300**. (Author's collection)

Necklace, sp brass, brass, red, blue glass cabochons, c. 1915, inverted triangular links of openwork foliate scrolls, centers set with a blue glass cab surmounted by a flowerhead, alternating with female heads above a red glass cab, joined with brass jump rings terminating in a hook clasp, ¾" w x 16" tl, **$100**. (Vickie Vega collection)

Necklace/Pendant, silver gilt, pink sapphires, rubies, green beryls, pearls, enamel, c. 1900, Hungarian, in the "neo-Renaissance" style, necklace of openwork scrolled links set with pink sapphires, rubies, and pearls, suspending a triangular surmount set with pink sapphires, green beryls and pearls, and a circ openwork pendant with a central mermaid motif and green-enameled foliage, bezel-set with rect and sq-cut beryls, circ-cut pink sapphires, and pearls, terminating in a rect-cut green beryl and pearl drop, Hungarian maker's mk and hmks (dog's head) on v-spring clasp, pendant 1¾" x 2⅝", 20" tl, **$1,200**. (Private collection)

Pendant, silver gilt, enamel, pink tourmaline, colored stones, fw pearl, c. 1900, Hungarian, in the "neo-Renaissance" style, enameled swan motif with f.w. pearl wing in the center of an openwork silver gilt mount bezel-set with a lg oval pink tourmaline cab and circ-cut and rect pink, blue and green stones, suspending a bezel-set oval pink tourmaline cab drop, 1" w x 2⅝" tl, **$600**. (Courtesy of Generations, La Verne, CA)

Pendant, silver gilt, enamel, seed pearls, rubies, sapphires, c. 1900, Austro-Hungarian, three-dimensional swan motif in the "neo-Renaissance" style, enameled on both sides, set with a row of sm sapphires on the wing, mounted within a chain of bezel-set rubies and a pearl drop, suspended from two seed pearl and silver chains joined to a silver bail, 1⅛" w x 2½" tl, **$500**. (Private collection)

Necklace, dog collar, sterling, garnets, c. 1900, links of slightly convex circ medallions, each with die-stamped S-scrolls, raised beads and radiating teardrop shapes encircling a millegrained bezel-set circ-cut garnet, alternating with scrolled vertical bars, oxidized recesses, flat backing, v-spring clasp mkd "J E CALDWELL & CO." (retailer), maker's mk for Gorham Mfg. Co, "STERLING," # 9675, 1¼" w x 13" tl, **$1,800**. (Janet Zapata collection)

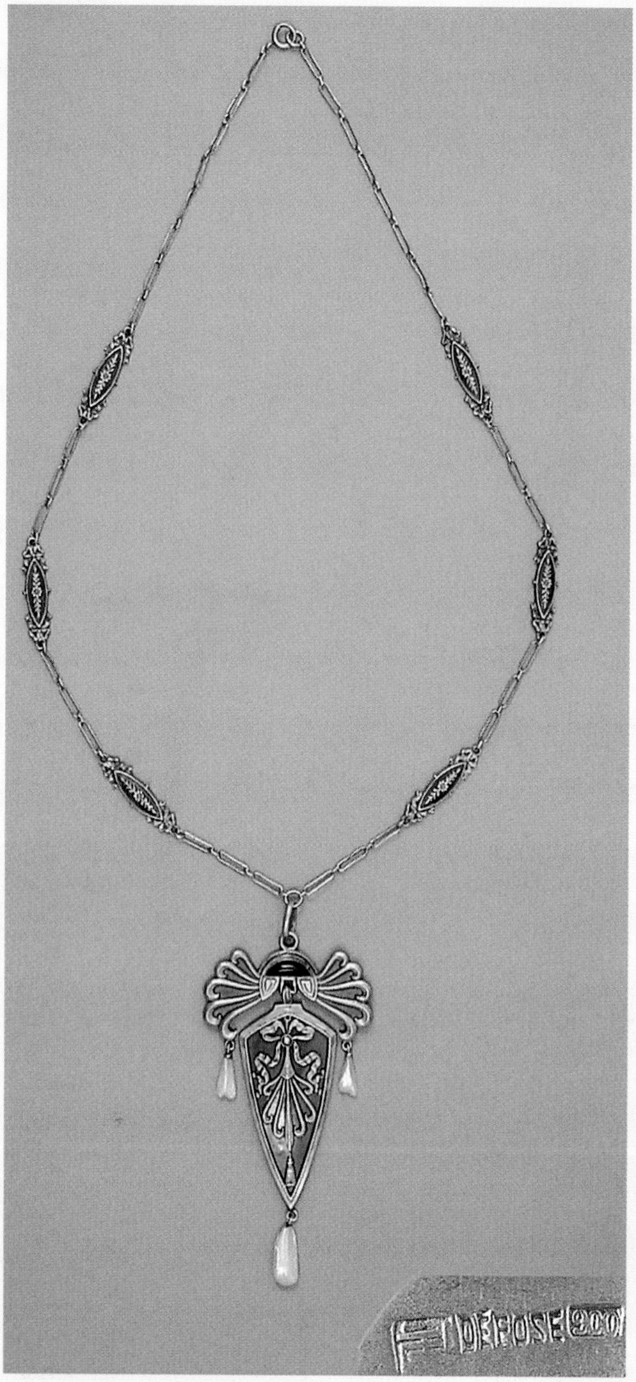

Pendant and Chain, 900 silver, enamel, f.w. pearls, bloodstone, c. 1900, Ger, an undulating ribbon bow set with a seed pearl, and tasseled scrolls surmounting a transparent green-enameled shield-shaped plaque suspended from a scrolled enameled surmount with a hemispherical bloodstone in the center, three f.w. pearl drops, linked to a fetter link chain interspersed with green-enameled navette-shaped plaques with floral/foliate decoration, spring ring clasp, pendant rev mkd "DÉPOSÉ 900," maker's mk for Heinrich Levinger, Pforzheim Ger, pendant 1½" x 3¾" tl, chain 19¾" tl, **$1,800**. (Courtesy of Xcentricities, Beverly Hills, CA)

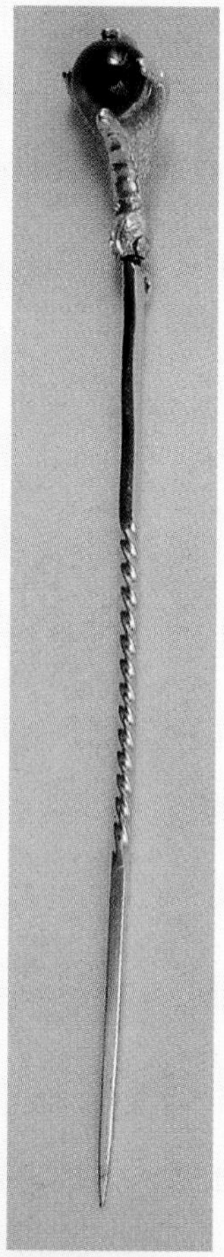

Scarf Pin/Stickpin, 14k yg, cabochon garnet, c. 1890, the head in the shape of a claw grasping a circ garnet cab, loop for safety chain on pinstem, ⅜" w x ⅝", 4" tl, **$175**. (Lisa Johnson collection)

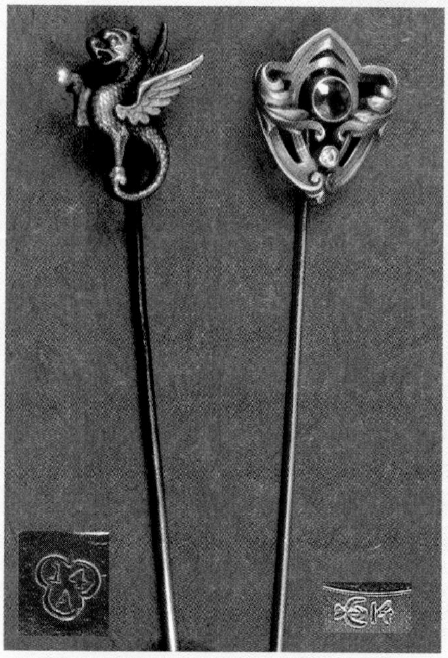

Scarf Pins/Stickpins, 14k yg, c. 1900-10, Am:
L, the head in the shape of a griffin in engr yg, a seed pearl set in upraised paw, maker's mk for Alling & Co, Newark, NJ on rev, ½" w x 2⅜" tl, **$225**.
R, an openwork shield shape with foliate scrolls on each side flanking a bezel-set syn ruby and a sm diamond, maker's mk for Whiteside & Blank, Newark, NJ on rev, ⅝" w, 2⅝" tl, **$200**.
(Bob and Diane Kusek collection)

Pendant and Chain, 14k yg, coral, diamond, c. 1910, sculpted and engr yg wings, the tips suspended from fetter and curb link chains, the center set with an om diamond in a pronged flowerhead mount, suspending three amphora-shaped coral drops, spring ring clasp, ⅞" w x 1¾", 15½" tl, **$475**. (Courtesy of Xcentricities, Beverly Hills, CA)

EDWARDIAN c.1890-1920

Historically, the Edwardian period lasted for only the nine years that King Edward VII was on the throne, 1901-1910. The *style* most often referred to as Edwardian, however, began to evolve more than 10 years earlier and continued to be seen for more than 10 years after Edward's death. By the time Edward and Alexandra became king and queen, they were past middle age, and the style they influenced was firmly entrenched.

The period was a time of social reform, but it also saw the rise of an incredibly wealthy upper class, even within the so-called "classless" democracy of the United States. Unlike Victoria, who was the people's queen, Edward and Alexandra set the tone for an international high society separated from the lower classes by a social whirl of balls, sporting events, yachting, and all the other accouterments of the well-to-do. Elegance and delicacy were the watchwords of the day. Jewels, of course, were an important part of the trappings.

Edwardian jewelry contrasts markedly with other concurrent styles. While Arts and Crafts and Art Nouveau were part of the aesthetic avant-garde, Edwardian jewelry clung to tradition. The former attracted the intellectual elite; the latter, the social elite. Arts and Crafts and Nouveau emphasized design and workmanship over intrinsically valuable materials. Edwardian emphasized diamonds, pearls, and platinum, in skillfully worked designs. Arts and Crafts and Art Nouveau jewelers used enamels and gemstones in a palette of colors. Edwardian jewels were monochromatic, mostly white or colorless.

Arts and Crafts was inspired by the medieval and Renaissance periods; Edwardian looked back to the Neoclassical and Rococo of the eighteenth century and the French courts of Louis XV and particularly, Louis XVI. Not so much the jewelry of that time, but rather the ornamental motifs found on furniture, architecture, and decorative objects: bows, tassels, lace, and the foliate wreaths and swags that gave the style a name: "the garland style."

One of the most distinctive aspects of Edwardian jewels is their lacy, delicate appearance, made possible by the use of platinum, an extremely strong and ductile metal. Although platinum had been used earlier (contrary to popular belief, decorative and utilitarian platinum objects were being made as early as the late eighteenth century), demand for it—and consequently its value—was not as high, nor was it worked in the same way as it was at the turn of the century.

For a while, jewelers continued to treat platinum as they had silver, laminating it to gold. This was unnecessary, because platinum does not tarnish, and is strong enough to be used alone. The speculation is that jewelers were striving to maintain the tradition of 19th century diamond jewels set in silver-topped gold. Later, in the teens and 20s, when platinum's value exceeded that of gold, platinum was once again layered with yellow gold in the manufacture of less expensive jewelry items, such as stamped filigree bar pins and flexible bracelets.

Platinum was not considered a precious metal until its advantageous qualities for setting diamonds were more widely recognized. Platinum wasn't *officially* recognized by the French government as a precious metal until 1910—years after platinum had become the metal of choice for setting diamonds. The French hallmark for platinum, a dog's head, wasn't introduced until 1912 (see appendix, Marks on Metals).

The Edwardian look is characterized by "knife-edge" platinum wires joining millegrained collet-set diamonds in openwork designs, and saw-pierced platinum plaques set throughout with diamonds. The colorless all-diamond and pearl-and-diamond jewels complemented the all-white and pale pastel feminine fashions of the period, which were made of lightweight fabrics and lace (see pendant/necklace this page).

While we are accustomed to referring to this style as Edwardian, as noted by Penny Proddow and Marion Fasel in their book, *Diamonds, a Century of Spectacular Jewels* (see References appendix), "Edwardian" is not an entirely accurate appellation. For one thing, the style has French derivations, and the French would *never* name a style after an English king! And while it's true that King Edward VII was a well-known patron of the delineator of the style, Cartier, whom he dubbed "the king of jewelers and the jeweler of kings," he himself would not have called the style Edwardian. As Proddow and Fasel note, other names, while French, are also found lacking: *belle époque* (beautiful era) covers a much longer period, and includes Art Nouveau. *Fin de siècle*, turn of the century, must also include other styles. "The garland style," *style guirlande* in

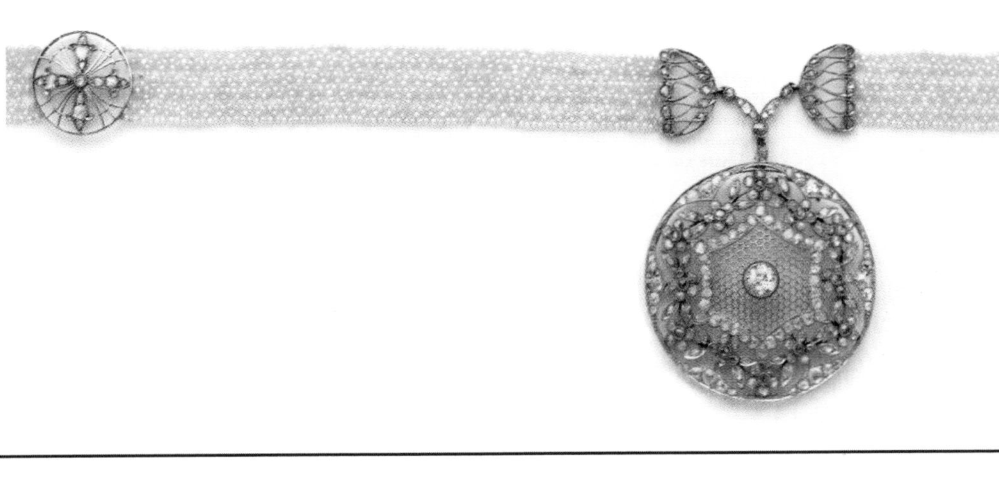

Pendant/Necklace, platinum, diamonds, seed pearls, gold, c. 1910, circ pendant centering a collet-set oe diamond, approx 0.75 ct, in a honeycomb filigree plat ground framed by rc diamonds in floral motif settings, suspended from a woven seed pearl ribbon necklace with circ diamond and platinum filigree spacers, connectors and clasp with yg v-spring, pendant 1¾" dia, 24" tl, **$4,406** [A]. (Photo courtesy of Butterfields, San Francisco and Los Angeles, CA, 12/11/01)

French, is perhaps the most appropriate or evocative name, but there is certainly no consensus on its use.

We usually think of what to call a style after some distancing of elapsed time has occurred. It should come as no surprise then, according to Judy Rudoe in the exhibition catalog, *Cartier 1900-1939*, that it was Hans Nadelhoffer, author in 1984 of the comprehensive book, *Cartier, Jewelers Extraordinary*, who first christened diamond and platinum Louis XVI-inspired jewelry "the garland style." Cartier was at the forefront in developing the style, introducing it in 1899. But it was not alone.

The style's emphasis on diamonds coincided with improvements in diamond-cutting technology, which gave rise to new cuts, such as the marquise or navette, the emerald cut, and the baguette. The term "calibré cut" was used to refer to any stone cut to a special shape to fit a setting. The briolette cut, a three-dimensional teardrop shape, was often used for stones meant to be suspended, e.g., in earrings or lavaliers. All of these cuts were also used for other transparent gemstones. Colored stones were often combined with diamonds and pearls in Edwardian jewelry, particularly amethysts, peridot (Alexandra's and Edward's favorites, respectively), blue sapphires, demantoid (green) garnets, alexandrites, rubies, opals, and turquoise (see brooch on page 122, and brooch/pendants also on page 122).

The motifs of the garland style combined floral and foliate swags with bows, tassels, and lace motifs to produce the jewelry forms of the day: dog collars, fringe and festoon necklaces, brooches, corsage ornaments and larger bodice ornaments (also called "stomachers," as they were in the 18th century), tiaras, lavaliers, pendants, and earrings.

The *négligée* pendant and the *sautoir* were uniquely Edwardian jewels of the period. A variation on the lavalier, the defining feature of the *négligée* is a pair of pendent drops suspended from unequal lengths of fine chain, usually joined to a small gem-set plaque. The drops are often pear-shaped pearls or gemstones. The *sautoir* is a long necklace terminating in a tassel or pendant. The necklace can be a rope or woven band of seed pearls, or a platinum chain interspersed with diamonds; the tassels are usually of pearls with diamond-set caps, the pendants pierced diamond-set plaques (see below and page 119).

Brooch/Pin, sapphire, moonstones, platinum, gold, c. 1910-15, the center a lg cushion-cut sapphire within a scrolling frame of calibré-cut moonstones, outlined in a slightly grad row of circ-cut sapphires, suspending three moonstone drops with platinum filigree caps and detail, mounted in platinum and gold, designed by Louis Comfort Tiffany, sgd "TIFFANY & CO.," in original Tiffany & Co. fitted case, 1½" w x 2¼", **$52,875** [A]. (Copyright Christie's Images, New York 2002©, Christie's New York, NY, 10/22/01)

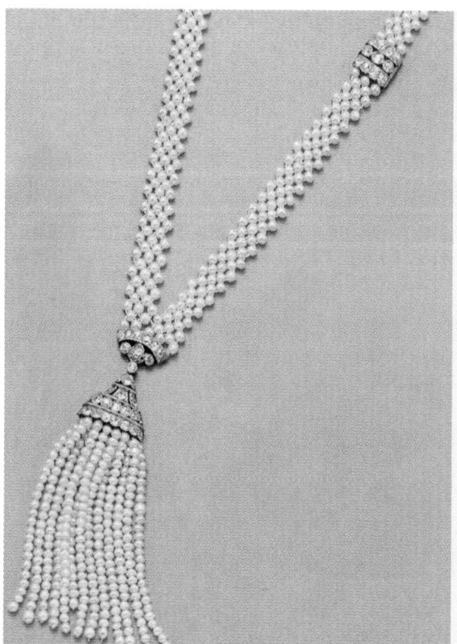

Necklace, sautoir, seed pearls, diamonds, platinum, c. 1915, a woven ribbon of seed pearls interspersed with scallop-edge bands of circ-cut and sc diamonds in millegrain settings, terminating in a seed pearl tassel with a circ-cut, sc and rc diamond-set cap, approx 30" tl, tassel 2¾" tl, **$5,414** [A]. (Photo courtesy of Sotheby's London, 11/27/01)

The probable originator of the garland style was Louis Cartier (1875-1942), who designed for an international clientele of the rich, royal, and famous. American bankers and industrialists, as well as French aristocrats and English nobility, commissioned jewels from Cartier's *atelier* in Paris. The firm was so successful with its new line of garland-style diamond and platinum jewelry, that it soon expanded, opening branches in London in 1902 and New York in 1909.

Other famous French houses working in the same mode were Lacloche Frères, Boucheron, Chaumet, and Mellerio. Georges Fouquet and Lucien Gautrait, also known for their Art Nouveau designs, made garland-style jewels as well.

Peter Carl Fabergé (1846-1920), the celebrated jeweler of the Russian Imperial court, was noted for his objects of vertu. Most of his jewels could be classified as Edwardian, but others have definite Art Nouveau lines and motifs. He was a master of enameling and a technical perfectionist, capable of great versatility. His clientele, however, tended toward the traditional in jewelry, and his jewels reflect a certain restraint. Because the Fabergé name on a piece brings high prices, there are many fakes and forgeries to beware of.

Although the style was predominantly white, pastel colors were also in fashion. Enameling played an important part in lending color to Edwardian jewels. Fabergé was the firm with which this type of enameling was most closely associated, called *guilloché* enamel, which was a transparent colored enamel over a machine-engraved repeating pattern. Cartier was also a proponent of enameling in the Russian taste—which was still very much in keeping with Louis XVI themes.

In the United States, by the first decade of this century, Tiffany & Co., Marcus & Co., Black, Starr & Frost, Udall & Ballou, and Dreicer & Co. all had retail establishments on Fifth Avenue in New York, where their garland-style jewels found favor with the wealthy denizens of that prestigious neighborhood (see brooch above by Louis Comfort Tiffany).

For those unable to afford the opulence of Cartier et al, more modest adornments were available. Even if she owned no other piece of fine jewelry, a woman might have a diamond and platinum or white gold ring in the elongated oblong or navette shape and pierced scrollwork of the Edwardian style (some of these date to the 1920s and early 1930s, see page 136). Bar brooches were very much in vogue; stars and crescents, sporting, and novelty jewelry continued to be popular, particularly reverse-carved and painted rock crystal intalgios (see pages 122 and 123), as were slim bangles, narrow flexible and link bracelets with pierced or filigree plaques; inexpensive gold lavaliers were prevalent. Most of these pieces were set with small diamonds and seed pearls. Moonstones, opals, peridots, demantoid garnets, pink tourmalines, and amethysts were also used. Synthetic rubies were introduced in 1902, and synthetic sapphires made their appearance after 1911. White gold came into common usage during World War I when platinum was appropriated for the war effort and banned for use in jewelry, and necessity prompted a search for a workable substitute. Karl Gustav Richter was granted a patent for his ternary (three-part) formula for white gold in 1915. The Belais Brothers of New York came out with their formula for white gold in 1917, dubbed "18k Belais.," which can sometimes be found marked on white gold jewelry of the late teens and 1920s (see ring, page 136, top center).

Less expensive still was "imitation" (the word "costume" had yet to be coined) jewelry in colorless rhinestones ("paste"), glass and silver made in exactly the same styles as "real" jewelry. It has been overlooked by many of today's costume jewelry collectors because of its small size and delicacy. Non-precious jewelry in the Edwardian or garland style has not survived in quantity. Whether little was made to begin with, or it was discarded, is unclear.

The latter part of the period, c. 1910-20, interrupted by war, saw both gradual and abrupt stylistic changes. It has been called a transitional period, from Edwardian to Art Deco, in both fine and costume jewelry. The transitional style continued through the 1920s, becoming more geometric, but retaining the open, lacy filigree and white or pale palette of high Edwardian, moving toward Art Deco's stronger contrasts in black and white, and red and white (see brooch/pendant page 122).

Aiding this change was what is considered a landmark event: the presentation in Paris of the Ballets Russes *Schéhérazade* in 1910. The ballet's Oriental-inspired costumes by Léon Bakst, stage design, and vibrant colors influenced trendsetters such as Paul Poiret, the progressive couturier, whose designs changed the fashion silhouette from curvilinear to vertical. Tassels and turbans were favorite Poiret accessories, and tasseled pendants and long pendent earrings were complementary jewelry forms. The sautoir evolved into long diamond-set geometric chain links and pendants, eventually reaching the masses as tasseled "flapper beads" in faceted glass.

At the same time that Paris was being swept away by the Ballets Russes, women in England and the United States were battling it out on the political front for women's suffrage. The suffragists had a secret color code which they translated into jewelry: green, white, and violet, which stood for "give women the vote." Green peridots, white pearls, and violet amethysts were all popular period gemstones. Many Edwardian and Art Nouveau-style jewels were made with these stones.

In the U.S., gold was sometimes used for the "g" instead of a green stone. Enamel was also used (see pendant on page 114).

Even today, it is difficult to say if a particular brooch or lavalier was meant for wear as a suffragist "badge," or is just a typical period piece.

Reproduction Alert

The open, lacy look of Edwardian jewels has been reproduced in recent renditions of the style in diamonds and white gold, which tend to be heavier and not as finely articulated as diamond and platinum pieces of the period. While the cut of the diamonds might be antique, the use of white gold is the tip-off that the piece is new.

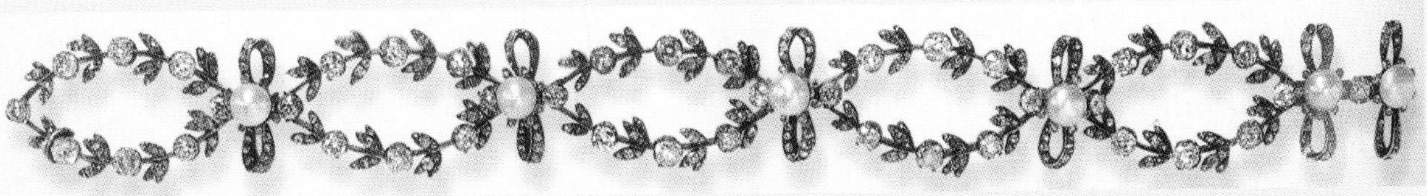

Bracelet, link, diamonds, pearls, st yg, c. 1895, Fr, five open navette-shaped links, each a laurel-leaf garland set throughout with om and rc diamonds, joined by rc diamond-set bows with pearl centers, Fr assay mks, maker's mk for Chaumet et Cie ("JC" with crescent above, five-pointed star below, in a vertically oriented lozenge), ⅝" w x 6¾" tl, **$23,500** [A]. (Copyright Christie's Images, New York 2002©, Christie's New York, NY, 10/22/01)

Bracelet, link, sapphires, diamonds, platinum, 18k yg, seed pearls, c. 1895-1900, Fr, navette-shaped links, seed pearl centers, set throughout with rc and table-cut diamonds in pierced plat, framed in yg, linked by collet-set circ-cut sapphires, Fr hmks and maker's mk on clasp, ⅜" w x 6¾" tl, **$1,998** [A]. (Photo courtesy of Butterfields, San Francisco and Los Angeles, CA, 6/19/01)

Bracelet, flexible, pearls, diamonds, platinum, c. 1900-10, openwork mesh panels of seed pearls and platinum wire with three openwork scrolled plat bar spacers, cusped quatrefoil centers set with oe diamonds and button pearls, terminating in an openwork ornamental clasp of similar design, 1¼" x 6¾" tl, **$3,525** [A]. (Photo courtesy of Skinner, Inc., Boston, MA, 3/17/02)

Brooch/Pin, sapphire, diamonds, platinum, yg, c. 1900, a cushion-shaped sapphire, approx 3.00 cts, encircled by oe diamonds, approx 6.00 cts tw, set within a pierced lacy foliate scallop-edged circ plaque set throughout with sm rc diamonds, mounted in plat-topped yg, with detachable pin assembly, 2⅞" dia, **$12,708** [A]. (Photo courtesy of Dupuis Jewellery Auctioneers, Toronto, ONT, Canada, 6/12/01)

Brooch/Pendant, calibré-cut rubies, rc diamonds, seed pearls, platinum-topped 18k yg, c. 1915-20, open circ form with a central lotus blossom and C-scroll motif set with two circ-cut, four triangular, and 17 calibré-cut rubies, 51 rc diamonds, surmounted by five seed pearls, suspending a pearl drop, set in plat-topped yg, 1" w x 1⅝" tl, **$1,150** [A]. (Photo courtesy of Beverly Hills Auctioneers, Beverly Hills, CA, 4/1/01)

Brooch/Pin, watch pin, 14k yg, pink sapphires, seed pearls, rc diamonds, c. 1900, crown motif set with three oval pink sapphires, 1.25 cts tw, five om diamonds approx. .20 ct, and 29 seed pearls, tubular C-catch, upturned hook on rev, 1¼" w x ⅞", **$1,400**. (Courtesy of Ocean Eyz Antique Jewelry, Orange, CA)

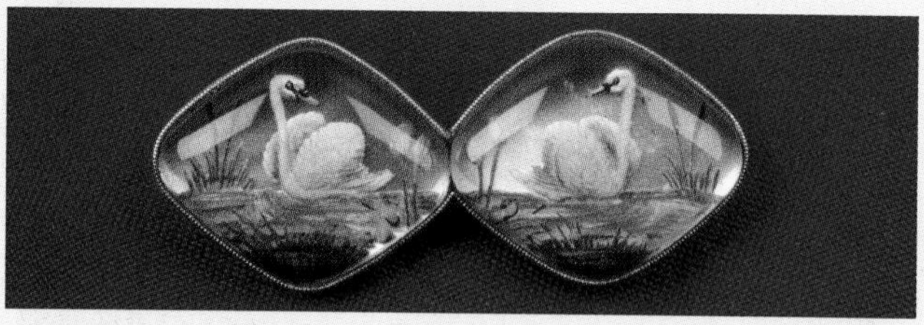

Brooch/Pin, reverse-painted crystal intaglio, platinum, c. 1900-1910, Am, two conjoined lozenge-shaped intaglios forming a bow shape with two images of swans in a lake with cattails and foliage, pierced cattail motif on rev, plat mount sgd "MARCUS & CO," New York, NY, 1⅝" w x ⅝", **$3,408** [A]. (Photo courtesy of Skinner, Inc., Boston, MA, 12/11/01)

Brooch/Pin, reverse-painted rock crystal intaglio, MOP, sc diamonds, platinum-topped yg, c. 1900-1910, depicting a shore bird on MOP background, within a scrolled diamond-set millegrained and pierced plat-topped yg frame, 1⅜" w x 1¼", **$2,585** [A]. (Photo courtesy of Skinner, Inc., Boston, MA, 12/11/01)

Brooch/Pin, bar, moonstone, om diamonds, 18k yg, c. 1900, a circ moonstone carved with the head of a classical warrior, encircled by six yg prong-set om diamonds, and flanked by 12 om diamonds on a yg bar, sgd "C. & CO." #7653, 1⅝" w x ⅝", **$2,070** [A]. (Photo courtesy of Skinner, Inc., Boston, MA, 9/25/01)

Brooch/Pin, bar, reverse-painted crystal intaglio, 22k yg, diamonds, MOP, c. 1900-1910, depicting the head of a dog, MOP backing, bezel-set, surmounting a narrow yg bar flanked by clusters of three circ-cut diamonds in millegrained bezels, tapered ends, lever catch, 1⅞" w x ⅝" T to B at center, **$900**. (Courtesy of Chris Enebo Antique Jewelry, Tualatin, OR)

Brooch/Pendant, peridot, rc, sc diamonds, st yg, c. 1905, Eng, the ribbon bow surmount set with rc diamonds suspending a garland decorated with rc and sc diamonds, set at the center with an oval peridot terminating in a pear-shaped peridot drop, on a later chain, detachable brooch fitting, fitted case by W. Battersby, 80 Newgate St, E.C., 1" w x 2¼" tl, **$2,352** [A]. (Photo courtesy of Sotheby's, London, 6/20/01)

Brooch/Pin, diamonds, platinum, yg, c. 1915, an openwork crescent of circ-cut diamonds, the largest stone at the center, bordered by sc, rc and circ-cut diamonds and terminating in an articulated icicle-like fringe of diamonds, one diamond deficient, 2¼" w x 1¾" T to B at center, **$11,760** [A]. (Photo courtesy of Sotheby's, London, 6/20/01)

Cuff Links, reverse-carved crystal, 14k yg, c. 1900, circ rev-carved and ptd quartz crystal links depicting a West Highland terrier, opposing gold disk link and bar link intersection, mounted in 14k yg, ⅝" dia, **$529** [A]. (Copyright Christie's Images, New York 2002©, Christie's Los Angeles, CA, 10/4/01)

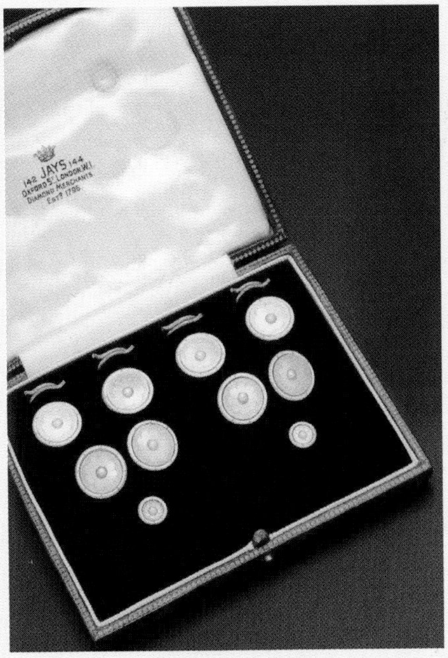

Dress Set, MOP, 9k yg, enamel, c. 1905, Eng, an engr MOP flower motif with raised center within a circ frame of white enameled yg, including four buttons, a pair of cufflinks and two shirt studs, in a fitted box stamped "JAYS DIAMOND MERCHANTS, 142-144 OXFORD ST., LONDON W1," buttons and links ½" dia, studs ⅜" dia, **$897** [A]. (Photo courtesy of Dupuis Jewellery Auctioneers, Toronto, ONT, Canada, 6/12/01)

Brooch/Pin, 9k yg, c. 1910, Eng, two swallows in flight, rev imp with Brit hmks (illegible) 9 375, with attached safety pin, 2" w x ¾", **$125**. (Vickie Vega collection)

Lavalier, diamonds, platinum, c. 1910, teardrop-shaped with scalloped edges, oe and rc diamonds set throughout in a pierced and millegrained plat mount, suspending an oe-diamond drop, detachable diamond-set bail, ⅝"w x 1⅞" tl, **$2,860**. (Photo courtesy of Karen Lorene, Facèré Jewelry Art, Seattle, WA)

Brooches/Pins, 9k yg, seed pearls, date letters for 1908-9, 1909-10, Eng, a pr of yg crescents, each with a slightly different floral/foliate motif set with seed pearls, maker's mk "T & G," Chester (Eng) hmks, 9 .375, each with a date letter for consecutive year on rev, C-catches, tube hinges, approx 1" dia, **$150/pr**. (Author's collection)

Earrings, drop, rc diamonds, plat-topped 18k yg, c. 1900, each with a prong-set rc diamond center encircled by smaller rc diamonds, suspended from a surmount set with two rc diamonds on a knife-edge wire, hinged post (Fr) backs with Fr import mks (owl and head of a bearded man), Fr import mks on loop surmounting drop, drops ⅜" dia, ⅞" tl, **$2,200**. (Lisa Johnson collection)

Earrings, pendent, jadeite, diamonds, platinum, c. 1915, each a green jadeite drop in a coiled rc and oe diamond-set snake surround, with a scalloped diamond-set cap, suspended from a line of three collet-set diamonds, # 316, in a fitted leather case, ⅜" w x 1½" tl, **$11,750** [A]. (Copyright Christie's Images, New York 2002©, Christie's New York, NY, 10/22/01)

Lorgnette, diamonds, platinum, seed pearls, c. 1900-1910, the openwork handle surmounted by two opposed bird motifs with ruby eyes, set throughout with oe and sc diamonds, a pearl above and below, opening to reveal a pair of oval-shaped spectacles with a diamond-set plat bridge, diamonds approx 3.00 cts tw, suspended from a platinum and seed pearl chain, 1⅜" w x 5¼", chain 18", **$7,050** [A]. (Photo courtesy of Butterfields, San Francisco and Los Angeles, CA, 9/25/01)

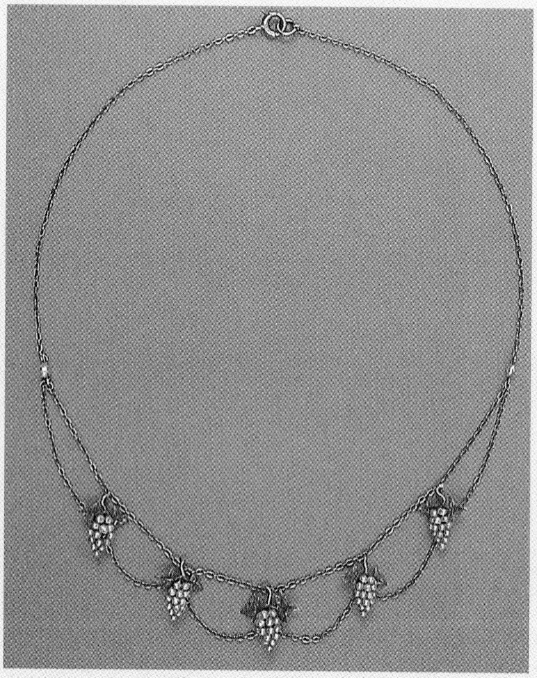

Necklace, festoon, yg, seed pearls, c. 1895-1900, fine yg chains suspending clusters of seed pearl grapes flanked by engr yg leaves, 15¼" tl, ⅝" T to B at center, **$300**. (Vickie Vega collection)

Necklace, festoon, synthetic rubies, low kt yg, c. 1905-1910, nine circ-cut prong-set flame-fusion syn rubies suspending 10 pear-shaped syn rubies from swagged yg chains, hook and eye clasp, 17" tl, 3½" at center, **$500**. (Courtesy of Generations, La Verne CA)

Necklace, fringe, citrines, 14k yg, seed pearls, c. 1900-1910, a grad line of 11 spectacle-set circ-cut citrines, the center stone suspending another circ-cut and a pear-shaped citrine alternating with seed pearls, flanked by three pearl and pear-shaped citrine drops on each side, joined to a fine yg cable link chain, tube clasp, 15" tl, 1¾" T to B at center, **$650**. (Private collection)

Necklace, festoon, pearls, platinum, wg, c. 1910-15, a plat filigree fleur-de-lis at center set throughout with white pearls (not tested for origin), eight drop-shaped natural pearls suspended from platinum chain swags continuing to a plat chain and wg clasp set with white bead (possibly of later date), 16" tl, 2⅛" T to B at center, **$2,938** [A]. (Photo courtesy of Butterfields, San Francisco and Los Angeles, CA, 9/25/01)

Pendant/Brooch, diamonds, turq, st yg, c. 1900, Fr, in the garland style, of delicate ribbon and swag design, set throughout with rc and om diamonds, suspending a pear-shaped diamond and turquoise drop, one small drop deficient, detachable brooch fitting with screwdriver, attributed to Chaumet, case by J. Chaumet, New Bond Street 154, London, Place Vendome 12, Paris, 2¾" w x 3½", **$14,784** [A]. (Photo courtesy of Sotheby's, London, 6/20/01)

Pendant and Chain, aquamarines, yg, rc diamonds, seed pearls, st yg, platinum, c. 1900, a pear-shaped aquamarine set in a millegrained yg bezel within a trefoil-shaped network of yg wires bordered by rc diamonds in st yg, suspending a sm oval and pear-shaped aquamarine drop, surmounted by a foliate branch of yg wires tipped with seed pearls and rc diamonds flanking a sm aquamarine, connected with three short plat and yg chains and pearls to an oval-cut aquamarine in millegrained yg bezel, continuing to a platinum and yg fetter and trace link chain, spring ring clasp, pendant 1¼" x 2¼", 15½" tl, **$1,500**. (Private collection)

Suite: Festoon Necklace and Earrings, pink tourmalines, 14k yg, c. 1910, seven bezel-set oval tourmaline cabochons linked with yg wire C-scrolls and quatrefoils, each suspending a pear-shaped tourmaline drop on a length of yg chain with swagged chain between, two drops converted to earrings with gf screwbacks, 1¾" T to B at center, 16" tl, **$1,500**. (Courtesy of Ocean Eyz Antique Jewelry, Orange, CA)

Suite: Necklace and Earrings, moonstones, platinum, diamonds, c. 1910, necklace set with graduated oval moonstones joined by baton links, suspending a diamond and moonstone drop supported by a trefoil diamond melee cluster, drop earrings, necklace 15¼" tl, drop 1⅜", earrings 1½" l, **$2,468** [A]. (Photo courtesy of Skinner, Inc., Boston, MA, 12/11/01)

Ring, diamonds, platinum, c. 1910, a collet-set oe diamond, approx 2.70 cts, in the center of an elongated oval pierced plat mount set throughout with oe diamonds, approx 4.30 cts tw, tapering from the diamond-set shoulders to a narrow engr plat shank, ½" w x 1⅛", **$18,775** [A]. (Photo courtesy of Butterfields, San Francisco and Los Angeles, CA, 12/11/01)

Part III
Twentieth Century Jewelry

The twentieth century truly began with World War I, a cataclysmic event that transformed society. Women would never be the same after "the war to end all wars." When the smoke cleared, the Gibson Girl had become Thoroughly Modern Millie. Her fashions, her attitude, her way of life, were marked departures from all that had gone before. The war, and—at last—the right to vote gave American women a stronger voice in the affairs of the country and a greater awareness of the affairs of the world. This worldly sophistication was aided by the advent of radio, the growth of fashion magazines and popular culture periodicals, and perhaps most importantly, the motion picture industry. Changes in fashion occurred at an ever-accelerating pace.

Although Paris continued to be regarded as a fashion Mecca through the mid-century, British and European royalty were no longer as influential as America's Hollywood elite. Movie stars were the new queens. What they wore was closely monitored, reported, and emulated. Purveyors to these new "royals" achieved instant fame and success by association. Names of designers attained new importance and "name-dropping" became a pastime of a new social class.

Indeed, "new" and "novelty" were watchwords of the day. The latest was considered the best. In jewelry, new designs and materials were incorporated into manufacturers' repertoires. Except for a hiatus during World War II, diamonds and platinum still ruled, but the avant-garde opted for chrome, rock crystal, glass, and that most novel of materials, plastic. Costume jewelry was given its stamp of approval by Coco Chanel and other haute couturiers. It was no longer looked down upon as a mere imitation of the real thing, although there were surely many rhinestone and rhodium-plated knockoffs masquerading as diamonds and platinum. Frankly fake jewels, however, were now being worn to complement one's outfit, or costume.

A method for producing dental castings, introduced in 1907, led to a new application of the ancient art of lost-wax casting in the 1930s: the mass-production of both fine and costume jewelry. Multiple copies of one design were made possible with the aid of vulcanized rubber molds, using the vulcanization process invented by Charles Goodyear in 1839, along with the development of an improved casting investment plaster in 1932.

Stylistic trends evolved more rapidly in the twentieth century. Whereas a nineteenth-century style could span several decades, after World War I, each decade was characterized by a different "look." And while the general term "modernism" can be applied to the entire era, we tend to group the changing styles within it by 10-year periods, i.e., the '20s, '30s, '40s, '50s, etc. This is not necessarily an accurate classification, nor are the appellations Art Deco, Streamline Moderne, or Retro Modern, correctly applied to each decade. These are styles, not periods, which, as always, tend to overlap and coexist along with revivals and traditions. It can be said, for example, that Art Deco was a popular style in the '20s, but certainly not the *only* style. Consequently, rather than label each of the following subdivisions of twentieth-century jewelry with a style name, they are divided by period, with a prefacing explanation of the predominant styles in each.

In this section, it is also necessary to introduce a separate classification based on certain materials from which some jewelry was made. "Costume jewelry" is too all-encompassing and unwieldy a term for the several types of non-precious jewelry that proliferated from the '20s onward. Therefore, there is a special category for plastic and novelty jewelry, the whimsical and "fun" costume jewelry that does not fall clearly into any other stylistic category. Costume jewelry that imitates fine jewelry is grouped separately in its respective periods. Because of its growth as a collectible in recent years, the classification of "designer signed" costume jewelry is divided into two sub-sections in this edition, with the chronological dividing line drawn at 1950.

FINE JEWELRY c. 1920-1935

After a period of wartime austerity, the '20s woman burst forth with a frenetic exuberance. She cut off her hair, her sleeves and her hems, bound her chest, and dropped her waistline to become *la garçonne*, the female boy. She celebrated her new post-war prosperity and freedom by piling on the jewels.

Bare arms and waistless dresses changed fashion's focus from the wide waist-cinching belts, sash, and corsage ornaments of the *belle époque* to multiple bracelets, and small plaque brooches or jeweled ornaments worn at the hips and shoulders. There were endless variations of the diamond and platinum bracelet variously referred to as the plaque, flexible link or box, strap, band, or straightline. Some were

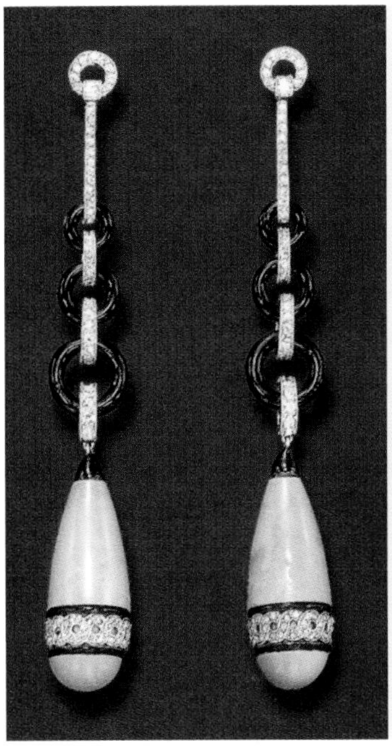

Earrings, pendent, enamel, diamonds, platinum, 18k wg, c. 1925, Fr, aqua enameled drops, each encircled by a double helix band of rc diamonds bordered with black enamel, suspended from a narrow line of om, oe, and sc diamond-set links alternating with grad black enameled annular links, diamond-set geo surmount, some enamel repair, Fr assay mks, maker's mks, #29373, ⅜" w x 3" tl, **$30,550** [A]. (Copyright Christie's Images, New York 2002©, Christie's New York, NY, 10/22/01)

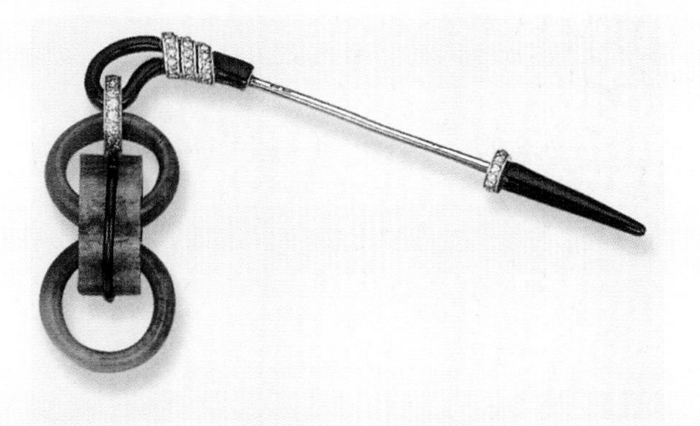

Jabot Pin, jadeite, diamonds, enamel, 18k wg, c. 1930, a black enamel loop surmounted by three bars with rc diamond accents suspending three carved jadeite interlocking rings, pinstem terminating in a black enameled tapered cap with rc diamond-set collar, mounted in 18k wg, Fr assay mks, 2⅞" w x 1⅝", **$7,050** [A]. (Copyright Christie's Images, New York 2002©, Christie's Los Angeles, CA, 10/4/01)

accented with natural or synthetic sapphires or rubies, or emeralds, or a combination of these. Platinum and gemstone link bracelets with charms depicting musicians—a reflection of the Jazz Age—were also popular (see page 130). Short hairstyles gave rise to long pendent drop earrings (see above and page 134). The screwback finding (called the "French back" by some in the trade), was now the norm, as most women no longer pierced their ears. Large hats, hatpins, and tiaras disappeared, to be replaced by bandeaux and cloche hats embellished with small hat ornaments.

The sautoir remained, but in modified "modernized" form, becoming more geometric. It was often made entirely of diamonds and platinum, terminating in a diamond-set drop instead of a tassel, and it was convertible, forming bracelets, choker, and a pendant. Lorgnettes continued to be fashionably suspended from long chains or cords; in the '30s, they adapted for wear as clips. Tasseled ropes of gemstone beads were also worn.

Pearls remained popular, worn as sautoirs or long ropes, or twisted about the wrist. The recently marketed cultured pearl was affordable to the middle classes, although it caused a furor among natural (oriental) pearl merchants. Dog collars narrowed to become short delicate necklaces, often worn in addition to a sautoir. The bar pin and plaque brooch continued to be worn as transitional jewels in addition to two news forms introduced by Cartier: the circle or ring brooch (Cartier called it *broche de ceinture*, "belt brooch," see page 132 for an example by Tiffany & Co.) and jabot pin, or *cliquet* (see above, right). Both could be worn as hat ornaments. Pierced platinum or white gold and diamond rings retained the elongated outline of the past two decades, but became increasingly geometric in design. New ring shapes were hexagonal or octagonal, with colored gemstones and diamonds set in domed or stepped mounts (see page 35).

The excesses of the '20s were sharply curtailed by the 1929 stock market crash and the onset of the Great Depression. But even though it was out of reach for most pocketbooks, and production diminished, precious jewelry continued to be made. The elite of Hollywood and New York could still afford it; women of wealth everywhere continued to wear their status symbols. Indeed, jewelry grew larger and more three-dimensional as fashions became less severe. During the early '30s, the waistline returned, sleeves grew longer and/or fuller, and a woman's curves were emphasized by bias-cut gowns in soft and satiny fabrics.

The dress clip became the most important jeweled accessory of the '30s (see below). Usually worn in pairs at the neckline, they were held in place by means of a flat-backed hinged mechanism that snapped shut over the fabric's edge. The story goes that Louis Cartier came up with the idea for the clip while watching a woman use clothespins to hang laundry out to dry. These versatile ornaments could also be worn on jacket lapels, hats, purses, belts, and, with the attachment of an additional pinback mechanism, a pair could be joined for wear as a brooch (see page 134).

The all-white look of diamonds and platinum that began with the Edwardians at the turn of the century persisted well into the 1930s, with the additional use of colorless rock crystal (see page 135; less expensive stamped filigree pieces were made with white gold). Over the years, geometric forms insinuated upon, then replaced, the garland style. By the early '20s, diamond cutting had advanced to

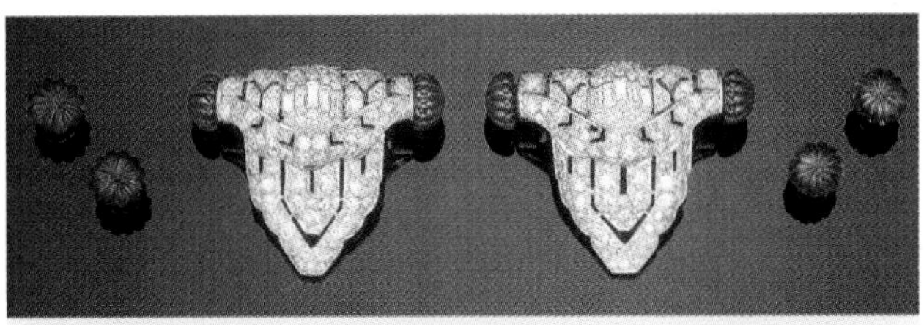

Dress Clips, diamonds, platinum, simulated rubies, sapphires and emeralds, c. 1930, Fr, a pr of geo pierced shield-shaped plaques pavé-set with circ-cut diamonds, with carved melon-cut simulated ruby, sapphire and emerald interchangeable terminals, Fr assay mks, 1⅝" w x 1⅜" each, **$17,625** [A]. (Copyright Christie's Images, New York 2002©, Christie's Los Angeles, CA, 10/4/01)

such a degree that unusual shapes, such as the half-moon, the obus or bullet (a narrow pentagon), the epaulet (a wide pentagon), the trapeze, and the triangle, could be produced for added geometric interest in all-white jewels. At the same time, color was injected into some jewelry designs in the form of rubies, emeralds, sapphires, jade, coral, lapis, onyx, and enamels, as the style which later came to be known as Art Deco exerted its influence.

Art Deco itself was influenced by a number of design sources: Oriental, Persian/Islamic, East Indian, ancient Egyptian and pre-Hispanic Mexican, African, American Indian, and, most directly, by turn-of-the-century Austrian and German Secessionist and *Jugendstil* designs.

While the commonly held view is that the Art Deco style arose as a result of the 1925 Paris exposition from which it derives its name, *L'Exposition Internationale des Arts Décoratifs et Industriels Modernes*, in fact, that date is more correctly a culmination of developments that occurred throughout the previous two decades. It should be noted that the outbreak of war forced the exposition's postponement. It was originally planned for 1916, the idea having been discussed since 1907, according to Sylvie Raulet in her book *Art Deco Jewelry*, listed in the References. So we see the seeds of modernism being planted at the turn of the century, and reaching full flower after World War I. Still, the popularization of the style was not widely felt in the United States until after the exposition—an event in which the U.S. did *not* participate. (Herbert Hoover, Secretary of Commerce at the time, was noted as saying this country did not have any "modern" decorative arts, and thus could not meet the entry requirements of newness and originality.)

The name Art Deco was not applied to what was then called "modernistic" or "moderne" until 1968, when it appeared in the title of a book by Bevis Hillier, *Art Deco of the 20s and 30s*. This probably explains why there are several different interpretations of what the style really is, and why there is debate over the period in which it flourished. For some, it is an all-encompassing label that includes what others separate into Art Deco, Zig-Zag Moderne, Streamline Moderne, and the International Style. Some say the style ended in 1925; others claim it spanned the entire period between the world wars. Mr. Hillier takes the inclusive, evolutionary point of view that although "there was a difference in character between the 'twenties and the 'thirties... Art Deco was a developing style...There was a strong continuity." (from the introduction to *The World of Art Deco*, catalog of an exhibition at the Minneapolis Institute of Arts, 1971).

The credo of the modernists was "form follows function," and all excess ornamentation was to be avoided, on a parallel with the tenets of the Arts and Crafts Movement. Unlike the purists of that movement, however, the modernists espoused and embraced the use of the machine. The style is characterized by the simplification and stylization of motifs from nature, and the introduction of abstract, nonrepresentational, structural, and geometric forms. Futuristic and speed-associated motifs were also part of the repertoire. Suffice it to say that whatever the label, there is general agreement that the design developments of the period between the wars were as much a departure from Victorianism as the chemise was from the hoop skirt.

In jewelry, too, one often hears the term Art Deco applied to everything from slight variations on Edwardian pierced platinum-and-diamond plaque brooches to starkly simple abstract metal and enamel pendants or bangles. The tendency is to call any piece from the '20s or '30s Art Deco—a matter of subjective interpretation. In fact, the evolution of the style in jewelry can be traced through several different lineages, from the traditional French *haute joailliers* to the avant-garde artist-designers, continuing to popular adaptations and modifications by American jewelers inspired by French designs.

Cartier is the most famous of the former for its version of Art Deco, which tended toward the figurative and exotic Eastern-influenced designs (see below). Notable were Cartier's use of carved gemstones in circular "belt brooches," jabot pins (called *cliquet* pins by Cartier), multicolored "fruit salad" arrangements of leaves and berries in flexible band bracelets, flower vase brooches, and double clip brooches (patented by Cartier in 1927). Having celebrated its 150th anniversary in 1997 with a major exhibition in New York and London, and accompanying catalog by Judy Rudoe (see References), the firm was once again in the spotlight, with newly documented pieces and information from the Cartier collection.

Van Cleef and Arpels also contributed a great deal to the genre. They were particularly known for their Egyptian Revival motifs executed in calibré-cut colored gemstones and pavé diamonds on strap bracelets, inspired by the discovery of Tutankhamen's tomb in 1922 (an event that launched a general mania for Egyptian motifs). The firm also excelled at creating convertible diamond and platinum jewels in the prevailing geometric forms, e.g., a sautoir necklace that separated into bracelets and a pendant.

Other famous French houses whose pieces come up for sale at important jewelry auctions include Boucheron, Mauboussin, Chaumet, and Lacloche. Less often seen is the work of the French avant-garde designers: Jean Desprès (1889-1980), Jean Dunand (1877-1942, see necklace on page 142), Georges Fouquet (1862-1957) and son Jean Fouquet (b.1899), Gérard Sandoz (b.1902), and Raymond Templier (1891-1968). When a significant piece by any of

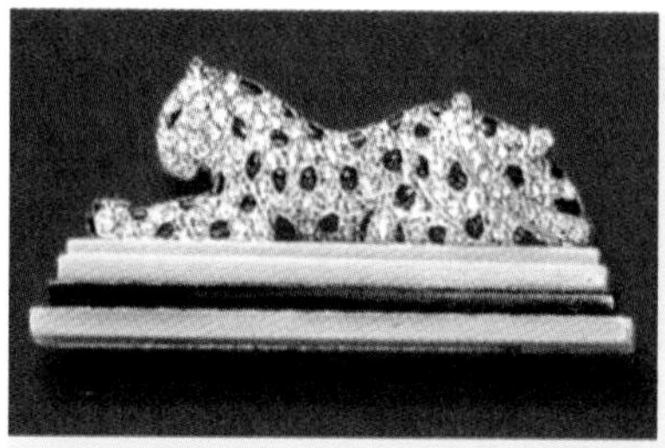

Brooch/Pin, diamonds, onyx, enamel, platinum, c. 1928, Fr, sculpted rc diamond panther with black enameled spots, reclining on an agate and onyx plinth, mounted in plat, Fr assay mks, sgd "*Cartier*, PARIS, MADE IN FRANCE," provenance: designed for Am boxer Gene Tunney by Cartier, made by the Lavabre workshop, 1½" w x ⅝", **$39,950** [A]. (Copyright Christie's Images, New York 2002©, Christie's New York, NY, 10/22/01)

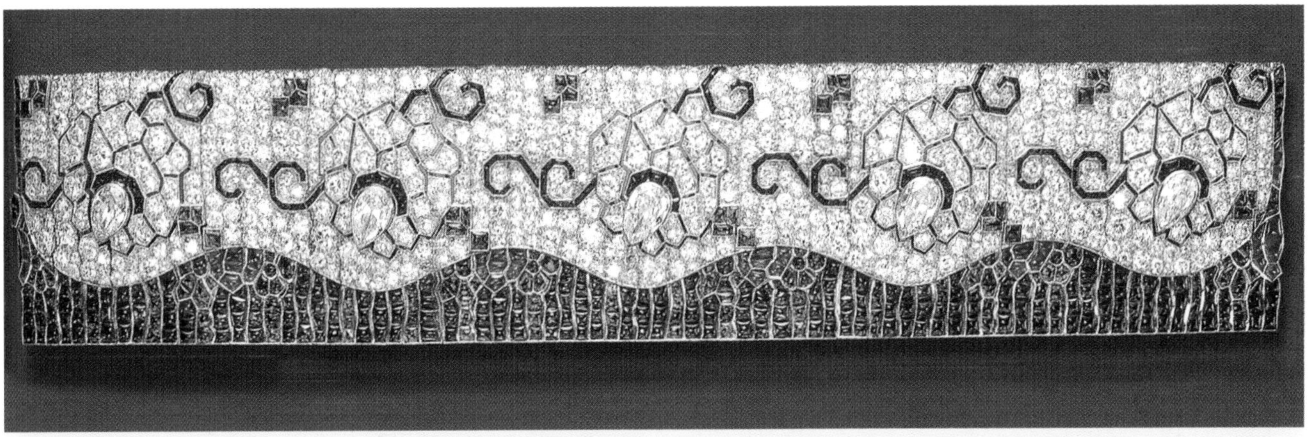

Bracelet, flexible, diamonds, onyx, sapphires, emeralds, rubies, platinum, c. 1925, Fr, a wide flexible band designed as a stylized garden, the undulating pavé-set diamond foreground accented with pierced flowerheads with calibré-cut onyx stems, buff-top calibré-cut emerald foliate motifs on a bg of buff-top calibré-cut emerald, ruby, and sapphire flowers, Fr assay mks, maker's mk for Rubel Frères ("R. FRÈRES," an oak leaf and an acorn cap), 1⅝" w x 7½", **$336,000** [A]. (Copyright Christie's Images, New York 2002©, Christie's New York, NY, 10/22/01)

these houses or designers is offered, it can realize five or six figures.

Several American firms made and sold noteworthy Art Deco jewels inspired by the French, especially after the 1925 exposition: the manufacturing jewelers William Scheer, Inc., and Oscar Heyman & Bros., retailers J.E. Caldwell & Co., Black, Starr & Frost, Tiffany & Co., Marcus & Co., C.D. Peacock, and the New York branches of Cartier and Van Cleef & Arpels. The French manufacturing firm Rubel Frères (see bracelet above), established in the U.S. in 1939 as John Rubel Co., was affiliated with VC & A until 1943.

Raymond C. Yard opened his own salon on Fifth Avenue in New York in 1922. He was known for catering to an elite clientele. In the late '20s and early '30s, he designed a series of whimsical anthropomorphic animals engaged in very human activities. His rabbit figures were especially charming (see page 133).

Many anonymous French and unsigned American-made pieces of the period are sold at auction. Price is often determined by the number, size, quantity, and quality of the gemstones used, as much as, if not more, than the design, which can be repetitious and unoriginal. Less-than-important commercial pieces signed by the famous houses are also auctioned regularly. Their names are often cause for an escalation in price, but astute buyers *always* evaluate a piece on its own merits before taking its marks into consideration.

Reproduction Alert

The Deco revival that began in the early 1980s has generated a plethora of knockoffs, and "Deco style" pieces that never existed during the 1920s and 1930s. Many of these come from Thailand and Hong Kong, where the workmanship is rarely as good as the originals, but European and American manufacturers are producing quality reproductions, some of which defy detection. Among them: Branca de Brito of Portugal, Hermes of Munich, Germany, and Authentic jewelry in New York City. A quantity of this jewelry is now coming onto the secondary market. Ask questions, read auction catalog warranties, conditions, and descriptions carefully—if a piece is described as "Art Deco *style*," it is not of the period—and examine pieces thoroughly. Be aware that descriptions are the *opinions* of the auction houses.

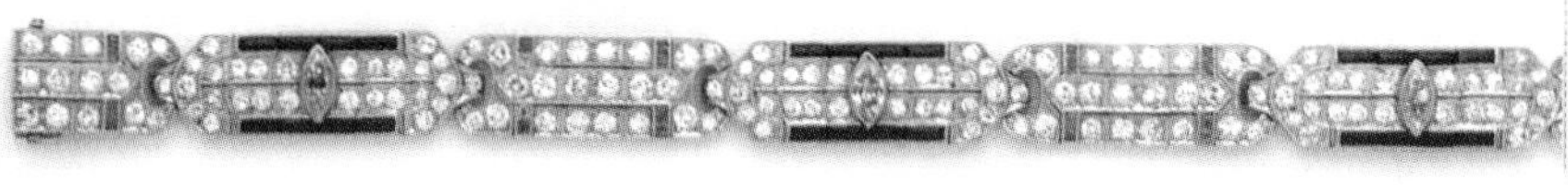

Bracelet, link, diamonds, onyx, emeralds, platinum, c. 1925, rounded rect plaques, bezel-set marquise-cut diamond centers bordered with calibré-cut black onyx and set throughout with oe diamonds, alternating with plaques set throughout with oe diamonds and vertical lines of square-cut emeralds, diamonds approx 10.50 cts tw, sgd *"Cartier,"* ⅜" w x 6⅞" tl, **$18,775** [A]. (Photo courtesy of Butterfields, San Francisco and Los Angeles, CA, 9/25/01)

Bracelet, flexible, diamonds, blue stones, platinum, c. 1920, geo pierced design tapering from the center, set with 48 oe and 16 sc diamonds, approx 4.75 cts tw, the center two diamonds flanked by two triangular-cut blue stones, in an engr and millegrained plat mount, band ¼" w, ½" w at center, approx 7" tl, **$6,900** [A]. (Photo courtesy of Beverly Hills Auctioneers, Beverly Hills, CA, 4/1/01)

Bracelet, flexible strap, diamonds, sapphires, platinum, c. 1925, a tapered band with a lg oe diamond center flanked by channel-set Fr-cut sapphires in geo bow and bracket motifs, within a geo pierced platinum mount pavé-set with 161 sc and oe diamonds, 5.60 cts tw, bisected by a channel-set tapering row of Fr-cut sapphires interspaced with diamond and sapphire X shapes, v-spring and box clasp, ¾" w at center, 7¾" tl, **$10, 575** [A]. (Copyright Christie's Images, New York 2002©, Christie's Los Angeles, CA, 3/6/01)

Bracelet, charm, diamonds, platinum, 18k wg, sapphires, rubies, emeralds, citrine, c. 1930, Fr, a line of triple diamond collet links alternating with baguette links suspending 11 calibré-cut and buff-top gem-set jazz band charms: band leader flanked by cellist, violinist, guitarist, banjo player, tuba player, flutist, saxophonist, trumpet player, French horn player, and drummer, mounted in plat and wg, Fr assay mks, unknown maker's mk, 1⅛" w x 6½", **$35,250** [A]. (Copyright Christie's Images, New York 2002©, Christie's New York, NY, 10/22/01)

Bracelet, charm, star rubies, diamonds, sapphires, platinum, c. 1930, charms depicting an orchestra, the conductor in the center flanked by a pianist, harpist, violinist, cellist, drummer, trumpeter, trombonist and a clarinetist, each figure set with a bc diamond head, star ruby body, joined by links set with sc and baguette-cut diamonds and calibré-cut sapphires, diamonds approx 7.00 cts tw, ⅞" w x 7¼" tl, **$12,925** [A]. (Photo courtesy of Butterfields, San Francisco and Los Angeles, CA, 9/25/01)

Bracelet, link, citrines, diamonds, onyx, platinum, c. 1925-30, four intaglio citrines depicting the heads and torsos of nude women as the four seasons, joined by flexible open rect links set with vertical onyx bars surmounted by double trefoils, set throughout with sc and oe diamonds, ⅞" w x 7" tl, **$8,519** [A]. (Photo courtesy of Skinner, Inc., Boston, MA, 12/11/01)

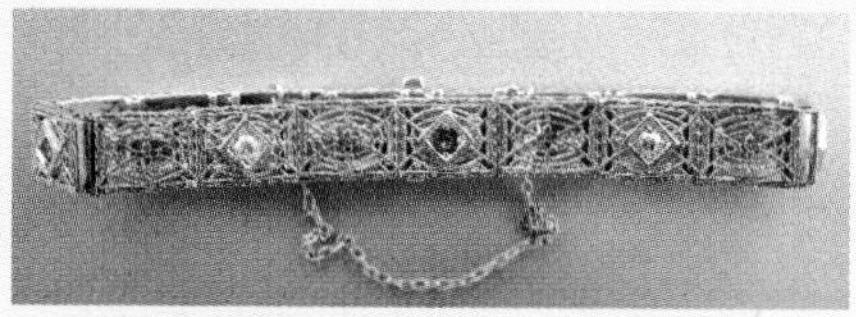

Bracelet, flexible, 14k wg, diamonds, syn sapphire, c. 1920-25, die-stamped filigree links, every other link alternately carré-set with a circ-cut diamond or a circ-cut syn sapphire, safety chain, ½" w x approx 7" tl, **$650**. (Photo courtesy of Karen Lorene, Facèré Jewelry Art, Seattle, WA)

Bracelet, flexible, diamonds, syn sapphires, platinum, c. 1920, set throughout with bc diamonds, the central buckle motif set with calibré-cut syn sapphires, engr gallery, diamonds approx 2.60 cts tw, ½" w at center, strap ¼", 6½" tl, **$5,875** [A]. (Photo courtesy of Butterfields, San Francisco and Los Angeles, CA, 6/19/01)

Bracelet, link, jadeite, diamonds, enamel, 18k yg, platinum, c. 1930, Fr, a rounded rect carved jadeite plaque flanked by a grad line of black enameled tapered sq links joined with rc diamond-set bars, mounted in 18k yg and platinum, Fr assay mks, 1⅛" w at center, 7" tl, **$3,760** [A]. (Copyright Christie's Images, New York 2002©, Christie's Los Angeles, CA, 10/4/01)

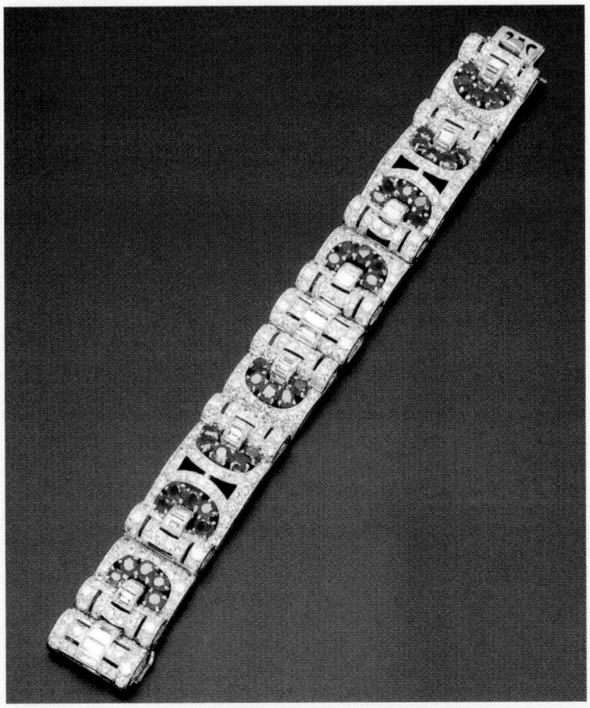

Bracelet, link, diamonds, rubies, platinum, c. 1930, pierced and scrolled panels pavé-set with circ-cut and rect diamonds, approx 27.00 cts tw, accented with crescents of cushion-cut rubies, approx 12.00 cts tw, mounted in plat, v-spring and box clasp with safety, ⅞" w, approx 7" tl, **$20,930** [A]. (Photo courtesy of Dupuis Jewellery Auctioneers, Toronto, ONT, Canada, 6/12/01)

Bracelet, strap, sapphires, diamonds, platinum, c. 1930, a rect cushion-cut sapphire, approx 18.50 x 14.00 x 10.00 mm, approx 26.40 cts, flanked by a flexible pierced plat strap in a honeycomb pattern pavé-set with bc diamonds, bordered with calibré-cut sapphires; diamonds approx 10.20 cts tw, orig box, engr gallery, ¾" w x 7⅜" tl, **$41,125** [A]. (Photo courtesy of Butterfields, San Francisco and Los Angeles, CA, 6/19/01)

Bracelet, flexible link, cab rubies, diamonds, platinum, c. 1935, the center set with a cab ruby of 16.00 cts within a baguette and circ-cut diamond openwork geo frame, flanked by four strands of ruby beads with baguette and circ-cut diamond bar spacers, diamond-set clasp, diamonds 6.75 cts tw, # 1384, provenance: from the estate of Lana Turner, 1" w at center, 7" tl, **$41,125** [A]. (Copyright Christie's Images, New York 2002©, Christie's Los Angeles, CA, 3/6/01)

Brooches/Pins, bar, diamonds, c. 1920-25:
T, five oe and 36 sc diamonds, approx 1.70 cts tw, set in a cusped navette-shaped pierced plat mount, wg pinstem, 2" w x ¾", **$978** [A].
C, eight oe and 59 sc diamonds, approx 1.75 cts tw, set in pierced and millegrained geo plat mount, Fr hmks, one diamond missing, 2" w x ½", **$1,150** [A].
B, one om and one oe diamond, approx 0.15 ct tw, and one colorless stone, set in a pierced and engr elongated elliptical wg mount, yg pinstem, 2" w x ⅜", **$259** [A].
(Photo courtesy of Beverly Hills Auctioneers, Beverly Hills, CA, 4/1/01)

Bracelet, flexible, diamonds, rubies, platinum, c. 1935, an articulated openwork plat band set throughout with baguette-cut diamonds, 15.50 cts tw, interspersed with bezel-set sugarloaf cab rubies, sgd "*Cartier*, London," mkd "PT 950," ¾" w x 7¼" tl, **$47,000** [A]. (Copyright Christie's Images, New York 2002©, Christie's Los Angeles, CA, 3/6/01)

Brooch/Pin, bar, 14k wg, diamonds, syn blue sapphires, c. 1920, a die-stamped filigree tapered and cusped bar, carré-set with three circ-cut diamonds, two Fr-cut syn sapphires in millegrained settings, lever catch, 2½" w x ½", **$300**. (Photo courtesy of Karen Lorene, Facèré Jewelry Art, Seattle, WA)

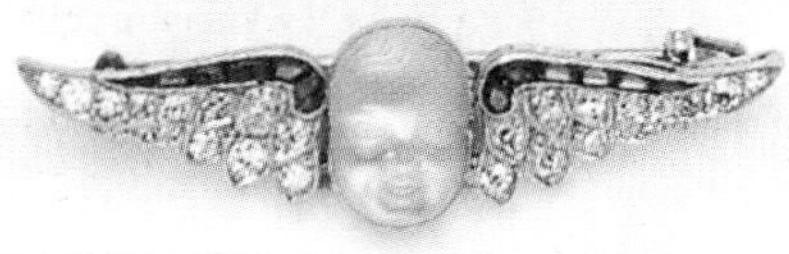

Brooch/Pin, bar, moonstone, diamonds, sapphires, platinum, c. 1920, a moonstone carved as the face of a cherub, flanked by wings set with oe and sc diamonds, the upper edges accented by channel-set calibré-cut sapphires, safety catch, sgd "*Cartier* NY," 1⅞" w x ½", **$6,463** [A]. (Photo courtesy of Butterfields, San Francisco and Los Angeles, CA, 6/19/01)

Brooch/Pin, circle, rock crystal, diamonds, platinum, 14k yg, c. 1920, a circle of floral etched crystal intersected by two pierced and millegrained plat plaques set with transitional-cut diamonds, yg findings, sgd "TIFFANY & CO.," 1½" dia, **$3,055** [A]. (Photo courtesy of Skinner, Inc., Boston, MA, 12/11/01)

Brooch/Pin, diamonds, sapphires, demantoid garnets, platinum, enamel, c. 1925, in the shape of a stylized geo butterfly with pavé-set diamond wings interspersed with buff-top calibré-cut sapphires and demantoid garnets, accented with black enamel, 90 baguette, shield, and circ-cut diamonds, 4.50 cts tw, lever catch (broken), one demantoid deficient, 2" w x 1½", **$12,925** [A]. (Copyright Christie's Images, New York 2002©, Christie's Los Angeles, CA, 3/6/01)

Brooch/Pin, bar, yellow diamond, sapphires, diamonds, platinum, c. 1925, an elongated oval plaque centering a yellow round bc diamond, approx 1.05 cts, bezel-set on a striped pattern of oe diamonds, approx 2.30 cts tw, and calibré-cut sapphires, 1⅞" w x ½", **$8,225** [A]. (Photo courtesy of Butterfields, San Francisco and Los Angeles, CA, 9/25/01)

Brooch/Pin, diamonds, demantoid garnets, platinum, onyx, c. 1927, in the shape of a wasp clutching an oe diamond, sc diamond body with calibré-cut onyx banding, extended table-cut diamond wings edged with calibré-cut demantoid garnets, with a marquise-cut diamond head, inscribed "Country of origin: France," sgd "VAN CLEEF & ARPELS, PARIS," #35122, NY, #255, 1⅜" x 1¼", **$25,850** [A]. (Copyright Christie's Images, New York 2002©, Christie's New York, NY, 10/22/01)

Brooch/Pin, diamonds, emeralds, platinum, wg, c. 1920, a pierced, lobed, and cusped navette-shaped plat plaque set throughout with 48 sm oe diamonds, approx 1.60 cts tw, with V-shaped calibré-cut emerald accents at compass points, the center set with an oe diamond, approx 1.00 ct, within a calibré-cut emerald frame, lever catch mkd "14k," one sm emerald missing, sm repair, 2⅛" w x 1", **$4,935** [A]. (Copyright Christie's Images, New York 2002©, Christie's Los Angeles, CA, 3/6/01)

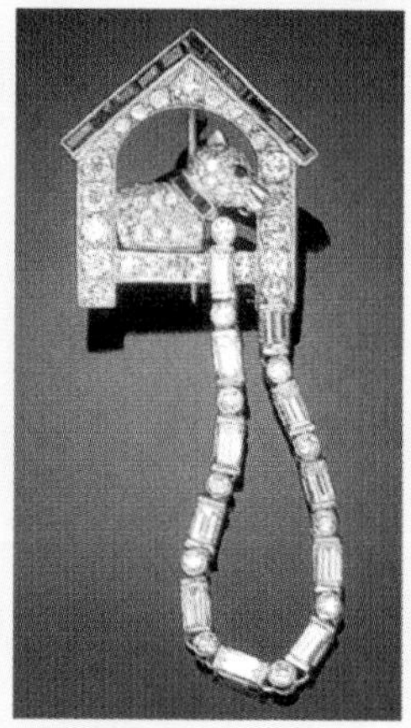

Brooch/Pin, diamonds, emeralds, rubies, platinum, c. 1925-30, in the shape of a doghouse enclosing a dog on a leash, pavé-set diamond dog with circ-cut emerald eye and baguette-cut ruby collar, baguette and circ-cut diamond leash, pavé-set diamond doghouse with baguette-cut emerald roof, ⅞" x ⅞", leash approx 3" tl, **$7,050** [A]. (Copyright Christie's Images, New York 2002©, Christie's Los Angeles, CA, 10/4/01)

Brooch/Pin, circle, diamonds, rubies, sapphires, emeralds, platinum, c. 1930-35, depicting a bird perched atop a branch set throughout with sc diamonds and calibré-cut rubies, sapphires, and emeralds, within a circ frame set with early modern bc diamonds, diamonds approx 2.10 cts tw, lever catch, modified tube hinge, 1½" dia, **$4,406** [A]. (Photo courtesy of Butterfields, San Francisco and Los Angeles, CA, 6/19/01)

Brooch/Pin, platinum, carved rock crystal, kunzite, topaz, amethyst, beryl, onyx, c. 1925-30, carved crystal flower basket bordered with sc and rc diamonds, bezel-set with eight gemstones in circ, cushion, and pear shapes, and sm onyx cabs in a pavé diamond-set millegrained platinum mount, Fr plat and gold standard guarantee stamps, 2½" w x 1½", **$6,463** [A]. (Photo courtesy of Skinner, Inc., Boston, MA, 12/11/01)

Brooch/Pin, diamonds, colored diamonds, rubies, platinum, c. 1930, in the shape of a flower basket in pierced plat set throughout with bc diamonds, the bouquet with one bloom centering an oval faceted ruby, approx 1.30 cts, encircled by bc diamonds, one set with a fancy yellow bc diamond, approx 0.75 ct, framed by bc diamonds, and one centering an oe diamond, approx 0.80 ct, surrounded by fancy yellow bc diamonds, accented by bezel-set circ-cut rubies, diamonds 5.00 cts tw, trombone catch, 1⅞" w x 2," **$10,575** [A]. (Photo courtesy of Butterfields, San Francisco and Los Angeles, CA, 6/19/01)

Brooches/Pins, diamonds, platinum, enamel, rubies, sapphires, emeralds, yg, c. 1930, set of four, in the sculpted shapes of rabbits, each pavé-set with circ-cut diamonds and mounted in plat, the bride with pavé-set veil, gem-set bouquet and cab ruby eye; the waiter with pavé-set jacket, calibré-cut ruby pants, black enameled bow tie, calibré-cut emerald cuffs and lapels, holding a black enameled tray with two triangular-cut diamond martini glasses, and articulated ice bucket decorated with sc diamonds, calibré-cut sapphires, and black enamel; the sea captain, with calibré-cut sapphire jacket, calibré-cut ruby lapel, black enameled tie, yg and black enameled hat, yg ship's wheel, and baguette-cut diamond deck; the butler with red and black enameled lapel, bow tie and cuffs, sc diamond and red enameled tray, bottle and glasses, and sc diamond and buff-top calibré-cut emerald napkin, all sgd "yard" for Raymond Yard, NY, each figure approx ¾"–⅞" w x 1⅝"–1¾", the set, **$88,125** [A]. (Copyright Christie's Images, New York 2002©, Christie's New York, NY, 10/22/01)

Dress Clip, diamonds, platinum, onyx, c. 1930, set with an om diamond, approx 1.00 ct within a circ onyx ground and centered within a rect frame of pavé-set diamonds decorated with a diamond-set arrow motif, the diamonds approx 2.80 cts tw, mounted in plat, flat-backed hinged clip on rev, ⅞" w x 1⅜", **$6,354** [A]. (Photo courtesy of Dupuis Jewellery Auctioneers, Toronto, ONT, Canada, 6/12/01)

Brooch/Pendant, diamonds, platinum, c. 1930, an oval pierced plat plaque with a central collet-set oe diamond, approx 1.85 cts, set throughout with smaller oe diamonds, retractable bail, lever catch, 1¾" w x 1¼", **$8,225** [A]. (Photo courtesy of Butterfields, San Francisco and Los Angeles, CA, 9/25/01)

Clip, diamonds, platinum, c. 1935, foliate design, leaves and branch set throughout with oe, circ-cut and baguette-cut diamonds, sgd "*Cartier*, PARIS," #07988, double-pronged hinged clip on rev, 1" w x 2⅞", **$11,163** [A]. (Photo courtesy of Butterfields, San Francisco and Los Angeles, CA, 9/25/01)

Cuff Links, sapphires, diamonds, platinum-topped 18k yg, c. 1920, each side of each double-sided circ link bezel-set with a sapphire cab encircled by 12 rc diamonds within a spoke pattern in plat-topped yg, ½" dia, **$1,725** [A]. (Photo courtesy of Beverly Hills Auctioneers, Beverly Hills, CA, 4/1/01)

Cuff Links, diamonds, rubies, platinum, c. 1925, each double link set with a baguette-cut ruby link opposite a circ-cut diamond link, joined by a bar link, sgd "*Cartier*," #2919776, one ruby deficient, in a Cartier red leather fitted case, 1⅜" w x ½", **$5,875** [A]. (Copyright Christie's Images, New York 2002©, Christie's Los Angeles, CA, 3/6/01)

Dress Clips, rock crystal, black onyx, diamonds, platinum, c. 1930, each with a central sq carved rock crystal panel with an oe diamond center, outlined by channel-set black onyx rods surmounted by a short vertical row of oe diamonds, the open half moon shape outlined in pavé-set oe diamonds, open hinged clip on rev conforms to shape, 62 oe diamonds, 5.00 cts tw, 1¼" w x ⅞" pr, **$5,875** [A]. (Copyright Christie's Images, New York 2002©, Christie's Los Angeles, CA, 3/6/01)

Double Clip Brooch, platinum, diamonds, wm, c. 1930, two triangular clips set throughout with 34 baguettes, two kite-shape, and 174 sc and bc diamonds, plat mount, detachable wm brooch mechanism, 3" w x 1⅛" (joined), **$3,408** [A]. (Photo courtesy of Skinner, Inc., Boston, MA, 12/11/01)

Double Clip Brooch, diamonds, platinum, 14k wg, c. 1930, each opposed mirror-image clip a symmetrical geo design of arcs and sprays set throughout with baguette-cut and bc diamonds, approx 6.40 cts tw, plat mount, open flat-backed hinged wg clips, detachable brooch mechanism, lever catch, 3" w x 1¼", **$8,225** [A]. (Photo courtesy of Butterfields, San Francisco and Los Angeles, CA, 6/19/01)

Double Clip Brooch, diamonds, platinum, wm, c. 1935, two clips forming a pierced ribbon and bow motif, pavé-set throughout with 152 oe and bc, 38 sc and 28 baguette-cut diamonds, approx 17.50 cts tw, in plat, with detachable wm brooch frame, accompanied by fitted box, 3" w x 1⅝", **$10,350** [A]. (Photo courtesy of Beverly Hills Auctioneers, Beverly Hills, CA, 4/1/01)

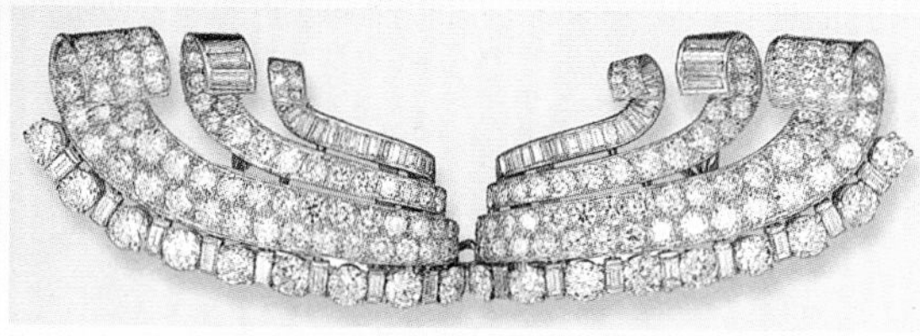

Double Clip Brooch, diamonds, platinum, c. 1935, Eng, a pr of clips forming a scrolled cascade of pavé-set circ-cut and baguette diamonds, with two removable brooch mechanisms for alternate configurations, mounted in platinum, Garrard & Co.(UK) fitted case, 2¼" w x 2⅜", **$25,850** [A]. (Copyright Christie's Images, New York 2002©, Christie's Los Angeles, CA, 10/4/01)

Double Clip Brooch, diamonds, platinum, rubies, wg, c. 1935, pr of shield-shaped double-pronged hinged clips, channel-set down the center with tapering square-cut rubies, set throughout with early modern bc diamonds, accented with baguette-cut diamonds; detachable wg frame and brooch mechanism, diamonds approx 7.00 cts tw, rubies approx 5.50 cts tw, 3⅝" x 1⅜", **$14,100** [A]. (Photo courtesy of Butterfields, San Francisco and Los Angeles, CA, 12/11/01)

Earrings, diamonds, c. 1920:
L, each set with one oe diamond, in a navette-shaped engr wg drop, suspended from an ear stud set with one oe diamond, approx 0.60 ct tw, evidence of repair, ⅜" w x 1⅛", **$403** [A].
R, each set with two om, two sc, and 30 rc diamonds in a pear-shaped pierced and engr plat mount, center stone enclosed with calibré-cut blue stones surmounted by a diamond-set plat V, suspended from a vertical diamond-set link, later-added yg posts, ⅜" w x 1¼", **$805** [A]. (Photo courtesy of Beverly Hills Auctioneers, Beverly Hills, CA, 4/1/01)

Double Clip Brooch, black opals, diamonds, platinum, wg, c. 1930, each shield-shaped clip centering an oval black opal measuring approx 20.70 x 15.00 x 4.40 mm, set throughout with bc and baguette-cut diamonds, approx 4.80 cts tw, openwork flat-backed hinged clips on rev, joined by a detachable 14k wg brooch mechanism, 3" w x 1½", **$8,225** [A]. (Photo courtesy of Butterfields, San Francisco and Los Angeles, CA, 9/25/01)

Earrings, coral, seed pearls, MOP, 10k yg, c. 1920, each surmount a flowerhead cluster of seed pearls strung with horsehair and mounted on a MOP plaque, suspending an articulated paired foliate motif seed pearl center and a coral drop with yg cap, screwbacks mkd "10k," ⅜" w x 2⅛" tl, **$325**. (Courtesy of Generations, La Verne, CA)

Earrings, star rubies, diamonds, platinum, c. 1930, Am, 56 oe and baguette diamonds in open shield-shaped panels, 5 cts tw, central star rubies, dress clips converted to post/clip earrings, sgd "TRABERT & HOEFFER-MAUBOUSSIN," ⅞" w x 1⅛", **$8,813** [A]. (Copyright Christie's Images, New York 2002©, Christie's Los Angeles, CA, 3/6/01)

Necklace, platinum, diamonds, rubies, enamel, c. 1925, fetter links interspersed with heart-shaped links suspending six sc pavé-set diamond charms: a monkey, a dachshund, a bulldog with ruby collar and eye, a swordfish with blue enamel fin, a pr of lovebirds with ruby eyes, and a rabbit coming out of a black enameled hat, continuing to a curb link chain and clasp (probably added to convert from orig bracelet), longest charm ⅞", 14" tl, **$2,938** [A]. (Photo courtesy of Skinner, Inc., Boston, MA, 12/11/01)

Pendant, rock crystal, 14k wg, diamond, sapphires, c. 1920, an oval frosted rock crystal plaque carved with radiating lines set in an engr geo wg frame, the center set with a circ-cut diamond, and two Fr-cut sapphires in a millegrained mount, suspended from a stamped and engr cusped bail mkd "14K DIANA" (Krementz trademark), ⅝" w x 2," **$650**. (Healy collection, photo by Bruce Healy)

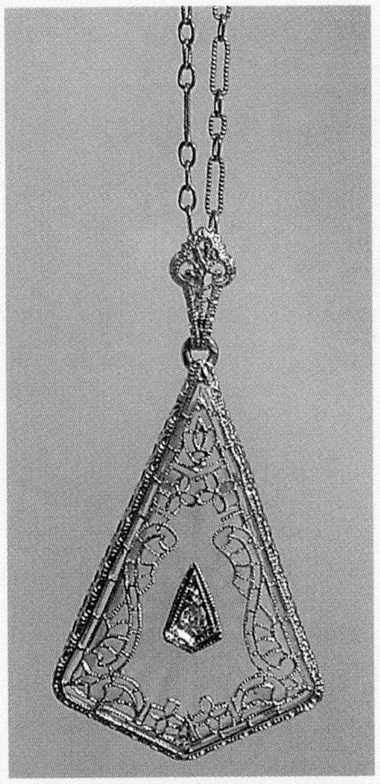

Pendant and Chain, rock crystal, 14k wg, diamond, c. 1920, a kite-shaped frosted rock crystal plaque set within a stamped filigree wg frame and border, a sm sc diamond in the center bead-set in a millegrained wg mount of conforming shape, suspended from a stamped filigree trefoil bail and orig wg fetter and trace link chain, spring ring clasp, ¾" w x 1½" tl, chain 16" tl, **$450.** (Private collection)

Rings, diamonds and platinum or wg, c. 1920-25:
TL, one oe diamond, approx 1.10 cts, in a sq pronged setting, surrounded by 16 sc diamonds, approx 0.30 ct tw, in a horizontally oriented plat mount, ½" w x ⅜" at center, **$3,163** [A].
TC, one oe diamond, approx 0.35 ct, in a sq mount framed by baguette-cut blue stones, tapering to a narrow shank, engr wg mkd "BELAIS" for Belais Bros.' trademarked 18k wg, ⅜"square center, **$460** [A].
TR, one oe diamond, approx .95 ct, in center of pierced and engr rounded navette-shaped plat mount set throughout with 14 oe and 20 sc diamonds, approx 1.60 cts tw, ¾" w x 1" at center, **$2,300** [A].
BL, 27 oe and sc diamonds, approx 1.20 cts tw, with eight calibré-cut blue stones, set in a pierced, millegrained and engr vertically oriented geo plat mount, ½" w x ¾"at center, **$1,265** [A].
BR, a vertical row of three oe diamonds, .75 ct tw, flanked above and below by four blue stone baguettes, set in pierced and engr 18k wg, slight damage, ⅜" w x ⅞" at center, **$489** [A]. (Photo courtesy of Beverly Hills Auctioneers, Beverly Hills, CA, 4/1/01)

Rings, c. 1920:
L:, c. 1920, central circ-cut diamond flanked by two smaller circ-cut diamonds, .22 ct tw, channel-set Fr-cut sapphires, pierced and millegrained setting, mkd "PLATINUM," ⅜" w x ¼", **$1,000.**
R, two large syn sapphires, pierced wg mounting mkd "14k," ⅝" w x ¼", **$350**. (Healy collection, photo by Bruce Healy)

Ring, diamonds, emeralds, platinum, c. 1925, an Asscher-cut diamond, approx 2.90 cts, in a rect frame set with sc diamonds, the prongs set with calibré-cut emeralds, tapering to a narrow engr shank set with a row of sc diamonds, diamonds approx 3.00 cts tw, ⅜" x ½", **$26,250** [A]. (Photo courtesy of Butterfields, San Francisco and Los Angeles, CA, 9/25/01)

Ring, diamonds, platinum, c. 1929, a prong-set rect-cut diamond, 4.58 cts, flanked by two trapeze and four marquise-cut diamonds, .40 ct tw, continuing to a narrow engr plat shank, inside engr "HARRY TO PEG, JULY 4, 1929," mkd "10% IR PLAT," size 6½, **$21,150** [A]. (Copyright Christie's Images, New York 2002©, Christie's Los Angeles, CA, 3/6/01)

Ring, sapphire, diamonds, platinum, c. 1930, an oval faceted sapphire, approx 17.10 x 14.00 mm, approx 20.00 cts, prong-set high in plat mount, the gallery set with bc diamonds; diamonds 2.00 cts tw, orig box, ¾" w x ⅞", sz 6, **$19,975** [A]. (Photo courtesy of Butterfields, San Francisco and Los Angeles, CA, 6/19/01)

Tie Pins, diamonds, emeralds, rubies, platinum, c. 1930, pr, each a devil's head motif, pavé-set with sc diamonds and calibré-cut emeralds and rubies, respectively, ½" w x ⅝", **$1,293** [A]. (Photo courtesy of Butterfields, San Francisco and Los Angeles, CA, 6/19/01)

Ring, 14k yg, glass, diamond, enamel, c. 1925-30, a sm collet-set circ-cut diamond in the concave center of a bezel-set circ faceted blue glass stone, encircled by a red, green and black enameled floral and geo design on an engr yg convex circ frame, continuing to a similarly decorated narrow shank, ¾" dia, sz 6½, **$575**. (Courtesy of Xcentricities, Beverly Hills, CA)

COSTUME JEWELRY c. 1920-1935

When Coco Chanel (1883-1971) reputedly declared in 1924, "It does not matter if they are real, as long as they look like junk!," costume jewels had already begun to enjoy widespread acceptance by women at all social levels. Both Chanel and her arch-rival, Elsa Schiaparelli, were foremost among Parisian couturiers in designing and promoting the wearing of *faux* jewelry as an accessory to clothing, and as a means of self-expression. Today we call it "making a statement."

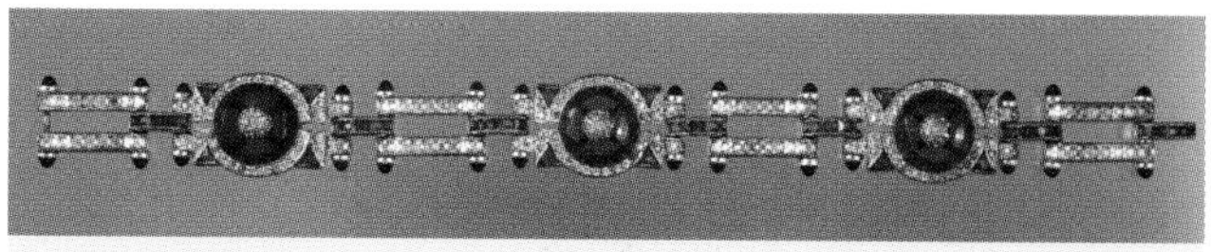

Bracelet, link, glass, rhinestones, rh pl wm, c. 1925, links of faceted red glass disks, each surmounted by a circ-cut colorless r.s., framed by r.s.-set semicircles, four triangular-cut red r.s. and r.s.-set bars capped with red glass cabs, alternating with open rect links set with calibré-cut colorless r.s. flanked by red cabs, connected with calibré-cut red r.s.-set bars and foldover clasp, ⅝" w x 7" tl, **$250.** (Courtesy of Generations, La Verne, CA)

Because they were made from non-precious materials, costume jewels gave manufacturers and designers a greater freedom to experiment with designs and the opportunity to cater to fashion's whims, trends, and fads. Consequently, we see a far greater diversity in costume jewelry of the period compared to fine jewelry.

To be sure, many directly imitative pieces were made, substituting "paste" or rhinestones and molded or cut glass, for gemstones, and silver or white "pot" metal (tin alloyed with lead) for platinum. Some of these pieces were remarkably well-made. The metal was often rhodium-plated for an even closer resemblance to platinum—rhodium is one of the six metals in the platinum group. Stones were prong- or bead-set; occasionally, millegrained settings were used. At a short distance, one would find it difficult to discern them from the "real" thing. Verbatim translations of the period style from fine to costume jewelry include flexible and linked plaque bracelets (see below and above right, and page 138), bead sautoirs (sometimes called "flapper beads"), pendent earrings, rings (page 143), geometric brooches and pendants (see circle brooch on page 139), dress clips and double clip brooches. (See page 140, mechanism patented 1936. Coro's version of the double- clip brooch, trade named the "Duette," was patented in 1931.)

As with fine jewelry, Art Deco costume pieces originated in Europe, where the *Jugendstil*, Bauhaus, Wiener Werkstätte, and Liberty styles had already made a case for modernism, emphasizing design over intrinsically valuable materials. But even in France, where *haute joaillerie* and Cartier reigned, the more adventurous Art Deco artist-designers turned to silver, chrome, glass, lacquer and enamel, and plastics (see necklace by Jean Dunand on page 142).

Some French Deco costume jewelry is of the *faux* diamond and platinum variety, usually referred to as "French paste," set in silver and, extremely well-made (see "fruit salad" brooches on page 140). The transitional path of Edwardian to Deco can be followed in these pieces, along the same route as fine jewelry. Similarly styled bracelets, clips, buckles, and brooches in rhinestones and white metal were made in the United States by costume jewelry manufacturers such as Trifari, Krussman and Fishel, later known simply as Trifari (see section on "Designer/Manufacturer Signed" costume). Ciner Mfg. Co., in business since 1892, made both fine and costume jewelry. They produced rhinestone and sterling pieces in the French mode during the '20s and '30s. The White Metal Casters' Association made inexpensive rhinestone and "pot" metal buckles and clips as dress accessories in the '30s, marked "WMCA."

The French and the Germans also excelled at designing modern-looking jewelry in sterling set with inexpensive gemstones and marcasites, small faceted bits of iron pyrite (see bracelet on page 138). Manufacturer Theodor Fahrner, already famous for its early twentieth-century *Jugendstil* designs, (as mentioned in the Arts & Crafts section), kept up with fashion by producing fine quality Deco pieces in high-grade silver set with marcasites combined with amazonite, smoky quartz, rock crystal (see page 139), onyx, carnelian, chrysoprase, "Swiss lapis" (dyed jasper, see page 140), coral, or matte enamel (see ring on page 143). Other less well-known German manufacturers also made jewelry in this style, most commonly using dyed blue, green (imitating chrysoprase), or black chalcedony with marcasites and sterling (see page 143).

Most accounts of fashion history tend to focus on what was original about the '20s and '30s, but all was not geome-

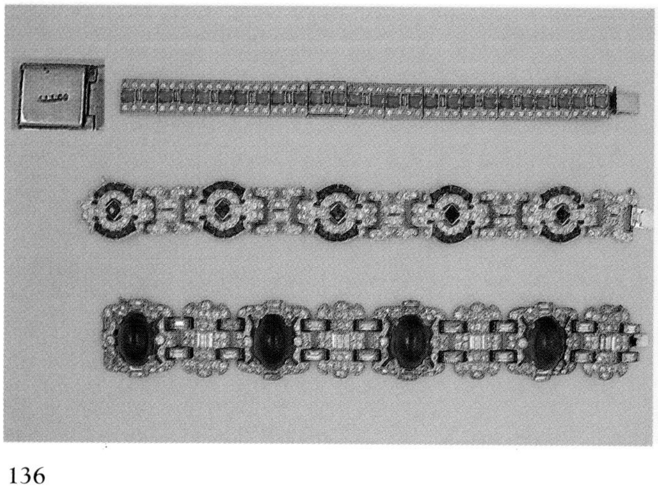

Bracelets, link, glass and rhinestones:
T, c. 1920, line of rect links, each with central green baguette r.s. flanked by sq red r.s. and edged with rows of circ-cut colorless r.s. in wm, v-spring and concealed box clasp, rev mkd "ALLCO," ½" w x 7" tl, **$150.**
C, c. 1925, five openwork links, each with a central sq green r.s. encircled by colorless circ-cut r.s. and flanked top and bottom by arcs of sq green r.s., the sides with cusped and lobed convex plaques pavé-set with colorless r.s. and joined to double bracket-shaped links and double crossbars pavé-set with colorless r.s. in rh pl wm, v-spring and concealed box clasp, safety chain, ¾" w x 7½" tl, **$300**.
B, c. 1930, four cushion-shaped openwork links with lg prong-set central green glass cabs pavé-set with circ and baguette colorless r.s., joined by double bar links of baguette r.s. to geo cusped and lobed plaques pavé-set with baguette and circ colorless r.s. in rh pl wm, v-spring and concealed box clasp, safety chain, 1" w x 6¾", **$350**.
(Courtesy of Denese Strand, Laguna Hills, CA)

Brooch/Pin, butterfly wing, glass, gp brass, c. 1930, rev-painted polychrome scene with palm trees backed with yellow butterfly wing, set in a stamped gp brass frame, closed back, safety catch, 1¾" w x 1", **$35**. (Courtesy of Ocean Eyz Antique Jewelry, Orange, CA)

try and streamline. The Victorians did not have a monopoly on revivals; in fact, Victorian fashion and historicism itself were revived beginning in the late '20s, and growing in popularity in the '30s and early '40s. Period films and their stars helped set the mood: Mae West in "She Done Him Wrong" (1933), Greta Garbo in "Camille" (1936) and "Conquest" (1937), Bette Davis in "Juarez" (1939), and of course, Vivien Leigh in the immortal "Gone With The Wind" (1939). The clothes and the jewelry (much of the latter created by Eugene Joseff, aka Joseff of Hollywood—see section on "Designer/Manufacturer Signed" costume) may not have always been authentically of the period portrayed, but they inspired a 1930s trend for softer, more romantic dresses with longer hems, peplums, and puffy sleeves, and such Victorian staples as cameos and jet (imitated in glass and plastic), gold-filled hinged bangles, ornate metal filigree, and flower jewelry.

A unique type of collectible jewelry, which appears to be attracting a growing number of collectors, originated in England. However, its primary component, the wings of the Morpho butterfly, came from South America. Several British firms made these pieces, which usually consist of a reverse-painted scene or a white sulphide bas-relief (reminiscent of Wedgwood jasperware) backed with an iridescent blue butterfly wing ground, a domed glass cover, and usually, a sterling silver frame and back. The backs are often marked with a British patent number, granted to Shipton & Co. of Birmingham, England, in 1923. Note that the wings ... or the iridescence can flake off if exposed ... nt, espe- ... usual *yel-* ... ated the ... nd wide- ... ll. The ... of King ... od films

(e.g., "Cleopatra" in 1934), caused Egyptian motifs to be particularly conspicuous. Enameled silver or gold-plated metal winged scarabs, falcons, vultures, and other motifs were produced in several European countries and the U.S., as well as in Egypt itself for export or the tourist trade (see bar brooch on page 139). The "slave" bracelet, of enameled metal or sterling links set with glass cabochons or molded scarabs, was an extension of the craze (see bracelet by Coro on page 138). One of the primary sources for Egyptian-themed pieces was Czechoslovakia. Here, the medium was usually glass, but celluloid and metal pieces, or a combination of materials, were also made.

After World War I, Bohemia, long renowned for its glasswork, beads, and garnet jewelry, became part of the new country called Czechoslovakia, created in 1918. In the period between the wars, quantities of glass beads, faceted and molded glass stones and stamped metalwork were produced and exported, some in the form of finished jewelry, some for use in jewelry manufactured in other countries. The center of this production was a town called Gablonz, now known as Jablonec. Because the country was taken over by the Germans during World War II (exports were curtailed in 1939), the glass and jewelry makers were dispersed to other areas, such as Neugablonz in Germany. Today, the boundaries have been redrawn once again, and Czechoslovakia is now divided into the Czech Republic and Slovakia. Jewelry marked "Czechoslovakia" is easily circa-dated, and has become quite sought-after. Prices have risen accordingly.

Czechoslovakia was the source of several types of costume jewelry. Stamped gilt metal filigree necklaces, bracelets, brooches, buckles, clips, earrings, and rings were set with glass cabochons, sometimes embellished with enameled foliate motifs, resulting in an ornate look that was more Victorian Revival than Art Deco (see sautoir on page 140).

The Deco style was not ignored, however. Geometric-cut pieces of glass resembling gemstones were prong-set in short necklaces and pendent earrings (see pages 140 and 141). Glass buckles, clasps, and clips were made in simple modern designs. Small faceted glass stones were often silver-plated to imitate marcasites.

Oriental-inspired pieces were made with molded and pierced glass plaques imitating carved jade and carnelian. Glass bead sautoirs were another Czech product (see page 142). Some Czech pieces are marked in difficult-to-read places, like the circumference of a jump ring. Other unmarked pieces are so characteristic of Czech glass and metalwork that they are unmistakable. Still others may have Czech components, but were assembled elsewhere, and may be hard to identify.

...eproduction Alert

... tume as ... r, which ... , quality varies widely. Some British and German exports are very well-made. Wholesalers specializing in reproductions advertise in antiques trade papers and on the Internet.

Bracelets, link, silver, c. 1925, European:
T, nine openwork circ links, each bezel-set with four circ-cut green glass cabs and two seed pearls, five links with rect-cut green beryl centers alternating with four links with pearl centers, each circ segment joined by two oval silver jump rings, Hungarian hmks (lion's head, 4 for 750 silver, mint-mark P for Hungary) imp on v-spring, concealed box clasp, ⅝" w x 7½" tl, **$300**.
C, five cusped oval openwork plaques, each with a central bezel-set circ-cut red stone within a scrolling floral motif edged with black and white enameled arcs, alternating with high-domed bezel-set dyed green chalcedony cabs joined with wide silver straps, v-spring and box clasp, safety chain, rev mkd "STERLING GERMANY," ½" w x 7¼" tl, **$200**.
B, in the Fahrner style, matte purple enameled rect links, each set with three oval dyed green chalcedony cabs within a swirled pattern of silver wires flanked by textured semicircles, alternating with textured biconcave/convex links with black enameled centers, terminating in a v-spring and box clasp with safety, rev mkd "STERLING GERMANY 935," ⅝" w x 8" tl, **$500**. (Private collection)

Bracelet, link, silver, carnelian, marcasites, c. 1925, seven pierced openwork rect links with oxidized ground, raised engr gallery set with marcasites in geo foliate motif, raised edges set with a row of marcasites, each link with two opposed half-round carnelian cabs separated by a line of marcasites, v-spring and concealed box clasp, mkd "MADE IN FRANCE," ⅝" w x 7½" tl, **$500**. (Courtesy of Denese Strand, Laguna Hills, CA)

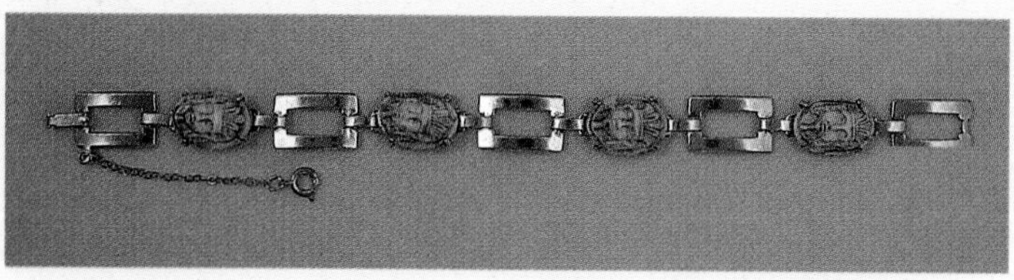

Bracelet, link, sterling, marbled opaque glass, c. 1925, Egyptian Revival, open rect ster links alternating with molded green glass pharaoh's heads, probably imported from Czechoslovakia, mkd "STERLING Coro," safety chain, ⅜" w x 7½" tl, **$50**. (Courtesy of Ocean Eyz Antique Jewelry, Orange, CA)

Bracelet, link, sterling, c. 1920, baby bracelet, links of cutout and engr Beatrix Potter animal characters, spring ring clasp not orig, ⅝" w x 5½" tl, **$85**. (Charlotte Healy collection, photo by Bruce Healy)

Bracelet, link, 800 silver, c. 1930, Fr, four truncated lozenge-shaped openwork hinged links, each with a central curved, lobed quatrefoil enclosed by prs of tapered bars, grooved borders with raised beads and U-shaped patterns, v-spring and box clasp, Fr hmks (crabs), illegible maker's mk, "H. TEGUY," on fronts of terminal links, 1⅛" w x 7⅜" tl, **$250**. (Courtesy of Andrea Fatell, Wellsley, MA)

Bracelet, 935 gp silver, citrines, beryls, pastes, enamel, c. 1930, Hungarian, central pierced navette-shaped plaque, center bezel-set with an octagonal faceted citrine, flanked top and bottom by two arcing rows of circ-cut pink beryls, four flowerheads and beads at corners, flanked by black-enameled C-scrolls set with four lt green circ-cut pastes, continuing to four smaller pierced scrolled plaques set with octagonal citrines flanked by two circ-cut pink beryls, foliate motifs, and lt green enameled edges, plaques joined by pairs of oval jump rings, v-spring and concealed box clasp mkd with Austro-Hungarian export mk (a caduceus) and "935," 1¼" T to B at center, 7¾" tl, **$850**. (Courtesy of Xcentricities, Beverly Hills, CA)

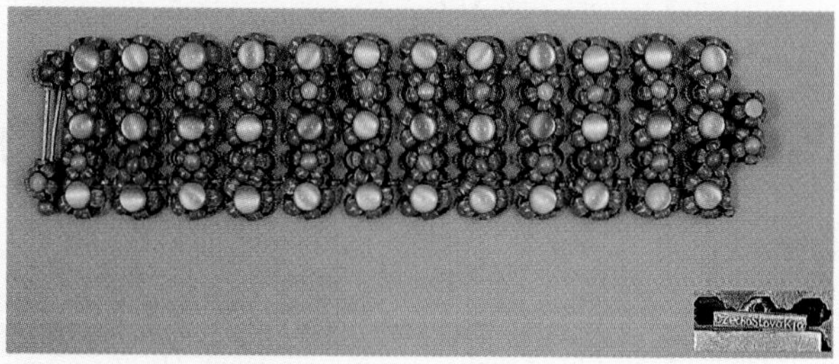

Bracelet, link, brass, glass, ptd enamel, c. 1930, 12 die-stamped openwork elongated rect plaques with scalloped edges, surmounted by vertical rows of alternating red and blue ptd enamel flowerheads with yellow and green accents, each flowerhead center bezel-set with adularescent ("moonstone" effect) circ glass cabs in pastel blue, pink, yellow, and green, flat hook and bar clasp, appl plaque on rev mkd "CZECHOSLOVAKIA," 1¾" w x 7¼" tl, **$450**. (Courtesy of D. Brett Benson, Inc., Chicago, IL)

Bracelets, hinged bangles, 10k gf, c. 1930-40, Victorian Revival, Am:
L, domed surface with allover stamped foliate texturing and central floral motif, smooth raised edge, mkd "1/20 10K GOLD FILLED, DUNN BROS.," ⅝" w, 2¼" inside dia, **$85**.
R, stamped geo and scrolling floral motif, raised and engr edges flanked by taille d'épargne enameled border, mkd "T&D" for Troob & Degnan Jewelry Co., Providence, RI (in business 1922-43), and "1-20-10k GOLD FILLED," ½" w, 2⅜" inside dia, **$85.** (Lisa Johnson collection)

Brooch/Pin, bouquet pin, sterling, glass, r.s., c. 1920, Am, narrow bar with bowed-out center section set with colorless r.s., surmounted by appl circ plaque with central bezel-set circ colorless r.s. encircled by calibré-cut dk blue glass stones, spike extending from back of central stone, mkd "STER" inside maker's mk for Fishel Nessler & Co., New York, NY (a fish with an L in its mouth), C-catch, 3½" w x ½" at center, 1" bow front to back, **$150**. (Courtesy of Denese Strand, Laguna Hills, CA)

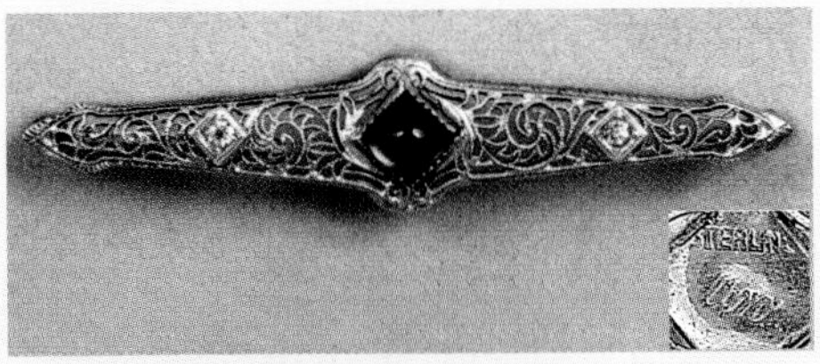

Brooch/Pin, bar, rh pl sterling, glass, rhinestones, c. 1920, stamped ster filigree tapered and cusped bar, a sq blue glass cab in the center flanked by two colorless r.s., pierced gallery, rev mkd "STERLING Coro," 2½" w x ½", **$90**. (Author's collection)

Brooch/Pin, rock crystal, sterling, turq, marcasites, pearl, c. 1920, a circ frosted rock crystal disk overlaid with an openwork ster floral pattern set with marcasites, a pearl center encircled by sm turq cabs, within a marcasite-set ster frame, rev mkd with maker's mk for Theodor Fahrner, "STERLING GERMANY," 1¼" dia, **$900**. (Private collection)

Brooch/Pin, circle, lead crystal, molded glass, r.s., wm, c. 1920, "fruit salad" motif, a colorless crystal annulus (ring shape) with faceted edges, flanked by openwork bows pavé-set with circ and baguette colorless r.s., each bow surmounted by three prong-set molded glass leaves in blue, green, and red, safety catch, unmkd, 2½" w x 1¾", **$200**. (Courtesy of Pat Seal, Treasures From Yesterday, Fort Worth, TX)

Brooch/Pin, lapel watch, sterling, black onyx, guilloché enamel, marcasites, c. 1920-25, bombé-sided rect plaque with marcasite-set stepped geo design framing a prong-set central oval onyx cab, surmounting a marcasite-set bracket suspending three articulated tapered rect plaques bezel-set with rect onyx cabs in marcasite-set frames, terminating in an elongated hexagonal watch case with geo-patterned blue, black, and tan basse-taille enameled sections outlined in orange, terminal winding stem, blue enameled rev, circ watch face mkd "ALBRUSE," safety catch, rev mkd "STERLING," 1¼" w x 4", **$1,500**. (Courtesy of Xcentricities, Beverly Hills, CA)

Brooches/Pins, glass, rhinestones, "fruit salad," c. 1925-30, Fr:
TL, in the shape of a potted plant, molded colored glass stones in the shapes of leaves, shells, and acorns flanking prong-set faceted colorless pentagonal pastes, interspersed with sm circ-cut r.s. above a geo pierced and millegrained "pot" set with colorless circ and rect-cut pastes, rev mkd "MADE IN FRANCE," Fr hmk for 800 silver (boar's head), Fr maker's mk in a lozenge, trombone catch, ¾" w x 1¾", **$300**.
TR, in the shape of a flower basket with molded colored glass flowers, leaves and acorns interspersed with colorless r.s. above an openwork basket set throughout with colorless r.s. in sp wm, rev mkd "FRANCE," 1¼" w x 1⅜", **$225**.
B, a stylized outdoor scene, a cluster of molded colored glass in the shapes of leaves, shells, acorns and flowers flanked by two towers with melon-cut glass bead turrets, the center and corners set with calibré-cut colorless pastes in millegrained mounts, the frame pavé-set with sm circ-cut r.s., rev mkd "MADE IN FRANCE," Fr hmk for 800 silver (boar's head), Fr maker's mk in a lozenge, trombone catch, 1⅞" x 1⅜", **$375**. (Photo courtesy of Lisa Mercer, Deja Vu Antiques, Portland, OR)

Brooch/Pin, bar, 800 silver gilt, enamel, faience, date letter for 1926, Egyptian Revival vulture with plique à jour wings flanking an Egyptian faience scarab, rev mkd "800," #5, Egyptian hmks, date letter "B" on pinstem, C-catch, tube hinge, 2¾" w x 1", **$300**. (Scott Grodsky collection)

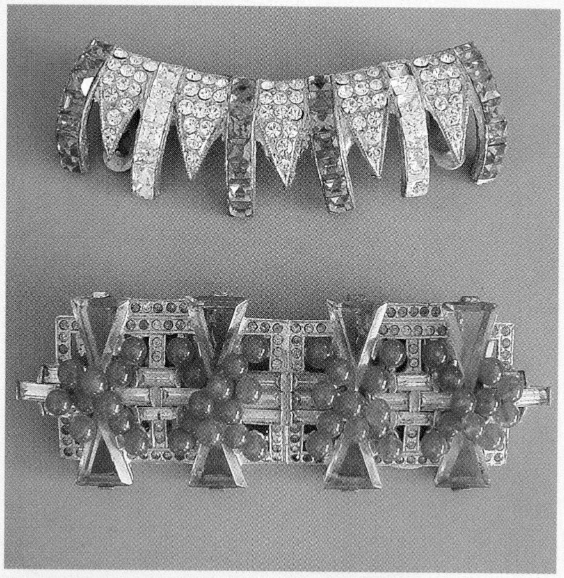

Dress Clips, glass, rhinestones, wm, c. 1930:
T, curved rect plaque, geo saw-tooth design of curved perpendicular bars of sq-cut lt pink and colorless r.s. alternating with triangular plaques of pavé-set colorless r.s., two flat-backed hinged clips on rev, 3½" w x 1⅛", **$275**.
B, wm rectangular plaque base with geo openwork lattice design of colorless horizontally-set baguette r.s. and colorless vertically pavé-set r.s., surmounted by four sets of opposed pink triangular glass stones with central pink glass bead clusters, two flat-backed hinged clips on rev, 3⅞" w x 1½", **$275**. (Photo courtesy of Morning Glory Antiques, Albuquerque, NM)

Double Clip Brooch, rhinestones, rh pl wm, c. 1935, two asymmetrical clips of geo fan and scroll design, pavé-set with colorless circ-cut and baguette rhinestones, flat-backed hinged clips on rev, detachable brooch mechanism mkd "U.S. PAT 2034129 [1936], OTHER PAT. PEND." patent issued to Marcel Boucher (filed Nov. 1, 1935) for a "brooch assemblage," 2½" w x 1⅞" (joined), **$175**. (Courtesy of Generations, La Verne, CA)

Necklace, sautoir, sp brass, glass, c. 1920, die-stamped openwork oval plaque with highly textured scroll and bead motif, bezel-set with a central oval mottled green glass cab encircled by one lg and seven smaller circ glass cabs, suspending two foxtail chain tassels from double oval links, plaque suspended from an oval green glass link, continuing to circ and oval green glass links alternating with openwork spherical sp brass beads joined to a box-link chain section, then to curb link chain and spring ring clasp, unmkd, probably Czech, pendant 2¼" w x 7", 28½" tl, **$175**. (Nancy Shadforth collection)

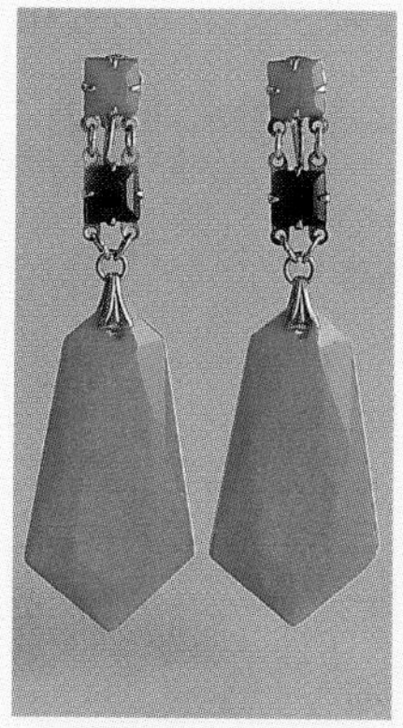

Earrings, pendent, glass, wm, c. 1925, faceted tapered hexagonal opaque vermilion glass drops, each suspended by a triangular bail from two vertical links of prong-set sq faceted vermilion and black glass stones, screwbacks, unmkd, possibly Czech, ⅞" w x 2½", **$185**. (Courtesy of Xcentricities, Beverly Hills, CA)

Earrings, pendent, sterling, gemstones, by Theodor Fahrner, c. 1920-25:
T, elongated dyed jasper ("Swiss lapis") drops suspended from navette-shaped sterling surmounts set with black onyx and maracasites, screwbacks, one mkd with maker's mk for Theodor Fahrner, ¼" w x 1⅝" tl, **$350**.
B, each articulated sq wire rod suspending a rounded triangular frame enclosing concentric arcs on matte green enameled ground, terminating in a hemispherical hematite disk, from enameled arc surmounts, screwbacks, appl rect plate on rev mkd "TF 935" for Theodor Fahner, ½" w x 1¾" tl, **$1,000**. (Private collection)

Earrings, pendent, Czech glass, gp wm, c. 1935, elongated faceted opaque glass beads with floral design in black with pastel pinks, blues, and greens, suspended from textured conical circ disk gp surmounts with openwork wire backing, clipbacks imp with pat #1967965 (1934), ½" w x 2¼" tl, **$50**. (Courtesy of Martha Exline, Metique, Laguna Hills, CA)

Necklace, sterling, amethysts, rhinestones, enamel, seed pearls, c. 1920, three central oval links with oval amethyst cab centers encircled by sm circ-cut purple glass r.s. in a geo patterned lavender, yellow and black basse-taille and champlevé enameled frame, alternating with cut-corner sq plaques with geo pattern enamel and seed pearl centers, linked to pairs of slightly convex lavender-enameled bars, continuing with alternating linked sqs and bars to an enameled box clasp, rev imp with maker's mk for Wolcott Mfg. Co., Providence, RI, 7/8" at center, 14 3/8" tl, **$600**. (Author's collection)

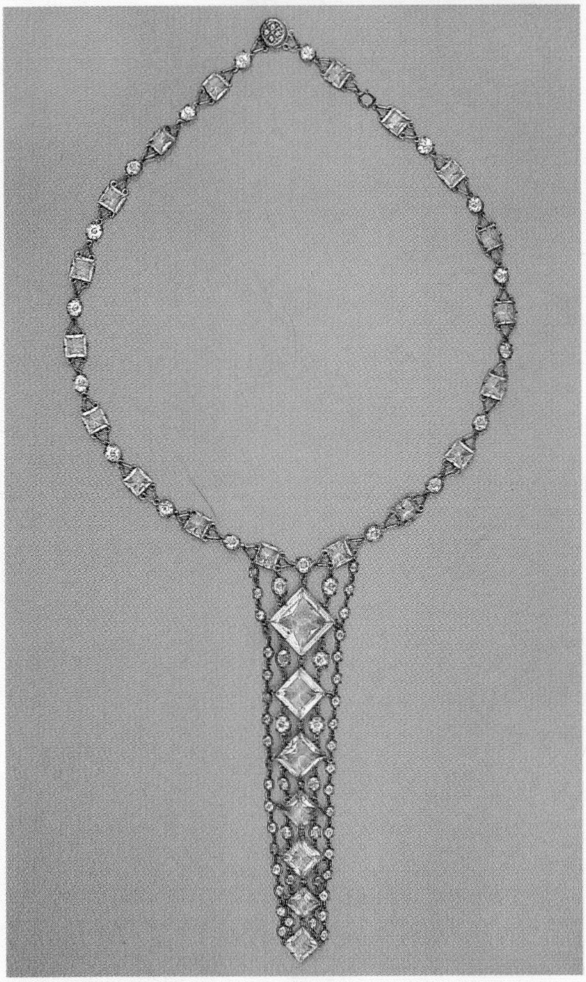

Necklace, lead crystal, silver, c. 1925, alternating links of sq and circ-cut colorless faceted stones prong-set in open-backed frames, joined with pairs of jump rings forming triangles, suspending a long tapered articulated central drop with a grad row of seven sq faceted stones turned 45 degrees flanked by double rows of chains of sm circ-cut stones, filigree snap closure mkd "GERMANY," 16" tl, 4½" T to B at center, **$200**. (Gail Eastman collection)

Necklaces, glass, gp brass, c. 1925, Czech:
T, geo stepped blue glass prong-set in gp brass links, spring ring clasp, mkd "CZECHO" on jump ring, ½" w x 16" tl, **$85**.
B, central shield-shaped pink and white glass cab flanked by gp brass links each set with two marquise-shaped prong-set pink and white glass stones, spring ring clasp, mkd "CZECHO" on rev of central element, 7/8" w at center, 15" tl, **$95**. (Marisela Doria collection)

Necklace, glass, gp brass, c. 1930, a central truncated pentagonal fuchsia glass cab in a gp beaded frame flanked by shell-shaped green glass stones in gp brass geo and foliate motif settings accented with faux pearls, linked to bezel-set triangular fuchsia cabs alternating with green shell shapes in gp and faux pearl mounts, probably Czech, 16" tl, 1⅜" at center, **$200**. (Courtesy of Generations, La Verne, CA)

Necklace, *arraché* (eggshell) lacquer, gilt base metal, c. 1935, rounded inverted triangular plaques joined with double rows of sm sq plaques coated with light blue eggshell lacquer and mounted on gp metal backs of conforming shapes, strung on chain, continuing to a single row of squares, lobster claw clasp, sgd (incised block letters) "JEAN DUNAND" on rev; provenance: the Dunand estate, 1⅛" T to B at center, 19" tl, **$5,000**. (Courtesy of Didier Antiques, London)

Necklace, bead sautoir, glass beads, c. 1925, Egyptian Revival, probably Czech, molded gray glass scarab, round, and sm indented bicone beads with ptd gilt and dk green accented details, interspersed with sm round red beads, hand-knotted continuous strand, 41" tl, **$75**. (Author's collection)

Pendant, glass, silver, rhinestones, enamel, c. 1920, bezel-set tapered rect cobalt blue glass surmounted by a r.s. within an open polychrome *plique à jour* enameled frame set with r.s., suspending a chain tassel, 1¾" w x 2¾" tl, chain 15" tl, **$300**. (Private collection)

Pendant, black onyx (dyed black chalcedony), marcasites, sterling, black enamel, seed pearls, c. 1925, a cusped black onyx plaque outlined in marcasites with a marcasite-set foliated urn motif in the center, ster frame mkd "GERMANY 935" (wg, enamel and pearl chain, not orig), 1⅜" w x 2", **$250**. (Courtesy of Generations, La Verne, CA)

Ring, rhinestones, silver, c. 1925, convertible, single rows of channel-set sq-cut red blue, and colorless r.s. in engr silver mount, hinged half hoops swivel to change face-up color of center band, ⅜" w, sz 7, **$175**. (Courtesy of Denese Strand, Laguna Hills, CA)

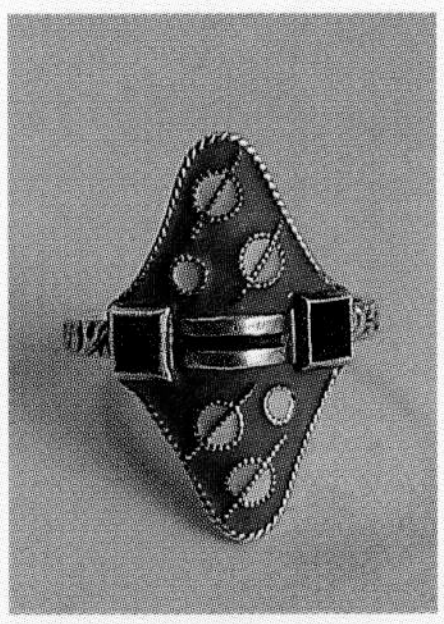

Ring, 935 silver, enamel, square syn stones, c. 1925, rounded lozenge shape, matte blue enamel ground decorated with yellow enameled disks and blue and yellow "Saturn" shapes, surmounted by a divided horizontal bar flanked by two bezel-set sq dk blue stones, mounted on a narrow shank, mkd "935, DÉPOSÉ," maker's mk for Theodor Fahrner, ⅝" w x 1⅞," sz 8, **$1,200**. (Private collection)

Suite: Necklace and Pendent Earrings, 800 silver gilt, glass, seed pearls, c. 1920, Hungarian, necklace of openwork silver gilt links set with circ-cut dk blue glass and seed pearls suspending a pear-shaped pendant of openwork floral/foliate motifs, an oval-cut blue glass stone in the center encircled with seed pearls and sm circ-cut blue glass stones, a vertical line of seed pearls above, a C-scroll of seed pearls below, terminating in a blue glass-set drop, replaced spring-ring clasp, pendent earrings of similar design set with blue glass and seed pearls, orig screwbacks imp with Hungarian hmk (dog's head in reserve with P mint-mark, #3), "800," pendant ⅝" x 2¼", 16¼" tl, earrings ⅝" x 2½" tl, **$750**. (Private collection)

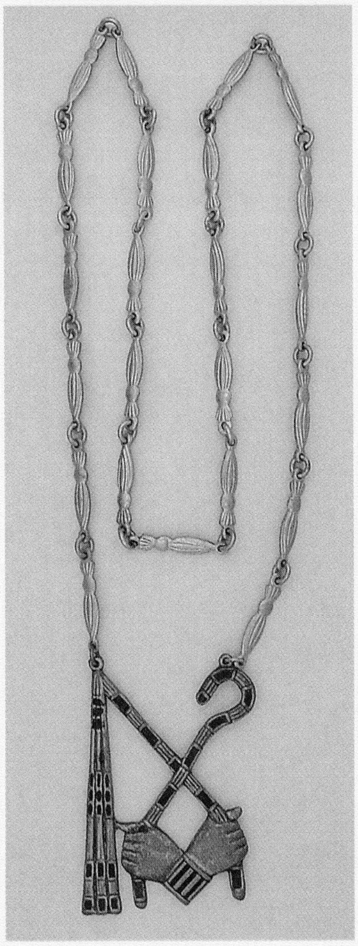

Pendant and Chain, gp brass, enamel, c. 1925, Egyptian Revival, die-stamped gp brass pendant in the shape of hands holding the crook and flail (symbols of a pharaoh's rule) with dk blue *champlevé* enameled accents (plating worn), suspended from a continuous lotus motif and circ jump ring chain, pendant 2" w x 2¾", **$75**. (Author's collection)

Suite: Necklace and Earrings, rock crystal, sterling, c. 1920, necklace of sixteen 15mm quartz crystal beads, each drilled for a U-shaped link at both ends securing ornamental scallop-edged ster caps, joined with swiveling links, matching drop earrings, each with an 11mm bead, ster surmount, screwbacks mkd "STERLING," necklace 17½" tl, earrings 1¼" tl, **$275**. (Courtesy of Ocean Eyz Antique Jewelry, Orange, CA)

Suite: Hinged Bangle Bracelet and Brooch/Pin, rhodium-plated wm, glass, enamel, r.s., c. 1925, brooch a tapered scallop-edged lozenge-shaped plaque with stamped wm filigree foliate and geo design, central millegrained bezel-set lt blue circ-cut stone encircled by a quatrefoil with enameled geo floral pattern in lt blue, black, yellow, and white, sm fleur-de-lis in blue-enameled lobed corners, flanked by two circ-cut colorless r.s.; matching stamped filigree hinged bangle with central scalloped section, lt blue circ-cut stone and enameled frame flanked by circ-cut r.s. and similarly enameled panels of overlapping navette shapes, v-spring and box clasp with safety chain, unmkd, bangle 1" w at center, 2⅛" inside dia, brooch 2⅜" w x 1¼", **$300**. (Courtesy of Pat Seal, Treasures From Yesterday, Fort Worth, TX)

PLASTICS and OTHER NOVELTY JEWELRY c. 1920-1970

In her introduction to the chapter on jewelry in *Art Plastic*, Andrea DiNoto remarks, "If one word were needed to summon up the spirit of the twenties and thirties, 'novelty' would do nicely." For the first time, the idea of wearing jewelry for *fun* caught on. The ideal material for creating this new type of jewelry was plastic—lightweight, inexpensive, and colorful. Although jewelry had been made from celluloid, the earliest semi-synthetic plastic, as far back as 1875, it was limited in style, made mostly in the form of imitation ivory, coral, amber, and tortoiseshell for naturalistic ornamental and utilitarian pieces (see Early Celluloid in the Late Victorian section). It was worn primarily by those who could not afford "the real thing." It wasn't until the reckless, lighthearted attitude of the flapper came on the scene that we begin to see whimsical and flamboyant items appear, in decidedly *unnatural* colors.

In the first half of the twentieth century, many types of plastic were developed and given trade names by the manufacturers that produced them. Numerous different trade names were given to the same generic substance, as each manufacturer strove for proprietary identification of the material. Over the years, certain names came into generic usage in spite of the fact that they were registered trade names (like Kleenex and Xerox). The three names in most common usage today are celluloid (the word is now seldom capitalized) for pyroxylin-camphor thermoplastic, Bakelite (sometimes written lowercase) for thermosetting phenol formaldehyde resin, and Lucite (seldom lowercase) for thermoplastic polymethacrylates or acrylics. Sometimes these labels are erroneously applied to other, related but not chemically identical, plastics. For example, cellulose acetate (trade name "Lumarith") is often incorrectly called celluloid, and casein plastic, a thermoset (trade name "Galalith"), is commonly confused with Bakelite. Accurately identifying these materials requires a variety of tests, some of which are potentially destructive.

Some collectors believe that a piece of plastic jewelry is collectible and has value because of other factors, such as design and craftsmanship, and that the type of plastic used is of secondary importance. They feel that knowing exactly what a piece is made of is not worth the risks involved in testing. Others consider correct material identification an important part of classifying, circa-dating, and putting a piece in historical context, all of which serves to enhance the value of their collection. Furthermore, the escalating values of Bakelite jewelry over the past few years have made some collectors regard testing as mandatory before purchase, which has generated the use of a variety of products never meant to be used for such "tests" to "prove" a piece to be Bakelite. The middle ground—the one taken here—is making educated guesses based on *non*-destructive sensory tests, and grouping plastics by generic types—thermoplastics and thermosets—and their related trade names. Although there are now dozens of different plastics on the market, for most collectible jewelry purposes, the ones covered here are celluloid, casein (Galalith), Bakelite, cellulose acetate (Lumarith), and Lucite.

Thermoplastics are those that will soften or melt with the application of heat. Once cooled, they will again become solid. Thermosets are liquid (resinous) before they are molded or cast, but once they solidify, they remain solid. Thermoplastic scraps can be recycled. Thermosets cannot. All plastics can be classified in one or the other of these two categories.

Celluloid and cellulose acetate

Celluloid, the first successful *semi*-synthetic thermoplastic, is part natural fiber, or cellulose. Its generic names, pyroxylin-camphor thermoplastic, sometimes referred to as cellulose nitrate, are clues to its makeup: cellulose fiber mixed with nitric acid (nitrated) to which camphor is added, and subjected to heat. Celluloid was first used as a substitute for natural materials, but its versatility, coupled with imaginative designs and new processes, later yielded a variety of forms. In 1902, a patent was granted for a process of setting rhinestones or metal into celluloid, thereby enhancing its decorative potential. In 1923, a synthetic pearl essence was invented, called "H-scale." It replaced the more expensive fish scale type of pearl essence (the coating on simulated pearls) for celluloid, and was used on toilet articles, decorative accessories, and jewelry.

One of the major drawbacks of celluloid was its flammability, due to the nitrocellulose it contained. In 1927, the Celluloid Corporation introduced Lumarith, its trade name for cellulose acetate, which substituted acetic acid (vinegar) for nitric acid and camphor. Except for its bright colors, in appearance and use, cellulose acetate is the same as Celluloid, but non-flammable. It is often labeled celluloid, but technically and chemically, this is incorrect. When warmed in hot water, the two materials can be differentiated: Celluloid smells like camphor; cellulose acetate, like vinegar. (This test should not be used on a piece set with rhinestones or other materials susceptible to water damage, nor should any piece be immersed in water for more than a few seconds.) The use of cellulose acetate coincided with the development of the injection-molding process, which made mass-production of inexpensive plastic items possible. In the 1960s and 1970s, an extensive line of large and small pins, bangles, and "stretchy" bracelets was made from laminated cellulose acetate by Lea Stein of Paris. These colorful figural and geometric pieces now have a large collector following (see brooches on page 154).

Celluloid articles should be stored carefully, in a dry and ventilated place. They are subject to disintegration if exposed to extremes of temperature, constant moisture, or corroding metal. Cracks, crystallization, and discoloration are signs of decomposition. Already damaged pieces are "contagious" and should be kept separate from others.

Much of the foregoing information on celluloid was brought to light by Julie P. Robinson, celluloid historian, who is co-author of a book on collectible celluloid and its inventor, John Wesley Hyatt (see References in the back of

Bracelets, bangles, celluloid, rhinestones, c. 1925-30:
L, ivory-colored, in the form of a coiled snake with its head joining and draped around the tail, inlaid with rows of circ colorless r.s., red r.s. eyes, ½" w at center, 2¼" inside dia, **$300**.
R, transparent celluloid, outside ptd dk pink and inlaid with diag rows of lavender r.s., ½" w, 2½" inside dia, **$195**. (Courtesy of Deja Voodoo, Santa Cruz, CA)

Bracelets, bangles, celluloid, rhinestones, c. 1925, group of six: blue r.s. on amber-colored, blue r.s. on green, deep yellow r.s. on yellow, green r.s. on amber-colored, colorless r.s. on ivory-colored, ⅛" to ½" w, all approx 2½" inside dia, each, **$60-125**. (Courtesy of Generations, La Verne, CA)

the book). She has obtained copies of U.S. patents and perused the archives of the Celluloid Corporation and other pyroxylin plastics manufacturers, and the Smithsonian Institution. Most material on collectible plastics published within the last 15 years has focused on Bakelite and later plastics, with sketchy—and sometimes conflicting—details about plastic's earliest developments. Therefore, the information on celluloid that Ms. Robinson has researched from original archival material has been the primary technical source for this section.

Hair combs and hatpins were among the earliest items of personal adornment made of celluloid, following fashion's currents at the turn of the century. (Leominster, Massachusetts, was a center for hair comb production, first in natural materials, then plastics. It is now the center for a plastics museum, see References). But when fashions changed, these fell by the wayside. Hatpins shrank to become hat ornaments, with a threaded metal pinpoint that was pushed through the hat and secured with a second ornamental "head" (similar to fine jewelry's "jabot" or "*cliquet*" pins, see page 155 for a whimsical version of a jabot pin).

Famous dancer Irene Castle cut her hair in a "bob" in 1914, prompting thousands of her fans to follow suit, thus signaling the demise of the hair comb. Surprisingly, hair combs didn't completely disappear when "the bob" became the predominant hairstyle. Large and ornate Spanish-style back combs, often embellished with rhinestones and painted enamel, were still occasionally worn, bound to the head, in the late '20s, when the tango was all the rage, and Spanish lace, fringed shawls, and flounced skirts were part of a dancer's costume. A more typical '20s head ornament was the headband, or bandeau. These too, were made of rhinestone-studded celluloid. Because the material is flexible, the headbands are adjustable, held by an ornamental celluloid clasp. Today, these are rare finds. Celluloid bangles, many ivory- or amber-colored, but in other colors as well, were worn from wrist to elbow, in the fashion made popular by heiress Nancy Cunard. The ones most sought-after today have painted designs and/or geometric patterns of pavé rhinestones set into them (see above right). Another unusual treatment was the layering of silver foil in patterns over the celluloid, similar to silver overlay glass (see page 149). Whimsical figural pins, buckles, dress clips, and short chain necklaces with dangling floral or figural motifs were also made of celluloid. Celluloid (pyroxylin plastics) continued to be used for jewelry well into the 1940s (post-WW II molded figural pieces marked "Occupied Japan" can still be found), but with the development of other less flammable and more easily mass-produced plastics, celluloid fell out of favor. After the Celluloid Corp. became part of Celanese in 1947, U.S. production was discontinued. Japan continued to make pyroxylin items during the '50s.

Bakelite and casein:

The first entirely synthesized plastic was invented by Leo H. Baekeland in 1908 (patented 1909). As with many inventions, it was accidental. He was searching for a formula for synthetic shellac, at which he failed miserably. Instead, he came up with "the material of a thousand uses," as the advertisers called it: thermosetting phenol formaldehyde resin. He christened it Bakelite. Other companies started manufacturing similar phenolics, and came up with their own trade names, among them: Catalin, Marblette, Durez, and Prystal. Bakelite is the name that has stuck with collectors, although some purists insist upon calling it by the generic name "phenolic" or the trade name "Catalin" (most jewelry made from this material was made by the Catalin Corporation).

Jewelry was not the first of the thousand uses. The Depression created a market for it, because it was cheap to manufacture, colorful, and lent itself to a wide range of styles and manufacturing techniques. It gave women a much-needed lift, to both their outfits and their spirits. Bakelite was well-suited to the chunky, heavy jewelry styles of the '30s. It could be laminated into geometric shapes (polka dots were a popular motif), set with rhinestones, clad or inlaid with metal, carved on a lathe, made into the shapes of animals, fruits, or other realistic figurals. Colorless Bakelite, (introduced in 1935 by the Catalin Corp., whose trade name for it was Prystal,) was carved on the back side with floral or figural designs. The carving was sometimes enhanced with paint. From the front, the designs look three-dimensional. "Reverse-carved" is today's name for this technique. Over

Brooches/Pins and Dress Clips, rev-carved "apple juice" Bakelite, paint, c. 1935-45:
L, circ plaque of rev-carved floral motif, surrounded by a circ frame of laminated, translucent "root beer" Bakelite, 2" dia, $325.
LC, crescent-shaped plaque, rev-carved and ptd floral motif, 3" w, **$225**.
T, rect bar with rev-carved and ptd floral motif with butterscotch-colored Bakelite laminated caps, 3" w x ¾", **$375**.
RC, bell-shaped dress clip, rev-carved and ptd daisy floral motif, 1¾" w x 1", **$75**.
R, triangular plaque dress clip, rev-carved and ptd geo houndstooth pattern, 1¾" w, **$125**. (Photo courtesy of Matthew Burkholz, Route 66 Antiques, Chatham, NY)

time, the pieces have oxidized to a light amber color, which collectors call "apple juice." (see above and pages 150 and 154). Reverse-carved fish and aquarium motifs are particularly desirable (see bangle on page 151).

Bracelets of all types—solid and hinged bangles, link, elastic "stretchies," cuffs, and charm bracelets—brooches, dress clips, shoe clips, buckles, earrings, rings, necklaces, beads, and pendants were all made from Bakelite. Bakelite jewelry and objects have been avidly collected for the past 20 years. Several books and magazine articles have covered the subject quite thoroughly (see References in the back for some of them). Over the past several years, a number of books on Bakelite jewelry and related objects have been published (see References), an indication of Bakelite's heightened popularity (and escalating prices). "Themed" figurals (patriotic, school, sports, animals, people, fruits and vegetables, Mexican motifs, etc.), and multi-colored laminated geometrics (especially bangles, solid and hinged) are among today's most sought-after Bakelite items. Of particular interest to many collectors are designs attributed to Martha Sleeper (1910-1983), an actress turned designer whose work has been documented in several of the books on Bakelite jewelry listed below. Sleeper and her jewelry made headlines in 1938, but after World War II, she went on to other things. Examples of Martha Sleeper designs are pictured on pages 151 and 152).

Casein plastic has received relatively little attention compared to Bakelite, the material it is often confused with. Most pieces made of casein plastic generate relatively little collector interest or value, with one exception. Not much plastic jewelry is signed or even attributed, but certain casein plastic pieces were: Auguste Bonaz, whose company is known for its geometric necklaces of the early '30s, which are now rare and sought-after. According to Ginger Moro in *European Designer Jewelry*, these necklaces were always made of Galalith, the trade name for casein. A more typical use of casein can be seen in the Egyptian motif belt on page 149.

Lucite

Although the German manufacturers Röhm and Haas are credited with being the first to formulate acrylic resin (1928), their trade name for it, Plexiglas, seems to be used mainly in reference to utilitarian and decorative objects. Lucite, introduced by DuPont in 1937, is the trade name most often heard in reference to jewelry. Lucite is water clear in its original form, but it is often tinted in a wide range of transparent to opaque colors. Jewelry made entirely of Lucite has only recently been recognized as collectible. Molded, tinted, and reverse-carved Lucite figurals are becoming nearly as sought-after as their early '40s Bakelite contemporaries. After the war, Bakelite was no longer cost-effective to produce, but Lucite, a thermoplastic, continued to be manufactured and is still in use today. Post-war jewelry forms, however, are quite different from earlier pieces.

Some circa 1940s novelty jewelry was made of Lucite combined with other materials like Bakelite, wood, leather, and metal. One of the hottest items amongst costume jewelry collectors a few years ago, "jelly bellies," have Lucite as the center, or "belly," of sterling animal pins. These were made in the '40s by Trifari and other American manufacturers (see "Designer/Manufacturer Signed Costume, c. 1935-50" section). In the '50s, "pearlized" Lucite bangles and button earclips, often rhinestone- studded, were popular accessories, as were laminated or reverse-carved and painted brooches (see page 153), bracelets, and earrings encasing flowers, or embedded with pastel-dyed shells and glitter. In the 1960s, Lucite was often used in colorless form for chunky rings, necklaces, and bracelets. These were also laminated with colored layers forming reflective stripes (see rings below).

Sensory tests can reveal a plastic's identity without being destructive. The aforementioned hot water test works for Bakelite, Lucite, and casein, as well as celluloid and cellulose acetate. See References: *What's it Made Of?*, by Sheryl G. Shatz, for various sensory tests for each. It is not necessary to use any chemical products for testing, some of which do not give consistently positive results, and which may be destructive.

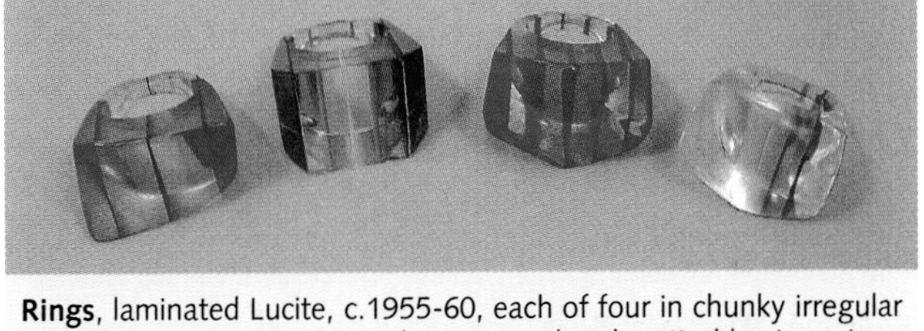

Rings, laminated Lucite, c.1955-60, each of four in chunky irregular angled transparent Lucite with narrow colored vertical laminae, in combinations of blue, orange, red, yellow, green or purple, ⅞" T to B at center, sz 7½, **$15 each**. (Courtesy of Patrick Kapty, Mad Jewelry, Palm Springs, CA)

Bracelet, hinged bangle, wood, leather, paint, c. 1940-45, carved wood horse's head with ptd eye and leather bridle surmounting a leather-topped circ wood disk, leather laced through punched holes and wrapped around border, mounted on a hinged shaped wood bangle with leather lacing through center holes, top 1¾" dia, 2⅛" inside dia, **$200**. (Diane White collection)

As prices of collectible plastics, especially Bakelite, have skyrocketed over the past few years, it is important to remember that plastics, unlike gold and gemstones, are not intrinsically valuable. The material itself is not collectible; what was made from it is. An unimaginative, plain, or downright ugly piece—even though it is "genuine" celluloid, Bakelite, or Lucite—will have little collector interest or value.

Other materials were used concurrently with plastics to produce whimsical novelty articles. In the 1940s, carved wood was a favorite material, alone or in combination with other materials. Western motifs were all the rage in wood, as well as plastic, due once again to the movies' influence. Horses' heads are the most prevalent motif (see bracelet above and brooches on page 153).

During wartime shortages, with factories given over to military production and European sources cut off, a kind of "make do" novelty jewelry was made, using readily available non-rationed materials to create amusing pieces. Many of these were hand-constructed. Ceramic or plaster composition, felt, yarn, leather, feathers, and sequins were combined to make fashion- head brooches, some of them resembling popular movie stars. These have been nicknamed "Victims of Fashion" by collectors. Others had exotic Oriental or African faces, some of which were also carved in wood. Wooden heads were also painted with "politically incorrect" cartoon-like features (see page 153). The Sears catalog of 1944 advertised "lapel 'pin-ups' in gay hand-painted ceramics"—caricatures of animals and people—with Lucite and yarn details. Once the war was over, this type of jewelry faded into oblivion. In the '50s, "cute" replaced "whimsical," and gold-plated metal and rhinestones were the usual materials of choice.

World War II also gave rise to the popularity of "sweetheart" jewelry: lockets and lapel pins representing the armed forces worn by wives and girlfriends of soldiers, sailors, and Marines fighting overseas. These often bore the insignia of the different military branches (see below).

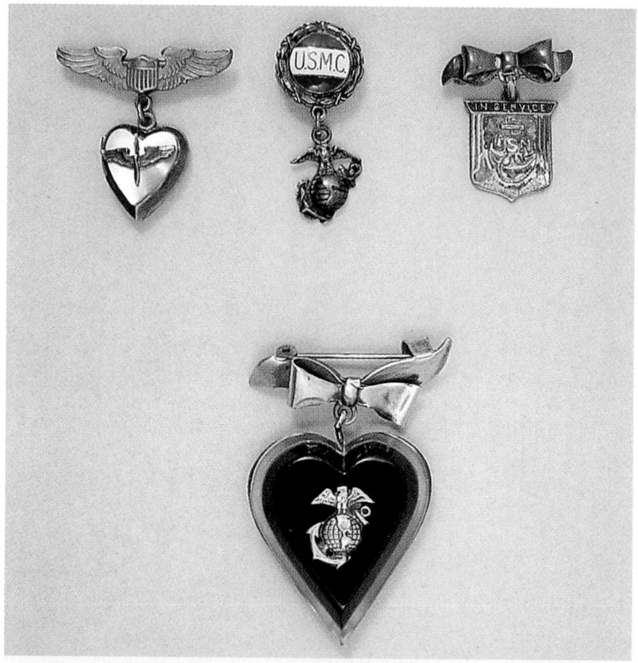

Brooches/Pins, World War II Armed Forces "sweetheart" pins, c. 1943:
TL, locket/pin, a pr of wings flanking a shield suspending a heart-shaped gp ster locket topped with MOP surmounted by the Army Air Corps insignia (propeller with wings), pin assembly with safety catch on rev of wings, mkd "AMICO [American Insignia Co., New York NY], STERLING + 1/20 10K," 1⅛" w x 1⅛", **$50**.
TC, circ wreath bordering a disk with red, white and blue enameled center, "U.S.M.C." on white ground, suspending a Marine Corps insignia charm, both pcs mkd "STERLING," pin assembly on disk rev, C-catch, ½" w x 1¼", **$30**.
TR, sterling, enamel, c. 1943, ster bow with pin assembly, safety catch, suspending a die-stamped shield with enameled "IN SERVICE" over Navy insignia with enameled letters "USN," rev mkd "STERLING," ⅞" w x 1", **$25**.
(Author's collection)
B, laminated black and colorless Lucite heart surmounted by a ster Marine insignia, suspended from a ster bow mkd "STERLING" on rev, 1⅛" w x 2", **$38**. (Courtesy of Gilly Phipps, Philadelphia, PA)

Reproduction Alert

As with anything that becomes highly collectible and expensive, Bakelite jewelry is once again being made, in both new and reproduction designs. The one saving grace for collectors is that producing a desirable piece is extremely labor-intensive, and requires a certain amount of craftsmanship. Some of today's makers are not attempting to deceive, and their work has become collectible in its own right. Marriages of old parts, and "fakelite" imitations (made of plastics other than Bakelite) are more commonly marketed as "vintage." Comparing a piece with a known old one, and buying from reputable dealers who stand behind their merchandise, are a collector's best protection.

Belt, Galalith (casein), wm, c. 1925, Egyptian Revival, mint green circ alternating with cut-corner rect Galalith plaques linked with wm serpent motif knots and lg circ wm jump rings, wm hook and eye closure riveted to terminal rect plaque and lg disk surmounted by a sq wm plaque stamped with a seated pharaoh motif, suspending two pear-shaped Galalith drops on unequal lengths of wm chain, center disk 1½" dia, 33½" tl, **$175**. (Author's collection)

Bracelets, bangles, celluloid with silver overlay, c. 1925-30, $195 each:
T, brown with foliate pattern, ⅝" w, 2¼" inside dia.
C, amber-colored with foliate pattern, ⅞" w x 2¼" inside dia.
B, dk brown with floral and foliate pattern, ¾" w x 2½" inside dia. (Photo courtesy of Morning Glory Antiques, Albuquerque, NM)

Bracelets, bangles, Bakelite and plated brass, matched pairs, c. 1930-35:
T, translucent yellow-green and amber-colored, each flat surface surmounted by a single row of lg faceted circ brass studs (some plating wear), ¾" w, 2½" inside dia, **$75 each**.
C, one red and one black, each with two lengthwise grooves, two wide brass bands flanking rounded centers, ⅞" w, 2½" inside dia, **$175** each.
B, one opaque yellow, one black, with repeating pattern of two brass bars, followed by one circ stud, 1" w, 2½" inside dia, **$250 each**. (Courtesy of Patrick Kapty, Mad Jewelry, Palm Springs, CA)

Bracelets, bangles, Bakelite, c. 1935-45, four prs of polka-dot bangles, each six-dot pr with opposed ground and inlaid dot colors, in black, yellow, marbleized green, marbleized red, and translucent "root beer," ½" w x 2½" inside dia, **$900-$950 each**. (Photo courtesy of Matthew Burkholz, Route 66 Antiques, Chatham, NY)

Bracelet, hinged bangle, Bakelite, paint, c. 1935, butterscotch-colored, deeply carved and painted roses, some wear to paint, 2½" inside dia, 1⅝" w, **$650**. (Courtesy of Ocean Eyz Antique Jewelry, Orange, CA)

Bracelet, hinged bangle, Bakelite, c. 1935-45, "Philadelphia" style, serrated design, butterscotch-colored Bakelite base with geo design laminated Bakelite fins in black, red, green, and yellow, 2" w, **$11,975**. (Photo courtesy of Matthew Burkholz, Route 66 Antiques, Chatham, NY)

Bracelets, bangles, rev-carved "apple juice"-colored Bakelite, c. 1935-45:
T, floral motif, ¾" w, **$875**.
C, ptd leaf, vine and floral motifs, ⅝" w, **$1,175**.
B, ptd geo crosshatch pattern, ¾" w, **$1,975**. (Photo courtesy of Matthew Burkholz, Route 66 Antiques, Chatham, NY)

Bracelet, bangle, Bakelite, paint, c. 1935-45, "apple juice" Bakelite with rev-carved and ptd fish motifs, medium wall thickness, ¾" w, **$1,975**. (Photo courtesy of Matthew Burkholz, Route 66 Antiques, Chatham, NY)

Bracelet, stretchy, Bakelite, elastic cord, paint, c. 1935-45, an oval central plaque of a rev-carved and ptd pansy motif in "apple juice" framed in laminated butterscotch, flanked by half-round and lozenge-shaped butterscotch segments strung on elastic cord, 1¾" at center, **$1,875**. (Photo courtesy of Matthew Burkholz, Route 66 Antiques, Chatham, NY)

Bracelets, bangles, carved Bakelite, c. 1935-45:
L, blue-green, carved lilypad floral decoration, medium wall thickness, ⅜" w, **$225**.
CL, yellow, with carved scallop and floral pattern, medium wall thickness, 1½" w, **$575**.
TC, red, carved with circ cross-hatched detail, medium wall thickness, ¾" w, **$475**.
CR, black, intricately carved with central flower and leaf design, medium wall thickness, 1½" w, **$875**.
R, intricately carved foliate motif in "root beer," medium wall thickness, ⅝" w, **$375**.
(Photo courtesy of Matthew Burkholz, Route 66 Antiques, Chatham, NY)

Brooch/Pin, wm, c. 1925, cutout wm depicting a flapper with a dog on a chain, C-catch, flapper ⅞" w x 2⅛", chain 2¾", dog 1" w x ½", **$50**. (Nancy Shadforth collection)

Brooches/Pins, carved Bakelite, c. 1935-45:
L, oval plaque of deeply carved and pierced butterscotch-colored Bakelite, flowerheads with burnt and ptd detail, 2¾" w x 2½", **$225**.
TC, carved and pierced tapered bar of red Bakelite, central butterfly motif flanked by flowers and leaves, 3" w x 1", **$175.**
BC, oval of deeply carved black Bakelite with floral and foliate motifs, 3" w x 2", **$275**.
R, rect plaque of deeply carved blue-green Bakelite with floral and foliate motifs, 2½" w x 1½", **$175**.
(Photo courtesy of Matthew Burkholz, Route 66 Antiques, Chatham, NY)

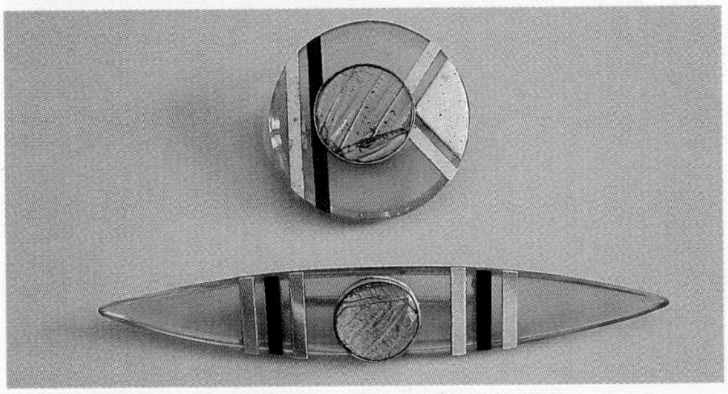

Brooches/Pins, Bakelite, butterfly wing, wm, glass, c. 1930:
T, circ plaque of "apple juice" Bakelite with black Bakelite and wm inset geo designs, a central circ disk of royal blue butterfly wing under a crystal cover, C-catch pin assembly attached with screws, 1⅝" dia, **$145**.
B, lenticular plaque of "apple juice" Bakelite with black Bakelite and wm inset geo designs, a central circ disk of royal blue butterfly wing under crystal cover, C-catch pin assembly attached with screws, 4" w, **$165**. (Photo courtesy of Morning Glory Antiques, Albuquerque, NM)

Brooches/Pins, figurals, Bakelite, paint, c. 1940-45:
L, in the shape of a turtle, dk orange Bakelite with ptd eye and carved feet, 2½" w x 1¼", **$275**.
C, carved and pierced "apple juice" Bakelite, an open circ "porthole" framing a carved sailfish with brown ptd accents, carved waves, 2" dia, **$475**.
R, in the shape of a lobster, overdyed rust-colored Bakelite with vinyl-coated string antennae and ptd glass eyes, 3" w x 1", **$975**. (Photo courtesy of Matthew Burkholz, Route 66 Antiques, Chatham, NY)

Brooches/Pins, fruit motifs, Bakelite, cellulose acetate, c. 1935-45:
L, five drops in the shapes of pears in butterscotch Bakelite with green and yellow cellulose acetate leaves, on a cellulose acetate chain with yellow links, suspended from a rect butterscotch Bakelite bar, 2" w x 4", **$975**.
C, five carved strawberries of red and lt green Bakelite with dk green cellulose acetate leaves, on cellulose acetate chain with red links, suspended from rect red Bakelite bar, 2" w x 4", **$975**.
R, five mixed fruit shapes of red and butterscotch Bakelite with dk green cellulose acetate leaves, on cellulose acetate chain with marbleized red and yellow links, suspended from rect red Bakelite bar, 2" w x 4", **$1,750**. (Photo courtesy of Matthew Burkholz, Route 66 Antiques, Chatham, NY)

Brooches/Pins, Bakelite, paint, c. 1940, attributed to Martha Sleeper:
L, carved yellow zebra, ptd stripes and eye, leather ears, two pcs, head riveted to body, 3" w x 2", **$975**.
C, carved pink overdyed squirrel, ptd detail, 2" w x 1¼", **$475**.
R, dog in overdyed butterscotch-colored Bakelite, with carved and ptd detail, floppy leather ears, 1" w x 1¼", **$675**. (Photo courtesy of Matthew Burkholz, Route 66 Antiques, Chatham, NY)

Brooch/Pin, Bakelite, wood, vinyl-coated string, c. 1940, branch-shaped, carved brown Bakelite surmounted by three bird figures in red, yellow, and green Bakelite with string tails, attributed to Martha Sleeper, 3" w x ¾", **$1,375**. (Photo courtesy of Matthew Burkholz, Route 66 Antiques, Chatham, NY)

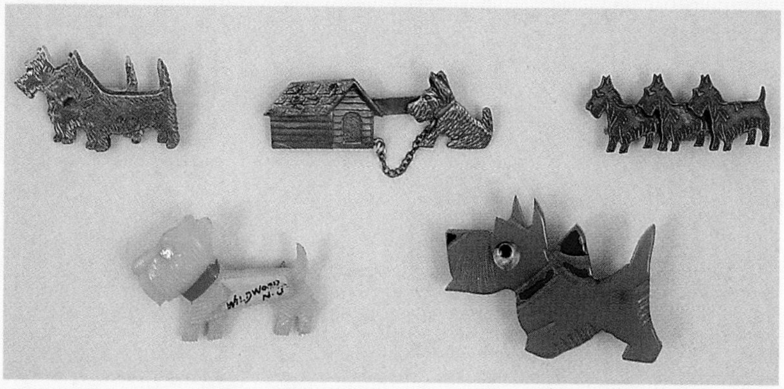

Brooches/Pins, Scottie dog motifs, c. 1940:
TL, stamped wm plaque in shape of two Scotties standing shoulder-to-shoulder, engr detail, 1⅜" w x ⅞", **$25**.
TC, two stamped brass plaques, a Scottie attached by a chain to a doghouse and by flat brass strip attached to rev of each plaque, engr detail, ⅞" w x ¾", **$35**.
TR, standing Scottie dog trio, overlapping stamped brass plaques, engr detail, 1½" w x ⅝", **$25**.
BL, molded plastic Scottie dog, ptd red collar and hand ptd black lettering "Wildwood N.J." colorless r.s. eye, 1⅝" w x 1⅛", **$25**.
BR, green Bakelite Scottie dog with dk red painted bow and black ptd nose, glass eye, some chipping of ptd details, 1⅝" w x 1¼", **$145**.
(Courtesy of Gilly Phipps, Philadelphia, PA)

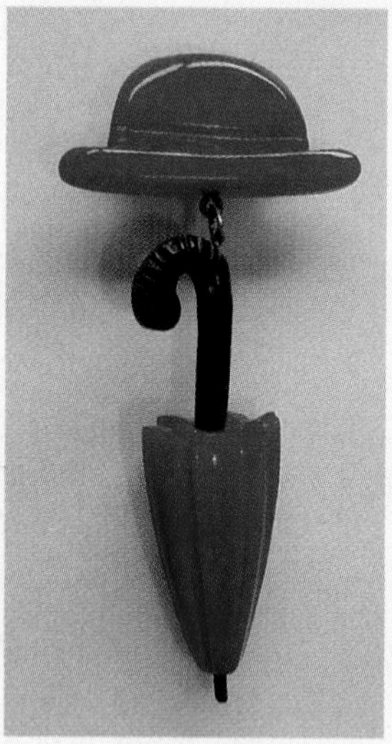

Brooch/Pin, Bakelite, wood, c. 1935, carved red Bakelite bowler hat suspending a carved red Bakelite umbrella with wood handle and tip, inset pin assembly on rev of hat, 2⅛" w x 4½" tl, **$700**. (Courtesy of Diane Richardson, The Gold Hatpin, Oak Park, IL)

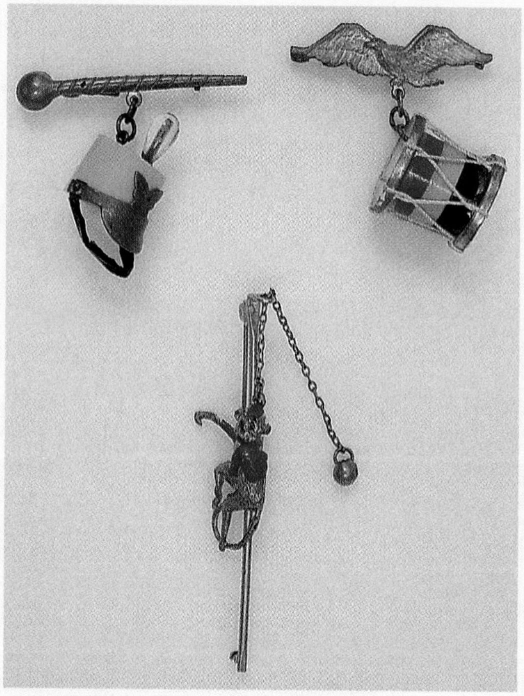

Brooches/Pins, figural novelties, c. 1935-40:
TL, brass marching baton suspending a majorette's hat in opaque yellow Bakelite, brass detail, a colorless glass bead "plume," and black fabric chinstrap, 1¾" w x 1¼", **$85**.
TR, stamped brass eagle in flight suspending a Bakelite drum with red, yellow (oxidized white), and dk blue stripes, brass top and bottom, and string details, 1⅝" w x 1¾", **$95**.
(Courtesy of Deja Voodoo, Santa Cruz, CA)
B, brass rod with sliding brass monkey figure with red ptd hat, eyes, and jacket, moves up and down rod when chain is pulled, ¾" w x 3", **$45**.
(Diane White collection)

Brooch/Pin, Bakelite, paint, metal, c. 1935-45, in the shape of a hand, butterscotch-colored Bakelite with ptd fingernails and cuffed wrist with a metal link bracelet, 4" w x 2", **$1,375**. (Photo courtesy of Matthew Burkholz, Route 66 Antiques, Chatham, NY)

Brooch/Pin, Bakelite, paint, c. 1935-45, cartoon animal carved in overdyed butterscotch Bakelite, pivoting arm holding a sword, moves when worn, ptd details, 2" square, **$2,475**. (Photo courtesy of Matthew Burkholz, Route 66 Antiques, Chatham, NY)

Brooch/Pin, celluloid, rhinestones, brass, c. 1940-45, transparent celluloid plaque in the shape of an eagle, one wing set with red r.s., body set with colorless r.s., and other wing set with blue r.s., red r.s. eye, suspending a V-shaped plaque from celluloid rings, banded sections set with red, colorless and blue r.s., 2⅝" x 2⅝", **$350**. (Courtesy of D. Brett Benson, Inc., Chicago, IL)

Brooches/Pins, wood figurals, c. 1940-45:
L, carved wood Longhorn steer head with ptd black eyes, green felt ears and black yarn forelock, inset pin mechanism, safety catch, 4½" w x 3½", **$30**.
C, carved cartoon-like wood giraffe head with ptd black, yellow, and white features, green felt ears, red felt tongue, and black felt eyelashes, inset pin mechanism, safety catch, 1½" w x 4", **$30**.
R, carved wood cartoon-like donkey with black bead eye, ptd red and white features, and jute tail, riveted pin mechanism, C-catch, 4" w x 4½", **$35**. (BeeGee McBride collection, photo by John Borgstrom)

Brooches/Pins, figurals, wood, plastic, paint, c. 1940-45:
L, carved cartoon-like wood horse with ptd white features and brown plastic-coated wire tail, mane, and forelock, inset pin mechanism, safety catch, 2" x 3", **$55**.
R, carved wood scarecrow with ptd red and black features, yellow plastic hat, dangling white plastic hands and red plastic shoes, jute "straw" accents, inset pin mechanism, safety catch, 3" w x 4", **$75**. (BeeGee McBride collection, photo by John Borgstrom)

Brooches/Pins, "politically incorrect" caricatures, wood, c. 1940-1945:
L, cutout wood plaque in the shape of a cartoon-like native's head, ptd red and black features, celluloid "googly" eyes, Bakelite bead nose, appl red wire earrings, bow tie, and topknot decoration, riveted pin mechanism, C-catch on rev, 2¼" w x 3½", **$40**.
C, cutout wood plaque in the shape of a scimitar surmounted by a cartoon-like frowning face with glass eyes, ptd yellow and black features, brass link chain attached between handle and blade of scimitar, 1⅛" w x 3¼", **$30**.
R, cutout wood plaque in the shape of a cartoon-like frowning native's head, ptd red features, beard and topknot of appl fur, inset C-catch on rev, 2¼" w x 3½", **$30**. (BeeGee McBride collection, photo by John Borgstrom)

Brooch/Pin, plastic, brass, c. 1945, molded black plastic old-style telephone with moving brass dial, white plastic dial face, and ptd black numbers, coiled cord spells out "Call," 2⅜" w x 1½", **$50**. (Courtesy of Gilly Phipps, Philadelphia, PA)

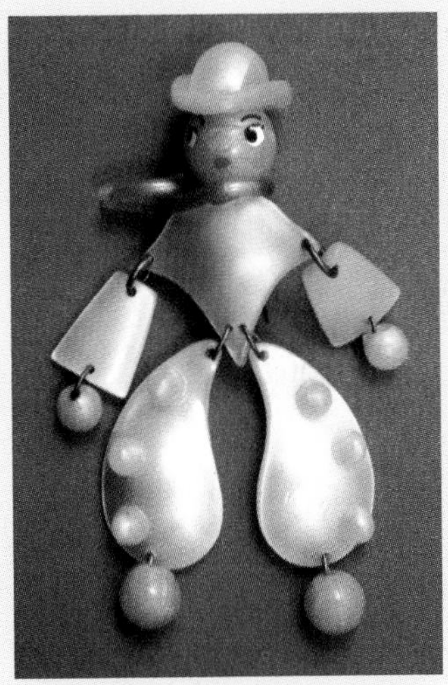

Brooch/Pin, polyethylene, paint, brass, c. 1950, an articulated cartoonlike cowboy in pastel colors, ptd face, arms and legs terminating in round beads for hands and feet, all joined with brass jump rings, 1⅞" w x 4" tl, **$95**. (Author's collection)

Brooches/Pins, rev-carved flower motifs, Lucite, paint, c. 1955-60:
TL, octagonal faceted colorless Lucite plaque with rev-carved and ptd orange hibiscus and green leaves, flat backing, 1⅜" dia, **$25**.
TR, tapered rect colorless Lucite plaque with rev-carved and ptd red roses and green leaves, 1⅝" w x 1¼", **$15**.
BC, oval colorless Lucite plaque, rev-carved and ptd black ground with central white rose and leaves, 2¼" w x 1", **$15**. (Ellie Laubner collection)

Brooch/Pin, cellulose acetate, wm, c. 1965, in the shape of an Airedale ("Ric the Terrier"), heat-set pin-back mkd "LEA STEIN, PARIS," 2¼" w x 3¾", **$100**. (Courtesy of Gilly Phipps, Philadelphia, PA)

Brooches/Pins, cellulose acetate, wm, Lea Stein, c. 1965:
TL, blackbird with white patterned wings and beak, pin back mkd "LEA STEIN, PARIS," paper label mkd "MADE IN FRANCE," 1¾" w x 1", **$75**.
BL, foliate motif in red plastic with colorless berries, pin back mkd "LEA STEIN PARIS," 2½" w x 1½", **$65**.
(Sue James collection)
R, laminated, in the shape of a female figure with black hair, white arms, legs, and face, pearlized red dress, pin back mkd "LEA STEIN PARIS," 1½" w x 2¼", **$75**. (Mary Williamson collection)

Buckles, celluloid, paint, c. 1930:
T, oval oxidized colorless celluloid with openwork entrelac quatrefoil motif, ptd green, blue, and red sections with inlaid matching r.s., flat celluloid bar for belt on rev, 3½" w x 2½", **$30**. (Vickie Vega collection)
B, ivory-colored open rectangle with molded ivory tulips, lt green ptd leaves, and lavender ptd dahlias in relief on pebbled-texture ground, wm center bar, 3½" w x 2½", **$60**. (Diane White collection)

Dress Clips, celluloid, paint, wm, c. 1930, made in Japan:
TL, pr of irreg tapered oval ivory-colored plaques with molded rose, daisy, and foliate motifs, daisies ptd yellow and leaves ptd blue-green, flat-backed wm hinged clips on rev, 1" w x 1⅞", **$40**.
TR, pr of rounded triangular laminated ivory-colored plaques, with pierced and molded stylized floral motif, red-orange and yellow ptd accents, flat-backed hinged clips, rev ink-stamped "MADE IN JAPAN," 1¾" w x 1½", **$45**.
BL, shield-shaped, pierced and molded lt yellow celluloid plaque with dahlia, daisy, and foliate motifs, lt orange and green ptd accents, flat-backed hinged clip on rev, 1¾" w x 2", **$15**.
BC, tapered oval ivory-colored celluloid plaque with carved dahlia and foliate motifs, pearlescent ptd pink and green accents, flat-backed hinged clip on rev, 1¼" w x 2", **$20**.
BR, shield-shaped, pierced and carved lt yellow celluloid plaque with lg central rose, daisy, and foliate motifs, lt green ptd accents, flat-backed hinged clip and ink-stamped "JAPAN" on rev, 1¾" w x 2", **$10**. (Diane White collection)

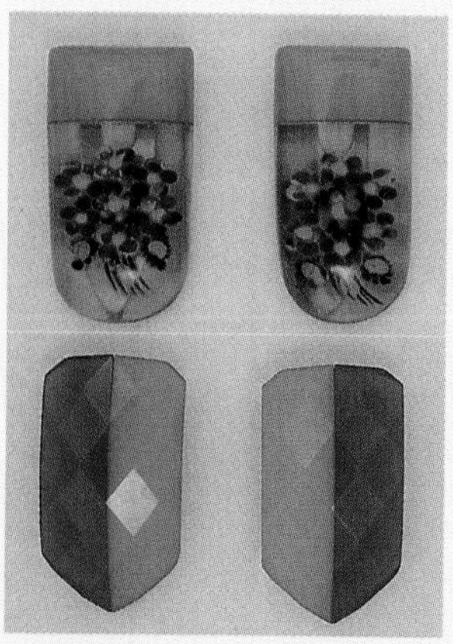

Dress Clips, Bakelite, wm, c. 1935-40:
T, pr of convex rounded-end oblong plaques, transparent "apple juice" Bakelite with rev-carved and painted floral motif, surmounted by laminated butterscotch-colored Bakelite tapered convex rect sections, flat-backed hinged clips on rev, 1" w x 1¾", **$75**. (Diane White collection)
B, two-tone pr, each with one half "root beer" and the other half "butterscotch" laminated and faceted Bakelite forming slightly convex elongated pentagons, flat-backed wm hinged clips on rev, 1" w x 1¾", **$65**. (Author's collection)

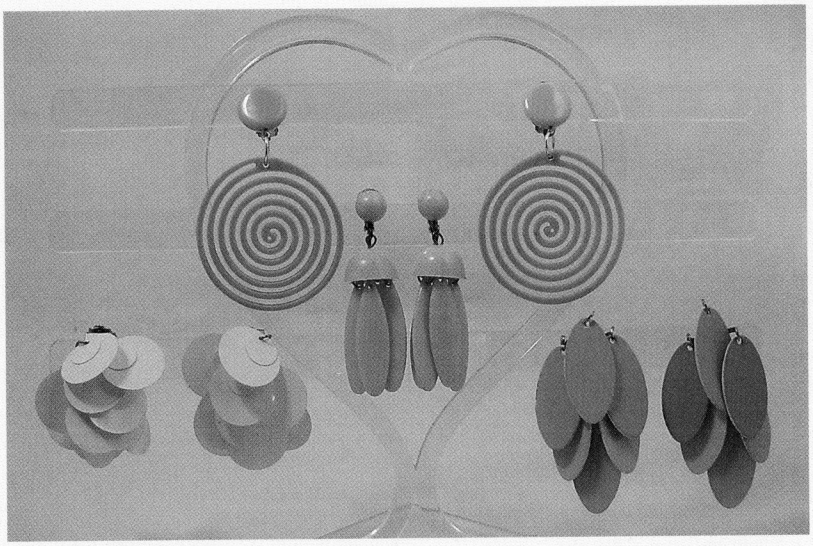

Earrings, plastic, metal, c. 1960:
T, spiral-patterned turq discs suspended from circ turq plastic surmounts, clipbacks, 1¾" w x 2⅝", **$25**.
C, each a cluster of flat lenticular pink plaques suspended from a domed plastic cap, spherical plastic surmounts, clipbacks, 2⅜" tl, **$25**.
BL, clusters of lg and sm white plastic disks attached to gp clipbacks, disks ¾" dia, **$25**.
BR, clusters of elliptical turq disks attached to gp clipbacks, ovals ⅝" w x 1¼", **$25**.
(Courtesy of Patrick Kapty, Mad Jewelry, Palm Springs, CA)

Jabot Pin, or Hat Ornament, celluloid, paint, wm, c. 1925, in the shape of a football player kicking a football, football detaches from pinstem, 3" w x 1½", **$75**. (Courtesy of Patrick Kapty, Mad Jewelry, Palm Springs, CA)

Necklace, Bakelite, cellulose acetate, c. 1940, political party motif Bakelite charms, cream white elephants, blue donkeys, and red stars, suspended from colorless cellulose acetate chain, 26" tl, animals 1½", **$225.** (Photo courtesy of Morning Glory Antiques, Albuquerque, NM)

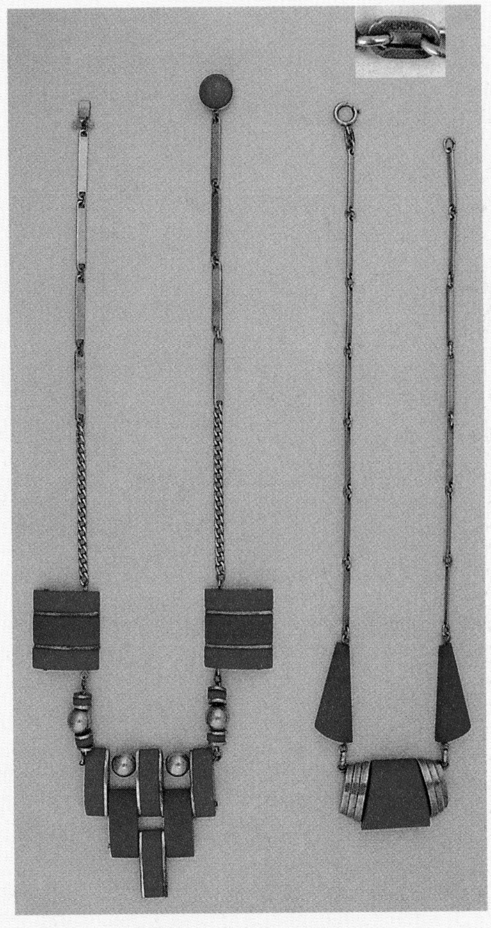

Necklaces, Bakelite, chrome, c. 1935:
L, articulated inverted ziggurat of rounded red Bakelite rectangles with chrome frames in a tank-track pattern flanked by round chrome bead spacers, red Bakelite and chrome rondels, and segmented Bakelite and chrome rect plaques, continuing to a wm curb link chain and rect bar links, v-spring and circ box clasp surmounted by a circ red Bakelite cab, 17¾" tl, 1⅞" T to B at center, **$250**.
R, central rounded convex red Bakelite trapezoid flanked by chrome stepped half cylinders linked to two truncated rounded red Bakelite triangles, continuing to a flat rect wm bar link chain, flat oval jump ring mkd "GERMANY" linked to spring ring clasp, 17" tl, ⅞" T to B at center, **$175**.
(Courtesy of Deja Voodoo, Santa Cruz, CA)

Necklace, Bakelite, cellulose acetate, brass, vinyl-coated string, c. 1935-45, red cellulose acetate link chain suspending various-sized carved red Bakelite cherries with green vinyl-coated string stems and dk green cellulose acetate leaves from brass jump rings, 30" tl, **$675**. (Photo courtesy of Matthew Burkholz, Route 66 Antiques, Chatham, NY)

Necklace, Bakelite, cellulose acetate, c. 1935-45, a fringe of grad-length, red cellulose acetate chains suspending red Bakelite heart-shaped plaques in grad sizes, 22" l, **$575**. (Photo courtesy of Matthew Burkholz, Route 66 Antiques, Chatham, NY)

Pendant and Chain, celluloid, paint, rhinestones, c. 1920-25, pear-shaped mottled green celluloid drop, incised geo design with two sections of ptd lt, med, and dk blue overlapping semicircles inlaid with colorless, lt and dk blue r.s., r.s.-set celluloid bail, suspended from an oval link ivory-colored celluloid chain, pendant 1¾" w x 3⅝" tl, chain 24" tl, **$200**. (Courtesy of Generations, La Verne, CA)

FINE JEWELRY c. 1935-1945

The stylistic developments of the 1930s started taking a markedly different path about half-way through the decade. By the mid-'30s, the all-white look of diamonds and platinum that had been a mainstay of fine jewelry fashion since the turn of the century began to fade. Colored gold and gemstones gradually became more prominent, encouraged by changes in clothing styles and later, by wartime shortages and restrictions. The repeal of Prohibition and the abandonment of the gold standard in 1933 may have precipitated the change. Although the Depression had the nation, and Europe as well, in its grip for the duration of the decade, these two events could have sparked hope for better days ahead. Nightclubs were once again in business and gold jewelry was once again in fashion, as publicized by Hollywood and its stars, the epitome of glamour. Jewelry was still desirable to own in hard times, not only as personal adornment, but also as portable wealth, a concept which remained viable throughout the war years. In the "make-do" spirit of the period, however, fewer and less expensive gemstones were used, including synthetic rubies and sapphires, and less expensive gold took the place of platinum, which became totally unavailable for jewelry during the war.

A resurgence of romanticism in the mid- to late-'30s generated a desire for femininity in fashion and a return to "old-fashioned" Victorian sentimentality. There was even a reprise of British royal influence, which nearly upstaged all of Hollywood. The abdication of King Edward VIII in 1936, and his subsequent marriage to Wallis Simpson, was the "the most famous love story of modern times." Jewelry played a well-publicized, prominent, and sentimental role in that story. (Not to be outdone, Margaret Mitchell and Hollywood gave us "Gone With The Wind," the most famous love story of Victorian times.) The Duke and Duchess of Windsor, as they became known, were the equal of Victoria in their influence on the jewelry-buying public. The most famous of the Duchess' jewels were made by Cartier and Van Cleef & Arpels, but designs by Suzanne Belperron, Harry Winston, Verdura, David Webb, and Seaman Schepps were also part of her collection. (All of these were sold by Sotheby's in Geneva at its renowned record-breaking auction of April 1987.)

Retro Modern is the somewhat controversial name recently coined for the fluid 1940s jewelry style that began to emerge around 1935. It is an appropriately contradictory term, carrying the suggestion of looking back and forward at the same time. The style's characteristics were truly an infusion of past and futuristic themes. The Machine Age, streamlined look of the late '20s and early '30s continued to evolve, becoming larger and more three-dimensional. But geometric severity was tempered by curvilinear softness, asymmetry, and a return to naturalistic motifs, usually interpreted on a larger scale and in more stylized forms than their Victorian counterparts. In the gradual move away from abstraction, flowers, animals, and birds became increasingly popular. Buckles, bows, ribbons, and fabric-like folds were often executed in combined contrasting colors of gold alloys in overtones of pink (rose) and green, as well as yellow (called bicolor and tricolor gold). Pieces were massive-looking, but hollow and, especially during wartime, the gold was of a thin gauge. In German-occupied France, the customer supplied the gold and gemstones, and the government took a percentage of the gold's value. While the U.S. was under no such restriction on gold, patriotism dictated restraint. Patriotism itself was a prevalent theme in wartime jewelry, both in colors (rubies and sapphires, often synthetic, accented with small diamonds) and motifs (flags, eagles, and military insignia).

Elements of the Machine Age style were reinterpreted in yellow and rose gold, including large geometric link and wide strap bracelets in "tank track" and other repeating patterns. In 1934, Van Cleef & Arpels designed a flexible strap of honeycomb or brickwork patterned segments with a large ornamental buckle-shaped clasp. They christened it the "Ludo" bracelet, after Louis "Ludovic" Arpels, but it appears to have been inspired by Victorian gold mesh *jarretières*, or "garter" bracelets (see below). The design was copied by many others, and remained popular throughout the '40. Bangles were wide and three-dimensional, often with a single large rectangular-cut gemstone (aquamarine and citrine were favored) in the center of a scroll or bow of gold with small colored stone accents (see page 160). Sentiment was expressed in charms of personal significance, some suspended from the traditional link bracelet, others mounted on wide hinged bangles or cuffs (see page 159). Charms were also fine jewelry's form of whimsy. Disney cartoon characters became popular, especially after the appearance of the first feature length animated film, "Snow White and the Seven Dwarfs," in 1937.

Dress clips, the ornamental mainstay of the early '30s, became even more versatile as the central removable decoration of bangle bracelets, and as the "*passe-partout*"—

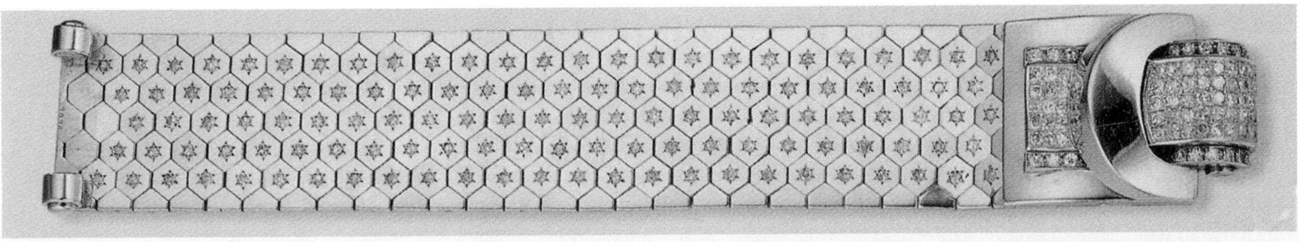

Bracelet, 18k yg, diamonds, c. 1940, Fr, "Ludo *Hexagone*," a flexible strap of honeycomb patterned links, each star-set with a sc diamond, terminating in a pavé-set diamond buckle clasp, Fr assay mks, maker's mk for Van Cleef & Arpels, 1" w x 6½" tl, **$23,500** [A]. (Copyright Christie's Images, New York 2002©, Christie's Los Angeles, CA, 10/4/01)

another Van Cleef & Arpels invention, introduced in 1938—an enhancer for a snakechain necklace. The ubiquitous double clip brooch also continued to be worn through the '40s. Early '30s pairs of clips were flat, geometric, symmetrical twins; later they became more three- dimensional and asymmetrical mirror images, or figurals. The double-pronged hinged clip finding took the place of the flat-backed clip by the end of the '30s. This type of fastening continued to be used on fine jewelry, often with the addition of a safety catch for one or both prongs.

During the war years, clothing fashions grew more severe and masculine, but jewelry, especially brooches, became more feminine. Large floral sprays were prevalent, worn high on a square-shouldered jacket, like a corsage of real flowers. Bicolor gold ribbon bows were another favorite, as were gem-set birds and butterflies. Necklaces became a focal point, shortened to collarbone or choker length. The flexible, slinky flattened gold tube, known variously as snake chain, gas pipe, or mouse tail, first exhibited in 1934, remained popular throughout the '40s (see page 162). Earrings became earclips with the introduction of the clip-back finding, patented in 1934. The emphasis was on the lobe rather than below it. Multi-petaled flowerheads, scrolls, and cornucopia were popular motifs (see pages 160-161). Pendent earrings continued to be worn at night, but were usually wider at the top and, narrower at the bottom. Rings were massive, generally set with a large central colored gemstone flanked by scrolls of gold or small gemstones of contrasting color (see page 161). Suites and demi-parures returned to favor after a hiatus of several decades, in matched brooches and earrings, clips and earrings, and necklaces, bracelets, and earrings (see pages 161 and 162).

French jewelers continued to be innovative and influential designers until 1940, when France fell under German occupation. Suzanne Belperron (1900-1983) was a celebrated French artist-jeweler whose distinctive style must be studied to be recognized, because she seldom signed her work. She favored inexpensive gemstones like citrine and rock crystal, often sculpturally carved or set in clusters (see page 160). She worked briefly for Cartier, and also ran her own shop; from 1921-32, she worked for René Boivin. She joined Bernard Herz in 1933. Her longest association was with Herz's son, Jean, with whom she formed the partnership Herz-Belperron in 1945, which lasted until her retirement in 1974. Belperron designs continue to be made in Paris and offered for sale at the Verdura salon in New York.

Although the firm of René Boivin was founded by its namesake in the 1890s, it was the work of his wife Jeanne (née Poiret, daughter of the famed couturier) and their daughter Germaine, that caused a stir in the early to mid-20th century. Retaining her husband's name for the company after his death in 1917, Jeanne Boivin established herself as the first female to head a jewelry firm in the 20th century. Along with a third partner, Juliette Moutard, they designed unique jewels, often with stylized themes from nature (see above and page 160). Jeanne Boivin died in 1959, but the Maison Boivin continues in business today.

Brooch/Pin, diamonds, sapphires, demantoid garnets, cabochon emeralds, yg, c. 1940, Fr, in the shape of a longhorn skull in yg, pavé-set with circ-cut near-colorless and yellow diamonds, polished yg horns, one wrapped in a calibré-cut purple sapphire ribbon, the other in an articulated calibré-cut demantoid garnet and cab emerald foliate wreath, the ribbon and wreath cascading over and through the skull, a one-of-a-kind commissioned piece by Maison Boivin, Paris, 2⅞" w x 4¼", **$58,750** [A]. (Copyright Christie's Images, New York 2002©, Christie's New York, NY, 10/22/01)

Van Cleef & Arpels was one famous firm whose designs came to prominence during the prewar period. In addition to the aforementioned creations, they are credited with the invention of the "invisible setting" of calibré-cut gemstones, used primarily for sapphires and rubies. Another of the firm's well-known designs was the ballerina clip or brooch (see page 160). This design actually originated in the U.S., executed in the early '40s by John Rubel Co. for Van Cleef & Arpels, New York. It inspired a host of female figurals, which remained popular through the 1950s.

Cartier, long renowned for its impeccably crafted original designs, continued to produce distinctive, mostly figural pieces before the war. Cartier even managed to create some new designs during wartime. Its famous "Bird in a Cage" and "Liberated Bird" brooches, executed in 1942 and 1944 respectively, symbolized the Occupation and the Liberation of Paris.

After 1940, most European jewelry production was curtailed, although the large French houses managed to stay afloat with a limited output of mostly prewar designs. By contrast, having been cut off from Europe during World War II, and with no Paris fashions to emulate, American jewelers and their designs came to the fore. Some of these jewelers were transplanted Europeans, others were "homegrown." One house, which became particularly well-known for its Retro Modern designs, was a merger of American and French firms: Trabert & Hoeffer-Mauboussin. Joining forces just after the stock market crash in 1929, the company became famous for its line of Retro-styled jewels, named "Reflection" in 1938. Its slogan was, "Reflection— your personality in a jewel." The unique feature of this line was a standardized array of elements that the customer could arrange and combine to suit her fancy. Trabert & Hoeffer-Mauboussin were among the first to take advantage of the recently developed method of mass-production using lost-wax casting with vulcanized rubber molds, which facilitated the making of interchangeable components for the Reflection line. While the firm of Trabert & Hoeffer, Inc. continues today, the association with Mauboussin was terminated in the 1950s.

Texas-born Paul Flato (1900-1999) opened his first salon in New York in the late '20s. His fame and fortune seemed assured when he opened a second establishment in Los Angeles in 1937, catering to Hollywood's elite. He was known for a wide variety of original, whimsical, naturalistic, and surrealistic designs. Fame and fortune were fleeting, however. His business closed in the early 1940s. He was "rediscovered" in Texas a few years ago, where he died in 1999. Consequently, more information about him and his work is now available. Portfolios of his designs were auctioned by Christie's Los Angeles in November, 1995.

One of Flato's designers, a European émigré who had already made a name for himself working for Chanel in Paris, was Fulco Santostefano della Cerda, duc di Verdura (1898-1978), known simply as Verdura. After leaving Flato in 1939, he opened his own shop in New York. He was known for his bold and imaginative designs and figural conceits. He emphasized design rather than large gemstones, the importance of which he dismissed, reputedly saying that "mineralogy is not jewelry." He occasionally incorporated shells and pebbles in his work. The firm founded by Verdura is still in business, under the ownership of Edward J. Landrigan, who continues to produce original Verdura designs (see page 185).

Seaman Schepps (1881-1972), a native American, opened his first shops in California, but he moved to New York in 1921, where his establishment remained, except for a five-year hiatus from 1929 to 1934. His work reflects influences by Belperron, Flato, and Verdura in his sculptural and figural pieces. His most -often seen design is for clip earrings, a pair of gem-set turbo (snail-shaped) shells, inspired by Verdura, which continue to be a popular item (see page 182). Schepps' namesake firm continues in business today.

Less well-publicized perhaps than their prestigious New York competitors, manufacturers in Newark, New Jersey, continued to produce well-made and affordable gold jewelry in the prevailing style of the period. Geared to conservative tastes, the pieces were more restrained examples of the "tailored" look that was popularly worn with suits at the time.

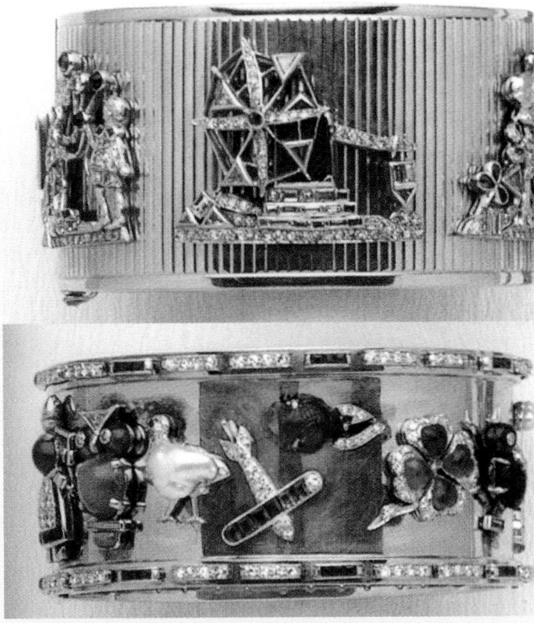

Bracelets, hinged gold bangles with appl charms, c. 1940:
T, ribbed 18k yg surmounted by six appl plat charms set with baguette, marquise, triangular and sc diamonds, calibré-cut rubies, sapphires, and emeralds, including a girl with kite, windmill, boy with balloon-seller, diamonds approx 3.75 cts tw, 1⅜" w, 2⅜" inside dia, **$7,638** [A].
B, diamonds, rubies, sapphires, pearls, 15 gem-set plat charms attached with rivets to the polished 14k rose gold surface, including birds, milkmaid, fish, four-leaf clover, airplane, key, heart lock, house, purse, tree, and balloon seller, raised borders decorated with short rows of sc diamonds and calibré-cut rubies, diamonds approx 4.00 cts tw, 1¼" w, 2⅜" inside dia, **$7,638** [A]. (Photo courtesy of Butterfields, San Francisco and Los Angeles, CA, 9/25/01)

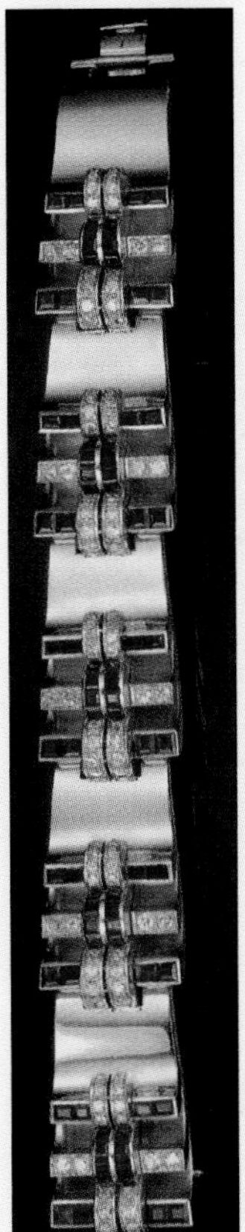

Bracelet, flexible, 18k rose gold, diamonds, simulated sapphires, c. 1940, five scrolled hinged plaques set with alternating rows and convex crossbars of calibré-cut simulated sapphires and circ-cut diamonds, v-spring and box clasp, 1" w x 6¼" tl, **$9,400** [A]. (Copyright Christie's Images, New York 2002©, Christie's Los Angeles, CA, 10/4/01)

Bracelet, hinged bangle, 14k rose and yg, citrine, rubies, c. 1940, a rect-cut citrine, 29.00 x 24.00 mm, prong-set within concave pierced fan shapes outlined with sm prong-set rubies, flanked by looped and ruffled yg ribbon and mounted on a smooth polished rose gold bangle, 2⅜" x 2⅜", 2⅜" inside dia, **$3,231** [A]. (Photo courtesy of Butterfields, San Francisco and Los Angeles, CA, 3/19/02)

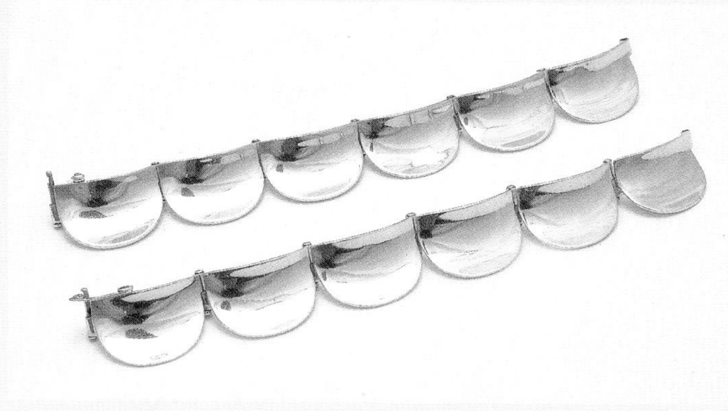

Bracelets/Necklace, link, 18k yg, c. 1940, each a series of six linked concave hemispherical plaques forming a scalloped edge, can be joined to form a necklace, unmkd, possibly by Paul Flato, each 1" w x 6⅞" tl, **$5,500**. (Private collection, photo by Fabrizio Rubeca, Rome, Italy)

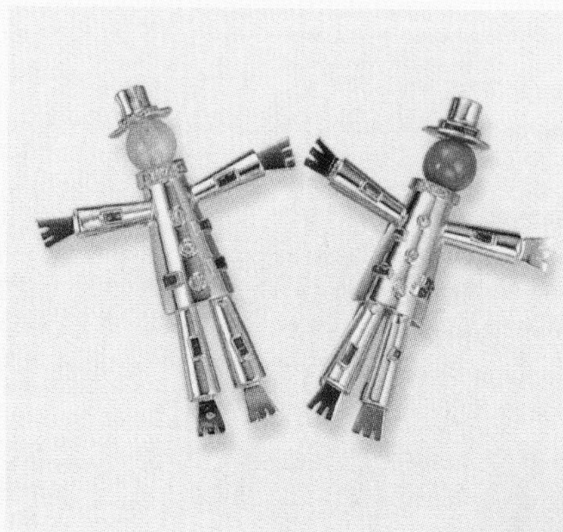

Brooches/Pins, 18k yg, sapphires, rubies, diamonds, coral, rose quartz, c. 1940, Fr, in the shapes of scarecrows, yg bodies and hats set with baguette-cut sapphires and rubies, rc diamond buttons and collars, coral and rose quartz heads, sgd "LACLOCHE," Fr assay mks, pr, 1⅜" w x 1⅞", **$4,113** [A]. (Copyright Christie's Images, New York 2002©, Christie's Los Angeles, CA, 10/4/01)

Brooch/Pin, onyx, diamonds, 18k gold, platinum, c. 1935, Fr, a series of tapering carved onyx scrolls with diamond accents, oe, om, rc diamond trim, Fr assay marks, in its orig B. Herz fitted case, designed by Suzanne Belperron, maker's mk for Sté Groene et Darde, 1¼" w x 2⅝", **$44,650** [A]. (Copyright Christie's Images, New York 2002©, Christie's New York, NY, 10/22/01)

Brooch/Pin, 14k gold, red stones, c. 1940, a whimsical depiction of songbirds playing instruments surmounting five knife-edge wires (a musical staff) with treble clef in yg, wg, pink gold, birds with red stone eyes, 2⅛" w x ¾", **$2,500**. (Courtesy of Apriori Antiques, San Francisco, CA)

Brooch/Pin, yg, diamond, rubies, turquoise, c. 1944, "Danseuse Hawaii," a ballerina accented with headdress and flowers of circ-cut rubies and turq cabs, with rc diamond face, sgd "VAN CLEEF & ARPELS, N.Y.," #6029, 2½" w x 3," **$21,150** [A]. (Copyright Christie's Images, New York 2002©, Christie's New York, NY, 10/22/01)

Earrings, 14k yg, white star sapphires, rubies, c. 1940, each a swirl motif curving around an oval-shaped bezel-set star sapphire, six prong-set circ-cut rubies at the edges, evidence of repair, clip backs, ¾" w x 1", **$460** [A]. (Photo courtesy of Beverly Hills Auctioneers, Beverly Hills, CA, 4/1/01)

Clip, rock crystal, sapphires, platinum, wg, c. 1935, Fr, two rounded rock crystal arcs flanking three rows of 43 grad circ-cut and oval-cut blue sapphires bead-set in plat, 18k wg findings, Fr assay mks, maker's mk for René Boivin, 1¼" w x 1¾", **$23,500** [A]. (Photo courtesy of Skinner, Inc., Boston, MA, 3/17/02)

Earrings, 14k yg, rubies, c. 1940, each round domed yg ear clip with seven circ-cut star-set rubies, clip backs, 1" dia, **$509** [A]. (Photo courtesy of Beverly Hills Auctioneers, Beverly Hills, CA, 4/1/01)

Earrings, clip, 14k rose and yg, citrines, rubies, c. 1940, each prong-set with a rect-cut citrine flanked on one side by three sm prong-set circ-cut rubies, mounted within a bicolored gold scrolling ribbon with ruffled terminal, ¾" w x 1½", **$881** [A]. (Photo courtesy of Butterfields, San Francisco and Los Angeles, CA, 3/19/02)

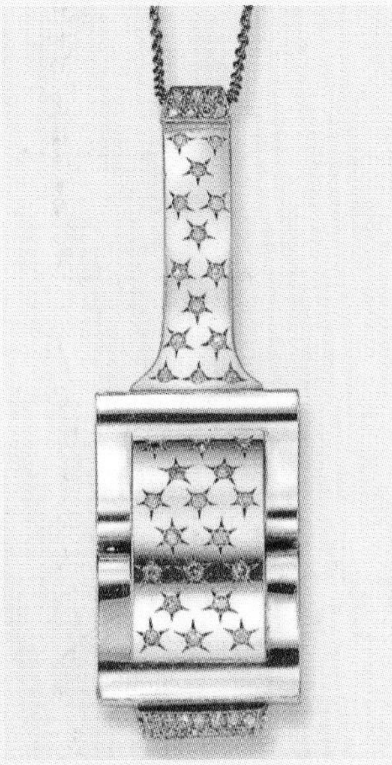

Lorgnette, 14k yg, diamonds, platinum, c. 1940, rectilinear, star-set diamond handle and cover, pavé-set sc diamonds at terminals, joined to a pr of folding lenses, mounted in 14k yg and plat, 1" w x 3⅛" tl, **$3,760** [A]. (Copyright Christie's Images, New York 2002©, Christie's Los Angeles, CA, 10/4/01)

Suite: Hinged Bangle and Ring, aquamarine, 14k yg, c. 1940, an emerald-cut aquamarine, approx 37.00 cts, set in a wide, tapering, stepped polished yg bangle, matching ring set with an emerald-cut aquamarine, approx 25.00 cts, bangle 1⅛" T to B at center, ring sz 6½, **$7,638** [A]. (Photo courtesy of Butterfields, San Francisco and Los Angeles, CA, 9/25/01)

Ring, 14k yg, rubies, c. 1940, wide polished yg band, slightly convex, set throughout with 14 circ-cut rubies in star-cut settings, ⅜" w, sz 7, **$115** [A]. (Photo courtesy of Beverly Hills Auctioneers, Beverly Hills, CA, 4/1/01)

Ring, amethyst, diamonds, 18k yg, c. 1940, square-cut amethyst, diamond at each corner, ribbed setting with wiretwist detail, ⅞" at center, **$2,800**. (Private collection, photo by Fabrizio Rubeca, Rome, Italy)

Ring, kunzite, rubies, 18k yg, c. 1940, a step-cut kunzite, approx 100.00 cts, the arched shoulders channel-set with sq-cut rubies, 1⅜" T to B at center, sz 6, **$4,994** [A]. (Photo courtesy of Butterfields, San Francisco and Los Angeles, CA, 9/25/01)

Ring, citrine, rubies, diamonds, 18k yg, platinum, c. 1940, a prong-set rect-cut citrine, 25.00 x 19.35 x 13.40 mm, flanked by split yg shoulders set with sq-cut rubies above and below plat arcs set with sc diamonds, continuing to a narrow yg shank, 1" T to B, 1⅛" w at shoulders, approx size 5, **$940** [A]. (Photo courtesy of Butterfields, San Francisco and Los Angeles, CA, 3/19/02)

Suite: Necklace and Earrings, 9k yg, rubies, diamonds, c. 1940-45, a lariat-style necklace, the central three-quarter round ribbed and notched ornament set with 12 circ-cut rubies and seven bc diamonds, completed by a fringed and fancy link double chain, with matching ear clips, diamonds approx 1.00 ct tw, necklace 1½" w x 2¾" at center, earrings 1" dia, **$1,380** [A]. (Photo courtesy of Beverly Hills Auctioneers, Beverly Hills, CA, 4/1/01)

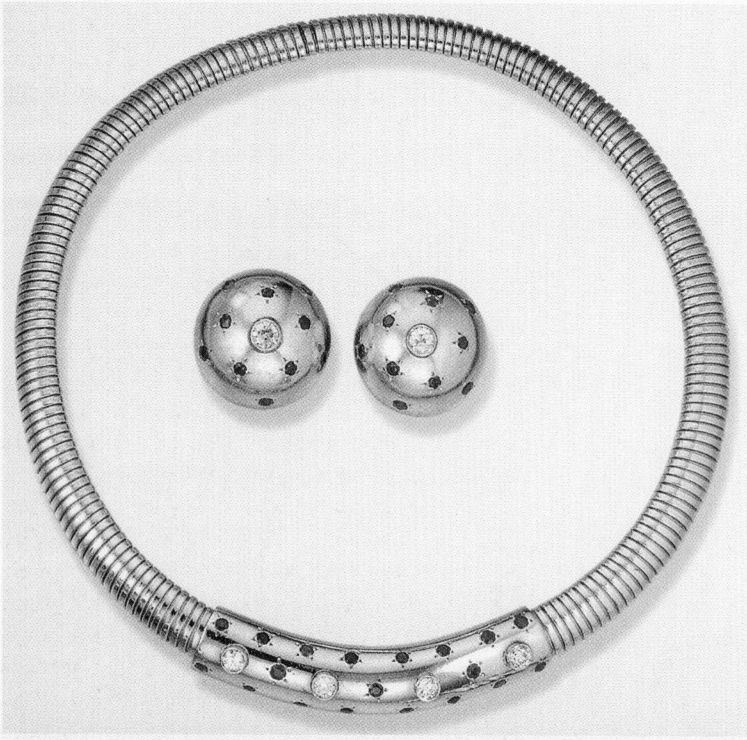

Suite: Necklace and Earrings, 14k yg, diamonds, rubies, sapphires, c. 1940-45, necklace with an adjustable front clasp in a tubular yg panel with star-cut set rubies and sapphires, and six bezel-set oe diamonds, 1.46 cts tw, on a "gas-pipe"-style band; adjustable front clasp, matching circ dome earrings, clipbacks mkd "14k," necklace ½" w, 16"-18" tl, earrings 1" dia, **$3,525** [A]. (Copyright Christie's Images, New York 2002©, Christie's Los Angeles, CA, 3/6/01)

Suite: Clip and Earrings, 18k yg, rubies, diamonds, c. 1945, starburst design with a cluster of circ-cut rubies in the center of ridged yg rays, set with five radiating rows of circ-cut and sc diamonds with circ-cut ruby terminals, diamonds .55 cts tw, double-pronged hinged clip with safety sgd "TIFFANY & CO." at the top of clip, matching earrings mkd "18k," in their original Tiffany & Co. black suede fitted cases, clip 1⅝" dia, earrings ⅞" dia, **$5,875** [A]. (Copyright Christie's Images, New York 2002©, Christie's Los Angeles, CA, 3/6/01)

Suite: Necklace and Earrings, 18k yg, diamonds, platinum, c. 1945, necklace a flexible tapering band of polished yg scrolling ribbons, interspersed with grad pavé-set sc and oe diamond florets, sgd "VAN CLEEF & ARPELS," #59567, Fr hmks, matching earrings, clipbacks not mkd, possibly later, diamonds 3.42 cts tw, ⅞" w x 15½" tl, earrings 1" dia, **$37,600** [A]. (Copyright Christie's Images, New York 2002©, Christie's Los Angeles, CA, 3/6/01)

MID-CENTURY MODERN-AMERICAN STUDIO JEWELRY, c. 1945-1965

Just as the adherents of the Arts & Crafts movement rebelled against mainstream tradition at the turn of the century, so too did studio artists of the mid-century follow a path of their own. They reinterpreted the earlier movement's guiding principles in new forms, with new approaches to design, creating a new definition of the word "modern," with which the 1950s came to be identified.

True to the Arts & Crafts philosophy, the emphasis was on design, hand-craftsmanship and accessibility to the public. Gold and precious stones were used on occasion, but sterling was the preferred metal, alone or in combination, most often with stones of the quartz family, cultured pearls, wood, brass, copper, and enamels. Although the jewelry was meant to be affordable for most people, the audience for these pieces was not wide. As was also the case at the turn of the century, this was not jewelry for the masses, but rather for an intellectual elite—the "Beat Generation"—that congregated primarily in urban centers on the East and West coasts. The "beatniks" were more ready and willing to accept the "far-out" designs that artist-jewelers produced than the average suburban housewife.

Still, as the crafts movement gathered momentum, demand did grow, and some jewelers attempted to manufacture more commercialized production pieces. Many of their hand-crafted designs were not well-suited to mass production, however, and when demand increased, prices for one-of-a-kind pieces by well-known artists went up. Today these pieces—by important designers such as Sam Kramer and Margaret De Patta—command thousands.

The mid-century modernist movement had its roots in pre-war Europe, under the influence of the Bauhaus and fine and applied arts "isms" such as Dadaism and Surrealism, Cubism, Biomorphism, and Constructivism. Several European painters and sculptors of these artistic schools also designed jewelry, among them: Salvador Dalí, Pablo Picasso, Jean Cocteau, and Georges Braque. In crossing the Atlantic, however, these influences were translated into a uniquely American idiom by artists who were jewelry *makers*, as well as designers. This was the case even when the European influences were more direct. Some American metalsmiths studied under leaders of the movement who had come to the United States just before the war and set up schools of design, or became directors of design programs at established schools and universities. Among them were Walter Gropius, Marcel Breuer, and László Moholy-Nagy of the Bauhaus. Other influences came from Scandinavia, where modernism flourished under the auspices of several important designers and their companies (see Scandinavian section under Special Collectibles).

Still another source of education came, surprisingly, from the U.S. government. After World War II, returning veterans entered into government-sponsored "rehab" programs. Workshops were led by metalsmith Margret Craver Withers (b.1907) from 1947 to 1951. These helped to generate interest in pursuing the study of crafts further through the G.I. Bill. In response to this growing interest, a number of "how-to" books on jewelry-making were published from the late '40s through the '60s. Today these books are invaluable resources for the historian, because they picture and give information about the work of modernist jewelers (see References).

The overriding concepts characterizing the modernists' work were abstraction and nonobjective form, but each of them interpreted these concepts in different ways with a variety of techniques. Artist-jeweler Philip Morton (1911-2001), author of a "how-to" book, *Contemporary Jewelry, a Studio Handbook*, in evaluating the work of mid-century metalsmiths, divides design into two groups, or "expressive modes": "rational" and "nonrational." Within each mode he names several forms and techniques: "plate-shape," "linear," "strip-plate," "constructed," "fused," "forged," and "cast." Each approach yielded a unique design, and yet for all their differences, there is an identifiable cohesiveness uniting the overall body of work by these artists. Space does not permit discussing the finer points of the work of every one of them here. Mention should be made, however, of the seminal, influential, and important American studio jewelers whose work is collected today. Pieces by some of them are included in this section. A longer, but of necessity still incomplete, list can be found in the appendix, Mid-century Modern American Studio Jewelers. Examples of these artists' work and that of many others, as well as biographical information can be found in two substantial articles by Marbeth Schon for Modern Silver online magazine (see References).

Harry Bertoia (1915-1978) was born in Italy, and came to the United States in 1930. He made his first pieces of jewelry in Detroit, at the age of twenty-one. He attended Cranbrook Academy of Art beginning in 1937, and emerged a multimedia artist, particularly fluent in metalworking. His jewelry, mostly executed in hammered brass, became something of a sideline to his primary focus on furniture, and later, sculpture. It is never signed. Bertoia lived in Los Angeles, California, for a while in the '40s, where he worked with Charles and Ray Eames before moving to Bally, Pennsylvania, in 1950 to design furniture for Knoll Associates.

Sam Kramer (1913-1964), another one of the first, and perhaps the most avant-garde studio artist of them all, also began making jewelry in 1936, a full decade before the crafts movement was truly established. He opened a shop in New York City's Greenwich Village in 1939. His work, and his personality, were a decided departure from the ordinary, a fact that he emphasized in advertising his wares as "fantastic jewelry for people who are slightly mad." He was called a "surrealistic jeweler" by *New Yorker* magazine. Kramer was known for incorporating bizarre materials like taxidermists' glass eyes and found objects into even more bizarre biomorphic fused, cast, and constructed designs that have been given such names as "Creature Brooch," "Skeletal Cuff," and "Pterodactyl Brooch." He trained his wife Carol to design and make jewelry, which she continued to do after his death until 1970. His mark, a mushroom inside a lobed circle, gave

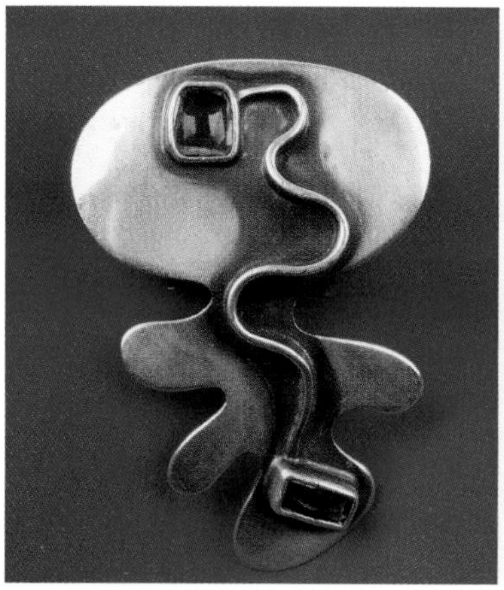

Brooch/Pin, sterling, pink and green stones, c. 1950, biomorphic abstract sterling plaque surmounted by a raised, curvilinear flat wire line terminating in bezel-set rect faceted green and pink stones, partially oxidized finish, maker's mk for Sam Kramer, New York, NY on rev, 1⅞" w x 2⅝", **$1,116** [A]. (Photo courtesy of Skinner, Inc., Boston, MA, 12/11/01)

him the nickname "Mushroom Sam"; like some of his pieces, the mushroom had erotic implications. Not all of Kramer's work was one-of-a-kind oddities. He did make some multiples of designs in a constructivist mode. Perhaps they were meant for his slightly less mad customers, but today these pieces bring slightly less money (see above and page 170).

Several other studio artists set up shop in Greenwich Village in the 1940s and 1950s, taking advantage of the favorable intellectual climate there. Among them, Paul Lobel (1900-1983) successfully maintained a commercial production operation from about 1945 to 1964, making large cuff bracelets and brooches from cutout silver sheet and soldered forged wire. He was known for both nonobjective designs and abstract figurals such as musical instruments, animals, fruit, and leaf forms, all of which were given names in his catalogs (see pages 168, 170, and 173). Art Smith (1917-1982), also worked in sheet and forged silver wire, as well as brass and copper, and although he was influenced by Lobel, his work was more sculptural and biomorphic; he used the human body as a point of departure or supportive armature for his designs. In 1948, Smith opened a shop in the Village, a few doors down from Lobel's. He signed his name in script on some, but not all, of his pieces (see below and page 173).

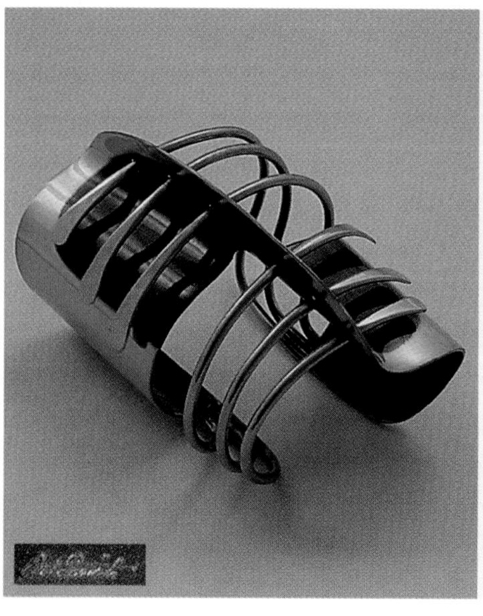

Bracelet, cuff, copper, brass, c. 1948, titled "Modern Cuff," composed of copper sheet and partially flattened round brass wire, oxidized and clear lacquered top surface, black lacquered inner surface, inside edge imp "Art Smith" in script (New York, NY), 2¾" x 4⅛", **$6,000**. (Courtesy of Gudrun Baxter)

Ed Wiener (1918-1991), began working in his own shop in 1946, in Provincetown, Massachusetts, but opened a store in New York City soon after, in 1947, called "Arts and Ends." His long career, ending only with his death, encompassed a succession of stylistic approaches, wrought or cast in silver and gold, often with the addition of gemstones. His signature is his name in lowercase print or block letters, but his jewelry is not always signed. Some later pieces are marked "E.W." His earlier work (1940s-50s) is generally more sought-after than his later pieces. He didn't start working in materials of high intrinsic value until the mid-1960s (see pages 168, 169, 171, and 174).

Ronald H. Pearson (1924-1996) was one of the founding fathers of Shop I in Rochester, New York. Opened in 1952, Shop I was the first independent gallery to exhibit and sell modern crafts exclusively. Pearson's work in forged or cast silver or gold is characterized by graceful simplicity of form, reminiscent of Scandinavian design. Pearson resided and worked in Deer Isle, Maine, until his death.

Paul H. Ackerman (1900-1968) grew up in Phillipsburg, New Jersey, where his father ran a jewelry store. He took over the business when his father died. But he was also a silversmith with modernist leanings, and he maintained a shop in New Hope, Pennsylvania, a crafts-oriented town. He exhibited at the "American Jewelry and Related Objects" traveling exhibition in 1955. His talent for enameling can be seen in the brooches on page 168.

Other East Coast artist-jewelers of note whose work is included here (New York City unless otherwise specified): Betty Cooke (b. 1924, Baltimore, MD, see Marbeth Schon's interview in Modern Silver, Aug-Sept. 2001, and pages 169 and 171); Joan Hurst and Jill Kingsbury (see page 171); Ed Levin (b. 1921, also Bennington, VT, see pages 170 and 173); Frank Miraglia (page 168); Frank Rebajes (1907-1990, page 168); and Olaf Skoogfors (1930-1973, Philadelphia, PA, buckle on page 169).

On the opposite coast, in northern California, Margaret De Patta's "rational" approach was the opposite of Sam Kramer's "nonrational" one, but her influence on others was seminal, and possibly greater than his. A modernist pioneer, De Patta (1903-1964) began jewelry-making in 1930, and had her own workshop by 1935. She established a studio in the San Francisco Bay Area in 1941, after studying with László Moholy-Nagy at his Bauhaus-oriented School of Design in Chicago. In 1946, disturbed by the fact that demand had driven up prices so that her jewelry was becoming inaccessible to the average person, De Patta and husband Eugene Bielawski responded by going into limited production of some of her designs using lost-wax casting methods. Each piece sold for under $50. The energy and time-consuming tasks required to run the business caused the couple to abandon this endeavor in 1958.

De Patta's constructivist techniques yielded jewelry with optical effects achieved by combining specially cut or faceted transparent stones with metal rods, wire, sheet, or textured surfaces. Her pieces were three-dimensional spatial studies. She worked in both silver and gold, occasionally

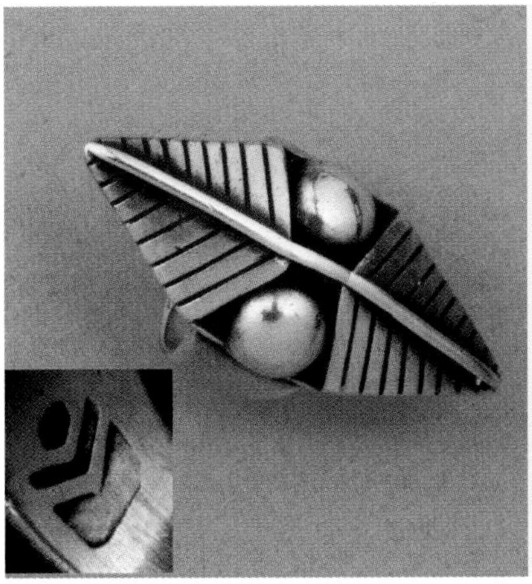

Ring, sterling, c. 1950, lozenge-shaped plaque with appl incised pyramidal shapes at each end flanking two beads, creating a mask-like effect, mounted on tapered shank, maker's mk for Margaret De Patta, San Francisco, CA imp on rev, ⅝" w x 1½", approx size 8, **$1,200**. (Janet Zapata collection)

using diamonds, more often rock crystal and rutilated quartz and other inexpensive gemstones. In the late '50s, she began incorporating pebbles picked up during walks on the beach, foreshadowing the "found object" trend of the late '60s and '70s. Her mark is a stylized M surmounted by a dot; she sometimes used her last name, with or without her mark. (see ring above).

In 1951, De Patta initiated the organization of the Metal Arts Guild in San Francisco, a resource, information, and support network for local metalsmiths. Joining this group were several artists who made names for themselves in the '50s and '60s. All of them give credit to De Patta as an inspirational and influential mentor. Some of them are still living and working today. Irena Brynner (b. 1917), who lived in San Francisco until 1956, started making jewelry in 1950. Her work there was constructivist and geometric (see brooch on page 168). In 1956, she moved to New York, where she changed her techniques to lost-wax casting and welding, and her style became looser and more organic. She signs her pieces with her first initial and last name, alternately spelled with one or two n's.

One of Irena Brynner's early influences was Claire Falkenstein (1908-1997). While not a member of M.A.G., Ms. Falkenstein was an inspiration to several members of that group (she lived in San Francisco before moving to Paris in 1950). She was a painter, and a metal sculptor who utilized the same linear forging techniques applied to her larger works for her jewelry. Her work was exhibited at the Louvre in Paris, as well as several galleries and museums in the U.S. She made her first piece of jewelry in the mid-'40s. During the 1950s, she made a series of large neckpieces of forged silver or gold wire, including unusual inverted U-shaped and C-shaped pieces with undulating organic lines. Her mark is a superimposed "CF." In 1997, at the age of 89, Ms. Falkenstein died in Venice, California, where she had worked and lived since 1965.

Peter Macchiarini (1909-2001) made his first piece of jewelry in 1937, but it wasn't until after the war that he was able to set up a studio and workshop in the North Beach neighborhood of San Francisco. He was one of the founding members of the Metal Arts Guild, and worked in the constructivist mode with a variety of materials, including ivory, ebony, brass, and copper. He signed his pieces with his first initial and last name, or last name alone (see brooches on page 169). Smaller items, like rings, are sometimes signed MACC (see ring on page 173). Macchiarini died in 2001, but his son Daniel continues to work in the same vein in his father's studio.

Merry Renk (b. 1921), another Metal Arts Guild founding member, has explored a number of techniques and forms, including *plique à jour* enamel, forged wire, lost-wax cast folded fabric, and solderless interlocking shapes. In 1947, she studied at the Institute of Design in Chicago, where she first exhibited in a gallery opened with two other students. Ms. Renk moved to San Francisco in 1948, where she still lives and works as a watercolorist, but she is no longer making jewelry. She signed her work with her last name in lowercase script (see earrings on page 170).

Southern California artists were the subject of recent articles by Toni Greenbaum for *Metalsmith* magazine (see References). Although their work is pictured in a number of "how-to" jewelry-making books, until now very little biographical information had been published on any of them. This section includes work by Philip Paval and Esther Lewittes of Los Angeles, and James Parker and Barney M. Reid of San Diego.

Philip Paval (1899-1971), according to Toni Greenbaum, citing his autobiography, catered to Hollywood stars more than to Venice Beach Bohemians. He was born and trained in Denmark. He came to Los Angeles and set up shop in the early 20s. He participated in many group exhibitions, including the well-known "American Jewelry and Related Objects" shows in 1955 and 1956. Greenbaum comments that "his jewelry could be quite eccentric." This is evident in the pendant and chain below.

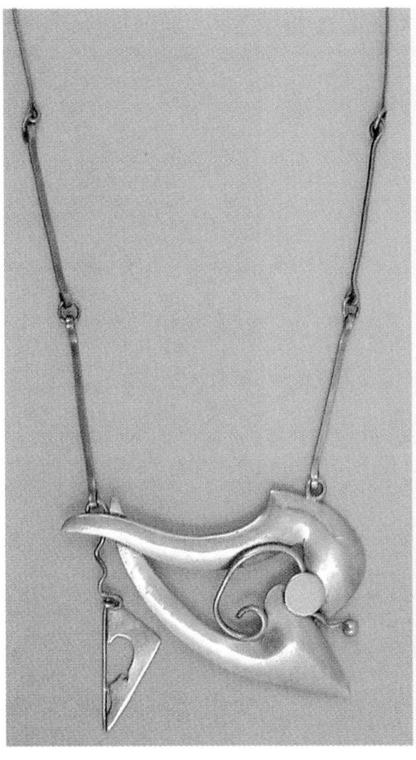

Pendant and Chain, sterling, c. 1950, a sculptured pendant constructed from two convex abstract shapes surmounted by a bead-tipped round wire volute and a disk, and a smaller cutout flat triangle suspended from undulating round wire, a chain of flat wire rods and circ jump rings, rev imp "STERLING," partially illegible maker's mk "Paval" for Philip Paval, Los Angeles, CA, 3" w x 3", 22" tl, **$750**. (Courtesy of Julia Stayden, Los Angeles, CA)

"Eccentric" is a word that could also be used to describe Esther Lewittes (1904-1990), or, as Greenbaum quotes Lewittes' friend Bernard Kester of the L.A. County Musuem of Art, "a real 'nut.'" Originally from New York, Lewittes began making jewelry in the early '50s, opening a gallery in Los Angeles around 1961. She studied at Columbia University and City College in New York, and some of her work, such as the cuff bracelet on page 168, is reminiscent of several Constructivist New York artists, e.g., circa 1950s pieces by Ed Wiener and Paul Lobel.

James Parker (1915-1987) was a San Diego craftsman who was one of many World War II veterans to study jewelry-making on the GI Bill. Having earned his teaching credential before the war, he taught high school in San Diego into the 1970s, but continued to make jewelry. His earlier pieces were all silver; he began adding colored gemstones in the early '50s, and enameled elements in the '70s. His work has generated a great deal of collector interest since the sale of his estate a few years ago, after his wife died. His mark is a distinctive conjoined JP, but not all of his pieces are signed. There are several examples of his work pictured in this section (see pages 172 and 174).

Barney M. Reid (1913-1992) was a craftsman who made objects as well as jewelry. He exhibited his jewelry nationally in the 1950s, and was president of the Allied Craftsmen of San Diego in 1953. He was an accomplished enamelist, as can be seen in the pendant below, which is signed "BMReid" in the counterenamel.

Other West Coast artist-jewelers whose work can be found pictured here include, Milton Cavagnaro (1915-1993, Mill Valley, California, see pendant on page 172, Everett MacDonald (1924-1991, Laguna Beach, California, page 172, Jack Nutting (San Francisco, California, see hair comb above), Polly Stehman (Ellensburg, Washington) and Byron Wilson (b. 1919, Oakland, California), see cuff links, page 170).

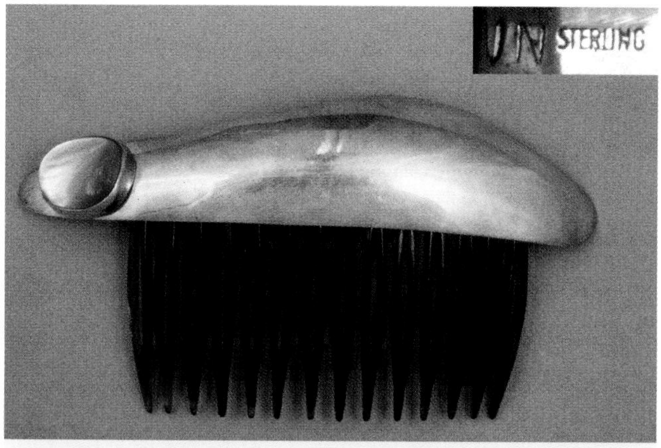

Hair Comb, sterling, abalone, plastic, c. 1955, freeform convex ster top, concave oval pink abalone bezel-set on left side, attached with wire to a tortoiseshell-colored plastic hair comb, top mkd "JN STERLING" for Jack Nutting, San Francisco, CA, 4" x 2⅛", **$150**. (Almunir Meghji collection)

Pendant, sterling, enamel on copper, c. 1955, enameled abstract design in shades of gray, brown, yellow and black, suspended free swinging within an angular flared three-sided flat wire ster frame, two U-shaped round wires appl at right angles on each side (cord not orig), counter-enameled, sgd in the enamel "BMReid" (script) for Barney M. Reid, San Diego, CA, 1⅞" x 3" tl, **$400**. (Almunir Meghji collection)

Because the concentration of studio artists is on the East and West coasts, artists from other parts of the country are often overlooked. Ruth Roach of Plainfield, Iowa, and Naples, Florida, is not well-known today, although beginning in 1955 (at the Walker Art Center in Minneapolis, Minnesota) and through the 1960s, her work was in a number of exhibitions, was awarded prizes, and is owned by several museums. Some of her pieces are pictured in Oppi Untracht's *Jewelry Concepts & Technology* (see References). A 1964 local newspaper review of an exhibit at the State College of Iowa enthused: "Anyone who has seen her work longs to own some." Perhaps the brooch on page 169 and the articulated pendant on page 172 will inspire other collectors to "long to own some." Ruth's son, Bill Roach, and his wife Patsy also made jewelry, and signed it "ROACH2." Marbeth Schon's interview with Patsy Roach is on the Modern Silver Web site, along with a number of photos of Ruth Roach's work.

Elsa Freund (1912-2001) developed her unique style of jewelry-making in the mid-1940s in Arkansas. A well-rounded student of the arts, she studied ceramics, and taught college craft and design courses. She began making glazed ceramic beads, which led to the creation of jewelry made with fused glass over ceramic "stones" and forged metal wire. Once she established her trademark style, she started selling her pieces in retail shops around 1953. Both she and her husband, painter Louis Freund, taught at Stetson College in Florida in the '50s and '60s, then moved back to Arkansas in 1967. Her style varied little throughout her career, and her pieces are instantly recognizable. They are signed "Elsa" in the clay. The necklace and earrings suite on page 174 is an early example of her work.

In 1956, H. Fred Skaggs (d. 1983) moved from Kansas City, Missouri, where he made traditional fine jewelry, to

Suite: Necklace and Earrings, sterling, amethysts, peridots, pink tourmalines, c. 1956-60, center section of nine irregularly shaped, tumble-polished gemstones, bezels formed around stones and mounted on cut-to-shape backplates linked with circ round wire jump rings, continuing to flat oval and circ round wire links, appl plate on rev mkd "STERLING HAND MADE H. FRED SKAGGS," Scottsdale, AZ, matching circ domed clip earrings, each bezel-set with three stones, same mks, necklace ½" at center, 14½" tl, earrings 1" dia, **$400**. (Author's collection)

Scottsdale, Arizona. He opened a shop with his wife at the Lloyd Kiva Craft Center, a prestigious collection of shops which included prominent Native American artists such as Charles Loloma. (In fact, it is to Skaggs that Loloma gave credit for inspiring and teaching him to make jewelry. The influence is evident in the earrings by Loloma on page 215 and by Skaggs on page 170.)

Skaggs turned to handcrafting silver upon his arrival because, according to his wife, "This is silver country...He loved working in silver and he loved working with wire. He was very good and fast." Even though he loved silver, he also made many designs in gold. He usually incorporated a variety of gemstones into his designs. His wife still runs the shop they opened in 1966, across the street from the Kiva Craft Center, which is where adviser Shari Miller conducted an interview with her. Skaggs' work is known to a few discriminating collectors, but perhaps because he shunned publicity while he was alive, not many are aware of his accomplishments. (see also the suite above).

Ray Graves (b. 1921) is another Scottsdale, Arizona, artist. He opened his shop in 1959. He worked in a variety of media, creating both stylized figural and abstract designs (see the brooch on page 169). The shop's name, "Gra-Wun" is a combination of his last name and that of an early business partner, Berta Wunderlich, but Graves continued to use the name for the shop and on his jewelry after his partner left. The Gra-Wun studio closed in 2001. This information is courtesy of Shari Miller.

There are many other lesser-known and unknown studio artists whose work has found its way into the collectibles marketplace. Because many studio artists supplemented their income by teaching classes in jewelry-making, their students' work, much of it unsigned, has also filtered into the secondary market. Some unsigned pieces are very well- made and designed, others are quite amateurish and imitative. A practiced eye will separate the wheat from the chaff.

Modernist mid-century jewelry is a specialized genre that does not appeal to everyone. But a dedicated and burgeoning corps of astute collectors, who, like the makers themselves, tend to be outside the mainstream, have caused interest to grow and prices to rise. Because the jewelry was mostly hand-made and one or few of a kind, a limited quantity is available for sale today.

Pieces by the most sought-after artists occasionally come up at twentieth-century decorative arts, rather than fine jewelry, auctions (Skinner's in Boston is the exception). Dealers who sell this type of jewelry are most often found at twentieth-century design shows and galleries in large cities.

Reproduction Alert

According to Steven Cabella, owner of The Modern i Gallery in San Anselmo, California, plagiarism does exist in modernist jewelry; there are some outright fraudulent copies being made. There are also "authentic limited reproductions" which are openly advertised as such, as well as newly made pieces by the original artist being sold as old ones. These are not fakes, but most collectors prefer pieces to have the "historical patina" (Cabella's words) of the artist's earlier work. The usual caveats apply: When paying a substantial price for a piece, make sure there is substantial documentation for it as well, or that the dealer from whom the piece is purchased is reputable and knowledgeable enough to guarantee the authenticity and circa date of his or her merchandise.

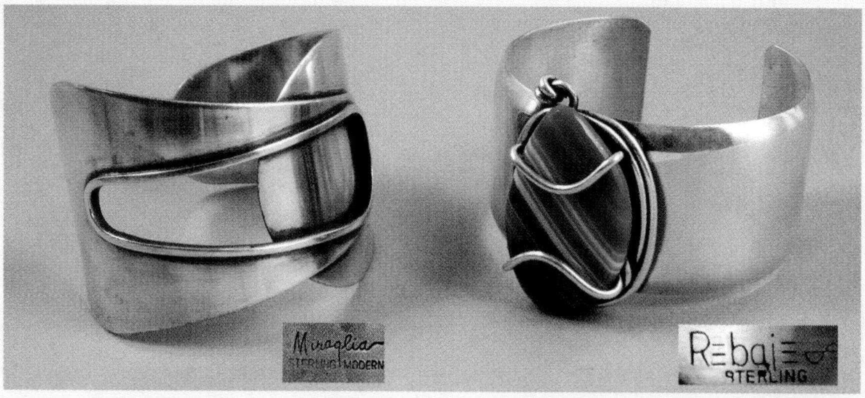

Bracelets, cuff, sterling, c. 1950:
L, formed from two overlapping ellipses, one with a cutout elongated tapered oval bordered by sq wire, sgd "Miraglia [in script] STERLING MODERN" for Frank Miraglia, New York, NY, 1¾" w, 2⅜" inside dia, **$250**.
R, rounded band surmounted by wire-wrapped irreg oval slab of rust-orange banded agate, sgd "REBAJES STERLING" on outer back edge for Frank (Francisco) Rebajes, New York, NY, band 1¼" w, agate 1½" x 1", **$350**.
(Almunir Meghji collection)

Bracelets, cuff, sterling, by Paul Lobel, New York NY, c. 1950:
L, a flat cusped and tapered cuff, one side formed from sheet, the other from round wire in parallel lines partially overlapping the sheet, oxidized around each wire, tapering to the back, rev imp "LOBEL STERLING," 1½" at center, 2¼" inside dia, **$450**. (Author's collection)
R, shaped from two irregular overlapping cutout pieces of sheet, a loop of round wire arcing from the center, the flattened end curving back over the cuff, rev imp "LOBEL sterling," 2¼" in dia, 2¼" T to B at center, **$550**. (Courtesy of Andrea Fatell, Wellsley, MA)

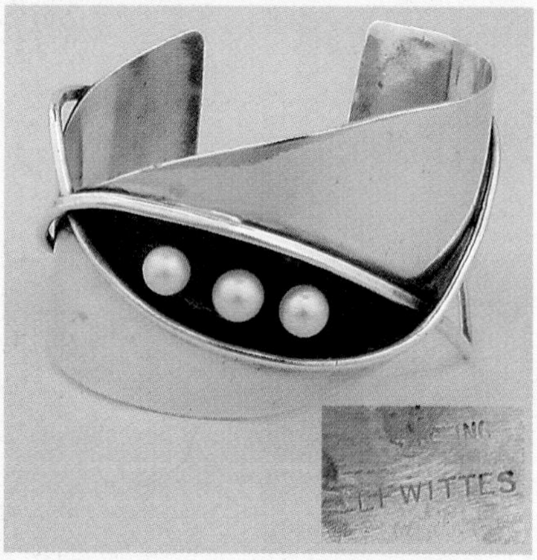

Bracelet, cuff, sterling, cultured pearls, c. 1950, cutout curved and angled sheet surmounted by curved and angled round wire forming a slightly off-center navette shape, a row of three cultured pearls mounted in the center of the oxidized ground, rev imp "STERLING LEWITTES" for Esther Lewittes, Los Angeles, CA, 1½" w, 2⅛" inside dia, **$700**. (Author's collection)

Brooch/Pin, sterling, c. 1955, polished triangular plaque with three grad lengths of sq wire appl at one end on oxidized ground, mkd "I. BRYNER STERLING" for Irena Brynner, San Francisco, CA, 1¼" w x 2¾", **$500**. (Courtesy of Before Antiques, Santa Monica, CA)

Brooch/Pin, sterling, wood, c. 1950, "musanga branch" (advertised as "ancient wood of an exotic tree") twig wrapped with ster wire vine, round ster bead and stylized ster leaves, rev mkd "REBAJES STERLING" for Frank (Francisco) Rebajes, New York, NY, 3" w x 2½", **$650**. (Francine Coles Collection, photo by Shari Watson Miller)

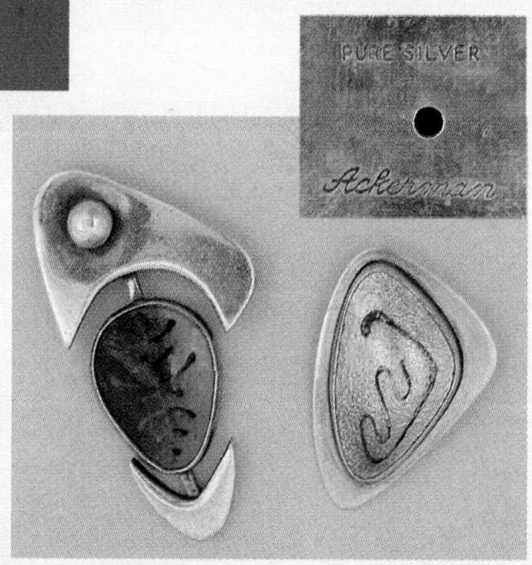

Brooches/Pins, sterling, fine silver, enamel, by Paul H. Ackerman, Phillipsburg, NJ, c. 1955:
L, bezel-set domed pear-shaped plaque, "sgraffito" enameled abstract design of short curved lines perpendicular to a long straight line, black to green on a green to rust-colored ground, plaque flanked by lg and sm cusped C-shaped silver plaques mounted on short sq wire bars, lg plaque surmounted by lg silver bead, rev sgd in script "Ackerman" in two places, "STERLING" on one plaque and "PURE SILVER" on the other, 1⅜" w x 2⅝", **$300**.
R, a rounded triangular plaque surmounted by a bezel-set domed rounded triangle with an abstract design in foil-backed enamel in shades of yellow, deep pink, and black, rev mkd "PURE SILVER," sgd "Ackerman" in script, 1¼" x 1¾", **$200**. (Author's collection)

Brooch/Pin, sterling, moonstone, c. 1945-50, an oxidized heart-shaped ster plaque within a polished frame surmounted by a polished ster U-shaped plaque with a trident shape on one end, the other end surmounted by an oval bezel-set moonstone, rev imp "STERLING, ED. WIENER" (New York, NY), 1" w x 1½", **$650**. (Tela Palmer collection)

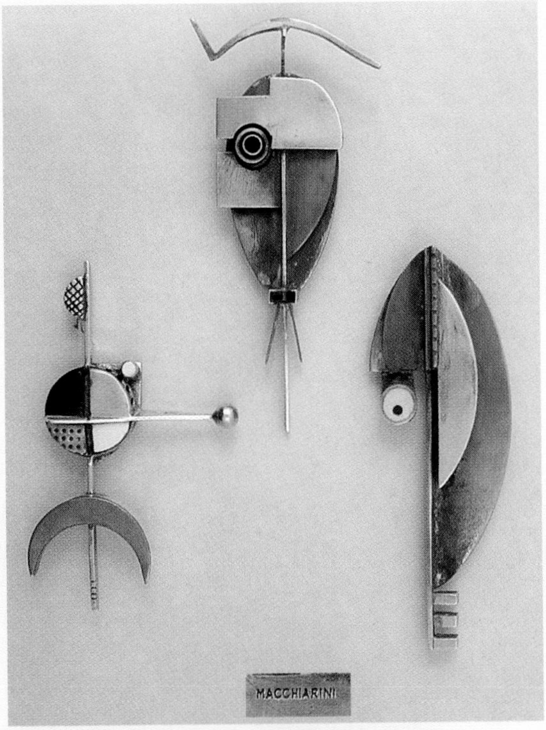

Brooches/Pins, imp "MACCHIARINI" for Peter Macchiarini, San Francisco, CA, commissioned by owner c. 1999, angled pinstems without hinges soldered to rev:
L, brass, silver, copper, ebony, ivory, an assemblage of smooth and textured geo shapes mounted on flat wire, forming a stylized figure, safety catch, 2⅛" w x 3⅞", **$850**.
TC, silver, copper, brass, a stylized mask constructed of layered, overlapping and concentric geo shapes mounted on flat wire, surmounted by a curved and angled brass strip, 2⅛" w x 4½", **$850**.
R, a stylized mask (or fish if turned sideways) constructed of a cutout brass plaque surmounted by silver, copper, and brass shapes mounted on a flat wire, an ivory and ebony "eye," 1⅜" w x 4½", **$1,000**. (Jill Crawford collection)

Brooch/Pin, silver, enamel on copper, c. 1960, layered circ disk, stylized bird motif enameled in blue and green on copper, rev imp "COOKE" for Betty Cooke, Baltimore, MD, 1" dia, **$225**. (Almunir Meghji collection)

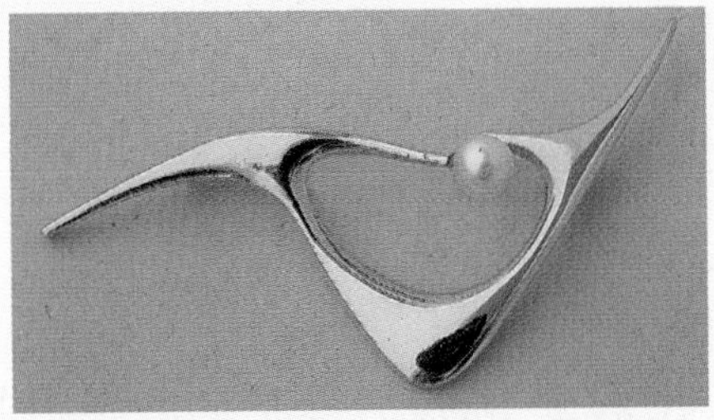

Brooch/Pin, 14k yg, cultured pearl, c. 1960, curv triangular freeform, a cultured pearl surmounting the open center, rev mkd "ED WIENER 14K," New York, NY, 2⅛" w x 1½", **$500**. (Victoria Palzkill Bonanno collection)

Brooch/Pin, opal, sterling, 14k yg, c. 1965, abstract insect figure with a bezel-set opal head, yg wire antennae, rounded sq yg plaque abdomen, mkd "GRA-WUN 14K STERLING" for Ray Graves, Scottsdale, AZ, 1" w x 2", **$250**. (Watson Miller collection, photo by Shari Watson Miller)

Buckle, bronze, 1971, rect plaque with chamfered sides, the center a textured convex quatrefoil on oxidized ground within a sq frame, a central sm circ opening enclosing a short rod with quatrefoil cross-section, four vertically mounted short round rods at compass points and in corners of quatrefoil, side mkd "OLAF SKOOGFORS," one of a kind in a series of 10 unique buckles that Skoogfors made in 1971, has original 1970s' gallery price tag of $2,500 on underside, 3" w x 2" x ⅞" h, **$3,500**. (Courtesy of Patrick Kapty, Mad Jewelry, Palm Springs, CA)

Brooch/Pin, sterling, cultured pearl, c. 1965, a tapered curv convex plaque folded over on itself, the back curving upward and terminating in a lg cultured pearl surmounting a disk, three cusped projections along the lower front edge, each suspending two convex lenticular drops, lines of texture and granulation on the front surface of the plaque and drops, rev imp "ROACH STERLING" for Ruth Roach, Plainfield, IA, approx 2" x 2", **$650**. (Courtesy of Shari Watson Miller, Phoenix, AZ)

Cuff Links, sterling and wood or pearls, c. 1950-55:
L, triangles formed with inlaid ebony sections flanking ster quadrangles, ster backing mkd "LEWITTES" for Esther Lewittes, ⅞" x 1⅛", **$150**.
CL, rect plaques with oxidized ovoid centers, a pearl set in the center of each, sgd "Lewittes" (in script) for Esther Lewittes, ⅞" x ¾", **$150**.
CR, wood bisected by ster strip forming rectangles with ster backing mkd "BOYER" for Merle N. Boyer, Honolulu, HI, ¾" x ⅝", **$100**.
R, narrow rectangles, one half wood with ster rivets, the other half ster, incised "M. N. BOYER" in wood rev, 1" x ⅜", **$100**. (Almunir Meghji collection)

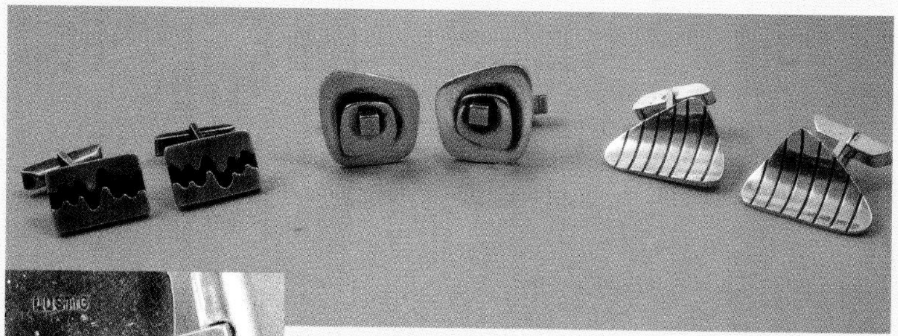

Cuff Links, sterling:
L, c. 1960, rect plaques, undulating cutout centers with oxidized ground, mkd "STERLING polly" for Polly Stehman, Ellensburg, WA, ¾" x ½", **$75**.
C, c. 1950, rounded quadrangles surmounted by concentric smaller quadrangles and sq centers, mkd "LUSTIG" for Nita Lustig, Chicago, IL, ⅞" x ⅞", **$145**.
R, c. 1950, concave rounded triangles with incised parallel lines, mkd "STERLING," sgd "byron" for Byron Wilson, Oakland, CA, 1" x ¾", **$125.** (Almunir Meghji collection)

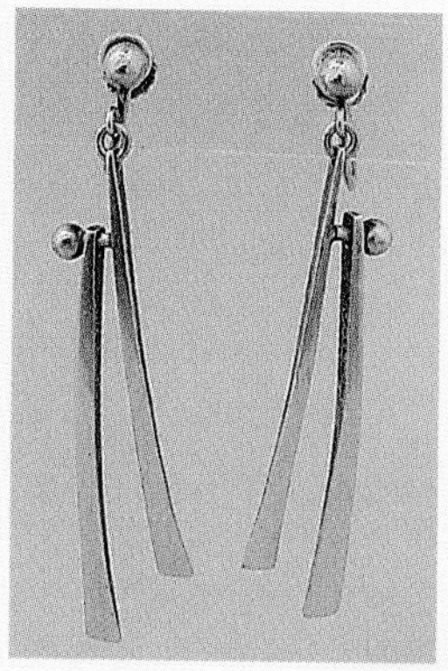

Earrings, pendent, sterling, c. 1950, each with two forged flattened lengths of sq wire, one suspended from the other on a bead-tipped wire, mkd "renk" in lower case script for Merry Renk, San Francisco, CA, "STERLING" along one side, bead-tipped surmount on screwback finding, ¼" w x 2⅛" tl, **$350**. (Author's collection)

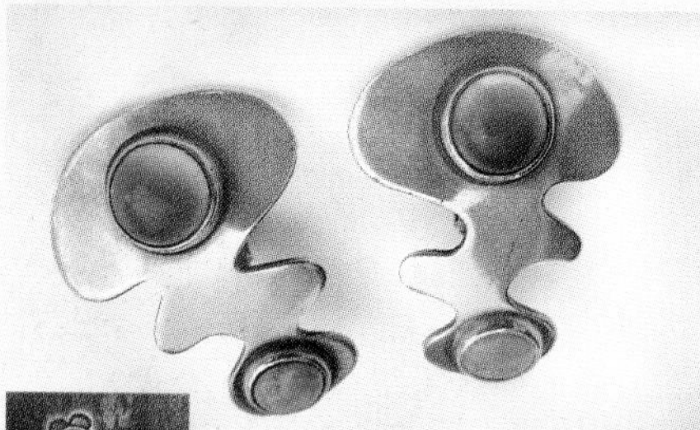

Earrings, sterling, moonstones, turquoise, c. 1950, biomorphic ster plaques of tapering undulating form, each bezel-set at the top with a circ moonstone cab, and at the bottom with a circ turquoise cab, clip backs, maker's mk for Sam Kramer, New York, NY, 1½" w x 1¼", **$475**. (Photo courtesy of M. Schon Antiques, Bay St. Louis, MS)

Earrings, pendent, sterling, c. 1950, inverted triangular surmounts vertically bisected by appl wire, suspending triangular bent wire open drops, mkd "LOBEL STERLING" for Paul Lobel, New York, NY, screwbacks, ⅞" w x 2½", **$300**. (Courtesy of Patrick Kapty, Mad Jewelry, Palm Springs, CA)

Earrings, sterling, turquoise, c. 1956-60, each a rounded triangular plaque, two corners bent downward, one bent upward, surmounted by a bezel-set irregular tumble-polished turq within an oxidized circle with a round wire rim, clip backs, rev imp "STERLING HAND MADE, H. FRED SKAGGS," 1⅜" x 1⅜", **$95**. (Author's collection)

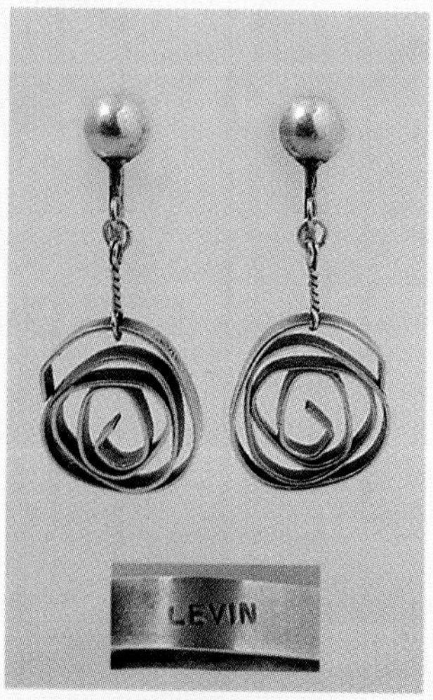

Earrings, drop, sterling, c. 1955-60, irregular volutes of coiled flat wire suspended by twisted wire shank from domed surmounts with screwbacks, side of one volute imp "STERLING," the other "LEVIN" for Ed Levin, Bennington, VT, ⅝" dia, 1½" tl, **$175**. (Author's collection)

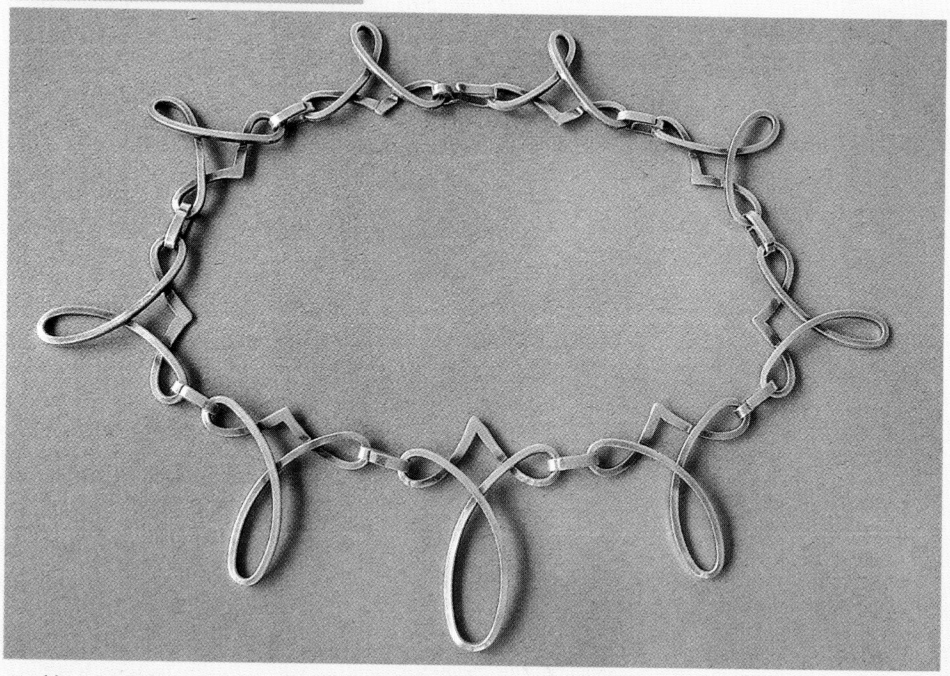

Necklace, sterling, c. 1950, each grad modular unit fabricated from sq wire loops with flattened cusped centers, joined with oval sq wire links, mkd "LOBEL STERLING" for Paul Lobel, New York, NY, 2¼" T to B at center, 16½" tl, **$1,500**. (Victoria Palzkill Bonanno collection)

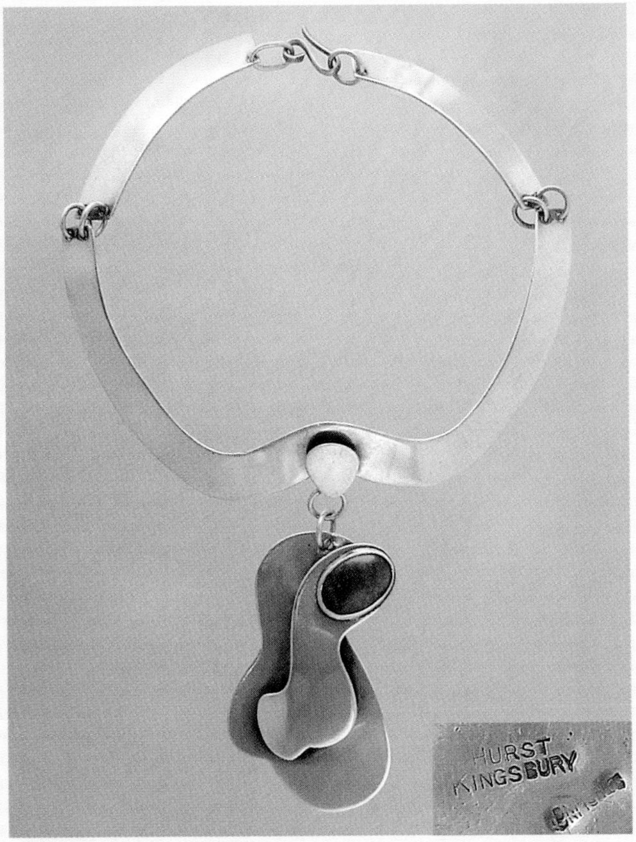

Necklace, sterling, labradorite, c. 1955, a collar of three curved segments of sheet silver joined with circ wire rings and a hook clasp, the center front surmounted by an ovoid plaque suspending a biomorphic pendant of irregularly shaped plaques, the smaller sumounting the larger and bezel-set with an oval labradorite cab, rev imp "HURST KINGSBURY, STERLING" for Joan Hurst and Jill Kingsbury, New York, NY, 4¾" dia, pendant 3¼" l, **$1,500**. (Courtesy of D. Brett Benson, Inc., Chicago, IL)

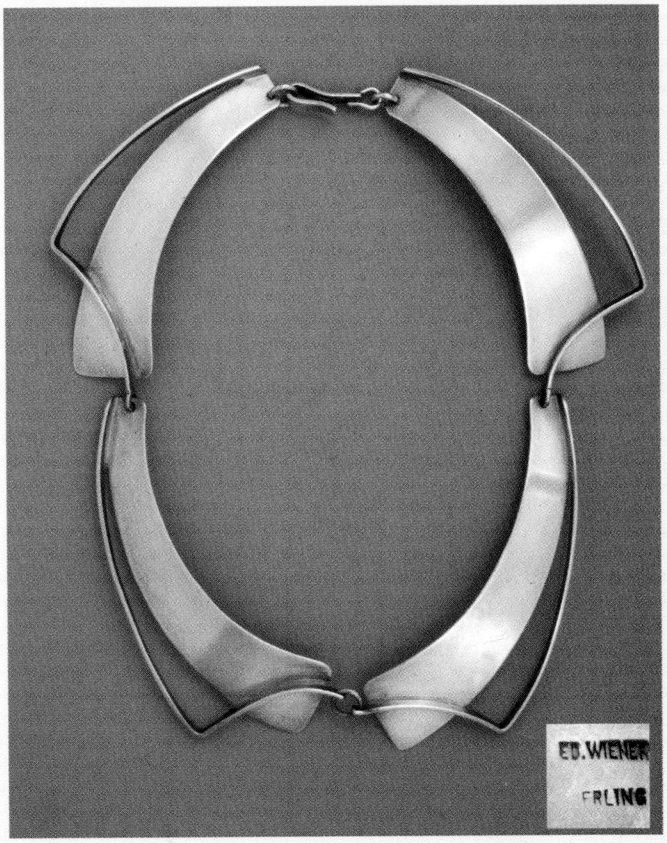

Necklace, sterling, c. 1950, a collar of four curved tapered oblong plaques, each surmounted and linked by appl flat L-shaped wire turned on edge, attached by rings through pierced openings at end of each plaque, hook and ring closure, mkd "ED. WEINER STERLING," 1⅛" T to B at center, 13½" tl, **$1,000**. (Courtesy of Shari Watson Miller, Phoenix, AZ)

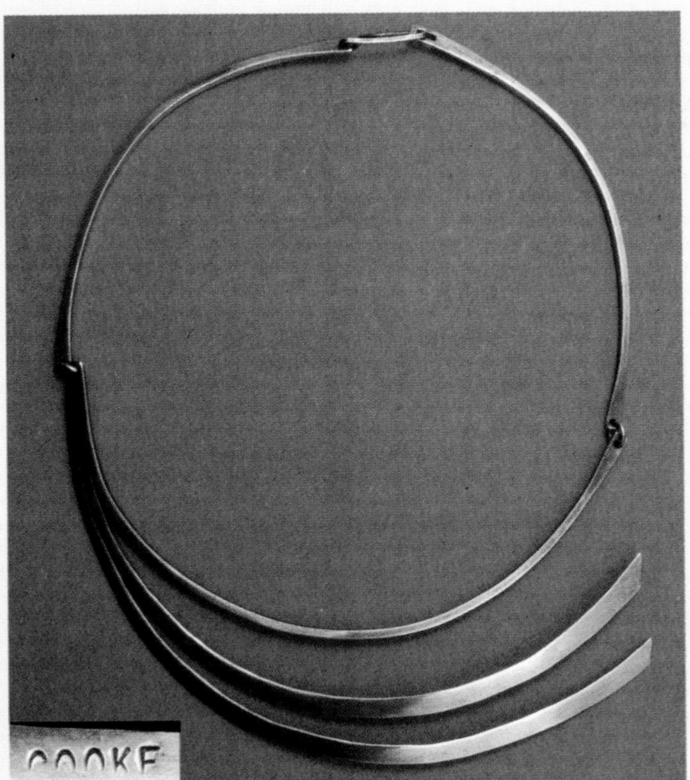

Necklace, sterling, c. 1955-60, collar of three forged sq wire segments joined with jump rings, a forged, partially split curved strip suspended from one side jump ring, rev imp "COOKE STERLING" for Betty Cooke, Baltimore, MD, approx 1½" T to B at widest point, 15¼" tl, **$800**. (Courtesy of Shari Watson Miller, Phoenix, AZ)

Pendant, sterling, c. 1955, biomorphic design, cutout oxidized plaque surmounted by a short rod and pierced cutout polished freeform, overlapping an open flat wire frame, suspended from cord (not orig), rev mkd "STERLING MACDONALD" for Everett MacDonald, Laguna Beach, CA, 1⅞" x 3" tl, **$500**. (Almunir Meghji collection)

Pendant and Chain, sterling, c. 1955, eccentric layered disks, lg with textured ground surmounted by smaller polished disk, off-center oxidized circ cutout surmounted by sm disk with engr stylized sun motif, rev mkd "HANDMADE," maker's mk, conjoined JP for James Parker, San Diego, CA, suspended from handmade oval link chain, pendant 2⅛" dia, chain 18" tl, **$450**. (Almunir Meghji collection)

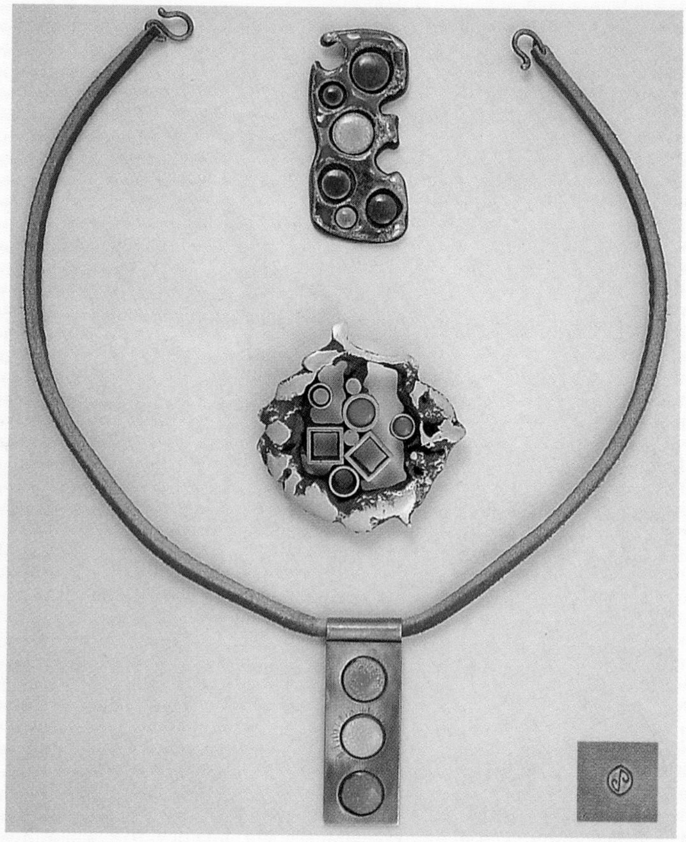

Pendants by James Parker, San Diego, CA, silver, enamel, c. 1970:
T, an irregular rect plaque with cutout indentations, red and green enameled surface with blue, red and green enameled circ disks within oxidized cutout circles, bail mounted on rev, unsgd, provenance: the James Parker estate, 1" w x 2¼", **$150**. (Courtesy of Patrick Kapty, Mad Jewelry, Palm Springs, CA)
C, a cast irregular circ brass disk with irregular openings surmounted by open sqs, short tubes, and rods, two tubes containing red-enameled disks, bail mounted on rev imp with maker's mk for James Parker, San Diego, CA, 2¼" dia, **$200**.
B, rect plaque with a vertical row of three enameled disks, tubular bail, suspended from a leather thong with wire hook clasp, rev imp with maker's mk for James Parker, pendant ¾" w x 2¼", 17½" tl, **$250**. (Courtesy of Postmodern, Oceanside, CA)

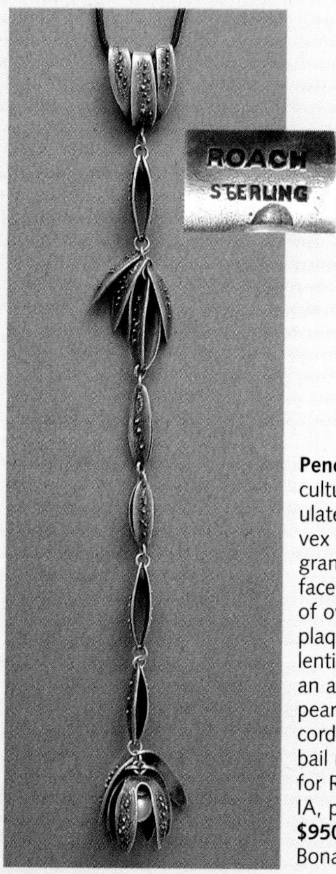

Pendant and Cord, sterling, cultured pearl, c. 1965, articulated pendant, linked convex lenticular plaques with granulated and textured surface terminating in a cluster of overlapping lenticular plaques and a four-part lenticular "cage" enclosing an approx 10mm cultured pearl, suspended from a 14" cord and silver wire clasp, bail rev imp "ROACH STERLING" for Ruth Roach, Plainfield, IA, pendant 1" w x 9½", **$950**. (Victoria Palzkill Bonanno collection)

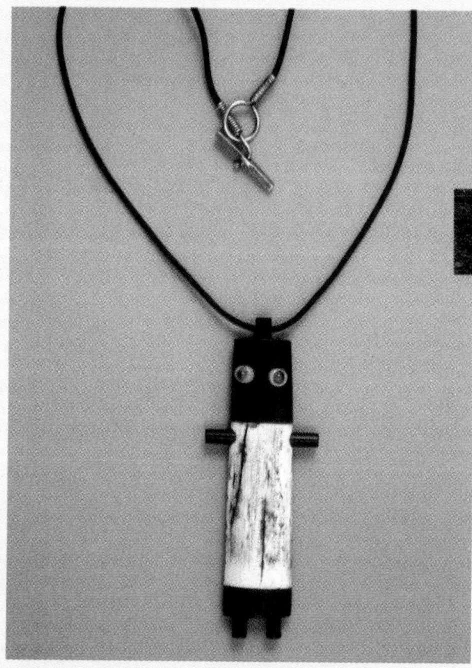

Pendant and Cord, bone, wood, ceramic, c. 1950, a stylized stick figure of bone and wood with ceramic eyes, rev imp "CAVAGNARO" for Milton Cavagnaro, Mill Valley, CA, suspended from a cord (orig) with ster T-bar clasp, 1⅛" x 4", cord 18" tl, **$350**. (Almunir Meghji collection)

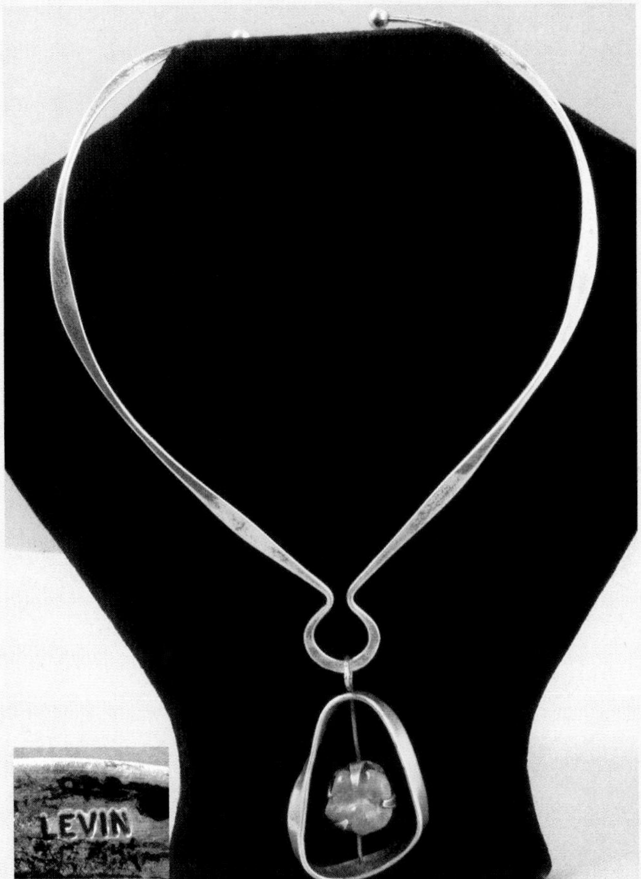

Pendant and Neckring, sterling, turquoise, c. 1960, hand-forged neckring with ball tips suspending a pendant with a tumble-polished turq prong-set and mounted on vertical wire within an open irregular ovoid frame, neckring mkd "STERLING LEVIN" for Ed Levin, Bennington, VT, pendant 1¼" x 1⅝", neckring 4½" x 6", **$450**. (Almunir Meghji collection)

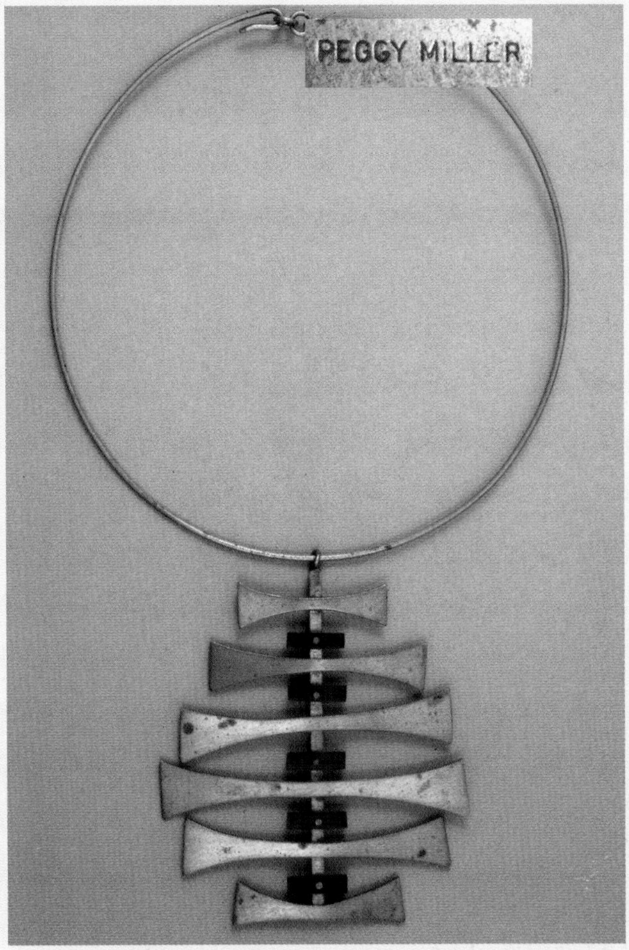

Pendant and Neckring, brass, wood, c. 1960, pendant of six grad flat brass waisted rect bars alternating with five sm wood rectangles, mounted on a vertical sq bar, rev mkd "PEGGY MILLER," pendant 3⅛" x 3⅝", neckring 5¼" dia, **$250**. (Almunir Meghji collection)

Ring, sodalite, turquoise, amethyst, sterling, c. 1955, three oval cabs bezel-set within S-curved borders on oxidized ground, tapering to form shank, imp "Art Smith" in script inside shank, 1" x 2⅛", approx sz 7½, **$2,250**. (Almunir Meghji collection)

Ring, sterling, 14k yg, amethyst, c. 1955-60, cutout curv indented "swoosh" surmounted by a capsule-shaped amethyst within a yg wire "cage" of grad loops, meant to be worn on pinky finger (conforms to side of hand), rev imp "Art Smith" in script, "14K STERLING," 1½" w x ¾", approx size 4½, **$2,000**. (Author's collection)

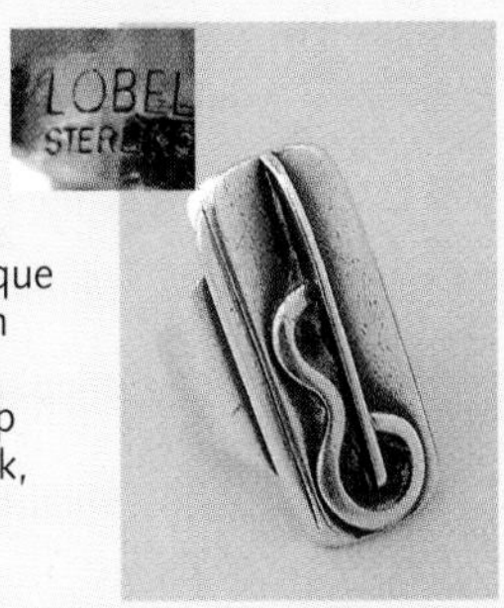

Ring, sterling, c. 1950, a rounded rect plaque with beveled side edges surmounted by an abstract guitar design on oxidized ground, mounted on a wide tapered shank, rev imp "LOBEL STERLING" for Paul Lobel, New York, NY, ⅝" w x 1½", approx size 6, **$250**. (Author's collection)

Ring, bloodstone (jasper), sterling, brass, copper, c. 1955-60, circ bloodstone cab set in wide brass bezel, flanked by short lengths of alternating ster and copper wire appl to shoulders, mounted on plain ster band, mkd "MACC" for Peter Macchiarini, San Francisco, CA, ⅞" dia, approx size 9, **$600**. (Author's collection)

Rings by James Parker, sterling:
L, c. 1965-70, a concave sq plaque surmounted by a convex sq plaque centering a circ bezel-set syn pink stone encircled by appl silver beads, surmounting a slightly tapered shank, maker's mk for James Parker (conjoined JP), "HANDMADE STERLING," sz 7½, ¾" sq at top, **$400**.
CL, c. 1970-75, irregularly-shaped top composed of high polished wire over dk bg with sm disk of bezel-set yellow enamel to one side, surmounting an irregular textured and patinated shank, maker's mk for James Parker, "HANDMADE STERLING," sz 7, ⅝" w x 1⅛", **$500**.
CR, c. 1975, tapered rounded rect plaque with design of meandering wire, one pennannular terminal encircling a disk of orange enamel and an eccentric sm disk of mauve enamel, another sm disk of pink enamel at other end, mounted on a tapered band, rev imp with maker's mk for James Parker, "HANDMADE STERLING," sz 7½, 1½" w x 1", **$650**.
R, c. 1955, rect plaque with rounded edges of tapering thickness and two circ cutouts surmounting the ends of a thick gauge round wire shank with three coils, top at an angle to shank, unmkd, provenance: the estate of James Parker's wife, sz 10, ¾" w x ⅛", **$350**. (Courtesy of Patrick Kapty, Mad Jewelry, Palm Springs, CA)

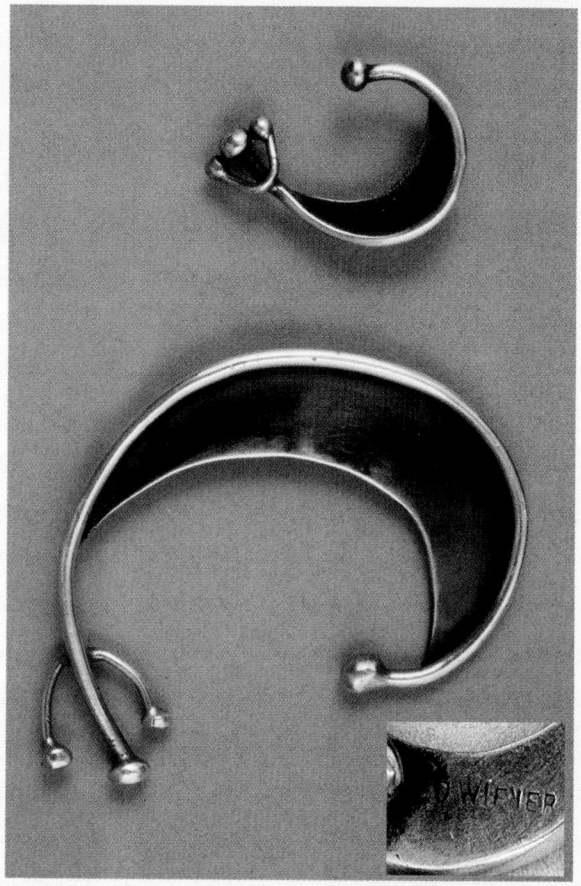

Suite: Bola Tie and Brooch/Pin, sterling, c. 1955, oxidized crescents framed by round wire, bead-tipped terminals, brooch sgd "ED WIENER," New York, NY, bola $2\frac{3}{8}$" x 1¾", brooch 1⅛" x ⅞", **$350**. (Almunir Meghji collection)

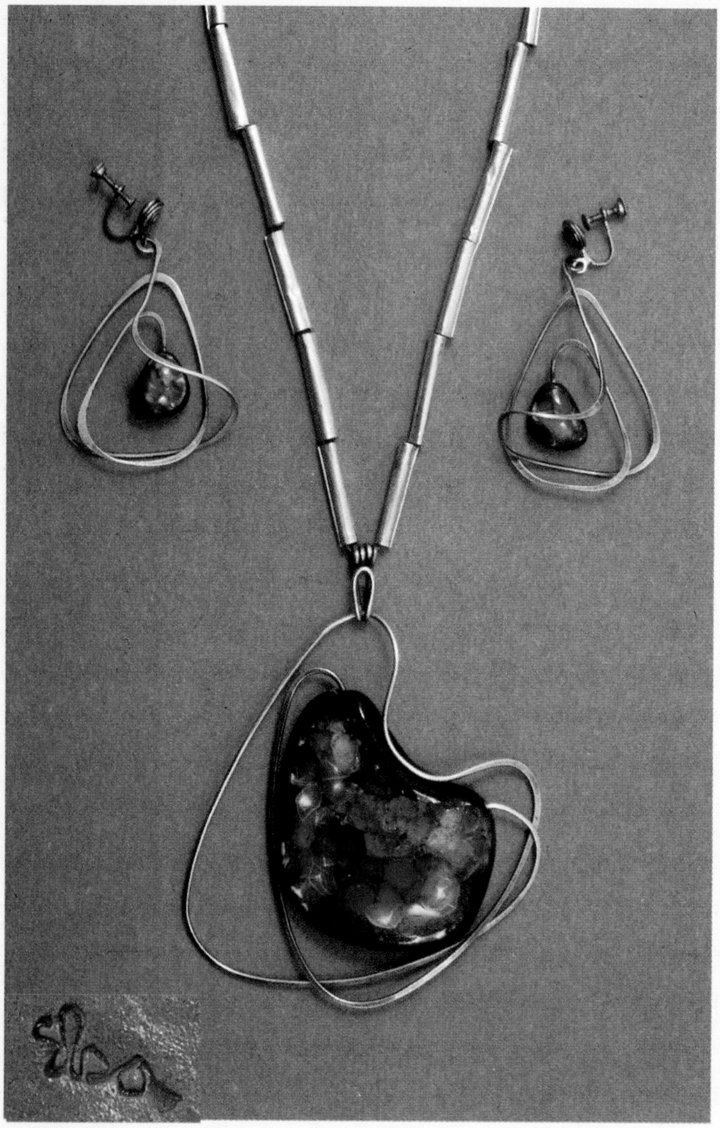

Suite: Pendant/Necklace and Earrings, ceramic, glass, silver, aluminum, c. 1955, pendant a rounded irregularly shaped "stone" of ceramic and fused glass enclosed in forged and shaped curv silver wire suspended from a cord strung with aluminum tubes, 14" tl, sgd "Elsa" in script imp into clay on rev for Elsa Freund, FL and AR, matching pendent earrings suspended from volute surmounts, screwback findings, unsgd, 1½"w x 2½"tl, pendant 3¾" w x 3½", **$1,200**. (Courtesy of Shari Watson Miller, Phoenix, AZ)

FINE JEWELRY c. 1945-1960

History records wars as lines of demarcation. What happens after them is usually a radical departure from what was happening before and during wartime. World War II was no exception. Post-war prosperity unleashed an indulgence in luxury long frustrated by deprivation. All aspects of popular culture changed, including a marked change in fashion. Christian Dior introduced his "New Look" in 1947: long full skirts, nipped-in waist, unpadded, sloping shoulders, tight bodices, and décolleté necklines. Femininity was back in style. To complement the look, jewelry had to change, too. In fact, jewelry design took off in two divergent directions, that of the "traditionalists" of fine jewelry, including the large houses and those who designed for them, and that of the new modernist designs of avant-garde studio artists (see section on Mid-Century Modern American Studio Jewelry). Among the former group, there was a return to an extravagant display of all kinds of gemstones, but especially, diamonds were a girl's best friend once again. In 1948, De Beers Corporation set the tone for the era with its their now-famous slogan, "a diamond is forever." A nearly imperceptible flexible platinum wire setting (said to have been inspired by a holly wreath), pioneered by diamond magnate Harry Winston around 1946, allowed clusters of stones to dominate a jewel. Fancy cuts, such as marquise and pear, were particularly favored in diamond jewelry. (see brooch below).

The motifs and forms of traditional jewelry in the '50s and early '60s were not a radical departure from those of the '40s, but their execution was decidedly different. Where '40s pieces had a heavy, solid, and smooth polished look (even though they may have been hollow and light in terms of actual weight), '50s pieces were open and airy with textured surfaces such as Florentine (brushed metal), ropetwisted or braided wire, mesh, reeding, fluting, and piercing (see bracelet by Van Cleef & Arpels on page 176 and "*passementerie*" necklace by Tiffany & Co. on page 178). Yellow gold was predominant except for all-diamond jewels, for which the preferred metal was once again platinum.

Following the trend for matching accessories, the suite returned in force as a full *parure* of necklace, bracelet, earrings, and brooch. Floral motifs were still in vogue, as well as a variety of leaf shapes, with increasing emphasis on gemstones and texture. Necklaces remained short as chokers, collars, or bibs. These could be draped, swirled, or fringed, in gold or entirely gem-set. Diamond necklaces typically featured a row or fringe of baguette and/or marquise diamonds flanked by scrolled or draped side elements (see page 179). Bracelets were primarily of the flexible sort, often gemstone-encrusted. Charm bracelets also maintained their popularity. Earrings were usually circular, floral, or foliate yellow gold clips for day, long fringes of gemstones, usually diamonds, for evening wear. Upswept styles that enveloped the ear were also common. Brooches in the forms of animals and people continued to amuse, more often stylized or cartoon-like caricatures than realistic portrayals (see page 177). Stylized foliate sprays entirely set with numerous baguette, marquise, and pear-shaped stones were another often-seen form. Modernism exerted its influence in the form of starburst and "atomic" shapes. Rings were domed clusters of gemstones, or one large stone surrounded by smaller stones, usually marquise or other fancy-cut diamonds.

The famous *haute joaillerie* houses—Cartier, Van Cleef & Arpels, et al—continued to produce opulent jewels in new designs, as well as reprising pre-war "classics" which were finding a wider audience among the newly prosperous. One French house that began making its mark in the early 1950s was Sterlé, founded by Pierre Sterlé (1905-1978) in 1934. Most famous among his designs is a fantastic "Bird of Paradise" brooch—a bird, not a plant, with a carved amethyst head, textured yellow gold body, fringes of foxtail chain (called *fil d'ange*) for tail and wings, set with turquoise, with diamond-set edges and beak. Another Sterlé bird design is pictured below. The company was purchased by Chaumet in 1976.

American jewelry firms began achieving greater recognition in the 1950s. Harry Winston (1896-1978), a retailer, broker and manufacturer since the 1930s, made an even bigger name for himself with his touring "Court of Jewels" exhibit, which opened in 1949, the same year he purchased the Hope Diamond. (He donated it to the Smithsonian Institution in 1958.) For obvious reasons, Winston became known as the "King of Diamonds."

Julius Cohen (d. 1995) began working for Harry Winston in 1942 (after leaving his uncle's firm, Oscar Heyman & Bros.). He opened his own salon in New York in

Brooch/Pin, diamonds, platinum, c. 1950, an asymmetrical arrangement of baguette and circ-cut diamond-set plat loops surmounted by two clusters of pear-shaped diamonds, 2" x 2," **$9, 988** [A]. (Copyright Christie's Images, New York 2002©, Christie's, Los Angeles, CA, 10/4/01)

Brooch/Pin, coral, turquoise, diamonds, 18k yg, c. 1955, Fr, in the shape of a stylized bird with an oval cab coral body, cabochon turq and circ-cut diamond crown feathers, textured yg and yg foxtail chain ("*fil d'ange*") tail feathers, mounted on a yg branch, sgd "STERLÉ, PARIS," #807 A, Fr assay mks, accompanied by orig design rendering, 2½" w x 3", **$8,225** [A]. (Copyright Christie's Images, New York 2002©, Christie's, Los Angeles, CA, 10/4/01)

Brooch/Pin, 18k yg, rubies, emeralds, sapphires, diamonds, c. 1955, Am, in the shape of a turtle, textured yg shell of flowerheads with ropetwist borders, each center prong-set with a faceted gemstone, cab ruby eyes, mkd "18 KT," conjoined "HB" on leg rev for Hammerman Bros., New York, NY, 1⅝" w x 1", **$525**. (Courtesy of Gilly Phipps, Philadelphia, PA)

Bracelet, flexible, diamonds, platinum, c. 1950, Fr, seven flexible rounded rect panels, each with a central circ-cut diamond, bisected by a row of baguette diamonds, within a pavé-set diamond frame, 140 baguette and 483 circ-cut diamonds, 46 cts tw, Fr maker's mks on v-spring and box clasp, 1¼" w x 6¾" tl, **$52,875** [A]. (Copyright Christie's Images, New York 2002©, Christie's, Los Angeles, CA, 3/6/01)

1955. Perhaps because of his association with Winston, he continued to incorporate large diamonds in his original designs. The "Fantasy of the Phoenix" brooch on page 177 is an example of a collaboration between jeweler Cohen and client Robert Tobin. The firm continues in business on Madison Ave., now run by Cohen's son-in-law.

Hammerman Bros., founded in New York in 1946, is a manufacturing jewelery firm still run by the founding family. They are known for fine quality mainstream jewelry. Their mark is a conjoined HB (see above brooch), which is sometimes confused with a similar mark used by Oscar Heyman & Bros., another prestigious New York jewelry manufacturer, founded in 1906.

Although it comes up for sale at auction from time to time, no written documentation has yet been discovered for a distinctive type of oxidized steel jewelry made for an Oriental art and antiques store, G.T. Marsh & Co., in Monterey, California.

San Francisco antique jewelry dealer Lynne Arkin provided the following information: "Founded by George Turner Marsh in 1876 in San Francisco, it became familiarly known as Marsh's. It is recognized as the oldest retail business in the U.S. dealing in Japanese and Chinese art. In 1927, the Marsh family built the architectural landmark in Monterey, California, that was their shop until February 2001.

"The senior Mr. Marsh had a jeweler-craftsman who worked for him, and created the unique black matte finish steel jewelry set with pearls, diamonds, gold...etc. in the 1940s, '50s, and '60s."

Several examples of Marsh jewelry are pictured in this section (see below and pages 177, 178, and 179). Marsh pieces are not always signed, but the style and materials are characteristic enough to safely attribute them.

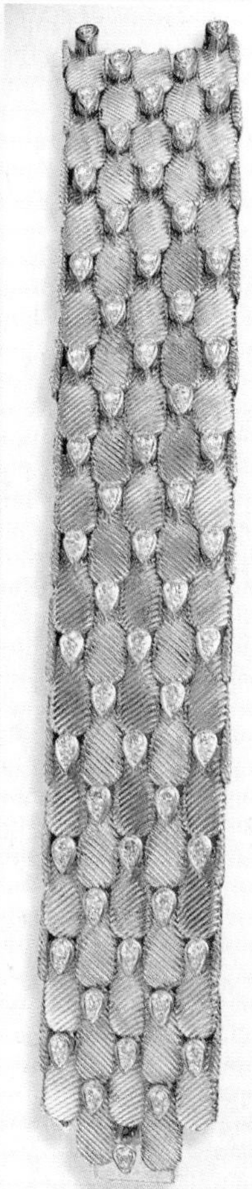

Bracelet, flexible, 18k yg, diamonds, c. 1950, Fr, a wide band with five rows of overlapping reeded gold foliate links, each alternating with circ-cut diamonds in pear-shaped wg collets, sgd "VAN CLEEF & ARPELS," France, #30798, 1⅛" w x 7¼", **$15,275** [A]. (Copyright Christie's Images, New York 2002©, Christie's, New York, NY, 10/22/01)

Bracelet, link, oxidized steel, wg, pearls, diamonds, c. 1945-50, Am, angular figure-8 shaped links, each surmounted by a row of three cultured pearls, joined with diamond-set wg links, attributed to Marsh, San Francisco, CA, ⅜" w x 7½" tl, **$2,400**. (Lynne Arkin collection)

Bracelet, flexible, 18k yg, rubies, sapphires, c. 1955, a flexible strap with appl textured yg disks, interspersed with flowerhead clusters of rubies and sapphires, Ital hmks on v-spring clasp, safety lock, ⅞" w x 7½" tl, $3,500. (Private collection)

Brooch/Pin, colored diamonds, diamonds, emeralds, 18k yg, platinum, c. 1958, a stylized phoenix with table-cut colored diamond wings, overlapping pear-shaped colorless diamonds in the breast, and tail feathers of varied-cut emeralds, colorless and colored diamonds, mounted in 18k yg and platinum, with a detachable 18k yg tree stand, sgd "Julius Cohen," in fitted leather case, commissioned and designed by Robert Lynn Batts Tobin, 3¾" w x 2⅜", **$54,050** [A]. (Copyright Christie's Images, New York 2002©, Christie's, Los Angeles, CA, 10/4/01)

Brooches/Pins, cabochon emeralds, rock crystal, sapphires, rubies, 14k yg, c. 1947, pr of "Rajah" brooches in openwork gold with emerald pantaloons, rc diamond faces, accented with circ-cut sapphires and rubies, one figure holding a crystal ball (#15030), the other a lute (#13489), both sgd "VAN CLEEF & ARPELS, N.Y.," 1⅛" w x 2½", **$19,975** [A]. (Copyright Christie's Images, New York 2002©, Christie's, New York, NY, 10/22/01)

Double Clip Brooch, diamonds, platinum, wg, c. 1950, opposed asymmetrical clips with looping ribbons set with bc and baguette-cut diamonds, gathered by a channel-set arc of baguette-cut diamonds, the ends set with bc diamonds, double-pronged hinged clips joined with a detachable 14k wg frame; diamonds approx 12.50 cts tw, 3" w x 1½", **$9,988** [A]. (Photo courtesy of Butterfields, San Francisco and Los Angeles, CA, 6/19/01)

Earrings, clip, oxidized steel, c. 1945-50, attributed to Marsh, San Francisco, CA:
L, hinged oval oxidized steel hoops, each inlaid with a wg flower set with four sm diamonds, a free-swinging cultured pearl suspended within a circ cutout, ¾" w x 1" l, **$900**.
R, each inlaid with a yg flower, a round yg bead suspended within a circ cutout, ½" w x ¾" l, **$750**. (Lynne Arkin collection)

Necklace, oxidized steel, wg, pearls, diamonds, c. 1945-50, a collar of linked curved oxidized steel bars, the wg links set with sm diamonds, a row of cultured pearls surmounting three front segments, attributed to Marsh, San Francisco, CA, ¼"w x 16" tl, **$3,500**. (Lynne Arkin collection)

Necklace, 18k yg, c. 1950, a series of interlaced woven yg tassels resembling and inspired by *"passementerie"* (braided cord trimming), sgd "TIFFANY & CO., ITALY," 1⅝" T to B at center, 16" tl, **$11,750** [A]. (Copyright Christie's Images, New York 2002©, Christie's, Los Angeles, CA, 10/4/01)

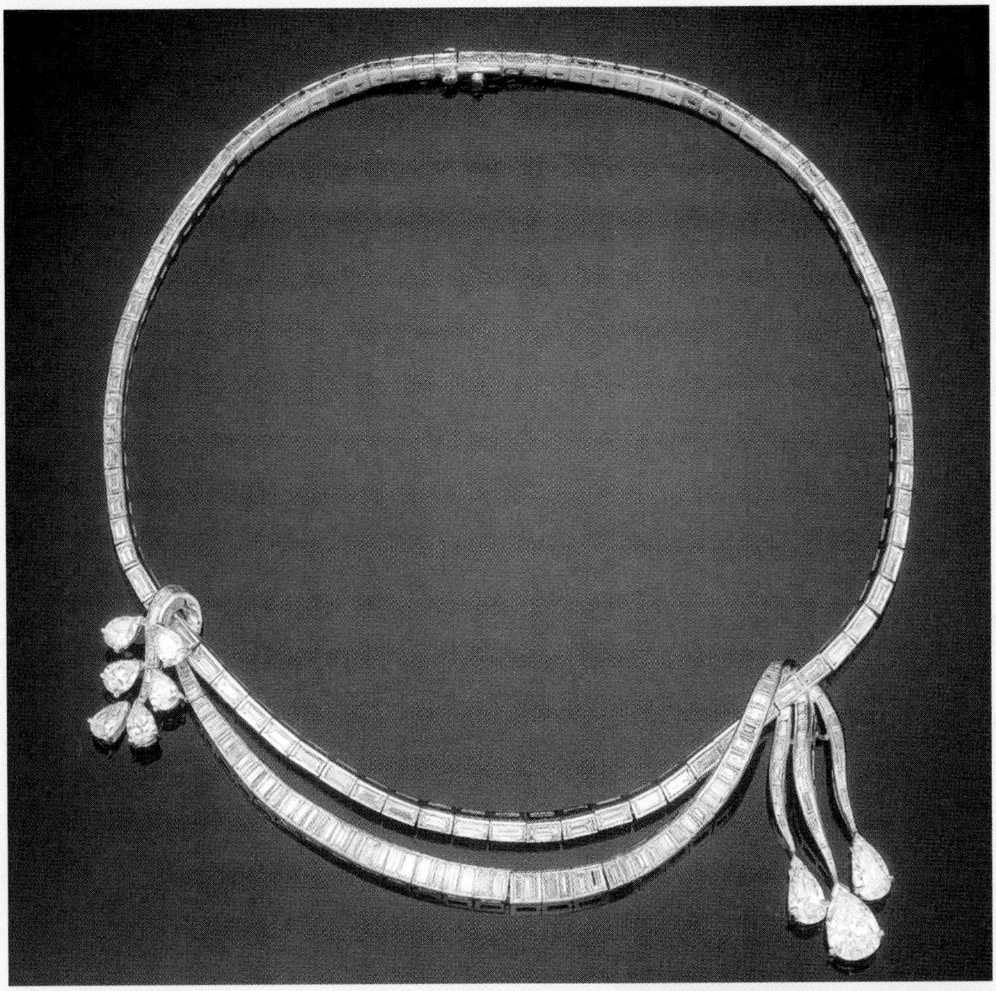

Necklace, diamonds, platinum, c. 1950, a flexible plat band of horizontally set grad baguette-cut diamonds, the front section draped with a grad row of vertically set baguettes on a flexible band terminating in pear-shaped diamonds, a fringe of three on one side, the largest weighing 1.65 cts, a cluster of six on the other, ½" at center, 14¼" tl, **$18,800 [A]**. (Copyright Christie's Images, New York 2002©, Christie's, Los Angeles, CA, 10/4/01)

Rings, oxidized steel, c. 1945-50, attributed to Marsh:
L, a rounded tapered oxidized steel hoop surmounted by a yg bead flanked by inlaid yg flowers, sz 6½, ½" T to B, **$750**.
R, oxidized steel hoop surmounted by a cultured pearl, flanked by inlaid wg flowers, each set with four sm diamonds, sz 5, ⅜" T to B, **$800**. (Lynne Arkin collection)

Suite: Brooch/Pin and Earrings, 18k yg, diamonds, c. 1955, Fr, the brooch a textured spiral radiating from a central twist, surmounted by a random sprinkling of sm circ-cut diamonds, matching clip earrings, Fr assay mks, sgd "STERLÉ, PARIS," #s 4673, 4684, brooch 2⅜" x 2¼", earrings, 1¼" x 1⅜", **$9,400** [A]. (Copyright Christie's Images, New York 2002©, Christie's Los Angeles, CA, 10/4/01)

FINE JEWELRY c. 1960-1975

Beginning in 1955 under Walter Hoving's directorship, Tiffany & Co. gained new distinction with designs by Jean Schlumberger (1907-1987), a former associate of Elsa Schiaparelli. Known for his use of colored gemstones, enamels, and animals and other motifs inspired by nature, Schlumberger became the first Tiffany designer whose jewels bore his signature (see earrings below). American-born Donald Claflin (d.1979), noted for his whimsical animal designs, joined Tiffany's in 1965. Claflin had previously worked for David Webb.

After opening an office in New York in 1946, and a salon in 1963, David Webb (1925-1975) came to prominence in the mid-1960s, when both clothing and jewelry styles were undergoing a significant change. He fostered, if not initiated, a trend for wearing quantities of large-scale, flamboyant jewels of Renaissance and fantasy-inspired design. Webb's animal motifs were influenced by Jeanne Toussaint of Cartier, creator of the famous panther jewels for the Duchess of Windsor and other wealthy clients. Today, pieces by Webb come up for sale regularly at auction, and generally do very well. This is no doubt partly due to the fact that Webb's "make a statement" jewels are so readily identifiable as his (see pages 181 and 182).

Designers Verdura, Seaman Schepps (see pages 185 and 182), and Suzanne Belperron remained active through the '60s. Companies founded by Verdura, Schepps, Herz-Belperron, and Webb continue in business today.

In the late '50s and '60s, the fashion world turned its eyes to Italy, where clothing designers like Emilio Pucci were garnering attention. Italian jewelers were also creating a stir.

Earrings, baroque cultured pearls, diamonds, 18k yg, c. 1960, Am, each surmount an outstretched polished yg wing, the lower portion pavé-set with circ-cut diamonds, suspending a detachable baroque cultured pearl pendant with a pavé-set diamond cap, sgd "TIFFANY SCHLUMBERGER" for Jean Schlumberger, Tiffany & Co., NY, ⅞" w x 2¾" tl, **$38,775** [A]. (Copyright Christie's Images, New York 2002©, Christie's New York, NY, 10/22/01)

The fashion for yellow gold created a new demand for Italian goldsmiths' talents. Foremost among Italian jewelers are the two family-run houses of Bulgari and Buccellati. The former house is famous for its Renaissance-inspired colored gemstone pieces, and classical designs incorporating ancient coins with heavy gold chains (see page 185). Buccellati is known for its patterned textured engraving using a *bulino* graver, a technique also inspired by Renaissance goldwork, particularly that of Benvenuto Cellini. Both firms expanded to international branches, including the United States in 1952 (Buccellati) and 1970 (Bulgari).

The 1960s were indeed a time of extreme changes, in fashion and in society at large. "Flower power" and the "sexual revolution" were watchwords of the day. There was a rejection of "the establishment" in favor of radical ideas and behavior. The mid-1960s also signaled the beginning of a renaissance of international style and multi-cultural consciousness, incorporating American, French, English, Italian, Islamic, and East Indian motifs, materials, and artistry. "Ethnic" looks became fashionable. New trends in art also inspired fashion and jewelry design: the black-and-white geometry of "Op Art" and the colorful irreverence of "Pop Art" found expression in jewelry and fabrics.

New practitioners of a new jewelry style emerged in the mid-1960s as well. Although conventional precious materials continued to be used, the designs themselves were decidedly *un*conventional, and large in scale. Abstract, textured, jagged-edged, and amorphous organic forms took shape in yellow gold, sometimes accented with diamonds or colored gemstones, and/or pearls (see suite by Boucheron, page 184, earrings and ring by Meister, page 186. Other more unusual stones were also used, including clusters of rough crystals, nodules and irregularly polished colored stones, and organic materials. In England, the master of this style is Andrew Grima (b. 1921), who opened his own business in 1965. His company now has shops all over the world (see ring on page 184). Arthur King (1921-1986), based in New York, also worked in a similar vein (see suite below), as did Gilbert Albert in Switzerland. Like the Modernists of the 1950s, these and other European and American designers of the period all followed a similar path, but each had his or her own individual mode of expression.

Wendy Ramshaw's (b. 1939) mode of expression is a

Suite: Hinged Bangle, Ring, Earrings, baroque pearls, diamonds, 18k yg, c. 1968, Am, irregular organic openwork design of cast yg interspersed with colorless and fancy orange-brown diamonds, freeform prongs enclosing baroque pearls, earrings with detachable drops and butterfly fittings, mkd 18 Kt, sgd "KING" for Arthur King, New York, NY, bangle 6" tl, earrings 1¾" tl, ring 1⅛" at center, **$9,000**. (Private collection, photo by Fabrizio Rubeca, Rome, Italy)

decided departure from other jewelry designers of the late 20th century. The London jeweler's work straddles the line between the artistic and the commercial. Her "Picasso's Ladies" series is perhaps the most well-known of her signature styles, particularly the stacks of multiple gold and gemstone rings mounted on lathe-turned Perspex (acrylic) stands that become part of the design. See page 184.

The firm of Kutchinsky was founded in London by Polish immigrant jewelers in 1893, but although it was successful from the beginning, it wasn't until after World War II that its international reputation was established. Kutchinsky jewels of the 1960s reflect a cosmopolitan approach to design (see page 183).

More traditionally designed jewels of the late '60s and early '70s also display a unique period twist: the setting of diamonds in yellow gold, rather than a white metal (platinum, white gold, or silver). Diamonds were often combined with colored gemstones, especially turquoise and rubies, or emeralds and rubies, typically framed in textured yellow gold or corded yellow gold wire (see clip by Van Cleef & Arpels on page 182). These stone combinations were also worked into Mogul-inspired pendants, necklaces and suites.

William Ruser (1908-1994?) was a mainstream jeweler whose Beverly Hills salon catered to Hollywood stars, including Joan Crawford and Loretta Young. He was noted for incorporating freshwater pearls into his whimsical poodle and cherub designs, some of which were actually created by the husband and wife team of Cy and Vera Wood (known as "Cyvra") of Topanga, California. One of the most popular series they designed was the "child of the week," based on the well-known nursery rhyme, ("Monday's child is fair of face, Tuesday's child is full of grace," etc., (see page 182). When Ruser retired in 1969, his Rodeo Drive location was taken over by Van Cleef & Arpels, which is still located there.

A few auction houses have recognized the 1950s as a "period," including circa dates in their descriptions; others do not. Most 1960s and 1970s jewelry is still described as contemporary, or simply not dated. Auction house catalogs of "important" or "magnificent" (i.e., very high-end) jewelry usually include biographical information on designers and manufacturers, which can be quite helpful. The second edition of *Understanding Jewellery* includes an additional chapter on 1960s and 1970s jewelry. Daniela Mascetti's and Amanda Triossi's *Earrings* and *The Necklace* both cover styles up to the present, as does Proddow and Fasel's *Diamonds, A Century of Spectacular Jewels*. Now that the twenty-first century is here, historians will undoubtedly acquire a clearer perspective on later twentieth century styles (perhaps someone will even come up with names for them), and more reference material will continue to be published.

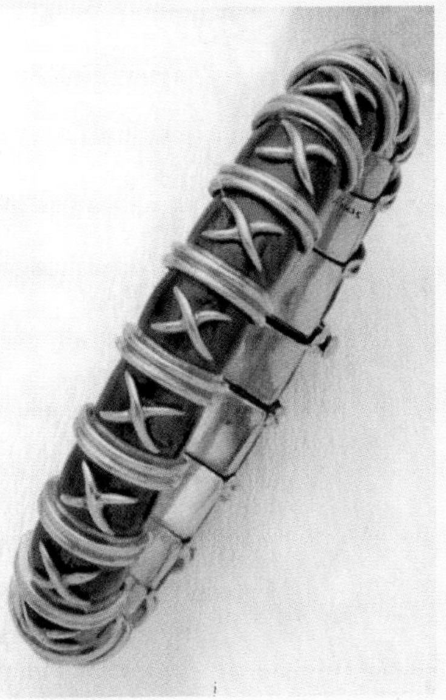

Bracelet, hinged bangle, 18k yg, enamel, c. 1960, Fr, articulated, each translucent red enameled segment separated by gold ribs, surmounted by appl gold X shapes, sgd "SCHLUMBERGER, PARIS," Fr hallmarks, ¾" w x 6¾" tl, **$5,875** [A]. (Photo courtesy of Butterfields, San Francisco and Los Angeles, CA, 9/25/01)

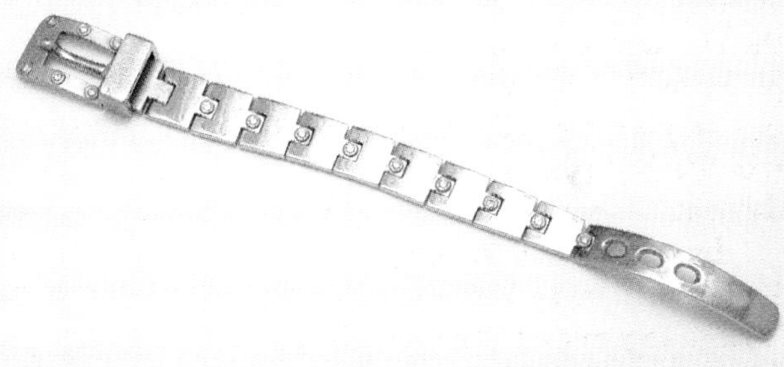

Bracelet, 18k wg, diamonds, c. 1975, Eng, belt and buckle design, each articulated link bezel-set with a circ-cut diamond, buckle with six circ-cut diamonds, mkd "750," UK 18k import assay mks, date letter U for 1975, sgd "LARRY," unknown maker, 9" tl, **$6,000**. (Private collection, photo by Fabrizio Rubeca, Rome, Italy)

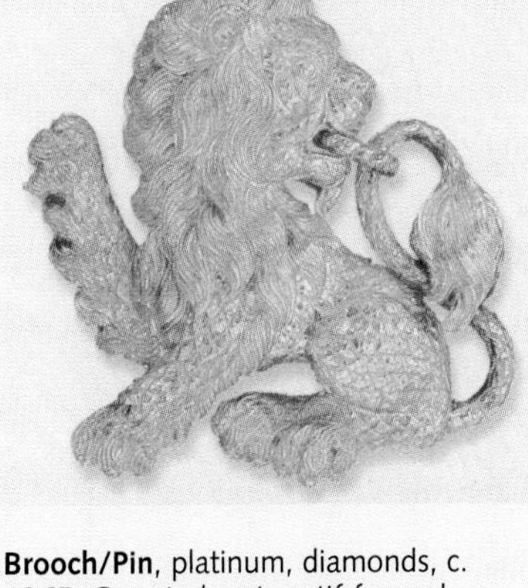

Brooch/Pin, 18k yg, c. 1965, Am, in the shape of a lion in textured yg, sgd "WEBB" for David Webb, New York, NY, 3¼" w x 3⅛", **$3,525** [A]. (Copyright Christie's Images, New York 2002©, Christie's Los Angeles, CA, 10/4/01)

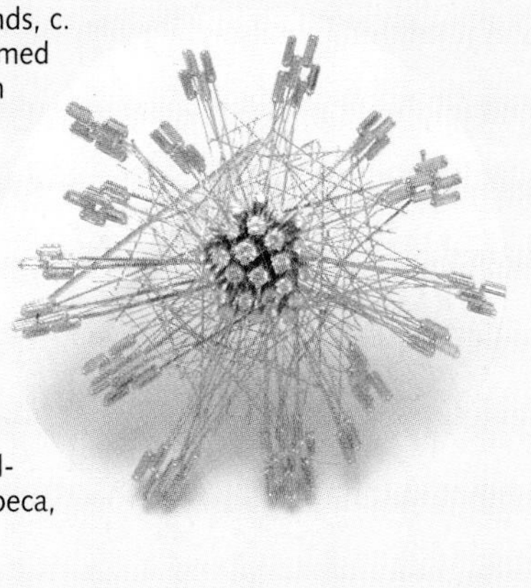

Brooch/Pin, platinum, diamonds, c. 1965, Ger, starburst motif formed of crisscrossing plat wires with a grouping of prong-set circ-cut diamonds in the center and clusters of baguette diamonds at the terminals, mkd "PLATIN," sgd "W" for Wipperfeld of Berlin (Heinz Wipperfeld 1945-87, active in Berlin, awarded "*Die Goldene Muschel*" [The Golden Shell] prize, 1970), 2¾" dia, **$12,000**. (Private collection, photo by Fabrizio Rubeca, Rome, Italy)

Brooch/Pin, pearls, jade, yg, c. 1965-70, a branch motif, five pale green jade cab leaves interspersed with pearl berries, textured yg stems, sgd "MING'S" for Ming's of Honolulu, HI, 1½" w x 2½", **$1,200**. (Photo courtesy of Joanne Valentine, Almost Antiques, Honolulu, HI)

Brooch/Pin, pearls, 14k yg, c. 1970s, berry and vine motif with a cluster of pearls surmounted by engr yg vines and leaves with appl yg beads, sgd "MING'S," 1½" w x 2¼", **$550**. (Photo courtesy of Joanne Valentine, Almost Antiques, Honolulu, HI)

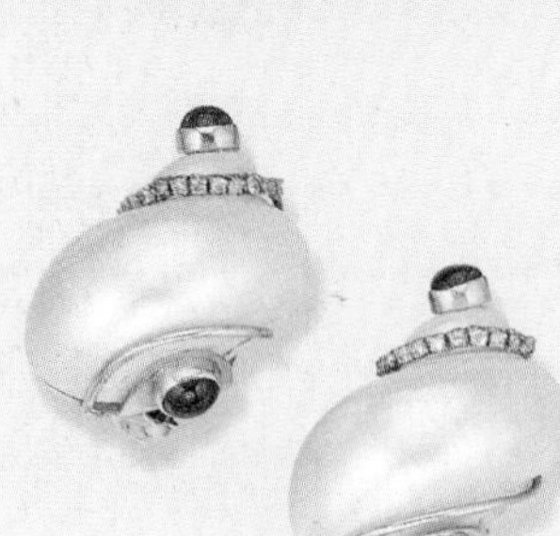

Earrings, turbo shells, diamonds, cab rubies, 14k yg, c. 1960-70, Am, each shell set in a gold spiral mounting with a row of circ-cut diamonds, bezel-set ruby terminals, omega clipbacks, rev mkd "SEAMAN SCHEPPS," clips mkd "14k," 1⅜" w x 1½", **$1,998** [A]. (Copyright Christie's Images, New York 2002©, Christie's Los Angeles, CA, 3/6/01)

Charm, 14k yg, baroque pearl, blue stones, c. 1960, Am, depicting "Saturday's Child" (one of the "children of the week" series: "Saturday's child works hard for a living") as a cherub with a broom surmounting a baroque pearl "cloud," blue stone eyes, rev mkd "©Ruser [incised script] 14k" for William Ruser, Los Angeles, CA, orig design drawing by Cy and Vera Wood ("Cyvra"), Topanga, CA, ⅜" w x 1⅛", **$200**. (Author's collection)

Clip, sapphires, turq, 18k yg, c. 1960, Am, teardrop-shaped turq cabs alternating with rays of cushion-cut sapphires, accented with gold cone decoration, double-pronged hinged clip with lever catch on rev, sgd "TIFFANY & CO.," 2¼" dia, **$12,925** [A]. (Copyright Christie's Images, New York 2002©, Christie's Los Angeles, CA, 3/6/01)

Clip, turq, diamonds, 18k yg, c. 1970, Fr, a circ-cut diamond and turq cab flowerhead or four-leaf clover mounted in textured yg, double-pronged hinged clip with trombone catch on rev, Fr assay mks on pinstems, sgd "VAN CLEEF & ARPELS © FRANCE," 2¼" dia, **$4,700** [A]. (Copyright Christie's Images, New York 2002©, Christie's Los Angeles, CA, 3/6/01)

Earrings, pendent, diamonds, platinum, cultured pearls, 18k wg, c. 1970, Fr, surmounts of tapered and narrow rect plat batons channel-set with rect-cut and circ-cut diamonds interspersed with prong-set circ-cut diamonds, mounted at various projecting angles, suspending similarly constructed detachable drops, each terminating in a gray pearl, hinged post and clip backs, Fr plat and gold assay mks, maker's mk for Chaumet, 2¾" tl, **$10,000**. (Private collection, photo by Fabrizio Rubeca, Rome, Italy)

Earrings, clip, rock crystal, diamonds, enamel, 18k yg, platinum, c. 1965, Am, each faceted crystal hoop tapering to a central pavé-set diamond bar with black enamel borders, 48 circ-cut diamonds, 3.20 cts tw, sgd "©DAVID WEBB®," 1⅛" dia, **$5,875** [A]. (Copyright Christie's Images, New York 2002©, Christie's Los Angeles, CA, 3/6/01)

Necklace, sautoir, dyed green chalcedony, diamonds, 18k yg, platinum, c. 1970, Fr, teardrop-shaped chalcedony pendant, textured yg center with three circ-cut diamonds set in plat, textured yg frame, may be worn as a brooch with provided additional fitting, chain of chalcedony and diamond-set plat and textured yg links divides into four sections, Fr export assay mks for gold and platinum, sgd "VC&A," #NY 43321, "MADE IN FRANCE," maker's mark "AV" for Vassort, Paris, brooch fitting sgd "VAN CLEEF & ARPELS," #NY 433529, chain 26¾" tl, pendant 2" w x 2¾", **$16,000.** (Private collection, photo by Fabrizio Rubeca, Rome, Italy)

Necklace, sautoir, red coral, onyx, diamonds, 18k wg, c. 1970, Fr, circ disk pendant divided into open segments of coral and onyx, surmounted by four quadrangular coral and onyx plaques, each edged in yg with a row of circ-cut diamonds along one side, suspended from a strand of alternating coral and three onyx beads with sq yg spacers, pendant detachable, mkd "MADE IN FRANCE," Fr export assay mks for 18k, indistinct Fr maker's mk, necklace mkd "FRANCE," Fr 18k export assay mk, maker's mk "STÉ G," design attributed to Kutchinsky, necklace 29⅛" tl, pendant 2⅜" dia, **$6,500**. (Private collection, photo by Fabrizio Rubeca, Rome, Italy)

Pendant and Neckring, 18k yg and wg, diamonds, 18k wg, c. 1970, Belgian, detachable pendant a textured yg convex disk suspended from an inverted Y of overlapping wg batons and rods of varying lengths interspersed with sm circ-cut diamonds, wg neckring, pendant mkd with Belgian 18k assay mk (lozenge reserve and 0750), maker's mk for Wolfers (head of a wolf and a W beneath in a barrel-shaped reserve), pendant 2½" w x 5," **$2,500**. (Private collection, photo by Fabrizio Rubeca, Rome, Italy)

Pendant and Neckring, 18k wg, MOP, cultured pearls, diamonds, 1976, Ger, titled "Symphony in White," a dished circ MOP disk, the center surmounted by an arrangement of cultured pearls of varied size and color interspersed with prong-set circ-cut diamonds and mounted on a network of wg wire, a slightly curved and tapered wg ribbon pavé-set with circ-cut diamonds mounted along the notched upper left edge, suspended from a round wg wire neckring, by Gunter Krauss, Stutgart Germany, winner of the award for best pearl jewel, "*Die Goldene Muschel* 1976" (The Golden Shell), pendant 3⅛" dia, **$12,000.** (Private collection, photo by Fabrizio Rubeca, Rome, Italy)

Ring, amethyst, diamonds, 18k yg and wg, c. 1965, Eng, a hemispherical amethyst cab in a spiral textured feather motif yg setting accented by sm diamonds in wg, sgd "GRIMA" for Andrew Grima, London UK, 1⅛" at center, **$3,500**. (Private collection, photo by Fabrizio Rubeca, Rome, Italy)

Ring, onyx, diamonds, 18k yg and wg, c. 1970, annular onyx center, flanked by plain yg and diamond set horseshoe-shaped bands, pavé diamond and yg center, 1⅛" w x 1", **$3,000**. (Private collection, photo by Fabrizio Rubeca, Rome, Italy)

Ring, 14k yg, c. 1970, "Flowers of the Four Seasons," convex oval pierced and engr plaque depicting four different flowers, mounted on a narrow shank, sgd "MING'S" for Ming's of Honolulu, HI, sz 7½, ⅝" w x 1" at front, **$350**. (Photo courtesy of Joanne Valentine, Almost Antiques, Honolulu, HI)

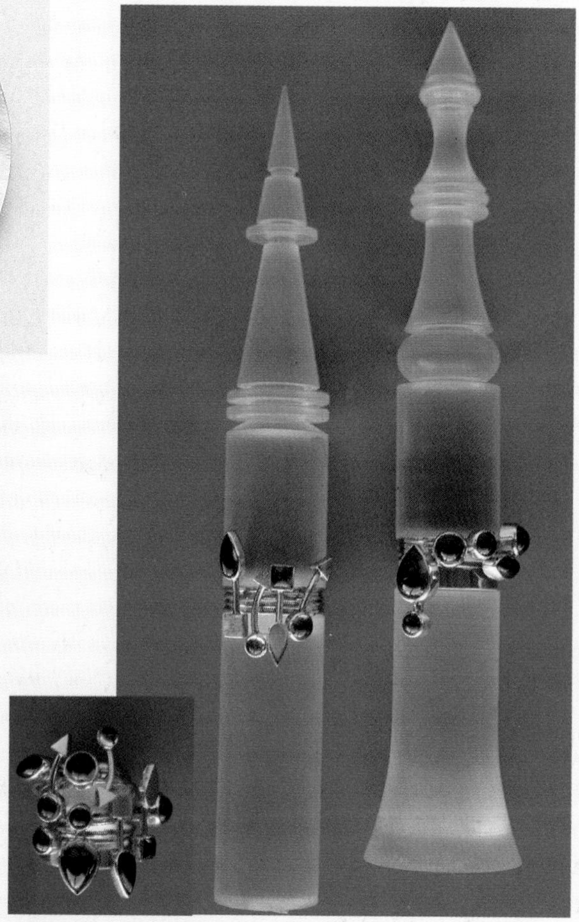

Rings and stands by Wendy Ramshaw, London, 18k yg and gemstones, 1970-71:
L, amethyst, moonstone, citrine, set of four rings on a lathe-turned Perspex (acrylic) stand, each ring with geo-shaped yg and bezel-set cab gemstones at the terminals of short yg wires surmounting a narrow band, forming an interlocking set, each mkd "WR," London hmks, date letter for 1970-71, stand ¾" w x 6", the set, **$2,500**.
R, garnet, ruby, amethyst, set of five rings and Perspex stand, each narrow band surmounted by a bezel-set circ or pear- or navette-shaped gemstone cab, wider band surmounted by a pear-shaped garnet and a circ amethyst on a short yg rod, each mkd "WR" with London hmks, stand 1" w x 6", the set, **$3,000**. (Shari Watson Miller collection, photo by Shari Watson Miller)

Suite: Brooch/Pin, Earrings, Ring, 18k yg, sapphires, diamonds, emeralds, c. 1965, Fr, textured openwork spiky freeform design in yg with circ-cut gemstone accents, Fr assay mks, maker's mk, each pc sgd "BOUCHERON, PARIS," brooch #17340, earrings (clipback) #37140, ring #49568, brooch 1⅝" dia, earrings 1" dia, ring ¾" w at front, **$7,050** [A]. (Copyright Christie's Images, New York 2002©, Christie's New York, NY, 10/22/01)

Suite: Necklace and Earrings, citrines, diamonds, 14k yg, platinum, c. 1960, a grad line of oval-cut citrines alternating with pavé-set diamond floral/foliate motifs, matching clip-back earrings, mkd "585," necklace clasp sgd "VERDURA," mkd "585, pt 950," necklace ⅝" w at center, 15" tl, earrings ⅞" w x 1⅛", **$52,875** [A]. (Copyright Christie's Images, New York 2002©, Christie's Los Angeles, CA, 3/6/01)

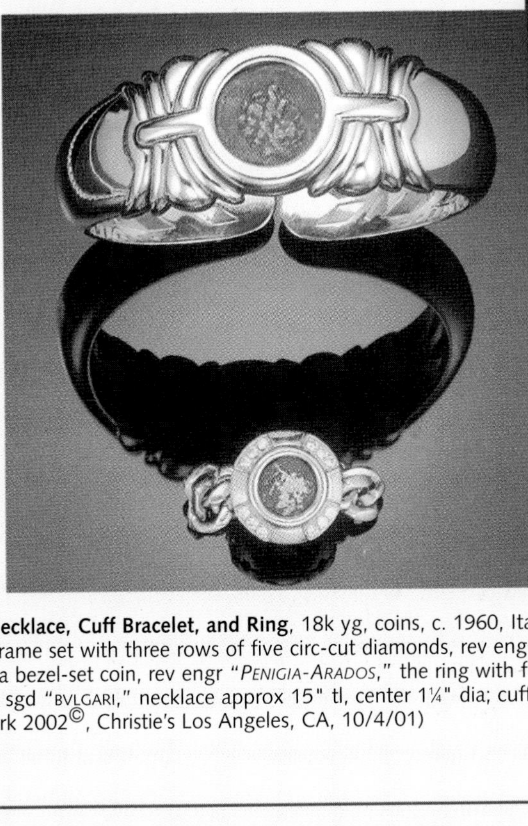

Suite: Necklace, Cuff Bracelet, and Ring, 18k yg, coins, c. 1960, Ital, the necklace a heavy curb link chain suspending a bezel-set Roman coin in a gold frame set with three rows of five circ-cut diamonds, rev engr "*Siracusa Pirro 278-276 a.c.*," the tapered cuff with a raised ribbed pattern around a bezel-set coin, rev engr "*Penigia-Arados*," the ring with flexible curb link shank, bezel-set coin in a diamond-set frame, necklace and bracelet sgd "BVLGARI," necklace approx 15" tl, center 1¼" dia; cuff 2⅛" inside dia, ¾" w, ring ⅝" dia, **$7,050** [A]. (Copyright Christie's Images, New York 2002©, Christie's Los Angeles, CA, 10/4/01)

Suite: Necklace and Earrings, white coral, diamonds, 18k wg, c. 1975, Fr, penannular hinged necklace with detachable element, a ring of coral cabs and a semicircular diamond link, which may be worn separately, assay mk for French 18k, JC with crescent and star in lozenge (maker's mk for Chaumet), sgd "CHAUMET PARIS," earclips, one mkd with Belgian 18k assay (lozenge and .0750), sgd "CHAUMET PARIS," necklace approx 17⅜", pendant 3" w x 2", earrings 1⅜" dia, **$9,500**. (Private collection, photo by Fabrizio Rubeca, Rome, Italy)

Suite: Necklace, Hinged Bangle Bracelet, and Ring, onyx, jadeite, *pâte de verre*, rubies, diamonds, 18k yg, c. 1970, collar of double lengths of yg round wire with a central ornament of a three-sided black onyx bracket surmounted by an asymmetrical arrangement of jadeite and green *pâte de verre* convex disks with concave centers surmounted by sm bezel-set ruby cabs, interspersed with yg bezel-set circ-cut diamonds, flanked by similar ornamentation on the yg wires, matching hinged bangle of open wirework surmounted by a convex rect onyx plaque and nine disks with rubies and diamonds, and a ring with a split yg shank and rect onyx plaque surmounted by four disks with rubies and diamonds, each pc mkd "H," "750," necklace approx 15," bracelet 7" tl, ring ⅞ " w x ¾" at center, **$11,000**. (Private collection, photo by Fabrizio Rubeca, Rome, Italy)

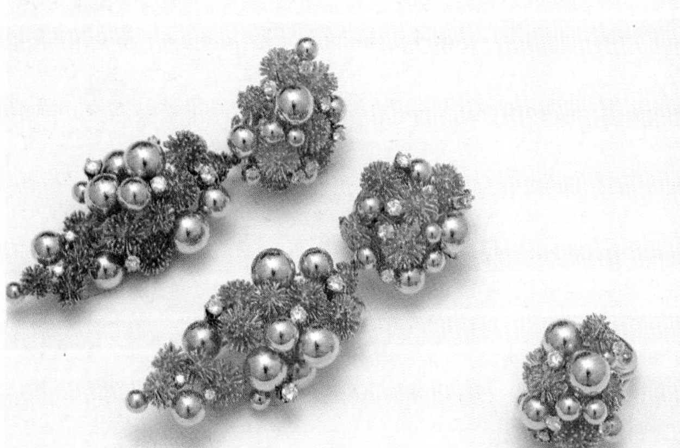

Suite: Pendent Earrings and Ring, 18k yg, diamonds, c. 1971, Swiss, earring surmounts and drops of clusters of polished smooth yg spheres in varied sizes and spiky "sea urchin" motifs interspersed with prong-set circ-cut diamonds; detachable drops can be worn as dress clips (a later modification), post and clip findings, matching ring with split shank, all pcs mkd "750," sgd "E M" for Meister of Zurich, Switzerland, ring ⅝" w x 1" at center, earrings 3⅛" tl, **$8,000**. (Private collection, photo by Fabrizio Rubeca, Rome, Italy)

Suite: Brooch, Earrings, Ring, jade, pearls, yg, c. 1960-70, flowering branch motif with clusters of round multicolored jade beads (5.5 mm to 6.5 mm) and pearls, engr yg leaves and stems, sgd "MING'S" for Ming's of Honolulu, HI, brooch 2¾" w x 1½", earrings ½" w x 1", ring ¾" w x 1", **$1,200**. (Photo courtesy of Joanne Valentine, Almost Antiques, Honolulu, HI)

COSTUME JEWELRY *(Designer/Manufacturer Signed and Other)*

Section One: c. 1935-1950

A few years ago, no one would have believed that a brooch made of rhinestones and base metal could be worth more than one made of diamonds and platinum. Up until almost 20 years ago, that same old rhinestone brooch probably would have been tossed in a drawer or thrown away. That was before costume jewelry collectors, price guides, and more recently, the Internet, entered the picture. Now, it seems that everyone knows and recognizes the "name" pieces—and knows their value, or at least knows better than to throw them away. Costume jewelry was elevated to an even higher level with the opening of an exhibition that toured museums in Europe and the U.S., from 1991 to 1993, called "Jewels of Fantasy, Costume Jewelry of the 20th Century." The exhibit's accompanying catalog (see References) has become an important resource and a sought-after collectible in its own right, now that it is out of print.

In this edition, the designer/manufacturer signed section has been divided chronologically, for two reasons. First, to more closely parallel the fine jewelry sections so that the evolution of styles can be compared between precious and non-precious pieces of the same periods. Second, because pre-1950 costume jewelry has a special place in the hearts of some collectors, while post-1950 costume jewelry is gathering its own group of followers. Furthermore, the sheer quantity of what is being collected has grown considerably since the publication of the second edition, and dividing the category at 1950 makes it more manageable.

Expanded though it may be, it is still not possible to go into great detail in even two sections of this book about the many manufacturers and designers whose history and products have already been amply documented by a plethora of entire books on signed and unsigned costume jewelry. New books on the topic in general, as well as monographs on specific makers, continue to be published. Some of them are better than others. The References in the back of the book list a few of the recommended ones. While these are recommended for the examples, marks, and information they contain, readers should be aware that it is not uncommon to find conflicting information in different sources. Furthermore, it is not likely that the "true story" will ever be known. Most companies did not keep detailed records of their jewelry lines. At the time it was produced, costume jewelry was thought to be as ephemeral and disposable as the fashions it was meant to complement. Much of the recent research on costume jewelry has of necessity been based on recollections of company executives, designers, and other employees, patent and trademark searches, and advertising and articles in consumer and trade periodicals of the times.

A listing of American costume jewelry manufacturers, including dates of operation if documented, can be found in an appendix at the end of this book. Since the second edition of *Warman's Jewelry*, dates have been added, and revised in some cases, as a result of information recently discovered by researchers in the field, including the advisers named in the References. Their Web sites, which they are able to update much more quickly than printed publications, are also listed.

Even though much has already been written by others, a few salient points should be made here, especially as they relate to the specific examples in the photos that follow.

The bulk of the "name" jewelry that collectors seek was produced from circa 1935 through the 1960s (1970s costume jewelry is beginning to generate collector interest as well). The few manufacturers who were making costume jewelry before 1935, e.g., Ciner, Coro, Miriam Haskell, Hobé, Napier, Trifari, and designer/couturiers Chanel, Hattie Carnegie, and Schiaparelli, did not consistently mark their pieces, if they signed them at all (the collector terminology for manufacturers' markings is "signed"). Their attributable circa 1920s (and some early 1930s) designs are rare and usually expensive.

As mentioned in the introduction, attribution of unsigned pieces and circa-dating of any piece should be backed up by printed evidence, or provenance. Because they assist in circa-dating, patent numbers found on the backs of pieces are given in the captions, with the year the numbers were issued in parentheses (which is the earliest year the piece could have been made), as well as the name of the person to whom they were issued or assigned, when known. Other aspects of a piece, such as style and other elements, may date it later. For example, Coro patented the mechanism for the double clip brooch with Coro's tradename "Duette" in 1931, when the clips were flat-backed and the motifs were geometric. However, figural motif Duettes with double-pronged hinged clips (often called "fur clips") bearing this same patent number were made in the late '30s and early '40s (see Duette in "Day and Night" grouping on page 188).

Recently, an extensive amount of research has been done on design patents for specific pieces by particular makers, predominantly by Trifari and Coro. Carla Genelli Brunialti and Roberto Brunialti, in their two books cited in the References, and N & N Vintage Costume Jewelry's Web site, trifari.com, include copies of design patents, as well as photos of the pieces themselves. Lucille Tempesta, publisher/editor of *Vintage Fashion & Costume Jewelry*, and her contributors' articles on several of costume jewelry's most well-known makers have added information based on interviews with their still-living designers; Liz Bryman has also interviewed designers for her Web site articles (see References).

In 1930, Trifari hired its most celebrated and prolific designer, Alfred Philippe, who designed many now sought-after pieces until 1968. A Frenchman trained in fine jewelry design—he produced designs made by William Scheer for Cartier and Van Cleef & Arpels—Philippe was known for creating molded glass and rhinestone pieces for Trifari which resembled Cartier's "fruit salad" or "tutti frutti" carved gemstone and diamond jewels from the late '20s and early '30s.

Suite: Link Bracelet, Earrings, Double Clip Brooch, ptd enamel, rhinestones, gp wm, c. 1940, "Day & Night" floral motif, with pink and red ptd enamel flowers, flower petals move to open and close around domed pavé-set colorless r.s. and red glass cab centers, bracelet with pavé-set colorless r.s. and ptd green gp metal leaves, red glass berries, clip/screw earrings each a single flowerhead with moving petals, findings mkd "PAT NO 1649187 [1927]," (for a "safety back device for ear ornaments" issued to Philip Reiter of New York, NY), bracelet 1¼" w x 7", **$695**, earrings 1⅛" dia, **$195**, double clip brooch, flower centers *en tremblant*, petals on clips do not move (design pat #115,852 issued to Adolph Katz, July 25, 1939,), removable pinback frame mkd "Coro Duette, pat no 1798867 [1931]," open flat-backed hinged clips unmkd, 3⅝", **$525**. (Photo courtesy of Morning Glory Antiques, Albuquerque, NM)

He was also the apparent designer of many of Trifari's painted enamel pieces of the late '30s and early '40s. There are a number of examples in this section for which design patents have been found that were issued to Philippe (see below and pages 192, 193, 194, and 195).

However, it should be noted that allegations have recently been made that the inventors/assignees who signed the patent applications, or had them signed by their attorneys, may not have always been the actual designers of the pieces attributed to them. The question of attribution to individual designers is a controversial one that may never be resolved, especially where large manufacturers who employed many designers are concerned. The companies themselves often controlled the ownership of patents and copyrights of designs, which at times were purchased from freelancers "off the street" (this is known as "work for hire" in copyright parlance. For further information on copyright, see Edward Samuels' *The Illustrated Story of Copyright*, Thomas Dunne, 2000). In e-mail discussions with several of the advisers for this section, it became clear that the matter is open to interpretation, and there is no definitive answer. Many industrial designers who may well deserve credit for their creations worked anonymously. At the time these designs were created, no one could have predicted how important their attribution would become!

During World War II, base metals were restricted for the war effort, as was platinum. Costume jewelry factories were called into service to make munitions and other military equipment. Jewelry production was diminished, but not curtailed. Feelings of patriotism were at an all-time high, and everyone wore jewelry with patriotic themes and/or colors (see page 192. Since the terrorist attacks of September 11, patriotic motifs are once again in vogue). With the rationing of base metals beginning in mid-1942, sterling silver was used as a substitute. Fewer rhinestones were used because supplies from Czechoslovakia and Austria were cut off, as were simulated ("faux") pearls from Japan. Manufacturers made do with existing stock and with "stones" of Lucite and other plastics. Although base metal restrictions were lifted after the war, some manufacturers continued to use sterling for their higher-end lines until the mid-'50s.

A relatively unknown American manufacturer, Rice-Weiner, was recently discovered to have been the maker of pieces designed by (and signed) McClelland Barclay (1893-1943), who was a well-known artist killed in action during World War II (see brooch on page 192). Founded in 1938, Rice-Weiner also produced jewelry by other designers who worked for the company. They were the manufacturer of licensed designs inspired by the films of Alexander Korda ("Thief of Bagdad," 1940, and "The Jungle Book," 1942). According to the Brunialtis in *A Tribute to America* (p. 39, see References), Korda himself had nothing to do with designing these pieces—the marks found on these pieces, "© Alexander Korda" or "Thief of Bagdad Korda ©," refer to the license agreement and the films' copyrights. Likewise, the company named "Barclay," which split from Rice-Weiner in 1946, had nothing to do with the artist McClelland Barclay (see bracelet on page 202).

Mid to late '30s and early '40s Retro Modern costume pieces made of rhinestones and gold-plated or rhodium-plated white metal or sterling silver were often larger in scale than precious stone, gold, and platinum equivalents, but many of the overall designs were quite similar (see Retro Modern brooches on page 191). Some costume jewelry designers, such as Miram Haskell, also took inspiration from earlier styles, especially during the Victorian Revival of the late '30s and early '40s.

Fashion jewelry *forms* also paralleled those of precious jewels. In the '30s and '40s, clips were just as stylish in rhinestones and white metal as they were in diamonds and platinum, moving to gold-plating and colored glass stones as fine jewelry changed to colored gold and gemstones. Gold-plated

Clip, imitation pearls, rhinestones, paint, rh pl wm, c. 1940, lily of the valley floral motif, ptd green enameled leaves and stems with colorless r.s. accents, faux pearl flowers, double-pronged hinged clip on rev mkd "TRIFARI," stem mkd "PAT PEND," (design pat #119,101 issued to Alfred Philippe, Feb. 20, 1940), two-part construction joined with rivets and screws, 2¾" w x 3½", **$200.** (Courtesy of Martha Exline, Metique, Laguna Hills, CA)

costume pieces of the late '30s and early '40s were often bicolored rose and yellow to resemble their fine jewelry counterparts.

Although the majority of the jewelry in this section and the one that follows is American-made, two of the genre's most important influences came from Europe in the persons of designers Gabrielle "Coco" Chanel (1883-1971) and Elsa Schiaparelli (1896-1973). While their influence was felt in the early years of costume jewelry manufacture (see Costume Jewelry c. 1920-1935), their early pieces, many of which are not signed, are rarely seen today. Chanel closed her business in Paris in 1939 with the advent of World War II, and reopened in 1954, coming out of retirement at the age of 71 and working until she died. It is during this later period that the multi-colored glass, faux pearl, and gold-plated metal necklaces, bracelets, brooches, and pendants most familiar to collectors were made. Chanel's company, under Karl Lagerfeld's supervision, continues producing costume jewelry designs today.

The biggest revelation to rock the costume jewelry collecting world recently is documented in the Brunialtis' book, *A Tribute to America* (p. 28). The authors discovered that costume jewelry marked with the script signature "Chanel" has nothing to do with Coco; it is the mark of the Chanel Novelty Co. of New York, New York, which changed its name to Reinad Novelty Co. The Chanel script mark was in use for only one season, spring 1941 (during the German occupation of France, when Coco Chanel's atelier was closed), which explains the scarcity of pieces so marked (a brooch with *both* marks, Chanel and Reinad, was displayed on a Web site soon after this important discovery was made public). A painted enamel seahorse brooch by the Chanel Novelty Co. is pictured below.

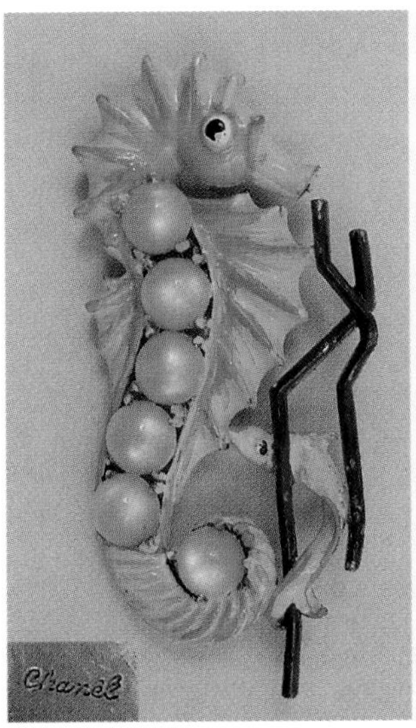

Brooch/Pin, ptd enamel, wm, plastic cabochons, c. 1941, seahorse scene with coral and sm fish, a row of lg circ yellow plastic "adularescent" (moonstone effect) cabs down the center, rev sgd "Chanel" (script signature) for the Chanel Novelty Co., New York, NY (no relation to "Coco" Chanel of Paris), later Reinad Novelty Co., 1½" w x 3¼", **$275**. (Courtesy of Ocean Eyz Antique Jewelry, Orange, CA)

Elsa Schiaparelli's avant-garde and surrealistic touch is evident in her 1930s jewelry designs, which are usually unsigned (see necklaces on page 198). Some late 1930s pieces are signed "schiaparelli" in lower-case block letters (see bar brooch on page 191). She opened an office in New York in 1949 and licensed her name for mass production of costume jewelry and accessories made by the David Lisner Co., which was also the authorized American agent and distributor for earlier French-made pieces.

Chanel and Schiaparelli also helped launch the careers of fine jewelry designers Verdura and Schlumberger, both of whom designed costume pieces for their respective employers in the '30s (see Fine Jewelry sections).

Some European designs are not signed, but merely marked with country of origin, or in the case of some French jewelry, "DÉPOSÉ" (registered). This mark is not a guarantee of French manufacture—some German makers also used it for their exports to France and England—but if found on a stylistically correct *pâte de verre* piece, for example, it offers further evidence of its origin (see clip on page 195, attributed to the House of Gripoix, one of several French makers of *pâte de verre* costume jewelry).

Other currently sought-after designs include circa late 1930s and early 1940s sterling vermeil (gold-plated) or rhodium-plated white metal and painted enamel figural brooches and clips by Marcel Boucher, bearing the mark now known to be a "Phrygian cap" from the French Revolution, not a bird's head, see pages 193, 194, and 196); Coro, including sterling and white metal figural Duettes, although demand for these has fallen off a bit; and Corocraft, De Rosa, Eisenberg Original, Hobé, Mazer Bros., Pennino, Réja, Staret, Trifari, and well-made unsigned examples. Among these are the now-famous animal "jelly bellies" with clear Lucite centers, most signed Trifari, Coro, or unsigned; see two examples by Trifari on page 193). Knockoffs and fakes have now cooled the jelly belly market considerably. Genuine rarities still command a premium, however.

Vintage '40s and '50s Miriam Haskell necklaces, bracelets, and suites continue to have a following, particularly the designer's more elaborate creations. The demand for Haskell has increased since a book devoted solely to her jewelry was published (see References). Thanks to author Deanna Farneti Cera's documentation and research, as well as that of collectors/advisers Jane Clarke and Pat Seal, some of Haskell's early unsigned work, designed primarily by Frank Hess, has been identified. A few examples are included in this section (see pages 190, 195, 197, 198, and 199).

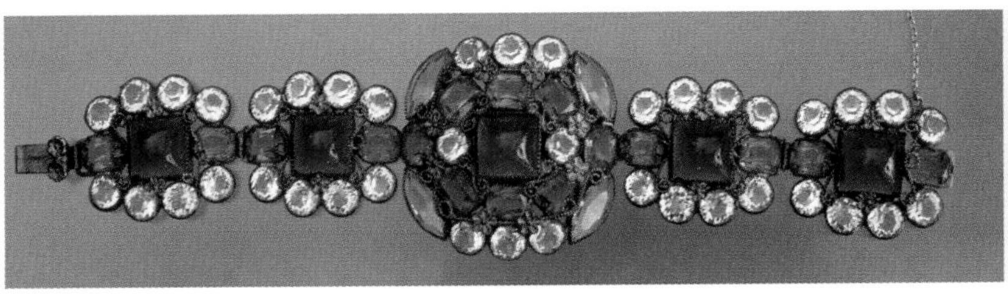

Bracelet, flexible, lead crystal, ym, c. 1935, a lg central plaque flanked by four smaller plaques set with green sugarloaf glass cabs encircled by rect-cut pink and circ-cut colorless lead crystal, set in ym filigree with wiretwist scrolls and sm flowerheads, unsgd, possibly by Hobé, v-spring and box clasp, safety chain, 1⅝" at center, 7" tl, **$300**. (Courtesy of Generations, La Verne, CA)

Bracelet, flexible, glass, gp wm, c. 1935, central openwork oval plaque with scrolling gp wirework throughout, centering a lg oval faceted amber-colored glass stone set à jour, encircled by two concentric rows of circ-cut pale amber-colored, green, and colorless r.s., with two green pear-shaped r.s. at top and bottom, all stones unfoiled and set à jour, flanked by straps of braided gp foxtail chain, terminating in a matching ornamental oval clasp and v-spring with green r.s. on thumbpiece, safety chain, appl rect plaque mkd "HOBÉ" on center rev, 2" w at center x 6½", **$500**. (Courtesy Sam Kusler, Studio City, CA)

Bracelets, flexible, glass, rhinestones, gp wm, attributed to Hobé:
T, c. 1940, lg octagonal royal blue stones set in ropetwist frames, linked by circ red and colorless r.s. with gp scrolling wiretwist decoration throughout, v-spring and hidden box clasp, safety chain, 1¾" w x 7", **$495**.
C, c. 1935, lg center plaque with central lt blue oval r.s. surrounded by pink and colorless marquise r.s., graduated width links on either side of central plaque set with circ and marquise pink and colorless r.s., gp wm hinges between links, v-spring and hidden box clasp, 1½" w at center, 6-3/4", **$665**.
B, c. 1940, lg octagonal green stones set in ropetwist frames, linked by circ pink and colorless r.s. with gp scrolling wiretwist decoration throughout, v-spring and hidden box clasp, no safety chain, 1¾" w x 7", **$545**.
(Photo courtesy of Morning Glory Antiques, Albuquerque, NM)

Bracelets, coil, glass beads, rhinestones, unmkd, 6½" to 7½", $650 each:
TL, c. 1940, berry cluster motif, multi-strand, with individually affixed and movable red glass beads, two star-shaped, wm plaques with pavé-set colorless r.s. and red glass bead centers, and smaller wire-strung red glass beads, attributed to Miriam Haskell.
TR, c. 1940, multi-strand wristband of turq blue glass beads surmounted by individually affixed and movable grad glass beads, wm pavé-set colorless r.s. leaves, smaller wire-strung turq blue glass beads coils, attributed to Miriam Haskell.
C, c. 1950, central decoration of two wire-strung white seed bead daisies with yellow seed bead centers, multiple wire-strung strands of green seed beads flanking the central flowers, dk and lt blue seed bead accents, two large purple glass bead accents.
BL, c. 1940, braided pink cotton cord wristband with two rows of lt pink glass beads attached with thread, surmounted by translucent pink and lt purple glass flowers with colorless r.s. centers and white glass leaves, wm endcaps.
BR, c. 1950, gp ym wristband surmounted by a lg central cylindrical marbled pink and blue glass bead flanked by clusters of small, individually attached, marbleized pink and lt blue beads surmounting a gold filigree circ plaque. (Photo courtesy of Morning Glory Antiques, Albuquerque, NM)

Bracelet, hinged bangle, gp wm, rhinestones, c. 1940, Retro Modern, buckle and floral motif, wide buckle strap surmounted by a gp flowerhead with a center cluster of circ green r.s encircled by baguette colorless r.s., petals edged in colorless r.s., surmounted by a crown with two rows of seven circ-cut colorless r.s. flanked by two gp leaves with r.s. edges, and on one side by radiating ribbons of polished metal and pavé-set colorless r.s., rev mkd with unknown maker's mk "A," some dk r.s., gp wear, 2¼" in dia, 1¾" at center, **$195**. (Vickie Vega collection)

Brooch/Pin, molded glass, rhinestones, oxidized wm, c. 1935, basket of flowers, an openwork foliate and floral motif frame surmounted by three flowerheads of circ red, yellow, and blue r.s. with colorless r.s. centers, prong-set green molded glass leaves, and prong-set oval unbacked faceted glass stones in purple, red, and blue, basket base of pavé-set colorless r.s., unmkd, 3" w x 2⅞", **$110**. (Courtesy of Pat Seal, Treasures From Yesterday, Fort Worth, TX)

Brooch/Pin, brass, glass, c. 1935, grape cluster motif, a thin rect bar surmounted by overlapping cutout stamped brass leaves, wire tendrils, and textured brass stems, three stems suspending articulated clusters of green and purple round glass beads from wire eyepins, unmkd, 3¼" w x 2⅜", **$85**. (Courtesy of Pat Seal, Treasures From Yesterday, Fort Worth, TX)

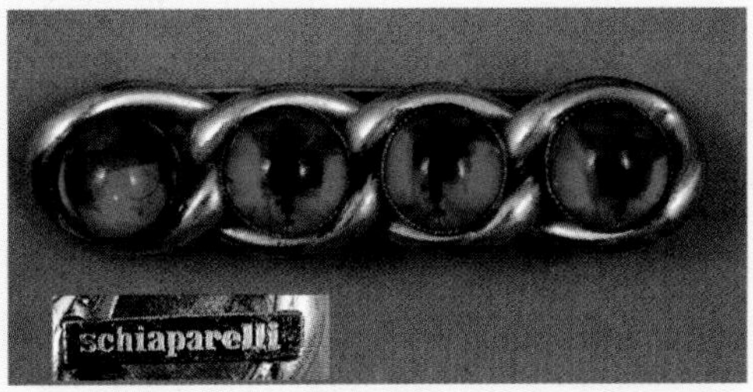

Brooch/Pin, bar, glass, gp brass, c. 1938, four saw-tooth bezel-set circ red glass cabs surmounting four joined tubular gp brass curb chain links, appl rect plaque on rev mkd "schiaparelli" in lower-case block letters, a similar necklace advertised in Women's Wear Daily Aug. 19, 1938 (distributed in U.S. through D. Lisner & Co.), 2½" w x ⅝", **$200**. (Courtesy of Martha Exline, Metique, Laguna Hills, CA)

Brooch/Pin, circle, rhinestones, sterling, c. 1935-40, two facing lovebirds with pavé-set colorless r.s. bodies and red r.s. eyes, perched on and encircled by a circ branchlike frame pavé-set with colorless r.s., appl wire branches with r.s. terminals, rev imp "STERLING," 1¾" w x 2½", **$200**. (Courtesy of Pat Seal, Treasures From Yesterday, Fort Worth, TX)

Brooch/Pin, rhinestones, rh pl wm, c. 1939, late 18th-early 19th C-inspired *"en tremblant"* design, openwork lozenge-shaped floral and foliate motif plaque pavé-set throughout with circ-cut colorless r.s., one central and two side flowerheads attached by springs to plaque, triangular cutout at the bottom of lozenge suspending a floral openwork drop, lg r.s. settings have appearance of cut-down collets, unmkd, attributed to Trifari, 3⅝" w x 3¼", **$600**. (Courtesy of D. Brett Benson, Inc., Chicago, IL)

Brooches/Pins, rhinestones, wm, Retro Modern, c. 1940:
T, openwork shield-shaped plaque with a scrolling intertwined ribbon motif pavé-set with colorless r.s., around a baton-shaped bar with channel-set royal blue sq r.s. and circ-cut royal blue r.s. terminals, ribbons interspersed throughout with circ-cut, baguette, oval, and octagonal royal blue r.s., rev mkd "STARET" for Staret Jewelry Co., Chicago, IL, 2½" w x 3", **$600**. (Courtesy of Xcentricities, Beverly Hills, CA)
BL, polished scrolled gp wm ribbons alternating with circ-cut and pavé-set colorless r.s. ribbons, a prong-set lg dk blue oval glass stone at the top, surmounted by a cascading floral/foliate spray of polished gp leaves with wire stems radiating from the center and terminating in dk blue marquise r.s. flowerheads, rev mkd "CORO," 3¾" w x 3¼", **$125**.
BR, floral spray with polished and pavé-set colorless r.s. leaves and stems, seven iridescent pink oval-cut unbacked r.s. prong-set at flowerhead terminals radiating from the center stem, unmkd, attributed to Réja, most gp worn off, 3" w 3½", **$140**. (Diane White collection)

Brooch/Pin, brass, glass, c. 1940, shield-shaped openwork floral and foliate motif plaque with lg bezel-set, central oval open-backed purple glass stone, surmounted by a circ colorless r.s. and a trefoil of three marquise purple r.s., suspending a foxtail chain tassel with openwork foliate cap surmounted by three elongated hexagonal purple stones, appl plaque on rev mkd "JOSEFF HOLLYWOOD," 2¼" w x 6" tl, **$250**. (Kathleen Peterson collection)

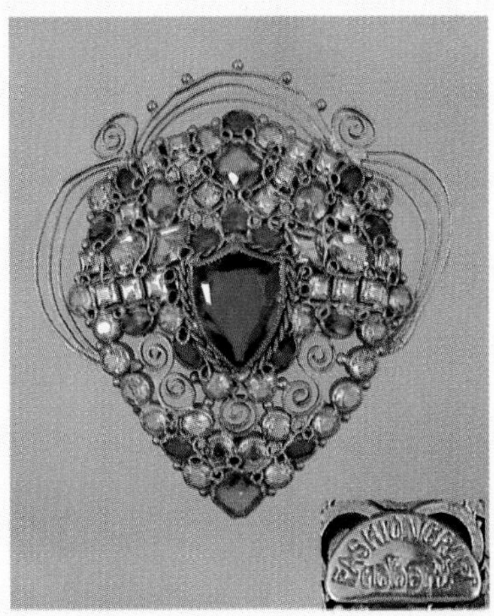

Brooch/Pin, glass, rhinestones, gp wm, c. 1942, large shield-shaped openwork frame of scrolled, swagged and looped ropetwist wirework, the top with appl beads and volutes, the cusped base outlined in colored r.s., a lg central shield-shaped red glass stone set within a ropetwist frame, flanked on each side by horizontal rows of sq colorless r.s., surmounted and encircled by pink, red, and colorless sq, circ, lozenge, and cushion-shaped r.s., all stones unfoiled and set *à jour* in millegrained bezels, appl semicirc plaque on rev mkd "FASHIONCRAFT robert," 3⅛" w x 3," **$250**. (Courtesy of Pat Seal, Treasures From Yesterday, Fort Worth, TX)

Brooch/Pin, gp wm, glass, rhinestones, c. 1941, a rect gp frame with concave chamfered corners, a central pierced geo plaque and corner-to-corner cross of sm circ pavé-set colorless r.s. and horizontal center ros of lg amber-colored step-cut r.s., a step-cut amber-colored r.s. in each corner, rev mkd "McClelland Barclay," 2" w x 1⅞", **$300**. (Courtesy of Charles Pinkham, Pomona, CA)

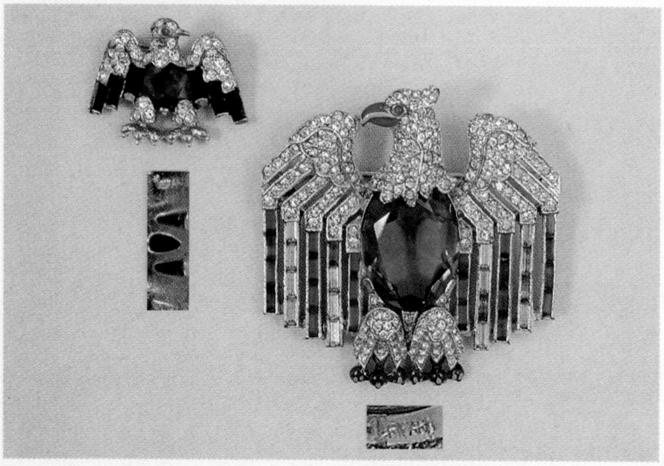

Brooches/Pins, lg and sm eagles by Trifari, rhinestones:
L, c. 1942, sm baby eagle with pavé-set colorless r.s. on head, wing tops, and legs, lg red pear-shaped r.s. body, blue glass cab eye, and dk blue baguette r.s. feathers, mkd "Trifari, Sterling," 1" w x ¾", **$150**.
R, rh pl wm, c. 1940, in the shape of an eagle with geo pierced spread wings, lg blue unbacked faceted oval glass body, rows of pavé-set colorless r.s. on head, upper wings, and legs, vertical rows of red and colorless baguette r.s. on lower wings, circ red glass cab eye, red ptd enamel beak and blue ptd enamel talons, rev mkd "Trifari, Pat Pend," (design pat #122,220 issued to Alfred Philippe, Aug. 27, 1940), 1¾" x 1¾", **$600**. (Courtesy of D. Brett Benson, Inc., Chicago, IL)

Brooches/Pins, figurals, rhinestones, glass, painted enamel, rh pl wm:
L, c. 1940, in the shape of a leaping fish, pavé-set colorless r.s. body, surmounted by two rows of high-domed circ blue and green glass cabs, red glass cab eye, ptd blue and white enamel fins and ptd red and white enamel mouth, arc-shaped cutout in gill area, unmkd, 2¼" w x 1⅝", **$125**.
R, c. 1941, a flying plumed bird with pavé-set colorless r.s. body, head, and wing edges, the neck interspersed with sm circ red glass cabs, a blue glass cab eye, red ptd enamel feet, baguette r.s. tail, openwork wings prong-set with molded translucent red and frosted colorless floral/foliate glass, rev mkd "Trifari, Pat Pend," (design pat #125,165 issued to Alfred Philippe, Feb. 11, 1941), some dk r.s., 3⅛" w x 2⅛", **$225**. (Courtesy of Richard Fauteux, San Pedro, CA)

Brooches/Pins, rhinestones, wm, ptd enamel floral bouquets, colorless r.s. centers, c. 1935-40, unmkd:
L, central flowerhead with oval dk green r.s. petals, two fronds of green ptd enamel with oval dk green r.s. bracts, pavé-set colorless r.s. ribbon leaves, green and brown ptd enamel stems, 2½" w x 4", **$185**.
C, two flowerheads with oval dk red r.s. petals, one frond with oval dk red r.s. bracts and pavé-set colorless r.s. center, pavé-set colorless r.s. leaves, green and brown ptd enamel stems, 3" w x 4", **$195**.
R, three flowerheads with lt pink navette r.s. petals, pavé-set colorless r.s. leaves, green and brown ptd enamel stems, 2⅜" w x 4", **$195**.
(Photo courtesy of Morning Glory Antiques, Albuquerque, NM)

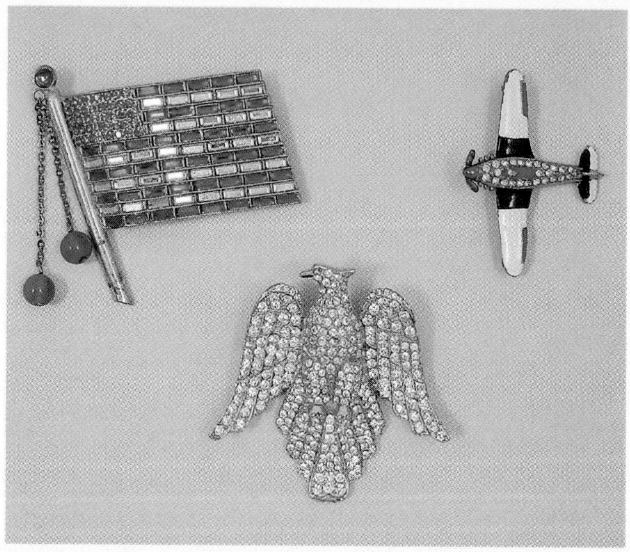

Brooches/Pins, patriotic, rhinestones, wm, c. 1940, unmkd:
TL, in the shape of an Am flag set with stripes of red and white baguette r.s., stars of circ-cut blue r.s., wm angled flagpole topped with circ blue cab and suspending two short gp chains with round red glass bead terminals, 2¼" w x 2½", **$100**.
TR, in the shape of an airplane, red, white, and blue ptd enamel on body, wings and tail, gp wm body with circ colorless r.s. accents, some wear to enameled edges, 2⅛" w x 1½", **$75**.
B, in the shape of an eagle with wings spread and fanned tail, pavé-set colorless r.s. throughout, circ red r.s. eye, yellow ptd enamel feet and beak, 2⅜" w x 2¼", **$200**.
(Courtesy of Pat Seal, Treasures From Yesterday, Fort Worth, TX)

Brooches/Pins, lapel watches, rh pl wm, rhinestones, c. 1940:
L, in the shape of a bird on a branch, pavé-set with colorless and red r.s., a watch mounted in the branch, mkd "LATHAM," 2⅝" w x 2", **$175**.
R, a pavé-set r.s. bird on a ptd enamel branch with ptd enamel plumage and beak, watch mounted in branch with leaves, mkd "COQ D'OR," 1⅞" x 3¼", **$375**. (Courtesy of Generations, La Verne, CA)

Brooches/Pins, hands holding flowers, wm, ptd enamel, rhinestones, c. 1940, mkd "STARET" for Staret Jewelry Co., Chicago, IL:
L, a hand holding a lily, sm colorless r.s. pavé-set on lily body, pink enameled lily petals, yellow enameled stamen set with sm colorless r.s., turq enameled curling leaves with sm colorless r.s. tips, green enameled stems, lt skintone ptd enameled hand with pink fingernails, wearing a colorless r.s. "ring," white cuff, 2¼" w x 4¼", **$950**.
R, a hand holding two flowers, wm stems and branches set with sm colorless r.s., flowerheads of lg prong-set, colorless oval r.s. with pink enameled bases, green enameled leaves, lt skintone ptd enameled hand with pink fingernails, wearing a red r.s. "ring," gray and white cuff, 1¾" w x 3⅛", **$650**. (Photo courtesy of Morning Glory Antiques, Albuquerque, NM)

Brooches/Pins, "jellybellies" by Trifari, sterling vermeil, Lucite, rhinestones, c. 1943:
L, , penguin, Lucite body framed in gp ster, pavé-set r.s. head, wings and legs, red glass cab eye, mkd "TRIFARI [CROWN]" on rev of head, "DES.PAT NO 135,189" (issued to Alfred Philippe, March 9, 1943) on rev of wing, "STERLING" on rev above feet, 1¼" w x 2¼", **$300**. (Author's collection)
R, sailboat, gp ster boat (plating worn), mast and rope, Lucite sail in ster frame, pavé-set r.s. flag and prow, mkd "STERLING, TRIFARI [CROWN], PAT. PEND," (design pat #135,174 issued to Alfred Philippe, March 2, 1943), 1½" w x 2½", **$460**. (Courtesy of Sam Kusler, Studio City, CA)

Brooches/Pins, fruit and flowers by Marcel Boucher, rh pl wm, ptd enamel, rhinestones, c. 1940, rev imp with maker's mk, "Phrygian cap" with initials MB:
TL, in the shape of a lily, orange and yellow ptd enamel petals, green ptd leaves with pavé-set colorless r.s. stem and accents, 3¼", **$320**.
TR, in the shape of a sweet peas, lt and dk pink ptd enamel petals, lt and dk green ptd leaves with pavé-set colorless r.s. stems and accents throughout, 3⅜" w, **$495**.
BC, in the shape of a cluster of cherries, pink, red, and yellow ptd enamel fruits, lt and dk green ptd leaves with pavé-set colorless r.s. stems and accents throughout, 2¼", **$525**. (Photo courtesy of Morning Glory Antiques, Albuquerque, NM)

Brooch/Pin, sterling vermeil, faux pearls, rhinestones, enamel, c. 1944, in the shape of a stylized dolphin, the gp ster body set with three rows of faux pearls, the tail, top of head, mouth and fin pavé set with colorless r.s., red and black ptd enamel mouth, faux pearl eye, rev imp "EISENBERG ORIGINAL STERLING," 2½" w x 2¼", **$465**. (Photo courtesy of Morning Glory Antiques, Albuquerque, NM)

Brooch/Pin, sterling, c. 1950, in the shape of a Hawaiian bird on a flowering branch, appl plate on rev mkd "GUMP'S, STERLING, DESIGNED BY G. CINI," for Guglielmo Cini, Boston, MA, 3" w x 1⅝", **$250**. (Courtesy of Generations, La Verne, CA)

Brooches/Pins, figurals, sterling vermeil, glass, rhinestones, c. 1945:
L, in the shape of a tree frog, faceted oval purple glass center, green r.s. eyes, mkd "REJA STERLING" on underside of outstretched leg, 1½" w x 2¾", **$175**. (Author's collection)
C, pr of ants with polished bodies and engr details, both ants with single inset circ-cut colorless r.s. in head and single yellow oval r.s in body (one lt, one dk), rev mkd "STERLING," 1⅛" w x 2¼", **$300/pr**. (Courtesy of Pat Seal, Treasures From Yesterday, Fort Worth, TX)
R, c. 1944, in the shape of a stylized cockatoo, a faceted oval fuchsia glass stone prong-set in the open center, pavé-set colorless r.s. along the wing, rev mkd "STERLING," maker's mk for Marcel Boucher (Phrygian cap MB), 1⅞" w x 3½", **$125**. (Author's collection)

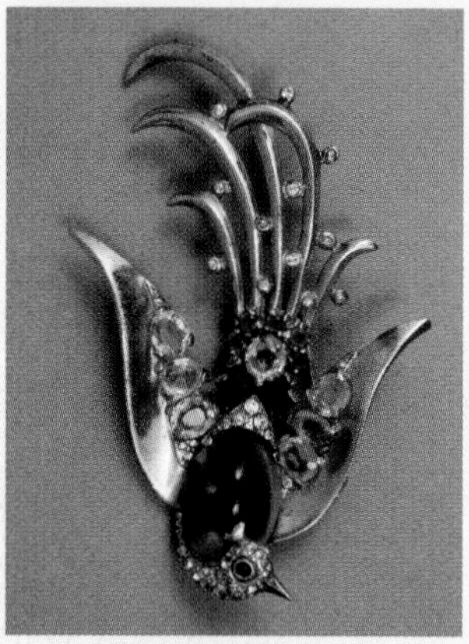

Brooch/Pin, sterling vermeil, rhinestones, glass, c. 1945, in the shape of a "lyre bird" in flight, the body an oval amber-colored glass cab, the head pavé-set with colorless r.s., green r.s. eye, the wings bordered with oval-cut yellow glass stones and colorless r.s., circ-cut red and yellow r.s. and blue baguettes at the base of the ster vermeil tail interspersed with colorless r.s., rev mkd "STERLING, TRIFARI [CROWN MK], PAT. PEND" (design pat #142,659 issued to Alfred Philippe, Oct. 23, 1945), 2" x 3", **$300**. (Courtesy of Generations, La Verne, CA)

Brooches/Pins, mkd "MAZER" for Mazer Bros., gp wm, rhinestones:
TL, c. 1947, bowknot motif with circ-cut colorless r.s.borders, curved edges prong-set with radiating pink marquise r.s., terminating in a grad fringe tipped with prong-set grad pink marquise r.s., segments of brooch joined with screws on rev, minor gp wear, 3¼" w x 1¾", **$250**.
TR, c. 1945-50, polished freeform scrolled and looped ribbons, ribbons segments set with colorless baguette r.s. and one faux pearl, circ colorless r.s. accents, segments of brooch joined with screws, 2⅝" w x 1¼", **$150**.
B, c. 1941, two scrolled branches with three prong-set translucent red molded glass floral/foliate motifs, circ colorless r.s. accents, wm pavé-set colorless r.s. ribbon tie screwed to back, gp worn, 3½" w x 2¼", **$275**. (Vickie Vega collection)

Brooch/Pin, gp sterling, rhinestones, c. 1947, bird in a cage (Cartier-inspired?) suspended from a gp bow brooch with pavé-set colorless r.s. undersides, gp bird with pavé-set colorless r.s. wings and red glass cab eye perched on a polished gp branch with circ-cut red r.s. terminals, cage with horizontal polished bars and pavé-set colorless r.s. base, sides, and top, most gp worn off outer surfaces, rev mkd "GARMAN, STERLING PAT PEND," (design pat #146,564 issued to Frank J. Gargano of Providence, RI, April 22, 1947), 1⅝" w x 2¾", **$130**. (Elaine Sarnoff collection)

Brooch/Pin, sterling vermeil, rhinestones, glass, c. 1948, articulated, in the shape of a monkey hanging by its tail from a branch set with pink, green, and colorless oval and circ-cut r.s., monkey's tail, head, and body studded with circ-cut colorless r.s., blue glass cab eyes, hands holding a lg prong-set, yellow unbacked faceted glass stone, pinstem on rev of branch, safety catch, rev mkd "TRIFARI, STERLING," #31, (design pat #148,563 issued to Alfred Philippe, Feb. 3, 1948), 1⅛" w x 2¾", **$1,200**. (Courtesy of D. Brett Benson, Inc., Chicago, IL)

Brooch/Pin, gp wm, rhinestones, c. 1949, polished gp stylized mini poodle with tapered baguette red r.s. muzzle, lg oval-cut red r.s. chest, and a circ red r.s. on each leg, rev imp "TRIFARI," (design pat #153,391 issued to Alfred Philippe, April 12, 1949), ⅞" w x ¾", **$85**. (Vickie Vega collection)

Clip, gp wm, rhinestones, red glass, c. 1935-40, plaque of two overlapping semi-circ tiers with colorless r.s. borders, surmounted by two domed rect centers channel-set with vertical rows of sq pink r.s. and circ-cut colorless r.s., double-pronged hinged clip on rev, appl rect plaque mkd "CALVAIRE," 1⅝" w x 1⅞", **$85**. (Courtesy of Pat Seal, Treasures From Yesterday, Fort Worth, TX)

Clips, chatelaine, brass, c. 1935-40, Victorial Revival, a pr of clips, one oval with stamped floral and geo pattern and cusped scalloped edge, the other shield-shaped with crenelated edges and stamped floral center, suspending two lengths of reeded flat and circ link chain, and a double-sided circ disk with scrolled foliate pattern, a double-sided rect plaque with stamped floral and foliate pattern, and a circ drop-shaped fob with openwork stamped sides and floral disk bottom, double-pronged hinged clips on rev, unmkd, 13" tl, clips 1" w x 1¼", **$75**. (Courtesy of Pat Seal, Treasures From Yesterday, Fort Worth, TX)

Clip, rhinestones, rh pl wm, c. 1939, late 18th-early 19th C-inspired design, floral and foliate openwork pavé-set with colorless r.s. throughout, lg central flowerhead, circ r.s. in stamen (a few r.s. missing), and lg circ r.s. center, lg r.s. settings have the appearance of cut-down collets, rev mkd "COPR. PAT. PEND." double-pronged hinged clip mkd "TRIFARI," possibly one of a pr, 1½" w x 2⅜", **$125**. (Vickie Vega collection)

Clip, glass, imitation pearls, gp brass, rhinestones, c. 1940, Fr, heart-shaped dk reddish amber-colored *pâte de verre* in a gp brass textured frame, outlined with lg oval faux pearls with r.s.-set gp terminals, suspending a dk amber-colored pear-shaped glass cab with bow-shaped colorless r.s.-set gp cap, gp brass backing, double-pronged hinged clip on rev mkd "*DÉPOSÉ*," attributed to Gripoix, 2¼" w x 3½", **$550**. (Courtesy of Sam Kusler, Studio City, CA)

Brooches and Clip, unmkd, attributed to Frank Hess for Miriam Haskell, c. 1935-40:

L, ptd blue, green, red, and tan star-shaped wood beads with blue bead centers wired to perforated rect metal plaque with pin assembly, multiple articulated strands of ptd blue, wire-strung round wood beads terminating in ptd wood bells, 2¾" w x 3", **$445**.

C, molded green glass leaves and two clusters of tan, flower-shaped wood beads with black bead centers wired to perforated rect metal plaque with attached pin assembly, chain link swag attached to plaque suspending two glass leaves and three articulated pinecones made from stacked flower-shaped flat wood beads separated by black seed beads, 2" w x 2⅞", **$445**.

R, green and gold ptd enamel and gp brass leaves, gp brass flowerheads, and clusters of round translucent green glass beads mounted on a circ gp brass disk, suspending gp chain strung with oblate and round yellow, oblate coral-colored, and round green glass beads with flowerhead gp brass spacers and gp brass bead terminals, double-pronged hinged clip on rev, 2¼" w x 2⅞", **$425**. (Photo courtesy of Morning Glory Antiques, Albuquerque, NM)

Clips, flower motifs, ptd enamel, rhinestones, wm, c. 1940, designed by Alfred Philippe, double-pronged hinged clips mkd "TRIFARI":

TL, floral bouquet of yellow ptd enamel flowerheads with colorless r.s. centers, green and brown ptd enamel leaves and stems, colorless r.s. accents, 1½" w x 2¾", **$148**.

TR, floral bouquet of red ptd enamel flowerheads and buds with colorless r.s. centers and accents, green ptd enamel leaves with pavé-set colorless r.s. undersides, green and brown ptd stems (design pat #121,253 issued to Alfred Philippe, June 25, 1940), 2" w x 3", **$148**.

C, a nosegay, two red and yellow ptd enamel flowerheads with flower centers of yellow ptd enamel and colorless r.s., green ptd enamel leaves with pavé-set colorless r.s. undersides, green and brown ptd stems with colorless r.s. accents (similar to design pat #118,758 issued to Alfred Philippe, Jan. 30, 1940), 2" w x 3", **$165**.

BL, floral bouquet of ptd enamel flowerheads in pastel blue, pink, and yellow, colorless r.s. centers and accents, green ptd enamel leaves, green and red-brown ptd stems, "tied" with pavé-set colorless r.s. "bow," 2⅜" w x 3", **$158**.

BC, in the shape of a poppy, red ptd enamel flowerhead, blue ptd enamel center surrounded by colorless r.s. set in wm, petal edges with pavé-set colorless r.s., green and brown ptd stem and leaves, colorless r.s. accents (design pat #120,573 assigned to Alfred Philippe, May 14, 1940), 1⅝" w x 2¾", **$165**.

BR, in the shape of a red tulip viewed from the side, ptd enamel flowerhead with cluster of colorless r.s. in center, S-curve stem and leaves in green and brown ptd enamel with pavé-set colorless r.s. accents (design pat #125,422 issued to Alfred Philippe, Feb. 25, 1941), 1⅝" w x 3", **$185**. (Photo courtesy of Morning Glory Antiques, Albuquerque, NM)

Clips, glass, rhinestones, ptd enamel, gp wm, c. 1940:
L, basket of flowers motif, basket an amber-colored trapezoidal glass stone, pavé-set colorless r.s. stems and flower petals with green ptd enamel leaves, central flowerhead of four purple heart-shaped glass stones with colorless r.s. center, double-pronged hinged clip mkd "LILLIAN" on rev, 2½", **$1,000**.
C, floral vase and peacock motif, gold enameled vase set with central purple trapezoidal glass stone, the base set pavé-set with colorless r.s., pavé-set colorless r.s.branches with green ptd enamel leaves, purple enamel floral clusters and faux pearl flowerheads scattered throughout, an enameled peacock with red, blue, and gold enamel accents perched on the left edge of the vase, peacock wings inlaid with red baguette r.s. and pavé-set colorless r.s., double-pronged hinged clip mkd "R DEROSA" on rev, 3" w x 2¼", **$1,200**.
R, basket of flowers motif, basket a garnet-colored trapezoidal glass stone, with lt green and gold ptd enamel basket base, flower stems, and leaves, seven flowerheads of tapering calf's-head shaped garnet-colored glass stones with pavé-set colorless r.s. buds, six smaller flowerheads with colorless r.s. petals and red r.s. centers, double-pronged hinged clip mkd "R. DEROSA" on rev, 2⅝", **$1,000**. (Photo courtesy of Morning Glory Antiques, Albuquerque, NM)

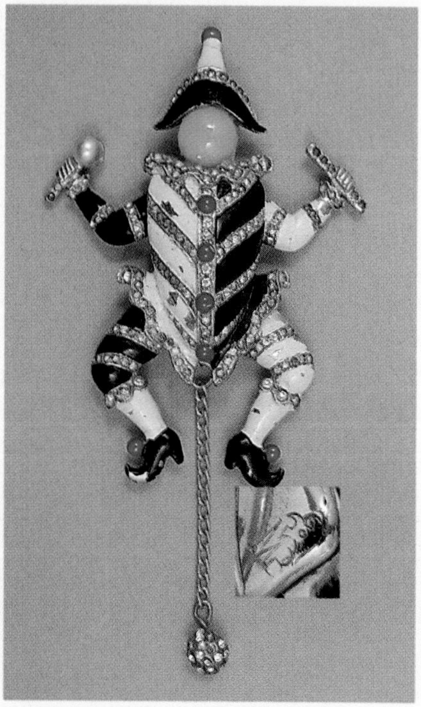

Clip, rh pl wm, ptd enamel, rhinestones, c. 1940, "Punchinello" jester figure, arms and legs move when chain is pulled, white, black, and red ptd enamel features, costume striped with pavé-set colorless r.s., circ pink glass cab head, figure holds a rattle with a faux pearl head and a baton set with circ colorless r.s., link chain with a colorless r.s.-set round wm bead terminal, double-pronged hinged clip on rev, backing plate attached with screws and imp with "Phrygian cap" MB maker's mk for Marcel Boucher, moderate wear to enamel, 2" w x 4" tl, **$1,500**. (Courtesy of Sam Kusler, Studio City, CA)

Clip, ptd enamel, gp wm, c. 1940, Am, circ multi-looped bow (a cockade) ptd red, white and blue, surmounting three ptd white notched ribbons inscribed with the words "*Liberté, Egalité, Fraternité*" (Fr Revolutionary motto: Liberty, Equality, Brotherhood) in raised script, sponsored by the American Friends of France, which received a percentage of sales, rev mkd "SILSON PAT. 120967" (design pat issued to Victor Silson, June 4, 1940), double-pronged hinged clip, 1½" w x 2¾", **$125**. (Courtesy of Charles Pinkham, Pomona, CA)

Clip, gp sterling, rhinestones, c. 1942, in the shape of a wishing well with a bucket on a moveable chain, roof and sides of well with imp grid pattern, roof supports with pavé-set colorless r.s., a floral/foliate spray at the base, with four flowerheads of prong-set circ-cut red and blue r.s. with colorless r.s. centers, and colorless r.s. accents, rev mkd "CoroCraft STERLING" [Pegasus logo], double-pronged hinged clip mkd "STERLING," some darkened r.s., 1" w x 1¾", **$275**. (Vickie Vega collection)

Clip, sterling vermeil, rhinestones, ptd enamel, c. 1942, in the shape of an American eagle with ptd enamel feathers and beak, colorless r.s.-set breast and eye, surmounting scrolled ribbon and a cluster of arrows with V-shaped tips set with red and blue r.s. baguettes and colorless circ-cut r.s., double-pronged hinged clip on rev mkd "STERLING," appl plate mkd "Coro Craft STERLING," 2⅜" w x 2¾", **$350**. (Author's collection)

Clip, ivory, silver, beryls, citrine, pink tourmaline, amethysts, gp wire, nephrite, c. 1940 (circa date uncertain) a carved ivory Chinese figure (Confucius?), a circ nephrite jade cab prong-set in center, surmounted by two faceted amethysts and a citrine, the base wrapped in corded gp wire, a cluster of various prong-set carved and faceted gemstones below, double-pronged hinged clip on rev, imp "HATTIE CARNEGIE" on base of silver frame holding the figure, possibly custom-made, 1½" w x 3¼", **$450**. (Courtesy of Ocean Eyz Antique Jewelry, Orange, CA)

Clip, rhinestones, ptd enamel, gp wm, c. 1942, floral motif, three-, four-, and five-petaled flowerheads of lg faceted oval amber-colored r.s., single circ-cut amber r.s. in center, sm colorless r.s. accents, green ptd enamel leaves, curv gp stems, double-pronged hinged wm clip on rev, mkd "EISENBERG ORIGINAL" and "X" (in a circle), 2¾" w x 4", **$500**. (Private collection)

Dress Clips, glass, gp brass, unmkd, attributed to Frank Hess for Miriam Haskell, c. 1935-40:

L, two overlapping circ gp brass floral filigree disks centered with multicolor striped turq-colored round glass beads, suspending four irreg pear-shaped, multicolor striped turq-colored glass drops with calyx-shaped scroll-patterned gp brass caps, sm turq-colored round bead spacers; disks, drops, and flat-backed hinged clip attached with wire to a perforated bullet-shaped translucent plastic backing, 1½" w x 2½", **$400**.

R, an asymmetrical layered arrangement of irregular lobed turq-colored glass disks, surmounted by three flowerheads with curved gp petals stamped with circles of raised dots, circ mottled turq-colored glass cab centers enclosed in gp brass, each flower in a different stage of blooming from bud to fully opened, flat-backed hinged clip mounted on circ gp brass disk on rev, 1¾" w x 2", **$400**. (Courtesy of Pat Seal, Treasures From Yesterday, Fort Worth, TX)

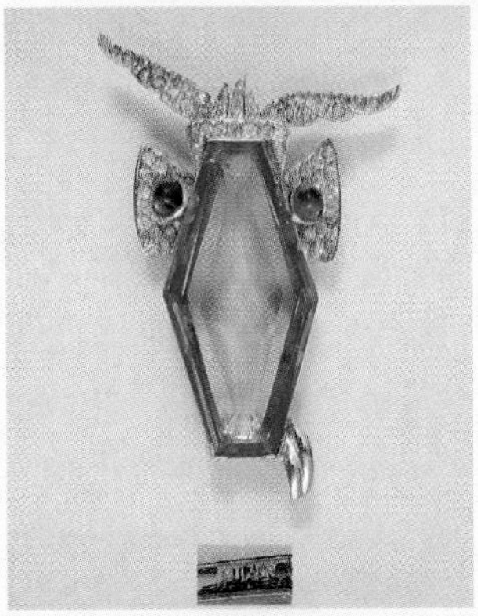

Clip, glass, rh pl wm, rhinestones, c. 1945, stylized bull's head, lg unbacked elongated hexagonal blue glass center, rh pl wm extended tongue at the base, with pavé-set colorless r.s. on horns and ears, red glass cab eyes, double-pronged hinged clip on rev, frame mkd "MAZER" for Mazer Bros., 1¾" w x 2½", **$850**. (Courtesy of D. Brett Benson, Inc, Chicago, IL)

Earrings, clip, 935 silver, dyed green chalcedony, marcasites, c. 1940, each earring an open scrolled ribbon motif set with a row of marcasites, ribbon terminals prong-set with two, teardrop-shaped chalcedony cabs, clipbacks, unmkd, possibly Ger, ¾" w x 1" tl, **$85**. (Private collection)

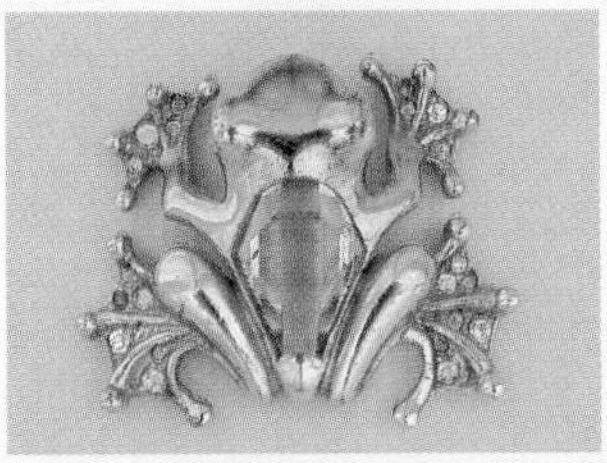

Clip, faceted glass, rhinestones, gp wm, c. 1945-50, stylized frog with gp body, foot webbing set with circ colorless r.s., body center with inset curved calf head-shaped colorless glass stone, unknown maker, serif "T" mk, double-pronged hinged clip on rev, 1¾" w x 1½", **$95**. (Vickie Vega collection)

Earrings, copper:

T, c. 1940, cutout copper sheet with appl copper wire and bead design and oxidized outlines forming masks for comedy and tragedy, screwbacks, unmkd, attributed to Frank Rebajes, New York, NY, 1" w x 1", **$60**.

B, c. 1950, titled "Curtain Call," stamped masks of comedy and tragedy motifs, clipbacks, one clip mkd "Renoir" in script, ⅝" w x 1", **$45**. (Courtesy of Terrance O'Halloran, San Pedro, CA)

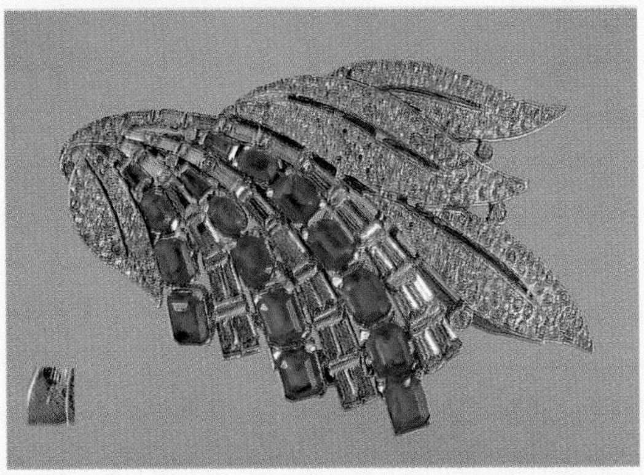

Dress Clip, rhinestones, glass, rhodium-plated wm, c. 1935, foliate spray motif, openwork plaque with curved spray of alternating rows of colorless baguette r.s. and emerald-cut red glass stones, flanked by four pavé-set colorless r.s. cutout leaves, circ colorless r.s. accents, open flat-backed hinged clip on rev in the shape of the front, "TKF" monogram maker's mk for Trifari, Krussman, & Fishel, 2¾" w x 2", **$125**. (Courtesy of Pat Seal, Treasures From Yesterday, Fort Worth, TX)

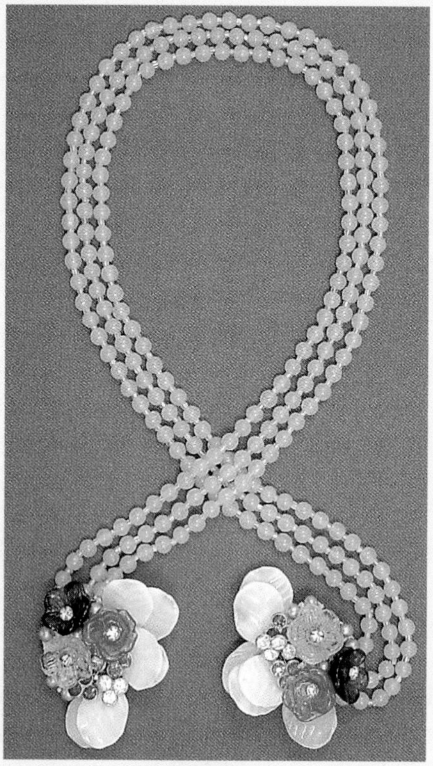

Necklace, molded glass, glass beads, wm, imitation pearls, c. 1935-40, three strands of translucent pink round glass beads with sm colorless round bead spacers suspending two circ wm disks with flat-backed hinged clips on rev, each surmounted by clusters of circ opaque white molded glass leaves, three molded glass flowerheads in pink, dk purple, and seafoam green with circ colorless r.s. centers, multiple faux pearls and pink, amber, and colorless circ r.s. accents, clips attach to neckline of dress, unmkd, attributed to Frank Hess for Miriam Haskell, 26" tl, clips 2¼", **$650**. (Courtesy of Pat Seal, Treasures From Yesterday, Fort Worth, TX)

Necklace, glass beads, rhinestones, ym, wm, c. 1940, a torsade of multiple twisted cranberry-colored bugle bead strands loosely encircled by a twisted rope of prong-set circ-cut colorless r.s., terminating in two round cranberry-colored beads, a v-spring and oval box clasp surmounted by five cylindrical cranberry-colored beads wired in the shape of a flower, clasp rev mkd "MADE IN FRANCE," 16½" tl, **$850**. (Courtesy of D. Brett Benson, Inc., Chicago, IL)

Necklaces, ptd metal, velvet ribbon, glass beads, c. 1938, two necklaces from the "Circus Collection" designed by Jean Schlumberger for Elsa Schiaparelli: **T**, two ptd metal winged chimera flanking a floral/foliate drop, continuing to polychrome floral and foliate motifs suspended from a shocking pink velvet ribbon; **B**, two ptd metal ostriches decorated with blue and pink round glass beads suspended from dk blue velvet ribbon mkd "MADE IN FRANCE," floral/foliate approx 2" T to B at center, 6" l; ostriches 1½" w x 2", **$11,500** [A]. (Photo Courtesy of William Doyle Galleries, New York, NY

Pendant, cross, sterling, amethyst, c. 1940, bezel-set oval faceted amethyst in the center of a raised foliate scroll design on oxidized ground, rounded terminals flanked by hemispherical beads, wide tapered bail with incised S-scroll design, bail and cross rev mkd "PERUZZI BOSTON STERLING" (Italian silver jewelry manufacturer with locations in Florence Italy and Boston, MA), 1½" w x 2¾", **$175**. (Courtesy of Generations, La Verne, CA)

Suite: Brooch/Locket and Earrings, gp brass, c. 1935-40, Victorian revival style, a die-stamped cusped bar suspending an oval locket with quatrefoil and scroll motifs, opens to glazed compartments, loop for wear as a pendant, later-added safety catch, matching earrings with later-added shepherd's hook earwires, locket 1½" w x 3⅝", earrings 1" w x 1½" l, **$135**. (Courtesy of Martha Exline, Metique, Laguna Hills, CA)

Suite: Necklace, Brooch, Bracelet, Clip, Earrings, molded glass, rhinestones, gp brass, c. 1940, floral/foliate motifs made with clusters of pink and purple "poured glass" petals, sm colorless r.s.-set flowerheads and stamped gp brass sm flowers and leaves, double-pronged hinged clip with gp foxtail chain tassel terminating in faux pearl drops, necklace and bracelet each with three strands of gp brass foxtail chain flanking floral centers, filigree clasps, clipback earrings each a floral cluster, all pcs unmkd, attributed to Miriam Haskell, necklace 15", bracelet 2¼" T to B at center, 6½" tl, brooch 3¼" w x 2", earrings 1¼", clip 2" w x 4" tl, **$2,400**. (Photo courtesy of Morning Glory Antiques, Albuquerque, NM)

Suite: Bracelet and Clip, gp wm, sterling, rhinestones, c. 1940, bracelet a "Ludo"-style strap with gp brickwork mesh terminating in a buckle motif pavé-set with r.s. on wm, rev mkd "CINER," sliding clasp with safety lock and chain, matching clip in gp ster, mkd "STERLING," double-pronged hinged clip on rev, bracelet ⅞" w x 8" tl, clip ⅞" w x 2", **$300**. (Courtesy of Martha Exline, Metique, Laguna Hills, CA)

Suite: Bracelet, Earrings, and Clip, gp wm, rhinestones, ptd enamel, faux pearls, c. 1940, stylized peacock motif, the double-headed clip with enameled details in green, pink, and blue, peacock tail set with green glass cabachons and faux pearls, a lg pear-shaped faux pearl drop suspended between two peacock heads, each with a smaller faux pearl drop in its beak, double-pronged hinged clip on rev; matching clipback earrings and link bracelet with pavé-set colorless r.s. along bottom edges, bracelet with four openwork links, peacock motifs set within rect chevron-textured frames, each link joined by reeded half-cylinders, box clasp and safety chain, each pc mkd "R. DEROSA" on rev, bracelet 6½" tl, clip 3", earrings 1⅛", **$1,800**. (Photo courtesy of Morning Glory Antiques, Albuquerque, NM)

Suite: Brooch and Earrings, gp wm, rhinestones, c. 1945, stylized openwork tulip motif formed of oval looped and S-shaped flat wires, petals surmounted by short rows of sq colorless r.s., leaf tips surmounted by single colorless r.s. baguettes, matching clipback earrings, all pcs mkd "PAT PEND, TRIFARI [CROWN]," brooch 2⅛" w x 3½", earrings ¾" w x 1", **$125**. (Lisa Johnson collection)

Suite: Bracelet, Brooch, and Earrings, sterling, c. 1940, stamped and chased realistic orchid motifs, brooch a single lg flower, matching earrings, bracelet with seven orchid-shaped links joined by curved bar links, v-spring and box clasp, part of Hawaiiana Series made for Gump's of Honolulu, mkd "GUMP'S, STERLING, DESIGNED BY G. CINI," for Guglielmo Cini, Boston, MA," bracelet ¾" w x 8", brooch 2½", earrings ¾", **$575**. (Photo courtesy of Joanne Valentine, Almost Antiques, Honolulu, HI)

Section Two: c. 1950-1975

Aside from the novelty items covered in the Plastic and Other Novelty section, most costume (or fashion) jewelry continued to follow fine jewelry trends until the late '50s, when "fabulous fake" pieces became more exaggerated and glitzier than their fine jewelry counterparts. Hollywood had perhaps even more influence on non-precious jewelry than on fine jewelry. Joseff of Hollywood outfitted many stars with fabulous fakery for their roles in "period" films. Marilyn Monroe's "diamonds are a girl's best friend" jewels were really rhinestones, as were Audrey Hepburn's "Breakfast at Tiffany's" baubles. It was also a profitable and common practice for manufacturers to produce costume jewels imitating the precious ones worn by the stars, so that even a woman of modest means could afford to emulate her favorite glamour queen.

The use of design patents gradually disappeared after Congress amended the copyright law in 1947, including the notice of copyright and the use of the copyright symbol © on specified works. This made the process of design protection much easier (and of longer duration) than what had been required for design patents. By the mid-1950s, most jewelry manufacturers were adding the copyright symbol to their mark on a piece of jewelry to indicate that the design was copyrighted, and protected by law. This explains why design patents are seldom found for costume jewelry after circa 1955.

As is the case with the earlier costume jewelry covered in Section One, only a small number of maker names will be mentioned here. Further information on some of these and other makers can be found in the References.

Concurrent with fine jewelry, the late '40s and '50s saw the return of the parure, or suite of necklace, bracelet, earrings, and brooch, or two or three of these. It should be noted that only one or two components of a suite may be marked with a manufacturer's name. If the pieces are separated, identification may prove difficult.

In the '50s, the crafts movement influenced commercial production of modernist copper and enameled copper designs, notably by Rebajes of New York and Renoir/Matisse of California (see pages 197 and 204). Though mass-produced and inexpensive, this "copper art" jewelry was usually hand-made or hand-finished. Frank Rebajes' status has recently been elevated to that of "studio artist," his work having been included in the "Messengers of Modernism" exhibition of studio artists' jewelry (see Mid-Century Modern section). Two of his sterling pieces are shown in that section. One known German maker is Perli, which specialized in matte enamels with modernistic tendencies (see bracelet below).

Some c. 1960s and later pieces, by Boucher, Stanley Hagler, Jomaz, Kenneth Jay Lane, Schreiner, and couturiers Christian Dior, Givenchy, Nettie Rosenstein, Yves St. Laurent, Pauline Trigère, as well as Carnegie, Chanel, and Schiaparelli, have a collector following. Sixties and early '70s designs tended toward the large and the dramatic. The more "over the top" it is, the more desirable to collectors.

French designer Robert Goossens is the creator of many "over the top" costume jewels. He began designing costume jewelry for Chanel when she came out of retirement in 1954 (he had already been working for other big-name couturiers). On November 15, 2000, Christie's East held a sale of Goossens' "couture" jewelry; more than 380 lots were pictured in the accompanying catalog, including many Chanel pieces.

Schiaparelli's later jewelry was still bold and imaginative, but it lacked the "off-the-wall" look of her earlier work. Chunky suites set with molded iridescent glass stones (sometimes called "watermelon" or "oil-slick") and "aurora borealis" rhinestones (developed by Swarovski in 1955), or large faceted colored glass stones, were mid-'50s Schiaparelli trademarks, signed with her famous script signature (see pages 202 and 203). Schiaparelli retired in 1954, but American manufacturers continued producing her designs through the remainder of the decade.

Designer Lyda Coppola (married name Toppo) designed pieces for Schiaparelli early in her career. The Italian maker's own company, Coppola e Toppo, was founded in 1946, but her dramatic faceted glass and plastic bead jewelry gained prominence in the 1960s (see necklace on page 205 and clip and earrings suite on page 210; see also *European Designer Jewelry*, cited in References, pp.197-206). The company closed in 1986.

Recent collector attention has been given to a circa late '50s to early '60s style called "Juliana." The name is derived from a paper hang-tag found on some pieces, which are unsigned—speculation is that it was made by wholesale "jobbers" and sold to several different companies. Most often seen are chunky flexible link bracelets or suites of clustered multicolored rhinestones, some with "aurora borealis" iridescence. Paper tags marked "Gloria" or "Tara" are also sometimes found on this type of costume jewelry. The construction and "look" are similar (see bracelets on page 202, and suite on page 209). More examples and information on Juliana style jewelry can be found in Morning Glory Antiques' online magazine, Jewel Chat (www.morninggloryantiques.com/JewelChatJul.html).

Jonné is a name found on circa 1950s costume jewelry

Bracelet, link, enamel, silver, c. 1950, slightly convex rect plaques with *cloisonné* matte enameled abstract foliate motifs in shades of brown, yellow, rust, and amber, wide oval links, counter-enameled black, mkd "MADE IN GERMANY," box clasp imp "PERLI," ⅞" w x 7¾" tl, **$500**. (Elaine Sarnoff collection)

Brooch/Pin, ptd ivory, vermeil, c. 1960-65, carved ivory double hibiscus, lt pink painted center, two pieces of ivory joined to form flower surmounting vermeil stems and leaves, rev of one leaf imp "MING'S STERLING," ivory mkd "Ming's" in India ink, 3" w x 3½", **$525**. (Photo courtesy of Joanne Valentine, Almost Antiques, Honolulu, HI)

that bears some resemblance to Miriam Haskell pieces of the same era, including the use of glass beads and "*roses montées*" (flat-backed) rhinestones. As is often the case with matched suites of this period, some pieces are not marked (see suites on page 208). No information or documentation on the company has yet been discovered.

Ming's of Honolulu, a Hawaiian jeweler in business from circa 1940 to 1999, made jewelry for a niche market with crossover appeal for Hawaiiana collectors, as well as jewelry collectors. Its trademark designs were created by founding artist Wook Moon (d. 1989), whose renditions of Hawaiian flora, such as birds of paradise, orchids, hibiscus, and anthuriums, appealed to Hawaiian locals and tourists alike. Most of these were made of carved and dyed ivory and sterling silver (see brooch above, and suites on page 208). At the height of its production, Ming's maintained shops in cities throughout the mainland, as well as several on the islands. It began closing the mainland stores in the 1960s. Now that the entire business has closed its doors, collector interest in all types of Ming's jewelry has grown (including gold and gemstone jewels, see Fine Jewelry c. 1960-75).

Gump's of San Francisco was a retailer for sterling designs by Guglielmo Cini (1903-1979), which also found their way to the company's store in Honolulu. According to a source at Gump's, the company's Honolulu location was in business from 1929 to 1950 (see brooch on page 193 and orchid suite on page 199), but the San Francisco store carried Cini jewelry until the mid-1960s. The Cini Jewelry company continues in business today in California under the direction of Guglielmo Cini's granddaughter, Amy Milner (www.cinijewelry.com).

Notes on Sections One and Two: Today, many costume jewelry collectors and dealers tend to focus on the name of the manufacturer or designer, rather than on the jewelry itself. Novice dealers often price a piece high because it is "signed," not because of its overall design and craftsmanship. It is true that certain manufacturers and designers have reputations for high-quality production and innovative design, and their names do make an upward difference in price compared to similar unsigned pieces. However, the same caveats apply to this genre of jewelry as to any other: A maker's mark is not a guarantee of quality. Be sure to evaluate a piece on its own merits *before* you turn it over to look for a mark.

Condition is an especially important factor in costume jewelry, because costume pieces are more easily damaged than fine jewelry and difficult to repair well. Major damage *or* major repairs lower value considerably. Replaced rhinestones and some wear are acceptable to most collectors, but replating, re-enameling, and soldering often are not. If badly done, the piece is ruined, and even if done well, it may end up not looking "right." Proper restoration of a worn or broken piece is a job for a skilled professional who specializes in costume jewelry.

Note on prices in these two costume jewelry sections: This is one area of jewelry collecting that is comparable to other collectibles, e.g. dolls or glassware, because the pieces were mass produced, and many of them are well-known, identifiable designs by recognized manufacturers and/or designers. Although the quantity, quality, and variety of costume jewelry are much greater than that of most other collectibles, certain designs, particularly the most desirable ones, have that "name recognition" factor. A collector can say "Trifari pearl belly swan," and another collector will know exactly what he or she is talking about. Some pieces are common and some are rare; rarity and demand drive this segment of the market in particular, as reflected by four-figure prices for the most sought-after pieces. A few examples of such rarities are pictured here. However, prices are less stable than for collectibles like Depression glass, for example.

In spite of the fact that the Internet has globalized the marketplace, regional differences do exist and can affect prices, and what's hot and what's not is constantly changing in different parts of the country. Collectors' attitudes can go from "gotta have it" to "been there, done that" in a very short time! In urban areas where the market is strong for particular designs by certain "names," prices may be higher than those listed here. Outside of these markets, however, prices will be comparable or lower.

Reproduction Alert

Knockoffs of Eisenberg Originals, Trifari jellybellies (the frog, turtle, stork, fish, and pig), and other big-name and pricey pieces have been infiltrating the market for the past several years. The most problematic are the ones which have been cast from the original pieces or molds, signatures intact. Some manufacturers, notably Cini, Eisenberg, Miriam Haskell, and Trifari, are "reissuing" their vintage designs, now that they are so collectible. In some cases, only a side-by-side comparison of old with new will reveal subtle differences. Other reproductions are clearly market, sometimes with dates. Many designers/manufacturers, such as Kenneth Jay Lane, never discontinue a line or design as long as it sells, which can be many years. As usual, the best defense is a buyer's knowledge and a seller's reputation.

Bracelets, charm, sterling, c. 1950-55:
T, six charms of Cub Scout emblems, labeled "CUB SCOUTS BSA" (one also reading "DEN MOTHER," another "BOBCAT") in circ, sq, and rect shapes on a ster chain, spring ring closure, all pcs mkd "STERLING," chain 7¾" tl, **$75**.
B, 20 charms of travel-related themes, including a nut that opens to become a boat with a man pushing a pole, a UN Building, a U.S. Capitol Building, a cruise ship, a submarine, a razor, an enameled maple leaf, a plaque reading "MADE IT PIKE'S PEAK, COLO.," ice skates, a statue, etc, some pcs mkd "STERLING," ster chain with spring ring closure, 7" tl, **$200**. (Sue James collection)

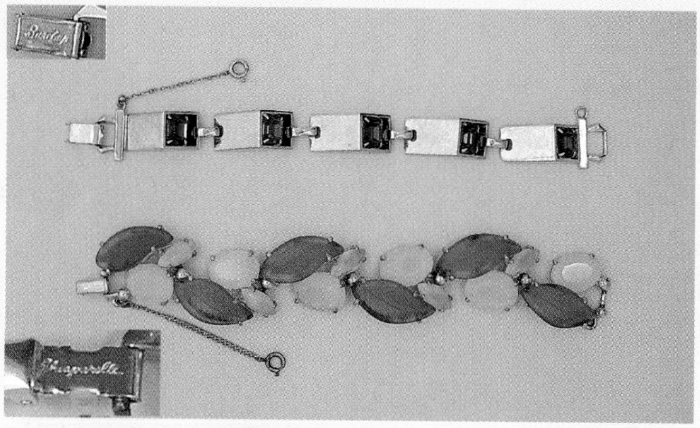

Bracelets, link, c. 1950-55:
T, three-dimensional hollow triangular chrome-pl wm links, one angled face of each prong-set with a sq-cut royal blue glass stone, joined with flat rect links, fold-over clasp on bracketed wm bars, rev mkd "Barclay" in script (Providence, RI, company founded in 1946, after split with Rice-Weiner), safety chain, ½" w x 7½" tl, **$60**.
B, gp base metal, alternating opposed links, each prong-set with a dk amber-colored molded satin glass leaf, a lg oval-cut white-yellow opalescent glass stone, a transparent marquise cab with yellow striations, and a gp bead, rev of foldover clasp mkd "Schiaparelli" in script, safety chain, 1⅛" w x 7¼" tl, **$125**. (Diane White collection)

Bracelets, flexible, rhinestones, glass, gp wm, c. 1955-60, unmkd, "Juliana" style:
T, lg oval multicolored irridescent glass stones surrounded by orange r.s., red, elliptical r.s. encircling a central green r.s., green molded glass leaves with central orange r.s. connect each link, gp wm foldover clasp with safety chain, ¾" w x 7", **$145**.
T2, five links, each with a large diagonally set, variegated color glass stone surrounded by lt and dk green r.s., gp wm foldover clasp with safety chain, 1¼" w x 7", **$135**.
B2, set with a repeating pattern of topaz-colored marquise r.s. and lg and sm circ lt green-blue aurora borealis r.s., gp wm foldover clasp with safety chain, 1" w x 7", **$95**.
B, blue, pink, and green aurora borealis and "watermelon" r.s., a repeating pattern of lg elliptical red-green stones, each flanked by two circ blue r.s. and one circ pink r.s., interspersed with large circ pink r.s. and green marquise r.s., gp wm foldover clasp with safety chain, 1½" w x 7", **$375**. (Photo courtesy of Morning Glory Antiques, Albuquerque, NM)

Brooches/Pins, glass seed beads, gp metal, c. 1950:
L, multiple strands of looped, wire-strung white glass seed beads supported by backing wire forming a white flowerhead with yellow glass seed bead center, flanked by looped, wire-strung strands of green, lavender, and yellow glass seed beads in a foliate and floral motif, terminating in a white seed bead tassel, oval gp filigree backing with pin assembly on rev with appl metal oval plaque mkd "HATTIE © CARNEGIE," 2¼" w x 4" tl, **$135**.
C, glass seed beads, c. 1950, multiple strands of looped white glass seed beads supported by wire forming a white flowerhead with yellow glass seed bead center, mounted on gp filigree backing, appl oval plaque on rev mkd "MIRIAM HASKELL," 3¼" dia, **$120**.
R, glass seed beads, gp metal, c. 1950, multiple strands of looped white glass seed beads supported by wire forming a white flowerhead with green glass seed bead center, flanked by multiple strands of green and pink seed bead accents, mounted on gp oval filigree plaque, appl metal oval mkd "HATTIE © CARNEGIE" on rev, 3" w x 2½", **$145**.
(Photo courtesy of Morning Glory Antiques, Albuquerque, NM)

Brooches/Pins, poodle figurals, c. 1955-60:
TL, silvertone metal, posing poodle sitting up on hind legs with raised paws, polished torso, textured legs and top of head, rev mkd "GERRY'S ©," ¾" w x 1½", **$15**.
TC, ster, standing poodle figure with smooth body and tail, scrolling patterned "fur" on legs and top of head, dog collar and drooping ears set with marcasites, rev mkd "STERLING SILVER GERMANY," 1" sq, **$25**.
TR, wm, oxidized finish, running poodle with polished torso and oxidized pebbled texturing on legs, muzzle, and top of head, unmkd, 1⅝" x 1¼", **$10**.
BL, rhodium-plated, paint, front-facing textured poodle with ptd red neck bow, unmkd, ⅝" w x 1⅞", **$10.**
BC, gp metal, r.s., poodle with gp stippled body and polished face, paws, and hair bow, circ blue r.s. eyes and colorless aurora borealis r.s. nose, unmkd, 1⅝" w x 2", **$10**.
BR, wm, r.s., paint, shyly posing poodle standing up on two legs with crossed front paws, brushed wm finish, ptd red bow on neck, green r.s. eye, unmkd, ¾" w x 1½", **$15**.
(Ellie Laubner collection)

Brooches/Pins, glass, japanned metal, rhinestones, c. 1955, a pr in the shapes of butterflies, each with japanned metal wire openwork frame set with various colored and aurora borealis navette and circ cabs, marquise and circ-cut r.s., lg brooch sgd "REGENCY," sm brooch unsgd, large 1½" w x 1¾", small 1¼" x 1¼", **$145**. (Photo courtesy of Morning Glory Antiques, Albuquerque, NM)

Brooch/Pin, rhinestones, wm, c. 1955, convex patinated wm plaque in the shape of a pineapple set with marquise r.s. in shades of dark and lt amber, and pale yellow, crossover top fronds with pink, amber, and colorless r.s., rev mkd "Schiaparelli" in script, 1¾" w x 2⅞", **$200**. (Elaine Sarnoff collection)

Brooch/Pin, sterling, pearls, c. 1955-60, irregular layers of textured cast ster wires arranged in the shape of a five-pointed star, surmounted by six randomly placed cultured pearls, appl plate on rev with maker's mk for Theodor Fahrner, "925 GERMANY," 2" dia, **$350**. (Private collection)

Brooches/Pins, fruit motifs, gp metal, painted enamel, c. 1960-65:
T, circ gp plaque in the shape of a cross-sectional orange slice, raised gp segment divisions and seeds, ptd orange outer rind and translucent orange wash over inner fruit segments, imp plaque on rev mkd "TRIFARI©," 2" dia, **$30**.
BL, gp metal, ptd enamel, c. 1960, red ptd apple with green ptd top stem and leaves, small ptd beige worm on lower apple body, appl palette-shaped plaque on rev mkd "Original by Robert©" [script], 1½" w x 2", **$25**.
BR, gp and sp metal, ptd enamel, imitation pearl, c. 1960, two red ptd cherries with lt green ptd top stems and leaves, faux pearl in center of leaves, appl palette-shaped plaque on rev mkd "Original by Robert©," 2", **$45**. (Diane White collection)

Brooches/Pins, gp metal, imitation pearls, beads, rhinestones, c. 1955, mkd "ART©":
L, in the shape of a fleur de lis with raised bead surface, vertical plumes pavé-set with faux seed pearls, side C-shaped plumes pavé-set with turq-colored circ glass cabs, center horizontal bar set with red r.s., 1½" w x 2⅛", **$30**.
R, in the shape of a crown, base with gp ropetwist border flanking a foliate pattern interspersed with imitation pearls and lt blue r.s., surmounted by pierced textured gp metal forming nine convex tapering strips with alternating rows of bezel-set circ-cut red r.s. with clusters of three circ turq-colored cabs at the base, and grad faux seed pearls, outermost edges set with colorless r.s. and turq cabs, lg circ-cut red r.s. at top of crown, 1½" w x 1½", **$30**. (Diane White collection)

Brooches/Pins, chick figurals:
TL, c. 1950, flapping, gp wm squawking chick wearing overalls with suspenders, colorless r.s. cuffs, red ptd eye, unmkd, moderate wear to gp, 1¼" w x 2⅛", **$45**.
TR, c. 1970, chick stepping out of a white ptd enamel egg, gp textured metal features on chick body, red r.s. eyes, appl plaque on rev mkd "TRIFARI©," 1⅝" sq, **$65**.
BL, c. 1970, left profile with colorless r.s. eye seated inside bottom half of a cracked eggshell with gp interior, white ptd enamel exterior with yg flower accents ptd at the base, appl oval plaque on rev mkd "ALICE CAVINESS," some wear to white enamel on pin front, 1¼" w x 1¾", **$75**.
BC, c. 1950, colorless Lucite head and body, black ptd eye, set in gp wm frame, seated inside bottom half of gp eggshell, moderate wear to gp on pin front, unmkd, 1¼" w x 1⅞", **$60**.
BR, c. 1970, faux pearl with colorless r.s. eye, emerging out of its cracked-open egg, exterior pavé-set with colorless r.s., sm pink r.s. flower at the chick's feet, appl plaque on rev mkd "NOLAN MILLER," 2¼" w x 1½", **$60**. (Vickie Vega collection)

Brooches/Pins, gp metal, plastic, rhinestones, Asian figures with ivory-colored carved plastic faces, c. 1960, sgd "Nettie Rosenstein":
TL, a fisherman holding a large fish, gp wm hat, intricately textured gp wm body, sleeves, collar, and fish scales set with colorless r.s., 1¼" w x 1¾", **$195**.
TR, a musician playing a lute, with gp wm hat, intricately textured gp wm body, sleeves, collar, and lute set with pavé-set colorless r.s., 1" w x 1⅞", **$195**.
BL, a kimono-clad lady holding an iris, textured gp wm body , kimono sleeves and collar set with colorless r.s., turquoise-colored bead accents throughout, 1¼" w x 2⅜", **$245**.
BR, a Siamese dancer, gp wm headdress set with rows of green and colorless r.s., crosshatch patterned gp wm body set with green and colorless r.s., 1⅝" w x 2½", **$235**. (Photo courtesy of Morning Glory Antiques, Albuquerque, NM)

Earrings, pendent, glass, wm, rhinestones, c. 1980, "fruit salad" motif, surmounts of molded dk blue glass flower buds with sm red glass cabs flanked by colorless r.s. at the base, each suspending an open lobed tapered drop pavé-set with colorless r.s., terminating in a lg molded green glass bud center stone flanked by a sm dk blue and a sm red molded glass bud, rev of drop mkd "©Givenchy," post and clutch findings for pierced ears, ⅞" w x 2⅞", **$175**. (Courtesy of Xcentricities, Beverly Hills, CA)

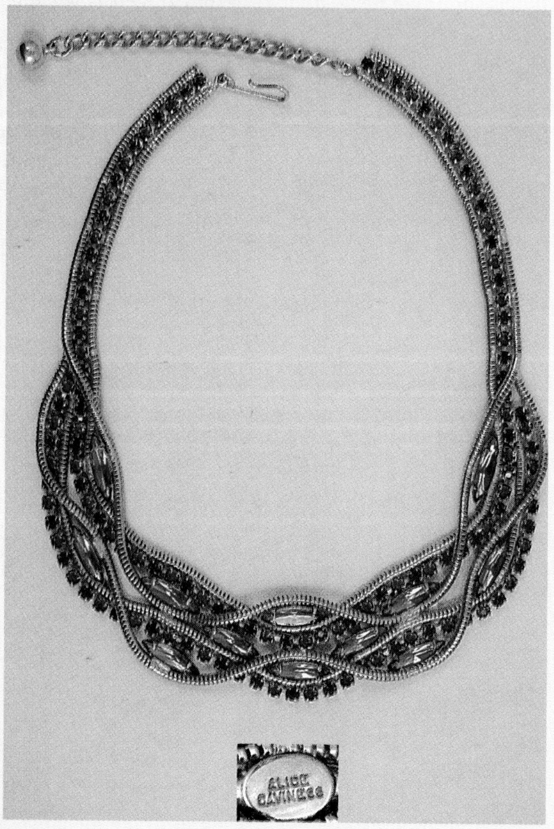

Necklace, rhinestones, gp metal, c. 1950, undulating crossover design, two rows of double snake chain with lg blue marquise r.s. centers and sm circ blue r.s. accents, continuing to single row of sm blue r.s., hook and chain closure, mkd "ALICE CAVINESS," 1" w at center, 16" tl, **$70**. (Diane White collection)

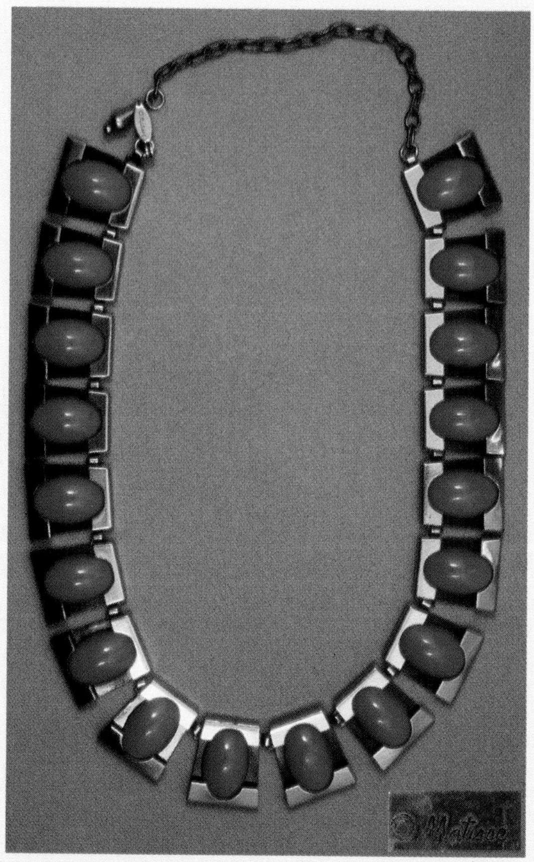

Necklace, copper, enamel, c. 1955, slightly tapered rect links, folded edges top and bottom enclosing red oval enamel cab centers on oxidized bg, chain and hook clasp, mkd "© Matisse" [script] on rev, ⅞" w x 18¾" tl, **$125.** (Courtesy of Patrick Kapty, Mad Jewelry, Long Beach, CA)

Necklace, bib, glass, rhinestones, gp brass, c. 1960, articulated openwork design of two separate strands, pattern-stamped multi-pronged gp bezels set with iridescent dk blue oval glass cabs, the central oval cab in the shorter strand framed by a flowerhead cluster of purple and turq circ-cut and marquise aurora borealis r.s., continuing to oval cabs and smaller flowerhead clusters, the center of the longer strand with two oval cabs drops framed by circ-cut and marquise r.s., continuing to a fringe of similarly set articulated drops with lg and sm oval cabs framed and interspersed with marquise and circ-cut r.s., strands joined at the back, terminating in a hook and jump ring closure, rev mkd "MADE IN FRANCE," long strand 18," short strand 14" tl, 3½" T to B at center, **$1,500**. (Courtesy of D. Brett Benson, Inc., Chicago, IL)

Necklace, glass, gp brass, c. 1960, five strands of grad round faceted glass beads shading from colorless to smoky gray, lg rect snap-together ornamental clasp, rev mkd "MADE IN ITALY BY COPPOLA E TOPPO," 1⅞" T to B at center, longest strand 22¼" tl, **$400**. (Courtesy of Martha Exline, Metique, Laguna Hills, CA)

Pendants and Chains, c. 1965-70:
L, five-pointed star motif in textured gp wm with scalloped ropetwist edging, studded with collet-set, circ and oval r.s. in a variety of colors, some with aurora borealis finish, textured bail set with a circ r.s., mkd "ART©," suspended from gp wm double-link chain, spring-ring clasp, star 2½", chain 24" tl, **$135**.
R, medallion with a central rect plaque of pavé-set colorless r.s. surmounted by a blue enameled Maltese cross with a gold crown center, encircled by striated gp wm rays surmounted by pavé-set colorless r.s. fleur-de-lis alternating with r.s.-set trapezoid shapes, rev sgd "Nettie Rosenstein [script]," suspended from a curb link gp wm chain, cross 2", chain 22" tl, **$165**. (Photo courtesy of Morning Glory Antiques, Albuquerque, NM)

Pendant, silver, enamel, c. 1950, ovoid plaque with yellow and blue-green matte cloisonné enameled abstract design, counter-enameled mottled white, mkd "MADE IN GERMANY," Perli style, 1⅛" w x 1⅞" tl, **$175**. (Private collection)

Pendant, enamel, silver, c. 1950, pear-shaped plaque with matte cloisonné enameled stylized foliate design in shades of black, dk brown, rust, yellow, gray, and cream, counter-enameled black, stamped "MADE IN GERMANY," chain not orig, 1½" w x 1⅞", **$250**. (Elaine Sarnoff collection)

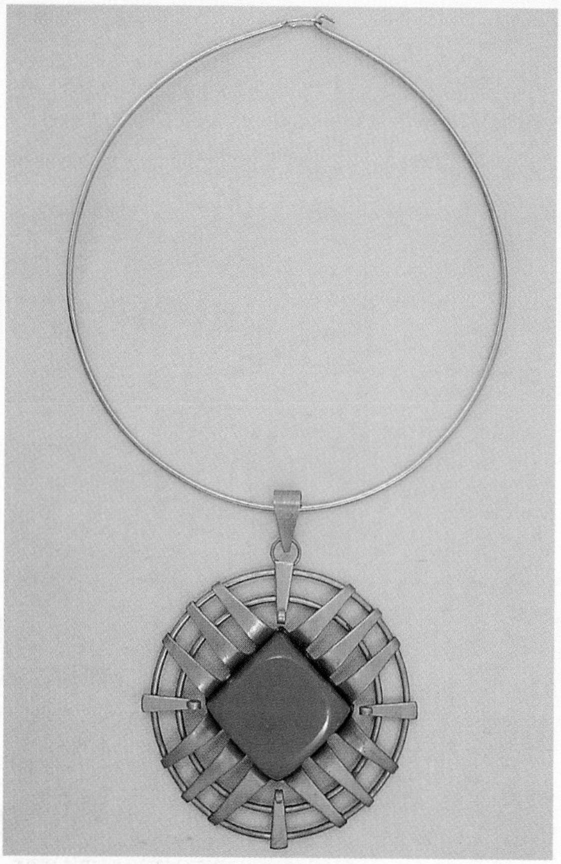

Pendant and Neckring, Bakelite, brass, c. 1960, circ medallion of two concentric wire rings centering a sq orange Bakelite tile turned 45°, framed by tapered convex brass strips radiating from the center and bent around outside ring, strips at compass points with upward-curled terminals, suspended by jump ring and triangular bail from brass neckring, unmkd, pendant 2⅞" diam, neck ring 4⅛" dia, **$75**. (Courtesy of Patrick Kapty, Mad Jewelry, Palm Springs, CA)

Suite: Necklace, Brooch, and Earrings, faceted crystal, molded glass, rhinestones, faux pearls, gp brass, c. 1950, necklace with central and side floral/foliate decorations of purple faceted crystal beads, chartreuse glass teardrops, and lt green poured glass leaves, colorless r.s., faux seed pearl, and gp brass filigree accents, suspended from multiple gp brass chains with ornamental clasp, matching clipback pendent earrings each with a faceted purple glass bead drop, all pcs unmkd, attributed to Miriam Haskell, brooch created from vintage parts by former Haskell employee, necklace 14" tl, 3" T to B at center, brooch 2½" dia, earrings 1¾" tl, **$2,000**. (Photo courtesy of Morning Glory Antiques, Albuquerque, NM)

Suite: Necklace, Bracelet, and Earrings, glass beads, faux pearls, molded glass, rhinestones, ym, c. 1950, eight-strand necklace with four strands of light blue glass beads and four strands of faux pearls, all strands with sm gp seed bead spacers, terminating in a bar-shaped floral/foliate motif clasp with circ blue and white aurora borealis glass beads, pink flower-shaped glass beads, colorless r.s., and gp leaf-shaped glass beads, matching four-strand bracelet with ornamental clasp, glass bead and *"roses montées"* r.s. cluster clipback earrings, all pcs sgd "MIRIAM HASKELL," necklace 14", clasp 1¾", earrings 1⅛", bracelet 7", **$2,000**. (Photo courtesy of Morning Glory Antiques, Albuquerque, NM)

Suite: Necklace, Brooches/Pins, Ring, rhinestones, gp metal, c. 1950, cluster of multi-colored r.s. in lavender, pink, turquoise, blue, green and yellow around lg pink oval center r.s., suspended from "antiqued" goldtone rope chain, r.s.-set clasp, matching pr of sm brooches, lg cluster ring, all pcs mkd "Hollycraft Copr. 1950," necklace 16½" tl, 1½" w x 1½" at center, brooches, ⅞" w x ¾", adjustable ring 1" w x 1⅛", **$300**. (Sandra Willard collection)

Suite, Brooch/Pin, and Earrings, rhinestones, rh pl wm, c. 1955, brooch an openwork shield shape with three lg oval lavender crinkle foiled glass cabs surrounded by lt blue marquise r.s., circ and pear-shaped pink aurora borealis r.s., and dk lavender circ and pear-shaped r.s., suspending two sm drops of circ and pear-shaped pink aurora borealis r.s. from each side, and a lg central openwork kite-shaped drop with matching stones, safety catch, matching circ openwork clipback earrings, all pcs mkd "WEISS," brooch 2¾" w x 4¼" tl, earrings 1¼" dia, **$185**. (Photo courtesy of Morning Glory Antiques, Albuquerque, NM)

Suite: Brooches and Earrings, rhinestones, gp wm, c. 1950, Christmas tree brooches in three sizes, prong-set green r.s. branches, red and pink circ r.s. ornaments, colorless baguette and circ yellow r.s. candles, surmounted by colorless pear-shape r.s. top, amber r.s. base, brooches rev mkd "© WEISS" on appl oval plate, matching earrings mkd "WEISS" on clip backs, lg 1⅝" w x 2⅝", med 1¼" w x 2⅛", sm 1⅛" x 1¾", earrings ¾" w x 1⅛", **$750**. (Courtesy of Generations, La Verne, CA)

Suite: Brooch/Pin and Earrings, rh pl wm, rhinestones, enamel, c. 1950, three-dimensional lily motif, curling petals of honeycomb mesh with ptd blue matte metallic finish, riveted construction, petals edged with pavé-set colorless r.s., central circ prong-set colorless r.s., stems with calibré-cut colorless baguette r.s., matching earrings, each with a flexible wire that wraps behind the ear and terminates in a lily on one end, a pavé-set circ-cut colorless r.s. C-scroll on the other, some wear to ptd finish on earrings, brooch and earrings rev mkd "BOUCHER," brooch #3459 and one earring #3509, brooch 2" w x 3," earrings 1" x 2¾" tl, **$150**. (Private collection)

Suite: Necklace, Bracelet, and Earclips, rhinestones, glass, rh pl wm, c. 1955-60, necklace in purple, lavender and aurora borealis circ and marquise r.s. linked clusters, sm purple r.s. chain, hook clasp, oval plate mkd "REGENCY" appl to rev center, matching flexible bracelet, linked r.s. clusters, mkd on rev, box and v-spring clasp, safety chain, matching earclips with lg center circ faceted purple glass encircled by circ lavender and marquise aurora borealis r.s., not mkd, necklace 1⅛" w at center, 16" tl, bracelet 1" w x 7⅛" tl , earrings 1¼" dia, **$275**. (Sandra Willard collection)

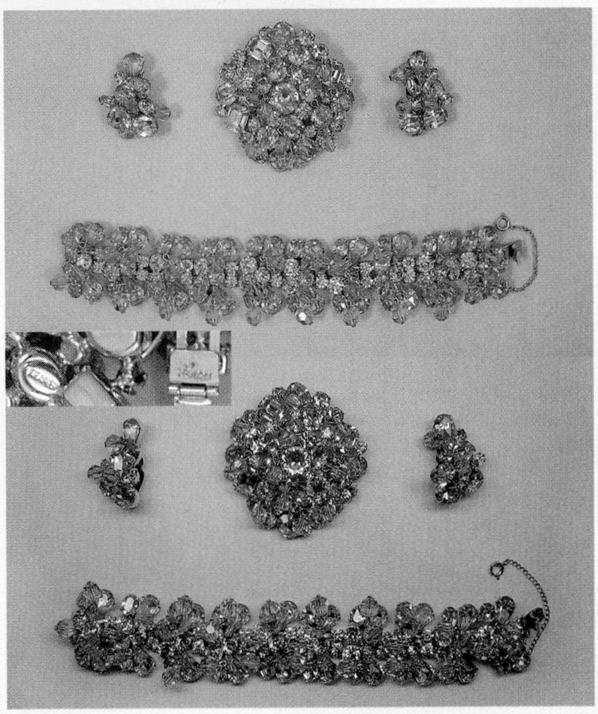

Suite: Bracelet, Brooch/Pin, and Earrings, glass beads, rhinestones, rh pl wm, c. 1955, brooch an openwork cushion-shaped plaque with prong-set circ, oval, and emerald-cut "alexandrine" glass (change of color, lavender to aqua, in incandescent and fluorescent light) r.s., round faceted "alexandrine" glass beads suspended from wm loops throughout, triangular clipback earrings with clusters of circ-cut and pear-shaped "alexandrine" r.s. and articulated round beads, matching bracelet with flexible base of two articulated wm "rails" surmounted by prong-set circ-cut r.s. flanked by clusters of oval and pear-shaped r.s. and articulated round beads, foldover clasp, all pcs mkd "KRAMER" on rev, bracelet 7" tl, brooch 2" dia, earrings 1" w x 1¼", **$300**. (Courtesy of Pat Seal, Treasures From Yesterday, Fort Worth, TX)

Suite: Bracelet, Brooch, Earrings, ptd ivory, sterling, c. 1950s, Bird of Paradise flower motif, carved and ptd ivory in teal, purple, pink, blue, yellow, and orange, ster leaves, bracelet with six links surmounted by birds of paradise and foldover clasp, matching clipback earrings, rev of brooch hand-lettered "MING'S HONOLULU, IVORY, BIRD OF PARADISE" on the ivory, rev of ster leaf imp "MING'S STERLING," bracelet, clasp imp "MING'S STERLING," 1¼" w x 7½", brooch 2" w x 3", earrings 1¼" w x 1¾", **$1,800**. (Photo courtesy of Joanne Valentine, Almost Antiques, Honolulu, HI)

Suite: Brooch and Earrings, ptd ivory, c. 1950s, chrysanthemum motif, carved and ptd with lt pink and yellow accents, paper label mkd "MING'S IVORY" on rev of brooch, brooch 2½" dia, screwback earrings 1" dia, **$600**. (Watters O. Martin, Jr. collection, photo by Joanne Valentine)

Suites by Jonné, glass beads, seed beads, rhinestones, ym, c. 1955:
L, three-strand necklace of grad round pink glass beads and r.s. rondelles flanking a central floral decoration with lt pink seed beads on the five outer petals and "roses montées" r.s. on each inner petal, adjustable hook and bead chain clasp, floral decoration repeated on the four-strand coil bracelet and clipback earrings, clipback mkd with patent #2,583,988 (assigned to F. A. Ballou Jr. et al, Jan. 29, 1952), and "Jonné" in script, necklace 16" longest strand, 2" at center, earrings 1½", bracelet 6"-7", **$900**.
BL and R, "grand parure": a three-strand necklace of grad round aqua glass beads and r.s. rondelles flanking a central floral decoration with aqua seed beads on the five outer petals and "rose montées" r.s. on each inner petal, adjustable hook and bead chain clasp, matching four-strand coil bracelet, brooch, and two prs of clipback earrings (1½" and 2") with "roses montées" r.s. petals, earclips sgd "Jonné [script]," necklace 16" longest strand, 2" at center, brooch 2¾", bracelet 6"-7", **$1,400**. (Photo courtesy of Morning Glory Antiques, Albuquerque, NM)

Suite: Necklace, Earrings, Brooches, Bracelet, glass, r.s., gp metal, c. 1955-60, "Juliana" style, necklace of circ colorless aurora borealis r.s. with suspended swags of sm circ colorless r.s., linked in centers by lg oval marbled glass cabs and lg green pear-shaped r.s. surrounded by circ orange, lt green, and colorless aurora borealis r.s., matching wide link bracelet, two circ brooches, and two sets of clipback earrings, one circ set and one oval set, all with same assortment and colors of r.s. and glass cabs as the necklace, bracelet with gp wm foldover clasp, safety chain, orig tag mkd "Gloria, FASHION CREATORS" on necklace, earrings on orig card with drawing of a street light/sign mkd "Gloria 5th AVE," necklace 14½", round brooch 2½" dia, oval brooch 2¼" w x 2", circ earrings 1⅜" dia, oval earrings 1¼", **$995**. (Courtesy of Emerald's Vintage Costume Jewelry, Garland, TX, photo by Jane Clarke)

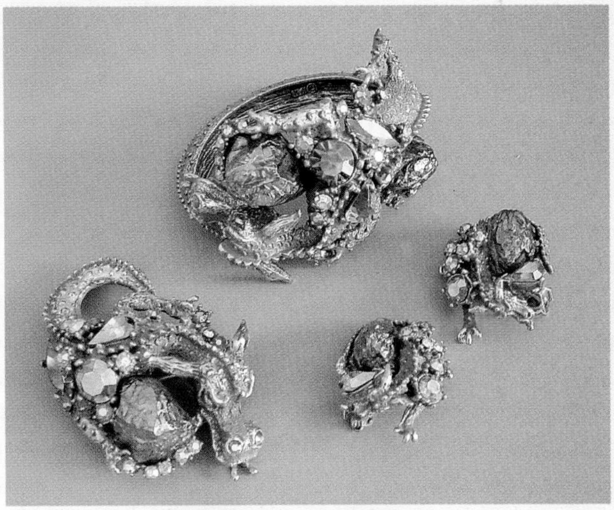

Suite: Bracelet, Brooch/Pin, and Earrings, gp wm, glass, rhinestones, ptd enamel, c. 1955-60, whimsical green dragon motif, green and gold ptd enamel with green, pink, and blue aurora borealis r.s. and irregular iridescent glass stones, hinged bangle with stippled green and gold ptd enamel surface, clipback earrings, all pcs mkd "© HAR" on rev, bracelet 7½", earrings 1½", brooch 2⅞", **$1,250**. (Photo courtesy of Morning Glory Antiques, Albuquerque, NM)

Suite: Necklace, Bracelet, and Earrings, rhinestones, japanned metal, c. 1955-60, pink, purple, and lt purple aurora borealis r.s. necklace with central flowerhead of oval r.s. around central circ r.s., flanked on each side by double rows of r.s. in a repeating diag pattern of each color stone, matching bracelet with four r.s. per row, circ clipback earrings set with circ r.s. in flowerhead motif, unsgd, necklace 1⅜" at center, 16½" tl, earrings 1⅛" dia, bracelet 1⅜" w x 7" tl, **$275**. (Courtesy of Generations, La Verne, CA)

Suite: Ring and Bracelet, gp wm, c. 1965, acorn motif, hinged bangle bracelet with open gp frame surmounted by grad projecting conical "acorns" of textured woven gp mesh, matching ring, imp plaque on rev of bracelet mkd "K. J. L." for Kenneth J. Lane, bracelet 2¼" inside dia, acorns 1½" l, **$175**. (Courtesy of Patrick Kapty, Mad Jewelry, Palm Springs, CA)

Suites: Brooches/Pins and Earrings, fruit figurals, aurora borealis and colored rhinestones, glass, gp metal, c. 1955-60, mkd "ART©," each suite, $75:
L, brooch and earrings in the shapes of strawberries, textured gp metal pierced plaque pavé-set with circ dk and lt pink r.s., gp top stem flanked by two lt green and one dk green marquise r.s., one marquise r.s. missing, brooch 1⅜" w x 1⅞", clipback earrings 1" w x 1¼".
TR, earrings in the shapes of apples, each textured gp metal pierced plaque pavé-set with circ-cut mint green r.s. and a navette-shaped iridescent mint green glass cab, each gp top stem flanked by a green marquise r.s., ⅞" w x 1".
BR, brooch in the shape of a pear, textured gp metal pierced plaque pavé-set with grad circ mint green r.s., two navette-shaped iridescent mint green glass cabs, gp top stem set with a green marquise r.s., 1⅜" w x 2⅛". (Diane White collection)

Suite: Brooch and Earrings, glass cabochons, aurora borealis, wm, c. 1960, brooch in the shape of a lyre, the antiqued wm wire frame set with branching pink and colorless aurora borealis marquise r.s., surmounted by a lg sawtooth bezel-set circ pink glass cab suspending another lg pink circ glass cab with three pink marquise r.s. prong-set along the bottom, terminating in a larger circ pink glass cab drop with aurora borealis r.s. fringe; adjustable screw/clipback earrings, each a single lg pink glass cabachon flanked on one side by pear-shaped colorless and circ pink aurora borealis r.s., sgd "Vendôme," brooch 2¼" w x 4" tl, earrings 1¼", **$325**. (Photo courtesy of Morning Glory Antiques, Albuquerque, NM)

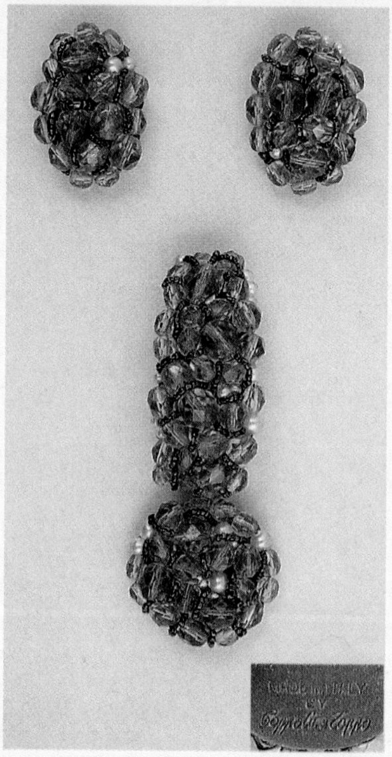

Suite: Dress Clip and Earrings, glass beads, seed beads, imitation seed pearls, brass, c. 1960, dress clip a rect brass plaque suspending a circ brass plaque, both surmounted by clusters of round faceted gray crystal beads and black seed beads strung on wire, tightly wrapped and clustered together, interspersed with faux pearls, matching circ clipback earrings, clips with star cutouts, rev of flat-backed hinged clip and earrings mkd "MADE IN ITALY BY COPPOLA E TOPPO," clip 1¼" w x 3¼" tl, earrings 1" w x 1⅜", **$250**. (Courtesy of Martha Exline, Metique, Laguna Hills, CA)

Suites: Brooches and Earrings, glass, rhinestones, gp metal, c. 1960, sgd "SCHREINER NEW YORK," each suite, $285:
L, brooch an aqua-colored fan-shaped, faceted stone encircled by concentric rows of opaque, lt blue circ cabachons, circ blue-green r.s., and dark aqua r.s., semi-circ clipback earrings with oval and circ blue-green r.s. with central opaque, lt blue cabachon accents, brooch 2¼" w x 2", earrings ¾".
R, brooch a dk rose-colored fan-shaped faceted stone encircled by concentric rows of circ colorless r.s., circ lt purple r.s., and dark rose r.s., semi-circ clipback earrings with oval and circ lt purple r.s. and central colorless r.s. accents, brooch 2¼" w x 2", earrings ¾". (Photo courtesy of Morning Glory Antiques, Albuquerque, NM)

Suite: Necklace and Bracelet, glass cabochons, aurora borealis rhinestones, wm, c. 1960, each pc with three rows of oval glass cabachons in pastel colors of green, purple, white, pink, blue, and amber alternating with circ aurora borealis r.s., adjustable hook and r.s. chain clasp on necklace, v-spring, hidden box clasp and safety chain on flexible bracelet, both sgd "Vendôme," bracelet 1⅜" w x 7½" tl, necklace 1⅜" w x 15" tl, **$800**. (Photo courtesy of Morning Glory Antiques, Albuquerque, NM)

Suite: Necklace, Bracelet, Brooches, Earrings, and Ring, glass cabochons, rhinestones, ym, c. 1965, necklace with a central decoration of two concentric circles, the lower half pavé-set with colorless r.s., the upper half with alternating pink and green oval glass cabs, surmounting multiple strands of gp wm chains terminating in a tassel, foldover clasp pavé-set with colorless r.s. and pink and green oval glass cabs; circle brooch with multiple rows of alternating pink and green glass cabs surmounted by leaf-shaped plaques of pavé-set colorless r.s., butterfly motif brooch with gp wm body and antennae, multiple rows of alternating pink and green glass cabs on wings surmounted by leaf-shaped plaques of pavé-set colorless r.s., matching hinged bangle bracelet, domed ring, and pendent hoop clipback earrings, all pcs sgd "TRIFARI©," necklace 24" tl, 6" T to B at center, circle brooch 1¾" dia, butterfly 2⅝" w x 2½", bracelet ½" w x 6½", ring 1" at center, earrings 2" w x 2⅜", **$1,200**. (Photo courtesy of Morning Glory Antiques, Albuquerque, NM)

Suites, Brooch/Pin and Earrings, rhinestones, ym and wm, from Trifari's "Starflight" series as illustrated in the Trifari Fall/Winter 1966 Catalog, all pcs signed Trifari©":

TL, star-motif earrings with multiple rows of circ green r.s. radiating from centers of six-pointed stars set with colorless r.s., 1" dia, **$54**.

BL, brooch in the shape of a shooting star, the eight-pointed star pavé-set with colorless r.s., surmounting nine grad rays set with champagne gold-colored r.s., 1⅝" w x 3½", **$145**.

C, brooch in the shape of a shooting star, a lg eight-pointed star pavé-set with colorless r.s., nine grad rays set with green r.s. radiating from one side, each clipback earring a domed oval, pavé-set green r.s. plaque surmounted on one side by four rays of pavé-set colorless r.s., brooch 1⅝" w x 3½", earrings 1", **$185**.

R, brooch a bursting comet motif with seven pavé-set colorless r.s rays surmounting eleven grad rays pavé-set with red r.s., star-shaped clipback earrings set with circ red r.s. surmounted by six-pointed stars set with colorless r.s., brooch 1¾" w x 2¾", earrings 1", **$185**. (Photo courtesy of Morning Glory Antiques, Albuquerque, NM)

Part IV
Special Collectible Jewelry

The three special collectibles categories in this section, Native American, Mexican, and Scandinavian, are based on country of origin. While jewelry-making traditions date back to earlier periods in all three areas, availability and collector interest are concentrated in the twentieth century. Most examples are from the 1920s or later. It is interesting to note that the three have certain features in common: the metal most often used is silver, the work is most often done by hand, and there was a certain amount of cross-cultural exchange of ideas and techniques between them. During the 1940s and 1950s, all three enjoyed a period of popularity in the U.S., brought about in part by World War II.

NATIVE AMERICAN JEWELRY

In the late 1960s and early 1970s, the booming popularity of Southwestern American Indian jewelry was at its peak. The volume of poor quality machine-made knockoffs, imported fakes, and "white man's work" had become so great that potential collector interest soured; most people were afraid to buy, for fear a piece was not "authentic."

As a result, over the past 30 years, the market for Indian jewelry, both old and new, has changed considerably. Today, there are two kinds of collectors: those who collect only traditional old pieces, preferably dating before World War II, and those who buy the traditional and contemporary work of recognized "name" artists.

The first type of collector makes a distinction between jewelry made for tribal wear and jewelry made for the tourist trade, although old examples of both are considered collectible. The second type is primarily concerned with quality of workmanship and originality of design. The following section concentrates on older, traditional Native American pieces. However, the work of some post-World War II artists is now considered "period," and is certainly highly collectible.

The pioneers of the "new Indian art"–a phrase coined by one of its practitioners, Preston Monongye–are for the most part no longer living, including Monongye, Charles Loloma, and Kenneth Begay. The individual styles they developed are considered the "turning point" in Native American art, and it is to them that contemporary Native American artists give credit for inspiration. Consequently, several examples of these seminal artists' work are included here.

For readers interested in the work of today's Native American artists, Dexter Cirillo's *Southwestern Indian Jewelry* (see References), which also includes a substantial amount of historical background, is recommended. As there are many caveats to be aware of, and much study required in order to fully understand the differences between old and new, authentic and imitation, readers are also directed to other reliable resources on traditional and old Indian jewelry.

Although other tribes in other parts of the U.S. made jewelry, the work of the silversmiths and lapidaries of the Southwest–the Navajo, and the Santo Domingo, Zuni, and Hopi Pueblo tribes–is the best known and most sought-after. What follows here is a basic introductory summary of the history, materials, techniques, and identifiable characteristics of typical traditional jewelry made by the major Southwest Native American tribes.

Many people are surprised to learn that silversmithing is a relatively new development in Native American arts, first practiced by the Navajo during the last quarter of the nineteenth century. However, other jewelry forms and materials, such as beads made from stone or shell, date to prehistoric times. Today, most of the oldest pieces are in museum collections. Ancient jewelry, and silver jewelry made before 1900 (the period 1868-1900 is known as "first phase") rarely comes up for sale, and is usually priced in the five-figure range when it does.

The earliest silverwork was made strictly for tribal use as symbols of status, portable wealth, and for ceremonial purposes. During lean times, the Indians would take some of their jewelry to the trading post and pawn it for credit. There are common misconceptions about the term "old pawn," one being that pawn jewelry is somehow more valuable because it has been pawned. In fact, the opposite is true. The Indians would pawn only expendable less-important pieces that they were willing to risk losing. The pawn system is still is use today, but only pieces made before 1900 are correctly called "old" pawn.

The influence of the trader and burgeoning tourism should not be underestimated. Traders mentored many a tribal silversmith and encouraged the development of distinctive styles, providing designs, as well as an outlet for the selling of finished goods. In addition to tools, the traders also

Brooch/Pin, silver, turquoise, c. 1930-35, "Fred Harvey" style, arrow-shaped stamped silver plaque surmounted by a cutout horse motif with a green oval turq cab body, stamped decoration throughout, safety catch, illegible mark on rev, 2¼" w x ½", **$125** (Nancy Shadforth collection)

brought in otherwise unavailable materials.

The building of the railroad (the Atchison, Topeka & Santa Fe, which ran from Chicago to Southern California via Albuquerque, New Mexico, was completed in 1880) led to the appearance of Harvey Houses—restaurants and rest stops constructed along the rail routes during the late nineteenth century. The commercialization of American Indian jewelry began in 1899, when the Fred Harvey Company placed its first order for silver jewelry to be made for the general public and sold in Harvey House "curio shops." (See above and page 217).

The company provided the silversmiths with sheet silver, machine-drawn wire, and precut stones. To appeal to tourists, they required the jewelry to be lighter in weight and decorated with stampings of arrows and other "symbols" that they thought souvenir buyers would associate with American Indian culture. Many of these "symbols" had no actual meaning to the silversmiths themselves. One symbol, however, the swastika, was taken from Navajo sand paintings. Although this ancient sign, representing the sun and infinity, had nothing to do with Nazism, its use was discontinued around 1930. Today, pieces stamped with swastikas are understandably a "tough sell."

Turquoise is a gemstone which has been used since ancient times in Southwest Native American cultures, as the mines are indigenous to the area. Highly prized turquoise is often labeled with the name of the mine from which it came, and turquoise from an identifiable mine raises the value of a piece set with it. Most of these mines are not active today.

The cost of extracting the turquoise from some of them has become prohibitive, and others have been exhausted. High-quality turquoise has also been imported from Persia since the turn of the twentieth century, and is now coming from China. Porous and soft low-grade turquoise is often subjected to one of several alterations to enhance its appearance: it can be stabilized with the injection of polymer resin (plastic) to increase hardness, treated with dyes to alter its color, or completely reconstituted and formed into shaped "stones" from turquoise powder and particles mixed with resin. Stabilized turquoise is considered acceptable if identified as such, but its value is not as high as natural turquoise. Other types of treated turquoise, along with synthetics and dyed substitutes such as howlite, are usually found in lesser quality jewelry, imitations, and foreign imports of low value.

Other than turquoise, materials used in Native American jewelry, such as coral and shell, have been obtained through traders and imported. Several varieties of shell, brought in from the Gulf of California and the Pacific, have been used since prehistoric times. Coral, called "red gold," was first brought to the Zuni by traders around 1938 and later used by the Santo Domingo and Navajo. Silver was never mined by the tribes. U.S. coins were used until they were prohibited in 1890, although illegal use since that time is not unheard of. Mexican coins continued to be used until the 1920s. Sterling silver sheet and wire were then purchased from traders.

The Navajo were the first to use turquoise in combination with silver, in the late nineteenth century. However, most of their early work was all silver, with the occasional addition of a stone or two. The Navajo traded with Mexican *plateros* (silversmiths), from whom they learned silversmithing beginning in the 1870s.

In the first phase period, prior to commercialization, the Navajo forged their own ingots from coin silver, which they then hammered into sheets and rods and drew into wire. They preferred making heavy pieces of simple design for tribal wear, and continued to do so after they began using pre-formed sheet silver and machine-drawn wire for commercial tourist production. Therefore, Navajo jewelry from the so-called transitional or second phase period, 1900-1930, is a mixture of first phase style and early tourist pieces.

Certain forms and techniques are associated with Navajo silver jewelry. The "squash blossom" necklace with "naja" pendant is one of the most familiar forms (see pages 219 and 220). The squash blossom is actually a pomegranate motif taken from Spanish and Mexican clothing ornaments, and the crescent-shaped or penannular naja was a bridle ornament for horses copied from the Spanish, who copied it from a Moorish amulet. Early squash blossom necklaces are heavy and simple with little if any turquoise, and entirely handmade from ingot coin silver. "Squashes" from the '60s and '70s are larger and gaudier, often composed of machine-made elements and elaborately decorated with turquoise.

Concha belts are another early Navajo ornament. Simple circular disks with lozenge-shaped cutout centers, minimally decorated and threaded on leather straps, date from the first phase period. Later conchas are oval with more stamping and other decorative elements, including turquoise (see page 216). Concha belts were also made by Zuni and Hopi silversmiths.

Some jewelry forms are relative newcomers to the Native American idiom. Brooches did not appear until the 1930s. Bola ties and slides (the correct word is bol*a*, not bol*o*) were "invented" and popularized by an Anglo Arizonan, Vic Cedarstaff, in 1949, although Indian antecedents from the 1920s are known but rare. The Bola Tie Society of Phoenix was formed in 1966, and bolas became the official Arizona state neckwear in 1971 (see pages 214, 216 and 221).

Tufa casting is a Navajo technique used since the first phase period to make najas, "ketohs" (ornamental wrist bowguards), buckles, rings, and bracelets. Sometimes

Bola Tie, sterling, turq, lapis lazuli, c. 1970-79, Zuni, keystone-shaped slide, central plaque with thin edges and cross-bars of channel inlaid turq and lapis lazuli and center grids of crosshatched silver design, bola leather thongs terminate in long tubular silver cones with flattened tips, sgd "A. WALLACE" for Anselm Wallace, slide 1½" w x 2", **$220** [A]. (Photo courtesy of R. G. Munn Auction, San Diego, CA, 10/12/01)

referred to as sand casting, the technique involves carving a pattern for a mold in tufa, a porous rock formed from volcanic ash (more correctly known as "tuff"), then pouring molten metal into the mold. The hardened piece is then shaped, decorated, and polished.

Early decoration techniques included "rocker engraving" with a short-bladed chisel, and stamped designs similar to those used by Mexican leather workers, using a hand-held punch. In general, the early pieces had simple decorations (see page 216); pieces made for tourists were more elaborately stamped and embellished. The Navajo taught silversmithing to other tribes, who copied their designs, so it is often difficult to determine tribal origins of earlier pieces.

The Pueblo tribes, particularly the Santo Domingo, are known for their bead, shell, and mosaic work. The disk-shaped shell beads strung on string known as "heishi" (alternately spelled "heishe"), are a Santo Domingo specialty and a 1,500-year tradition. The shells are individually cut into squares, drilled, strung, and then rolled by hand or machine to make thin circular disks. The word "heishi" is also erroneously used to refer to a similar type of bead made of turquoise or other stone. The Santo Domingo are also known for their mosaics, patterns of stone, jet, coral, and shell applied to a shell, wood, or bone base (see page 219).

During the 1930s and '40s, the Depression and the war forced artisans to use car battery casings and 78 rpm phonograph records for bases and as jet substitutes. Pieces of old plastic toothbrush handles were used as substitutes for coral and turquoise. Depression-era necklaces strung with tubular shell beads interspersed with tabs and suspending thunderbird motif pendants, battery-backed with mosaic overlay, are now collectible (see page 219). Prices range from $200 to $1,000, depending on quality. The necklace is the most common form of jewelry made by the Santo Domingo, but they also produce pendants, earrings, rings, and bracelets. The ancient tradition of fetish-carving is still carried on by the Santo Domingo and the Zuni. Fetishes are animals and birds carved from stone or shell. Small ones are strung on necklaces, often in combination with shell heishi.

The Zuni are another Pueblo tribe known for their lapidary work, but early Zuni silver jewelry is difficult to distinguish from that of the Navajo. Zuni began establishing their own style of jewelry-making around 1915. They are noted for bezel-setting stones in clusters and patterns, and channel inlay of stone into silver. Numerous small, narrow navette-shaped turquoise slivers set in patterns are called needlepoint; somewhat larger pear-shaped or oval stones are called petit point. Zuni cluster work evolved during the 1920s, petit point and needlepoint were developed in the 1940s (see below and page 218). Channel inlay is a technique that the Zuni began using just prior to World War II (see page 218). All of these techniques were made possible by the introduction of more sophisticated tools and equipment, supplied by traders.

The Hopi were the last tribe to develop their own identifiable style, beginning in the late 1930s. Until that time, the jewelry they made was copied from Navajo and Zuni designs. The all-silver layered technique that the Hopi are now noted for is called overlay, introduced by the founders of the Museum of Northern Arizona in 1938, using Hopi pottery and textile patterns. Abstract and/or figural designs are cut out from a piece of silver, which is then soldered to another piece. The background is oxidized and textured to bring out the design. The earliest Hopi overlay was not signed, but later silversmiths began using marks, either symbols or their names.

In general, pre-World War II Native American jewelry is not signed; early shop and trader marks include the "horn moon" symbol for Navajo Arts & Crafts Enterprises, and "U.S. Navajo 2" for one of the Dept. of the Interior's Indian Arts & Crafts Board traders (see bracelets on page 217). Since the '60s, many artists have been marking their work. Barton Wright's *Hallmarks of the Southwest* is an excellent

Bracelet, cuff, sterling, turquoise, c. 1950, Zuni, lg circ central plaque with concentric circles of petit point turq cabs, twisted wire, and silver crescent and bead decorations, surmounting a cuff set with alternating petit point turq cabs and silver beading, 3" w x 2⅝" inside dia, **$925**. (Jon Bonnell collection, photo by Shari Watson Miller)

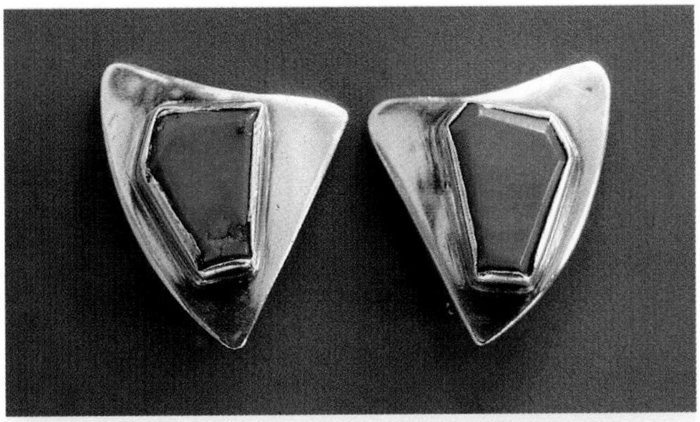

Earrings, sterling, chrysocolla, c. 1968, Hopi, rounded triangular plaques, each bezel-set with irregular, angular stones, mkd "STERLING," maker's mark for Charles Loloma, clipbacks, 1" x 1", **$1,750**. (Courtesy of Faust Gallery, Scottsdale, AZ, photo by Shari Watson Miller)

source for Native American marks identification (see References).

World War II was a turning point in the history of Native American jewelry-making. For the first time, Native Americans were drafted into the armed forces and sent overseas. They were exposed to cultures other than their own, and returned with a broader view of the world, cash in their pockets, and an opportunity to further their education through the GI Bill. Like many other American veterans, they attended classes in jewelry making, learning new techniques using modern equipment. They formed guilds that enabled them to market their own goods. For some Native Americans, making jewelry became more than a traditional tribal occupation. They became *artist-jewelers*.

A paragraph in the article "American Expressions" by Lane Coulter, in *American Craft* magazine, Oct/Nov, 1997, sums it up nicely:

"A few artists had established fresh directions for jewelry at mid-century. The Navajo metalsmith Kenneth Begay (1913-1977), working out of the White Hogan Shop in Scottsdale, Arizona, in the late 1940s, created strong, simple forms utilizing the Navajo techniques of stamped and chased silver...The best-known modern Native American jeweler, the Hopi artist Charles Loloma (1921-1991) served in the armed forces during World War II and trained as a ceramist in the 1950s on the GI Bill at the School for American Craftsmen in Alfred, New York. He pioneered the use of gold, ivory, lapis lazuli, and other materials while teaching at the Institute of American Indian Arts in Santa Fe in the 1960s. He also created new imagery and textures and a distinctive sense of scale in his jewelry designs. Loloma's work was widely published, particularly in the 1970s, influencing a generation of Native American jewelers. A third artist who opened up avenues for today's jewelers was Preston Monongye (1927-1987), who was of California Mission ancestry, but was raised on the Hopi Reservation. His small cast containers and jewelry emphasized line drawings and retained the coarse texture of the tufa stone molds while incorporating beautiful colored stone and shell inlays. The importance of these innovators cannot be overstated. Both Begay and Loloma taught and Monongye was often quoted and his work reproduced in numerous articles [Preston's son Jesse learned silversmithing from his father, see page 217]. Their efforts at individualizing designs while retaining the 'Indianness' of their work has given other Native jewelers the impetus to experiment further with materials, techniques, and forms."

Pieces by Kenneth Begay are on pages 217, 218, and 220. See examples of Charles Loloma's work above left and on pages 217, 218, and 221.

Two other artists whose work is sold through The White Hogan Shop, (still in business,) is are brothers Allen (d. 1976) and George Kee. Their silver designs are sleek, simple, and polished, appealing to modernists, as well as Native American jewelry collectors (see cuff by George Kee on page 218).

The Patanias, Frank Sr. (1899-1964), Frank Jr. (b. 1932), and Sam (b. 1961), are a family of "Anglo" silversmiths who have come to be associated with Native Americans in their adopted Southwestern homeland. Examples of their work are now on display at the Smithsonian's Renwick Gallery in Washington, D.C. Their marks are listed in Barton Wright's Hallmarks of the Southwest. A few examples of their work are shown on pages (217, 218, and 220). For additional information and examples, see Shari Watson Miller's articles for *Modern Silver Magazine*, cited in the References.

Today, Native American silversmiths' work, both traditional and contemporary, is sought-after for its unique designs and superb quality. The market is strongest in the Southwestern United States. The best pieces can be priced in the thousands to ten thousands. Many artists exhibit and sell at the annual Indian Market, a tradition since 1922, held every August in Santa Fe, New Mexico.

Reproduction Alert

Low-quality imitation Indian jewelry is mass produced in Taiwan and the Philippines. Some skilled Anglo craftspeople copy old techniques and designs well enough to fool the experts. "Old pawn" may be neither old nor pawn (fake pawn tickets can be easily attached to any piece). Treated turquoise and simulants may be difficult to identify. *Caveat emptor*: know your sources, and obtain written documentation.

Belt, concha, sterling, turquoise, c.1930-40, Navajo, seven oval conchas, each with central oval turq cabs encircled by radiating repoussé lines and scalloped stampwork edging, alternating with seven butterfly-motif plaques with central circ turq cabs and similar repoussé and stampwork decorations, fluted rect buckle with a central oval turq cab flanked by two smaller oval turq cabs, repoussé "S" and teardrop-shaped decorations, and scalloped stampwork, 32" l, conchas 2¾" w x 2¼", **$660** [A]. (Photo courtesy of R. G. Munn Auction, San Diego, CA, 10/14/01)

Belt, concha, sterling, turq, c. 1970-89, Navajo, four oval conchas, each with central oval turq cabs encircled by radiating repoussé lines and scalloped stampwork edging, alternating with five butterfly-motif plaques with central oval turq cabs and similar repoussé and stampwork decorations, fluted oval buckle with open rect center framed by incised line edging flanked by four oval turq cabs, repoussé "S" decorations with incised lines, and scalloped stampwork edging, 38"-44" l, conchas 5" w x 4", **$605** [A]. (Photo courtesy of R. G. Munn Auction, San Diego, CA, 10/14/01)

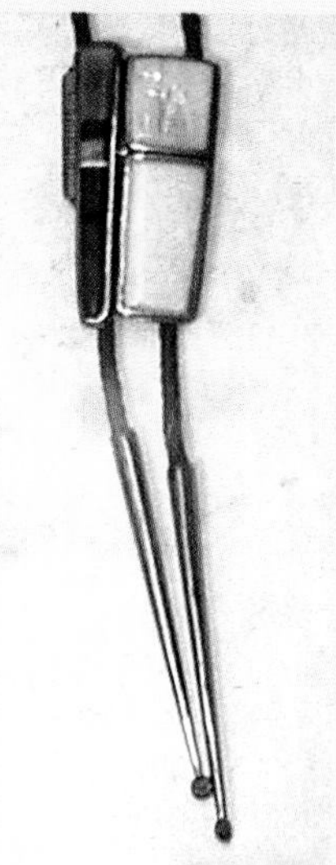

Bola Tie, fossilized ivory, sterling, c.1970-80, rect slide of four carved fossilized ivory cabs in shades of cream and brown, bezel-set in silver, bola leather thongs terminate in long tubular silver cones with bead tips, sgd "Eveli," 1½" w x 2½", **$578** [A]. (Photo courtesy of R. G. Munn Auction, San Diego, CA, 10/14/01)

Bracelets, cuff, Navajo:
L, sterling, c. 1935, flat, with four lengthwise grooves, an incised central zigzag design, and diagonally incised edges, 1" w x 2¼" inside dia, **$350**.
C, steel, c. 1920, stamped ridged grooves along edges and a central band of helical ridged stampwork, 1" w x 2¾" inside dia, **$1,500**.
R, sterling, c. 1930, flat cuff with incised diag grooves in center and on edges, mkd with horn moon symbol for Navajo Arts and Crafts Enterprises, 1¼" w x 2¼" inside dia, **$350**. (Jon Bonnell collection, photo by Shari Watson Miller)

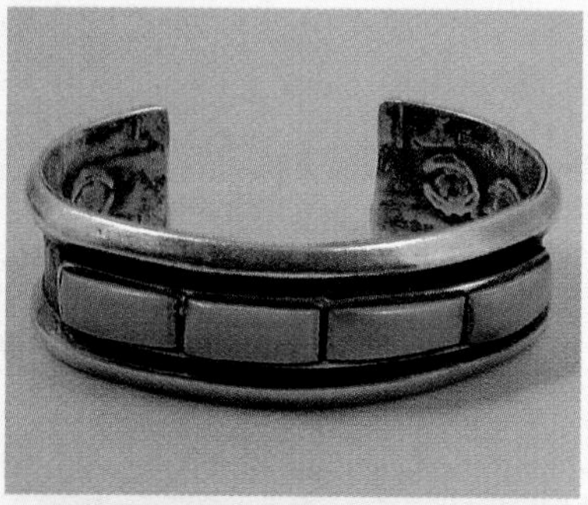

Bracelet, cuff, turquoise, silver, c. 1920, Navajo, raised edge and center oxidized ground inlaid with four bezel-set rect turq cabs set end-to-end, stamped eye motif decorations along cuff sides, ¾" w, 2¼" in dia, **$350**. (Lisa Johnson collection)

Bracelets, cuff, sterling, c. 1935, Navajo, mkd "US NAVAJO 2" for U.S. Dept. of Interior, Indian Arts & Crafts Board, $2,000 each:
L, rounded grooved edges flanking two equidistant pairs of grooves forming ribs, 1½" w x 2⅜" inside dia.
R, borders with parallel rows of sawtooth-edged stampwork, incised pairs of diagonal grooves forming a central geo design, 1¼" w x 2⅜" inside dia. (Jon Bonnell collection, photo by Shari Watson Miller)

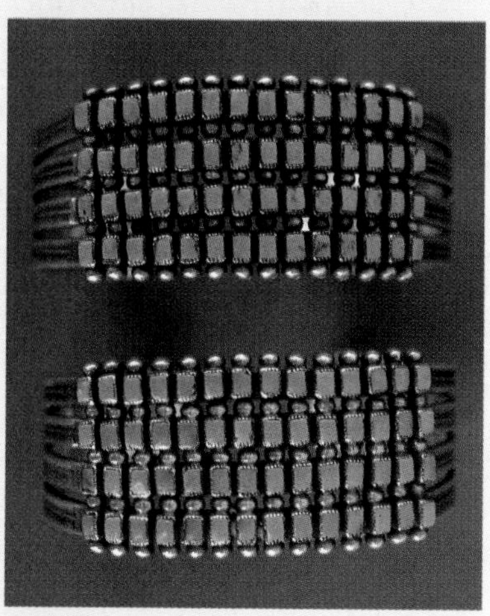

Bracelets, cuff, sterling, turq, c. 1940, Zuni, matched pair, each with four rows of sawtooth bezel-set rect turq cabs interspersed with silver bead decorations on four strips of silver with center ridge joined at terminals, 1" w x 2½" inside dia, **$750**. (Jon Bonnell collection, photo by Shari Watson Miller)

Bracelet, cuff, sterling, turquoise, c. 1950, Navajo, Cochiti tribe, oxidized ground, central lg ovoid Blue Gem turq cab set in notched bezel , elaborate appl scrolling wirework and beading throughout, 2" w x 2½" inside dia, **$600**. (Watson Miller collection, photo by Shari Watson Miller)

Bracelets, cuff, "Fred Harvey"" tourist jewelry, c. 1930-40:
L, Zuni style, two openwork rows of sawtooth bezel-set sq green turq cabs, flanked by appl silver beads, sides stamped with thunderbird and crossed arrow motifs, rev imp "STERLING," ¾" w x 2¼" inside dia, **$175**. (Kim Lord collection)
R, cuff, Navajo style, tapered cuff with central bezel-set oval green turq cab flanked by appl thunderbird and arrow motifs, stamped decoration throughout, unmkd, ⅝" w x 2¼" inside dia, **$150**. (Nancy Shadforth collection)

Bracelet, cuff, sterling, turq, c. 1960, Navajo, floral motif, three ster flowerheads with convex navette-shaped silver petals and central spider-web turq cabs, stamped sun motif between flowerheads, mkd "STERLING HAND MADE," mk for White Hogan, maker's mark "KB" for Kenneth Begay, 1¾" w x 2⅜" inside dia, **$1,400**. (Jon Bonnell collection, photo by Shari Watson Miller)

Bracelet, cuff, turquoise, sterling, c. 1955, Navajo, curv outline, central channel with oxidized ground bezel-set with a row of 15 circ turq cabs, mkd "STERLING HAND MADE," mk for White Hogan, maker's mk "KB" for Kenneth Begay, 1¾" w x 2⅜" inside dia, **$1,400**. (Watson Miller collection, photo by Shari Watson Miller)

Bracelets, cuff, by Jesse Monogye, sterling, turquoise, c. 1970, Navajo:
L, oxidized textured ground with flared edges, surmounted by three irregularly-shaped Morenci turq cabs set in deep bezels with incised parallel lines, maker's mk (mirror image M inside a rectangle), 1¾" w x 2¼" inside dia, **$950**.
R, geo zigzag-shaped cuff bracelet with oxidized textured ground, featuring one lg and one sm irregularly-shaped Morenci turq cab bezel-set with geo incised edging, maker's mk, 1¾" w x 2¼" inside dia, **$1,250**. (Watson Miller collection, photo by Shari Watson Miller)

Bracelet, cuff, sterling, turquoise, c. 1965, Navajo, oxidized ground surmounted by three lengthwise strips mounted on edge, flanking a central bezel-set oval Morenci turq cab, rounded borders interspersed with four rows of incised lines forming ridges, rev imp with mk for White Hogan, maker's mk conjoined "JMB" for Jonny Mike Begay, 1" w, 2¼" inside dia, **$600**. (Jon Bonnell collection, photo by Shari Watson Miller)

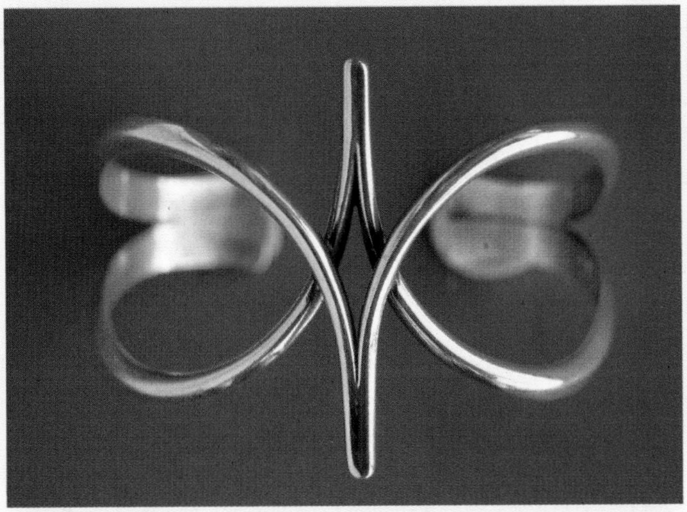

Bracelet, cuff, sterling, c. 1975, two opposed curv wire "wishbone" motifs, one surmounting the other, joined at flattened terminals, maker's mark "FP" with vertical bar of P crossed, for Frank Patania Jr., 1¾" w x 2½" inside dia, **$450**. (Shari Watson Miller collection, photo by Shari Watson Miller)

Bracelet, cuff, 18k yg, lapis lazuli, turq, coral, chalcedony, c. 1980, Hopi, composed of varying heights of parallel fitted stones including lapis lazuli, turquoise, coral, and chalcedony, the solid yg band tapered from 11.5 to 3.5 mm in width, maker's mk for Charles Loloma, 2⅜" inside dia, **$1,121** [A]. (Photo courtesy of Dupuis Jewellery Auctioneers, Toronto, ONT, Canada, 6/10/01)

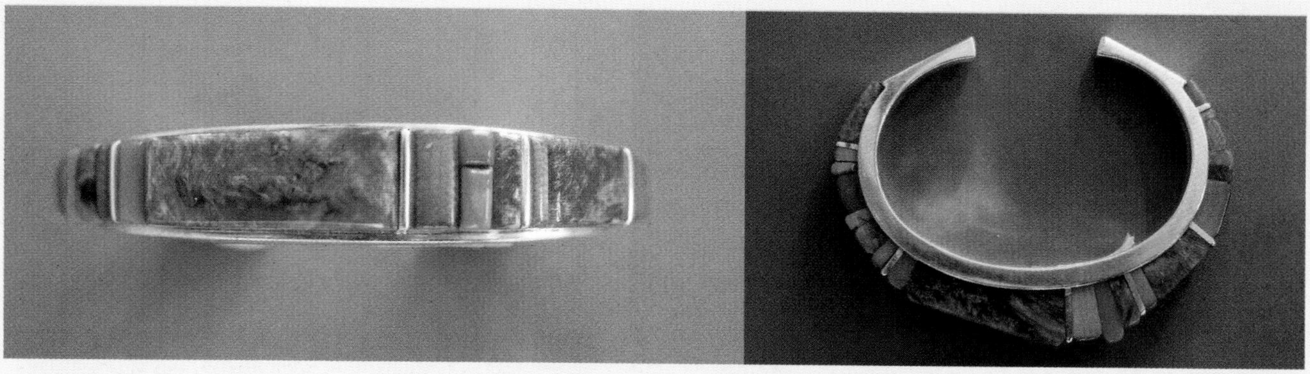

Bracelet, cuff, 14k yg, sugilite, turq, coral, tiger's eye, c. 1980, Hopi, varied size rect cabs of sugilite, turq, coral, and tiger's eye arranged in an irregular block design, mkd "14k," maker's mark for Charles Loloma, ½" w x 2¾" inside dia, **$11,000**. (Courtesy of Faust Gallery, Scottsdale, AZ, photo by Shari Watson Miller)

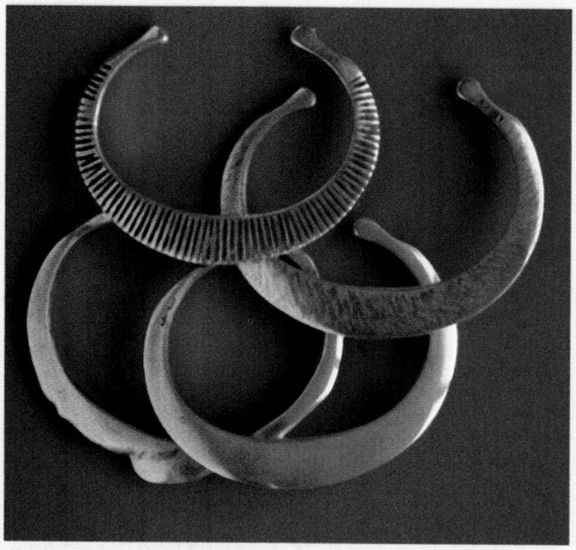

Bracelets, cuff, sterling, c. 1980, four crescent shapes to be worn together or separately, one with a smooth finish, one with vertical incised marks throughout, one with striated texturing, and one with a smooth finish with scalloped edge shape, each mkd with conjoined offset "FP," and a bar over "S" for Samuel Patania, Tucson, AZ, ¼" w x 2¼" inside dia, **$140** each. (Shari Watson Miller collection, photo by Shari Watson Miller)

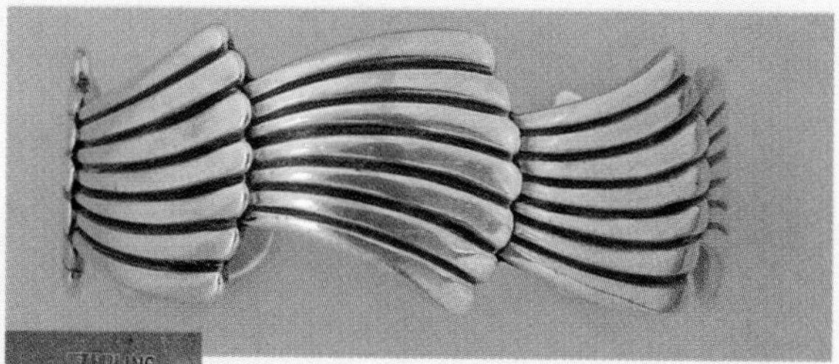

Bracelet, cuff, sterling, c. 1955, Navajo, overlapping curv scallop shell motifs with oxidized incised grooves, mkd "STERLING HAND MADE, GK" for George Kee, White Hogan mk, ⅞" w x 2⅛" inside dia, **$250**. (Author's collection)

Brooch/Pin, sterling, jet, MOP, turq, coral, shell, c. 1935-40, Zuni, knifewing god motif inlaid with jet, MOP, turq, coral, and colored shell, attributed to Leo Poblano, 3" w x 2½", **$1,250**. (Jon Bonnell collection, photo by Shari Watson Miller)

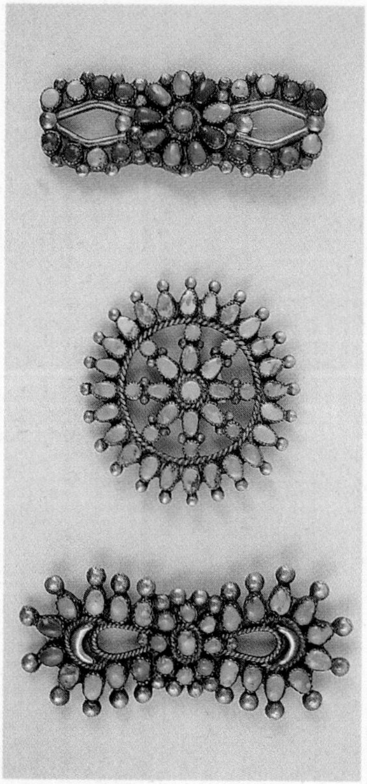

Brooches/Pins, turquoise, silver, c. 1940, Zuni:
T, in the shape of conjoined openwork lozenges outlined with circ turq cabs and appl silver beads, flanking a central floral decoration of clustered oval turq cabs, 2⅝" w x 1", **$250**. (Lisa Johnson collection)
C, openwork circle with a central eight-pointed star of circ and teardrop-shaped turq cabs framed in ropetwist wire, outer circle of teardrop-shaped turq cabs and appl silver bead terminals, 2" dia, **$210**.
B, in the shape of a figure 8 with central floral decoration of clustered circ turq cabs with an oval cab center, outlined with teardrop-shaped turq cabs and lg appl silver bead terminals, 3" w x 1½", **$220**. (Diane White collection)

Earrings, turquoise, silver, c. 1960, convex slightly tapered rectangles, inlaid with turquoise in a grid pattern, each suspending two undulating flat silver wires with stamped snake motifs, appl shepherd's hook earwires on rev, ½" w x 2⅜" tl, **$275**. (Lisa Johnson collection)

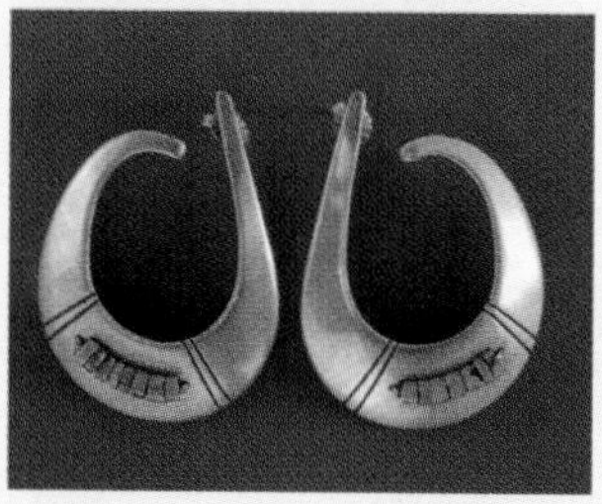

Earrings, sterling, turq, c. 1960, Navajo, penannular hoops, each with a row of eight small turq beads strung on wire flanked by a pair of parallel incised lines, post and clutch findings, mkd "STERLING HAND MADE," mk for White Hogan, maker's mark "KB" for Kenneth Begay, 1" w x 1½", **$450**. (Jon Bonnell collection, photo by Shari Watson Miller)

Zuni-style machine-made tourist jewelry, silver, Bakelite, c. 1925-30:
T, pendant, cross, and chain, six circ turq-colored cabs, each encircled by appl silver beads, suspended from a silver link chain, 1¼" w x 2½", **$50**.
B, necklace, crescent-shaped central section with a line of oval turq-colored cabs and appl silver beads, suspended from a chain of bowtie-shaped links with geo stampwork and appl silver beads, 14½" tl, **$125**. (Jon Bonnell collection, photo by Shari Watson Miller)

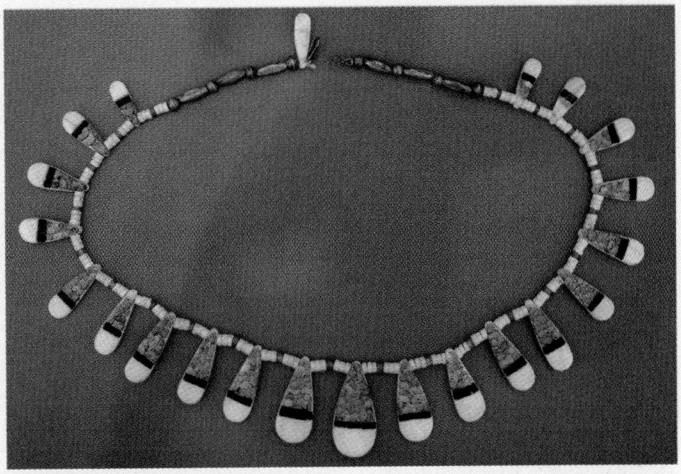

Necklace, bone, turquoise, jet, gypsum, silver, c. 1935, Santo Domingo, grad lengths of teardrop-shaped bone plaques with encrustations of turq and bands of jet, interspersed with tubular gypsum and turq beads, later restrung with added terminal silver beads, 24" tl, 1½" T to B at center, **$300**. (Jon Bonnell collection, photo by Shari Watson Miller)

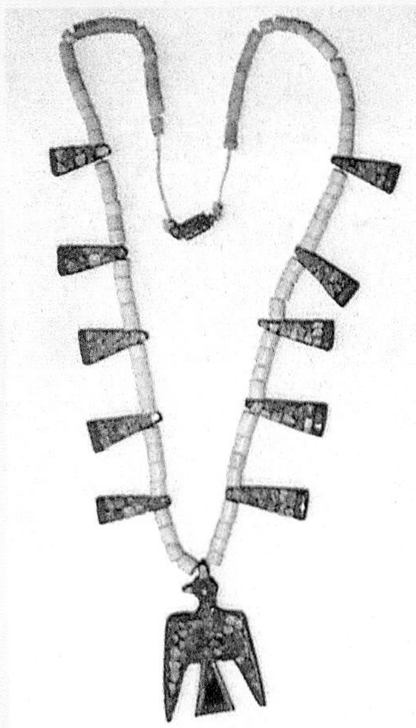

Necklace, turquoise, bone, Bakelite, plastic, c. 1940, Santo Domingo, a central thunderbird motif pendant flanked by triangular plaques, red plastic with inlaid mosaic turq and black Bakelite backs, interspersed with tubular bone beads, 22" tl, **$248** [A]. (Photo courtesy of R. G. Munn Auction, San Diego, CA, 10/12/01)

Necklace, silver, c. 1930, Navajo, cast central naja with three sets of radiating ridges, suspended from necklace of machine-stamped hollow beads interspersed with cutout Thunderbird motifs with stamped decoration, hook closure, 22¾" tl, 2¼" at center, **$500**. (Lisa Johnson collection)

Necklace, sterling, turquoise, c. 1950, Navajo, squash blossom motif, central double-row naja with lozenge-shaped stampwork and circ turq cab, suspended from lg silver beads interspersed with ten silver squash blossom-shaped beads, hook closure, 24" tl, **$250**. (Jon Bonnell collection, photo by Shari Watson Miller)

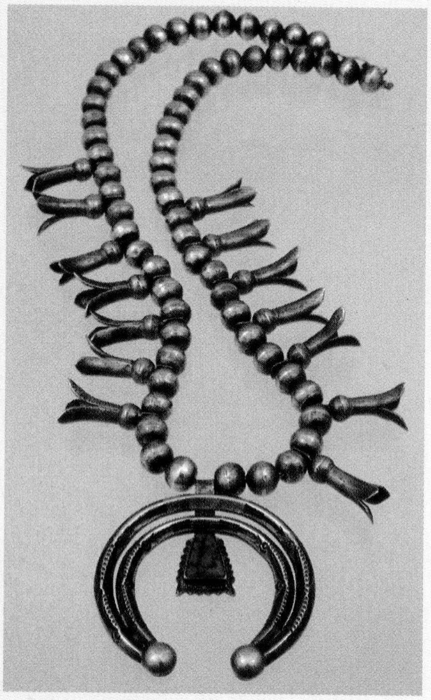

Necklace, sterling, turquoise, c. 1955, Hopi, a bezel-set tapered rect Fox turq with a saw-tooth-edged frame in the center of a bead-tipped double naja with stamped decoration, suspended from a necklace of hollow spherical beads interspersed with 14 squash blossom motifs, maker's mk for Morris Robinson (an H over a snake symbol with arrow-shaped head), 24" tl, **$1,800**. (Watson Miller collection, photo by Shari Watson Miller)

Necklace, sterling, coral, turq, c. 1955, reversible grad fringe, one side with top row of rect oxidized plaques set with lg oval #8 spider web turq, a middle row of square floral motif plaques with oval turq cabs and appl silver bead centers, bottom row of suspended melon-shaped coral beads with silver end caps, rev set throughout with coral, by Frank Patania Sr., 2½" w x 15" tl, **$10,000**. (Courtesy of Patania's Photographic Archive, photo by Sam Patania)

Necklace, sterling, c. 1960, Navajo, an articulated row of overlapping flat volutes suspended from a curb link chain, hook closure, mkd "STERLING," mk for White Hogan, 15" tl, **$300**. (Watson Miller collection, photo by Shari Watson Miller)

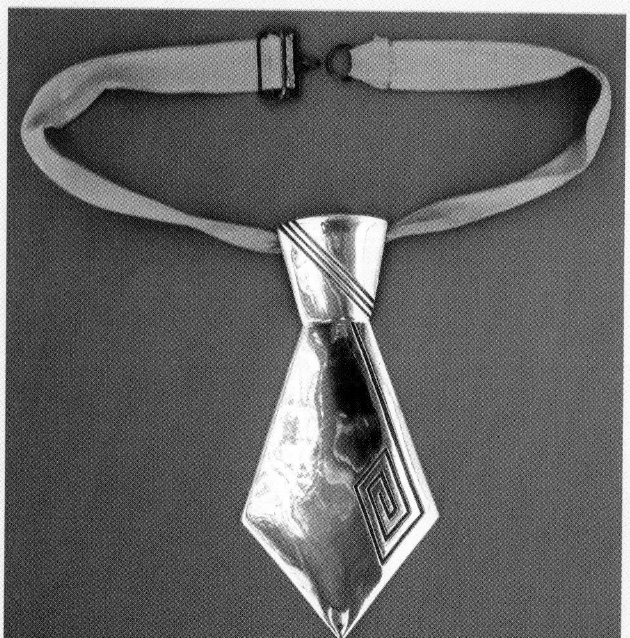

Pendant/Neckpiece, sterling, grosgrain ribbon, c. 1953, Navajo, in the shape of a necktie, slightly domed sterling plaque, geo incised lines, suspended from beige grosgrain ribbon with buckle clasp, mkd "STERLING HAND MADE," mk for White Hogan, maker's mk "KB" for Kenneth Begay, 3" w x 5½", **$750**. (Jon Bonnell collection, photo by Shari Watson Miller)

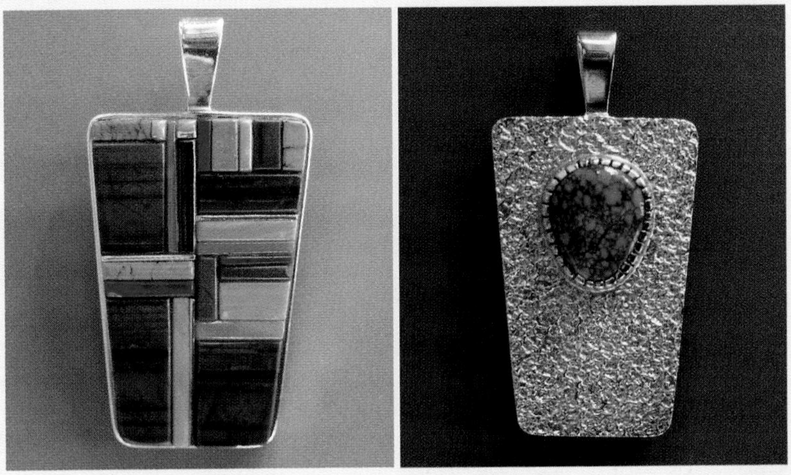

Pendant, 14k yg, sugilite, turquoise, coral, ironwood, lapis lazuli, c. 1980, Hopi, double-sided (reversible) keystone shape, inlaid with varied sizes of stone quadrangles on one face, a notched bezel-set ovoid turq cab on textured yg rev, maker's mk for Charles Loloma, "14k," 1½" w x 3" tl, **$7,600**. (Courtesy of Faust Gallery, Scottsdale, AZ, photo by Shari Watson Miller)

Rings, Hopi, maker's mk for Charles Loloma:
TL, sterling, coral, turq, c. 1968, tufa cast, flat rect face with oxidized ground and raised textured ridges, the center set with one rect coral cab and one rect turq cab, mounted on a wide brushed silver shank, ½" w x 1", **$2,100**.
TR, sterling, turquoise, tiger's eye, lapis lazuli, ironwood, malachite, c. 1980, raised center inlaid with a row of rect cabs channel-set in a ster band, ½" w, **$2,700**.
BL, 14k yg, coral, c. 1980, oval coral cab set in notched-edge bezel, mounted on a tapered smooth polished shank, ½" dia, **$1,750**.
BR, 14k yg, coral, c. 1980, an elongated elliptical coral cab in a notched bezel, one end mounted on a flat yg band with a polished shank, ½" w x 2¼", **$6,800**. (Courtesy of Faust Gallery, Scottsdale, AZ, photo by Shari Watson Miller)

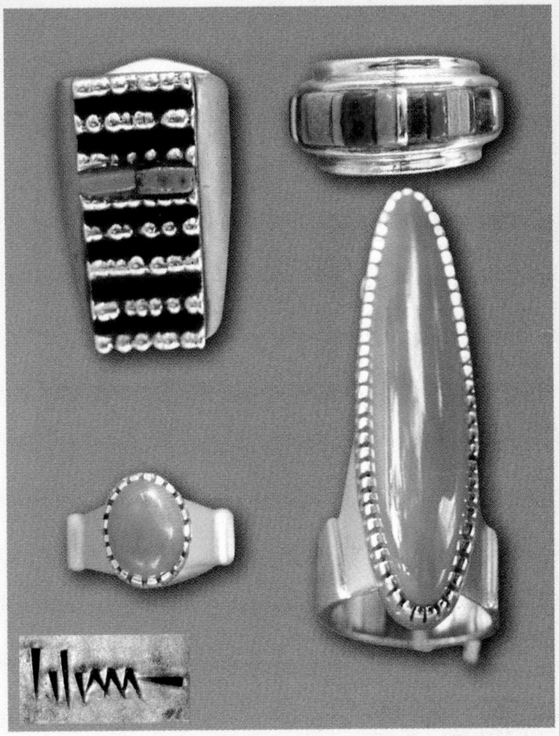

Suite: Bola tie and ring, coral, silver, c. 1970-79, Navajo, bola tie slide a lg oval central plaque with stamped, scalloped silver edge, set with kidney-shaped oxblood coral cabs in concentric circles edged in silver, matching ring, sgd "J.R.," slide 3" w x 4", ring 1" w x 2" at front, **$220** [A]. (Photo courtesy of R. G. Munn Auction, San Diego, CA, 10/13/01)

MEXICAN JEWELRY (TAXCO SCHOOL, c. 1930-1970)

Brooch/Pin, silver, amethyst, turquoise, c. 1940, a repoussé angelfish with amethyst cab body and sm turq cab eye, safety catch, flat back imp with maker's mk for Frederick Davis (conjoined FD) and "SILVER MEXICO," 2¾" w x 2⅜", **$2,500**. (Courtesy of D. Brett Benson, Inc., Chicago, IL)

Metalsmithing is a centuries-old Mexican tradition. Mexican plateros had already been practicing their craft for generations when they taught silversmithing to the Navajo in the 1870s. There are those who collect the traditional, regional, religious, and "folk art" jewelry of Mexico, which fall into the category of true "ethnic" jewelry, a subject covered in the first six chapters of Davis' and Pack's *Mexican Jewelry* (referenced in the back of the book). The last chapter, which up until recently was virtually the sole source of information for collectors, is on the product of a unique, 20twentieth-century multicultural amalgam of Mexican, U.S., and European cultures, centered in the town of Taxco (pronounced TAHS-co). This is the place where one man and a serendipitous combination of events founded an industry in 1931.

The story really begins in the 1920s in Mexico City, where another man, an American named Frederick Davis, began designing jewelry and small objects as a sideline to his main occupation as manager of the Sonora News Company. His designs were based on ancient pre-Hispanic motifs, which he had made up in silver, sometimes adding obsidian, a native volcanic glass, or amethyst quartz, a stone which is also indigenous to Mexico (see above right). Some of Davis' designs reflect the modernity of the period in smooth shaped plaques which were quite compatible with his use of the geometric motifs found in the clay stamps of pre-Conquest (before 1520) native Mexican tribes.

During a time when most Mexican jewelry was based on colonial, religious, or regional designs, and usually made of gold, Davis' work was unique, and seminal to later developments in Taxco. His simple, stylized obsidian face design, which he set into necklaces, bracelets, brooches, and clips, was the precursor to what would become ubiquitous tourist-souvenir carved stone face jewelry in the '40s and '50s.

In 1933, Davis went to work for Sanborn's as the manager of the antiques and handcrafts shop housed in the restaurant-cum-gift store in downtown Mexico City that still operates today in the historic House of Blue Tile. He continued designing jewelry, which was made and sold alongside Sanborn's own more conventional line of silver articles. Perhaps catering to the burgeoning tourist trade of the time, some Davis designs are of traditional Mexican motifs, like bullfighters and sombrero-clad *paisanos*; others are of then-popular floral sprays. Davis was not a prolific designer, so his pieces are relatively scarce, and important to collectors because they were the first of their kind.

Meanwhile, in 1929, in a little mining village in the mountains southwest of Mexico City, another American had arrived. As an architect from Tulane University in New Orleans, he had come to Taxco to study Spanish Colonial architecture. As a writer, he was to write a book about Mexico (*Little Mexico*, published in 1932). As an artist, he made sketches of the local scenery. But in fact, it was as a designer and the proprietor of a little shop selling trinkets to tourists that this twentieth-century Renaissance man, William Spratling (1900-1967), became most famous. Responding to a comment from a friend, U.S. Ambassador Dwight Morrow, Spratling conceived the idea of working the silver that had been mined in the area for centuries, along with other native materials, such as amethyst, obsidian, and rosewood. He created jewelry and objects that were a strikingly original synthesis of Mexican and cosmopolitan design.

When Spratling opened his shop, later called *Taller de Las Delicias* (the Delights Workshop), in 1931, he had one master silversmith executing his ideas, and a few young local boys as apprentices. They made pieces entirely by hand with the crudest of implements. Spratling's earliest designs were necessarily simple: the plainest of button earrings, traditional buckles with incised decoration, and plaque brooches based on pre-Hispanic and ranchero motifs, all made of heavy gauge, high- grade silver (early Spratling pieces are sometimes marked "980"–containing only 2 percent alloy). These were offered for sale, along with other regional handicrafts such as textiles, tinware, and furniture, in the old abandoned customs house that became Taxco's first workshop.

In 1927, the road from Mexico City to the popular resort of Acapulco had reached Taxco, which was conveniently located half-way between the two cities. With the growth of auto travel and tourism, Spratling's timing was perfect. His shop became a favorite tourist stop, his pieces sold well, and his business grew. By 1940, he had more than 300 artisans working for him. He had made Taxco a major tourist destination, famous for its silverwork. It became a single-industry town, with successive generations carrying on the work of their predecessors.

Today there are more than 10,000 silversmiths working in the area. While the craftsmanship of some of them rivals that found in any other country, many continue to make the cheap tourist trinkets known as *chácharas*, or they merely copy the designs of others, a common practice since the 1940s. Only a few of the best and most original designers and work-

Bracelet, cuff, sterling, amethyst, c. 1940, zig-zag design with incised line decoration, open center with a row of five bezel-set circ amethyst cabs, 1940-45 maker's mk for William Spratling, 2¼" w x 2⅝" inside dia, **$2,000**. (Jill Crawford collection)

shops have survived the test of time. Their work, marks, and names have become well known to collectors. Identification of marks is especially important with Mexican silver in determining values, which have escalated as interest has grown over the past few years (see appendix, Marks and Names on Mexican Silver). This is because plagiarism of original designs was (and is) rampant. Spratling's work is understandably the most widely copied. Spratling used a number of different marks, most of them incorporating a conjoined WS (one notorious copyist, Serafín Moctezuma, used his own conjoined initials, which look like WS upside down). He took his first mark from his ranch's brand for his horses.

Around 1940, Victor Silson, a businessman with whom Spratling had been in partnership, "appropriated" and patented some of his designs and manufactured them in the U.S., in pewter and silverplate. He used Spratling's conjoined WS mark with "Silson, Inc." under it. These have limited collector interest and do not bring the high prices of Spratling originals.

During World War II, business in Taxco was booming. Spratling exported quantities of silver to U.S. stores cut off from European trade, including Neiman Marcus, Saks Fifth Avenue, Macy's, Lord & Taylor, and Montgomery Ward. Even Ward's catalogs pictured Spratling silver objects and jewelry with hefty pricetags for the time. A 980 silver and carved amethyst Spratling cuff bracelet was originally priced at $45.95 in 1943. The mark found most often on Spratling pieces from the early 1940s was used for those that were sold through Ward's (see above).

Spratling changed his mark in 1949, after he had moved his shop to his ranch outside of town, where he lived and worked until his accidental death in 1967. The jewelry of Spratling's later period is more refined and stylized than his early work (see buckle on page 228). He was influenced, as were many others, by abstract modernism and Scandinavian design. Some later pieces were also made in 18 karat gold.

Spratling established a hierarchical training system still in use today. As his apprentices moved through the ranks to become master silversmiths, some of them showed a talent for creativity, as well as skill in executing Spratling's ideas. Their *patrón* (boss) encouraged them to open their own shops and produce their own designs. Many of them did; some were very successful at making names for themselves and establishing individual styles. They are recognized today as the innovators of the Taxco School begun and inspired by William Spratling.

The four brothers Castillo were among the first to go out on their own, opening their shop, Los Castillo, in 1939. The family business became one of the largest, expanding to stores in Mexico City, as well as Taxco. They are still in operation today, with second and third generations turning out both old and new designs. Don Antonio Castillo, the sole survivor of the first generation, died in 2000. The Castillos' contributions include innovative metalworking techniques and many original designs. Their most famous design, *Perfil de Perico* (profile of parrot) incorporates the techniques of *metales casados* (married metals) and *mosaico azteca* (stone inlay), which are actually refinements of ancient Mexican Indian methods. Jorge "Chato" Castillo was the brother who developed these and other techniques. Some of Chato's designs bear his personal mark (see bracelet on page 226). See examples of Los Castillo's wide-ranging talents on pages 226, 227, 228, 229 and 230.

Héctor Aguilar (1905-1986) was the manager of the Spratling shop until 1939, when he opened his own *Taller Borda* in the center of town. Aguilar was influenced by Spratling's early work with ranchero motifs. He usually used 940 silver without stones, but his earliest work was almost pure silver (980 or 990), as were the decorative elements on some of his later belts and bracelets in leather. In the mid-1960s, Aguilar closed the *taller* and moved with his wife to the resort town of Zihuatanejo. Always sought-after, Aguilar's pieces are in even greater demand now that a book focusing primarily on his work has been published, *Silver Masters of Mexico* (see References). See below and page 226for examples by Aguilar.

Antonio Pineda, another early Spratling apprentice, opened his shop in 1941. His mark, "Antonio Taxco" in the shape of a crown, first used circa 1950, is an important one to know, as his work is sought-after and often copied. He is a favorite among modernists, because of the sleek simplicity

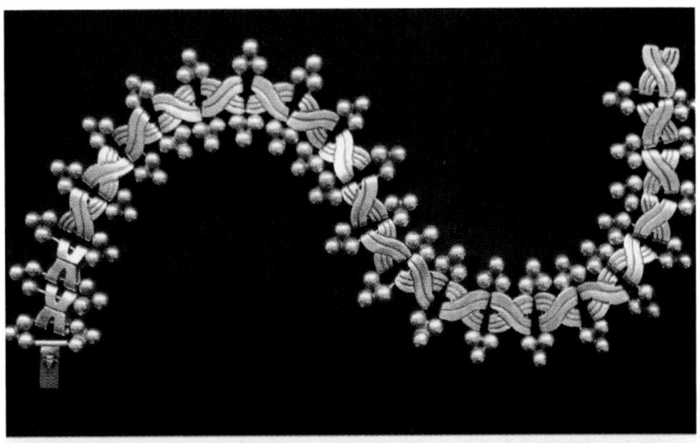

Necklace, sterling, c. 1948, repeating design of crossover X-shaped links with flat-chased decoration alternating with triple bead clusters at either side of hinges, v-spring and box clasp, maker's mk for Hector Aguilar (conjoined HA), 1" w x 13" tl, **$2,500**. (Jill Crawford collection, photo by Spencer McDonald)

and superior craftsmanship of his designs. He preferred to use high-grade (970) silver and often incorporated gemstones in his work, some not usually found in Mexican silver, such as moonstones, chrysocolla, and topaz. Antonio lives in Taxco in semi-retirement. Pieces by Antonio are on pages 226, 227, 228, 230, and 231.

Margot van Voorhies Carr Castillo, whose mark was "Margot de Taxco," was one of the few women who owned their own shops. She was married to Antonio Castillo and designed for Los Castillo before opening her shop in 1948. Margot was an artist and world traveler who is known for a wide variety of styles and motifs inspired by Art Deco, Egyptian, Arts and Crafts, Art Nouveau and Mexican designs. She is most noted for the use of polychromatic champlevé and basse-taille enamels, which allowed the painterly expression of her love of color. Margot died in 1985. Margot designs are pictured below and on pages 228 and 231.

Another woman whose work is unmistakably distinctive (and often copied) is Matilde Poulat. She began working in Mexico City in 1934, and opened a retail shop in 1950. Her pieces are typically repoussé silver set with amethysts, turquoise, or coral (or a combination). Her motifs are often figural—birds, fish, butterflies, or religious figures and crosses (see pages 226 and 229). Her larger items tend to be quite ornately decorated. Matilde (mark: "Matl") died in 1960, but her nephew, Ricardo Salas Poulat (mark: "Matl" over "Salas"), continues to make jewelry in a similar style.

In the 1950s, the next generation of silversmiths began opening their own shops. These were silversmiths who had trained under Spratling and also worked for his first protégés. Each of the ones whose jewelry and objects are collected today had a distinctive approach to design, but the influence of 1950s modernism can be clearly seen throughout their work.

Enrique Ledesma was the first of this generation to have his own establishment, which he opened in 1950. Until then, he had worked for Spratling and Los Castillo. One of Ledesma's signature techniques was to inlay stone into silver and shape the two materials together as a unit. The units were then linked for bracelets and necklaces, or used singly for a brooch or an earring (see bracelets above). Ledesma also used silver alone in shaped and oxidized hinged bangles and brooches. His mark is his last name with an elongated L underlining it. Ledesma died in 1979.

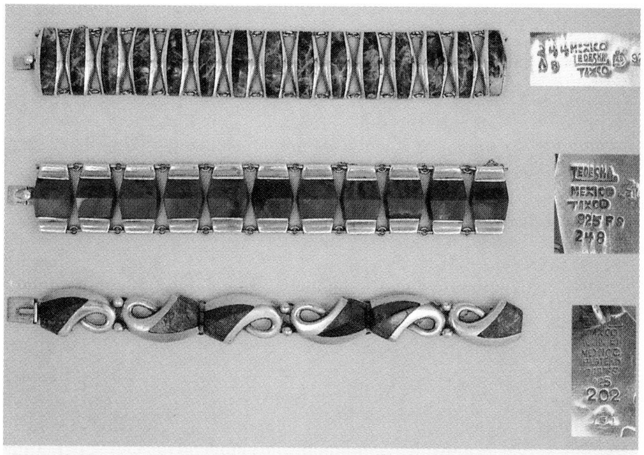

Bracelets, link, sterling and gemstones, by Enrique Ledesma, c. 1955:
T, 15 tapered oblong links with squared ends, each inlaid with a ridged rect sodalite cab, all connected with sm circ jump rings, v-spring and box clasp, safety chain, mkd "LEDESMA MEXICO 244 TAXCO 925 AB" and Mexican government assay mk #60, 1" w x 7" tl, **$275**.
C, 11 convex rect links centering red jasper and quartz ridged truncated lozenge-shaped plaques with concave ster terminals, joined with sm circ jump rings, v-spring and box clasp, safety chain, mkd "LEDESMA TAXCO MEXICO 925 FS" #248 and Mexican government assay mk #3, 1" w x 7" tl, **$325**.
B, six tapered swirl links with inlaid ridged cusped azur-malachite triangles at wide end of each link, forming opposed prs with a double sphere interlink, v-spring and box clasp, safety chain, mkd "LEDESMA 202 TAXCO HECHO EN MEXICO PLATERA CORTÉS 925" and Mexican government assay mark # 3, ¾" w x 7¼" tl, **$350**. (Author's collection)

Felipe Martinez was another Fifties Generation silversmith whose shop, also opened in 1950, was called *Piedra y Plata* (stone and silver). True to the name, most of Martinez's designs are combinations of silver and turquoise, obsidian, azurmalachite, or other opaque stone inlaid in smooth geometric patterns, or bezel-set and joined to silver shapes. Martinez also made stone carvings which Hubert Harmon and others in Taxco incorporated into their jewelry designs.

Salvador Terán was a cousin of the Castillos, for whom he worked until the opening of his own shop in Mexico City in 1952 (he was also one of Spratling's apprentices in the '30s). Davis and Pack called him "original, inventive, and versatile" (*Mexican Jewelry*, p.213), and indeed his imagination seemed to know no bounds. He designed some strikingly modern pieces, and others that display a fanciful sense of humor. One of his trademarks was creating a three-dimensional effect with cutout motifs mounted on pegs above an oxidized surface. He signed his pieces "Salvador" in script. Salvador died in 1974. See earrings on page 229, tie bar on page 231.

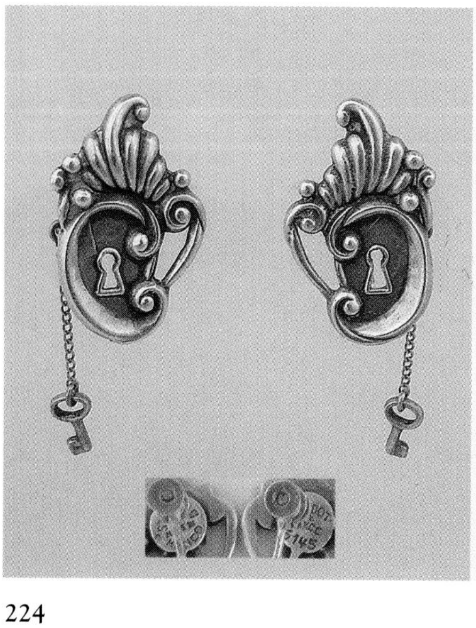

Earrings, sterling, c. 1945-50, repoussé design of ear-shaped plaques, each with scrolled decoration at top and a key-hole center, suspending a key charm on a chain to one side, mkd "MARGOT DE TAXCO," #5145, "STERLING MADE IN MEXICO," ⅝" w x 1¾" tl, **$175**. (Author's collection)

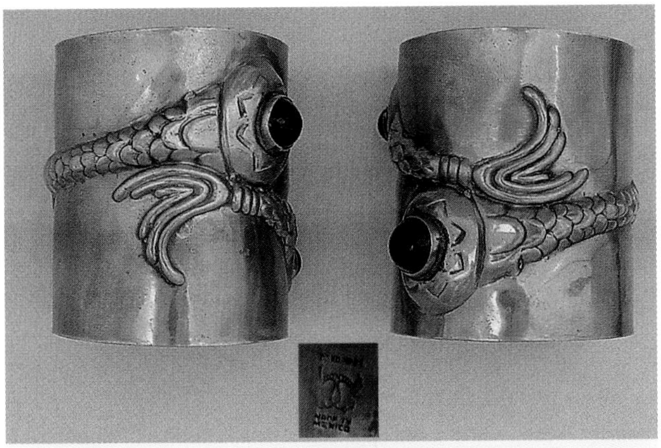

Bracelets, cuffs, brass, obsidian, c. 1945, slightly tapered brass cuffs with repoussé stylized fish motifs with single lg circ obsidian cab "eye," imp with maker's mk for Hubert Harmon, "HAND MADE, MADE IN MEXICO," 3" w x 2⅜" inside dia, **$3,500/pr.** (Author's collection)

The sole survivor of the Fifties Generation of silversmiths is Sigi (pronounced SEE-hee, b. 1929), who opened his shop in Taxco in 1953, after working for Los Castillo and for Margot as her shop foreman. Sigi was the only Mexican silversmith out of the 22 who were awarded prizes in a flatware design contest sponsored by International Silver in Connecticut in 1960. His designs reflect both American and Scandinavian modernist influence, yet they are identifiably his own. Sigi recently resumed designing and making new pieces, which are crafted with the same careful attention to detail and finishing as his earlier work. His signature is "Sigi Tasco" (the alternate spelling of Taxco). See pages 228, 231.

Hubert Harmon (1913-2002) was an eccentric American artist who lived and worked in Taxco, where his taller produced his designs from c.1943 to 1948. A few years ago, he was "rediscovered" living in Mexico, where he was interviewed by Penny Morrill for her article, cited in the References. He designed out-of-the-ordinary pieces which are scarce and highly collectible today. He had a bizarre sense of humor, as well as an imaginative eye. Whimsical motifs were his specialty—including his mark, a pair of winged feet (see brass cuffs above).

Penny Morrill has also written about another recent "rediscovery," the identity of the designer who signs with the mark "Ric" in script. Erika Hult de Corral began using this mark in her own workshop in 1965, after having worked for Sigi and Enrique Ledesma. Morrill's article for *Silver* magazine (see References) contains several photographs from the collection of Fred and Stella Krieger, as well as biographical information (see brooch page 228 and earrings page 229).

Morill is also curator of an important traveling exhibition, "William Spratling and the Mexican Silver Renaissance: *Maestros de Plata*," which opened at the San Antonio (Texas) Museum of Art in October 2002. She edited the accompanying information-filled catalog (see References), which is sure to generate greater interest in pieces by recognized Mexican designers, both past and present.

Many other Taxco designers and silversmiths have worked in relative obscurity. Only their output and their marks are known. Of the literally hundreds, and at present, thousands, who have worked or are working there, only a few, in addition to the ones mentioned above, have been identified and referenced in any book or catalog. These include: Manuel Altamirano, Carmen Beckmann, Ana Nuñez Brilanti (shop name and mark "Victoria"), Isidro García (shop name and mark, "Maricela"), Bernice Goodspeed, Los Ballesteros, Gerardo López, Emma Melendez and Miguel Melendez, and Valentín Vidaurreta.

Little written documentation is available on those whose pieces surface repeatedly, which are well-made, with distinctive maker's marks, and others whose initials are all that is known (the recently published *Little Book of Mexican Silver Trade and Hallmarks* by Bille Hougart is the most thorough compilation to date; it includes many of these unknown makers' marks). In addition, there are many pieces of excellent quality with no identifying marks at all, other than "sterling, *Hecho en* (or) Made in Mexico" (or variations). Because of this lack of documentation, attribution, and name recognition, values are comparatively low. As with any jewelry, however, both signed pieces by known makers and unsigned or unknown work should be evaluated with the same criteria. Even some Spratling pieces are less than exemplary, and certainly there is a great quantity of Taxco silver made by unknowns who deserve to remain so.

Reproduction Alert

Between 1946 (or thereabouts) and 1979, the Mexican government required the stamping of a "spread eagle" assay mark on any piece that was made of 925 (sterline) silver or above. In 1979, the eagle mark was abandoned, and since then all workshops have been required to use individually assigned registry marks of two letters and two or three numbers, separated by a hyphen. Although some pieces escape marking, any item taken out of exported from Mexico should be marked. This is one way to differentiate new from old pieces by the same workshop. Since Spratling's death in 1967, his designs have been produced by the current owner of his estate. The recently-made pieces bear the later WS maker's mark, along with the registry number TS-24. Copies of Spratling designs, unsigned or signed by others, were also commonly made during Spratling's lifetime, as they continue to be today. Antonio Pineda and Margot de Taxco fakes regularly appear on the market. Unsigned Frederick Davis designs are common. Los Castillo and Héctor Aguilar designs are reproduced somewhat less frequently. Of the Fifties Generation, Salvador and Ledesma are seldom copied, but Sigi's pieces often are.

Bracelet, link, sterling, turquoise, coral, c. 1945, central convex rect openwork plaque decorated throughout with wire volutes and S-scrolls around an urn motif flanked by two repoussé birds, each surmounted by a curved row of five sm turq cabs, the center with three lg circ turq cabs above a curved row of five sm circ coral cabs, and sm circ turq cabs in bottom corners, joined on each side to four rounded rect pierced plaques, each a pr of volutes with three central coral cabs and a sm circ turq cab in volute centers, v-spring and box clasp, clasp rev mkd "MATL *HECHO EN MEXICO*" in a circle around "0.925" for Matilde Poulat, opposite terminal link engr "Matl" in lg script, 1⅞" w x 8" tl, **$1,500**. (Courtesy of D. Brett Benson, Inc., Chicago, IL)

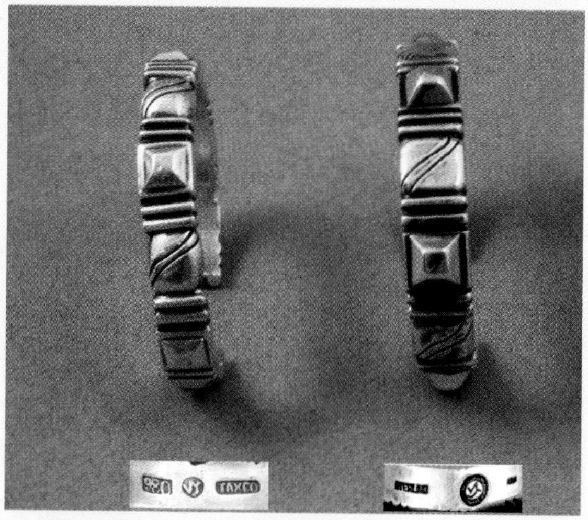

Bracelets, cuff, by William Spratling, variations of "pyramid" design:

L, 980 silver, c. 1935-40, shaped ster bar with geo design of pillow shapes, each with two incised diagonal undulating parallel lines, alternating with appl truncated pyramids and flanked by deep ridges, maker's mk for William Spratling (serif WS), "980 TAXCO," ½" w, **$1,400**.

R, sterling, 18k yg, c. 1945, appl 18k yg truncated pyramids, mkd "STERLING" and "18K," 1940-1945 maker's mk for William Spratling, ⅝" w, **$1,800**. (Jill Crawford collection)

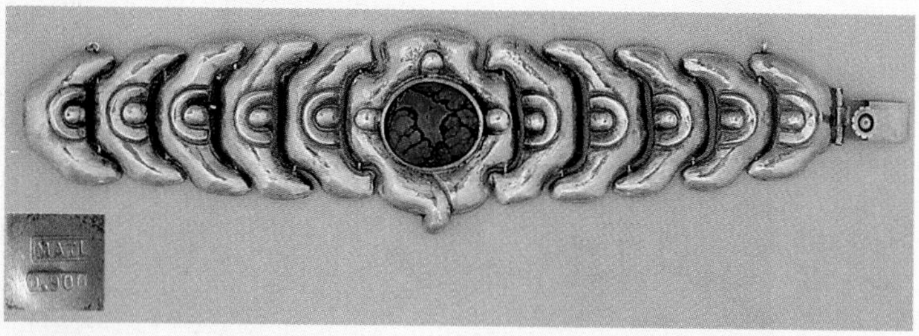

Bracelet, link, 900 silver, malachite, c. 1945, repoussé design with an equilateral cross-shaped center bezel-set with an oval malachite cab, flanked by five flattened U-shaped repoussé sections each with a central raised bead, v-spring and box clasp, safety chain, mkd "MATL" for Matilde Poulat, "0.900," 1⅝" w x 6½" tl, **$650**. (Author's collection)

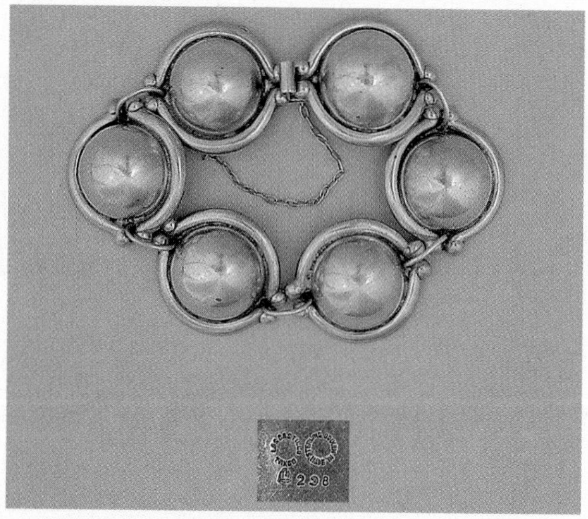

Bracelet, link, sterling, c. 1955, links of polished domes, each encircled by ball-tipped round wire, v-spring and box clasp, safety chain, mkd "LOS CASTILLO TAXCO" in a circle, "STERLING MADE IN MEXICO" in a circle, #298 and eagle assay mk #15, 7⅛" tl, links 1" dia, **$375**. (Courtesy of Gilly Phipps, Philadelphia, PA)

Bracelet, link, sterling, turquoise, coral, pearls, c. 1955, alternating convex sq and concave circ links, each sq plaque with four elongated cutout prongs centering a baroque pearl, each circ link centering an irregular turq held by two prongs set with pieces of branch coral and linked to sq plaques, v-spring and box clasp, mkd "CHATO CASTILLO, TAXCO MEXICO, 925," ¾" w x 8" tl, $850. (Watson Miller collection, photo by Shari Watson Miller)

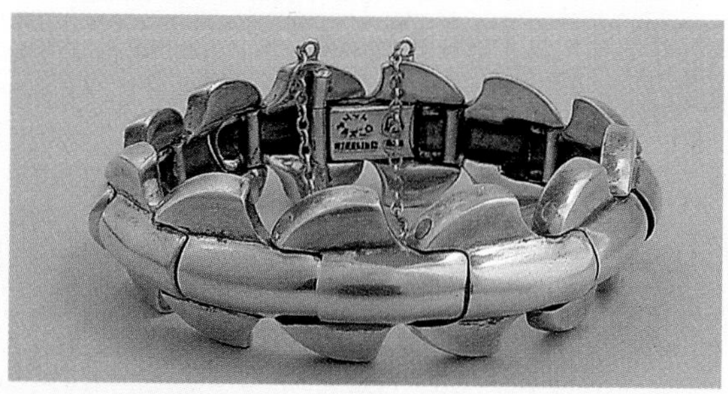

Bracelet, link, 970 silver, c. 1955, design by Antonio Pineda of interlocking wrench-shaped links, v-spring and box clasp, safety chain, illegible maker's mk, mkd "TAXCO 970" and eagle assay mk #208, ⅞" w x 8½" tl, **$1,000**. (Courtesy of Patrick Kapty, Mad Jewelry, Palm Springs, CA)

Bracelet, link, 940 silver, c. 1950, pre-Hispanic motifs of alternating stylized X-shaped and lozenge-shaped links, with flat-chased decoration and appl indented spheres, appl beads above and below, maker's mk for Hector Aguilar (conjoined HA), "TAXCO 940" and eagle assay mk #9, 1" w x 6⅞", **$1,000.** (Author's collection)

Bracelet, link, sterling, aventurine quartz, pearls, c. 1960, seven lyre-shaped links, each center bezel-set with an oval aventurine quartz cab, each hinge surmounted by a bezel-set pearl, imp with maker's mk (crown) for Antonio Pineda, illegible eagle assay mark, "TAXCO" and illegible three-letter craftsman's mk, v-spring and box clasp, 2⅜" inside dia, 1⅛" w, **$3,500**. (Courtesy of D. Brett Benson, Inc., Chicago, IL)

Bracelet, hinged wraparound bangle, sterling, c. 1950, hollow repoussé design with opposed double-scrolled terminals and raised bead accents, oxidized recesses and polished raised areas, imp with maker's mk for Gerardo Lopez, "TAXCO" and eagle assay mk #26, 3¼" T to B at center, 2½" inside dia, **$1,200**. (Courtesy of D. Brett Benson, Inc., Chicago, IL)

Bracelet, hinged bangle, sterling, synthetic alexandrite-like corundum, c. 1965, seven concentric ovals of round silver wire encircling a lg bezel-set oval faceted gemstone, forming a conical design, joined to a tapered ster back mkd "STERLING TAXCO 925" in a circle around unknown maker's mk "LC," #147, eagle assay mk #3, v-spring and box clasp, safety chain, 2⅛" inside dia, **$950**. (Courtesy of D. Brett Benson, Inc., Chicago, IL)

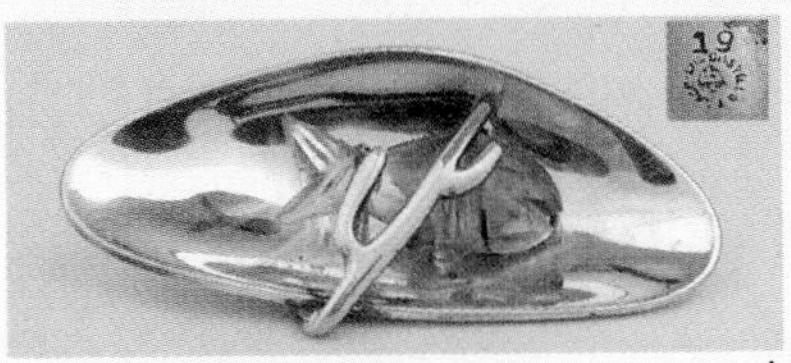

Brooch/Pin, sterling, carved amethyst, copper, c. 1955, concave elongated irregular oval ster plaque with two sm *metales casados* copper fish shapes flanking a lg carved amethyst fish at center surmounted by a copper "coral" branch, safety catch, imp "LOS CASTILLO TAXCO" in a circle around illegible eagle assay mk, #19, 2½" w x 1¼", **$295**. (Courtesy of Andrea Fatell, Wellsley, MA)

Bracelets, sterling

L, hinged bangle, amethysts, smokey quartz, synthetic gemstones, c. 1960-70, slightly tapered rect plaque forming each side of bangle, allover design of incised four-pointed stars alternating with faceted oval gemstones in high pronged bezels, mkd "LOS BALLESTEROS TAXCO GRO" in a circle around the stylized lg "B" maker's mk, "STERLING 925 *HECHO EN MEXICO*," 1⅝" w x 2½" inside dia, **$395**. (Courtesy of Andrea Fatell, Wellsley, MA)

R, c. 1950, four lg rounded sq hinged links, each with an overlaid pre-Hispanic motif and chased border, v-spring and box clasp with safety chain, maker's mk for Pedro Castillo (superimposed PC), eagle #103, "TAXCO," 1⅝" w x 2⅜" inside dia, **$400**. (Caren Fine collection)

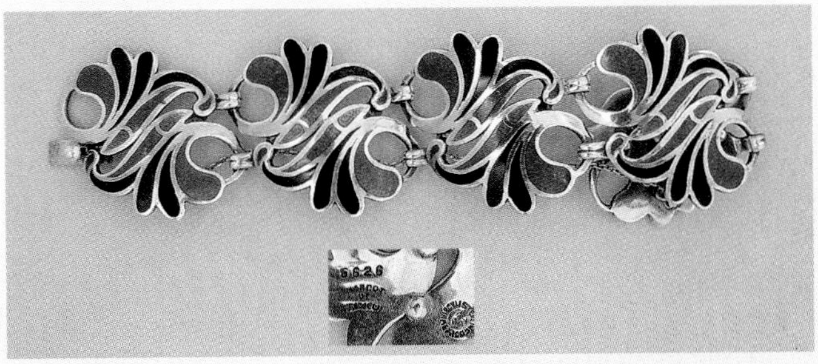

Bracelet, link, sterling, enamel, c. 1960, links of opposed lobed segmented scrolls, black champlevé and rust-brown *basse-taille* enameled lobes, sgd "MARGOT DE TAXCO," #5626, "MADE IN MEXICO STERLING" around eagle #16, 1⅜" w by 7¼" tl, **$600**. (Author's collection)

Brooch/Pendant and Brooch/Pin by Antonio Pineda, sterling, amethysts, c. 1950:

L, repoussé ster in the shape of a turbaned woman's head with carved amethyst face, a circ opal cab bezel-set within a starburst appl to turban, suspending two drops with teardrop-shaped earrings and carved circ amethyst cabs in the shapes of breasts bezel-set in starburst frames, rev mkd "SILVER BY TOÑO" in a circ for Antonio Pineda and "MEXICO PR 241," safety catch, two appl rings on rev for chain, 1½" w x 4⅛", **$3,500**.

R, a three-dimensional repoussé knot motif surmounted by a chased ridged swirl, suspending a fringe of five articulated tubular drops of irregular lengths with flared ends and drop-shaped amethyst cab terminals, safety catch, maker's mk (crown) for Antonio Pineda, eagle assay mk #17 and "PR 517 *HECHO EN MEXICO* SILVER," 1¼" w x 4¼", **$1,200**. (Courtesy of D. Brett Benson, Inc., Chicago, IL)

Brooch/Pin, sterling, c. 1955, boomerang shape, layered with a polished section surmounting an oxidized backing, imp "Sigi Tasco, STERLING *HECHO EN MEXICO*" #248, illegible eagle assay mk, 2¼" x 2⅛", **$175**. (Almunir Meghji collection)

Brooch/Pin, sterling, amethysts, c. 1975, overlapping three-dimensional biomorphic shapes in brushed silver with appl silver plaque through center bezel-set with four sm circ amethyst cabs, mkd "Ric" in script for Erika Hult de Corral, "TAXCO STERLING 925," #48 and eagle assay mk #3, 2½" w x 2", **$225**. (Photo courtesy of M. Schon Antiques, Bay St. Louis, MS)

Brooch/Pin, sterling, glass and stone beads, c. 1970, starburst design in hammered textured cutout silver sheet with five silver bead-topped columns of alternating pink glass beads and black stone beads, central volute surmounted by a silver bead-topped black stone, mkd "STERLING TAXCO" in a circle around "AC" and "*HECHO EN MEXICO* TOÑO 925," 4" w x 3½", **$2,500**. (Courtesy of D. Brett Benson, Inc., Chicago, IL)

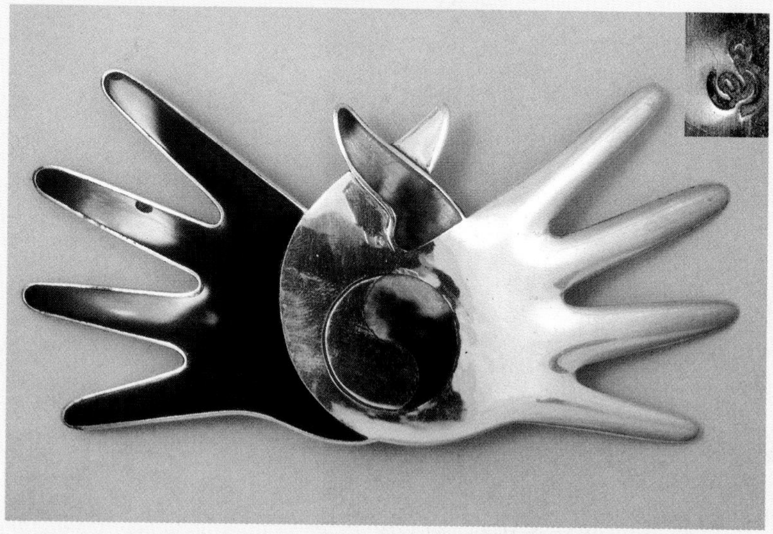

Buckle, sterling, tortoiseshell, c. 1950-55, two opposing open hand shapes with interlocking thumbs centering a yin-yang symbol, one hand in tortoiseshell inlay, the other in polished silver, maker's mk for William Spratling (script), 5¾" w x 2½" T to B, **$2,500**. (Jill Crawford collection)

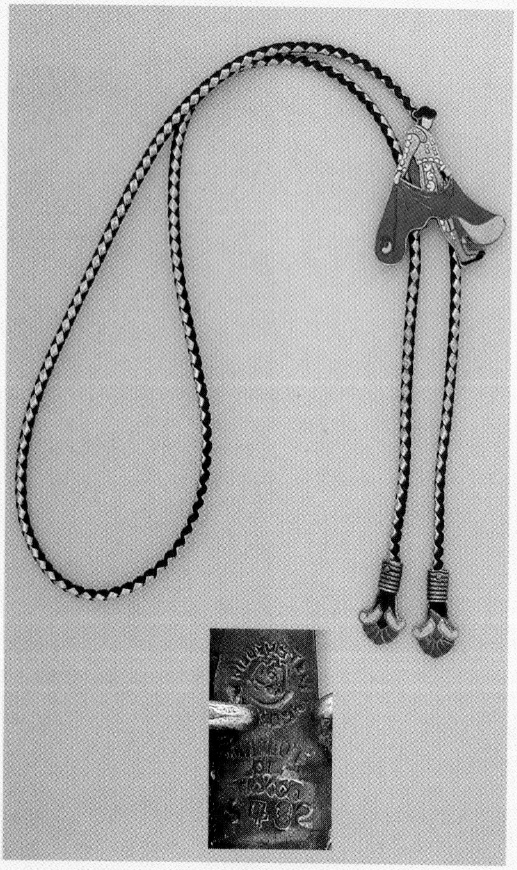

Bola Tie, sterling, enamel, leather, vinyl, c. 1955, slide a polychrome enameled matador figure in black, red, yellow, blue, white, and brown, with enameled stylized floral motif tips mounted on a braided gold vinyl and black leather tie, rev of slide imp "MARGOT DE TAXCO 5482" and "MADE IN MEXICO STERLING" in a circle around eagle assay mk #16, slide 1¾" w x 2" l x 16¼" tl, **$300**. (Author's collection)

Cuff Links, sterling, c. 1955, toggle findings:
L, irregular rectangles with dark bg and polished boomerang raised section to one side, mkd "Sigi" and "TASCO" in overlapping ovals, "STERLING *HECHO EN MEXICO*" in a circle, "01," and eagle assay mk #35, ½" x ⅞", **$100**.
C, two crescent-shaped sections, one with black enamel and a post-set pearl, the other in polished silver with a black enamel dot, centering an eye-shaped cutout section, maker's mk (crown) for Antonio Pineda and eagle assay mk #17, ¾" x 1⅛", **$200**.
R, concave kite-shaped oxidized sections with three appl polished spheres, rev mkd "Sigi" and "TASCO" in overlapping ovals, "STERLING *HECHO EN MEXICO* 48" and eagle assay mk #3, ⅞" x ¾", **$100**. (Almunir Meghji collection)

Earrings, silver, coral, turquoise, c. 1940, each an elaborate chased and repoussé bird motif with a sm circ coral cab eye, suspending a cutout cloud-shaped plaque with appl wire, spheres, and a row of five sm circ turq cabs, further suspending a fringe of three teardrops with circ terminals set with sm circ turq cabs, circ jump rings connecting each part, screwbacks, appl plaque on rev of one earring imp "Matl" in script for Matilde Poulat, 1" w x 2⅛", **$300**. (Diane White collection)

Earrings, white metal, feathers, c. 1960, two-sided circ flat disks with cutouts on brushed front surface forming a stylized peacock over an interior of polychrome feather inlay, two layers joined with rivets, screwbacks, mkd "PLUMA AZTECA" in a circle and "LOS CASTILLO TAXCO" in a circle around #2, "*HECHO EN MEXICO*," 1⅛" dia, **$105**. (Author's collection)

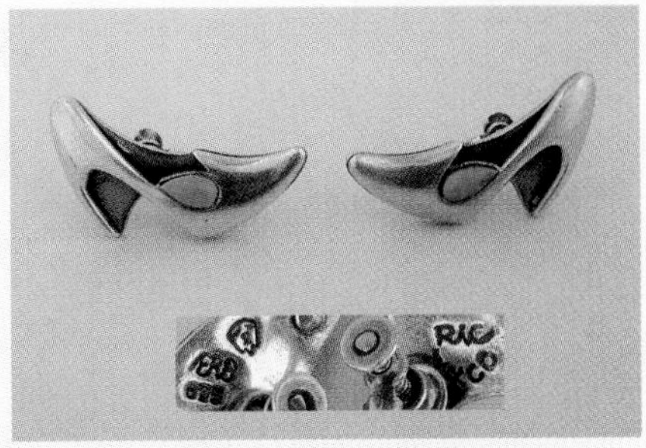

Earrings, sterling, turquoise, c. 1975, in the shapes of stylized high-heeled shoes, each with an off-center teardrop-shaped turq cab, mkd "RIC TAXCO" for Erika Hult de Corral on one earring, the other mkd "ERE 925" and eagle assay mk #3, adjustable screw/clip findings,1¼" w x ⅞", **$125**. (Courtesy of Patrick Kapty, Mad Jewelry, Palm Springs, CA)

Earrings, sterling, black onyx, c. 1955, abstract curv design, each with an onyx center inlaid with two offset opposed curved ster bars, flanked by two sets of three short ster wires radiating from ster frame, screwbacks, mkd "LOS CASTILLO, *HECHO EN MEXICO*" #43 and eagle assay mk #15, 1½" w x 1¼, **$75**. (Photo courtesy of M. Schon Antiques, Bay St. Louis, MS)

Earrings, sterling, c. 1955-60, each with a tapered triangular surmount suspending opposed elongated hollow pyramids with angled bases from a fold at the top, screwbacks, maker's mk "Salvador" in script for Salvador Terán, "STERLING MEXICO," #145, eagle assay mk #16, 2¾" T to B, ⅞" w, **$175**. (Courtesy of Patrick Kapty, Mad Jewelry, Palm Springs, CA)

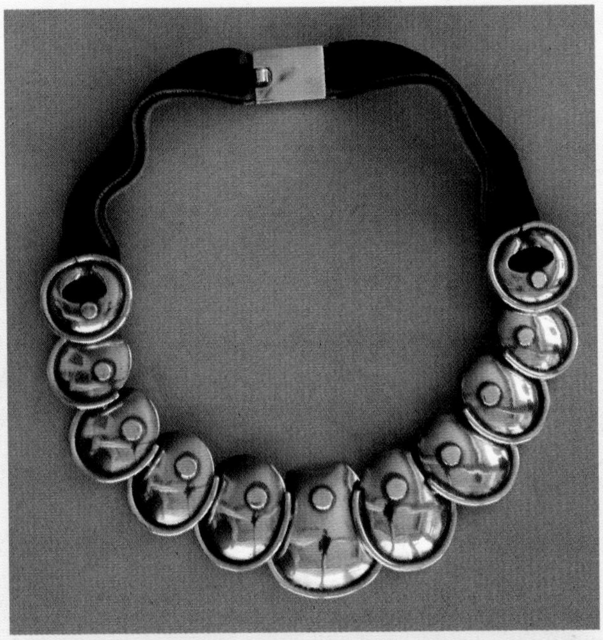

Necklace, sterling, velvet ribbon, c. 1945-50, "Armadillo" design by Valentín Vidaurreta of grad overlapping convex ovals, each with an off-center appl dot and partial round wire framing, continuing to a purple velvet ribbon with v-spring and box clasp, imp in two places with maker's mk "M ALTAMIRANO" in a circle for Manuel Altamirano, "TAXCO MEXICO 925," 1½" w x 16", **$500**. (Healy collection, photo by Bruce Healy)

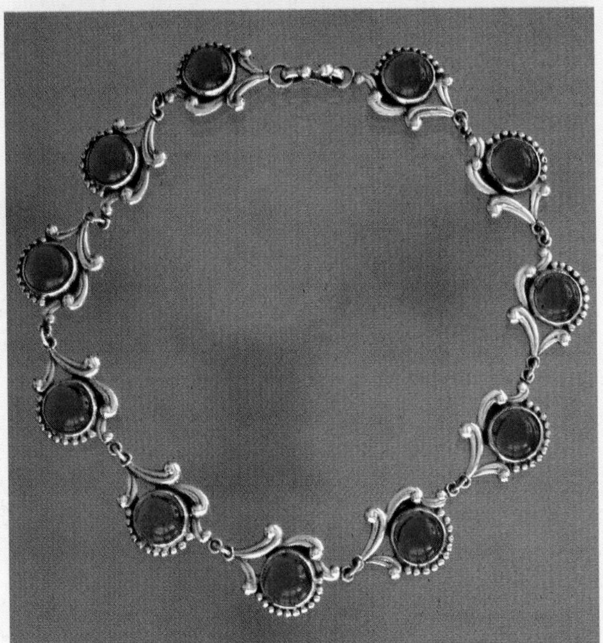

Necklace, sterling, glass, c. 1950, 11 repoussé floral and foliate motif links with lg circ blue glass bezel-set cabs, mkd "LOS CASTILLO TAXCO STERLING MADE IN MEXICO 60" and eagle assay mk #15, hook clasp, approx 15" tl, **$450.** (Healy collection, photo by Bruce Healy)

Necklace, gp sterling, c.1940-45, elaborate chased and repoussé design of two fish intertwined with waves and bubbles, flanked by articulated scrolled trefoil links, plating worn, mkd "LOS CASTILLO TAXCO MEXICO STERLING," #491, 6½" w x 3⅞" T to B at center, 16½" tl, **$4,500**. (Jill Crawford collection)

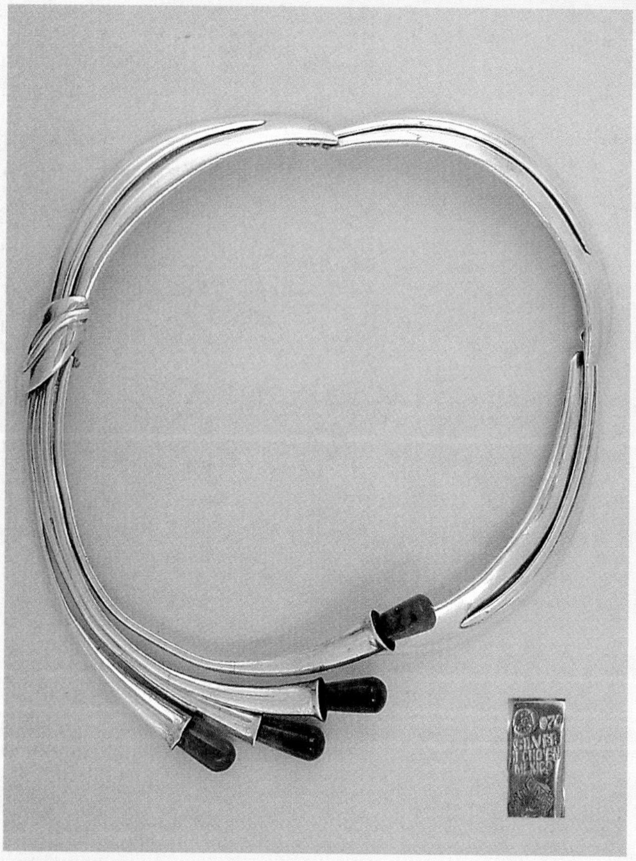

Necklace, 970 silver, amethysts, c. 1955-60, three linked curved repoussé sections of stylized leaf forms, one joined to a spray of four curved tubes with flared terminals set with rounded tapered cylindrical amethyst cabs, v-spring and box clasp concealed under a repoussé foliate motif, rev imp with maker's mk (crown) for Antonio Pineda, "970 Silver *HECHO EN MEXICO*" and eagle assay mk #17, 5¼" inside dia, approx 15" tl, **$3,500**. (Courtesy of D. Brett Benson, Inc., Chicago, IL)

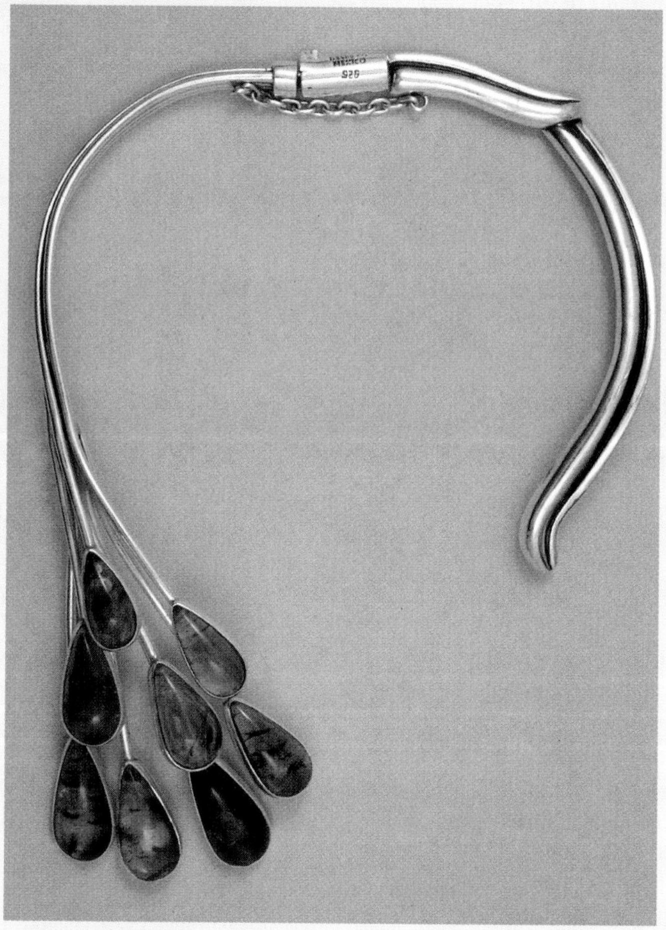

Necklace, collar, sterling, amethyst, c. 1955-60, sculptural design with chased line decoration and a spray of eight teardrop-shaped bezel-set amethyst cabs at one side, maker's mk for Antonio Pineda, "MEXICO 925," eagle assay mk #17, 4½" w at center, 4½" T to B, **$3,500**. (Jill Crawford collection)

Suite: Bracelet and earrings, sterling, c. 1950, bracelet of eight abstract cutout convex ovoid links with oxidized flat bg, alternating with vertical rows of three hemisphere, v-spring and box clasp; drop earrings of similar design and hemisphere surmount and terminal, screwback findings, mkd "VICTORIA MEXICO TAXCO" in circle for Ana Nuñez Brilanti, "STERLING" #53, eagle assay mk #12, bracelet ⅞" w x 8" tl, earrings 1" w x 1⅛", **$400**. (Elaine Sarnoff collection)

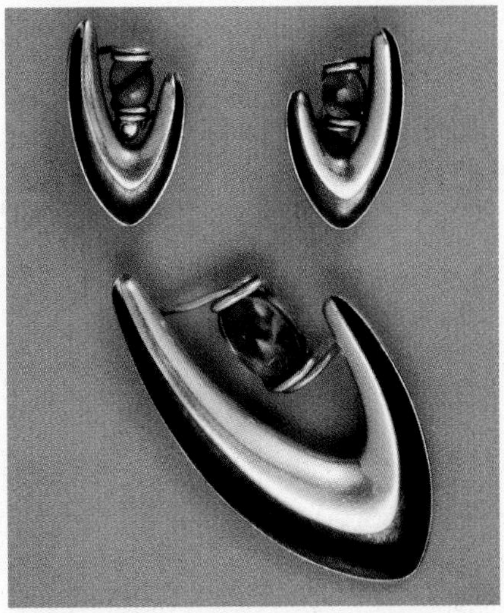

Suite: Earrings and Brooch/Pin by Sigi, sterling, amethysts, c. 1955:
T, three-dimensional boomerang with open oxidized interior and polished outer sections centering a wire-wrapped oval amethyst cab, screwbacks, imp with maker's mk for Sigi Pineda, "STERLING HECHO EN MEXICO," #87 and eagle assay mk #3, ¾" w x 1⅛", **$75**. (Author's collection)
B, matching brooch with safety catch, identical mks, 1⅜" x 2⅜", **$200**. (Almunir Meghji collection)

Suite: Brooch/Pendant and Chain, Bracelet, and Earrings, sterling, enamel, c. 1955, brooch/pendant of a feather-crowned Mayan/Aztec profile in polychrome enamel with black enameled face, removable S-shaped link polychrome enameled chain, polychrome enameled earrings with circ surmounts suspending sq plaques with curv design, each with three cutout segments at the base, polychrome enameled link bracelet in a Greek key design, chain unmkd, brooch/pendant and earrings mkd "MARGOT DE TAXCO STERLING MADE IN TAXCO" #5404, and eagle assay mk #16, bracelet mkd "STERLING MADE IN MEXICO" in a circle, #5376, and "MARGOT DE TAXCO" in a circle around eagle assay mk #16, enamel imperfect on bracelet and neckchain, brooch/pendant 2½" w x 3½", chain ⅜" w x 15½", earrings ¾" w x 1¾", bracelet 1" x 7¼", **$2,800**. (Author's collection)

Tie bars, sterling, c. 1955:
T, rect plaque with appl abstract geo design over oxidized bg, alligator clip mounted on rev, maker's mark (crown) for Antonio Pineda, "HECHO EN MEXICO 970" and eagle assay mk #17, ⅜" w x 1¼", **$100**.
B, irregular curv polished bar with cutout center over oxidized bg, mkd "Salvador [script] STERLING MEXICO 150," ⅝" w x 2", **$150**. (Jimmie Romero collection)

SCANDINAVIAN JEWELRY

Scandinavians have approached design in a way that differs from all other European countries, perhaps because of a culture that is rooted in a separate and unique Nordic tradition. Prior to the turn of the century, when historicism was rampant everywhere in the Western world, jewelry designs were derived from direct copies of ancient pieces from the Bronze, Iron, and Viking Ages.

Each of the four Scandinavian countries–Denmark, Norway, Sweden, and Finland–also produced regional "folk" jewelry which has remained virtually unchanged in appearance and technique for several centuries. During the nineteenth century, too, Danish fine jewelry often had a British-influenced Victorian look, no doubt coming from the fact that the Princess of Wales, Alexandra, was a Dane. The art of hair jewelry-making, another Victorian tradition, is said to have originated in Denmark and Sweden.

Scandinavians are noted for their metalwork, and silversmithing in particular has given expression to original design, most fully realized by twentieth century Scandinavian designers and manufacturers. Many of these designers applied their talents to more than jewelry. Some, like Georg Jensen (1866-1935) of Denmark, began as sculptors, transferring the three-dimensional art form to silver hollow ware, flatware, and jewelry. Others, like Tapio Wirkkala (1915-1985) of Finland, were multimedia artists: they designed glass, porcelain, and wood decorative objects, as well as silver.

Since the publication of the second edition of *Warman's Jewelry*, interest in Scandinavian jewelry has grown considerably. Many more examples have come onto the market, and additional information about makers and designers has been discovered. Consequently, in this edition, information on and examples of each Scandinavian country's jewelry are grouped separately, including references specific to each. A number of references include *all* of the countries' makers and products, and these are listed.

Numerous books have been published in their native languages on the designers and makers in each of the Scandinavian countries. Some have English translations. However, the books themselves have been difficult to find in the U.S. (book search sites on the Internet have made this task a bit easier). More readily available, recently published books and articles in English have now called American collectors' attention to Scandinavian jewelry. But some of it still goes unrecognized and underpriced in the marketplace. Identification of marks has become increasingly important. In addition to the Scandinavian marks appendix beginning on page 257, the actual marks as struck on the pieces themselves are included in the photos wherever possible in this edition.

As is the case with Mexican silver jewelry, well-made pieces of good design with unknown makers' and designers' marks appear on the secondary market quite regularly. The Danish, Norwegian, Swedish, and Finnish governments keep records of makers' marks in registries that are updated from time to time. The only information listed is the identity of the maker and the years the marks were registered. Often there is no way to obtain biographical information. The collector's only recourse is to evaluate the work on its own merits, and let it speak for itself. However, in a name-driven marketplace, the value of these pieces will likely remain lower than those by their better-known counterparts.

Denmark

At the turn of the century, the Arts and Crafts Movement found its way to Denmark, where it was called *skønvirke*, literally translated, "beautiful work" or "aesthetic activities." The word was coined in 1907, but the style and movement had earlier roots, as it did in other parts of Europe and Britain. (There is little published documentation in English about jewelry of this period from other Scandinavian countries, but evidence exists of similar work being done in Norway and Sweden.)

Though similar in form and inspiration to other European Arts and Crafts work, one of the unique qualities of *skønvirke* jewelry is its sculptural three-dimensionality, achieved with repoussage and chasing. Silver, of varying fineness (usually 826 or 830), was the most often-used material, sometimes set with cabochon gemstones such as amber, chrysoprase (or dyed green chalcedony), carnelian, lapis, or moonstones (see below). *Skønvirke* jewelry enjoyed widespread appreciation in Denmark, thanks in part to large-scale production by several manufacturing silversmithies, such as Bernhard Hertz (see pages 235 and 236). Like

Brooches/Pins, silver, c. 1910, *skønvirke*:
T, 826 silver, dyed green chalcedony, carnelian, a chased and repoussé lobed lozenge-shaped plaque in a floral and foliate motif, one lg central oval carnelian cab encircled by raised beads, and four sm circ chalcedony cabs at compass points, C-catch, tube hinge, imp "826 S" flanking maker's mk for C M Cohr, 1⅞" w x 1⅜", **$175**. (Courtesy of Gail Gerretsen, South Pasadena, CA)
BL, 900 silver, glass, open oval garland of repoussé silver floral and foliate motifs encircling a bezel-set lg oval faceted lavender glass stone (possible replacement), mkd "RBH, 900S" flanking an unidentified mk of a Viking helmet within a convex rect frame, 2" w x 1¾", **$400**.
BR, 830 silver, amber, open elongated oval with a chased and repoussé stylized foliate design centering a circ amber cab, tube hinge, replacement safety catch on flat backing imp with illegible maker's mk, "830S," *Dansk Arbejde* (Danish Handicraft guild) mk (D and A flanking a hammer inside a shield), 2½" w x 1½", **$500**. (Author's collection)

Liberty in Britain and Fahrner in Germany (see Arts & Crafts section), Danish manufacturers commissioned designs from independent artists and also made their own versions of others' work.

Mogens Ballin (1871-1914) was a pioneer of the *skønvirke* style. Inspired by the philosophy of the founders of the English Arts & Crafts movement, William Morris and John Ruskin, his desire was to create "everyday objects with a lovely form of...cheap metals...things which even the smallest purse can afford." However, his style was not influenced as much by the English as by his fellow countrymen, and by German silversmiths. In 1900, he opened a workshop that produced decorative objects and jewelry. From the beginning, he employed a sculptor, Siegfried Wagner, as a designer. In 1901, another sculptor joined the firm, by the name of Georg Jensen—now the most recognized and widely collected name in Scandinavian silver in the United States.

Even though his name recognition in the United States is not that of Jensen's, the work of Evald Nielsen is very well known in Denmark. He is admired as one of the best of the *skønvirke* designers. Nielsen opened his own shop in 1907. Nielsen's characteristic style of setting stones was to place them within a floral motif in an irregular bezel, so they looked as if they were "bursting forth" from the floral bud. Those who do know Nielsen's work in the U.S. recognize its value. There are many who may recognize the quality, but not the name (see page 236).

In 1904, Georg Jensen opened his own silversmithy and began designing and making the jewelry and silverware the company is now famous for. Over the past 90-plus years, a number of noted designers have created jewelry designs for the Jensen firm, many of which are familiar to today's collectors, including those by Sigvard Bernadotte (1907-2002), Torun Bülow-Hübe (b. 1927), Nanna (b. 1923) and Jørgen (1921-1961) Ditzel, Bent Gabrielsen (b. 1928), Henning Koppel (1918-1981), Arno Malinowski (1899-1976), and Harald Nielsen (1892-1977).

A designer's initials are sometimes added to the company marks on a piece, which can raise its value. Many early designs are still produced today, although production methods have changed, in some cases, from die-stamping to casting. Shop marks have changed as well. The mark currently in use, "GEORG JENSEN" inside a dotted oval, has been the same since 1945, but a number of different marks were used prior to that date. The earliest Jensen pieces, c. 1904 to 1914, are made of 826 silver. The grade of silver in pieces dating from the mid-teens through the 1920s is 830 or 925; after 1933, the company went to the sterling standard of 925 exclusively (see page 236). It should be noted that some jewelry designs were also made in 18 karat gold.

In spite of a long tradition in its native countries, Scandinavian design was not well known in the United States until Frederik Lunning opened a shop and agency for Georg Jensen in New York in 1924. The shop helped to popularize Scandinavian design in general, and Jensen designs in particular. Lunning was an important figure in promoting awareness and appreciation of Nordic decorative and

Brooch/Pin, iron, silver, c. 1940-45, "*jernsølv*," slightly convex quatrefoil iron plaque inlaid with dolphin, plant and water motifs, rev imp with an "A" over an "M" for designer Arno Malinowski, "GEORG JENSEN," #5002, 2" x 2", **$500**. (Author's collection)

applied arts. From 1951 to 1970, he funded the Lunning Prize, awarded each year to two outstanding Scandinavian designers working in various media.

Among the prizewinners were jewelry and silverware designers and metalsmiths Grete Prytz-Kittelsen (b. 1917), Norway; Henning Koppel, Denmark; Nanna and Jørgen Ditzel, Denmark; Torun Bülow-Hübe, Sweden; Bertel Gardberg (b. 1916), Finland; Börje Rajalin (b. 1933), Finland; Bent Gabrielsen, Denmark; Björn Weckström (b. 1935), Finland; and Helga (b. 1939) and Bent (b. 1932) Exner, Denmark. Tapio Wirkkala was one of the first two prizewinners in 1951. All of these designers are well- known in their own countries; some have achieved world-wide recognition. A number of them maintained their own studios and workshops. Most of them also designed for large manufacturing firms (see appendix, 20th Century Jewelry Designers and Manufacturers in Scandinavia).

The Nordic countries were hard-hit by World War II, which brought shortages of both workers and materials, along with the anxiety of invasion and occupation. Remarkably, the arts communities in each country sustained themselves through the hard times. Gold and silver were restricted to mostly settings and inlays. Silversmiths and jewelers began adding other more readily available materials, like glass and ceramics, and substituting other metals, such as iron and bronze. Georg Jensen's designers created a line known as *jernsølv* (iron silver), using patinated iron as a base with silver and gold inlay, similar to damascening or Japanese inlay. The designs themselves, first made by Arno Malinowski and then by others, were inspired by Japanese technique and tradition (see brooch above).

In the United States, when war came and supplies from Europe were cut off, Frederik Lunning turned to American manufacturers and produced a line for Jensen on his own, marked Georg Jensen, U.S.A. There was some controversy after the war concerning the U.S. production. The Copenhagen company disavowed any association with the U.S. designs. A special mark for the Copenhagen shop only, "Georg Jensen & Wendel A/S Denmark," was used for the period 1945-1951. Production of Jensen U.S.A. pieces ended around 1950. Today, they don't bring the prices that the Danish ones do, but they are still of interest to collec-

Earrings, sterling, enamel, c. 1955, "Eskimo boys" motif, enameled in blue, white, brown, black, and red, maker's mk for A. Dragsted, "DENMARK STERLING," 1" w x ⅞", **$35**. (Private collection)

tors. Alphonse La Paglia (d. 1953), Joan Polsdorfer (JoPol, see page 236), and Laurence Foss (b. 1920, see Arts & Crafts section) were three recognized American designers for Jensen U.S.A. (who also worked independently).

The post-war years gave Nordic artists the opportunity to display their talents as never before. For the first time, Scandinavian design was setting the pace for others to follow. Their work was highly influential in Europe and North America. Simplicity of line, adventurous abstract form, and flawlessness of execution were trademarks of Nordic products. For those used to seeing repetitious, derivative "traditional" styles, these designs were an exciting revelation.

The designers at Georg Jensen did not merely keep up with changing times, they were at the forefront of innovation. Collectors of modernist jewelry seek out their work, particularly that of Henning Koppel (see pages 235, 236, and 238), Sigvard Bernadotte, and the Ditzels (see pages 236 and 237).

But they were not alone. Others, too, produced sleek and bold pieces that were the epitome of what came to be known as Scandinavian Modern. Although Jensen is the most well-known in the U.S., several other Danish manufacturers are just as well-known in their own country, including A. Michelsen (see page 237), A. Dragsted (see above), and Hans Hansen.

Hans Hansen's silversmithy has manufactured the work of several highly regarded modernist designers, among them Karl Gustav Hansen (b. 1914), the founder's son (who designed a line called "Future" at the age of 18), Bent Gabrielsen (b. 1928), and Anni (b. 1926) and Bent (b. 1924) Knudsen.

The company's mark is its name in script, "HaH," or a superimposed double H (see appendix). Two variations of the script and HaH marks were used at different times. Individual designers are not identified on their pieces, but the HaH mark in use from 1937 to 1947 is most often found on Karl Gustav Hansen designs. Bent Gabrielsen designed for the company from 1953 until 1969, when he opened his own workshop. Hans Hansen is now under the ownership of the Royal Copenhagen Group, as is Georg Jensen.) See pages 235, 236, 237, and 238.

Just Andersen is another venerable firm that was founded by its namesake (1884-1943) in 1918. The workshop's style changed with the times, from *skønvirke* to "functionalism" to the sleek mid-century modern style that Denmark and the other Scandinavian countries became famous for (see necklace on page 238).

N.E. From, first opened in 1931 by Niels Erik From (d. 1982) as a repair shop, began wholesale production in the late '40s, and expanded to larger-scale production in 1955. In 1967, From built a large factory which at one time employed as many as 85 people, some of whom contributed designs for production. The firm exported a quantity of jewelry to the United States (and elsewhere) in the '50, '60s, and '70s; sterling pieces bearing the name, with modern lines or stylized floral and foliate motifs typical of the period, turn up frequently on the secondary market (see pages 238 and 239). Collectors in the U.S. and England are beginning to take notice of From pieces, although price levels continue to be moderate. The company ceased operations in the late 1990s. This information courtesy of Danish-born New York dealer Soren Jensen (www.jensen-silver.com).

Another familiar name, one that confuses dealers and collectors, is Jørgen Jensen (b. 1931), found on modern-looking Danish pewter pieces. The mark is a script signature (see appendix), totally different from but often mistaken for Georg Jensen, who is no relation, although Georg had a son Jørgen who worked for the company (both Jørgen and Jensen are common names in Denmark). The values on these pewter pieces are nowhere near the levels of Georg Jensen silver.

Reproduction Alert

Die-stamped copies of Georg Jensen and Jensen-inspired designs were made by Coro, Danecraft, and other American companies in the 1940s, but they are usually marked and easily identified because they are not backed with a flat plate as Jensen pieces are. Trade names like "Vikingcraft" and "Norseland" were used to evoke association with Scandinavian design. Pieces marked "Georg Jensen U.S.A." were first made and marketed by Frederik Lunning during World War II when sterling was in short supply in Denmark and trade routes were cut off. Lunning turned to American manufacturers and produced the Jensen line on his own, hence the U.S.A. mark. Values tend to be lower for these items, although interest has grown over the past few years since more information about U.S. designers for Georg Jensen U.S.A. has been published. According to Jensen dealer Caryl Unger of Imagination Unltd. in Miami, Florida, an Israeli firm was making knockoffs of Jensen jewelry about 20 years ago, taking molds of original pieces and leaving the marks intact. When purchasing on the secondary market, it's advisable to know your Jensen or know your sources.

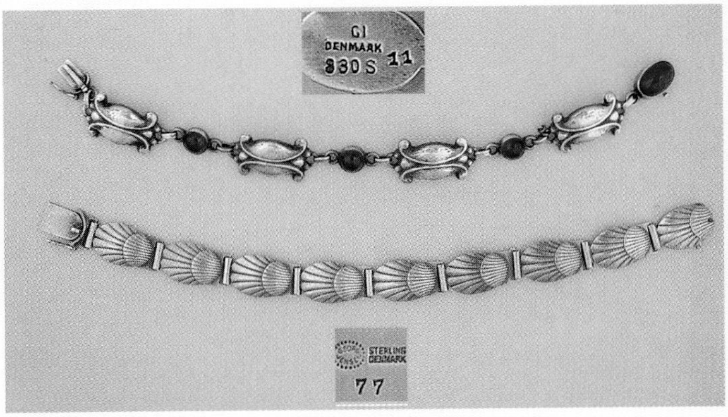

Bracelets, link, sterling, Georg Jensen:
T, 830 silver, dyed green chalcedony, c. 1935, four stylized foliate motif silver links alternating with three bezel-set circ green chalcedony cabs, box clasp with one lg oval green chalcedony cab, v-spring, safety lock, 1933-44 maker's mk for Georg Jensen, #11, inscribed "IBS from JAB Jr 12-4-35," ½" w x 7½" tl, **$900**. (Caren Fine collection)
B, sterling, post-1945 mark, a line of die-stamped scallop shell-shaped links, v-spring and box clasp, safety catch, mkd "GEORG JENSEN" in a dotted oval, "STERLING DENMARK" #77, ½" w x 7¾" tl, **$500**. (Courtesy of Gilly Phipps, Philadelphia, PA)

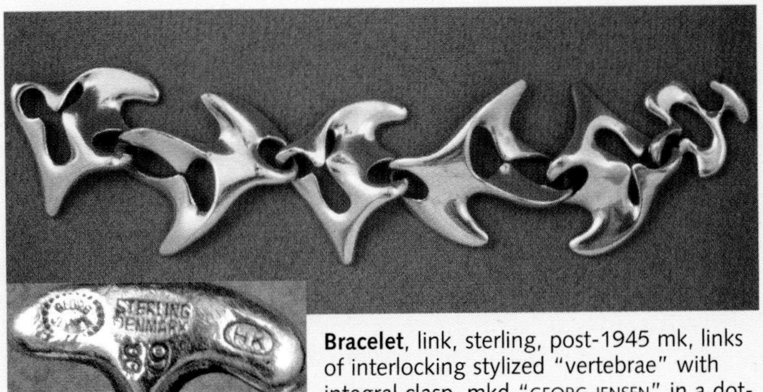

Bracelet, link, sterling, post-1945 mk, links of interlocking stylized "vertebrae" with integral clasp, mkd "GEORG JENSEN" in a dotted oval, "STERLING DENMARK" #89 and "HK" for designer Henning Koppel, ¾" w x 7¾" tl, **$1,250**. (Courtesy of Patrick Kapty, Mad Jewelry, Palm Springs, CA, 9/25/01)

Bracelet, link, sterling, date letter for 1963-64, linked three-dimensional interlocking fin-shaped modular units, v-spring and box clasp, post-1945 mk for Georg Jensen, #108, mkd "GJ LTD," British import mks and date letter, ¾" w x 8" tl, **$1,400**. (Healy collection, photo by Bruce Healy)

Bracelet, hinged bangle, sterling, c. 1965-70, tapered band with hinged ring ornamental top clasp, mkd "Hans Hansen [script] 925S DENMARK," top 1½" w x ¾", 2½" inside dia, **$300**. (Sue James collection)

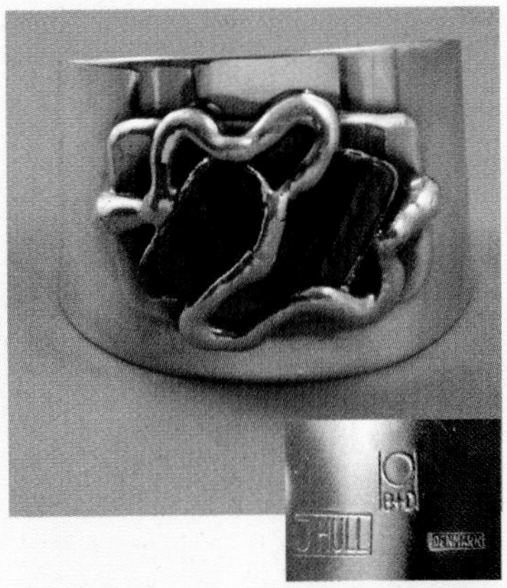

Bracelet, cuff, sp wm, tiger's eye, c. 1970, slightly tapered band centering an abstract motif with a cast wormlike form meandering over and around a bezel-set irregular flat tiger's eye plaque, mkd "J. HULL, B + D [below a circle flanked by vertical lines] DENMARK," designed by Jacob Hull, Buch & Deichmann mfrs, 1¾" w, 2½" inside dia, **$100**. (Almunir Meghji collection)

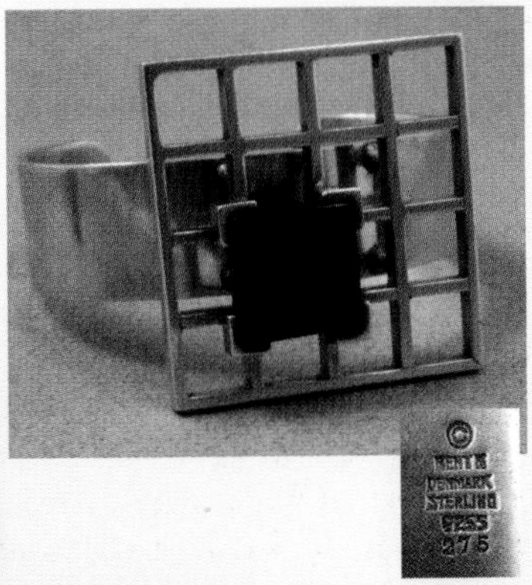

Bracelet, cuff, sterling, onyx, c. 1960-65, heavy gauge ster band surmounted by a grid of sixteen sm sqs within a sq frame, a bezel-set sq onyx plaque to one side surmounting the grid, designed by Anni and Bent Knudsen, imp "© BENT K, DENMARK STERLING 925s," #275, 2" sq, **$800**. (Courtesy Patrick Kapty, Mad Jewelry, Palm Springs, CA)

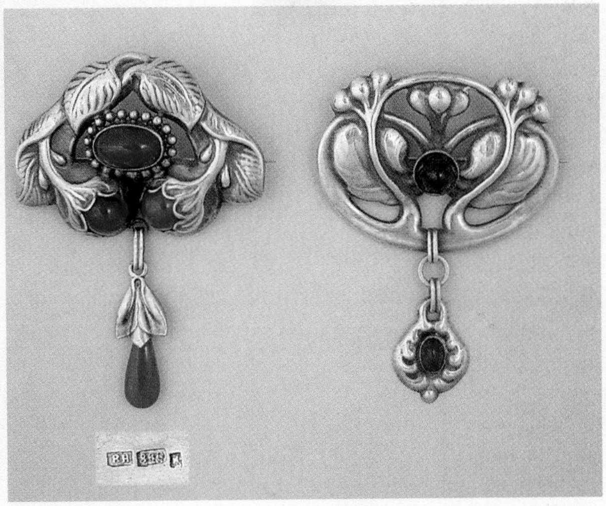

Brooches/Pins, silver, dyed green chalcedony, c. 1905-10, *skønvirke*, maker's mk "BH" for Bernhard Hertz:
L, 830 silver, die-stamped floral/foliate motif encircling one lg oval chalcedony cab bezel-set in a beaded frame, two circ chalcedony cab "buds," and one elongated teardrop-shaped chalcedony cab drop, center cab flat backing imp "830 S, BH" 2½" w x 3⅜", **$650**.
R, 826 silver, openwork die-stamped floral/foliate motif with a high-domed circ chalcedony cab bezel-set in the center flanked by stylized flowers and leaves, suspending three links with one raised foliate motif pear-shaped drop bezel-set with a sm oval chalcedony cab, C-catch, tube hinge, inside top edge mkd "BH 826 S," 2⅜" w x 3⅛", **$650**. (Courtesy of Gail Gerretsen, South Pasadena, CA)

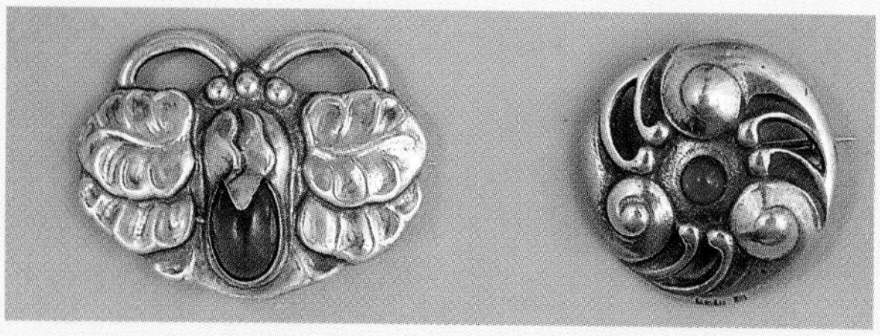

Brooches/Pins, 826 silver, c. 1905-10, *skønvirke*:
T, in the shape of a winged insect with floral/foliate details, the center bezel-set with an oval dyed green chalcedony cab surmounted by a leaf form, C-catch, tube hinge, mkd "826 S BH" for Bernhard Hertz, 2" w x 1½", **$250**.
B, openwork circ disk with die-stamped scrolls and volutes, the center bezel-set with a sm circ carnelian cab, mkd "826S" on outer lower edge, 1⅛" dia, **$200**. (Private collection)

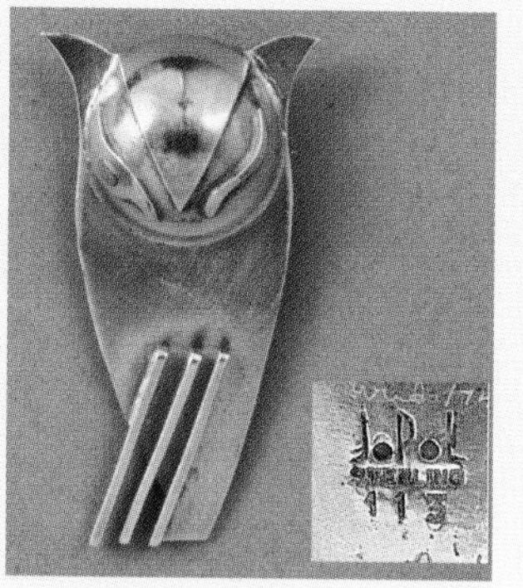

Brooch/Pin, sterling, enamel, c. 1948, in the shape of a stylized owl, one eye with red and yellow mottled enamel, three diagonal appl parallel sq wire bars at the base, rev imp "JoPol STERLING" for Joan Polsdorfer, New York, NY, #113, illustrated in a 1948 Georg Jensen USA catalog, 1⅛" w x 2", **$200**. (Author's collection)

Brooch/Pin, sterling, post-1945 mk, open biomorphic design by Henning Koppel, mkd "GEORG JENSEN" in a dotted oval, #322, "STERLING DENMARK," 1¾" x 1½", **$250**. (Almunir Meghji collection)

Brooch/Pin, 830 silver, amber, c. 1910, *skønvirke* oval repoussé floral/foliate plaque with opposed volutes encircling a hand-hammered ground, central floral bud set with a circ amber cab, suspending a teardrop-shaped amber cab in a bud-like setting from three oval links, unbacked, maker's mk "EN" for Evald Nielsen, "830s"on rev, C-catch, tube-hinge, 2¼" w x 3" tl, **$800**. (Nancy Shadforth collection)

Brooch/Pin, sterling, amethyst, c. 1960, in the shape of an openwork abstract eye, centering a sm circ sugarloaf amethyst cab, mkd "Hans Hansen" [script], #211, 1¾" w x 1⅛", **$264** [A]. (Photo courtesy of Skinner, Inc., Boston, MA, 12/11/01)

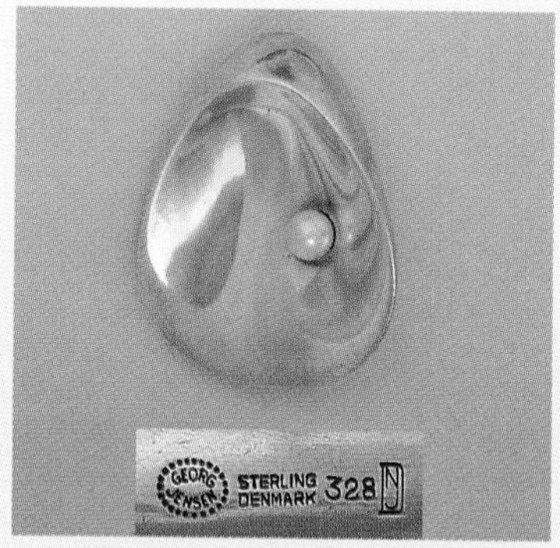

Brooch/Pin, sterling, pearl, c. 1955-60, three-dimensional hollow-shell shape surmounted by an off-center post-set pearl, design by Nanna and Jørgen Ditzel, safety catch, post-1945 maker's mk for Georg Jensen, "STERLING DENMARK," #328 and designers' mk N above J inside lg D, 2⅛" w x 1⅝", **$300**. (Courtesy of Gilly Phipps, Philadelphia, PA)

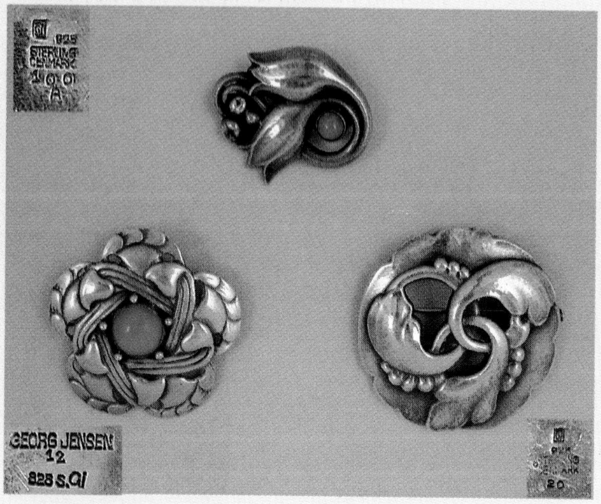

Brooches/Pins by Georg Jensen:
T, c. 1933-1944, die-stamped double tulip design with bezel-set amazonite cab, tube hinge, safety catch, flat backing imp with 1933-44 maker's mk for Georg Jensen, #100 A, "DENMARK STERLING 925," 1½" w x 1¼", **$400**. (Courtesy of Gilly Phipps, Philadelphia, PA)
BL, c. 1915, a die-stamped pierced five-lobed plaque with a stylized organic design, centering a bezel-set circ amber cab encircled by five appl silver beads, flat-backed, tube hinge, later-added safety catch, appl circ disk on rev mkd "GEORG JENSEN," #12, "828 S. GI," 1⅝" dia, **$500**. (Caren Fine collection)
BR, c. 1933-44, a slightly convex die-stamped pierced circ plaque with intertwined foliate and berry motifs, trombone catch, tube hinge, flat backing imp with 1933-44 maker's mk for Georg Jensen, "925 STERLING DENMARK" #20, 1¾" dia, **$300**. (Courtesy of Andrea Fatell, Wellsley, MA)

Brooch/Pin, sterling, dyed green chalcedony, c. 1960, open design of five criss-crossing silver wires with sphere terminals in varying sizes, one wire surmounted by an off-center bezel-set circ chalcedony cab , mkd "FROM 925s" for N.E. From, Denmark, 2⅜" x 1¾", **$175**. (Almunir Meghji collection)

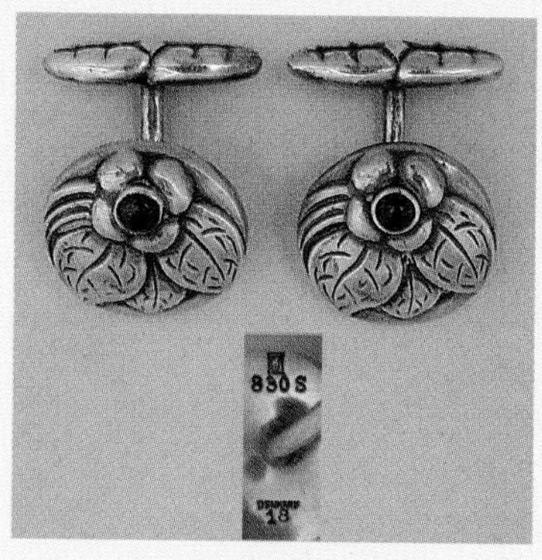

Cuff Links, 830 silver, sapphires, c. 1933, "dumbbell" style links, circ floral/foliate design, a cab sapphire bezel-set in center of each flowerhead, 1933-44 maker's mk for Georg Jensen, "830S DENMARK" #18, ½" dia, **$500**. (Courtesy of Gilly Phipps, Philadelphia, PA)

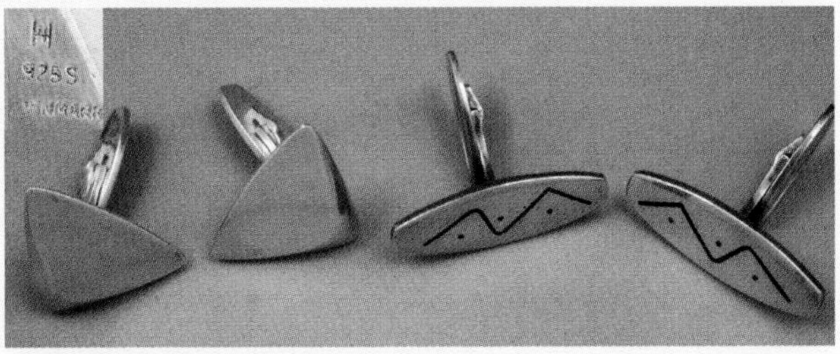

Cuff Links, sterling, Hans Hansen, mfr:
L, c. 1950, rounded triangular plaque, shaped and tapered from thick to thin edge, navette-shaped hinged back mounted on curved bar mkd "925 S DENMARK," maker's mk for Hans Hansen Silversmithy (superimposed lg and sm Hs), #640, design attributed to Bent Gabrielsen, 1" w x ¾", **$85**. (Bruce Healy collection)
R, c. 1940, elongated oval ster plaques with incised and oxidized zigzag and dot design, hinged oval back, maker's mk for Hans Hansen [script] and "925S DENMARK # 638," 1¼" w x ⅜", **$85**. (Courtesy of Terrance O'Halloran, San Pedro, CA)

Dress Clips, gp silver, c. 1935, each a triangular shape centering an oval bead within a geometric and curvilinear design mount, imp with 1933-44 maker's mk for Georg Jensen, "STERLING DENMARK" #232," 1⅛" w x 1⅜", **$588** [A]. (Photo courtesy of Skinner, Inc., Boston, MA, 12/11/01)

Dress Set, sterling, c. 1960, concave disk design by Nanna Ditzel, each pc mkd with post-1945 mk for Georg Jensen, "STERLING DENMARK," cuff links #74C, studs #74, cuff links ¾" dia, studs ⅜" dia, **$300**. (Healy collection, photo by Bruce Healy)

Earrings, sterling, c. 1950-60, clipbacks, maker's mk for A. Michelsen, "STERLING DENMARK":
TL, striated leaf design by Eigel Jensen, ⅝" w x 1⅜", **$100**.
TR, boomerang design by Eigel Jensen, ⅝" w x 1⅜", **$100**.
BL, c. 1955, "comma" design by Nanna and Jørgen Ditzel, imp with designers' mk (N J inside lg D), ⅝" w x ⅞", **$200**.
BR, coiled tube design with oxidized interiors, ⅜" w x 1", **$75**.
(Healy collection, photo by Bruce Healy)

Necklace, sterling, labradorite, moonstones, c. 1925-30, a chain of linked floral/foliate motifs, lobed rect foliate plaques centering bezel-set oval labradorite cabs alternating with paired scrolled leaves suspending floral moonstone "buds," joined with elongated oval links, imp with maker's mk for Georg Jensen, "DENMARK STERLING," #9, 1¼" at center, 16" tl, **$7,475** [A]. (Photo courtesy of Skinner, Inc., Boston, MA, 9/25/01)

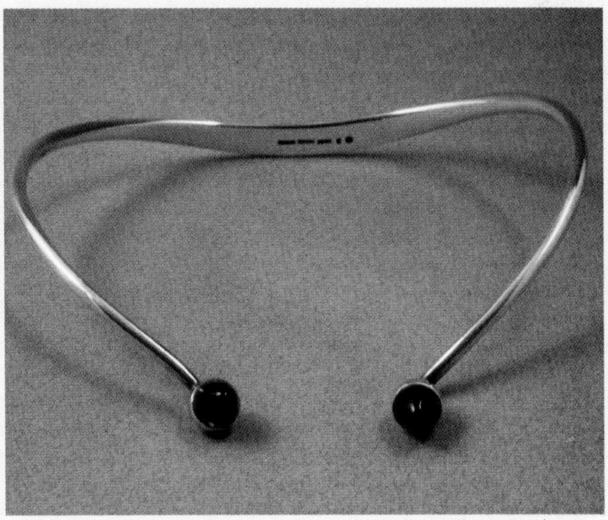

Necklace, torque, sterling, amethyst, c. 1956, forged band, slightly tapered width and thickness with a sm circ bezel-set high-domed amethyst cab at terminals, shown in open position, when closed the terminals overlap and lock, designed by Anni and Bent Knudsen, mkd "BENT K © DENMARK STERLING 925s," 5½" across at center, 4½" T to B, **$650**. (Courtesy of Patrick Kapty, Mad Jewelry, Palm Springs, CA)

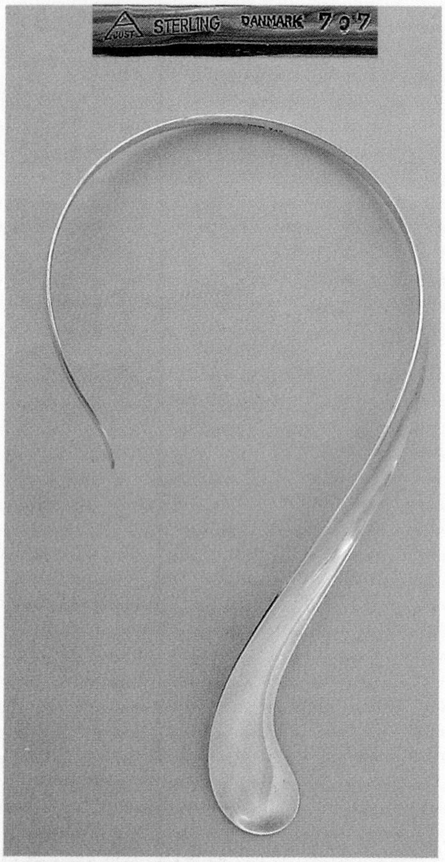

Necklace, sterling, c. 1965, an open-ended collar forged from a single piece of silver in the shape of a question mark, slightly concave surface tapering and curving around the neck, widening at the lobed base, maker's mk for Just Andersen, #707, "STERLING DANMARK," 4½" inside dia, 8½" T to B, **$475**. (Courtesy of Patrick Kapty, Mad Jewelry, Palm Springs, CA)

Pendants by N. E. From, sterling, rock crystal, c. 1965-70:
L, two vertically aligned open rings surmounting a tapered rounded bar, each with a bezel-set circ-cut rock crystal at the center, mkd "from 925s," ⅞" w x 2½", **$100**.
C, a polished circ disk with a cutout center surmounting an oxidized disk backing, a circ-cut rock crystal bezel-set off-center, suspended from a plain silver wire neckring, mkd "STERLING DENMARK N. E. FROM 925S," 2" dia, **$150**.
R, a lg oval lapis plaque flush-mounted in a ster frame, surmounted and bisected by a vertical silver bar, a bezel-set circ-cut rock crystal surmounting the bar off-center, rev mkd "NE From" in script, "925S DANMARK STERLING," 1" w x 2", **$100**. (Healy collection, photo by Bruce Healy)

Pendants and Chains, sterling, post-1945 maker's mk for Georg Jensen, "STERLING DENMARK":
L, c. 1960, deeply indented convex circ plaque suspended from two lengths of cable link chain, #337A, design by Torun Bülow-Hübe, pendant 2⅜"dia, chain 31", **$400**.
R, date letter for 1968-69, open-centered abstract bird with extended wings, design by Henning Koppel, #340, chain mkd "GJ LD," British import mks, pendant 2¾" x 1⅝", chain 28", **$350**. (Almunir Meghji collection)

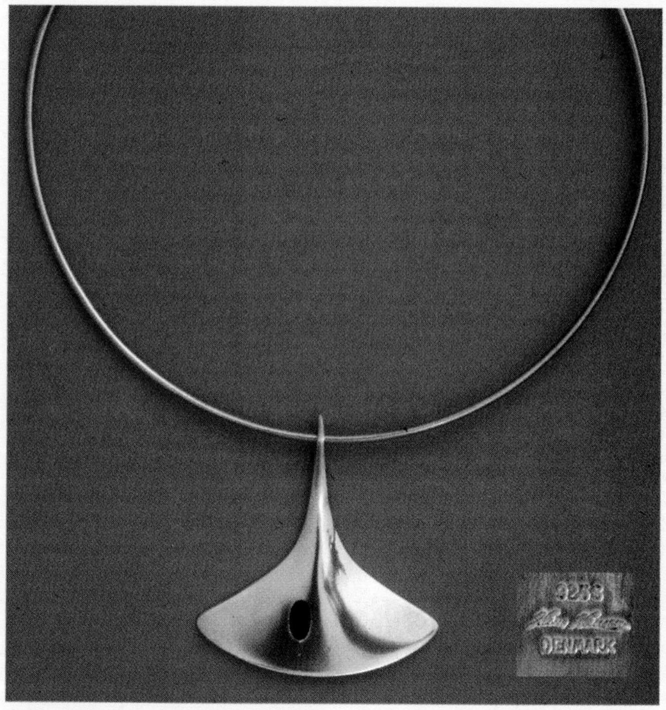

Pendant and Neckring, sterling, enamel, c. 1955-60, a tapered rounded triangular plaque with off-center black enameled oval dot, an abstract Thor's Hammer design by Bent Gabrielsen, suspended from plain wire neckring, plaque mkd "925S Hans Hansen [SCRIPT] DENMARK," neckring mkd "HaH 925," pendant 1⅞" w x 2" (with bail), **$450**. (Al Munir Meghji collection)

Rings, sterling and gemstones by Uwe Helmuth Moltke, c. 1965-75, all mkd 925S:
L, shank forged from a single piece of silver, curving up and out above the finger to enclose a lapis cylinder at terminals, mkd "UM STERLING," #757, ⅜" w x ½", **$125**.
C, a sq plaque centering an inset nephrite jade disk surmounting a squared shank with rounded corners, mkd "UM DENMARK," #771, ⅝", **$165**.
R, a curv U-shaped silver bar of varying thickness , curving up and out to encompass a nephrite jade cylinder at terminals, mkd "MOLTKE DENMARK," #702, 1⅜" w x ¾" x ⅜" h, **$145**. (Healy collection, photo by Bruce Healy)

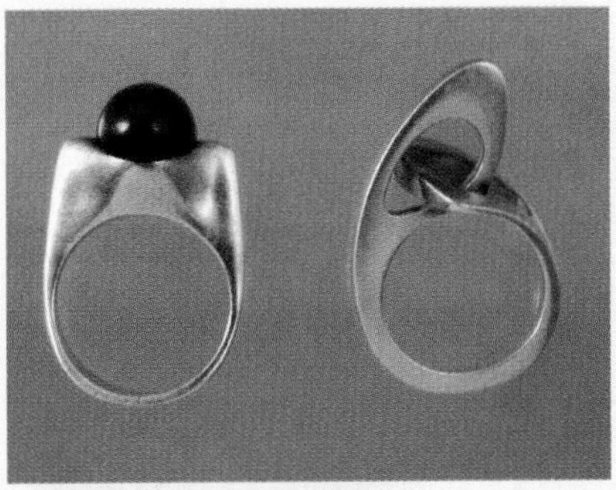

Rings by N. E. From, sterling, c. 1965-70:
L, tapered shaped shoulders with a central depression set with a dyed green chacedony sphere, narrow shank, mkd "FROM 925s," sz 7, **$100**.
R, narrow tapered shank curving up to rounded biomorphic terminals, one vertical, one horizontal, with interlocking cutout centers, mkd "FROM 925s," ½", sz 6, **$85**. (Almunir Meghji collection)

Ring, 18k yg, green tourmalines, c. 1965, a band of yg, forming a wide shank and continuing to form a V-shape projecting to one side, the flat surface bezel-set with two rows of three sq-cut green tourmalines, imp with post-1945 maker's mk for Georg Jensen, "18k 750," ⅞" w x ⅜" at front, sz 4½, **$1,500**. (Healy collection, photo by Bruce Healy)

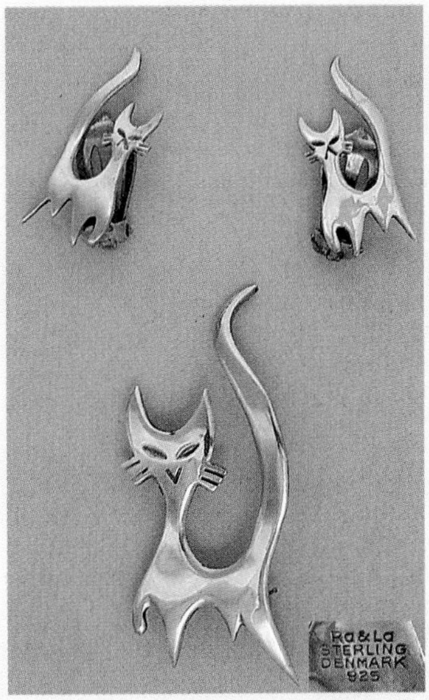

Suite: Brooch and Earrings, sterling, c. 1960, cutout stylized cat motif, mkd "RA & LA, STERLING DENMARK 925," for Rasmussen & Lassen of Copenhagen (in business 1960-70), earrings with clip-backs, brooch 1" w x 2⅛", earrings 1⅛", **$150**. (Courtesy of Gilly Phipps, Philadelphia, PA)

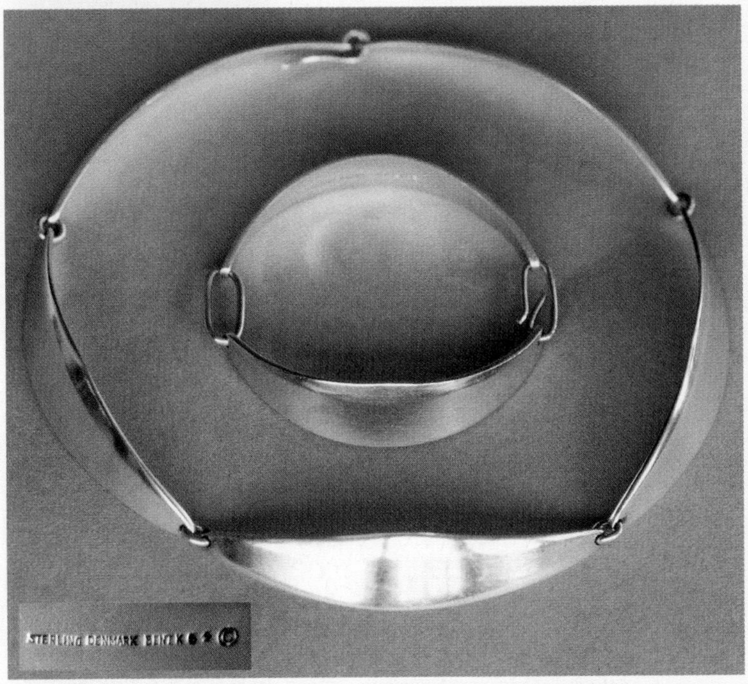

Suite: Necklace and Bracelet, sterling, c.1964, necklace with five, bracelet with two elongated navette-shaped curved plaques connected with jump rings, wire hook closures, Anni and Bent Knudsen design, both pcs mkd "STERLING DENMARK BENT K 64 ©," bracelet 2⅜" inside dia, necklace 5" inside dia, **$600**. (Healy collection, photo by Bruce Healy)

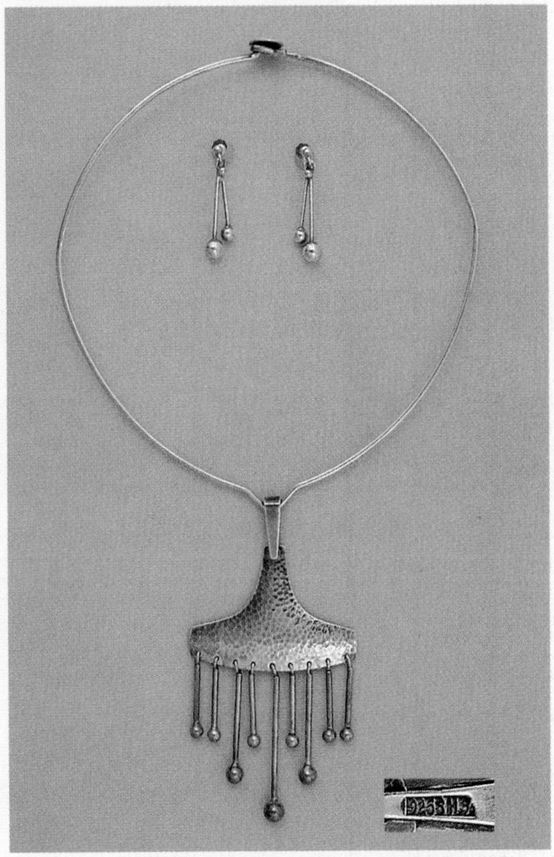

Suite: Pendant/Neckring and Earrings, sterling, c. 1965-70, pendant a simplified Thor's Hammer design with hammered finish, suspending a fringe of nine drops of varying length with sphere terminals from a neckring of simple wire construction with a hammered disk and hook closure, screw-back earrings with bead surmounts, each suspending uneven inverted V-shaped wires with sphere terminals, mkd "HS" for Hermann Siersbol of Copenhagen and "925S," neckring 4" dia, pendant 3¾" tl, earrings 1⅜" tl, **$350**. (Courtesy of Patrick Kapty, Mad Jewelry, Palm Springs, CA)

Norway

Very little early twentieth century (or earlier) Norwegian jewelry is found on the market today, other than the traditional filigree brooches with dangling concave disks known as *sølje*, which continue to be made. Other early jewelry that does turn up is usually enameled on silver. At the end of the nineteenth century, a variety of enameling techniques came to be closely associated with Norwegian decorative arts, especially *basse-taille* and *plique à jour*, which several firms were known for, among them: Marius Hammer, J. Tostrup, and David-Andersen. *Plique à jour* fell out of favor concurrently with the demise of Art Nouveau, before World War I, but transparent *basse-taille* and *guilloché*, and opaque *champlevé* enamels were adapted to changing styles throughout the twentieth century. J. Tostrup and David-Andersen continue in business today; Marius Hammer went out of business, but the years of the firm's operation are not documented.

Rings, sterling, enamel, titled "Domino," designed by Grete Prytz Kittelsen in 1952, stamped from a single piece and bent into shape, forming a curved rect top with *basse-taille* enameled front surface around eight sq dots of silver, adjustable shank, rev mkd "STERLING J.TOSTRUP NORWAY," 7/8" x 3/8", **$125** each. (Author's collection, Almunir Meghji collection)

A few examples of enamel and silver jewelry by Marius Hammer (1847-1927) of Bergen have surfaced. Hammer founded his company in the western Norwegian city in the late nineteenth century, specializing in *basse-taille* and *plique à jour* enamels on silver. They were particularly known for their elaborately wrought and enameled souvenir spoons. The firm sold spoons through Liberty of London in the 1890s, and also jewelry, most likely, since examples are found more frequently in England than in the United States (see buckle below, and necklace on page 242).

J. Tostrup, the oldest of the three firms (founded 1832), also produced some enameled jewelry in the early twentieth century, although at that time the firm was better known for its decorative objects. Later, more jewelry was produced, much of it designed (after World War II) by Grete Prytz (now Kittelsen, b. 1917), the granddaughter of Torolf Prytz, the company's production manager at the turn of the century (see her famous "Domino" rings above right). Gine Sommerfeldt (b. 1939) apprenticed at Tostrup and graduated from the National College of Arts, Crafts and Design in 1959. She worked for ONEIDA Ltd., New York, and has had her own workshop since 1964. Her jewelry is found in several museums, and has also been purchased by HM Queen Sonja of Norway. (The necklace on page 242 is a fine example of her work.) I thank Lennart Persson and Svein Josefsen of effie-graa.com for this information.

Buckle, sterling, enamel, c. 1910, two pc, *basse-taille* enameled foliate design, opposed five-lobed palmate leaves in medium green surmounting dk green enameled open ovals, flanking two spiked fruit shapes in yellow, red, and green enamel, surmounted by a sm floral motif disk in white, lt and dk green enamel, maker's mk for Marius Hammer, Bergen, "930S" on rev, 3¾" x 2⅛", **$500**. (Courtesy of Didier Antiques, London)

The biggest and most well-known Norwegian silver manufacturer is David-Andersen, established in 1876. Famous for its hollowware and flatware enameled in jewel-toned *basse-taille*, the company has also been making jewelry since the turn of the century, both with and without enamel. David-Andersen is still in business, and has been quite prolific (it might be called the Norwegian Georg Jensen), but relatively little information about the history of its production, especially its jewelry, has been recorded in English. (Information on turn-of-the-century Art Nouveau *objects* by Marius Hammer, J. Tostrup, and David-Andersen can be found in *Art Nouveau and Art Deco Silver*, cited in the References section. I thank Didier of Didier Antiques in London for calling the information on Hammer to my attention.)

Early David-Andersen jewelry is relatively scarce. It is also difficult to identify, because one of the early company marks (used c. 1888-1924) does not use its initials or name (see appendix).

Later (post-World War II) David-Andersen jewelry is much more commonly available, as the company began exporting to the U.S. in quantity after the war. Designs from this period fall into two categories: modernist abstract and figural.

In the 1950s and 1960s, David-Andersen had several recognized designers in its employ, who are best known for their flatware and hollowware. Two of them are Harry Sørby (1905-1988) and Bjørn Sigurd Østern (b. 1935), both of whom also designed jewelry. Sørby worked for the company from 1929-1970, Østern from 1961-1973, and 1974-1985. The latter often used the *basse-taille* enamel the company is famous for in his smoothly-cast and sleekly simple modern pendants and brooches. Both designers also set stones such as amazonite and rhodochrosite in their pieces. The company's marks usually include their initials after the abbreviation "INV," meaning "designer." Østern has also maintained his own workshop since 1960, and now has a Web site showcasing his designs (www.design-ostern.com). Examples by Østern for David-Andersen are pictured on pages 243 and 244.

Basse-taille enamel is also predominant in the David-Andersen sterling vermeil production pieces most often seen today: long slender curved leaves made into suites of necklace, bracelet, brooch, and earrings, die-stamped figural pins in a wide assortment of animals, birds, and fish, and "Viking Revival" scenes. The leaves are usually enameled in a single color, while the other pieces may be in subtle shades of a single color or multicolored. Circa 1950s abstract modern plaques and 1960s lost-wax cast biomorphic shapes are also enameled sterling vermeil. Some of these are signed "KOtteren" for designer Karl Jørgen Otteren. Company marks are varied, sometimes with "David-Andersen" written out, sometimes "D-A" with the company logo (in use since 1939), a pair of scales.

Like Georg Jensen, Hans Hansen, and many other Scandinavian silversmithies, David-Andersen is a family run business, handed down from generation to generation. The current president is the founder's great-grandson. His sister, Uni (b. 1930), continued working as a designer for the firm after starting her own workshop in 1959 with her own group of women designers, including Marianne Berg, designer of the pendant on page 243.

Colorfully enameled sterling vermeil pieces by smaller and lesser-known Norwegian makers also appear on the secondary market with regularity, including that of O.F. Hjortdahl of Oslo (see brooch at right), Aksel Holmsen of Sandefjord (right), Øystein Balle of Stavanger (page 242), and others whose marks have yet to be identified.

Tone Vigeland (b. 1938) is the most celebrated Norwegian designer of the twentieth century. Her work is in a number of museum collections, including the Museum of Modern Art and the Cooper-Hewitt National Design Museum in New York. A retrospective exhibition was held in 1995, with accompanying catalog (see References). Vigeland's earliest work was made at Plus, an arts and crafts center established in Fredrikstad, Norway, in 1958, where she apprenticed from 1958 to 1961 (see page 242). Vigeland and other budding young designers created pieces that were then put into production. The artist's initials are stamped on the pieces, along with the marks for Plus (see appendix for Tone Vigeland and Plus). Other artists who worked for Plus include Anna Greta Eker (b. 1928, see bracelet right and suite on page 244) and her husband Erling Christoffersen, whose designs are very much a part of the Scandinavian minimalist style of the late '50s and early '60s. Odvar Pettersen is another designer who only made two designs for Plus, a brooch (see page 242) and a pendant.

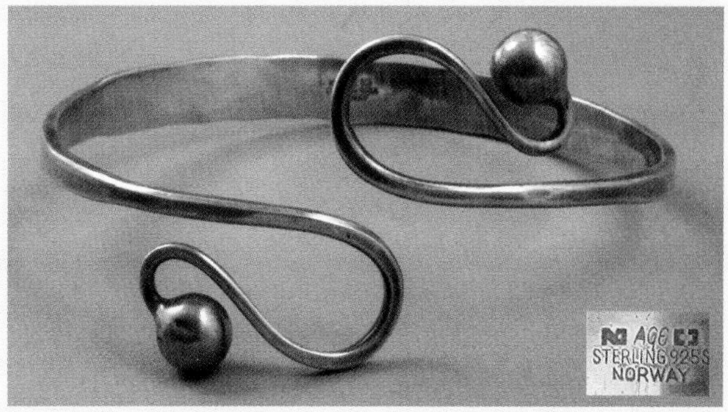

Bracelet, upper armband, sterling, c. 1960, hand-forged of curv tapered wire with sphere terminals, mkd for Norway Design Plus, "AGE" for Anna Greta Eker, "STERLING 925S NORWAY," 2" x 3⅜" inside dia, **$175**. (Almunir Meghji collection)

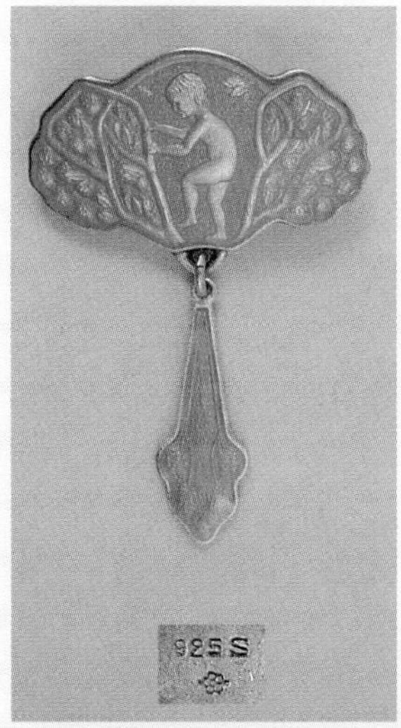

Brooch/Pin, sterling, enamel, c. 1915-20, irregular scallop-edged oval plaque with pale blue *basse-taille* enamel, depicting a child at play in a foliate setting, suspending an enameled scalloped teardrop-shaped drop, C-catch, tube hinge, plaque rev imp with maker's mk (five-petaled flower) for O. F. Hjortdahl, Oslo, "925S," 1¼" w x 1⅞", **$300**. (Courtesy of E. Foxe Harrell, New York, NY)

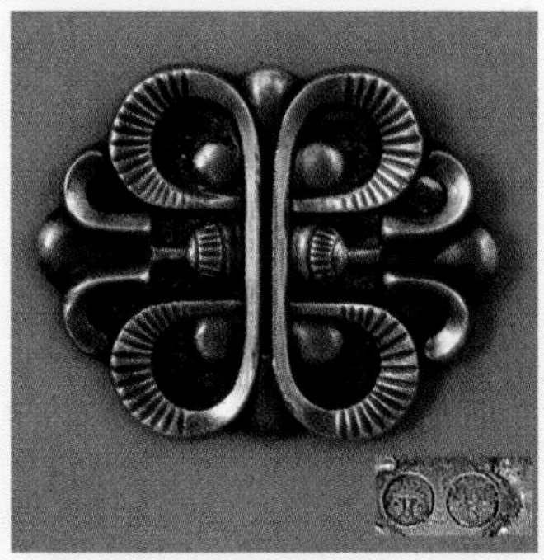

Brooch/Pin, 830 silver, c. 1940-45, one of the "Saga" series, an interlocking scrolled quatrefoil flanked by geo floral motifs, mk for David-Andersen after 1939 (scales), "830 S," 1⅝" w x 1¼", **$80**. (Diane White collection)

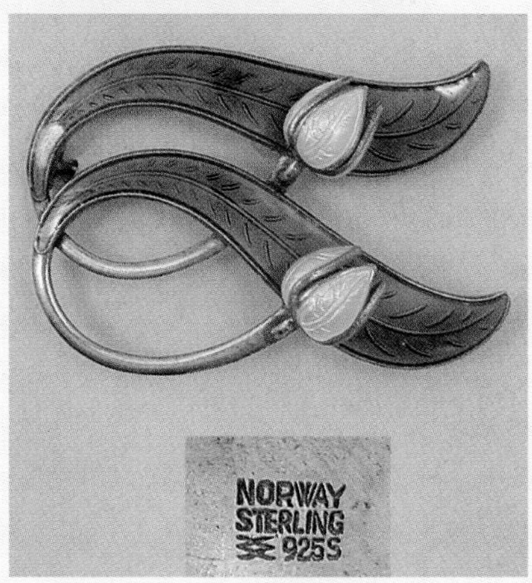

Brooch/Pin, sterling vermeil, enamel, c. 1950, basse-taille enameled curv floral/foliate motif, two yellow buds and two olive green leaves, rev mkd "NORWAY STERLING 925S," with maker's mk for Aksel Holmsen, 2¼" w x 1⅝", **$45**. (Gene Ratcliffe collection)

Brooches/Pins, gp sterling, enamel, c. 1955-60, mkd "BALLE NORWAY STERLING 925s," for Øystein Balle of Stavanger, $125 each:
T, rounded concave/convex quadrangular plaque with a yellow, orange, brown, white, blue, and mauve basse-taille enameled abstract design over a textured ground, safety catch, 1⅞" w x 1⅛".
B, rounded-corner rectangular plaque with a gp raised border and abstract wavelike design, recessed areas champlevé enameled in shades of white, blue, green, red, and yellow, C-catch, 1¾" w x 1¼". (Courtesy of Patrick Kapty, Mad Jewelry, Palm Springs, CA)

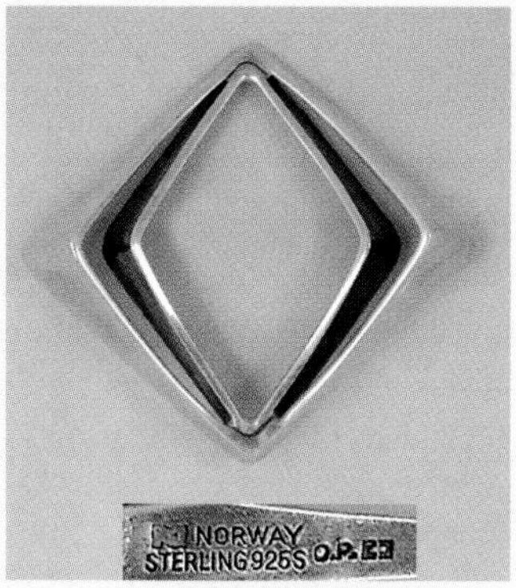

Brooch/Pin, sterling, c. 1960, titled "Amphi," open concentric lozenges with angled tapered sides, oxidized inner surface, maker's mk for Norway Designs Plus, "NORWAY STERLING 925s," designer's initials "O.P." for Odvar Pettersen, 2⅛" sq, **$150**. (Courtesy of Andrea Fatell, Wellsley, MA)

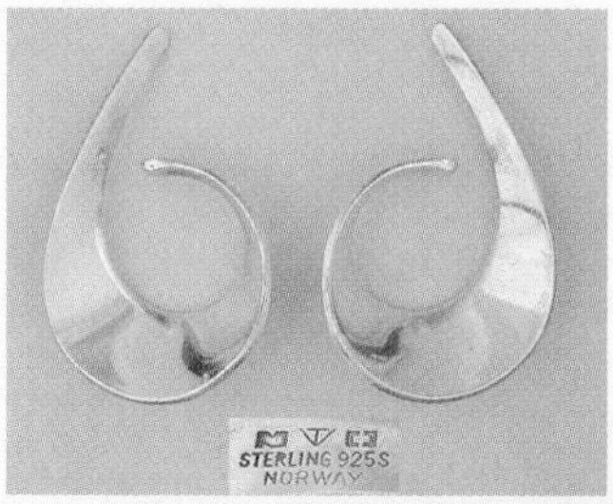

Earrings, sterling, c. 1958, titled "Sling," each an open tapered concave hoop with an extension for support behind the ear (hoop suspends from ear canal around the earlobe without findings), maker's mk for Norway Designs Plus, "STERLING 925S NORWAY," designer mk for Tone Vigeland (T within V), 1⅛" w x 1⅞", **$250**. (Author's collection)

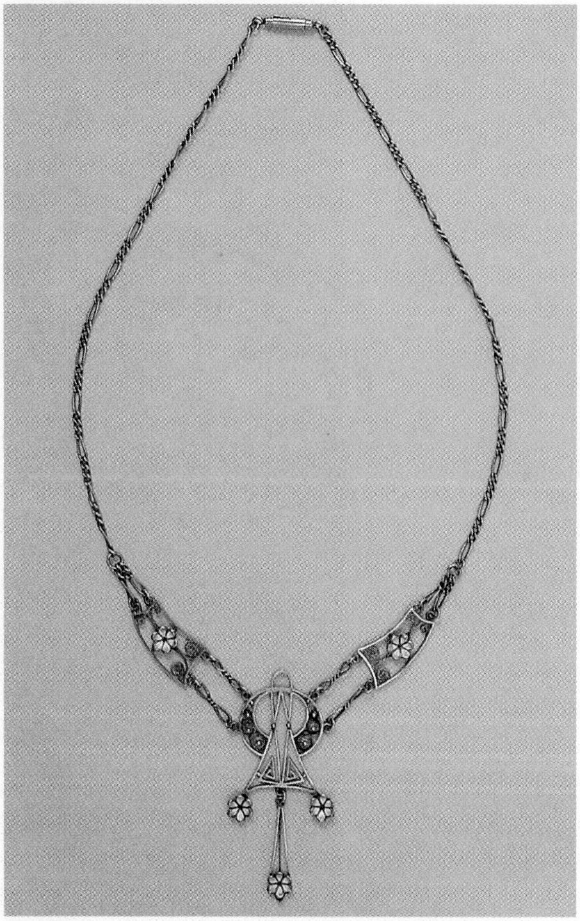

Necklace, gp sterling, enamel, c. 1905, central cusped and lobed openwork triangle with sm white and pale blue enameled flowerheads at bottom terminals, suspending an open cusped drop with enameled flowerhead terminal, top of triangle encircled by an open tapered oval with grad bead decoration suspended from double curb and fetter link chains linked to irregular open rectangles, each centering a sm enameled flowerhead flanked by wire volutes, continuing to a single chain and tubular clasp, unmkd, attributed to Marius Hammer, 2⅜" T to B at center, 17½" tl, **$600**. (Elaine Sarnoff collection)

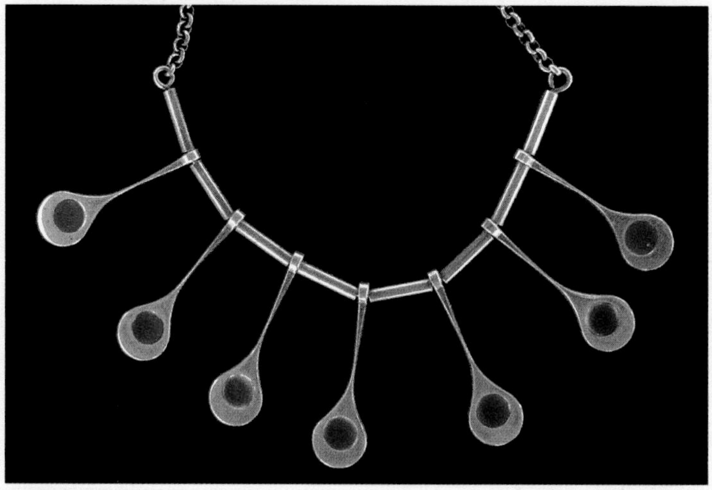

Necklace, sterling, enamel, c. 1960, a bib of eight hand-forged tubes alternating with seven elongated teardrop-shaped pendants with blue enameled discs in concave centers, suspended from cable link chain, designed by Gine Sommerfeldt for Tostrup, Norway, mkd "STERLING TOSTRUP NORWAY," and designer's mk of a sm S inside a lg G, 17" tl, drops approx. 1⅝", **$345.** (Photo courtesy of M. Schon Antiques, Bay St. Louis, MS)

Pendant, porcelain, sterling, c. 1955-60, a porcelain sphere, white ground decorated with blue and gold disks and abstract eye motifs with volutes, suspended from a cable link Y chain, rect plaque at terminal with maker's mk for Porsgrund Porcelain Factory (anchor flanked by Ps), "925S NORWAY STERLING," pendant 1¼" dia, chain 20½", **$125**. (Almunir Meghji collection)

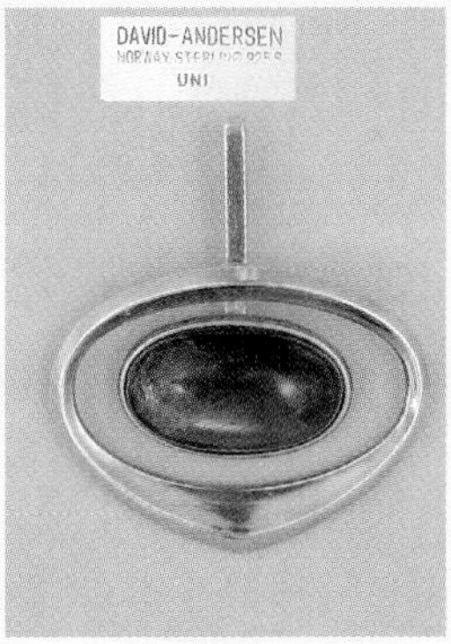

Pendant, sterling, labradorite, c. 1962, titled "Marianne's Heart," an open shaped cusped oval centering a lg oval bezel-set labradorite cab surmounted by a vertical bar with integral bail, mkd "DAVID-ANDERSEN NORWAY STERLING 925S UNI" for Uni David-Andersen, part of the "Troll" series designed by Marianne Berg, 2" w x 2" l, **$225**. (Author's collection)

Pendant, sterling, enamel, c. 1955-60, rectangular plaque with mottled olive green *basse-taille* enamel over an abstract grid design, appl half-sphere and twisted wire in lower right corner, surmounted by a flat bar with integral bail, rev imp with unidentified maker's mk of an H in a circle, "925S NORWAY STERLING," 1⅛" w x 2¼", **$245**. (Courtesy of Patrick Kapty, Mad Jewelry, Palm Springs, CA)

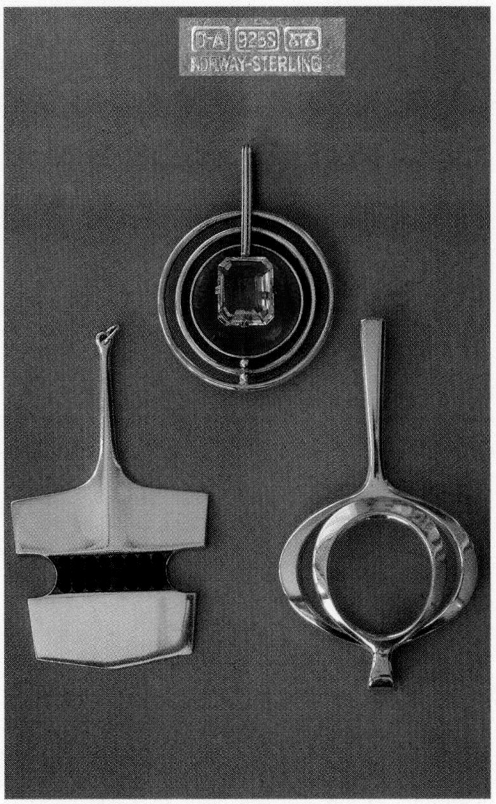

Pendants, sterling, designers for David-Andersen:
BL, enamel, c. 1965, a variation on Thor's Hammer design with a band of teal blue *basse-taille* enamel across the center, mkd "DAVID-ANDERSEN, NORWAY STERLING 925S, INV B.S.Ø" for Bjørn Sigurd Østern, designer, 2" w x 3¼" tl, **$225**.
TC, *guilloché* enamel, rock crystal, c. 1966, two concentric open circles centering a royal blue enameled disk vertically bisected by a reeded bar of silver with integral bail, surmounted by a cut-corner rect-cut prong-set rock crystal, attributed to Uni David-Andersen, maker's mk (scales) for David-Andersen, "D-A 925S NORWAY STERLING," 1¾" w x 2⅜" tl, **$225**.
BR, c. 1975, slightly convex open circle with projecting flared terminal surmounting an open oval surmounted by a tapered bar with integral bail, Toril Bjorg design, mkd "DAVID-ANDERSEN NORWAY STERLING 925S," 2" w x 3¼" tl, **$150**. (Healy collection, photo by Bruce Healy)

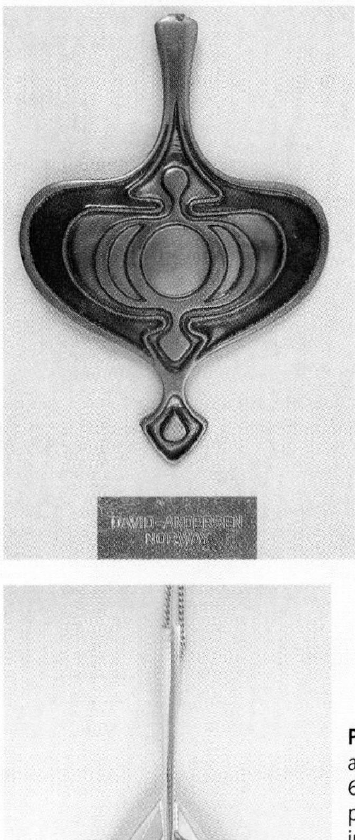

Pendant, bronze, enamel, c. 1960, spade-shaped, concentric curv design with cusped terminal, enameled in shades of light and dark blue, integral bail, mkd "DAVID-ANDERSEN NORWAY," enamel imperfect, 2½" w x 3½", **$95**. (Courtesy of Patrick Kapty, Mad Jewelry, Palm Springs, CA)

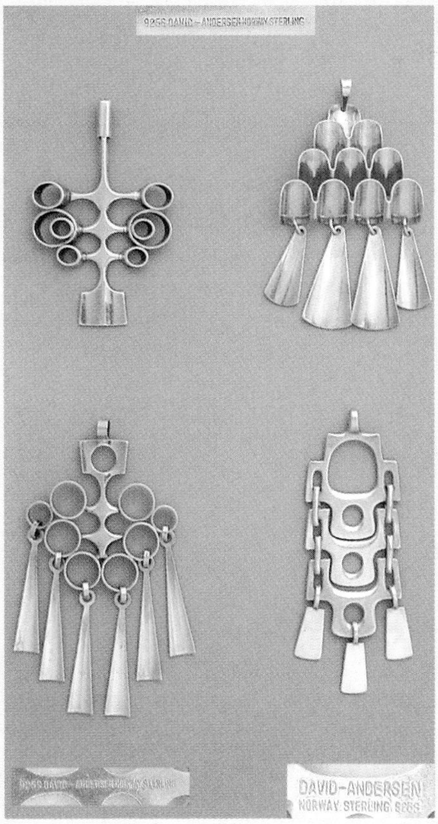

Pendants, sterling, c. 1960-65, David-Andersen, $175 each:
TL, central waisted plaque with projecting arms flanked by open ovals with a sm paddle-shaped terminal, surmounted by a shaped bar with integral bail, mkd "DAVID-ANDERSEN 925S STERLING NORWAY," 1⅝" w x 2½" tl. (Courtesy of Xcentricities, Beverly Hills, CA)
TR, three-dimensional design of four grad stepped rows of concave arched sections suspending two lg flanked by two smaller rounded concave triangular drops, integral bail, mkd "925S DAVID-ANDERSEN NORWAY STERLING," 1¾" w x 3" tl.
BL, six lg flanked by two smaller adjoining open circles suspending a fringe of six elongated concave triangular drops, flanking waisted center with circ cutout and integral bail, mkd "925S DAVID-ANDERSEN NORWAY STERLING," 1¾" w x 3⅜" tl.
BR, articulated open design of three fitted jigsaw puzzle-shaped plaques attached with lg jump rings and suspending three tapered rect drops, integral bail, mkd "DAVID-ANDERSEN NORWAY STERLING 925S," 1¼" w x 3¼" tl.
(Author's collection)

Pendant, 14k yg, amethyst, c. 1960-65, open concave pear shape centering a prong-set step-cut amethyst, continuing to a tapered bar with integral bail, design by Bjørn Sigurd Østern, mkd "D-A 585," 1" w x 2¼" tl, **$575**. (Victoria Palzkill Bonanno collection)

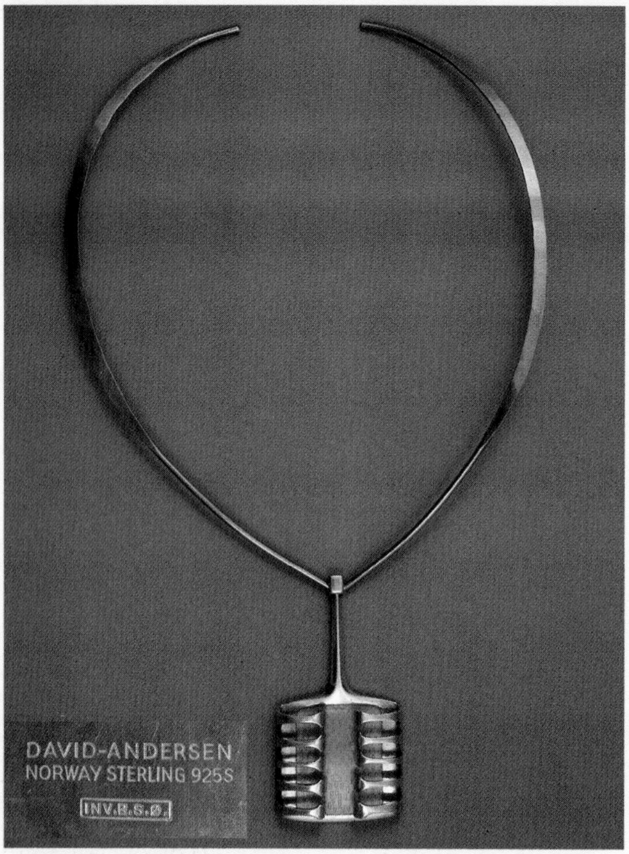

Pendant and Neckring, sterling, enamel, c. 1966, rect plaque with orange *basse-taille* enameled center flanked by overlapping silver "ribs," surmounted by a shaped tapered bar with integral bail and suspended from a hand-forged and hammered neckring, mkd "DAVID-ANDERSEN NORWAY STERLING 925S, INV. B.S.Ø" for Bjørn Sigurd Østern, designer, pendant 1⅜" w x 2½", neckring 15", **$300**. (Almunir Meghji collection)

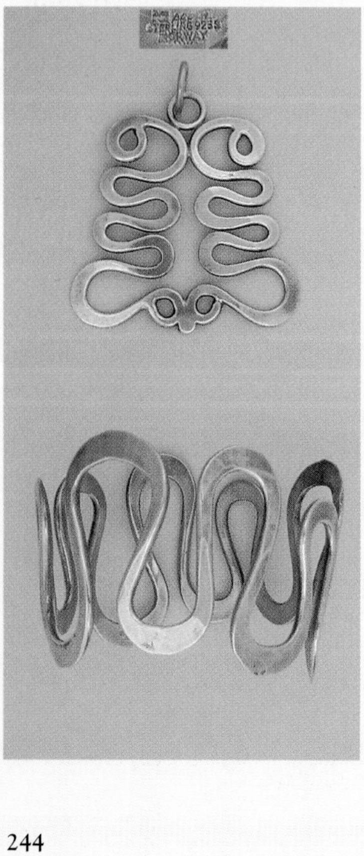

Suite: Pendant and Bangle Bracelet, sterling, c. 1960, pendant a hand-forged opposed abstract serpent design with hammered finish, bangle of undulating hammered loops, designed by Anna Greta Eker for Plus, Norway, maker's mark for Plus, "AGE NORWAY STERLING 925S," pendant 2½" w x 3", bracelet 2½" inside dia, 2" w, **$475/set**. (Courtesy of Patrick Kapty, Mad Jewelry, Palm Springs, CA)

Sweden

Wiwen Nilsson (1897-1974) was the first Swedish modernist, designing, in fact defining, the very essence of simplified form with impeccable precision. He worked briefly for Georg Jensen in Jensen's Paris studio before returning to Sweden to open his own shop in 1927. He was appointed a court jeweler in 1928. He is well- known in Europe, but has limited name recognition in the U.S., perhaps because so little of his work ever reaches our shores. In Europe, his designs in silver sell in the four- figure range.

Atelier Borgila is a well-known Swedish maker, founded by Erik Fleming (1894-1954) in 1920, still in business today. Fleming's son Lars was trained by his father and worked for the firm (see earrings and necklaces on page 246). Several other Swedish designers also worked for Borgila, including, early in his career, Sigurd Persson.

Sigurd Persson (b. 1914) is the most well-known Swedish metalsmith and jeweler of the mid-twentieth century. His widely lauded designs are noted for their strength, simplicity, and innovative concepts. Most of them are one of a kind or limited production. In 1953, Persson designed a series of modular link bracelets and necklaces for Atelier Stigbert, a Swedish production company, called "Bowl and Cube." (see page 245). In the 1960s, he created a series of rings, bracelets, necklaces, and earrings for Swedish retailer Nordiska Kompaniet that were remarkable for their originality and avant-garde style (see earrings below).

Very little Swedish jewelry has crossed the Atlantic, judging by its scarcity in the secondary market. (Swedish designers Sigvard Bernadotte and Torun Bülow-Hübe are more closely associated with the Danish firm of Georg Jensen. Danish manufacturer A. Michelsen ran a factory in Stockholm, where they marked their pieces with Swedish hallmarks and maker mark MIC from 1946 to 1963—see page 245.) There is also a paucity of information about it in print in English. The few pieces that do turn up are as well-made and designed as other Scandinavian work. Swedish jewelry is often hallmarked (see Marks on Metals appendix), with assay marks and date letters (see Tardy, *International Hallmarks on Silver*, in the References).

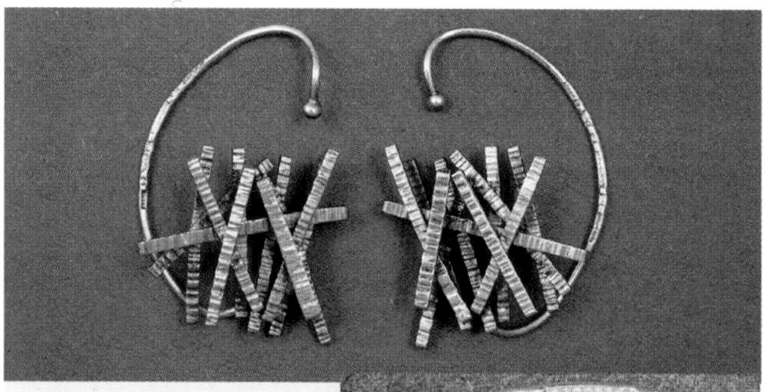

Earrings, sterling, gp sterling, date letter O9 for 1964, clusters of crisscrossing ridged gp matchsticks mounted at the base of bead-tipped over-the-ear wires, both wires imp with maker's mk "SIGP" for Sigurd Persson, Stockholm assay mk, Swedish hmks (three crowns S, date letter), "STERLING [Persson trademark] SWEDEN," 1½" w x 2⅛", **$650**. (Healy collection)

Bracelet, link, sterling, date letter for 1957, nine open-backed box-shaped links with concave tops joined with triangular wire loops, hook closure, mkd "STERLING SWEDEN," Swedish hmks, date letter G9, and mfr's signature "Stigbert" [script] for Atelier Stigbert imp on outside of two links, "Cube" design by Sigurd Persson, 1953, ½" w x 8" tl, **$150**. (Author's collection)

Bracelet, bangle, sterling, date letter X9 for 1972, irreg textured silver bands with appl vertical round wire bars alternating with appl wire circles, mkd "MARITSCHNIG, SWEDEN STERLING," maker's mk "ICO" in sq reserve for Galerie 22: an AB, Stockholm, Swedish hmks, 2⅝" inside dia, ⅞" w, **$150**. (Courtesy of Andrea Fatell, Wellsley, MA)

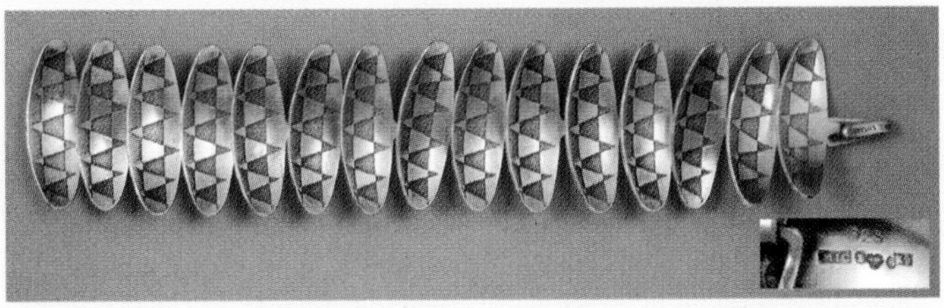

Bracelet, link, sterling, date letter K9 for 1960, fifteen elongated oval concave links with opposed triangles design, alternating textured dk and polished sections, rev of one link imp "925," "MIC" for Stockholm factory of Danish manufacturer A. Michelsen, Swedish hmks (Stockholm assay mk, three crowns in lobed reserve, S in hexagonal reserve, date letter), hook clasp mkd "STERLING SWEDEN," 1¼" w x 6¾" tl, **$200**. (Almunir Meghji collection)

Bracelet, link, sterling, dyed green chalcedony, c. 1960, overlapping concave spade-shaped links with parallel incised line borders, each centering a sm circ bezel-set green chalcedony cab, unmkd, possibly a removed link, Swedish provenance, ¾" w x 7¾" tl, **$225**. (Courtesy of Andrea Fatell, Wellsley, MA)

Earrings, sterling, date letter H9 for 1958, clusters of overlapping flat C shapes, some with hammered texture, some with polished surface, screwbacks, mkd "ABA," Swedish hmks, orig box mkd "ATELIER BORGILA, L. FLEMING" for Lars Fleming, son of founder Eric Fleming, trademark of a Viking ship within a circle, ⅞" w x 1", **$125**. (Healy collection, photo by Bruce Healy)

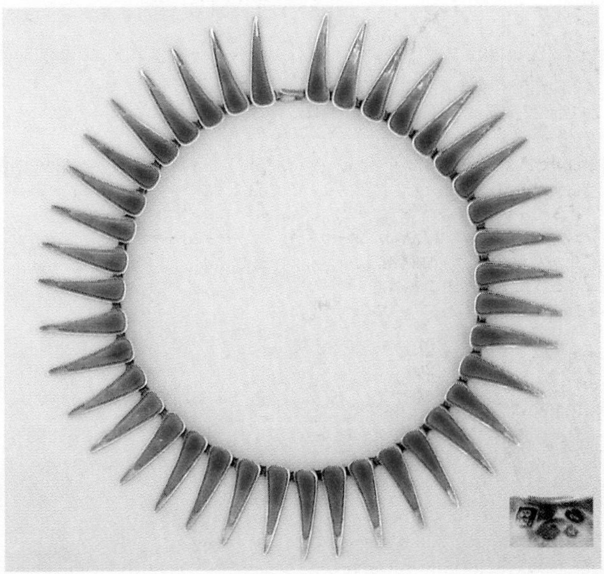

Necklace, sterling, enamel, date letter H9 for 1958, collar of radiating inverted rounded triangle concave links with teal blue enameled centers, terminal link rev imp with Swedish hmks (date letter, three crowns, S, Stockholm assay mk), maker's mk "ABA" for Atelier Borgila, hook clasp imp "STERLING SWEDEN," 1¼" w x 14" tl, **$350**. (Author's collection)

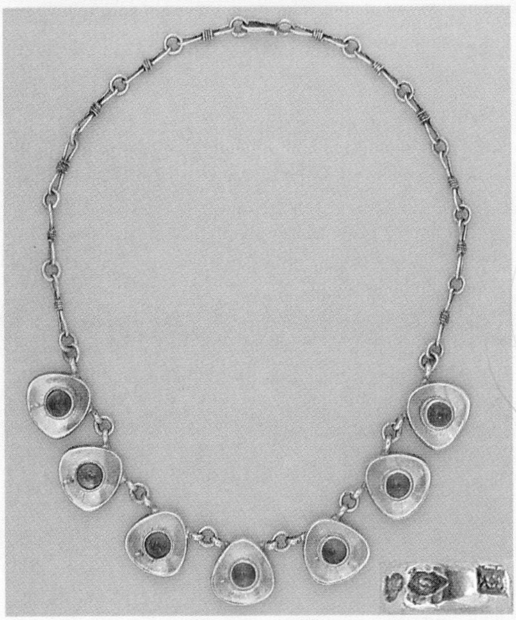

Necklace, sterling, amethysts, date letter C9 for 1953, a row of seven rounded concave triangular plaques each centering a bezel-set circ amethyst cab, joined with appl looped wires to circ jump rings, continuing to a chain of wire-wrapped bow-shaped links alternating with circ jump rings, hook clasp imp with maker's mk "CF" for Atelier Borgila, Stockholm assay mk, Swedish hmks (three crowns S, date letter), ¾" plaques, 16" tl, **$275**. (Author's collection)

Rings, sterling, 1960s:

T, date letter Q9 for 1966, four open-ended cubes forming a sq box, top surface showing two solid and two open sides, mounted at 45° on a narrow flat hexagonal shank, maker's mk "GK" for manufacturer Ge-Kå Smycken, G. Kaplan, Swedish hmks (date letter, Stockholm assay mk, three crowns, S), ⅝" sq, approx sz 7, **$85**. (Author's collection)

B, date letter S9 for 1968, flat-topped oval amethyst with tapered faceted sides set in a cupped bezel surmounting a tapered band, imp with maker's mk "ALTON" in a rectangle for manufacturer Alton Guldvaru AB, Swedish hmks (Falkoping assay mk, three crowns, S, date letter), approx ½" w x ⅞", **$125**. (Courtesy of Andrea Fatell, Wellsley, MA)

Finland

Mid-century Finnish silversmiths and jewelers were particularly adept at creating new, fresh concepts in both form and function. Although the Finns' silversmithing legacy goes back to the fourteenth century, Finnish jewelry design is a mid-twentieth century development. Shortage of silver during World War II led to the making of jewelry instead of larger objects from what little reclaimed metal was available. But forms remained traditional. A nationalistic revival of the ancient Iron Age epic, the *Kalevala* (c. 500-1100 A.D.), during the war yielded replicas of ornaments from ancient tombs, made and sold in a display of national solidarity. The company that made it, Kalevala Koru, went on to become one of the largest jewelry manufacturers in the country. After the war, the search for new ideas began in earnest, and it was then that talented artists began to emerge. But the Finns were slow to accept avant-garde design. Not until 1958, at an exhibitionexhibtion at the Galerie Artek in Helsinki, were the works of a quartet of designers—Bertel Gardberg (b. 1916, now referred to as the "father of modern silverworking in Finland"), Elis Kauppi, Börje Rajalin, and Eero Rislakki—finally appreciated.

Elis Kauppi (b. 1921) was the second of the Finnish avant-gardists to achieve recognition. He helped establish the company Kupitaan Kulta in 1945, but the initial output lacked originality. In 1952, Kauppi began designing original pieces incorporating the native Finnish gemstone spectrolite, also known as labradorite, a dark stone with an iridescent shimmering rainbow of color. Simplicity of form and innovative function, as well as the use of native stones, characterize Kauppi's and the others' work (see one of Kauppi's masterworks, a pendant/necklace titled "Mountain Stream," on page 249).

By this time, Finnish manufacturers and designers were beginning to venture into promoting Finnish products abroad. The Milan Triennale in 1951 was the first postwar international exhibition to display Finnish, as well as Danish and Swedish, decorative art. The modern designs found a receptive audience in Europe and the U.S. soon after. Triennales of 1954, 1957, and 1960 were likewise successful. Because of this warm reception, Finland began exporting in volume. Other Finnish designers and manufacturers were established in the '50s and '60s. They found a ready market for their wares overseas.

Kaunis Koru, opened in 1954, is known for its sleekly modern, deceptively simple designs. Springy silver bangles with unusual closure mechanisms seem to be a uniquely Finnish concept, which Kaunis Koru excelled at producing (see page 248). Several well-known designers' work has been produced by Kaunis Koru, including Jan Salakari, Paula Häiväoja, and Mirjam Salminen (see bracelet on page 247). Kaija Aarikka (b. 1929), a textile designer turned jewelry-maker, founded her own company in 1959, making wood and silver jewelry, as it continues to do today. The tradition of using bronze for jewelry was popularized by Kalelevala Koru in its wartime Iron Age reproductions. Pennti Sarpaneva (1925-1978) was known for his work in cast bronze in the '60s and '70s, which was made by Kalevala Koru and Turun Hopea (see bracelet on page 247). Seppo Tamminen also worked in cast bronze (see bracelet on page 247), but during the early part of his career in the '60s, he made some limited edition pieces in sterling (see necklace and bracelet below).

Björn Weckström (b. 1935) is considered one of the most innovative Finnish designers of the 1960s, and is still working today. He was one of the founders and the first designer for the well-known Finnish firm, Lapponia. He was a Lunning prizewinner in 1968. Cast jewelry was the new wrinkle of the '60, and in fact wrinkled is what some of Weckström's gold and silver jewelry looked like, sometimes combined with acrylic. When Yoko Ono wore one of his silver and acrylic ring designs on the Dick Cavett television show in 1972, Weckström's international fame was assured. In 1977, Carrie Fisher wore a necklace of his in her role as Princess Leia in the movie "Star Wars." Appropriately, this necklace was part of the design line Weckström created in

Suite: Necklace and Hinged Bangle, sterling, c. 1965-70, necklace with articulated lobed and cusped pendant cut from sheet, with layered wing-like projections, appl solid beads and punchwork, suspended from a chain of alternating rect and circ plaques with appl wire and perforations, bangle with a curv scalloped "tongue" designed to project over the back of the hand, continuing to a curv band, hingepin closure linked to safety chain, necklace mkd "HANDMADE FINLAND STERLING 925" and script signature "Seppo Tamminen," #2/25, bracelet with same mks, #7/25, necklace 3½" w x 7⅛" tl at front, 22¼" tl, bracelet 2⅜" inside dia x 3" T to B, **$650**. (Author's collection)

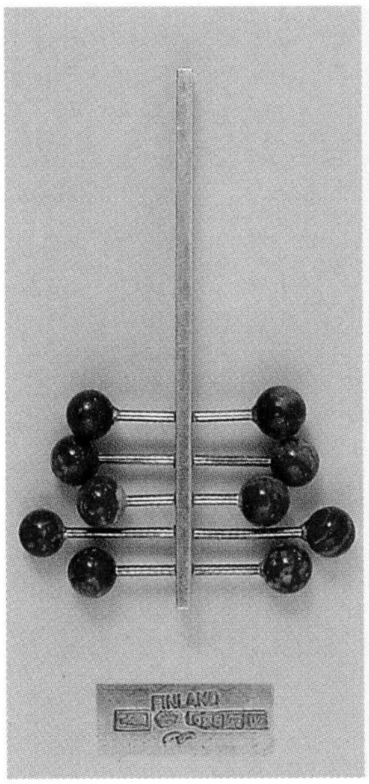

Pendant, sterling, lapis lazuli, date letter U7 for 1973, a single flat bar of silver turned on edge, with a rect cutout for suspension (from chain or neckring), the lower portion intersected at right angles by five lapis bead-tipped silver wires of unequal lengths, side of bar imp with maker's mk for Auran Kultaseppä, "FINLAND," Finnish hmks (crown in heart, 925, Turku assay, date letter), designer mk for Pekka Piekäinen (*PP*), 1⅝" w x 2⅝", **$250**. (Caren Fine collection)

sterling, (which sometimes incorporated tiny human figures), called the "Space Silver" series (see rings on page 249). In the '70s, another series made with chemically colored cast bronze was called the "Flame Bronze" series (see pendant on page 248 and rings on page 249). Each design in the Weckström oeuvre was given a name. Now that American collectors' attention has once again been called to his work in recent English-language publications, Weckström pieces have become well known and sought-after.

In the early '70s, a company called Kultateollisuus made a series of pendants and chains, all variations on a circular form, the centers set with a variety of native Finnish stones. During this same period, Pekka Piekäinen designed simple but elegant pendants and striking rings with projecting elements, sometimes incorporating lapis beads (see pendant above and rings on page 249), made by Auran Kultaseppä in Turku. He has come to be known as Finland's foremost designer of silver objects and jewelry.

It is possible to find pieces from the late '50s through the '70s on the secondary market in the U.S. made by the aforementioned makers and designers, as well as several others (see appendix for Finnish makers' marks). The names may seem strange and difficult to pronounce, but the quality of Finnish design and craftsmanship speaks for itself. The Finnish hallmark for local manufacture is a crown inside a heart (see Marks on Metals appendix). They use assay marks, date letters, and manufacturers' marks in a manner similar to the British, but unfortunately, some Finnish pieces are not fully hallmarked.

Bracelet, link, lacquered bronze, c. 1965, seven links of quadrate crosses with clusters of three sm disks at terminals, each surmounted by a pierced flattened sphere at center, v-spring and box clasp, safety chain, mkd "BRONZE SARPANEVA FINLAND" for Pentti Sarpaneva, 1½" w x 8⅛" tl, **$100**. (Author's collection)

Bracelet, hinged bangle, bronze, c. 1970, cast in two matching halves, each a curv open equilateral cross shape with appl central irregular convex disk and oblate beads with dimpled centers, hingepin closure linked to safety chain, mkd "SEPPO TAMMINEN, MADE IN FINLAND," 2½" inside dia x 2½" T to B, **$125**. (Author's collection)

Bracelet, bangle, sterling, amethyst, date letter U7 for 1973, flat band curving up and widening to a circ concave disk front terminal and a lg oval amethyst cab mounted in the opposing terminal, front closure on underside of amethyst hooks into underside of disk, inside imp with Finnish hmks, "925," maker's mk for Kaunis Koru, U7, designer's initials "OLW" for Olavi L. Wehmersuo, outside imp with Dutch import mks, 1¾" top to bottom at center, 2⅝" w when closed, 2⅜" inside dia, **$500**. (Author's collection)

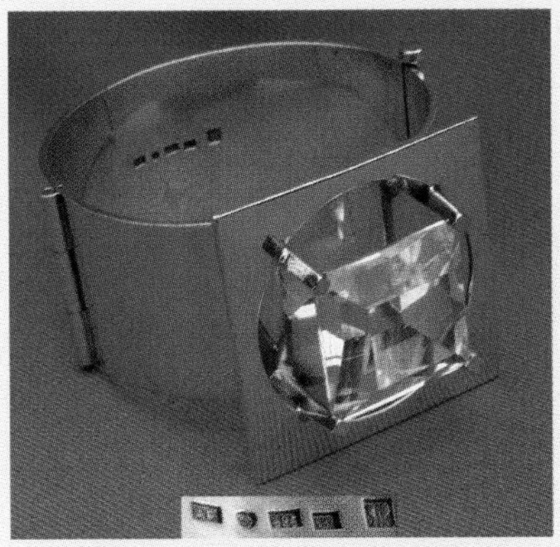

Bracelet, hinged bangle, sterling, rock crystal quartz, date letter U7 for 1973, design by Mirjam Salminen, geo architectonic design of a raised sq platform centering a lg sq faceted prong-set rock crystal elevated on sq rods over a circ opening surmounting a plain wide hinged band with sliding hingepin and tube closure, maker's mk "AP" for Kari Aarre Apell, and mfr's mk for Kaunis Koru, Finnish hmk (crown in heart), "925," 1⅝" w x ⅝" hgt at top, 2⅛" inside dia, **$750**. (Author's collection)

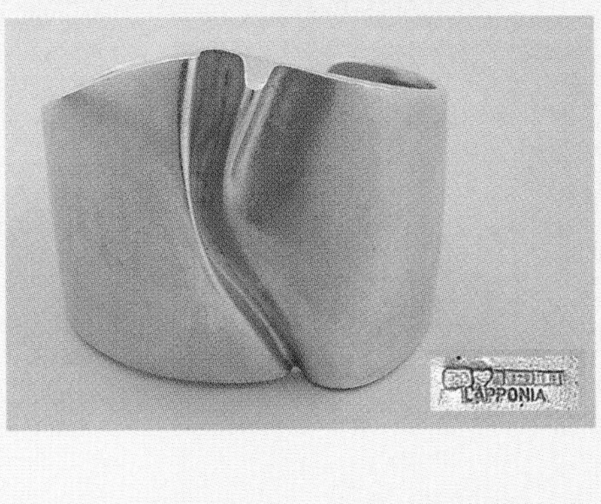

Bracelet, cuff, sterling, date letter I8 for 1986, "Ygol's Jewel" design by Björn Weckström, tapered band with a center curv "fold," textured surface and polished edges, imp with maker's mk for Lapponia Oy, Finnish hmks, "LAPPONIA," 1½" w at center, 2⅛" inside dia, **$550**. (Courtesy of Julia Stayden, Los Angeles, CA)

Brooch/Pin, sterling, rose quartz, c. 1960, in the shape of a stylized eye centering a sm circ high-domed rose quartz cab, rev imp with maker's mk for Kupittaan Kulta [anvil], "STERLING FINLAND," 2¼" x ⅞", **$125**. (Almunir Meghji collection)

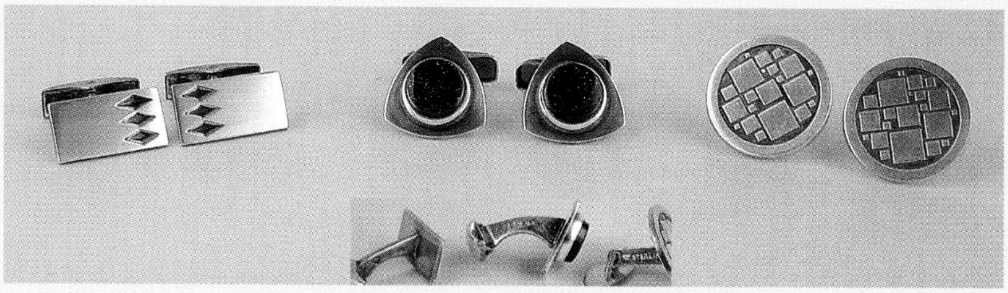

Cuff Links, sterling, c. 1960s:
L, date letter O7 for 1967, rect with a row of three oxidized lozenges on one side of each face, toggle findings, curved shank imp with maker's initials "EP" for Keravan Kultaseppä (E. Penttinen), Finnish hmks (crown in heart, 813H, Helsinki assay mk, date letter), ¾" w x ⅜", **$50**.
C, c. 1965, convex-sided concave triangles centering bezel-set circ dark blue "goldstone" glass disks, toggle findings on curved shanks imp with anvil mk for Kupittaan Kulta, "FINLAND, STERLING," ¾" x ¾", **$95**.
(Courtesy of Andrea Fatell, Wellsley MA)
R, c. 1960, circ disks, polished lg and sm flat squares slightly raised on oxidized ground, articulated oval plaque foot joined to rounded rect shank imp with maker's mk for Kupittaan Kulta Oy, "STERLING," ½" dia, **$85**. (Courtesy of Gilly Phipps, Philadelphia, PA)

Brooches/Pins, sterling:
TC, date letter R7 for 1970, irregular circ shape composed of varying sizes and heights of short tubes with oxidized concave disk centers, joined at the sides, maker's mk for Kaunis Koru, designer's mk (conjoined HN) for Helge Narsakka, Finnish hmks (crown in heart, 925, Lahti assay mk, date letter), 2" dia, **$200**.
BL, date letter H7 for 1961, shell-shaped concave plaque surmounted by an inverted appl convex shell shape centering three oval bezel-set rhodocrosite cabs, oxidized ground, rev imp with maker's mk (conjoined HN) for Helge Narsakka, Finnish hmks (crown in heart, 916H, Lahti assay mk, date letter), and "KASITYÖ" (handmade), 2" w x 1¾", **$175**.
BR, date letter U7 for 1973, a polished concave rounded ster crescent partially enclosing a lg circ bezel-set sodalite cab centrally mounted on a short bar, maker's mk for Auran Kultaseppä, Finnish hmks (crown in heart, 925, Turku assay mk, date letter), 1¾" w x 1⅝", **$175**.
(Author's collection)

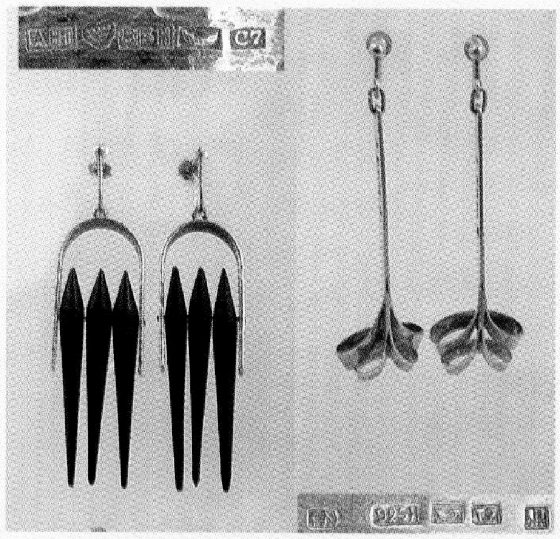

Earrings, pendent:
L, 830 silver, ebony, date letter C7 for 1956, arch of hammered silver centering three articulated ebony bicones, screwbacks, maker's mk AHI for Aatos Hauli, Finnish hmks (crown in heart, 813H, Helsinki assay mk, date letter), ⅝" w x 2½" tl, **$200**.
R, sterling, date letter T7 for 1972, each a single long flat ster bar shank opening to a curving backward double loop terminal, screwbacks, shank imp with designer's mk (conjoined HN for Helge Narsakka), Finnish hmks (925H, Helsinki assay mk, date letter), maker's mk for Kaunis Koru, ⅝" w x 2⅝" tl, **$175**. (Author's collection)

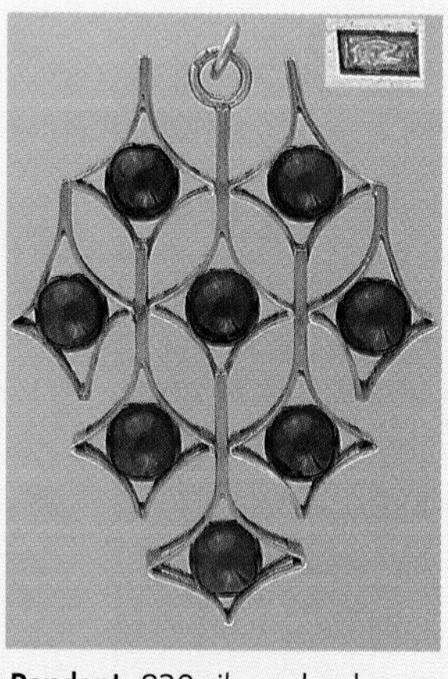

Pendant, 830 silver, dyed green chalcedony, c. 1970, a network of open cusped lozenges enclosing eight free-moving chalcedony spheres, joined to vertical bars forming a shield shape, maker's mk for Salovaara (bear) and "830H" on circ loop for bail, 2⅛" w x 3¼", **$245**. (Courtesy Patrick Kapty, Mad Jewelry, Palm Springs, CA)

Pendant and Chain, patinated bronze, c. 1971-1978, "General Motors" from the "Flame Bronze" series designed by Björn Weckström, rect section of intricate mechanistic design surmounting a three-dimensional semi-circ organic motif with appl purple and blue chemical coloration, suspended from a continuous chain with adjustment bracket, mkd "LAPPONIA BW FINLAND," 1⅞" w x 3⅛" l x 28" tl, **$300**. (Author's collection)

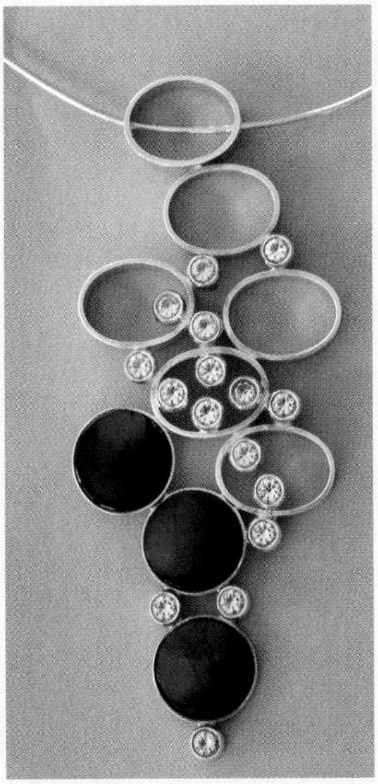

Pendant and Neckring, spectrolite, rock crystal, sterling, c. 1975, "Mountain Stream" by Elis Kauppi, a cascading abstract design of stylized bubbles, open ster ovals interspersed with sm circ-cut bezel-set rock crystals mounted inside and outside the ovals, terminating in a line of three lg circ bezel-set spectrolite disks and three bezel-set rock crystals, suspended from a plain wire neckring, imp with maker's mk for Kupittan Kulta [anvil], "925 FINLAND," 2" w x 4⅛" tl, **$1,200**. (Healy collection, photo by Bruce Healy)

Rings, sterling, 1970s:
L, date letter T7 for 1972, a sq plaque surmounted by a folded piece of silver resembling an open book, mounted on a plain band, imp with maker's mk for Auran Kultaseppä, Turku assay mark, "925H," ¾" square, sz 7½, **$65**.
C, date letter U7 for 1973, a convex disk with a deep concave slash from one side to just past the center surmounting a plain band, Turku assay mk, "MJH 925" for Sirokoru Ky Hyvarinen, designed by Matti Hyvarinen, 1¼" widest dimension, sz 5½, **$100**.
R, date letter X7 for 1975, three-dimensional design of three overlapping semi-circ disks, the lower layers oxidized, tapering to an adjustable shank, maker's mk for Kaunis Koru, "UJK 925," ⅞" widest, adjustable, **$100**. (Almunir Meghji collection)

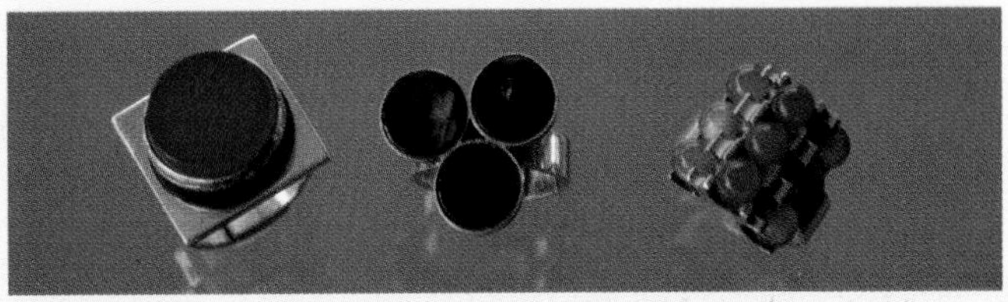

Rings, sterling and gemstones, maker's mk for Kupittaan Kulta [anvil], c. 1970:
L, bezel-set disk of carnelian on oxidized square base, mkd "925 S," ¾" square, **$150**.
C, three bezel-set spectrolite disks in a triangular shape surmounting a plain band, mkd "925 S FINLAND," ⅞", **$175**.
R, three vertical rows of alternating dyed blue and white chalcedony spheres in an interlocking three-dimensional grid of silver, surmounting a plain band, mkd "925 S FINLAND," ⅝" w x ¾", **$200**. (Healy collection, photo by Bruce Healy)

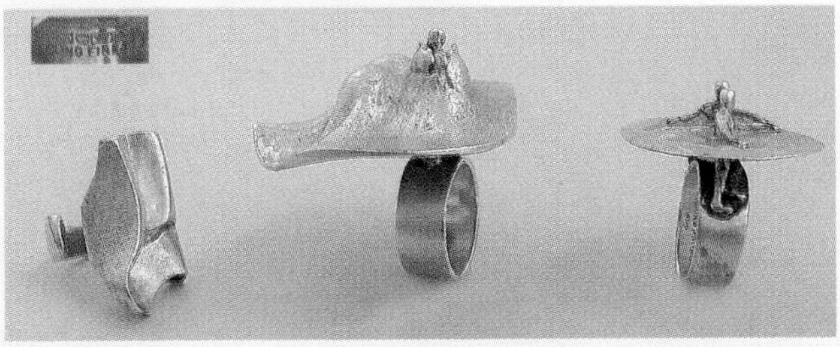

Rings designed by Björn Weckström, sterling, imp with maker's mk for Lapponia Oy:
L, date letter V7 for 1974, penannular, organic motif of continuous cast construction, mkd "925 LAPPONIA," Finnish hmk (crown in heart), sz 7, 1⅛" w at center, **$250**.
C, date letter R7 for 1970, "Man in Clouds" from the "Space Silver" series, circ shape of varying thickness, irregular "moonscape" with a sm embedded "moon man" surmounting a plain wide band, mkd "BW STERLING FINLAND 925H," Finnish hmks (crown in heart, Helsinki assay mk, date letter), sz 7, top 1½" x 1⅝, hgt 1⅛", **$700**.
R, date letter Q7 for 1969, "Dance in the Galaxy" from the "Space Silver" series, horizontal textured disk surmounted by two sm embedded "moonmen" in a dance posture, their lower bodies below the disk surmounting a plain wide band, mkd "925H," Finnish hmks (crown in heart, Helsinki assay mk, date letter), "STERLING FINLAND," Swedish import mks (three crowns in oval reserve, S), sz 7½, top 1¼" dia x ⅝" hgt, **$450**. (Courtesy of Julia Stayden, Los Angeles, CA)

Rings from the "Flame Bronze" series designed by Björn Weckström for Lapponia, patinated bronze, c. 1970-75, mkd "LAPPONIA BJORN FINLAND":
L, "Pentagon," a single penannular cast piece of a triangular top with open circ center, flanked on one side by a mechanistic motif, some wear to purple chemical coloration, ¾" x ½", sz 7, **$175**. (Courtesy of Patrick Kapty, Mad Jewelry, Palm Springs, CA)
C, "Henry J," three-dimensional circ shape with irregular broken center and interior with chemically colored purple mechanistic motif, 1⅛" dia, sz 4½, **$250**.
R, "Scarab," a continuous cast piece with one irregular bracket-shaped terminal enclosing the other narrow rounded terminal, chemical coloring worn, 1" x ⅞", sz 6½, **$175**. (Author's collection)

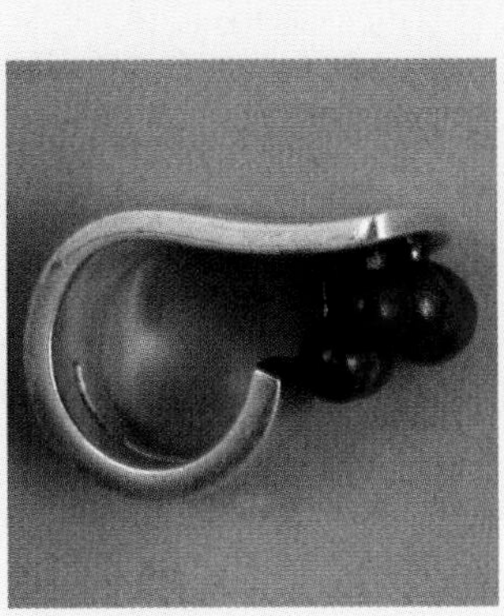

Ring, sterling, lapis lazuli, date letter V7 for 1974, continuous band of thick gauge silver forming shank and extending above the finger, with five post-set lapis beads of varying sizes mounted on the inner surface, inside shank imp with maker's mk for Auran Kultaseppä, Finnish hmks (crown in heart, 925, Turku assay, date letter), designer's mk "*PP*" for Pekka Piekäinen, "FINLAND," ⅞" T to B, sz 6, **$450**. (Almunir Meghji collection)

Ring, 830 silver, date letter N7 for 1966, a crown of bead-tipped sq wires enclosing a lg freely-moving spherical bead surmounting a plain tapered band, inside imp "E. GRANIT & CO," maker's mk for Eric Granit, Finnish hmks (crown in heart, 813H, Helsinki assay mk, date letter), sz 7, ⅝" w at top, **$100**. (Author's collection)

Rings designed by Matti Hyvarinen, sterling and gemstones, mkd "MJH" in a rectangle, maker's mk for Sirokoru Ky, Turku assay mk, date letter V7 for 1974:
L, dyed-blue chalcedony sphere held by a silver arc forming over-sized prongs, adjustable shank, mkd "925," ⅜" w x ⅝", **$125**.
C, onyx disk in a raised circ setting, adjustable shank, mkd "925 MADE IN FINLAND," ⅝" dia, **$145**.
R, upright amethyst disk held in an arc of silver forming over-sized prongs, adjustable shank, mkd "925 made in finland," ¾" w x ⅝" high, **$125**.
(Healy collection, photo by Bruce Healy)

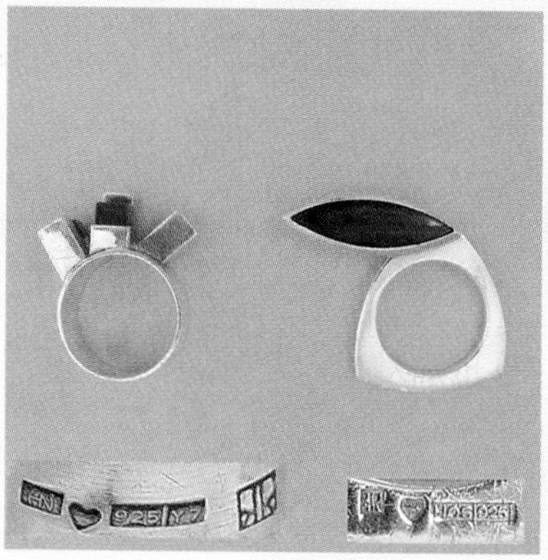

Rings, sterling, gemstones, maker's mk for Kaunis Koru:
L, date letter Y7 for 1976, plain wide band surmounted by three elongated sq bars of varying heights projecting at angles, and two elongated sq bezels set with dyed green chalcedony cubes, designer mk (conjoined HN) for Helge Narsakka, Finnish hmks (crown in heart, 925, date letter), maker's mk, sz 7, ⅞" w at top, **$150**.
R, c. 1985, rounded triangular flat shank surmounted by a navette-shaped spectrolite cab bezel-set flush in a ridged backing and mounted on edge, side of shank imp with maker's mk, Finnish hmk (crown in heart), "HOS" for Henri Sorensen Kultas of Turku, "925," sz 7, 1⅛" w at top, **$225**.
(Author's collection)

Rings, 830 silver, enamel, c. 1975, design by Liisa Vitali for Kultakeskus Oy of Helsinki, mkd "MADE IN FINLAND, 830 S," $200 each:
L, hollow double domed disks, the top surface with cutout circ openings revealing a blue enameled interior, surmounting a tapered shank, sz 8½, 1" dia x ½" h at top.
R, red enameled interior, sz 7. (Author's collection)

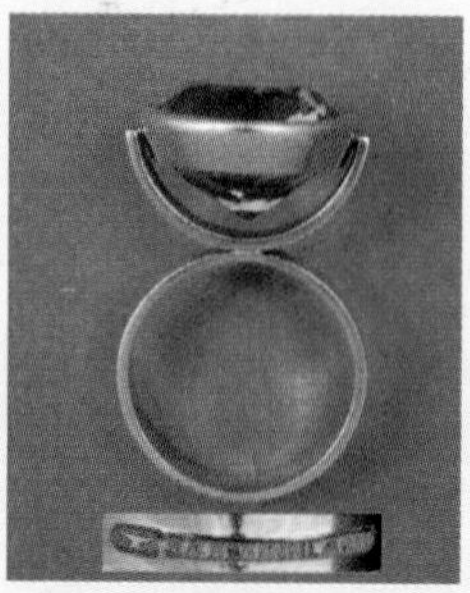

Ring, 14k yg, citrine, c. 1970, semi-circ yg band supporting a circ bezel-set faceted citrine, surmounting a plain circ yg band, inside imp with maker's mk for Kupittaan Kulta [anvil], "585, FINNLAND," sz 7½, ¾" across at top, **$400**. (Courtesy of Patrick Kapty, Mad Jewelry, Palm Springs, CA)

Suite: Bangle Bracelet, Pendant, and Earrings, sterling, green "chrome" chalcedony, date letter S7 for 1971, bangle a cluster of five open-backed wide triangular prong-set green chalcedony spheres mounted on a curved ster plaque joined by a hinge to a ster band, safety chain, pendant of similar cluster design with integral bail, earrings each a single drop with a chalcedony sphere terminal, screwbacks, bracelet imp with maker's mk (bear) for Salovaara Ky, Finnish hmks, (crown in heart, Turku assay mk, date letter), bracelet 2½" inside dia, pendant 1⅛" w x 2⅜", earrings 1¼" tl, **$550**. (Courtesy of Patrick Kapty, Mad Jewelry, Palm Springs, CA)

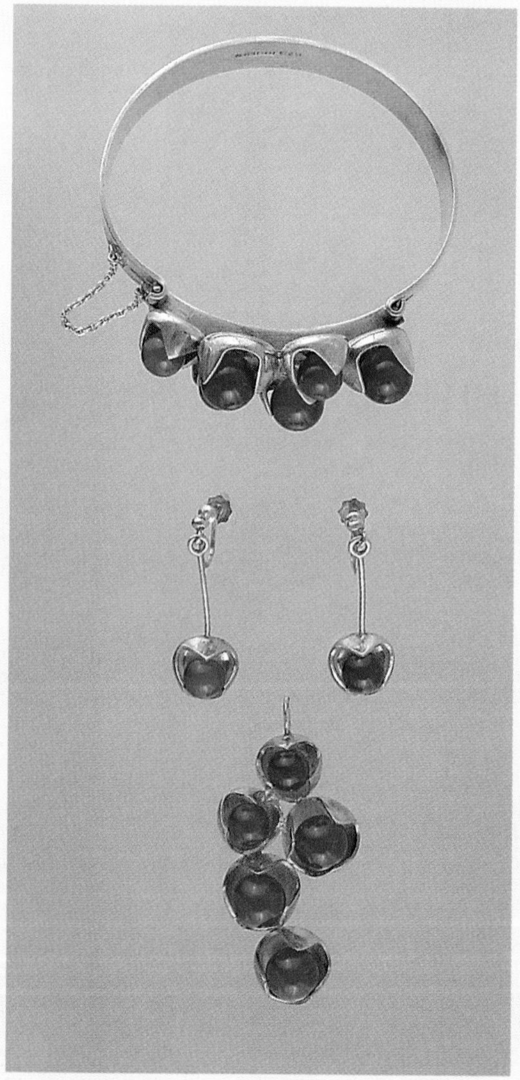

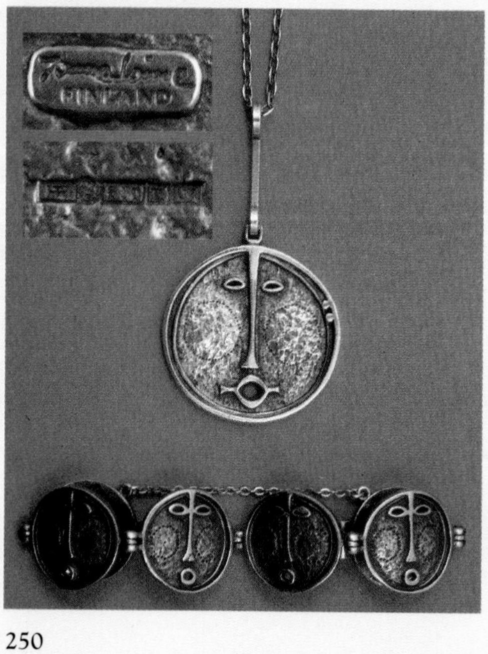

Suite: Pendant and Chain, Link Bracelet, 830 silver, date letter U7 for 1973, pendant a single lg disk with appl wire forming a stylized face with pierced mouth and textured bg, bracelet a series of six sm disks of similar design, safety chain, both pcs sgd "Jorma Laine [SCRIPT] FINLAND," maker's mk for Turun Hopea, Finnish hmks (crown in heart, 830, Turku assay mk, date letter), pendant 2" dia, chain 20" tl, bracelet 1¼" w x 7½" tl, **$550**. (Courtesy of Patrick Kapty, Mad Jewelry, Palm Springs, CA)

Marks On Metals

Marks listed shown larger than actual size

GOLD:

Solid karats:

9c/ct (Brit.)	15c/ct (Brit.)
10k	18k or 18c/ct
12k or 12c/ct	20k
14k	22kor 22c/ct

14KP = plumb (exact) [not used until c. 1976]

375 = 9c/ct

583 or 585 = 14k

750 = 18k

Eagle's head (French) = 18k

Eagle's Head

1/20 14k (or 12k) GF = gold-filled

RGP = rolled gold plate

HGE = heavy gold electroplate

PLATINUM:

900 Plat - 100 Irid
(alloyed with 10% iridium)

Dog's head (French after 1912)

Dog's Head

SILVER:

925 = sterling (92.5% silver)

British: lion passant = sterling

Lion Passant

French: boar's head or crab = 800

Boar's Head

Crab

Swedish: three crowns = 830 or higher (S after 1912, oval reserve for imports)

Sweden

Finnish: **813H** = 830; **916H** = 935

Finland

Austro-Hungarian: dog's or lion's head = 750 or higher (1866-1937)

.800
Dog's Head

.750
Lion's Head

800, 825, 830, 850 (European or continental), **900 standard** or **coin** (American before 1906) marked on silver = lower silver content than sterling or 925 (92.5% silver, 7.5% copper)

EPNS = electroplated nickel silver

German silver, nickel silver = NO silver content (copper, nickel, zinc alloy)

Alpaca = copper, zinc, nickel, 2% silver

American Manufacturer's Marks

NEWARK NJ

ALLING & CO.

ALLSOPP & ALLSOPP

BIPPART, GRISCOM & OSBORN

CARTER, HOWE (after 1915, GOUGH) & CO.

CRANE & THEURER

A. J. HEDGES & CO.

WILLIAM B. KERR & CO.

KREMENTZ & CO.

LARTER & SONS

ENOS RICHARDSON & CO.

RIKER BROS.

SLOAN & CO.

TAYLOR & CO. (for 10K)

UNGER BROS.

WHITESIDE & BLANK (HENRY BLANK, CRESARROW)

WORDLEY, ALLSOPP & BLISS

GEORGE W. SHIEBLER & CO., NEW YORK, NY

TIFFANY & CO., NEW YORK, NY

GORHAM MANUFACTURING, CO., PROVIDENCE, RI

Mid-Century Modern American Studio Jewelers

(Dates of birth/death where known)

PAUL H. ACKERMAN 1900-1968
CARLTON BALL 1911-1992
MILDRED LEE BALL
WARD BENNETT
FRANZ BERGMANN 1898-1977
HARRY BERTOIA 1915-1978
MERLE N. BOYER
JULES BRENNER 1917-1991
IRENA BRYNNER b. 1917
ALEXANDER CALDER 1898-1976
MILTON CAVAGNARO 1915-1993
BETTY COOKE b. 1924
MARGRET CRAVER (WITHERS) b. 1907
MARGARET DE PATTA 1903-1964

Margaret De Patta

JOSÉ DE RIVERA 1904-1985

Claire Falkenstein

CLAIRE FALKENSTEIN 1908-1997
FRED FARR b. 1914
LOIS FRANKE (WARREN)
ELSA FREUND 1912-2001
ARNOLD FREW b. 1922
RICHARD GOMPF b. 1928
RAY GRAVES b. 1921
CLIFFORD HERROLD
(JOAN) HURST & (JILL) KINGSBURY
ADDA HUSTED-ANDERSEN 1900-1990
MICHAEL JERRY b. 1937
SAM KRAMER 1913-1964

Sam Kramer

MARY KRETSINGER 1915-2001
ROBERT LASNIER
ED LEVIN b. 1921
ESTHER LEWITTES 1904-1990
PAUL LOBEL 1900-1983
NITA LUSTIG
PETER MACCHIARINI 1909-2001
EVERETT MAC DONALD 1924-1991
PHYLLIS MALDONADO (JACOBS) 1907-1990
FRANK MIRAGLIA
PHILIP MORTON 1911-2001
JACK NUTTING
HARRY OSAKI
EARL PARDON 1926-1991
JAMES PARKER 1915-1987

James Parker

PHILIP PAVAL 1899-1971
RONALD H. PEARSON 1924-1996
CORALYNN PENCE 1909-1994
ALVIN PINE
SVETOZAR (1918-1998) & RUTH (1920-1975) RADAKOVITCH
FRANCISCO (FRANK) REBAJES 1907-1990
MERRY RENK b. 1921
FLORENCE RESNIKOFF
BARNEY M. REID 1913-1992
RUTH ROACH 1913-1979
CAROLINE ROSENE
GEORGE K. SALO 1915-1990
CHRISTIAN SCHMIDT d. 1974
H. FRED SKAGGS d. 1983
OLAF SKOOGFORS 1930-1973
ART SMITH 1917-1982
POLLY STEHMAN
HENRY STEIG 1906-1973
BILL TENDLER 1924-1981
ED WIENER 1918-1991
BYRON WILSON b. 1919
BOB WINSTON b. 1915

20th Century American Costume Jewelry Manufacturers/Designers

For updates, additional info, manufacturers and designers, visit: www.illusionjewels.com/list.html

ccessocraft c. 1930-1998
ART c. 1950-1980
Avon 1971-present
McClelland Barclay c.1935-1943
Barclay 1946-c.1957
Beau (sterling) 1947-present
Bergère 1946-1979
Les Bernard 1962-1996
Bogoff [Spear Novelty Co.] c.1946-1959?
Boucher 1937-1971 ["Phrygian cap" mark in use 1937-1949]

Marcel Boucher

BSK c.1948-present [?]
Nadja Buckley c. 1940-1979
Calvaire c. 1920-c.1960
Hattie Carnegie 1918-1976 [first jewelry 1939]
Castlecliff c. 1918-1977
Alice Caviness 1945-? [Caviness died 1983]
Chanel 1914-1939, 1954-present (most early, some later pieces unmarked)
Chanel Novelty Co. 1941 [Reinad]
Ciner 1892-present [first costume, 1931]
Cini (sterling) 1922-1970, 1993-present
Coro 1901-1979
  Corocraft (sterling pre-1950) 1933-1979
  Francois 1938-c.1960
  Vendome 1944-1979
  (Coro, Inc. Canada, to present)
Sarah Coventry 1949-c.1984
Danecraft (sterling) 1939-1977 Felch-Wehr Co 1977-present
Deja 1939-1940 [changed to Reja 1941]
Wm de Lillo and Robert Clark 1967-?
DeMario 1945-1965
DeNicola 1957-1970
R.[Ralph] DeRosa 1934-1970
Christian Dior 1948-present [jewelry]
Eisenberg Original c.1935-1945 (sterling 1943-1948)
  E. (script mark) c. 1942-1945
  EISENBERG (block letters) c. 1945-1958
  EISENBERG ICE © (block letters) 1970-present
  (no mark 1958-1970, many pieces not marked 1970-1990)

Eisenberg "E" Mark

Eisenberg Ice (script) with year 1994 and 2000 (reissued "Classic" series)

Emmons 1949-1981

Eugene c. 1950-1960

Florenza c. 1950-1981

Gerry's c. 1950-c.1996

Givenchy 1952-present

Leo Glass 1928-1957

Stanley Hagler 1953-1996

HAR (Hargo Jewelry Co.) c. 1950-1960

Miriam Haskell 1924-present (most pieces not marked 1924-c. 1947)

Hobé 1927-present [under different ownership]

Hollycraft 1948-1971

Joseff of Hollywood 1938-present

Kramer 1943-c.1980

Krementz 1866-present [no costume after 1997]

KJL/Kenneth J. Lane 1963-present

Laguna 1944-c. 1980?

Lang (sterling) 1946-1977?

Ledo 1949 c. 1962/Polcini c.1960-c.1980?
(DBA Leading Jewelry 1911-1948)

Lisner 1938-c.1985 [mark; co. founded c.1904]

Marvella 1911-present
(1982-2000: a division of The Monet Group, 2000-present owned by Liz Claiborne)

Mazer Bros 1923-1951 [mark from1926]
Jomaz/Joseph Mazer 1946-81

Ming's of Honolulu c. 1940-1999

Monet 1937-present
(1989-1994: a subsidiary of Crystal Brands
Jewelry Group; 1994-2000: Chase Capital Partners, Lattice Holding, 2000-present, owned by Liz Claiborne)

Napier c. 1922-1999

Original by Robert 1942-1979
(Fashioncraft Jewelry Co.)

D'Orlan c. 1960-?

Panetta 1945-1995

Pell 1941-present ?

Pennino 1926-1961

Peruzzi c. 1900-present

Rebajes 1932-c. 1967

Regency c. 1950-1970

Reinad c. 1922-c.1955 [Chanel mark 1941]

Réja 1941-1953

Renoir 1946-1964/ Matisse 1952-1964/ Sauteur 1958-1963

Rice-Weiner 1938-1950? (Thief of Bagdad, Korda, McClelland Barclay, c.1940s)

Nettie Rosenstein c.1935-1975

Sandor c. 1938-1972

Schiaparelli 1931-1973
(most pre-1949 unmarked)

Schrager c.1925-c.1962? (Jonné, c.1950s)

Schreiner N.Y. 1939-1977

Silson Inc. 1937-c.1945?

Staret c. 1940-1947

Yves St. Laurent 1959-2002

Tortolani c. 1950-1976, reopened 2002

Trifari 1918-present [mark since 1920, sterling 1942-1947]
TKF (Trifari, Krussman & Fishel) 1925-1938
(mark in use from 1935)
(1975-1988: subsidiary of Hallmark; 1988-1994: Crystal Brands; 1994-2000: Chase Capital Partners, Lattice Holding, a division of The Monet Group; purchased by Liz Claiborne, 2000)

KTF.
Trifari, Krussman & Fishel

Van S Authentics c.1935-1969

Vogue 1936-c. 1975

Weiss 1942-1971

Whiting & Davis 1876-present?

Wiesner c. 1953-?

WMCA (White Metal Casters' Assoc.) 1930-?

Other Manufacturers: Dates of Operation Unknown

Garman

Gloria

Juliana

Ramé

Tara

Warner

Joseph Wiesner NY

References:

Joann Dubbs Ball, *Costume Jewelers, The Golden Age of Design*, Schiffer Publishing, 1990
Carla Ginelli Brunialti and Roberto Brunialti, *American Costume Jewelry, 1935-50*, Edizioni Gabriele Mazzotta, 1997 (Italian text), and *A Tribute to America, Costume Jewelry 1935-50*, Edita, 2002 (English text)
Matthew Burkholz and Linda Kaplan, *Copper Art Jewelry, A Different Lustre*, Schiffer Publishing, 1992
Deanna Farnetti Cera, ed., *Jewels of Fantasy*, Harry N. Abrams, 1992 (out of print)
Maryanne Dolan, *Collecting Rhinestone & Colored Jewelry*, 4th ed., Krause Publications, 1998
Harrice Simons Miller, *Official Price Guide to Costume Jewelry*, 3rd ed., House of Collectibles, 2002
Dorothy Rainwater, *American Jewelry Manufacturers*, Schiffer Publishing, 1988
Fred Rezazadeh, *Costume Jewelry, A Practical Handbook & Value Guide*, Collector Books, 1998
Lucille Tempesta, ed., *Vintage Fashion & Costume Jewelry Newsletter*, various quarterly issues
Back issues of *Vogue* and *Harper's Bazar* magazines (researched by Pat Seal)

Advisers: Pat Seal, Bobye Syverson, Lucille Tempesta.

Marks & Names on Mexican Silver Jewelry & Metalware c. 1930-2000

(Dates of operation/Marks in use)

FREDERICK DAVIS
(c.1925-1960)

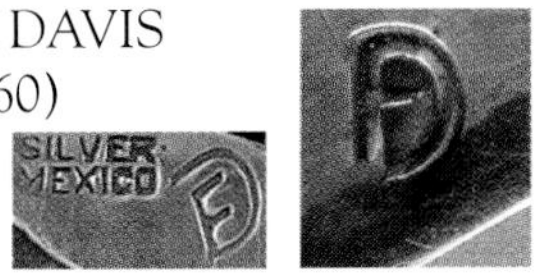

WILLIAM SPRATLING
c. 1931-1935 c. 1940-1945

c. 1940 c. 1949-1950

c. 1949-1967 c. 1955-1967

LOS CASTILLO
(1939-present)

HÉCTOR AGUILAR
(1939-1962)

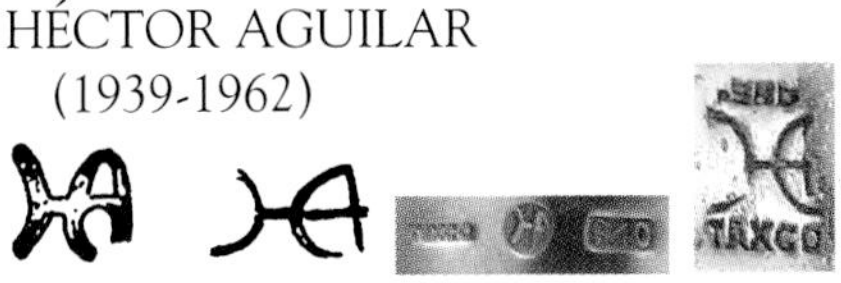

ANTONIO PINEDA**
(1941-present, crown mark in use since c.1950)

Antonio Pineda

MARGOT van VOORHIES CARR CASTILLO
(MARGOT DE TAXCO)
(1948-c.1975)

ENRIQUE LEDESMA
(1950-c.1980)

SALVADOR TERÁN
(1952-1974)

SIGI PINEDA
(1953-c.1975; c.1985-present)

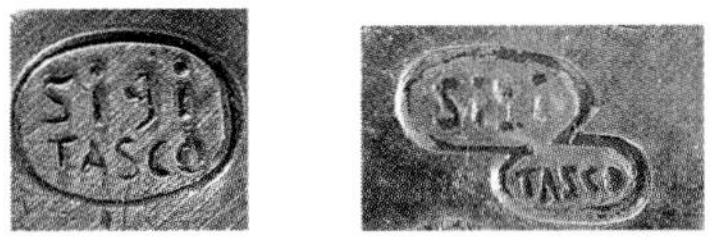

FELIPE MARTíNEZ
(PIEDRA Y PLATA)
(1950-?)

HUBERT HARMON
(c.1943-1948)

Hubert Harmon

ISIDRO GARCíA (MARICELA)
(1943-1986)

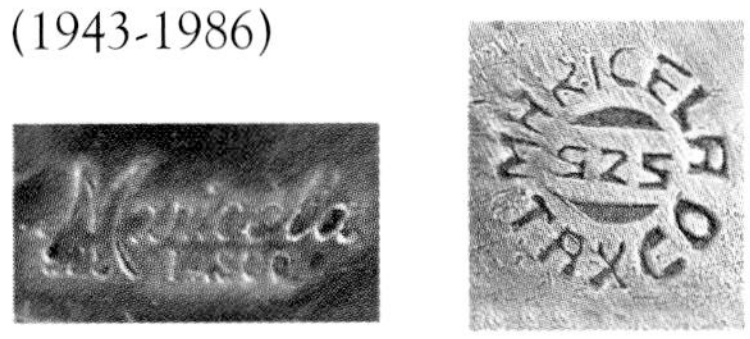

BERNICE GOODSPEED**
(1940-1972)

MATILDE POULAT
(mark since c.1950-1960)

RICARDO SALAS POULAT**
(c.1960-present)

LOS BALLESTEROS
(c.1940-present)

SPREAD-EAGLE MARK - 925
c.1948-1979 (assay mark)

Government Assay
"Spread Eagle" Marks

mark used on non-sterling (pewter or silverplate) copies of Spratling designs by Victor Silson, c. 1940

"Silson" Mark

SERAFÍN MOCTEZUMA
(WS IMITATOR)
(c. 1940-50)

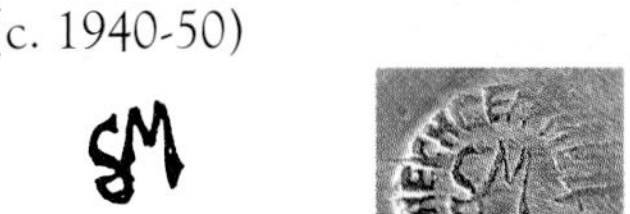

Serafin Moctezuma

[XX] - [00] GOV'T-ISSUED REGISTRY NO.

ASSIGNED TO WORKSHOPS SINCE 1979
(e.g., **TS-24** for Spratling workshop)

Lesser-known Workshops & Silversmiths

IN TAXCO & MEXICO CITY D.E.

(Dates of Operation/Marks in use if known)

MANUEL ALTAMIRANO**

CARMEN BECKMANN
(c.1960-1980)
[BECKMANN or BEKMANN]

PEDRO CASTILLO
(1948-present)

ERIKA HULT DE CORRAL (RIC)
(1965-present)

RAFAEL DOMÍNGUEZ
(1943-1980)
[RD in a circle]

DORIS
[block letters]

FAR-FAN
[FAR FAN in rounded block letters]

DÁMASO GALLEGOS**
(1941-1980)

GERARDO LÓPEZ**
(c.1950- ?)

MACIEL
(c.1930-1970)
[block letters]

EMMA MELENDEZ**
(1953-1971)

MIGUEL MELENDEZ**
(c.1955-present)

RAFAEL MELENDEZ**
(1939-1980)

POPOWSKI (Mexico DF)

RANCHO ALEGRE [block letters]
(c.1960-1980)

REVERI - REVERIANO & MARÍA CASTILLO
(1952-1989)

SANBORN'S [block letters]
(c.1930-present)

TANE [block letters]
(1953-present)

EZEQUIEL TAPIA [EXEL-TAPIA]
(1961-present)

JANNA THOMAS
(1965-1980)

VALENTÍN VIDAURRETA**
(1935-1955)

VICTORIA - ANA NUÑEZ BRILANTI**
(1940-1978)

ALFREDO VILLASANA
[conjoined AV or A. VILLASANA in block letters]

**marks drawings courtesy of Bille Hougart, *The Little Book of Mexican Silver Trade and Hallmarks*, published by the author, 2001

20th Century Jewelry Designers and Manufacturers in Scandinavia

Dates refer to births/deaths of individuals or founders of manufactories; initials of major companies follow names of designers who worked for them.

<u>DENMARK</u>

JUST ANDERSEN 1884-1943 (mfr)

MOGENS BALLIN 1871-1914 (mfr)

THORVALD BINDESBØLL 1846-1908

BUCH & DEICHMANN (mfr)

C.M. COHR (mfr)

NANNA & JØRGEN DITZEL (AM, GJ) NANNA b.1923-, JØRGEN 1921-1961

A.[AAGE] DRAGSTED 1886-1942 (mfr) [**AD** or **A.DRAGSTED** surmounted by a crown]

N.E. FROM (mfr) [**FROM, N.E. FROM**]

BENT GABRIELSEN (HH, GJ) b.1928

GRANN & LAGLYE (mfr)

HANS HANSEN 1884-1940 (mfr)

KARL GUSTAV HANSEN (HH) b.1914

BERNHARD HERTZ 1834-1909 (mfr)

PETER HERTZ 1811-1885 (mfr)

GEORG JENSEN 1866-1935 (mfr)

c.1904-1920 c.1915-1930 c.1915-1930

c.1933-1944 Post-1945

JØRGEN JENSEN (mfr)

JØRGEN JENSEN (GJ) 1895-1966

SØREN GEORG JENSEN (GJ) b.1917

ANNI (b.1927) & BENT (b.1924) KNUDSEN (HH)

HENNING KOPPEL (GJ) 1918-1981

HOLGER KYSTER 1872-1944 (mfr)

ERIK MAGNUSSEN 1884-1960 (DENMARK/U.S.)

ARNO MALINOWSKI (GJ) 1899-1976

A.[ANTON] MICHELSEN 1809-1877 (mfr)

UWE HELMUTH MOLTKE [**MOLTKE**]

EVALD NIELSEN 1879-1958

HARALD NIELSEN (GJ) 1892-1977

JAIS NIELSEN 1885-1961 (AD)

RASMUSSEN & LASSEN

JOHAN ROHDE (GJ) 1836-1935

HARALD SLOTT-MØLLER 1864-1937

KAREN STRAND (AD, AM) b.1924 [**STRAND**]

POUL WARMIND b.1929 [**WARMIND**]

<u>FINLAND</u> (Finnish mfrs' names after individuals who designed for them)

AURAN KULTASEPPÄ (mfr)

KAIJA AARIKKA b.1929 (mfr)

BERTEL GARDBERG (GJ) 1916- [**BRG** or **GARDBERG**]

E. [ERIK] GRANIT 1930-1988 (mfr) [**E. GRANIT**]

PAULA HÄIVÄOJA b.1929 (Kalevala Koru, Kaunis Koru)

MAUNO HONKANEN b.1931 (Tillander)

SAARA HOPEA-UNTRACHT 1925-1984 (Ossian Hopea [**OH**])

MATTI HYVARINEN (Sirokoru) [**MJH**]

KALEVALA KORU (mfr)

KAUNIS KORU (mfr)

KULTAKESKUS OY (mfr)

KULTATEOLLISUUS KY (mfr)

KUPITTAAN KULTA OY (mfr)

ELIS KAUPPI b.1921 (Kupittaan Kulta)

JORMA LAINE (Turun Hopea) [**Jorma Laine** in script]

LAPPONIA (mfr)

HELGE NARSAKKA (Kaunis Koru)

PEKKA PIEKÄINEN b.1945 (Auran Kultaseppä)

BÖRJE RAJALIN b.1933 (Kalevala Koru)

EERO RISLAKKI b.1924- (Kalevala Koru)

JAN SALAKARI b.1932 (Kaunis Koru)

MIRJAM SALMINEN b.1918 (Kaunis Koru)

PENTTI SARPANEVA 1925-1978 (Kalevala Koru, Turun Hopea)

SALOVAARA KY (mfr)

SEPPO TAMMINEN (Turun Hopea)

SIROKORU KY **(mfr) [MJH]**

TILLANDER (mfr)

TURUN HOPEA (mfr)

LIISA VITALI (Kultakeskus)

BJÖRN WECKSTRÖM b.1935 (Lapponia) **[BW** or **BJÖRN**

WESTERBACK OY (mfr)

TAPIO WIRKKALA 1915-1985 (Westerback, Kultakeskus)

<u>NORWAY</u>

DAVID-ANDERSEN (mfr)

UNI DAVID-ANDERSEN b.1930 (DA) **[UNI]**

MARIANNE BERG (UNI D-A) **[INV. M.B.]**

ØYSTEIN BALLE **[BALLE]**

ERLING CHRISTOFFERSEN (Norway Design Plus) **[EC]**

ANNA GRETA EKER (Norway Design Plus)

MARIUS HAMMER 1847-1927 (mfr)

O. F. HJORTDAHL

AKSEL HOLMSEN (mfr)

FRANK & REGINE JUHLS **[JUHLS]**

THORBJØRN LIE-JØRGENSEN (DA) 1901-1961

GRETE PRYTZ KITTELSEN b.1917 (Tostrup)

NORWAY DESIGNS PLUS (mfr)

BJØRN SIGURD ØSTERN b. 1935 (DA) **[INV. B.S.Ø]**

HARRY SØRBY 1905-? (DA) **[INV. H.S.]**

J. TOSTRUP (mfr) **[TOSTRUP** or **J.TOSTRUP]**

TONE VIGELAND b.1938

<u>SWEDEN</u>

ALTON GULDVARU AB (mfr) **[ALTON]**

SIGVARD BERNADOTTE (GJ) 1907-2002

W.A. BOLIN (mfr)

ATELIER BORGILA (mfr) **[ABA]**

INGA BRITT [IBE] DAHLQUIST (GJ) 1925-

ERIK FLEMING (ATELIER BORGILA) 1894-1954

WIWEN NILSSON (GJ) 1897-1974

SIGURD PERSSON b.1914 **[SIGP]**

ATELIER STIGBERT (mfr) **[Stigbert** in script]

TORUN [BÜLOW HÜBE] (GJ) b.1927 **[TORUN]**

Company codes:
AD = A. DRAGSTED
AM = A. MICHELSEN
DA = DAVID-ANDERSEN
GJ = GEORG JENSEN
HH = HANS HANSEN

Basic Hallmark Identification

Hallmarks have been in use in England and France since the fourteenth century. Most other European countries also use hallmarks. The United States has never used hallmarks per se. Indications of fineness or karat have been required since 1906, but fineness marks were sometimes stamped on silver jewelry in the nineteenth century ("coin" or "standard" for 900 silver, "sterling" for 925).

Hallmarks are most often found on objects made of precious metals. Jewelry is exempted from hallmarking under certain circumstances. However, when a piece of jewelry *is* hallmarked, the marks can yield clues to country of origin and, sometimes, date of manufacturer, as well as indicate the metal content of the piece. Makers' marks are not strictly considered hallmarks by themselves, although a maker's mark may accompany a hallmark on a piece (see Glossary for definition).

Every country has a different system of hallmarking, ranging from simple to complex. The most commonly found marks will be discussed here. Others can be found in Tardy's *International Hallmarks on Silver and Poincons d' Or et de Platine* (hallmarks on gold and platinum, French text).

FRENCH HALLMARKS

The French have what is undoubtedly the most complex system of hallmarks in the world, and the most difficult to read. If you learn to recognize the French marks for gold, silver, and platinum, you will have done well. The difficulty lies in the fact that the French never use numbers. Symbols in the form of animals and heads of animals and people, insects, and birds have been used to indicate fineness, place of manufacture, imports, and exports. These have changed over the centuries. Tardy's *Hallmarks on Silver*, in English, can help decipher most of these marks, and help with understanding the book on gold and platinum marks, which has not been translated from the French.

The most easily recognized and commonly seen French mark is the eagle's head, in use since 1838, indicating 18 karat gold. Assayed French gold is never lower than 18k. The mark can be found on jewelry in any number of places. Look for it on clasps, side edges, galleries, and pin stems, as well as on the back surface of a piece.

On French silver jewelry, the most often-seen mark is the boar's head, the mark of the Paris Assay Office, indicating a fineness of 800 or higher on small articles (such as jewelry). This mark was in use from 1838 to 1961, and since 1962, has also been used by the Paris Assay Office.

After 1838, a maker's mark in a lozenge (diamond shape with four equal sides) was also required on French silver and gold.

From 1829, items made of both gold and silver were stamped with a conjoined boar's and eagle's head.

Platinum was not officially recognized by the French government as a precious metal until 1910, at which time the eagle's head for gold was used for platinum. In 1912, a special mark for platinum was introduced, a dog's head.

OTHER EUROPEAN HALLMARKS

Many European countries mark silver and gold with numerical fineness marks in thousandths, e.g., 800, 830, 900, 935, etc. for silver, and 333, 500, 585, 750, 875, etc. for gold. Other symbols may be used in combination with these numbers.

Austro-Hungarian items may bear the head of a woman, animal, or bird with a number inside a cartouche or reserve. The most commonly seen mark on silver and silver-gilt jewelry is the dog's head with the number 3 inside a coffin-shaped reserve, indicating 800 silver, in use 1866-1937.

In Russia, two-digit numbers refer to *zolotniks*, which convert to thousandths, e.g. 56 = 583 (14k), 84 = 875 (silver or 21k gold). Between 1896 and 1908, the national mark was the left profile of a woman's head wearing a diadem ("*kokoshnik*"). From 1908 to 1917, a right-facing profile was used. After the Russian Revolution, the mark was a right-facing worker's profile with a hammer, and a fineness in thousandths.

Swedish hallmarks after 1912 include a triple crown mark, in a trefoil for local manufacture, and in an oval for imports, along with an S in a hexagon for silver indicating 830 or higher. Gold will bear a karat mark in a rectangle. There will also be a date letter and number, a city mark, and a maker's mark.

Finnish hallmarks are similar to Swedish. A crown inside a heart indicates local manufacture, a crown in an oval for imports. Place of assay, maker's mark, and date/letter number may be added.

BRITISH HALLMARKS

The British system of hallmarking is somewhat complex, but relatively easy to follow once the system is deciphered. British hallmarks include a fineness or purity mark, an assay office mark, a date letter, and usually, but not always, a maker's mark. A royal duty mark was added from 1784 to 1890 (not always found on jewelry of this period). The sequence of marks on a piece is arbitrary.

Fineness or purity marks:

On gold, a crown plus the karat (spelled with a "c" in Britain, abbreviated "c" or "ct") was used from 1789 until 1975 (22 ct was marked the same as sterling silver until 1844). In Scotland, a thistle was used instead of the crown. From 1798 to 1854, only gold assayed at 18 and 22 ct was permissible and hallmarked. In 1854, 15, 12, and 9 ct were legalized. The fineness in thousandths was added to these karat marks from 1854 to 1932.

In 1932, 15 and 12 ct were abandoned in favor of 14 ct, which was also marked 585; 9 ct continued to be legal, also marked 375. In 1975, all gold marks were standardized, and the crown mark and the fineness in thousandths became the only marks to be used in addition to place of assay and date letter.

On English silver, the lion *passant* (walking lion) is the symbol for sterling silver (925). Scottish silver before 1975, like gold, bears a thistle mark. A higher silver standard, Britannia silver (958.4) was required to be used for a short period at the end of the seventeenth century, bearing the figure of Britannia instead of the lion. Britannia silver is still legal, but has been seldom used since the reinstatement of the sterling standard in 1720. The lion *passant* was retained in the Hallmarking Act of 1975, but the Scottish thistle was changed to a rampant lion.

Place of assay marks:

Assay offices have been located in a number of British cities. The ones still in operation today are in London, Birmingham, Sheffield, and Edinburgh. Most jewelry will bear a London, Birmingham, or Chester place of assay mark (the Chester assay office closed in 1962). The mark for London is referred to as a leopard's head (crowned before 1821). The mark for Birmingham is an anchor. Most hallmarks books indicate an upright anchor for silver and a sideways anchor for gold, but this was not strictly adhered to. The mark for Chester is a shield bearing the town's arms, a sword and three sheaves of wheat.

Date letters:

Each place of assay has its own cycles of hallmarks which include a letter of the alphabet for each year, beginning with the letter A, and continuing through to Z (sometimes the lowercase letter j is omitted, and some cycles end with a letter before Z). The style of the letter and the shape of the reserve or shield background changes with each cycle. A letter can be upper or lower case and of differing type faces, in order to distinguish it from the same letter in an earlier or later cycle.

It is not necessary to memorize these letters. Pocket-sized editions of British hallmarks books make it possible to look up the date letter found on a piece "in the field." All that is necessary is to determine the place of assay from its mark and look up the date letter in the tables given for that city. It is important to remember to match the style of letter and shape of its surrounding shield. Occasionally there will be a discrepancy between what is in the books and the mark on the piece, in which case the style of the letter takes precedence over the shape of the shield. With practice, and book in hand, you can learn to read British hallmarks quickly and easily.

PSEUDO HALLMARKS

Because of the association of British sterling with quality, some American manufacturers emulated the British, making sterling objects and jewelry long before the United States government nationalized the sterling standard in 1906. Not only were British styles and metal quality imitated, some American maker's marks bear a striking resemblance to British hallmarks. The most well-known of these is the mark of Gorham Manufacturing Co., featuring a walking lion, an anchor, and an Old English style capital G, looking very much like a Birmingham hallmark for 1830. Most American maker's marks can be found in Dorothy Rainwater's *American Jewelry Manufacturers*.

MEXICAN HALLMARKS

After World War II, with the rising popularity of silver jewelry and objects make in Taxco, Mexico, the Mexican government issued an assay mark guaranteeing the fineness to be 925 or higher. This mark is referred to as the "spread eagle" mark. The original mark did look like an eagle, but with modifications over the years, the mark was simplified. The number inside the mark is a workshop or city designation. In 1979, this mark was abandoned in favor of a series of registry letters and numbers assigned to individuals and workshops.

MARKS REFERENCES

John Bly, *Miller's Silver & Sheffield Plate Marks* (English, Continental European, and American), Reed International Books, Ltd., 1993.

Jan Divis, *Guide to Gold Marks of the World* and *Guide to Silver Marks of the World*, English translation reprints, Promotional Reprint Co. Ltd., 1994.

Ian Pickford, ed., *Jackson's Hallmarks*, pocket edition (English, Scottish, Irish silver and gold marks), Antique Collectors' Club, 1991; and *Jackson's Silver and Gold Marks of England, Scotland and Ireland*, Antique Collectors' Club, 1989.

Dorothy Rainwater, *American Jewelry Manufacturers*, Schiffer Publishing, 1988.

Tardy, *International Hallmarks on Silver*, Tardy, Paris, 1993; and *Poincons d' Or et de Platine* (French text), Tardy, Paris, 1988.

Seymour B. Wyler, *The Book of Old Silver* (English, European, American), Crown Publishers, 1937 (still in print)

References and Other Sources for Further Information

For additional references and other sources, go to: www.center4jewelrystudies.org (Reference Request form).

PART I - *Late Eighteenth and Nineteenth Century Jewelry*

References (for all of Part I):

Vivienne Becker, *Antique and Twentieth Century Jewellery*, 2nd ed., N.A.G. Press, 1987 (out of print).

C. Jeanenne Bell, *Answers to Questions About Old Jewelry*, 5th ed., Krause Publications, 1999.

David Bennett and Daniela Mascetti, *Understanding Jewellery*, 2nd ed., Antique Collectors' Club, revised 2000.

Shirley Bury, *Jewellery, 1789-1910, The International Era*, 2 vols., Antique Collectors' Club, 1991 reprinted 1997.

Genevieve E. Cummins and Nerylla D. Taunton, *Chatelaines, Utility to Glorious Extravagance*, Antique Collectors' Club, 1994.

Ginny Redington Dawes & Corinne Davidov, *Victorian Jewelry, Unexplored Treasures*, Abbeville Press, 1991.

Priscilla Harris Dalrymple, *American Victorian Costume in Early Photographs*, Dover, 1991.

Martha G. Fales, *Jewelry in America 1600-1900*, Antique Collectors' Club, 1995.

Margaret Flower, *Victorian Jewellery*, A.S. Barnes & Co., 1951, revised 1967 (out of print), Margaret Flower and Doris Langley-Levy Moore, reprint published by Dover Publications, 2002.

Alison Gernsheim, *Victorian and Edwardian Fashion, A Photographic Survey*, Dover, 1981.

Kristina Harris, *Victorian and Edwardian Fashions for Women*, Schiffer Publishing, 1995

Duncan James, *Antique Jewellery: Its Manufacture, Materials and Design*, Shire Publications, 1998.

Arthur Guy Kaplan, *The Official Identification and Price Guide to Antique Jewelry*, 6th ed., House of Collectibles, 1990 (out of print).

Shena Mason, *Jewellery Making in Birmingham 1750-1995*, Phillimore, 1998.

Clare Phillips, *Jewels and Jewellery*, V & A Publications, 2000 (collection of the Victoria and Albert Museum).

Dorothy Rainwater, *American Jewelry Manufacturers*, Schiffer, 1988.

Diana Scarisbrick, *Jewellery in Britain 1066-1837*, Michael Russell, Publishing Ltd., 2000.

Henri Vever, *French Jewelry in the Nineteenth Century*, English translation of La Bijouterie Francaise au XIXe Siecle (originally published 1906-1908) by Brenda Forman, Ph.D., Antiquorum, 2001 (3 vols.); another translation by Katherine Purcell, Thames & Hudson, 2001 (1 vol., with additional color plates).

Museums: The Victoria and Albert and the British Museums, London. The *Musée des Arts Décoratifs*, Paris, has a collection of jewelry that was pictured in Vever's monumental work (see above). In the United States: the Newark Museum, Newark, NJ, the Toledo Museum of Art, Toledo, OH, the Peabody Essex Museum, Salem, MA, Museum of Fine Arts, Boston, MA, Walters Art Gallery, Baltimore, MD, Cooper-Hewitt Museum, New York, NY, and National Museum of American History, Smithsonian Institution, Washington, DC, all have some jewelry of the period in their collections. Mount Vernon in Virginia has a collection of Martha Washington's jewelry.

LATE GEORGIAN

References: M.D.S. Lewis, *Antique Paste Jewellery*, Boston Books and Art, 1970 (out of print).

Advisers: Sam Gassman, Daniela Mascetti, Barry Weber.

CUT STEEL, BERLIN IRON, SILESIAN WIRE WORK

References: Anne Clifford, *Cut Steel and Berlin Iron Jewellery*, Adams and Dart, 1971 (out of print).

Exhibition catalog: Derek Ostergard, ed. *Cast Iron From Central Europe*, 1800-1850, The Bard Graduate Center for Studies in the Decorative Arts, 1994 (essay on jewelry by Brigitte Marquardt, many photos of Berlin iron jewelry and wirework).

Museum: The Austrian Museum of Applied Arts, Vienna (MAK) has a collection of Berlin iron jewelry that was part of the Bard Center exhibition. Its Web site is www.mak.at.

MEMORIAL, MOURNING, and HAIR JEWELRY

References:

Ann Louise Luthi, *Sentimental Jewellery*, Antique Jewels of Love and Sorrow, Shire Publications, 1998.

Ruel Pardee Tolman, *"Human Hair as Pigment,"* Antiques, December, 1925.

Museum and Internet Web site: The Mendocino Museum of Mourning in Mendocino, CA, currently offers a "virtual tour" of its collection at ww.mourningmuseum.com.

Advisers: Lenore Dailey, Carmelita Johnson, Barry Weber.

MINIATURES

References: Robin Jaffee Frank, *Love and Loss: American Portrait and Mourning Miniatures*, Yale University Press, 2000.

Advisers: Elise Misiorowski, Elle Shushan, Barry Weber.

EARLY VICTORIAN (ROMANTIC PERIOD) c. 1837-1861

References:

The Crystal Palace Exhibition Illustrated Catalogue, reprint of the original Art-Journal publication, Dover, 1970.

Carolyn Goldthorpe, *From Queen to Empress, Victorian Dress 1837-1877*, Metropolitan Museum of Art, New York (exhibition catalog), 1988.

Trade catalogs: *C.D. Peacock*, Chicago, IL, 1912-1914.

Adviser: Sam Gassman.

CORAL

References: see Vivienne Becker, *Antique and Twentieth Century Jewellery*.

HAIRWORK

References: C. Jeanenne Bell, *Collector's Encyclopedia of Hairwork Jewelry*, Collector Books, 1998.

Collectors' Club: Hairwork Society, P.O. Box 1617, Orem, Utah 84059 (send SASE for newsletter).

Internet Web site: www.hairwork.com, site of Marlys Fladeland (e-mail: marlys@hairwork.com), who also maintains the newsletter.

Museum: Leila's Hair Museum, Independence, MO.

Adviser: Carmelita Johnson.

SCOTTISH JEWELRY

References: see Dawes & Davidov, op. cit.

MID VICTORIAN (GRAND PERIOD) c. 1861-1880

Reference: John Loring, Tiffany's 150 Years, Doubleday & Co., 1987, and Tiffany Jewels, Abrams, 1999.

BLACK JEWELRY

References:

Sheryl Gross Shatz, *What's It Made Of?, A Jewelry Materials Identification Guide*, 3rd ed., published by author, 1966.

Sylvia Katz, *Early Plastics*, Shire Publications, Ltd., 1999. Includes information on vulcanite and other Victorian compositions.

Helen Muller, *Jet Jewellery and Ornaments*, Shire Publications, Ltd., 2001, and *Jet*, Butterworths & Co. Ltd., 1987 (out of print). Both books contain extensive information on jet and its imitations, including history, sources, and identification.

Mike Woshner, *India-Rubber and Gutta-Percha in the Civil War Era*, published by author, 1999 (includes a few jewelry pieces).

Internet Web site: www.poesattic.com, Poe's Attic has an online "museum" of Victorian mourning jewelry.

Advisers: Colin Williamson (Victorian compositions), Mike Woshner (vulcanite and gutta-percha).

TORTOISESHELL and PIQUE

References: see Becker, op. cit., and Dawes & Davidov, op.cit.

REVIVALIST JEWELRY

Reference: Geoffrey Munn, Castellani and Giuliano, *Revivalist Jewellers of the Nineteenth Century*, Trefoil, 1984 (out of print).

Museum: Some of the ancient jewels that inspired the Castellani can be seen at the British Museum in London (www.thebritishmuseum.ac.uk), which has an extensive collection of Revivalist jewels.

CAMEOS and INTAGLIOS

Reference: Anna M. Miller, *Cameos Old & New*, 3rd edition, Gemstone Press, 2002.

Museums: see Anna Miller's book, above, for further information on these and other cameo collections.

Adviser: Anna Miller.

MOSAICS IN JEWELRY

Reference: Jeannette Hanisee Gabriel, *Micromosaics: the Gilbert Collection*, Philip Wilson Publishers, 2000.

Internet Web site: www.micromosaics.com

Museum: The Somerset House, London, houses the Gilbert Collection; Web site: www.somerset-house.org.uk/attractions/gilbert/index.html.

Advisers: Margot Conté, Laura Hiserote.

MANUFACTURED GOLD, GOLD-FILLED, GOLD-PLATED

References: see Dietz, ed., op. cit., Mason, op. cit.

Museum: Providence Jewelry Museum, Providence, RI.

Internet Web site: www.theassayoffice.co.uk/html/assay mainframe.html, the Birmingham Assay Office.

LATE VICTORIAN (AESTHETIC PERIOD) c. 1880-1901

Reference: Lillian Baker, *Baker's Encyclopedia of Hatpins & Hatpin Holders*, Schiffer Publishing, 2000.

EARLY CELLULOID

References:

Mary Bachman, *Collector's Guide to Hair Combs*, Collector Books, 1998.

Sylvia Katz, *Early Plastics*, Shire Publications, Ltd., 1999.

Keith Lauer and Julie P. Robinson, *Celluloid, A Collector's Reference and Value Guide*, Collector Books, 1998.

Internet Web site: www.plastics-museum.com, the site of the Plastics Historical Society and the Virtual Plastics Museum.

Advisers: Julie P. Robinson, Belva Green.

SILVER and MIXED METALS

References:

Scott V. Martin, *The Guide to Evaluating Gold & Silver Objects*, SM Publications, 1998.

Janet Zapata and D. Albert Soeffing, "Artistic Wares of George W. Shiebler, Silversmith," in *The Magazine Antiques*, July, 1995.

Periodical: *Silver Magazine*, Web site: www.silvermag.com.

Internet Web site: www.silvercollecting.com, includes an online encyclopedia of American silver marks.

Advisers: Benjamin Randolph, Janet Zapata.

DIAMONDS and GEM STONES

References:

Dietz, ed., op. cit, Fales, op. cit., vever, op. cit.

David Federman, "American Diamond Cutting: The Untold Heritage," Modern Jeweler, Vol. 84 #1 (January, 1985).

Wm. Revell Phillips and Anatoly S. Talantsev, "Russian Demantoid, Czar of the Garnet Family," Gems & Gemology, Summer, 1996.

Museums: Victoria and Albert and the British Museums, London; the Cooper-Hewitt and Metropolitan Museum of Art, New York, and the Smithsonian Institution, Washington, have noteworthy collections.

Advisers: Elise Misiorowski, Peter Shemonsky, Joseph W. Tenhagen.

PART II - Turn-of-the-Century Jewelry

References (for all of Part II):

Baker, op. cit., Becker, op. cit., Gernsheim, Op. cit., Harris, op. cit.

Terence Pepper, *High Society, Photographs 1897-1914* (exhibition catalog), National Portrait Gallery, London, 1998.

ARTS and CRAFTS c.1890-1920

References:

Vivienne Becker, Art Nouveau Jewelry, Thames & Hudson, 1998.

Malcolm Haslam, *Collector's Style Guide: Arts and Crafts*, Ballantine Books, 1988.

Jo-Ann Burnie Danzker, *Art Nouveau Buckles, 1896-1910*, The Kreuzer Collection, Arnoldsche Art Publishers, 2000 (includes Jugendstil, English, and Danish Arts & Crafts).

Sharon S. Darling, *Chicago Metalsmiths*, Chicago Historical Society, 1977.

Charlotte Gere and Geoffrey C. Munn, *Pre-Raphaelite to Arts and Crafts Jewellery*, Antique Collectors' Club, 1996.

Nancy Impasto, "Paye & Baker Silversmiths," *Silver Magazine*, October 1990.

Elyse Zorn Karlin, *Jewelry & Metalwork in the Arts and Crafts Tradition*, Schiffer Publishing, 1993.

Stephen A. Martin, ed., *Archibald Knox*, Academy Editions, 1995.

Ulrike von Hase-Schmundt et al, *Theodor Fahrner Jewelry, between Avant-Garde and Tradition*, Schiffer Publishing, 1991.

Janet Zapata, *The Jewelry and Enamels of Louis Comfort Tiffany*, Harry N. Abrams, 1993.

Periodical: *Fine Early 20th Century American Craftsman Silver, Jewelry & Metal* (semiannual catalog with prices), ARK Antiques, Box 3133, New Haven, CT 06515.

Museums: Birmingham Museums and Art Gallery, Birmingham, the Fitzwilliam Museum, Cambridge, and The Victoria and Albert Museum, London, England; The Schmuckmuseum (Jewelry Museum) in Pforzheim, Germany; Museum of Fine Arts, Boston, MA.

Advisers: Rosalie and Aram Berberian (American), Gail Gerretsen, Didier Haspeslagh (British, European), Susan Oakes Peabody, Ramona Tung, Janet Zapata (American).

ART NOUVEAU c.1895-1910

References:

Vivienne Becker, *Art Nouveau Jewelry*, Thames & Hudson, 1998; and *The Jewellery of René Lalique* (exhibition catalog), Goldsmiths' Company, London, 1987.

Yvonne Brunhammer, ed. *The Jewels of Lalique* (exhibition catalog), Flammarion, 1998.

Danzker, op. cit., Dietz, ed., op. cit., Vever, op. cit.

Dorothy Kamm, *Painted Porcelain Jewelry and Buttons Identification and Value Guide*, Collector Books, 2002.

Museum: The Calouste Gulbenkian Museum in Lisbon, Portugal, houses the René Lalique collection created for its namesake.

Advisers: Ulysses G. Dietz, Dorothy Kamm (porcelain), Elise Misiorowski, Janet Zapata.

BEAUX-ARTS and "NEO-RENAISSANCE" c.1890-1920

References:

Ulysses G. Dietz and Janet Zapata, "Beaux-arts Jewelry Made in Newark, New Jersey," *The Magazine Antiques*, April, 1997.

Dietz, ed., op. cit.

Ginger Moro, *European Designer Jewelry*, Schiffer Publishing, 1995 (chapter on Hungarian, including "neo-Renaissance" jewelry).

Trade catalog reprint: Daniel Low & Co. *Gold and Silversmiths*, Salem, MA, 1901 (includes designs by Unger Bros. and Wm. B. Kerr), Eden Sterling Co. (www.edensterling.com).

Museum: The Newark Museum, Newark, NJ.

Advisers: Ulysses G. Dietz, Janet Zapata.

EDWARDIAN c.1890-1920

References:

Bennett and Mascetti, op. cit., Dietz, ed., op. cit.

Franco Cologni and Eric Nussbaum, *Platinum by Cartier, Triumph of the Jewelers' Art*, Harry N. Abrams, 1996 (out of print).

Hans Nadelhoffer, *Cartier, Jewelers Extraordinary*, Harry N. Abrams, 1984

(out of print).
Penny Proddow and Marion Fasel, *Diamonds, A Century of Spectacular Jewels*, Harry N. Abrams, 1996.
Judy Rudoe, *Cartier, 1900-1939*, Harry N. Abrams, 1997.
Museum: The Virginia Museum of Fine Arts, Richmond, VA, has a sizable collection of Fabergé *objets de vertu* and jewelry.
Adviser: Elise Misiorowski.

PART III - Twentieth Century Jewelry
FINE JEWELRY c.1920-1935

References:
Sylvie Raulet, *Art Deco Jewelry*, Rizzoli Intgernational, 1985 (out of print), and *Van Cleef & Arpels* (abridged), Universe Publishing, 1998.
Rudoe, op. cit.
Suzanne Tennenbaum and Janet Zapatta, *The Jeweled Menagerie*, Thames & Hudson, 2001.
Museums: *Musée des Arts Décoratifs*, Paris; Toledo Museum of Art, Toledo, OH.
Adviser: Peter Shemonsky.

COSTUME JEWELRY c.1920-1935

References:
Deanna Farneti Cera, *Amazing Gems, An Illustrated Guide to the Worlds' Most Dazzling Costume Jewelry*, Harry N. Abrams, 1997; Deanna Farneti Cera, ed., *Jewels of Fantasy, Costume Jewelry of the 20th Century*, Harry N. Abrams, 1992 (out of print).
Sibylle Jargstorf, *Baubles, Buttons and Beads, The Heritage of Bohemia*, Schiffer Publishing, 1993, *Glass in Jewelry, revised ed.*, Schiffer Publishing, 19918 and *Glass Beads from Europe*, Schiffer Publishing, 1995.
Ellie Laubner, *Fashions of the Roaring '20s, with Values*, Schiffer Publishing, 1996 (chapter on jewelry), and *Collectible Fashions of the Turbulent 1930s*, Schiffer Publishing, 2000.
Moro, op. cit.
Penny Proddow, Debra Healy, and Marion Fasel, *Hollywood Jewels*, Harry N. Abrams, 1992.
Ulrike von Hase-Schmundt et al, *Theodor Fahrner Jewelry, Between Avant-Garde and Tradition*, Schiffer Publishing, 1991.
Museums: Glass and Costume Jewelry Museum, Jablonec andnad Nisou, Czech Republic; Providence Jewelry Museum, Providence, RI.
Adviser: Ellie Laubner.

PLASTICS and OTHER NOVELTY JEWELRY c.1920-1970

References:
Matthew L. Burkholz, *The Bakelite Collection*, Schiffer Publishing, 1997.
"Techniques and Materials" (Chapter 8), in Deanna Farneti Cera, ed., *Jewels of Fantasy, Costume Jewelry of the 20th Century*, Harry N. Abrams, 1992 (out of print).
Corinne Davidov and Ginny Redington Dawes, *The Bakelite Jewelry Book*, Abbeville Press, 1988.
Andrea DiNoto, *Art Plastic, Designed for Living*, Abbeville Press, 1984 (out of print).
Keith Lauer and Julie Robinson, *Celluloid, A Collectors' Reference and Value Guide*, Collector Books, 1998.
Moro, op. cit.
Karima Parry, *Bakelite Bangles*, Krause Publications, 1999, and *Bakelite Pins*, Schiffer Publishing, 2001.
Shatz, op. cit.
Collectors' Club: The American Plastics History Association (quarterly newsletter "APHA Notes"), G. Marshall Naul, founder, 534 Stublyn Road, Granville, OH 43023.
Museum: National Plastics Center and Museum, Leominster, MA.
Internet Web site: www.pastics-museum.com, the Virtual Plastics Museuuem, Web site of the Plastics Historical Society.
Advisers: Matt Burkholz (Bakelite), Julie Robinson (celluloid).

FINE JEWELRY c.1935-1945

References:
John Culme and Nicholas Rayner, *The Jewels of the Duchess of Windsor*, Vendome Press/Sotheby's London, 1987 (out of print).
Sylvie Raulet, *Jewelry of the 1940s and 1950s*, and *Van Cleef & Arpels*, Rizzoli International, 1987 (both out of print), and *Van Cleef & Arpels* (abridged), Universe Publishing, 1998.
Suzanne Tennenbaum and Janet Zapata, *The Jeweled Menagerie*, Thames & Hudson, 2001.
Adviser: Janet Zapata.

MID-CENTURY MODERN-AMERICAN STUDIO JEWELRY c.1945-1965

References:
Philip Morton, *Contemporary Jewelry, A Studio Handbook*, Holt, Rinehart, and Winston, 1970 (out of print).
Marbeth Schon, "Interview with Betty Cooke," Aug-Sept. 2001, "The Wearable Art Movement," Parts I and II, Dec-Jan. 2001-2002, and April-May 2002, in the library archives of Modern Silver online magazine (www.modernsilver.com).
Oppi Untracht, *Jewelry Concepts and Technology*, Doubleday, 1985.
Toni Greenbaum, *Messengers of Modernism*, Montreal Museum of Decorative Arts, Flammarion, 1996; "California Dreamin': Modernist Jewelers in Los Angeles, 1940-1970," *Metalsmith*, Winter 2002, and "Tea and Jewelry: Modernist Metalsmithing in San Diego, 1940-1970," *Metalsmith*, Summer 2002.
Periodical: *Metalsmith*, quarterly journal of the Society of North American Goldsmiths, 710 East Ogden Ave. Suite 600, Naperville, IL 60563-8603 (Web site: www.snagmetalsmith.org).
Internet Web site: The online magazine Modern Silver (www.modernsilver.com) is an excellent resource for collectors. The site is also the sponsor of the online discussion group SilverForum.
Museums: see Reference Request form, www.center4jewelrystudies.org.
Advisers: Steven Cabella, Al-Munir Meghji, Shari Miller, Patrick Kapty, Marbeth Schon.

FINE JEWELRY c.1945-1960

References:
Sylvie Raulet, *Jewelry of the 1940s and 1950s*, Rizzoli International, 1987 (out of print), and *Van Cleef & Arpels*, Rizzoli, 1987 (out of print), and Universe, 1998 (abridged).
Suzanne Tennenbaum and Janet Zapata, *The Jeweled Menagerie*, Thames & Hudson, 2001.
Adviser: Lynne Arkin (Marsh).

FINE JEWELRY c.1960-1975

References:
Bennett and Mascetti, op. cit.
Daniela Mascetti and Amanda Triossi, *Earrings from Antiquity to the Present*, Rizzoli International, 1990, reprinted 2001; *The Necklace from Antiquity to the Present*, Harry N. Abrams, 1997, and *Buvlgari*, Abbeville, 1996.
Penny Proddow and Debra Healy, *American Jewelry*, Rizzoli International, 1987 (out of print); Penny Proddow, Debra Healy and Marion Fasel, *Hollywood Jewels*, Harry N. Abrams, 1992, reprinted 1996 (out of print).
Penny Proddow and Marion Fasel, *Diamonds, A Century of Spectacular Jewels*, Harry N. Abrams, 1996, and *Bejeweled, Great Designers, Celebrity Style*, Harry N. Abrams, 2001.
Museum: Toledo Museum of Art, Toledo, OH.
Advisers: Elise Misiorowski, Amanda Triossi.

COSTUME JEWELRY
(Designer/Manufacturer Signed and Other)

References:
Carla Genelli Brunialti and Roberto Brunialti, *American Costume Jewelry, 1935-50*, Edizioni Gabriele Mazzotta, 1997 (Italian text), and *A Tribute to America, Costume Jewelry 1935-50*, Edita, 2002 (English text).
Deanna Farneti Cera, *The Jewels of Miriam Haskell*, Antique Collectors' Club, 1997, and Cera, ed., *Jewels of Fantasy*.
Maryanne Dolan, *Collecting Rhinestone & Colored Jewelry*, 4th ed., Krause Publications, 1998 (large section on makers' marks).
Roseann Ettinger, *Popular Jewelry 1840-1940*, Schiffer Publishing, revised ed., 2000, *Forties & Fifties Popular Jewelry*, Schiffer Publishing, 1994, and *Popular Jewelry of the '60s, '70s, and '80s*, Schiffer Publishing, 1997.
Harrice Simons Miller, *Costume Jewelry Identification and Price Guide*, 2nd ed., Avon Books, 1994; 3rd edition (new title: *Official Price Guide to Costume Jewelry*, House of Collectibles), 2002.
Moro, op. cit.
Cherri Simonds, *Collectible Costume Jewelry*, 2nd edition, Collector Books, 2000.

Periodical and Collectors' Club: Vintage Fashion & Costume Jewelry Newsletter/Club, P.O. Box 265, Glen Oaks, NY 11004, e-mail: VFCJ@aol.com, published quarterly, page on Web site: www.lizjewel.com (click on "VFCJ Club").

Museums: see Reference Request form, www.center4jewelrystudies.org.

Internet Web sites: N & N Vintage Costume Jewelry's site includes a collection of Design Patents (www.trifari.com/patentgallery/patentgallery.html), which allows you to view actual patents, including drawings, for many different pieces designed between 1937 and 1956.

Jewelcollect (www.jewelcollect.org) is an e-mail listserv for a very active costume jewelry discussion group, headed by Liz Bryman, who also maintains an informational site on costume jewelry collecting (http://jewelrycollecting.allinfo-about.com).

Advisers: Roberto Brunialti, Liz Bryman, Jane Clarke, Neil and Natasha Cuddy, Elayne Glotzer, Amy Milner (Cini), Charles Pinkham, Pat Seal, Sherry Shatz (Ming's), Bobye Syverson (Eisenberg), Lucille Tempesta, Joanne Valentine (Ming's and Gump's).

PART IV - *Special Collectible Jewelry*

References (for other categories not included in this section): **see** Reference Request form, www.center4jewelrystudies.org

NATIVE AMERICAN JEWELRY

References:

Allison Bird-Romero, *Encyclopedia of Native American Jewelry*, Oryx Press, 2000.

Dexter Cirillo, *Southwestern Indian Jewelry*, Abbeville Press, 1992.

Larry Frank and Millard J. Holbrook, *Indian Silver Jewelry of the Southwest, 1868-1930*, Schiffer Publishing, 1990.

Shari Watson Miller, "Patania: 70 Years of Excellence," Parts I and II, *Modern Silver Magazine* (www.modernsilver.com), Feb.-March and April-May, 2001.

Barton Wright, *Hallmarks of the Southwest*, Schiffer Publishing, revised 2nd ed., 2000.

Internet Web site: www.indianvillage.com/Indianarts/Jewelry.html.

Museums: see Reference Request form, www.center4jewelrystudies.com.

Adviser: Shari Miller.

MEXICAN JEWELRY (TAXCO SCHOOL), c.1930-1970)

References:

Mary L. Davis and Greta Pack, *Mexican Jewelry*, University of Texas Press, 1963, reprinted 1982, 1991, 1996.

Bille Hougart, *The Little Book of Mexican Silver Trade and Hallmarks*, TBR International, 2001 (www.cicatrix.com).

Penny Chittim Morrill and Carole A. Berk, *Mexican Silver, 20th Century Handwrought Jewelry & Metalwork*, 3rd edition, Schiffer Publishing, 2001.

Penny C. Morrill, *Silver Masters of Mexico*, Schiffer Publishing, 1996, "Hubert Harmon: Whimsy and Humor in Mexican Silver," *Jewelry, The Journal of the American Society of Jewelry Historians*, Vol. One, 1996-1997, "RIC: A Designer in Mexican Silver Makes Her Mark," *Silver* magazine, November/December, 1999.

Exhibition catalog: Penny Chittim Morrill, ed., *Maestros de Plata: William Spratling and Mexico's Silver Renaissance*, San Antonio Museum of Art (Harry N. Abrams), 2002.

Internet Web site: www.spratlingsilver.com, an information site for Spratling silver maintained by collector Phyllis Goddard.

Museum exhibition: "Maestros de Plata: William Spratling and Mexico's Silver Renaissance," San Antonio Museum of Art, San Antonio, TX, through January 2003 (other venues to follow).

Advisers: Jill Crawford, Patrick Kapty, Penny Morrill.

SCANDINAVIAN JEWELRY

General Scandinavian References:

Annalies Krekel-Aalberse, *Art Nouveau and Art Deco Silver*, Harry N. Abrams, New York, NY, 1989 (chapter on Scandinavian silversmithies, appendix of makers' marks, out of print).

Moro, op. cit. (chapters on Scandinavian).

Fred Rezazadeh, *Collectible Silver Jewelry*, (chapter on Scandinavian).

Schiffer, op. cit., Scandinavian included in several chapters.

Oppi Untracht, *Jewelry Concepts and Technology*, Doubleday, 1985 (many photographs of work by Scandinavian designers, especially Finns).

Internet Web site: effie-graa.com, a site administered by Norwegian dealers B. Lennart Persson and Svein G. Josefsen, includes information on a number of Scandinavian designers.

Advisers: Bruce Healy, Patrick Kapty, Ginger Moro, B. Lennart Persson and Svein G. Josefsen, Fred Rezazadeh.

Denmark References:

Janet Drucker, *Georg Jensen, A Tradition of Splendid Silver*, Schiffer Publishing, 2nd ed., 2001.

Jacob Thage, *Danske Smykker/Danish Jewelry* (Danish and English text), Komma & Clausen, 1990.

Museums: The Museum of Silver at Koldinghus in Kolding has a collection of works by Danish silversmiths, and a useful list of their names (including dates of birth/death and their years of production) on its Web site: www.koldinghus.dk/engelsk/frameset/Solv_fset.html.

Norway References: Anniken Thue, ed., *(The Jewelry of) Tone Vigeland, 1958-1995*, catalog of exhibition, Oslo Museum of Applied Art, Norway, 1995 (English text).

Museum: The Oslo Museum of Applied Art, Oslo, Norway. A (a virtual exhibition of Norwegian silver of the last 1,000 years is also on its Web site: http://kunst.uib.no/Art/Web/Exhibition/inglisj.html).

Sweden References:

Kersti Holmquist, *Wiwen Nilsson, Silversmeden*, Sweden, 1990 (Swedish text).

Ginger Moro, "Sigurd Persson, The Swedish Modernist," *Silver Magazine*, March-April, 1997.

Jan Von Gerber, *Erik Fleming, Atelier Borgila*, Sweden, 1994 (Swedish text, English summary).

Ann Westin, *Torun, Samtal med Vivianna Torun Bülow-Hübe (Conversation with...)*, Carlsson Bokförlag, Sweden, 1993 (Swedish/English text).

Dag Widman, *Sigurd Persson, en Mästare I Form (A Master of Design)*, Carlsson Bokförlag, Sweden, 1994 (Swedish text, English summary).

Museum: The Nationalmuseum, Stockholm, Sweden (Web site: www.nationalmuseum.se/enindex.shtml).

Finland References:

Tuula Poutasuo, ed., Michael Wynne-Ellis, English text, *Finnish Silver*, Teema Oy, 1989.

Finnish Modern Design, Marianne Aav and Nina Stritzler-Levine, eds., Bard Graduate Center for Studies in the Decorative Arts, 1998 (exhibition catalog, chapter on jewelry and metalwork).

Museum: Museum of Applied Arts, Helsinki, Finland.

Glossary

In order for us to understand each other when talking about antique and period jewelry, we must have a common vocabulary. A great many jewelry terms are French. French jewelers were the leaders of the jewelry industry, and so France is where the language of jewelry-making evolved. The terms used there were adopted by English and American jewelers and thus are part of our jewelry vocabulary today. Included in the list below are the most commonly used French jewelry terms, their *approximate* phonetic pronunciation (nasal and glottal sounds are difficult to transcribe) in brackets, and jewelry-related definitions. Words in SMALL CAPS are defined elsewhere in the Glossary, foreign words are italicized, and approximate phonetic pronunciations in brackets.

acrostic jewel a ring, brooch, or other jewel set with a ror or circle of gemstones, the first letter of the name of each stone spelling a word, such as "DEAREST" or "REGARD"

à jour [ah ZHOOR] an open setting which allows light to pass through

aigrette a jeweled hair ornament in the shape of a plume or feather, sometimes with a feather attached

Algerian knot a tubular knot motif, inspired by Algerian cord embroidery

alloy mixture of two or more metals

alpaca yellowish silver-colored metal composed of copper, zinc, nickel, and 2% silver

amber fossilized resin from extinct trees; lightweight and warm to the touch; can be translucent to opaque, imitated in plastics

amphora ancient Greco-Roman two-handled jar or urn with a tapered base, popular mid-Victorian Revivalist motif

annular ring-shaped

arraché eggshell lacquer decoration developed by French artist Jean Dunand

articulated having segments connected by flexible joints or jump rings

assay analytical test to determine metal content

Asscher-cut diamond named after diamond cutter Joseph Asscher, who developed a variation of the step cut in 1902, an octagonal stone (cut-corner square) with 74 facets, small table and high crown

attributed not SIGNED, but considered likely to have been made by a particular person or firm

aurora borealis an iridescent coating applied to faceted glass beads or rhinestones, developed by Swarovski Corp. in 1955

baguette narrow rectangular faceted stone

bail pendant loop finding through which a chain or cord passes

Bakelite trade name for thermosetting phenol formaldehyde resin, first entirely synthesized plastic, patented in 1909 by Leo H. Baekeland

balustered swelled section (as in the posts in a balustrade, or railing for a staircase)

bandeau ornamental band worn around the head

bangle rigid circular or oval bracelet

baroque in reference to pearls, having an irregular shape

base metal a non-precious metal

basse-taille [bas TIE yuh] enamelling technique: translucent or transparent ENAMEL applied over a decorated (engraved, chased, stamped) metal GROUNDPLATE, similar to *CHAMPLEVÉ*, but with a pattern or design visible through the enamel; when the groundplate has an "engine-turned" pattern, it is known as *GUILLOCHÉ* enamel

baton narrow, stick-shaped

bead set setting in which stones are held in place by beads raised from the surrounding metal

beauty pin small brooch/pin, also called *handy pin, lace pin*

bezel metal band with top edges burnished over to hold a stone in place

biomorphic amoeba-like, organic shape

blackamoor depiction of a dark-skinned man or woman

bloomed gold karat gold which has been treated with nitric acid, causing the alloy to dissipate from the surface, leaving a thin matte surface layer of pure gold (has a "frosted" appearance)

bog oak fossilized peat; found mainly in nineteenth century Irish jewelry

bola string tie of braided leather with a decorative slide and ornamental tips, usually silver

bombé having swelled or bulging sides

bookchain chain necklace with folded-over square or rectangular links, often engraved or stamped, popular mid to late 19th century

bouquet pin brooch with bowed-out center and a spike mounted on reverse, designed to hold a small flower bouquet

box clasp fastener for bracelets and necklaces, a slotted box into which a V-SPRING catch is inserted

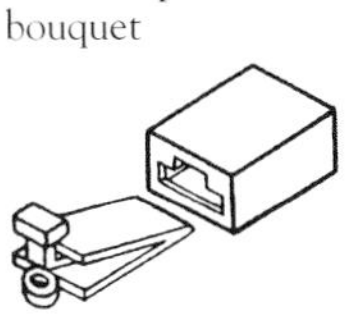

V-spring and Box Clasp

brilliant circular gemstone cut, especially for diamonds, with fifty-eight facets; the *modern brilliant* is a mathematically designed cut published in a treatise by Marcel Tolkowsky in 1919, also called the *American* or *ideal* cut; see also OLD MINE CUT and OLD EUROPEAN CUT

briolette gemstone cut, a three-dimensional faceted pear-shaped drop with small triangular facets

buff top gemstone cut, low cabochon top with a faceted pavilion (portion below the GIRDLE)

bulla ancient neck ornament made of two hinged convex plates, usually circular, suspended from a cord or chain; revived in the mid-Victorian period

bypass a bracelet or ring with open ends crossing parallel in front

cable link chain oval links formed of round wire

cabochon an unfaceted, domed cut for stones or glass, with a flat base (a *double cabochon* has a convex base)

calibré small faceted gemstones, usually four-sided, cut to fit a setting, often in rows or groups

cameo a design carved in relief, often (but not always) from stone or shell with layers of more than one color forming background and foreground; a cameo carved within a concave depression of a gemstone, with the highest part of the design level with the edge of the stone, is called a *chevet* or *chevée, curvette* or *cuvette* (British term: "dished")

cameo *habillé* [ah bee YAY] depicting the head or bust of a person wearing jewelry set with diamonds or other gemstones (literally, "dressed up")

cannetille [kan ne TEE yuh] a type of metal ornamentation using thin wires to make a filigree pattern, often in tightly coiled spirals or rosettes, used in the early nineteenth century

carat unit of weight for gemstones

carbuncle cabochon cut almandite garnet

carré set a circular stone set within a square, flat-topped setting

casting molten metal poured or forced into a mold made from a design model

catch closure finding for brooch/pin that holds the pointed end of the pinstem. A *C-catch* is a simple C-shaped hook. See also SAFETY CATCH

C-catch

celluloid trade name for semi-synthetic pyroxylin-camphor thermoplastic, invented by John Wesley Hyatt in 1868

Celtic knot also known as *entrelac*, an intricate interlaced motif common in ancient Celtic ornamentation, revived by the British Arts & Crafts movement

chamfered having cut or beveled corners

champlevé [chaw le VAY] enamelling technique: opaque or translucent ENAMEL fills recesses or depressions which are stamped, etched or engraved into a metal GROUNDPLATE

channel setting a row of same-size square or rectangular stones fitted into a continuous metal channel or trough which holds the stones in place

chasing technique of decorating metal from the front, usually by hand, without removing any metal, forming a relief design by raising and indenting

chatelaine ornamental clip worn at the waist from which implements or trinkets are suspended by chains

choker short necklace that fits snugly around the neck

circa within ten years before or after a given date; literally, "around"

clip a type of brooch with a hinged double-pronged mechanism for attaching to clothing, sometimes called a "fur clip" to differentiate from a DRESS CLIP

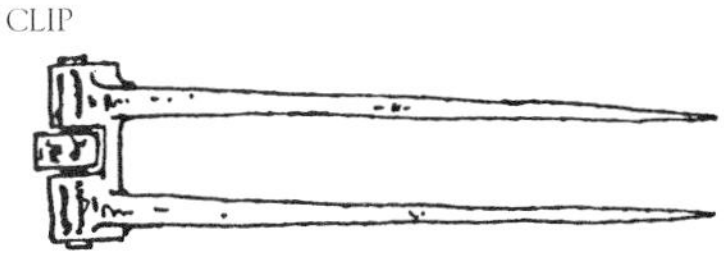

Clip

clipback earring finding for unpierced ear with a hinged clip for clamping earring to ear

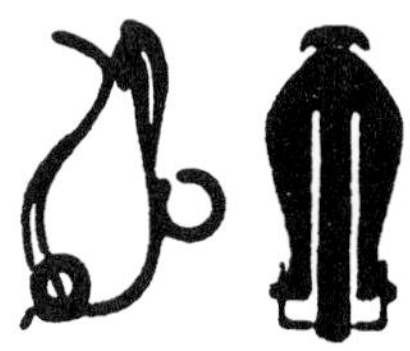

Clipback

cliquet [klee KAY] lit., catch. Type of pin having two ornamental terminals, one at each end of a pinstem, the pointed end having a snap closure or other mechanism for attachment. When worn, the pinstem is invisible. A.k.a. JABOT PIN, SÛRETÉ.

cloisonné [klwah son NAY] enamelling technique: a design or pattern is formed

of wire soldered on to a GROUNDPLATE, creating cells or *cloisons* which are filled with ENAMEL
collet a short tubular band or collar of metal enclosing a stone
compass points (North, South, East, West) to indicate position of stones or design elements: top, bottom, and two sides
costume jewelry made from nonprecious materials, esp. since c. 1920
counter-enameled enamel applied to the reverse of a piece for stability
crystal < see LEAD CRYSTAL, ROCK CRYSTAL>
cuff bracelet a PENANNULAR rigid bracelet, usually wide with rounded ends
cultured pearl pearl produced by insertion of an irritant (small glass or mother-of-pearl bead) into a mollusk (a *natural* pearl is formed around a foreign particle which occurs in nature)
curb chain twisted oval links forming a chain that lies flat
cushion cut rounded corner square faceted stone
cusped coming to a point, pointed end
cut-down collet or setting a method of setting gemstones in a collet or bezel with vertical ribs of metal holding the stone in place
cut steel small faceted steel studs, riveted closely together on a metal backing
damascening decorative technique, the embedding of gold and/or silver wire and/or cutout sheet metal shapes into a blackened iron or steel base (a.k.a. "inlaid metal")
demi parure [pah ROOR] two or three matched pieces of jewelry; a partial SUITE
déposé **[day poe ZAY]** registered (trademark or design), mark found on French items, and on items imported into or exported from France
die rolling repeating design created by rolling thin metal sheets between two steel rollers incised with a pattern
die striking or stamping method of mass production, a relief design produced from a flat sheet of metal with a two-part steel die forming the pattern under pressure
dog collar a wide ornamental choker necklace worn tightly around the neck
double clip brooch a pair of clips joined with a detachable pinback mechansim
dress clip an ornament attached to clothing by means of a hinged clip with a flat back and small prongs on the underside

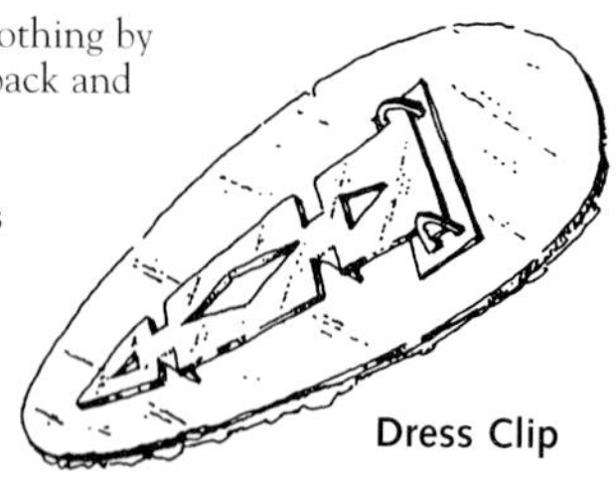
Dress Clip

ebonite <see VULCANITE>
échelle [ay SHELL] lit., ladder. Series of graduated gem-set brooches or dress ornaments (often a bow motif) worn vertically (large to small) down the front of a bodice, 17th - 18th centuries.
Egyptian faience a type of quartz-based glazed ceramic made by the ancient Egyptians
electroplating electrolytic process of depositing a layer of metal over another metal
embossing technique for creating a raised decoration on metal using punches and hammers on the reverse side; also known as REPOUSSÉ work
emerald cut square or rectangular cut stone, square table, chamfered corners, step cut sides
enamel powdered pigmented glass fired onto a metal GROUNDPLATE using a variety of techniques <see *BASSE-TAILLE, CHAMPLEVÉ, CLOISONNÉ, GRISAILLE, LIMOGES, PLIQUE À JOUR, TAILLE D'ÉPARGNE*>
engraving creating a design or pattern on a metal surface with incised lines ; differs from CHASING in that metal is removed with a tool called a graver, or a burin
en esclavage [awn es kla VAJH] lit., enslaved. A necklace or bracelet of identical or graduated plaques joined by swagged chains, usually three or more.
en résille [aw ray ZEE yuh] lit., in a hair-net. A flexible trellis or network, usually of diamonds and platinum, often forming a dog collar or other close-fitting necklace, originated by Cartier, early 20th century.
en tremblant [aw trã BLÃ] a brooch or other ornament with a motif (often a flower) mounted on a wire or spring, which trembles with movement of the wearer
equilateral all sides of equal length
estate jewelry previously owned, not necessarily antique, period or vintage
essence d'orient [door ee Ã] **(pearl essence)** coating used on glass or plastic to imitate pearls, made of fish scales
etching process for creating a design on metal or glass using acids
Etruscan jewelry ancient ornaments from central Italy (western Tuscany), usually of gold, reproduced in the nineteenth century
extended pinstem extends beyond the body of a brooch/pin; found on some nineteenth century brooches with C-CATCH closures, used to secure the brooch by weaving back into the clothing
fabrication hand construction using soldered sheet and wire
facet plane cut polished surface of a stone
faux [foe] French: false or fake
faux pearl artificial or imitation pearl, a glass or plastic bead coated with *ESSENCE D'ORIENT* (pearl essence)
fede ring from the Italian *fede* meaning "faith" or "trust," a ring depicting a pair of clasped hands, often given as a token of affection, dating as far back as the Romans; sometimes the hands are mounted on separate swiveling shanks that open and close, *see* GIMMEL RING
ferronière [fair own ee AIR] lit., blacksmith's wife. A narrow band, usually with a central jewel, worn around the forehead, originally worn in the 15th century, popular c. 1830.
fetter chain elongated oval or rectangular links, often combined with short lengths of TRACE, CABLE, or CURB link chain
fibula ancient style brooch, used to close garments, resembles a modern safety pin
filigree metal decoration made of twisted thin wires
findings the functional metal parts used in construction and wearing of jewelry: catches, clasps, clips, jump rings, spring rings, etc.

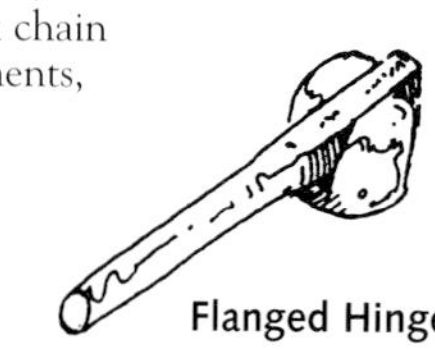
Flanged Hinge

fine jewelry made from PRECIOUS METAL and gemstones
flanged hinge brooch finding, a hinge (called a *joint* by jewelers) with projecting metal sides and a hingepin or internal posts to which pinstem is attached
Florentine finish textured brushed surface created by engraving crosshatched lines on metal
fob a decorative ornament or seal suspended from a watch chain; also, a ribbon or metal band attached to a pocket watch
foiled back a thin sheet of metal backing a gemstone or paste, sometimes colored to enhance the appearance of the stone, used in closed-back settings; also, in reference to a RHINESTONE with painted-on metallic backing, as on a mirror, which can be set in an open setting
foliate, foliated any leaf or plant design
forging the shaping of metal by heating and hammering
French cut a square, mixed cut with a square table turned 45 degrees and triangular crown facets, often used for small accent or CALIBRÈ gemstones
French jet black glass
gadrooned, gadrooning decorative oval beading on a border or edge
gallery a strip of metal with a pierced decorative pattern, used for settings
garter motif (Fr, *jarretière*) a strap with a buckle design
German silver an alloy of nickel, copper, and zinc, also known as NICKEL SILVER
gilding process by which a base metal is plated or coated with a thin layer of gold (called *gilt* metal)
gimmel ring a ring with two or more separate shanks which are joined together to form one ring; dating back to the 15th century, often worn as a betrothal ring
girandole [[jhee rahn DOLE] lit., chandelier. brooch or earring in which three pear-shaped drops are suspended from a center stone or motif
girdle widest part of a stone, part usually grasped by the setting; in a BRILLIANT-cut stone, the widest circumference where the crown (upper) and pavilion (lower) facets meet
gold filled a mechanical process using heat and pressure to join a layer of gold to a base metal; by law in the U.S., the gold layer must be at least 1/20th of the total weight of metal
gold plated layer of gold of less than 1/20th of total weight, can be applied by any process, but often ELECTROPLATED
gold wasH a very thin coating of gold over base metal
graduated arranged in ascending or descending order of size
granulation ancient decorative technique of applying minute spheres of gold to a gold surface without visible solder, used in ETRUSCAN JEWELRY, a technique approximated by Victorian goldsmiths
grisaille [aw gree SIGH yuh] painted enameling technique, monochromatic, usually in shades of gray and white and/or black
groundplate the metal base on which enamels are fired; the method of decoration determines the name given to the technique (see ENAMEL)
guilloché [gee oh SHAY] lit., engine-turned. Machine-engraved decoration on metal, over which a translucent enamel is often applied (called *guilloché enamel*)
gypsy setting a one-piece mount for a stone which is recessed into the metal, with the table (top facet) of the stone level with the metal surface; also called STAR SETTING when lines radiating from the stone are engraved in the metal
hair jewelry ornaments made of, decorated with, or containing human hair
hallmark the mark(s) stamped on gold, silver, or platinum indicating fine-

ness or karat; depending on country of origin, hallmarks can also include symbols for place of assay, date of assay (in the form of a letter or letter and number), maker's mark, and importation mark if applicable.
handy pin <see BEAUTY PIN>
Holbeinesque a pendant or brooch in the Renaissance style, usually a vertically oriented oval, enameled and gem-set with a pendent drop, named after Renaissance artist Hans Holbein the Younger
intaglio Ital.[in TAHL yo] an engraved stone, opposite of a cameo, with a recessed design carved into the surface, common for signet rings and fob seals
invisible setting (*serti invisible*) a type of CHANNEL SETTING using specially cut square or rectangular colored gemstones (usually rubies or sapphires) which are notched to slide onto metal tracks and fit closely together in rows; no metal is visible from the front of the piece

Kidney Wire

jabot pin [zhah BOW] a pin with ornamental elements at both ends of a long pinstem which is invisible when worn at the collar (formerly worn on a jabot, a front ruffle on a shirt), see also CLIQUET, SÛRETÉ
japonaiserie decorative motifs in the Japanese style
jarretière [jhar et TYAIR]<see GARTER MOTIF>
japanned black-lacquered metal
jet a type of fossilized coal, used primarily for mourning jewelry in the nineteenth century
jump ring a round or oval finding for linking or attaching other parts, made of round wire
karat 1/24th of the total weight in a gold alloy, a measure of fineness (24 karats is pure gold)
kidney wire <see SHEPHERD'S HOOK>
lace pin <see BEAUTY PIN>
lavalier, lavaliere, lavallière a neckchain suspending a gemstone or small pendant set with gemstones, popularly worn at the turn of the century
lead crystal colorless glass with a high percentage of lead added to enhance clarity and brilliance; resembles and is confused with ROCK CRYSTAL
Limoges [lee MOZH] enamelling technique: layers of finely ground colored ENAMEL fired after each application resulting in an image resembling a painting (without metal borders)
locket a two-part pendant or brooch with a hinge and cover, often containing a photo or lock of hair
longchain a very long metal chain worn around the neck with the end attached to the bodice, forming a swag, often terminating in a SWIVEL hook for suspending a watch or pendant
lorgnette [lorn YET] a pair of spectacles with an attached handle, usually suspended from a neckchain
loupe magnifying lens used by jewelers
lozenge an equilateral four-sided shape with corners at compass points; diamond-shaped (as in playing cards)
Lucite Du Pont trade name for acrylic thermoplastic
mabé pearl a pearl with a flat MOP bottom and rounded top (hollow, filled with epoxy or cement)
manchette [maw SHET] lit., cuff. bangle bracelet tapering out in the shape of a sleeve cuff
marcasite iron pyrite with a silver luster, cut in small faceted circular stones and often PAVÉ-set in silver or other white metal
marquise cut a gemstone cut that is oval or elliptical with pointed ends; the shape is also called NAVETTE
marriage a piece put together with two or more components from different sources, not as originally made
married metals: the creation of a design in contrasting colors of metal (e.g., silver, brass, copper), each metal piece cut out and put together like a jigsaw puzzle to form the design, the edges butted and joined using minimal amounts of solder to form a smooth solid surface (a.k.a. "metal mosaic")
melee a small cut diamond, under .20 carat
millegrain a method of setting stones using a tool around the top edge of a COLLET to form minute beads of metal which hold the stone in place; also a decorative technique
mosaic an object or jewel decorated with many small pieces of multicolored stone (called PIETRA DURA) or glass (TESSERAE) inlaid flush into stone or glass to form a design, motif, or scene; often called "*micromosaic*" when the glass tessarae are very small
mother-of-pearl the iridescent inside lining of mollusks
mourning jewelry jewelry worn in memory of a deceased loved one, most often black, sometimes containing the hair of the deceased
naja a horseshoe- or crescent-shaped silver pendant used in Navajo jewelry, often suspended from a SQUASH BLOSSOM necklace, sometimes set with turquoise or coral
nanny pin a brooch with a compartment, usually tubular, for holding sewing needles
navette <see MARQUISE>
neck ring a rigid circular metal ornament worn around the neck
négligée [nay glee ZHAY] lit., negligent, careless. a pendant or necklace with two drops suspended unevenly
nickel silver <see GERMAN SILVER>
nicolo a variety of onyx with a thin layer of bluish-white over black, from which a cameo or intaglio is carved
niello a metallic variation similar to vitreous enamelling using a powdered mixture of silver, copper, and lead which is fused by heat into an engraved design in silver, or occasionally gold, creating a grayish-black contrast with the metal ground
old European cut brilliant cut for diamonds with a circular GIRDLE, otherwise similar to OLD MINE CUT; the circular shape, developed c. 1860, was more easily produced with the invention of the power-driven bruting, or girdling machine in 1891
old mine cut old style brilliant cut for diamonds, a cushion-shaped stone with a small TABLE, high crown (top facets) and an open, or large culet (the small flat facet at the base, virtually eliminated in a modern BRILLIANT)
open back setting setting which permits light to pass through a transparent or translucent stone (same as À JOUR)
painted enamel enamel applied in liquid form and baked on at lower temperatures than required for firing powdered enamels; used on costume jewelry
pampille [pahm PEE yuh] articulated row of graduated gemstones or pastes terminating in a tapered pointed drop; grouping of *pampilles* also called *aiguillettes* [ay gwee YET], from *aiguille* (lit., needle)
parure [pah ROOR] a complete set or SUITE of jewelry, matching pieces of three or more
paste high lead content glass which has been cut (faceted) to resemble a gemstone; also known as *strass*
pâte de verre (lit., glass paste), molded colored glass used in jewelry, sometimes called "poured glass"
patina color change on the surface of metal, esp. silver, copper, bronze, resulting from age and exposure to the atmosphere; a type of oxidation. Patina may be artificially applied using acids and/or liver of sulphur; color is usually green, brown, or red on copper, brass, or bronze (called *patinated*), greyish-black on silver
pavé [pah VAY] lit., paved. Method of setting many small stones very close together (literally, paved)
peacock eye glass a glass cabochon or bead with blue and green foiling resembling the center, or "eye" of a peacock feather
pebble jewelry Scottish jewelry set with multicolored agates in silver or gold
penannular open-ended ring shape
pendeloque [paw d'LOKE] lit., drop or pendant. Pear-shaped drop earring, suspended from a circular or bow-shaped surmount
pendant (noun) decorative element suspended from a necklace, chain, or cord
pendent (adjective) hanging, suspended
pietra dura literally, "hard stone," a type of MOSAIC made of small pieces of stone which form a picture or scenic design, also known as *Florentine mosaic*
pinchbeck alloy of copper and zinc, developed in 1720 by Christopher Pinchbeck, a brass alloy used to imitate gold
piqué [pee KAY] lit., pricked**.** The inlaying of gold or silver in patterns, usually into tortoiseshell or ivory. *Piqué posé* [poe ZAY]: floral or ornate patterns of inlay; *piqué point* [pweh]: geometric shapes or dots.
plaque de cou [plak de KOO] lit., plate of the neck. Central ornamental plaque of a dog collar necklace.
plique à jour [pleek ah ZHOOR] enamelling process in which the GROUNDPLATE is removed after firing; the end result resembles stained glass, the translucent enamel framed in metal
polychrome three or more colors, multicolored
"pot" metal base white metal, tin and lead alloy, greyish in color, used in early twentieth century costume jewelry
precious metal gold, platinum, or silver
prong set stones held in place by metal claws or prongs
provenance the origin and history of a piece, including its former owners
quatrefoil decorative element having four lobes
regard ring finger ring set with a variety of gemstones, the first letters of which spell "regard" (ruby, emerald, garnet, amethyst, ruby, diamond), see ACROSTIC JEWEL
relief raised or standing out from the background
repoussé [ruh poo SAY] lit., pushed back or out. Raised design in metal. *Repoussage*: a technique of hand-raising a design in metal, working with punches and hammer from the back of the piece
rhinestone faceted colorless or colored glass, cut like a gemstone and usually with a fused metallic backing for light reflection (like silvering a mirror); used in costume jewelry

rivière [ree vee AIR] lit., river or stream. A short necklace of graduated gemstones of the same kind (e.g., diamonds), each stone COLLET-set and linked in a row without further decoration

rock crystal colorless quartz, occurring in nature as a six-sided (hexagonal) crystal

rolled gold a thin layer of gold fused over base metal

rondel, rondelle thin disk-shaped metal ornament, sometimes set with rhinestones, strung on a necklace between beads

rose-cut circular gemstone cut with triangular facets coming to a point at the top and a flat back

rose gold gold of a pinkish color (alloyed with copper)

rose montée small, flat-backed circular-cut rhinestones, usually colorless

safety catch brooch finding with a swiveling closure which prevents it from unintentionally opening

Safety Catch

safety chain a chain attached to a piece of jewelry which prevents loss if clasp opens

St. Andrew's cross an "X"-shaped motif, Scottish national emblem

sautoir [soTWAHR] a very long necklace or strand of beads or pearls, often terminating in a tassel or pendant

saw piercing decorative technique, the creation of an openwork design or pattern by cutting away metal, often used for platinum in the early 20th century

scarab Egyptian symbol of immortality, the *Scarabaeus* beetle, usually carved or molded in stone, clay, or glass

scarf pin, stickpin, tie pin decorative pin with a long pinstem and ornamental top, inserted into a scarf, cravat, or necktie

screwback earring finding for unpierced ear with a screw mechanism for securing earring to ear

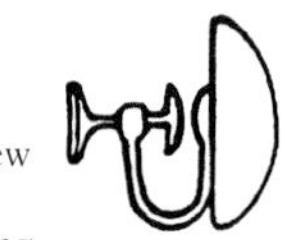

Screwback

seed pearl a natural, cultured, or artificial pearl weighing less than one quarter of a grain

sévigné [say veen YAY] a bow brooch set with diamonds, worn on the bodice (three or more worn *en échelle*), popular from the 17th century, named after the Marquise de Sévigné (1626-96), of the court of Louis XIV

sgraffito from the Italian *sgraffiato*, meaning "scratched." Enamelling technique: an unfired layer of enamel is scratched through to create a design revealing the layer of enamel or metal underneath

shakudo, Japanese alloy of copper with small amount of gold; ***shibuichi,*** Japanese alloy of copper with silver, tin, and lead or zinc

shank the part of a ring that encircles the finger

shepherd's hook, fishhook, kidney wire earring findings for pierced ears, primarily for pendent or drop earrings

Shepherd's Hook, Fishhook

shoulder area of a finger ring where the SHANK and BEZEL or head (top) meet

signed marked (engraved, stamped, impressed) with the name, initials, logo, or trademark of the maker, designer, or manufacturer

slave bracelet a link bracelet of glass and silver or brass, often enameled; also a bangle worn on the upper arm, popular 1920s

slide movable decorative and functional element of a LONGCHAIN which adjusts its opening; when longchains went out of fashion, collections of slides were strung together and made into bracelets

solder metal alloy used to fuse pieces of metal together with the use of heat; *hard* solder requires high temperatures, is made of an alloy of the same metal being joined, and creates the strongest bond; *soft* or *lead* solder fuses at a lower temperature; it is considered unsuitable (and damaging) for use on PRECIOUS METAL

solitaire the mounting of a single stone, usually in a ring

spacer decorative or functional element used to separate pearls or beads

spectacle setting a ring of metal around the girdle of a stone, like an eyeglass frame, often used for setting diamonds or other transparent stones linked at intervals on a chain

spring ring type of clasp finding used with a JUMP RING to connect one part to another

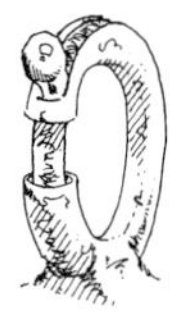

Spring Ring

squash blossom necklace Navajo, hollow silver beads interspersed with floral motifs resembling squash blossoms, sometimes set with turquoise, with a central NAJA pendant

sterling silver an ALLOY which is 925 parts pure silver and 75 parts copper

stomacher large, usually triangular, bodice ornament, also known as a *corsage ornament* or *devant de corsage*

strass <see PASTE>

stud or post & clutch or nut earring findings for pierced ears

Stud or Post & Clutch or Nut

suite several pieces of jewelry similarly designed to be worn together <see also PARURE>

surmount the decorative top part of an earring

sûreté [soor TAY] (pin) lit., safety, security. See *CLIQUET.*

swivel a type of finding, a hook with a hinged spring closure joined to a swiveling base with a jump ring for attaching watches, PENDANTS, or other items to chains

Swivel

synthetic gemstone laboratory-created gemstone which is chemically, physically, and optically identical to its natural counterpart; in contrast to an *imitation*, which is only similar in appearance (e.g., purple glass imitating amethyst)

table the top facet or surface of a cut stone

taille d'épargne [tie yuh day PARN] lit., saving (economical) cut. enameling technique: engraved design partially filled with opaque enamel, usually black (also known as *black enamel tracery*)

T-bar clasp a closure, usually for chain necklaces, consisting of a T-shaped bar that slips through a circular ring; when the chain is worn, the bar is held in place against the ring

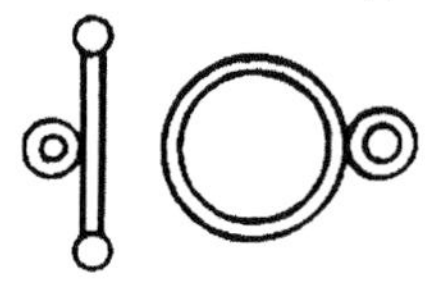

T-bar Clasp

tesserae [TESS er ee] tiny colored glass pieces used in MOSAIC (sometimes called *Roman mosaic)*

Tiffany setting a four- or six-prong elevated setting for a solitaire stone introduced by Tiffany & Company in 1886

torsade multi-strand twisted short necklace, usually beads or pearls; cabled or twisted cord

trace chain chain with oval links of equal size

trefoil decorative element having three lobes

trombone catch a two part sliding tubular closure finding for brooches

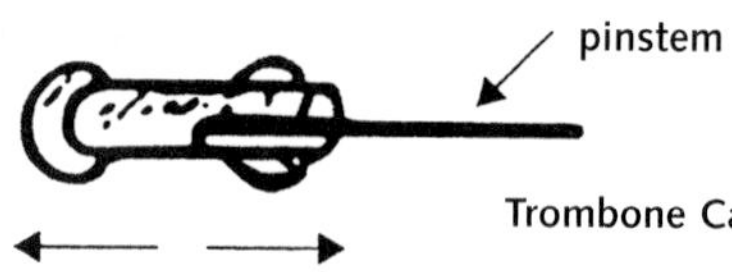

Trombone Catch

tube hinge brooch finding, an elongated tubular hinge (called a *joint* by jewelers) to which pinstem is attached

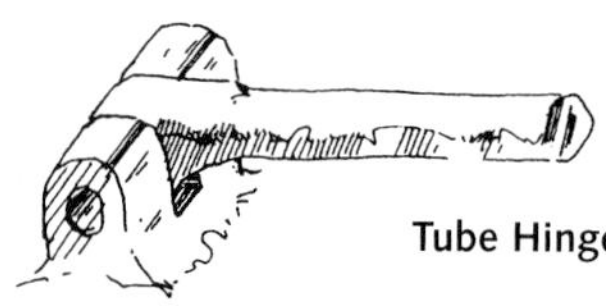

Tube Hinge

v-spring part of a BOX CLASP closure finding in which a wedge-shaped element fits into a metal box

vasiform vase-shaped

vermeil [ver MAY] gold-plated silver, silver gilt

volute spiral, snail shell-shaped

vulcanite vulcanized (hardened) rubber, used for mourning jewelry in the nineteenth century, also known as EBONITE

watch pin a small brooch/pin with a hook at the base of the reverse with its open end up, for suspending a small watch; worn on women's bodices at the turn of the century

white gold alloy of gold with nickel, palladium, or platinum (various formulae) which produces a silver-white color, approximating platinum, for which it is substituted

wirework twisted wire decoration applied to metal ground

yellow gold alloy of gold with silver and copper, most common color of gold

ziggurat stepped triangle or pyramid shape

Index

Aarikka, Kaija, 246
abalone shell, 98
acid-etched, 98, 101, 102, 106
Ackerman, Paul H., 164, 168
acorn motif, 209
acrostic jewelry, 26
Aesthetic Movement, 75, 77, 93
agate, 46, 47, 48, 59, 60, 83, 98, 128, 168
Aguilar, Héctor, 223, 225, 226
Albert, Gilbert, 37, 39, 49, 50, 78, 180
Alexandra, 74, 75, 119, 120, 232
Algerian knot motif, 35
Allco, 136,
Alling & Co., 108, 114, 115
Altamirano, Manuel, 225
Alton Guldvaru, 245
amazonite, 136, 236, 241
amber, 47, 98, 103, 145, 146, 147, 149, 190, 192, 194, 195, 196, 197, 198, 200, 202, 203, 207, 211, 232, 236
amethyst, 26, 27, 36, 40, 47, 64, 85, 100, 114, 132, 141, 161, 173, 175, 184, 198, 222, 223, 227, 228, 230, 231, 236, 237, 243, 245, 247, 250
anchor motif, 52, 73, 79
Andersen, Just, 234, 238
animal motif, 60, 75, 180
aquamarine, 39, 40, 44, 91, 125, 157, 161
Archaeological style, 55
arrow motif, 133, 217
Art, 43, 59, 72, 80, 84, 92, 93-106, 107, 108, 115, 119, 120, 121, 123, 126, 128, 129, 130, 131, 136, 137, 145, 163, 164, 166, 173, 180, 224, 201, 240, 241
Art Deco, 95, 121, 126, 128, 129, 136, 137, 224, 240
Art Nouveau, 92, 93, 94, 95, 97, 98, 107-114, 115, 119, 120, 121, 224, 240
Art Silver Shop, 98, 105
Arts and Crafts Movement, 92, 93, 94, 97, 107, 128, 232
Ashbee, C.R. 93, 95, 96
Asscher-cut diamond, 135
Atelier Borgila, 244, 245
Atelier Stigbert, 244, 245
Aucoc, Maison Louis, 107
Auran Kultaseppä, 247, 248, 249
Austrian Renaissance Revival, 56
aventurine, 227
Bacchante, 61
Bakelite, 145, 146, 147, 148, 149, 150, 151, 152, 153, 154, 155, 156, 206, 219
Baker, Oliver, 94, 105
Balle, Øystein, 241, 242
Ballin, Mogens, 233
Barclay, 188, 202
Barclay, McClelland, 188, 192
baroque pearls, 98, 180
bar brooch/pin, 73,
basket motif, 79
basse-taille enamel, 35, 108, 113, 139, 224, 227, 240, 241, 242, 243, 244
beads, 30, 31, 35, 41, 43, 44, 45, 46, 49, 51, 52, 54, 55, 58, 61, 62, 72, 73, 75, 83, 89, 99, 100, 101, 103, 104, 113, 114, 117, 121, 127, 131, 136, 137, 138, 140, 142, 144, 147, 153, 165, 166, 174, 182, 183, 186, 190, 191, 195, 197, 198, 201, 202, 203, 205, 206, 207, 208, 210, 212, 214, 217, 218, 219, 220, 228, 232, 236, 246, 247, 249
beauty pin, 74
Beaux-arts, 92, 115-118
Beckmann, Carmen, 225
Begay, Jonny Mike, 217
Begay, Kenneth, 212, 215, 217, 218, 220
Belais, 121, 135
Belperron, Suzanne, 158, 159, 180
belt, 51, 66, 69, 74, 89, 92, 102, 109, 111, 112, 113, 127, 128, 149, 154, 181, 216
Berg, Marianne, 241, 243
Berlin iron, 30, 31, 32, 33, 39
Bernadotte, Sigvard, 233, 234, 244
Bertoia, Harry, 163
bib necklace, 205, 242
bicolor gold, 158
Billiken, 98, 101, 104
Bing, Sigfried (Samuel), 107
Bippart, Griscom & Osborn, 108
bird motif, 169, 229
Birks, 62
Bjorg, Toril, 243
black enamel, 34, 35, 36, 43, 50, 51, 53, 68, 71, 85, 98, 127, 128, 130, 132, 133, 134, 135, 138, 143, 182, 228, 231, 238
black glass, 36, 51, 52, 65, 67, 76, 140
black onyx, 34, 50, 52, 57, 130, 133, 139, 140, 143, 186, 229
Black, Starr & Frost, 120, 129
blackamoor motif, 57, 59
blister pearls, 103
bloodstone, 47, 48, 118, 173
bog oak, 50, 51, 52, 53
Boivin, René,
bola tie, 213, 221
Bonaz, Auguste, 147
bone, 31, 172, 214, 219
bookchain, 69, 72
Boston Society of Arts and Crafts, 96
Boucher, Marcel, 140, 189, 193, 194, 196, 200
Boucheron, 56, 120, 128, 180
bow motif, 25, 28, 38, 62, 89, 134
Boyer, Merle N., 169
bracelet, 30, 31, 33, 34, 37, 39, 40, 43, 44, 47, 51, 54, 57, 61, 68, 69, 72, 78, 79, 84, 87, 89, 96, 99, 101, 109, 115, 121, 122, 129, 130, 131, 132, 134, 136, 137, 138, 144, 148, 149, 150, 152, 157, 159, 160, 164, 166, 168, 175, 176, 177, 181, 185, 186, 188, 189, 190, 199, 200, 206, 207, 208, 209, 211, 214, 216, 217, 218, 223, 226, 227, 231, 235, 239, 241, 244, 245, 246, 247, 250
bracelet, bangle, 40, 146, 149, 150, 247
bracelet, bangle, hinged, 37, 54, 56, 57, 68, 69, 77, 84, 115, 138, 148, 149, 150, 159, 150, 181, 190, 227, 235, 247
bracelet, charm, 79, 130, 202
bracelet, coil, 190
bracelet, cuff, 164, 168, 214, 215, 216, 217, 223, 225, 226, 235, 247
bracelet, flexible, 109, 122, 129, 130, 131, 159, 176, 177, 189, 190, 202
bracelet, link, 31, 40, 43, 47, 54, 61, 70, 79, 84, 96, 99, 121, 130, 131, 136, 138, 160, 176, 200, 202, 224, 226, 227, 235, 247
bracelet, Silesian wire, 31
bracelet, snake, 44
bracelet, strap, 131
bracelet, upper armband, 241
bracelet, wraparound, 56, 70
brass, 25, 28, 37, 47, 51, 52, 54, 63, 64, 65, 66, 67, 68, 69, 70, 72, 73, 75, 88, 93, 98, 100, 101, 102, 104, 106, 108, 111, 112, 115, 116, 137, 138, 140, 141, 142, 143, 149, 152, 153, 156, 163, 164, 165, 169, 172, 173, 191, 195, 197, 198, 199, 205, 206, 210, 225
Brassler Company, 116
Breuer, Marcel, 163
Brilanti, Ana Nuñez, 225
Brogden, John, 56, 57
bronze, 97, 106, 169, 232, 233, 243, 246, 247, 248, 249
brooch, 23, 27, 31, 33, 35, 37, 38, 39, 40, 41, 42, 43, 45, 46, 47, 48, 49, 50, 51, 53, 55, 56, 57, 61, 62, 63, 65, 66, 67, 68, 70, 71, 73, 76, 77, 79, 80, 82, 83, 84, 85, 87, 89, 92, 94, 95, 96, 97, 98, 99, 100, 101, 104, 106, 107, 108, 110, 111, 114, 115, 120, 121, 122, 123, 125, 127, 128, 131, 133, 134, 134, 136, 137, 139, 140, 144, 151, 152, 153, 154, 158, 160, 163, 164, 165, 166, 167, 168, 169, 174, 175, 176, 177, 179, 181, 182, 183, 184, 186, 187, 188, 189, 190, 191, 192, 193, 194, 198, 199, 200, 201, 203, 206, 207, 208, 209, 210, 211, 213, 218, 224, 225, 227, 228, 231, 233, 236, 239, 241, 242, 248
brooch/pendant, 37, 38, 62, 85, 97, 120, 121, 133, 231
brooch/pin, 25, 27, 31, 35, 37, 39, 41, 43, 45, 47, 48, 49, 51, 54, 57, 61, 65, 66, 71, 76, 79, 80, 83, 84, 85, 94, 97, 98, 99, 100, 101, 107, 108, 115, 122, 123, 131, 132, 133, 137, 139, 147, 148, 151-153, 154, 158, 160, 164, 168, 169, 175, 176, 177, 181, 182, 189, 190, 191, 192-194, 201, 202, 203, 204, 213, 218, 222, 227, 228, 232, 233, 235, 236, 241, 242, 248
Brynner, Irena, 165, 168
Buccellati, M., 180
Buch & Deichmann, 235
buckle, 41, 47, 50, 51, 80, 92, 94, 102, 108, 111, 130, 157, 164, 169, 181, 190, 199, 216, 220, 228, 240
buckle motif, 130, 199
Bulgari, 180
bulla, 55, 66
Bulow-Hube, Torun, 262, 268, 275
butterfly motif, 66, 151, 211
butterfly wing, 137, 151
Caldwell, J. E. Co., 117, 129
Calvaire, 195
cairngorms, 47, 48
cameos and intaglios, 30, 52, 55, 60-64, 68, 69, 108
cannetille, 26, 27, 40, 66, 68
carbuncle, 57, 88
Carence Crafters, 98
Carnegie, Hattie, 187
carnelian, 25, 64, 136, 138, 232
Carter, Gough & Co., 108
Carter, Howe & Co., 110
Cartier, 107, 119, 120, 127, 128, 129, 130, 131, 132, 133, 136, 137, 157, 158,175, 180, 187, 194
casein, 145, 146, 147, 149
cast iron, 30
Castellani, 24, 49, 55, 56, 58, 61, 65
Castillo, Chato, 223, 226
Castillo, Pedro, 223, 224, 227
cat motif, 239
Catalin, 146
Cavagnaro, Milton, 166, 172
Caviness, Alice, 203, 204
Cellini, Benvenuto, 180
celluloid, 54, 76, 110, 137, 145, 146, 147, 148, 149, 152, 153, 154, 155, 156
cellulose acetate, 145,147, 151, 154, 155, 156
Celtic and Celtic motif, 39, 47, 53, 55, 94, 103
Celtic Revival, 47
Centennial Exposition, 24, 49, 56
ceramic, 148, 166, 172, 174
chain, 25, 26, 27, 29, 32, 33, 35, 38, 39, 40, 41, 43, 46, 47, 50, 51, 52, 57, 58, 59, 61, 62, 63, 67, 69, 70, 71, 72, 73, 74, 75, 77, 78, 81, 83, 84, 86, 89, 90, 91, 92, 94, 95, 96, 98, 99, 102, 103, 104, 105, 106, 109, 113, 114, 117, 118, 120, 121, 122, 124, 125, 130, 134, 135, 136, 138, 140, 142, 143, 144, 146, 149, 151, 152, 153, 155, 156, 158, 161, 165, 172, 183, 185, 189, 190, 191, 195, 196, 199, 202, 204, 205, 206, 207, 208, 209, 211, 219, 220, 224, 226, 227, 231, 237, 238, 242, 245, 246, 247, 248, 250
chalcedony, 26, 41, 47, 50, 66, 98, 106, 136, 138, 183, 197, 217, 232, 235, 236, 245, 248, 249, 250
champlevé enamel, 100, 102, 108, 141, 143, 240, 242
Chanel, Coco, 126, 136, 159, 187, 189, 200
Chanel Novelty Co., 189
charm, 44, 47, 78, 81, 130, 134, 147, 148, 175, 182, 202, 224
chatelaine, 30, 32, 71, 74, 75, 80, 81, 195
Chaumet, 120, 121, 125, 128, 175, 182, 186
cherub, 25, 35, 43, 132, 181, 182
Chicago Arts and Crafts Society, 97
Child & Child, 88
chimera (mythical creatures), 56, 107, 116, 198
choker, 61, 72, 74, 127, 158
Christoffersen, Erling, 241
chrysoprase, 136, 232
Ciner, 136, 187
Cini, Guglielmo 193, 199, 201
circle pin or brooch, 139, 191, 211
citrine, 48, 49, 88, 106, 110, 112, 113, 114, 124, 130, 138, 157, 158, 160, 161, 184, 196, 250
claymore, 48
clip brooch, 136
cliquet, 127, 128, 146
cloisonné, 107, 200, 205
Cocteau, Jean, 163
Cohen, Julius, 175, 177
Cohr, C.M., 232
coin holder, 75, 81
collar, 49, 55, 59, 64, 74, 76, 92, 96, 103, 115, 117, 127, 132, 134, 152, 171, 178, 186, 202, 204, 230, 238, 245

collar button, 49
composition, 51, 148
concha belt, 213
Cooke, Betty, 164, 169, 171
Cooke, C. H. Co., 80
copper, 68, 69, 70, 77, 78, 93, 98, 163, 164, 165, 166, 169, 173, 197, 200, 204, 227
Coppola e Toppo, 200, 205, 210
copyright symbol, 200
coral, 23, 27, 31, 34, 39, 41, 43, 60, 61, 63, 98, 111, 116, 118, 128, 134 , 136, 145, 160, 175, 183, 186, 189, 195, 213, 214, 217, 218, 220, 221, 224, 226, 227, 229
Coro, Corocraft, 136, 137, 138, 139, 187, 188, 189, 191, 196, 234
corsage ornament, 82, 120, 126
cosmetic pot, 75
costume jewelry, 49, 56, 68, 121, 126, 136, 137, 147, 187, 188, 189, 200, 201
costume jewelry (c. 1920-1935), 136-144
costume jewelry (c. 1935-1950), 187-199
costume jewelry (c. 1950-1975), 200-211
Craftsman's Guild of Chicago, 98
cravat pin, 49
crescent shape, 218
cross, 26, 29, 30, 33, 43, 46, 48, 49, 50, 51, 52, 53, 59, 63, 66, 69, 72, 73, 77, 79, 150, 169, 192, 198, 204, 205, 212, 219, 226, 243, 247
crown motif, 31, 122
Crystal Palace, 24, 30, 39, 93
cuff links, 92, 237
cut steel, 23, 30, 31, 32, 33
Cymric, 93, 94
Czechoslovakia, 137, 138, 188
daisy motif, 147, 154
Dalí, Salvador, 163
Danecraft, 234
Dansk Arbejde (Danish Handicraft Guild), 232
David-Andersen, 240, 243, 244
David-Andersen, Uni, 240, 241, 243
Davis, Frederick, 137, 222, 225
De Beers Co., 82, 175
demantoid garnets, 83, 85, 88, 121, 132, 158
De Patta, Margaret, 163, 164-165
déposé, 95, 99, 118, 143, 189, 195
De Rosa, R., 189
design patents, 187, 188, 200
Desprès, Jean, 128
diamonds, 23, 24, 25, 26, 27, 28, 29, 30, 35, 37, 38, 39, 41, 43, 49, 55, 57, 59, 61, 62, 64, 69, 74, 77, 82, 83, 84, 85, 86, 87, 88, 89, 90, 91, 93, 103, 106, 107, 110, 112, 113, 114, 115, 119, 120, 121, 122, 123, 124, 125, 126, 127, 128, 129, 130, 131, 132, 133, 134, 135, 157, 158, 159, 160, 161, 162, 165, 175, 176, 177, 178, 179, 180, 181, 182, 183, 184, 185, 186, 187, 188, 200
diamonds and colored gemstones, 82-91
dirk, 47
Dior, Christian 175, 200
Ditzel, Nanna and Jørgen, 233, 236, 237
dog collar choker, 74, 92, 97, 103, 108, 117, 120, 127
dog motif, 152
dolphin motif, 109, 193, 233
double clip brooch, 128, 136, 158, 187, 188
doublé d'or (French rolled gold), 40, 68
dove motif, 36, 65, 66
dragon motif, 209
Dragsted, A. 234
Dreicer & Co., 120
dress clip, 127, 134, 136, 146, 147, 157, 186, 210
dress set, 123
Duette, 136, 187, 188
Dunand, Jean, 128, 136
Dunn Bros., 138
earring covers, 72
earrings, 24, 26, 27, 29, 30, 32, 40, 44, 45, 46, 47, 48, 49, 50, 52, 53, 54, 56, 57, 59, 60, 61, 63, 64, 65, 66, 67, 68, 69, 73, 74, 80, 85, 86, 89, 90, 91, 93, 96, 99, 106, 120, 121, 123, 125, 127, 134, 136, 137, 140, 143, 144, 147, 153, 155, 158, 159, 160, 161, 162, 165, 166, 167, 170, 174, 175, 177, 179, 180, 181, 182, 184, 185, 186, 188, 197, 198, 199, 200, 204, 206, 207, 208, 209, 210, 211, 214, 215, 218, 222, 224, 225, 227, 229, 231, 234, 237, 239, 241, 242, 244, 245, 248, 250
earrings, pendent, 27, 32, 45, 48, 52, 85, 123, 127, 140, 170, 182, 204, 248
Edwardian Period/Style, 83, 92, 119-125
Egyptian motif, 128, 137
Egyptian Revival, 128, 139
Eisenberg, 189, 193, 197, 201
Eker, Anna Greta, 241, 244
electroplating, 68, 69
elephant motif, 155
Elverhöj Colony, 97, 100
emerald, 26, 28, 29, 91, 120, 127, 129, 132, 133, 158, 161, 177, 197, 207, 209
enamel, 29, 36, 37, 38, 39, 55, 57, 59, 68, 73, 78, 94, 95, 97, 98, 99, 107, 110, 111, 113, 115, 120, 121, 127, 128, 134, 136, 138, 141, 143, 166, 168, 169, 174, 188, 192, 193, 195, 196, 197, 203, 204, 209, 228, 231, 240, 243
en esclavage, 25
en tremblant, 39, 82, 188, 191
Etruscan, 55, 56, 57, 61, 93
Etruscan Revival, 55, 61
eye miniature, 37, 38
Fabergé, Peter Carl, 120
Fahrner, Theodor, 94, 95, 136, 139, 140, 143, 203
Falkenstein, Claire, 165
Fashioncraft (Robert), 191
faux pearls, 142, 193, 195, 198, 199, 206
feathers (*pluma azteca*), 74, 85, 107, 114, 148, 175, 177, 192, 196, 229
female profile, 61, 62
festoon necklace, 92, 120
fibula, 55
fine jewelry (c. 1920-1935), 126-135
fine jewelry (c. 1935-1945), 157-162
fine jewelry (c. 1945-1960), 175-177
fine jewelry (c. 1960-1975), 180-186
Fishel, Nessler & Co., 112, 139
fish motif, 83, 150, 225
Flato, Paul, 159, 160
Fleming, Erik, 244
Fleming, Lars, 244, 245
fleur-de-lis motif, 29, 52, 58, 125, 144, 205
floral motif, 28, 34, 43, 52, 54, 59, 65, 66, 77, 99, 104, 106, 108, 111, 114, 119, 138, 147, 150, 154, 175, 188, 190, 197, 202, 217, 220, 228, 233, 240, 241
floral/foliate motif, 40, 49, 54, 62, 65, 66, 71, 73, 79, 99, 106, 123, 143, 185, 194, 199, 206, 235, 237, 241
flower basket motif, 132, 139
foil, foiled, 25, 40, 77, 82, 29, 41, 56, 94, 113, 146, 168, 207
Fontenay, Eugène, 55, 56
Forest Craft Guild, 98
forget-me-not motif, 41
Foss, Laurence, 96, 99, 234
Fouquet, Georges, 92, 107, 120, 128
Fouquet, Jean, 128
foxtail chain, 45, 61, 68, 140, 175, 190, 191, 199
French jet, 34, 50, 51, 52
Frères, Rubel, 129
freshwater pearls, 56,113, 115, 181
Freund, Elsa, 166, 174
Friedell, Clemens, 98
From, N.E. (Niels Erik), 49, 60, 69, 72, 78, 139, 144, 146, 190, 191, 192, 194, 195, 197, 198, 207, 233, 234, 238, 239
Froment-Meurice, 24, 56
Frost, George W., 98, 101, 106
fruit motif, 151, 203, 204
"fruit salad" motif, 139
Gabrielsen, Bent, 234
Gage, Mary, 96, 101
Gaillard, Lucien, 107
Galalith, 145, 147, 149
García, Isidro, 254
Gardberg, Bertel, 233, 246
garland motif, 79, 119, 120, 121, 122, 125, 127, 232
garland style, 119, 120, 121, 125, 127
garnet, 26, 27, 29, 35, 38, 42, 57, 83, 84, 88, 91, 96, 99, 106, 110, 117, 118, 137, 158, 184, 196
Gaskin, Arthur and Georgie, 94, 105
Gautrait, Lucien, 120
George III, 24
German silver, 101
Gerry's, 202
gesetz-gesch?zt, 115
Gibson, Charles Dana, 92
gilt metal, 28, 37, 137
girandole, 24, 26, 32, 45, 85
Giuliano, Carlo and Arthur, 55, 56, 58, 59
Givenchy, 200, 204
glass, 25, 29, 34, 35, 37, 38, 40, 43, 44, 46, 48, 49, 51, 52, 53, 56, 57, 58, 59, 60, 61, 63, 65, 71, 72, 73, 76, 78, 93, 121, 101, 102, 106, 110, 111, 112, 113, 115, 116, 126, 135, 136, 137, 138, 139, 140, 141, 142, 143, 144, 151, 152, 153, 146, 166, 174, 187, 188, 189, 190, 191, 192, 193, 194, 195, 196, 197, 198, 199, 200, 201, 202, 203, 204, 205, 206, 207, 208, 209, 210, 211, 222, 228, 229, 232, 233, 248
glass paste, 29, 121
Glessner, Frances, 98
"Gloria," 200, 202, 209
gold nugget, 70, 104
Gold Rush, 70, 104
gold-in-quartz, 70
goldstone, 248
Goodspeed, Bernice, 225
"googly" eyes, 153
Goossens, Robert, 200
Gothic Revival, 30
Gorham (Manufacturing Co.), 75, 78, 81, 98, 108, 115, 117
Gradl, Max, 95
Grand Period, 49, 69
Granit, Erik & Co., 249
grape and vine motif, 33, 57, 58, 100, 108, 124, 191
Graves, Ray ("Gra-Wun"), 167, 169
Greco-Roman Revival, 60, 93
Greek key motif, 89
green gold, 42, 71, 96, 103, 114
griffin motif, 63, 115, 116, 118
Grima, Andrew, 180, 184
Gripoix (House of), 189, 195
grisaille enamel, 38
Gropius, Walter 163
Guild of Handicraft, 93, 95, 96
guilloché enamel, 75, 120, 139, 240, 243
Gump's, 201
gunmetal, 75
gutta percha, 50
gypsy, American, 104
hair comb, 54, 76, 92, 108, 146, 166
hair jewelry, 34-36, 44, 232
hair ornament, 25, 93
hairwork, 44-46
Hale, Frank Gardner 96
hallmarks, 23, 56, 70, 78, 94, 214, 215, 225, 244
Hammer, Marius, 93, 238, 239, 240, 242, 243
hammered, 80, 98, 99, 100, 101, 102, 104, 106, 163, 213, 228, 236, 239, 244, 245, 248
Hammerman Bros., 176
Hanck, Matthias W., 98
handkerchief holder, 71
handkerchief pin, 34, 35, 83
hand motif, 23, 32, 39, 43, 51, 73, 81, 143, 152, 193, 228
hand-painted porcelain, 108, 111
handy pin, 74
Hansen, Hans, 234, 235, 236, 237,238, 241
Hansen, Karl Gustav, 234
hardstone, 60, 61, 62, 63, 64
Harmon, Hubert, 224, 225
Harvey, Fred, 213
Haseler, W.H., 93, 94, 103
Haskell, Miriam, 187, 188, 189, 190, 195, 197, 198, 199, 201, 206
hatpin, 76, 80, 112, 152
Häussler, Hermann, 102
heart motif, 38, 45, 47, 52, 54, 70, 75, 76, 77, 78, 79, 80, 104, 113, 134, 148, 156, 159, 168, 195, 196
Heintz Art Metal Shop, 97
Herpers, Ferdinand J., 82
Hertz, Bernhard, 232, 235, 236
Hess, Frank, 189, 195, 197, 198
Heyman & Bros., Oscar, 129, 175, 176
Hjortdahl, O.F., 241
Hobé, 187, 189, 190
Hoffman, Josef, 95
Holbeinesque design, 59
Hollycraft, 206
Holmsen, Aksel 241
Hopi, 212, 213, 214, 215, 217, 218, 220, 221
horn, 53, 114, 130, 214, 216
Horner, Charles, 93, 94
horse motif, 213
horsehair, 40, 42, 46, 83, 134
horseshoe motif, 84, 88

Huber, Patriz, 95
Hull, Jacob, 235
Hult de Corral, Erika, 225
Hungarian, 25, 28, 56, 114, 115, 117, 138, 143
Hurst and Kingsbury, 164, 171
Hyatt, John Wesley, 76, 145
Hyvarinen, Matti, 249, 250

imitation coral, 76
Indian Jewelry, 212, 213, 215
insect motif, 82, 111
intaglio, 25, 60, 64, 113, 122, 130
international exhibitions, 49, 75
iron, 30, 32, 136, 176, 233, 246
ivory, 34, 35, 36, 37, 38, 39, 60, 74, 76, 104, 114, 145, 146, 154, 156, 165, 169, 196, 201, 204, 208, 215, 216
jabot pin, 83, 127, 128, 146
jade, 128, 137, 182, 186, 196, 238
jadeite, 123, 127, 130, 186
Japanese metalwork, 77
Japanese motif, 75, 77
Japonaiserie, 71, 75, 77, 81, 93
jelly belly, 189
Jensen, Georg, 96, 232, 233, 234, 235, 236, 237, 238, 239, 240, 241, 244
Jensen Jørgen, 234
jernsølv, 233
jet, 36, 39, 50, 51, 52, 53, 60, 137, 214, 218, 219
John Rubel Co., 129, 158
Jomaz, 200
Jonné, 200, 208
JoPol, 234, 236
Joseff of Hollywood, 137, 200
Jubilee jewelry, 77
Jugendstil, 92, 94, 95, 114, 128, 136
"Juliana" style, 200, 202, 209
Kalevala Koru, 246
Kalo Shop, 98, 100
Katz, Adolph 188
Kaunis Koru, 246, 247, 248, 249, 250
Kauppi, Elis, 246, 249
Kee, George 215, 218
Kerr, William B., 108, 109, 112, 115
King, Arthur, 180
King, 65, 119, 137, 157, 175
King, Jessie M., 94
Kittelsen, Grete Prytz, 233, 240
Kleeman, Georg, 95
knot motif, 30, 89, 94, 103, 227
Knox, Archibald, 94, 103
Knudsen, Anni and Bent, 234, 235, 237, 239
Koppel, Henning, 233, 234, 235, 236, 238
Korda, Alexander, 188
Kramer, Sam, 163, 164, 170
Krauss, Gunter, 184
Krementz & Co., 108, 114
Kultateollisuus, 247
kunzite, 132, 161
Kultaseppä, Auran, 247, 248, 249
Kupitaan Kulta, 246
Kutchinsky, 181, 183
La Paglia, Alphonse, 234
labradorite, 171, 237, 243, 246
Lacloche Frères, 107, 120
lacquer, 136, 142
Laine, Jorma, 250
Lalique, René, 92, 107, 110, 112, 114
Lane, Kenneth J., 200, 201, 209, 215
lapis lazuli, 57, 66, 214, 215, 217, 221, 247, 249
Lapponia, 246, 247, 249
Late Georgian-Early Victorian, 23 24-38, 39-48, 68, 83
Late Victorian, 23, 30, 47, 54, 74-91, 145
lava, 60, 61, 63
lavalier, 92, 116, 120, 121, 123
lead crystal, 37, 114, 139, 141, 189
Lebolt & Co., 98
Ledesma, Enrique, 224, 225
Levin, Ed, 164, 170, 173
Levinger, Heinrich, 95, 99
Lewis Bros, 80
Lewittes, Esther 99, 165, 166, 168, 169
Liberty, Arthur Lazenby, 93
Liberty, 93, 94, 95, 102, 103, 104, 105, 136, 196, 233, 240
lily motif, 109, 207
Limoges enamel, 99
Lobel, Paul, 164, 166, 168, 170, 173
locket, 52, 55, 56, 69, 72, 77, 81, 108, 112, 116, 148, 198
López, Gerardo, 225
lorgnette, 69, 92, 102, 112, 116, 124, 161
Los Ballesteros, 225
Los Castillo, 223, 224, 225, 229
Lucite, 145, 147, 148, 153, 188, 189, 193, 203
Lumarith, 145
Lunning, Frederik, 233, 234, 246
Lustig, Nita, 170
Macchiarini, Peter, 165, 169, 173
MacDonald, Everett, 166, 172
Madison, Dolley, 24, 176
malachite, 47, 48, 66, 221, 224, 226
male head, profile, or figure, 27, 61
Malinowski, Arno, 233
Maltese cross, 26, 29, 53, 63, 205
Mann, Forest, 98
manufactured gold, gold-filled, gold-plated, 68-73
marcasite, 95, 102, 137, 139, 143
Marcus & Co., 97, 108, 110, 120, 129
Marsh & Co., G. T., 176, 177, 178, 179
Marshall Field & Co., 98
Martínez, Felipe, 224
mask, 63, 165, 169
match safe, 75
Matisse, 200, 204
Mazer Bros., 189, 194, 197
Meister of Zurich, 186
Melendez, Emma, 225
Melendez, Miguel, 225
memorial, 23, 34-36, 49, 83
Metal Arts Guild, 165
Mexican jewelry, 222-231
Michelsen, A. 97, 234, 237, 244
micromosaic, 65-67
Mid-century modern, 163-174
Mid Victorian Period, 49-73
Ming's of Honolulu, 182, 184, 186, 201
miniature, 34, 35, 37-38, 60, 65, 108
Miraglia, Frank, 164, 168
Moholy-Nagy, László, 163, 164
Moltke, Uwe Helmuth, 238
Monongye, Jesse, 215
Monongye, Preston, 212, 215
moonstone, 93, 101, 120, 122, 125, 132, 138, 168, 170, 184, 189, 237
mosaics, 25, 55, 56, 65, 66, 67, 214
mother-of-pearl, 39, 40, 60
mourning, 34-36, 39, 44, 49, 50, 51, 54, 74
Murrle, Bennett & Co., 93, 94, 95, 102, 103
Napier, 187
Napoleon, 24, 25, 30, 60
Narsakka, Helge, 248, 250
Native American, 167, 212-221
Navajo, 212, 213, 214, 215, 216, 217, 218, 219, 220, 221, 222
neckchain, 59, 102, 113, 231
necklace, 24, 26, 27, 28, 30, 32, 33, 34, 39, 41, 42, 45, 46, 54, 55, 57, 58, 59, 60, 62, 63, 64, 65, 67, 69, 72, 74, 86, 87, 88, 90, 91, 97, 102, 103, 113, 115, 116, 117, 119, 120, 124, 125, 128, 134, 136, 140, 141, 142, 143, 144, 155, 156, 158, 160, 161, 162, 166, 167, 170, 171, 174, 175, 178, 179181, 183, 185, 186, 191, 198, 199, 200, 204, 205, 206, 207, 209, 211, 213, 214, 219, 220, 223, 229, 230, 234, 237, 238, 239, 240, 241, 242, 245, 246
neckpiece, 220
négligée, 102, 120
Neo-classical, 25, 30, 60, 119
nicolo, 60
niello, 78, 79, 81
Nielsen, Evald, 233, 236
Nielsen, Harald, 233
Nilsson, Wiwen, 244
Nutting, Jack, 166

Oakes, Edward Everett, 96, 103, 106
Oakes, Gilbert, 96
obsidian, 222, 224, 225
Odd Krafters Shop, 106
Skoogfors, Olaf, 164
onyx, 50, 60,63, 128, 129, 130, 132, 133, 136, 139, 143, 160, 183, 184, 186, 229, 235, 250
opal, 57, 85, 94, 99, 100, 103, 105, 110, 134, 169, 227
Order of the Garter, 47
ore samples, 70, 71
Østern, Bjørn Sigurd, 240, 241, 243, 244
Otteren, Karl Jørgen, 241
painted enamel, 37, 107, 146, 188, 189, 192, 204
Panis, Stavre Gregor, 106
Paris Exposition, 24, 75, 82, 92
Parker, James, 165, 166, 172, 174
Parks Bros. & Rogers, 111
paste, pastes, 25, 26, 27, 28, 29, 39, 77, 121, 136, 138, 139
Patania, Frank Jr., 215, 217
Patania, Frank Sr., 215, 220
Patania, Sam, 220
patriotic motif, 147, 188, 192
Paval, Philip, 165
Paye and Baker, 98
peacock, 68, 107, 111, 112, 113, 114, 129, 196, 199, 229
Peacock, C.D., 129
peacock eye glass, 113
pearls, 25, 27, 29, 34, 37, 38, 40, 41, 42, 43, 51, 53, 56, 57, 59, 61, 63, 71, 73, 74, 83, 84, 87, 88, 89, 96, 98, 100, 102, 103, 104, 106, 110, 113, 114, 116, 117, 118, 119, 120, 121, 122, 123, 124, 125, 127, 134, 143, 145, 159, 163, 168, 169, 176, 178, 180, 182, 184, 186, 188, 193, 195, 198, 199, 203, 206, 226, 227
pearls, baroque, 98, 104, 107, 180, 182, 226
Pearson, Ronald H., 164
pendant, 24, 26, 28, 29, 30, 32, 33, 35, 37, 38, 43, 46, 55, 59, 61, 62, 63, 65, 67, 69, 71, 72, 81, 85, 86, 87, 88, 89, 94, 95, 96, 98, 102, 103, 104, 105, 106, 107, 108, 110, 111, 113, 114, 116, 117, 118, 119, 120, 121, 122, 125, 127, 128, 133, 135, 140, 142, 143, 156, 165, 166, 171, 172, 173, 174, 180, 183, 184, 186, 198, 205, 206, 213, 219, 220, 221, 227, 231, 238, 239, 241, 242, 243, 244, 246, 247, 248, 249, 250
pendant and chain, 59, 72, 75, 94, 95, 96, 105, 106, 114, 118, 125, 135, 143, 156, 165, 172, 205, 231, 238, 248, 250
pendant/brooch, 125
pendant and cord, 172
pendant and ribbon, 114
pendant and neckring, 173, 183, 184, 206, 244, 249
pendant/necklace, 26, 64, 117, 119, 174
pendant/neckpiece, 220
pendeloque, 24, 27
Pennino, 189
peridot, 99, 113, 120, 122
Perli, 200, 205
Persson, Sigurd, 240, 244, 245
Peruzzi, 88
Pettersen, Odvar, 241, 242
pewter, 223, 234
Philippe, Alfred, 187, 188, 192, 193, 194, 195
Phillips, Robert, 24, 41, 56, 91
photograph, 70
Picasso, Pablo, 163, 181
Piekäinen, Pekka, 247, 249
Pierre, Georges (GIP), 114
Pierret, Ernesto, 56
pietra dura, 65
Pinchbeck, Christopher, 69
Pineda, Antonio, 223, 225, 226, 227, 228, 230, 231
Pineda, Sigi, 225, 228, 231
pink gold, 38, 114, 160
"pinked" topaz, 40, 41
piqué, 54
plastic, 54, 126, 145-156, 166, 189, 197, 200, 204, 214, 219
platinum, 82, 90, 110, 114, 119, 120, 121, 122, 123, 124, 125, 126, 127, 128, 129, 130, 131, 132, 133, 134, 135, 136, 157, 160, 161, 162, 175, 176, 177, 179, 181, 182, 183, 185, 187, 188
plique à jour, 95, 99, 100, 106, 107, 114, 139, 142, 165, 240
Plus, Norway Designs, 241, 242, 244
Poblano, Leo, 218
polyethylene, 153
porcelain, 35, 111, 232, 242
Porsgrund Porcelain Factory, 242
portrait miniature, 37, 40, 49, 57
Potter Studios, 98
Poulat, Matilde, 224, 226, 229
pressed horn, 50, 51, 53
Pretz, Florence, 98

Prince of Wales plumes, 34, 37
Princess Royal Victoria, 31
Prutscher, Otto, 95
Prytz-Kittelsen, Grete, 233
Pueblo tribes, 212, 214
putti, putto, 38, 56
quartz, 70, 71, 123, 144, 160, 163, 165, 224, 227, 248
quatrefoil motif, 32, 51, 54, 57, 58, 66, 103, 122, 125, 138, 144, 154, 169, 198, 233, 241
Queen Victoria, 24, 31, 37, 39, 47, 49, 50, 74, 77, 119, 157, 169, 170, 172, 225, 243
rabbit motif, 129, 133, 134
Ramshaw, Wendy, 180, 184
Rasmussen & Lassen, 239
Rebajes, Francisco (Frank), 164, 168, 197, 200
REGARD, 26
Regency, 23
Reid, Barney M., 165, 166
Reinad, 189
Renaissance Revival, 49, 55-56, 57, 58, 59, 115
Renk, Merry, 165, 170
Renoir, 197, 200
repoussé, 39, 40, 50, 66, 67, 68, 69, 96, 98, 99, 103, 108, 216, 224, 225, 226, 227, 229, 230, 232, 236
Retro Modern, 126, 157, 158, 188, 190, 191
reverse-carved, 121, 123, 146, 147
reverse-painted (crystal) intaglio, 60, 75, 122
Revivalist, 49, 55-59, 65, 68, 115
rhinestone, 126, 136, 146, 147, 187
rhodochrosite, 241
rhodolite garnet, 27, 57, 86
Ric (Erika Hult de Corral), 154, 225, 228, 229
Rice-Weiner, 188, 202
Richert, Eugène, 55
Richter, Karl Gustav, 121
Riker Bros., 110, 115
ring, 29, 33, 35, 36, 39, 44, 46, 48, 51, 52, 53, 59, 63, 64, 67, 69, 71, 74, 81, 88, 96, 102, 106, 113, 114, 118, 121, 125, 127, 135, 136, 137, 138, 139, 140, 141, 143, 155, 161, 165, 171, 173, 180, 184, 185, 186, 193, 202, 205, 206, 209, 211, 221, 235, 239, 246, 249, 250
rivière, 87
Roach, Ruth, 166, 169, 172
Robinson, Julie P., 76, 145, 146, 220
Robinson, Morris, 220
rock crystal, 34, 35, 36, 60, 121, 122, 126, 127, 132, 133, 135, 136, 139, 144, 158, 160, 165, 177, 182, 238, 243, 247, 249
rock crystal quartz, 60, 247
Rogers, Margaret, 96, 106
Rokesley Shop, 98
Rosenstein, Nettie, 200, 204, 205
Roycrofters, 95
ruby, 25, 26, 29, 41, 85, 116, 118, 124, 127, 129, 130, 131, 132, 133, 134, 162, 176, 182, 184, 186
ruby, synthetic, 121, 124, 127, 157
Ruser, William, 181, 182
Ruskin, John, 93, 233

Salvador, 163, 224, 225, 229, 231
Salminen, Mirjam, 246
Salovaara, 248, 250
Sandoz, Gerard, 128
Santo Domingo, 212, 213, 214, 219
sapphire, 26, 57, 84, 91, 100, 103, 109, 120, 122, 127, 129, 130, 131, 133, 135, 158, 160, 236
sardonyx, 61
Sarpaneva, Pentti, 247
sash ornament/pin, 101, 11, 115
sautoir, 120, 121, 127, 128, 137, 140, 142, 183
Scandinavian jewelry, 232-250
scarf pin/stickpin, 38, 76, 88, 92, 98, 106, 108, 118
Scheer, William Inc., 129
Scheid, Georg Anton, 95
Schiaparelli, Elsa, 136, 180, 187, 189, 198, 200, 202, 203
Schlumberger, Jean, 180, 189
Schmidt, Wilhelm, 88
Schreiner, 200
Scott, James, 97, 100
Scottish jewelry, 47-48, 83
seed pearls, 27, 29, 37, 34, 38, 40, 41, 42, 43, 51, 52, 53, 59, 61, 71, 73, 75, 84, 88, 89, 102, 103, 106, 110, 114, 116, 119, 120, 121, 122, 123, 124, 125, 134, 138, 141, 143, 203, 210
sévigné, 25
shakudo, 77, 80
shamrock motif, 67, 80
Shaw, Josephine Hartwell, 96
shell, 54, 55, 56, 60, 61, 62, 63, 99, 142, 176, 181, 182, 184, 212, 213, 214, 215, 218, 235, 236, 248
shellac, 50, 51, 146
shibuichi, 77
Shiebler, George W., 75, 78
shield motif, 40, 58, 63, 71, 73, 84, 89, 94, 103, 104, 106, 108, 114, 116, 118, 133, 134, 141, 148, 154, 191, 195, 207, 248
shirt studs, 49, 123
Shreve, Crump and Low, 96
Siersbol, Hermann, 239
Sigi (Pineda), 225, 228, 231
Silesian wire, 30, 31, 33
Silson, Victor, 196, 223
silver gilt, 28, 29, 56, 58, 59, 116, 117, 139, 143
silver jewelry, 77-81, 97, 198, 212, 213, 214, 232, 240, 246
Sirokoru Ky Hyvarinen, 249, 250
Skaggs, H. Fred, 166, 167
skønvirke, 94, , 232, 233, 234, 235, 236
Skoogfors, Olaf, 169
Sleeper, Martha 147, 151, 152
sleeve buttons, 49
Smed, Dan, 97
Smed, Peer, 97
Smith, Art, 164, 173
snake motif, 34, 70, 83, 101, 111, 218
sodalite, 173, 224, 248
Sommerfeldt, Gine, 240, 242
Sørby, Harry, 240
spectrolite, 246, 249, 250
sporting jewelry, 60, 75
Spratling, William, 222, 223, 224, 225, 226, 228
squash blossom necklace, 213
St. Laurent, Yves, 200
Standard Button Co., 110
Stanhope, Lord Charles, 43
stanhope, 43, 53
star motif, 26, 33, 83, 205
Staret, 189, 191, 193
Stavre, Gregor Panis, 106
Strass, Georg Frédéric, 25
steel, 30
Stehman, Polly, 166, 170
Stein, Lea, 145, 154
Sterlé, Pierre, 175
sterling silver, 104, 137, 188, 201, 202, 213
sterling vermeil, 116, 189, 193, 194, 196, 241
Stickley, Gustav, 95
stickpin, 38, 71, 97, 118
strap and buckle motif, 47
Streamline Moderne, 126, 128
suffragist, 114, 121
suite, 29, 33, 40, 42, 46, 53, 63, 64, 66, 67, 73, 75, 89, 90, 91, 99, 106, 114, 125, 143, 144, 161, 162, 166, 167, 174, 175, 179, 180, 184, 185, 186, 188, 198, 199, 200, 201, 206, 207, 208, 209, 210, 211, 221, 231, 239, 244, 246, 250
sunburst motif, 84
swallow motif, 75, 80, 85, 123
swan motif, 117
"sweetheart" pin, 148
Swiss enamel, 37, 40, 41
"Swiss lapis," 136, 140
sword motif, 83
T.C. Shop, 98
taille d'épargne enamel, 35, 71, 73, 89, 138
Tamminen, Seppo, 246, 247
Taxco, Margot de, 224, 225, 227
Templier, Raymond, 128
Terán, Salvador,
thermoset plastic, 145, 146
"Thief of Bagdad," 199
tiara, 40, 42
tie pin, 49
Tiffany, Louis Comfort 92, 97, 120
Tiffany, 42, 78, 100, 200
Tiffany & Co., 24, 49, 50, 70, 75, 82, 97, 108, 120, 127, 129, 162, 175, 180
Tiffany Furnaces, 97
Tiffany setting for diamonds, 82
tiger's claws, 49
tiger's eye, 218, 221, 235
topaz, 24, 26, 40, 41, 91, 100, 132, 202, 224
Toril Bjorg, 243
Tortoiseshell and piqué, 54, 116, 145, 228
Torun, 233, 238, 244
Tostrup, J., 240, 242
tourmaline, 49, 100, 104, 105, 106, 117, 121, 125, 167, 196, 239
Trabert & Hoeffer, Mauboussin, 134, 158, 159
trefoil motif, 30, 40, 51, 52, 54, 71, 89, 125, 130, 135, 191
Trifari, 136, 147, 187, 188, 189, 191, 192,193, 197, 201, 211
Troob & Degnan Jewelry Co., 138
turquoise, 83, 213
Turun Hopea, 246, 250
Tyler, Julia, 24
Unger Bros., 108
urn motif, 143, 226
Van Cleef & Arpels, 129, 157, 158, 175, 181, 187
Vanderbilt, Consuelo, 74
Varley, Charles Fleetwood, 94
Vausch, Louis, 103
Vauxhall glass, 50, 52
Vendome, 125
Verdura, 157, 158, 159, 180, 189
Vernon, Frédéric Charles Victor de, 107, 114
Vever, Maison, 107
Victoria (Ana Nunez Brilanti), 225, 231
Victor Silson
Victorian Revival, 68, 83, 137, 138, 188
Vigeland, Tone, 241, 242
Vitali, Liisa, 250
Vogue Magazine, 92
vulcanite, 50, 52, 53
waist set, 75, 114
watch chain, 44, 80
watch pin, 122
watchcock, 69
watch chain, 81
watch fob, 59, 64, 73, 80
watch key, 73
watch pin, 122
water lily motif, 108, 109
Watson, Newell & Co., 108
Webb, David 157, 180, 181
Weckström, Björn, 233, 246, 247, 248, 249
Werkstätte, 95
Western motif, 148
white gold, 121, 127, 181
White Hogan, 215, 217, 218, 220
white metal, 136, 181, 188, 189, 229
Whiteside & Blank, 108, 116, 118
Wiener, Ed, 164, 166, 169, 174
Wiener Werkstätte, 95, 100, 136
Wièse, Jules, 56, 57
Wièse, Louis, 56
Wilson, Byron, 166, 170
Winn, James H., 98
Winston, Harry, 157, 175, 176
Wipperfeld, Heinz, 181
wirework, 30, 31, 32, 33, 35, 55, 56, 57, 59, 61, 72, 103, 105, 110, 186, 190, 191, 216
Wirkkala, Tapio, 232, 233
Withers, Margaret Craver, 163
WMCA, 136
Wolcott Mfg. Co., 141
Wolfers, 183
wood, 42, 147, 148, 152, 153, 163, 168, 169, 172, 173, 181, 182, 195, 214, 232, 246165, 167, 171, 172, 182, 188, 189, 192, 193, 203, 204, 220, 243, 261, 277
Wood, Cy and Vera ("Cyvra"), 181, 182
Wood and Hughes, 80
World War I, 92, 94, 95, 121, 126, 128, 137, 147, 148, 158, 163, 166, 175, 181, 188, 189, 212, 214, 215, 223, 233, 234, 240, 246
World War II, 126, 137, 147, 148, 158, 163, 166, 175, 181, 188, 189, 212, 214, 215, 223, 233, 234, 240, 246
Wynne, Madeline Yale, 98
Yard, Raymond C., 129, 133
yellow metal, 24, 49, 53, 63, 64, 110, 116, 189, 190, 198, 206, 208, 211
Zapata, Janet, 78, 79, 80, 97, 108, 115, 117, 165
Zuni, 212, 213, 214, 216, 217, 218, 219